The Motivated Mind

In the *World Library of Psychologists* series, international experts themselves present career-long collections of what they judge to be their finest pieces – extracts from books, key articles, salient research findings, and their major practical theoretical contributions.

In this volume Arie Kruglanski reflects on the development throughout his distinguished career of his wide-ranging research covering radicalisation, human judgement and belief formation, group and intergroup processes, and motivated cognition. This collection offers an invaluable insight into the key works behind the formation of Kruglanski's seminal theory of lay epistemics, as well as his important input into a diverse range of fields of social psychology. A specially written introduction gives an intimate overview of this career, and contextualises the selection in relation to changes in the field during this time.

With continuing relevance today, and of vast historical importance, this collection is essential reading for anyone with an interest in goals, belief formation, group processes, and social psychology in general.

Arie W. Kruglanski is a Distinguished University Professor at the University of Maryland in the US, a recipient of numerous awards, and is a Fellow of the American Psychological Association and the American Psychological Society. He has served as editor of the *Journal of Personality and Social Psychology: Attitudes and Social Cognition*, editor of the *Personality and Social Psychology Bulletin*, and associate editor of the *American Psychologist*.

World Library of Psychologists

The *World Library of Psychologists* series celebrates the important contributions to psychology made by leading experts in their individual fields of study. Each scholar has compiled a career-long collection of what they consider to be their finest pieces: extracts from books, journals, articles, major theoretical and practical contributions, and salient research findings.

For the first time ever the work of each contributor is presented in a single volume so readers can follow the themes and progress of their work and identify the contributions made to, and the development of, the fields themselves.

Each book in the series features a specially written introduction by the contributor giving an overview of their career, contextualizing their selection within the development of the field, and showing how their thinking developed over time.

Discovering the Social Mind
Selected Works of Christopher D. Frith
By Christopher D. Frith

Towards a Deeper Understanding of Consciousness
Selected Works of Max Velmans
By Max Velmans

Thinking Developmentally from Constructivism to Neuroconstructivism
Selected Works of Annette Karmiloff-Smith
By Annette Karmiloff-Smith

Acquired Language Disorders in Adulthood and Childhood
Selected Works of Elaine Funnell
Edited by Nicola Pitchford, Andrew W. Ellis

Exploring Working Memory
Selected works of Alan Baddeley
By Alan Baddeley

The Motivated Mind

The Selected Works of
Arie W. Kruglanski

Arie W. Kruglanski

LONDON AND NEW YORK

First published 2018
by Routledge
2 Park Square, Milton Park, Abingdon, Oxon OX14 4RN

and by Routledge
711 Third Avenue, New York, NY 10017

Routledge is an imprint of the Taylor & Francis Group, an informa business

© 2018 Arie W. Kruglanski

The right of Arie W. Kruglanski to be identified as author of this work has been asserted by him in accordance with sections 77 and 78 of the Copyright, Designs and Patents Act 1988.

All rights reserved. No part of this book may be reprinted or reproduced or utilised in any form or by any electronic, mechanical, or other means, now known or hereafter invented, including photocopying and recording, or in any information storage or retrieval system, without permission in writing from the publishers.

Trademark notice: Product or corporate names may be trademarks or registered trademarks, and are used only for identification and explanation without intent to infringe.

British Library Cataloguing in Publication Data
A catalogue record for this book is available from the British Library

Library of Congress Cataloging in Publication Data
Names: Kruglanski, Arie W., author.
Title: The motivated mind : the selected works of Arie W. Kruglanski / Arie W. Kruglanski.
Description: Abingdon, Oxon ; New York, NY : Routledge, 2018.
Identifiers: LCCN 2017060861 (print) | LCCN 2017061073 (ebook) | ISBN 9781315175867 (Ebk) | ISBN 9781351708029 (Adobe) | ISBN 9781351708012 (Epub) | ISBN 9781351708005 (Mobipocket) | ISBN 9781138039438 (hbk)
Subjects: LCSH: Motivation (Psychology) | Cognition.
Classification: LCC BF503 (ebook) |
LCC BF503. K78 2018 (print) | DDC 153.8—dc23
LC record available at https://lccn.loc.gov/2017060861

ISBN: 978-1-138-03943-8 (hbk)
ISBN: 978-1-315-17586-7 (ebk)

Typeset in Baskerville
by Keystroke, Neville Lodge, Tettenhall, Wolverhampton

Contents

Acknowledgments   vii

1 **Speaking in general: Reflections on my work**   1
KRUGLANSKI, A. W.

PART I
How people know   17

2 **Three decades of lay epistemics: The why, how, and who of knowledge formation**   19
KRUGLANSKI, A. W., DECHESNE, M., OREHEK, E., & PIERRO, A. (2009).

3 **Motivated closing of the mind: "Seizing" and "freezing"**   60
KRUGLANSKI, A. W. & WEBSTER, D. M. (1996).

4 **Intuitive and deliberate judgments are based on common principles**   104
KRUGLANSKI, A. W. & GIGERENZER, G. (2011).

5 **Political conservatism as motivated social cognition**   129
JOST, J. T., GLASER, J., SULLOWAY, F. J., & KRUGLANSKI, A. W. (2003).

PART II
How people want   205

6 **A theory of goal systems**   207
KRUGLANSKI, A. W., SHAH, J. Y., FISHBACH, A., FRIEDMAN, R., CHUN, W. Y. & SLEETH-KEPPLER, D. (2002).

PART III
How people act   251

7 The rocky road from attitudes to behaviors: Charting the goal systemic course of actions   253
KRUGLANSKI, A. W., JASKO, K., CHERNIKOVA, M., MILYAVSKY, M., BABUSH, M., BALDNER, C., & PIERRO, A. (2015).

8 To "do the right thing" or to "just do it": Locomotion and assessment as distinct self-regulatory imperatives   299
KRUGLANSKI, A. W., THOMPSON, E. P., HIGGINS, E. T., ATASH, M. N., PIERRO, A., SHAH, J. Y., & SPIEGEL, S. (2000).

9 To the fringe and back: Violent extremism and the psychology of deviance   344
KRUGLANSKI, A. W., JASKO, K., CHERNIKOVA, M., DUGAS, M., & WEBBER, D. (2017).

Index   367

Acknowledgments

I would like to thank Taylor & Francis for permission to include the following:

Kruglanski, A. W., Dechesne, M., Orehek, E., & Pierro, A. (2009). Three decades of lay epistemics: The why, how and who of knowledge formation. *European Review of Social Psychology*, 20, 146–191

I would like to thank the American Psychological Association for permission to include the following:

Kruglanski, A. W. & Webster, D. M. (1996). Motivated closing of the mind: "Seizing" and "freezing." *Psychological Review*, 103(2), 263.
Kruglanski, A. W. & Gigerenzer, G. (2011). Intuitive and deliberate judgments are based on common principles. *Psychological Review*, 118, 97–109.
Jost, J. T., Glaser, J., Kruglanski, A. W., & Sulloway, F. J. (2003). Political conservatism as motivated social cognition. *Psychological Bulletin*, 129, 339–375.
Kruglanski, A. W., Jasko, K., Chernikova, M., Milyavsky, M., Babush, M., Baldner, C., & Pierro, A. (2015). The rocky road from attitudes to behaviors: Charting the goal systemic course of actions. *Psychological Review*, 122, 598–620.
Kruglanski, A. W., Thompson, E. P., Higgins, E. T., Atash, M., Pierro, A., Shah, J. Y., & Spiegel, S. (2000). To "do the right thing" or to "just do it": locomotion and assessment as distinct self-regulatory imperatives. *Journal of Personality and Social Psychology*, 79(5), 793.
Kruglanski, A. W., Jasko, K., Chernikova, M., Dugas, M., Webber, D. (in press). To the fringe and back: Violent extremism and the psychology of deviance. *American Psychologist*.

I would like to thank Elsevier for permission to include the following:

Kruglanski, A. W., Shah, J. Y., Fishbach, A., Friedman, R., Chun, W. Y., & Sleeth-Keppler, D. (2002). "A theory of goal systems." *Advances in Experimental Social Psychology*, 34, pp. 331–378.

1 Speaking in general

Reflections on my work

Arie W. Kruglanski, University of Maryland

My tortuous way to social psychology: A personal history

"Life happens when you are busy doing other things," goes the saying. My way into the science of psychology illustrates how this can transpire, if you aren't careful. Fortuitous events, kind comments of friends and strangers, life's ups and downs, choices made, and paths pursued all conspired to miraculously bring me herein, looking back at already a long (and hopefully much longer) career as a psychological researcher and theorist.

Growing up in Poland and later Israel to a family whose business was textiles, it never entered my mind to consider a scientific career, though the seeds of my fascination with science were planted in my late teens by my uncle, a botanist. It was during my furloughs from the army (I served in the Israeli air force), while visiting the home of my aunt Sofia (Zuza) that uncle Zem (her spouse) treated me to articles from the *Scientific American* that he collected. The calm, systematic and serenely "serious" expositions of scientific research contrasted sharply with the rough and tumble of army life and a youth culture centered on music, entertainment, and "having a good time," superficially defined. It was this juxtaposition that instilled in me the notion of the "good" and worthy life as a life of serious study resistant to the "siren call" of the vanities to which I gladly (even if guiltily) succumbed at the time.

Fresh out of the military service and anxious to move forward, I enrolled in the school of architecture at the University of Toronto (the city where my mother resided). This decision was heavily influenced by aunt Zuza's advice and her (erroneous, it turns out) assumption that my (alleged) talent for drawing and my good grades at math held the promise of an illustrious architectural career. That was not to be, alas. My limited ability to imagine things in space, and my indifference (to say the least) to engineering details and the intricacies of construction, contributed to my "fish out of water" sense with architectural nitty gritty. What broke the proverbial camel's back was a summer job experience at a Toronto architectural firm. This outfit specialized in high-rise condos, and my mission as a junior draftsman was to draw the bathrooms for thousands of apartments. This unhappy experience brought me to the brink of despair or nearly so; to escape the morass I decided to cut my losses and change course sooner rather than later.

But what course to elect? was the question. This time, rather choosing rationally based on what I might be good at, I chose to study a subject that intrigued me the most: human behavior! Concretely, this meant enrolling in the department of psychology (at the University of Toronto), which I hoped would train me to become a wise psychoanalyst capable of interpreting the dreams of people, explaining the mysteries of their conduct, and unraveling the psychological knots that held them in bondage (just as was shown in Alfred Hitchcock's Freud-inspired films). That too wasn't to be, however: In the early 1960s, the department of psychology at the University of Toronto was as far from psychoanalysis as one might imagine. Instead, it was heavily populated by psychological super scientists. Animal learning types, including Abram Amsel the frustration theorist, Endel Tulving and Ben Murdock, both giants in the field of memory, George Mandler, a superstar in the realm of emotion, Daniel Berlyne, a leader in the domain of motivation, Jean Foley the perception expert, and other faculty of stellar scientific stature.

Though my hopes of a shining psychoanalytic career were dashed, I quickly fell in love with the rigors of scientific psychology taught and practiced in Toronto. It apparently hit a spot created by my uncle's *Scientific American* articles I had perused years ago and evoked a vision of scholarly pursuits and a life dedicated to ideas and research.

While I found behavioral learning theory (the rage at the time) fascinating, I was less enamored when it came to actual work with animals in the lab. The white rat I tried to educate and train to press a bar escaped from the cage and bit me, and while I was crawling on the lab floor trying to capture the escapee, a light went on in my head, and two words rang in my ears: Social Psychology! Fortunately, I found a wonderful mentor in this domain in the person of John Arrowood, whose encouragement, enthusiasm, and guidance made the study of social psychology seem like an exciting adventure. When the time came to apply to grad schools, John recommended that I work with Harold Kelley (his own mentor) at UCLA, and I did so. It turned out to be one of the most important decisions I ever made. Hal was a truly great scientist who inspired, challenged, and encouraged me like few others. From that point on, the Social Psychology community became my extended family, the group to which I was honored to belong and whose members came to be my role models, colleagues, and dear friends. As you will see below, I wasn't quite a prototypical member of the clan, and often found myself questioning some of the most basic tenets of its shared knowledge and received views. My excuse was that the problems I addressed were the major ones that social psychology has set for itself, and in tackling them in the best way I could I felt I was carrying out its scientific mission just as a "good" social psychologist was meant to do.

I. How People Know

The inferential process

Einstein is reputed to have quipped that "Everything should be made as simple as possible, but no simpler." When I look back on my work of almost 50 years, it seems that I have followed a kindred principle in trying to make "everything" as *general* as possible, though no more general. A good example of this approach has been my work on lay epistemics; a theory of the process whereby people acquire their subjective knowledge, that is, their beliefs on various topics. This theory, exemplified by a sample of articles in the first section of this volume, grew out of my work in attribution theory and the distinction between the *contents* of knowledge and the *process* of knowledge acquisition.

It seemed to me that whereas attribution theory purported to address the *process* of causal attribution, major theorists in this domain (the likes of Fritz Heider, Bernard Weiner, Edward (Ned) Jones, or Harold Kelley) dwelled instead on the *contents* of attributional categories. Heider (1958), for instance, and later Jones (e.g., Jones & Davis, 1965) talked about attributions to the *person* (referred to as internal attributions) versus to the *situation* (referred to as external attributions), Kelley (1967) distinguished between attributions to "entity," "consensus," and "time/modality," and Weiner (1985), addressing the achievement context, parsed the attributional domain into ascriptions to "ability," "luck," "effort," and "task difficulty."

Though these attributional categories are of great interest, and have illuminated important phenomena in specific domains, they do not (so I argued) describe the general process of causal attribution as such. They pertain to the *contents* of possible causal categories as did my own distinction between *endogenous* and *exogenous* attributions proposed as an alternative to the ubiquitous internal–external partition (Kruglanski, 1975).

In essence, the *process* of causal attribution should apply to all causal categories not just to the select ones identified by attributional researchers. On careful examination, it turns out that once stripped of their content elements that process embodies the principle of *covariation*. As Kelley (1973, p. 108) pointed out: "An effect is attributed to the one of its possible causes with which, over time, it covaries." Why is it so? Because that is precisely what the concept of "cause" (in part) means. A cause (as commonly understood) is something that covaries with the effect; therefore, something that covaries with the effect could well be its cause, whereas something that does not so covary could not possibly be its cause. Plain and simple. Because the concept of cause is what it is, we now know what evidence is relevant to the inference of causality. In other words, our "theory" of causality implies what the evidence for causality should consist of. This common "theory" of causality warrants a deduction of causal conclusions from evidence according to an "if–then" rule whereby: "if x covaried with y, then x is a possible cause of y."

But then it struck me that it is possible (and desirable) to carry this reasoning further. In the same way that notions like "internal," "external," "ability," "luck," and so on, are special contents of the "cause" category, so the "cause" category itself is a special instance of a "topic" category in which people may be interested. Of course, the set of "topics" is infinitely diverse and it encompasses anything that people may wish to address or to know. Yet while the *contents* of possible categories are quite open-ended and varied the *process* whereby their knowledge is validated appears to be uniform. And a critical aspect of that process, is the deductive "if–then" reasoning identified above in reference to causality.

Of course, whereas the (partial) evidence for causality is *covariation*, evidence for other concepts derives from the specific theories we may hold about these concepts and their properties. For instance, to discover whether a newly encountered animal is a dog one may investigate whether it barks; this process may be guided by the "if–then" rule (derived from our "theory" of dogs) whereby "if barks then dog," and so on. In short, my quest for generality led from specific causal contents to the process of causal attribution and, more generally yet, to the deductive process whereby all human knowledge (not only causal knowledge), both scientific and lay, is validated.

Epistemic motivations

My argument that the inferential principle of lay knowledge is of the "if–then" form was influenced by my immersion in the contemporary philosophy of science that was making exciting strides in the 1960s and the 1970s, as represented in the writings of Karl Popper (e.g., 1949, 1966), Thomas Kuhn (1962), Imre Lakatos (1971), Paul Feyerabend (1975), and their counterparts. One notion that their analyses made crystal clear is that the process of knowledge formation is never complete. It is always possible to test one's hypotheses again and again, to gather further information, or replicate one's former observations. Confidence is never conferred by an *objective* state of affairs. It constitutes a psychological state of mind rather than one uniquely determined by actual states of the world. How is it, I then wondered, that individuals are able to reach confident knowledge, and why is it that given the same amount of information some persons may experience supreme confidence, whereas others may feel uncertain and indecisive?

In my attempt to solve this puzzle, I proposed the notion of *epistemic motivations*. These are motivations concerning the features of desired beliefs. I distinguished in this regard between the needs for specific and nonspecific closure, the former representing the quest for (non-directional) certainty on a topic—the latter the need to reach judgments consistent with one's wishes. The function of these epistemic motivations is to serve as *stopping mechanisms* instilling in the individual the confidence that she or he has enough evidence to warrant a definite judgment. As mentioned earlier, such confidence constitutes a subjective experience and is in the eye of the beholder.

The work on the need for cognitive closure benefited from my collaboration with several outstanding researchers at diverse world locations: Antonio Pierro and Lucia Mannetti of the University of Rome, Malgorzata Kossowska of the Jagiellonian University in Krakow, Arne Roets of the University of Ghent, and Ying Yi Hong of the Chinese University of Hong Kong. This research resulted in scores of empirical articles including three theoretical analyses published in the *Psychological Review* (Kruglanski, 1980; Kruglanski & Webster, 1996; Kruglanski, Pierro, Mannetti, & De Grada, 2006). The most recent review of the closure work was published in 2015 authored by an international team headed by Arne Roets (Roets, Kruglanski, Kossowska, Pierro, & Hong, 2015).

Epistemic authority

The third facet of my theory of lay epistemics, concerned the source of the information. The source may often serve as evidence for the validity of a proposition; it may function as an antecedent in the inferential "if–then" rule according to a premise of the kind "if the information comes from source X, then it can be trusted." There are two quintessential sources that fulfill this evidential function. One is the individual's *own* epistemic "machinery," that is, her or his senses, perceived access to information and self-ascribed deductive ability, on all of which individuals may vary. In other words, individuals may attribute to themselves different degrees of *epistemic authority*, reflecting the degree of confidence they may have in understanding a given aspect of the world on their own.

For instance, individuals may differ in the acuity of their eyesight, some boasting 20/20 vision while others having impaired vision for various reasons. A person whose eyesight is weak would not trust the evidence of his or her eyes to the same degree as a person whose eyesight was good, for example. One's self-ascribed epistemic authority might also vary across domains, depending on one's extent of training and expertise in a given subject matter. A person might feel confident about his or her assessment of abstract art, but feel completely at a loss when it comes to plumbing, car mechanics, medicine, etc.

The other source of knowledge on which we may rely is *other people* assumed to have general or specific epistemic authority in various domains. It is to them that we turn for interpretation and elucidation when our own perceived self-authority in given domains is lacking. Little children rely in this way on their adult caregivers, as do adults in areas outside their sphere of expertise.

These three dimensions of lay epistemics, the *inferential*, the *motivational* and the *evidential*, are represented in Chapter 2, on the *how*, the *why* and the *who* of knowledge formation. Chapter 3, on "seizing" and "freezing," describes the extensive work on the need for cognitive closure carried out by my colleagues and me, looking at this motivation's implications for judgment and decision making at the individual level of analysis. Chapter 4 is written in collaboration with Gerd Gigerenzer and is devoted to an analysis of the inferential aspect of epistemics. This chapter argues that the basic inferential mechanism involved in what has been generally regarded as two qualitatively distinct modes of reaching judgments, that is, the "fast" and the "slow" ways of thinking (Kahneman, 2011) or the reflexive and reflective modes (Strack & Deutsch, 2004). Indeed, this Kruglanski and Gigerenzer chapter elaborates a parsimonious, evidence-based, alternative to the popular dual process theories known as the *unimodel*, whereby the different instances of judgment share the same underlying process and vary along quantitative parameters (e.g. on the *extent* of processing) rather than qualitatively.

Political ideology

The last chapter in this section is the most "famous" (i.e., most often cited) of the four. It applies the theory of lay epistemics to the realm of political behavior, and in particular to a significant motivational difference between conservatives and liberals on the need for cognitive closure. Specifically, a meta-analysis of the last fifty years of research (up until 2003) on the motivational make-up of these ideologies' adherents yields evidence that the conservatives are significantly higher on the need for cognitive closure than are the liberals. This relates to the assured decision-making style of many conservative politicians (George W. Bush comes to mind as a prototypical example), and to their apparent tendency to be more group-centric (i.e., more nationalistic, and supportive of cultural traditions and stereotypes) than are the liberals.

Of curious interest, the publication of the Jost, Kruglanski, Glaser, and Sulloway (2003) paper occasioned a flurry of intensely angered reactions on the part of conservative pundits and journalists as well as a fair share of hate mail, largely by individuals who didn't actually read the original paper but rather learned about it second-hand. This unwanted excitement about our work subsided when John Jost and I published an opinion piece in the *Washington Post* that explained that the need for cognitive closure isn't necessarily a bad thing and that in certain circumstances the confidence it instills is preferable to the indecision and lack of resoluteness that the need to avoid closure may confer. In addition, the tendency under high need for closure to be committed to one's group (to one's family, one's friends, one's nation, or one's values) is often considered a good thing, and uncommitted relativism fostered by a low need for closure is often frowned upon. So, as in nearly all domains of psychology, the consequences of a given variable or factor are neither "good" nor "bad" universally. There are no panacea or silver bullets in psychology, rather it is all a matter of tradeoffs.

II. How People Want

Goal systems

Throughout my whole career, I have been passionately interested in the topic of motivation. As my views of human psychology crystallized I was increasingly impressed by the central role that this aspect of our psyche plays in human behavior; this includes motivation's role in human cognition, which process is importantly driven and selectively directed by epistemic needs for nonspecific and specific closure. "Thinking is for doing," William James famously asserted (1890/1983, p. 18) and doing is guided by our wishes and desires; thus, ultimately thinking is "for" the gratification of our wants. In this sense motivation is the *dog* and cognition the *tail*, or to put it differently cognition serves as the *handmaiden* of motivation.

What makes things particularly intriguing is that motivation and cognition interweave as if in a twisting and turning Moebius strip (see Figure 1). Even as cognition is motivationally driven so motivation is cognitively represented; the two are 'connected at the hip' as it were and you can't have the one without the other. Throughout my career as a psychological scientist my work has invariably addressed a motivational problem of some sort. Early on, as an attributional researcher I was interested in the issue of intrinsic motivation; this is the aforementioned case where

Figure 1 Moebius strip.

an activity is perceived as its own end, being endogenously versus exogenously attributed (Kruglanski, 1975).

Subsequently, I explored the motivational underpinnings of knowledge formation, resulting in my theory of epistemic motivations alluded to earlier. The latter work may be described as representing a "motivation *and* cognition" paradigm that assigned separate roles to the two; motivation driving the extent and directionality of information processing and cognition representing the inferential logic of forming judgments from considered evidence. A subsequent phase of my interest in motivational phenomena represented a different "motivation *as* cognition" paradigm that addressed the mental representation of motivational entities; namely, *goals* and *means* and their various configurations. This work is featured in our theory of goal systems (Kruglanski et al., 2002), Chapter 6 in Part II of this book.

One of this theory's contributions lies in identifying and deriving the psychological implications of different cognitive architectures connecting goals and means; specifically, the configurations of (1) *equifinality* in which the same goal may be alternatively served by several different means, (2) *multifinality* in which the same means at once serves several goals, and (3) *counterfinality* in which a means that serves one goal at the same time undermines another goal.

Goal systems theory's second contribution concerns the allocation of resources to different goal pursuit systems and the finite and depletable pool of cognitive resources available for goal-driven cognition and behavior. The notion of depletable resources figures prominently in our theory of cognitive energetics (Kruglanski et al., 2012) and is exemplified by Part II, How People Want.

By now, fifteen years after its publication, the theory of goal systems has been applied to a variety of domains including addiction (Köpetz, Lejuez, Wiers, & Kruglanski, 2013), close relations (Orehek & Forest, 2016), intrinsic motivation (Kruglanski, Fishbach et al., 2017; Woolley & Fishbach, 2017), cognitive consistency phenomena (Kruglanski, Jasko, Milyavsky et al., 2017) and violent extremism (Kruglanski & Fishman, 2009; Kruglanski, Jasko, Chernikova et al., 2017). The reason for its broad applicability is its content-free generality that, as noted earlier, represents my preferred mode of thinking and theorizing about psychological phenomena.

Goal shielding

A paper by Shah, Friedman, and Kruglanski (2002) demonstrates the principle of finitude (or constant sum) in reference to attentional resources allocated to goal pursuit. Specifically, the greater the individual's commitment to one of several concurrent goals, the lesser is this person's commitment of resources to the remaining goals. This phenomenon is capable of occurring outside individuals' conscious awareness and manifests itself in such micro phenomena as retarded latency of responding to those alternative goals. Functionally, the reallocation of resources to a committed goal shields it from distraction and interference from other concurrent objectives. An interesting implication of the goal shielding phenomenon is the lessening or removal of constraints that the alternative goals may exercise on means to the focal (highly committed to) goal (see Köpetz, Faber, Fishbach, & Kruglanski, 2011). Specifically, to the extent that these alternative goals were active, means that the focal goal that undermined them would tend to be "disallowed," or avoided. For instance, a hungry person who at the same time was concerned about her or his health and figure would tend to abstain from fattening, unhealthy, foods that while satisfying the hunger-reduction goal were detrimental to the health goal. Under those conditions, the individual may be selective in what she or he chooses to consume and, should the appropriate foods be unavailable, be willing to bide her or his time and postpone food consumption until they were found. In other words, one's active concern about the health goal would constrain the means to the hunger reduction goal (foods one would allow oneself to eat) and restrict them to those which alongside satisfying hunger are also healthy and nutritious.

However, if hunger became particularly intense, commitment to the hunger reduction goal would be enhanced which (according to the goal shielding principle) would reduce the commitment to the health/figure goal. In turn, this would weaken or completely remove the constraints on means of hunger reduction, expanding the set of available means to that goal. In consequence, one might forego all constraints, pull out all the stops and be prepared to eat "anything that moves" as it were, including unhealthy, fattening, and disgusting foods.

III. How People Act

Extremism

Recently we applied this type of reasoning to understanding the phenomenon of *extremism* in general and the phenomenon of violent extremism in particular.

These are addressed in Part III, namely the work of Kruglanski, Gelfand et al. (2014) and Kruglanski, Jasko, Chernikova et al. (2017). Extremism can be defined as behavior, attitude, or opinion that runs counter to or deviates from what most people (in a given group) would engage in or endorse. The latter behaviors and attitudes characterizing a majority of persons represent *moderation*; they are constrained by a variety of goals one may attempt to satisfy. But when one of those objectives looms particularly large and becomes dominant, the others are suppressed, their constraints are, therefore, removed, allowing deviant (and hence 'extreme') behaviors/attitudes/opinions eschewed by most people to be embraced or enacted. In other words, I assume that people have a set of basic needs (cf. Ryan & Deci, 2000; Fiske, 2010; Higgins, 2012), defining goals they strive to attain. Such balanced striving defines moderation exhibited by most people. Only small minorities are capable and willing to let those basic concerns be unaddressed or frustrated; these are the people whose overriding commitment to one thing, their "*idée fixe*," prompts them to "forget all else." In this way, daredevils who pursue extreme sports (like bungee jumping, wingsuit flying, or rock skiing) are forgoing concerns about safety and survival; similarly, individuals committed (addicted) to various substances are willing (at certain moments) to relinquish their professional, or familial, obligations only to feed their habit, and so on.

In the case of violent extremism, the quest for *personal significance* and mattering (we argued) leads individuals to commit to various sanctified causes (e.g., their religion or their nation) whose defense lends them the venerated status of martyrs and heroes, and for which they are willing to risk life and limb (Kruglanski, Chen, Dechesne, Fishman, & Orehek, 2009; Kruglanski, Gelfand et al., 2014; Kruglanski, Jasko, Chernikova et al., 2017).

Our Part III chapter on violent extremism (Chapter 9, Kruglanski, Jasko, Chernikova et al., 2017) also addresses the question of means selection for serving best the goal of personal significance. This function is fulfilled by a violence-justifying narrative that identifies aggression and terrorism as the supreme road to personal significance. It is here, at the level of the narrative, that counter- and de-radicalization interventions may best succeed. The quest for personal mattering and significance is fundamental and difficult to uproot. Nor would one want to uproot it, for its immense motivating potential should not be wasted. What can be done, instead, is to redirect it toward pro-social and constructive means, rather than condoning violence and mayhem as representing the road to mattering.

Finally, understanding of violent extremism would be incomplete without appreciating the role in this phenomenon of violence supporting *social networks* (Sageman, 2004; 2007) and group dynamics that put individuals under the networks' spell. As discussed earlier, individuals' in-groups serve as revered epistemic authorities; they validate the violence-justifying narrative and dispense the significance (admiration, veneration) that the individual craves. Thus, they provide the shared reality (Hardin & Higgins, 1996) concerning values and what it means to matter, have significance, and lead a worthy life.

Between liking and doing

Thinking in *goal* terms turns out to have intriguing implications for one of social psychology's most persistent questions, concerning the relation between attitudes and behavior. Because prediction of behavior was hailed as one of psychology's main tasks (Watson, 1913, p. 158), and because attitudes were thought to lead to behavior (that is, of approaching things which one liked, and avoiding things one did not like), attitudes have become of central interest to social psychologists. But is it necessarily so? Should attitudes necessarily prompt behavior? Chapter 7 ("The rocky road . . .") questions the assumption of a direct link between attitudes and behavior and delineates the conditions under which attitudes will or will not promote behavior. The novelty of this contribution is the introduction of the *goal concept* as a critical moderator of conditions under which attitudes will or will eventuate in behavior. Prior theories of the attitude behavior relations (extensively reviewed in this "rocky road" chapter) did not explicitly mention goals though the empirical research cited in their support implicitly created conditions where goals were inevitably present. Unsurprisingly, this should have been so if we assume (as most psychologists do) that behavior is purposive, that is goal driven. Nonetheless, the goal construct was conspicuously absent from prior discussions of the attitude behavior nexus; a gap in knowledge we set out to redress.

So, when do attitudes lead to behavior and when don't they? They do so where liking of (a positive attitude toward) an object or a state of affairs is translated into an approach goal and disliking (or a negative attitude) is translated into an avoidance goal. Such translation does not invariably take place. But liking and wanting are hardly the same thing! Influential research by Kent Berridge and his colleagues (e.g., Berridge, Robinson, & Aldridge, 2009; Berridge & Aldridge, 2008), compellingly demonstrate the separateness of these concepts on the hormonal level. A commonsensical analysis echoes this distinction: You may like something but already have it, so not wanting it (in the sense of orienting toward a desirable future state) is engendered. Also, you may like something that you do not have but like it less than what you have, again without any implications for wanting. Or you may dislike something (say a root canal) but like something else even less (having one's tooth extracted). In this case, an approach goal would be formed toward a disliked procedure. To cut a long story short, wanting and consequent goal formation require a discrepancy between a present or impending (liked or disliked) state of affairs and another future state that is liked more or disliked less than that present (or impending state).

The psychology of looking and leaping

A different take on the problem of human action is represented in a theory of *regulatory mode* that Tory Higgins, Antonio Pierro, and I developed and extensively researched over the last (nearly) two decades (e.g., Kruglanski et al., 2000, 2013, 2016; Higgins, Kruglanski, & Pierro, 2003; Pierro et al., 2011) The attitude to behavior sequence described in the "rocky road" chapter portrays a sequence of (implicit or explicit) decisions that an individual makes *en route* to action: decisions concerning whether there is a discrepancy between one's liking for the present and possible future state of affairs, whether the discrepancy is sufficiently large, and whether the action involved (task) is worth the effort in light of other contemporaneous concerns, etc. (as discussed in our "Motivational Readiness" paper; Kruglanski, Chernikova, Rosenzweig, & Köpetz, 2014). In contrast, regulatory mode theory describes a tendency to dwell extensively and ponder painstakingly each of those decisions, versus "breezing" through them quickly and leaping headstrong into action.

The former, ponderous, mode is referred to as *assessment*; it entails a careful evaluation of alternatives, extensive comparisons between possibilities, and a reluctance to make a commitment for fear of making a mistake. The latter mode is called *locomotion*; it portrays individuals' proclivity to be in physical or psychological motion, to be "doing" things, experiencing and effecting change rather being stuck in a given status quo. As the theory has it (and extensive research supports it) the assessment and locomotion modes represent orthogonal dimension of individual differences, some people being higher on locomotion than on assessment, others vice versa, and yet others having balanced (high or low) degrees of each of those predilections. As with many other psychological states, those of assessment and locomotion may be also induced by appropriate psychological circumstances, that is, to be affected by the psychological situation. Chapter 8 ("To do the right thing" or to "just do it") represents a seminal paper that initiated what was to become a particularly fruitful and prolific line of research, yielding scores of papers in various domains of psychological science (including intrapersonal, interpersonal, group, and organizational phenomena) to which the fundamental dimensions of action are of relevance.

Epilogue

As I look back at this selection of papers and the body of my work more generally, I am struck that implicitly or explicitly I was guided by the principle of the "gist" (Kruglanski, 2004a), striving for the most general explanation of phenomena of interest, as noted earlier. Typically, this entailed stripping from the phenomena their enticing context and content, their so-called surface structure, and delving to unearth their deep structure, the general underlying mechanism that made them tick. This approach turned out to have several implications. Some of these were beneficial to the work and enhanced its contribution. Others were less advantageous and posed difficulties in communicating my ideas to colleagues.

A major advantage (at least, according to my philosophy of science) is that the gist-guided approach afforded integration of research domains that previously were considered foreign and unrelated to each other. For instance, cognitive consistency theories (e.g., Heider, 1958; Festinger, 1957) were typically viewed as having precious little to do with attribution theory (e.g., Jones & Davis, 1965; Kelley, 1967), yet from the epistemic perspective both have to do with the principle of knowledge validation (Kruglanski, 1989, chapters 4 and 5): consistency theories address the case where (desirable) knowledge is *invalidated* by information inconsistent with that knowledge, and attribution theory—where causal knowledge is *validated* by information consistent with a given pattern of causality (what Harold Kelley (1967) labeled as "attributional criteria").

For another example, consider the "unimodel" (e.g. Kruglanski & Gigerenzer, 2011; Kruglanski, Pierro, Mannetti, Erb, & Chun, 2007; Kruglanski & Thompson, 1999); it underscores the fundamental inferential commonality between what generally were considered two qualitatively distinct modes of judgment (i.e., the *central* versus *peripheral* modes, the *heuristic* versus *systematic* modes, *System 1* versus *System 2* ways of thinking, etc.). Instead, my colleagues and I proposed that in all cases of judgment, individuals are guided by "if–then" rules and the differences between instances of judgment reside in the *contents* of those rules (e.g., different heuristics versus statistical rules), the number of rules considered, their accessibility etc., the latter representing quantitative continua rather than qualitative dichotomies, as has been generally assumed.

For yet another example, consider our current work on intrinsic motivation, a topic that was rarely connected to behavioral learning theory (but see Eisenberger & Cameron, 1996). In a recent paper, however, we make the connection explicit by proposing a means-ends fusion model defining a continuum of intrinsicality, reflecting the degree of perceptual mesh between an activity and its goal (Kruglanski, Fishbach, et al., 2017) and reflecting the phenomenon of secondary reinforcement discovered long ago by animal learning researchers (cf. Hilgard, Kimble, & Marquis, 1961). In short, the "gist-quest" approach that has guided my research over the years led me to seek commonalities among rarely interconnected phenomena, thus fostering integration under shared principles and reaching across seemingly diverse topics highlighted at different periods in the history of psychological science.

The disadvantage of the gist approach resided in the difficulty of communicating the integrative ideas and abstract formulae to the research community and replacing in their terms familiar and cherished notions. Though I never intended, nor do I feel comfortable to be cast in the role of a scientific "rabble rouser," I may have been perceived as such by colleagues and reviewers committed to prior, more specific and contextualized, theories of phenomena. The theory of lay epistemics (Kruglanski, 1989; 2004b), by now an innocuous "classic," encountered considerable resistance on its first introduction, as Harold Kelley wisely presaged in his generous introduction to my 1989 volume. Similar was the fate of the unimodel that had to "fight" its way to the major journals over many years. And even as I write this, a paper of ours that questions the widely presumed "general need for cognitive consistency" is struggling against opposition by reviewers. In fact, it has been my distinct impression that the more important a given paper was (in my estimation of importance), the more "revolutionary" and integrative its message, the tougher was its road to acceptance.

To clarify, I am not complaining. In fact, I consider myself very lucky for having had the support I have had from colleagues and cherished students. Thus, basically I am a happy scientist and grateful for the excitement that new ideas have brought to my life. As for the struggles and the uphill battles, I relish them as well, and gladly (would you believe, reluctantly) accept that there is a price to be paid for having one's voice heard (cf. Popper, 1949), and to challenging the shared reality of one's scientific community. As in most of life's domains, the "no pain—no gain" dictum holds fast in the realm of ideas as well.

References

Berridge, K. C., & Aldridge, J. W. (2008). Decision utility, the brain, and pursuit of hedonic goals. *Social Cognition, 26,* 621–646.
Berridge, K. C., Robinson, T. E., & Aldridge, J. W. (2009). Dissecting components of reward: "liking," "wanting," and learning. *Current Opinion in Pharmacology, 9,* 65–73.
Eisenberger, R., & Cameron, J. (1996). Detrimental effects of reward: Reality or myth? *American Psychologist, 51*(11), 1153–1166.
Festinger, L. (1957). *A theory of cognitive dissonance.* Evanston, IL: Row & Peterson.
Feyerabend, P. (1975). Imre Lakatos. *The British Journal for the Philosophy of Science, 26*(1), 1–18.
Fiske, S. T. (2010). *Social beings: Core motives in social psychology.* Hoboken, NJ: John Wiley & Sons Inc.
Hardin, C. D., & Higgins, E. T. (1996). Shared reality: How social verification makes the subjective objective. In Sorrentino, R. M. & Higgins, E. T. (Eds.), *Handbook of Motivation and Cognition, Volume 3: The Interpersonal Context* (pp. 28–84). New York, NY: Guilford Press.
Heider, F. (1958). *The psychology of interpersonal relations.* New York, NY: Wiley.
Higgins, E. T. (2012). *Beyond pleasure and pain: How motivation works.* New York, NY: Oxford University Press.
Higgins, E. T., Kruglanski, A. W., & Pierro, A. (2003). Regulatory mode: Locomotion and assessment as distinct orientations. *Advances in Experimental Social Psychology, 35,* 293–344.
Hilgard, E.R., Kimble, G. A., & Marquis, D.G. (1961). *Conditioning and learning,* revised by Gregory A. Kimble. London, UK: Methuen & Co.
James, W. [1890] (1983). *The principles of psychology,* edited by George A. Miller. Cambridge, MA: Harvard University Press.
Jones, E. E., & Davis, K. E. (1965). From acts to dispositions: The attribution process in person perception. *Advances in Experimental Social Psychology, 2,* 219–266.
Jost, J. T., Glaser, J., Kruglanski, A. W., & Sulloway, F. J. (2003). Political conservatism as motivated social cognition. *Psychological Bulletin, 129*(3), 339–375.
Kahneman, D. (2011). *Thinking, fast and slow.* New York, NY: Farrar, Straus, & Giroux.
Kelley, H. H. (1967). Attribution theory in social psychology. *Nebraska Symposium on Motivation, 15,* 192–238.
Kelley, H. H. (1973). The processes of causal attribution. *American Psychologist, 28*(2), 107–128.
Köpetz, C., Faber, T., Fishbach, A., & Kruglanski, A. W. (2011). The multifinality constraints effect: How goal multiplicity narrows the means set to a focal end. *Journal of Personality and Social Psychology, 100*(5), 810–826.
Köpetz, C. E., Lejuez, C. W., Wiers, R. W., & Kruglanski, A. W. (2013). Motivation and self-regulation in addiction: A call for convergence. *Perspectives on Psychological Science, 8*(1), 3–24.
Kruglanski, A. W. (1975). The endogenous–exogenous partition in attribution theory. *Psychological Review, 82*(6), 387–406.

Kruglanski, A.W. (1980). Lay epistemologic process and contents: Another look at attribution theory. *Psychological Review*, *87*, 70–87.

Kruglanski, A. W. (1989). *Lay epistemics and human knowledge: Cognitive and motivational bases.* New York, NY: Springer.

Kruglanski, A. W. (2004a). The quest for the gist: On challenges of going abstract in social and personality psychology. *Personality and Social Psychology Review*, *8*(2), 156–163.

Kruglanski, A. W. (2004b). *The psychology of closed mindedness.* New York, NY: Psychology Press.

Kruglanski, A. W., Belanger, J. J., Chen, X., Köpetz, C., Pierro, A., & Mannetti, L. (2012). The energetics of motivated cognition: A force field analysis. *Psychological Review*, *119*, 1–20.

Kruglanski, A. W., Chen, X., Dechesne, M., Fishman, S., & Orehek, E. (2009). Fully committed: Suicide bombers' motivation and the quest for personal significance. *Political Psychology*, *30*(3), 331–357.

Kruglanski, A. W., Chernikova, M., Rosenzweig, E., & Köpetz, C. (2014). On motivational readiness. *Psychological Review*, *121*(3), 367.

Kruglanski, A. W., & Fishman, S. (2009). The psychology of terrorism: Syndrome versus tool perspectives. *Journal of Terrorism and Political Violence*, *18*, 193–215.

Kruglanski, A. W., & Gigerenzer, G. (2011). Intuitive and deliberate judgments are based on common principles. *Psychological Review*, *118*(1), 97–109.

Kruglanski, A. W., Gelfand, M. J., Belanger, J. J., Sheveland, A., Hettiarachi, M., & Gunaratna, R. (2014). The psychology of radicalization and deradicalization: How significance quest impacts violent extremism. *Political Psychology*, *35*(S1), 69–93.

Kruglanski, A. W., Fishbach, A., Woolley, K., Belanger, J. J., Chernikova, M., Molinario, E., & Pierro, A. (2017). A structural model of intrinsic motivation: On the psychology of means-ends fusion. [*Unpublished manuscript.*] University of Maryland, College Park, USA.

Kruglanski, A. W., Jasko, K., Chernikova, M., Dugas, M., & Webber, D. (2017). To the fringe and back: Violent extremism and the psychology of deviance. *American Psychologist*, *72*(3), 217–230.

Kruglanski, A. W., Jasko, K., Milyavsky, M., Chernikova, M., Webber, D., Pierro, A., & Di Santo, D. (2017). Epistemic and affective responses to cognitive inconsistency: The validation-satisfaction model. [*Unpublished manuscript.*] University of Maryland, College Park, USA.

Kruglanski, A. W., Pierro, A., & Higgins, E. T. (2016). Experience of time by people on the go: A theory of the temporality-locomotion interface. *Personality and Social Psychology Review*, *20*(2), 100–117.

Kruglanski, A. W., Pierro, A., Mannetti, L., & De Grada, E. (2006). Groups as epistemic providers: Need for closure and the unfolding of group-centrism. *Psychological Review*, *113*(1), 84–100.

Kruglanski, A. W., Pierro, A., Mannetti, L., Erb, H. P., & Chun, W. Y. (2007). On the parameters of social judgment. *Advances in Experimental Social Psychology*, *39*, 255–303.

Kruglanski, A. W., Pierro, A., Mannetti, L., & Higgins, E. T. (2013). The distinct psychologies of "looking" and "leaping:" Assessment and locomotion as the springs of action. *Social and Personality Psychology Compass*, *7*(2), 79–92.

Kruglanski, A. W., Shah, J. Y., Fishbach, A., Friedman, R., Chun, W. Y., & Sleeth-Keppler, D. (2002). A theory of goal systems. In M. P. Zanna (Ed.), *Advances in Experimental Social Psychology* (Vol. 34, pp. 331–378). San Diego, CA: Academic Press.

Kruglanski, A. W., & Thompson, E. P. (1999). Persuasion by a single route: A view from the unimodel. *Psychological Inquiry*, *10*(2), 83–109.

Kruglanski, A. W., Thompson, E. P., Higgins, E. T., Atash, M., Pierro, A., Shah, J. Y., & Spiegel, S. (2000). To "do the right thing" or to "just do it:" Locomotion and assessment as distinct self-regulatory imperatives. *Journal of Personality and Social Psychology, 79*, 793–815.

Kruglanski, A. W., & Webster, D. M. (1996). Motivated closing of the mind: "Seizing" and "freezing." *Psychological Review, 103*, 263–283.

Kuhn, T. S. (1962). *The structure of scientific revolutions*. Chicago, IL: University of Chicago Press.

Lakatos, I. (1971). History of science and its rational reconstructions. In R. C. Buck & R. S. Cohen (Eds.), *Boston Studies in the Philosophy of Science* (Vol. 8, pp. 91–136). Dordrecht, Netherlands: Springer.

Orehek, E., & Forest, A. L. (2016). When people serve as means to goals: Implications of a motivational account of close relationships. *Current Directions in Psychological Science, 25*(2), 79–84.

Pierro, A., Giacomantonio, M., Pica, G., Kruglanski, A. W., & Higgins, E. T. (2011). On the psychology of time in action: Regulatory mode orientations and procrastination. *Journal of Personality and Social Psychology, 101*(6), 1317–1331.

Popper, K. R. (1949). On the theory of deduction, part I: Derivation and its generalizations. *Journal of Symbolic Logic, 14*(1), 62–63.

Popper, K. R. (1966). Some comments on truth and the growth of knowledge. *Studies in Logic and the Foundations of Mathematics, 44*, 285–292.

Roets, A., Kruglanski, A. W., Kossowska, M., Pierro, A., & Hong, Y. Y. (2015). The motivated gatekeeper of our minds: New directions in need for closure theory and research. *Advances in Experimental Social Psychology, 52*, 221–283.

Ryan, R. M., & Deci, E. L. (2000). The darker and brighter sides of human existence: Basic psychological needs as a unifying concept. *Psychological Inquiry, 11*(4), 319–338.

Sageman, M. (2004). *Understanding terror networks*. Philadelphia, PA: University of Pennsylvania Press.

Sageman, M. (2007). *Leaderless jihad: Terror networks in the 21st century*. Philadelphia, PA: University of Pennsylvania Press.

Shah, J. Y., Friedman, R., & Kruglanski, A. W. (2002). Forgetting all else: on the antecedents and consequences of goal shielding. *Journal of Personality and Social Psychology, 83*(6), 1261–1280.

Strack, F., & Deutsch, R. (2004). Reflective and impulsive determinants of social behavior. *Personality and Social Psychology Review, 8*(3), 220–247.

Watson, J. B. (1913). Psychology as the behaviorist views it. *Psychological Review, 20*, 158–177.

Weiner, B. (1985). An attributional theory of achievement motivation and emotion. *Psychological Review, 92*, 548–573.

Woolley, K., & Fishbach, A. (2017). Immediate rewards predict adherence to long-term goals. *Personality and Social Psychology Bulletin, 43*(2), 151–162.

Part I
How people know

2 Three decades of lay epistemics

The why, how, and who of knowledge formation

Arie W. Kruglanski, Mark Dechesne, and Edward Orehek, University of Maryland
Antonio Pierro, University of Rome "La Sapienza"

The label *homo sapiens* by which humankind is designated translates into "the knowing person," hinting at the essential importance for human affairs of knowledge and its construction. As individuals we form new knowledge constantly and continually. To carry out even the most mundane activities we need to *know* a variety of things. Before embarking on a bit of intelligible behavior, no matter how small, we need to orientate ourselves in time and space, decide what our implementation intentions are for that particular instant, divine their feasibility under the circumstances, and so on. All these are types of knowledge that individuals need to formulate on a moment-to-moment basis.

Our social interactions are also suffused with prior knowledge. We quickly form a preliminary impression about our partners' identity (e.g., as regards their age, gender, nationality, or social status). We figure out what language they speak, what they know about a topic at hand, and what their attitudes and opinions are, so that we tailor our communications accordingly. In addition, our lives as group members and participants in larger collectivities (societies or cultures) are fundamentally guided by our shared knowledge of concepts, norms, and worldviews.

Given the ubiquity of knowledge formation concerns, and their essential psychological relevance to human thought, feeling, and action, understanding how knowledge is formed and changed defines a task of considerable importance for psychological science. Indeed, psychological researchers and theorists have examined epistemic processes in a variety of paradigms including those concerned with attitude formation and change (e.g., Maio & Haddock, 2007; Petty & Wegener, 1999), impression formation (Brewer, 1988; Fiske & Neuberg, 1990), judgment under uncertainty (Kahneman, 2003), and attribution (Hilton, 2007). Typically too, such endeavors, though insightful and useful, have addressed localised issues *specific* to a given content domain of knowledge (for a review see Kruglanski & Orehek, 2007).

More than 20 years ago, a paper published in the *Psychological Review* (Kruglanski, 1980) became the first in what was to become a long string of research reports and essays on the psychological factors involved in a *general* knowledge formation process. A more elaborate theory on this topic was featured in a volume called *Lay Epistemics and Human Knowledge* published nearly a decade later (Kruglanski, 1989). Whereas the initial theoretical effort centered on a generalized, lay epistemic interpretation of attribution theory, subsequent work extended the approach to further topics, including cognitive consistency theories, attitudes and attitude change, cognitive therapy, social comparison processes, and the social psychology of science.

Subsequent to this early publication, extensive empirical and conceptual developments in lay epistemics took place under the aegis of three fairly separate research programs, namely those on *closed-mindedness* (see Kruglanski, 2004), the *unimodel* (see Kruglanski et al., 2007), and *epistemic authority* (see Kruglanski et al., 2005). The purpose of the present chapter is to offer an integrative, up-to-date synopsis of this work, affording a bird's eye perspective on knowledge formation processes and their ramifications for a broad variety of social psychological phenomena.

In what follows we first briefly recapitulate the theory of lay epistemics and describe the three separate research programs it inspired, including the description of substantial novel data not covered in prior reviews. We conclude with a conceptual integration of these research programs and indicate how the processes that they address form an integral part and parcel of the knowledge formation enterprise of potentially considerable real-world relevance.

The theory of lay epistemics

The theory of lay epistemics concerns the process of knowledge formation. It outlines a general framework designed to pertain to all kinds of knowledge, scientific and lay, including personal knowledge of people and the world, religious knowledge, political knowledge, etc. Its point of departure has been Karl Popper's (1959) famous assertion that scientific knowledge is formed in the same general manner as lay knowledge, and hence that science is "common sense writ large". Popper and other philosophers of science (e.g., Paul Feyerabend, or Imre Lakatos) have noted that whereas knowledge formation is guided by the ideal of Truth, one can be never certain that this ideal has been realized. This implies that the concept of "knowledge" is best understood in its subjective sense, as a *belief*. This hardly implies that knowledge must be solipsistic or idiosyncratic. On the contrary, knowledge typically is socially shared, and knowledge construction (whereas scientific or lay) is accomplished via a communal process (Hardin & Higgins, 1996).

According to our theory that regards knowledge as tantamount to belief, to have *knowledge* in which one does not *believe* is a contradiction in terms. However, some authors (e.g., Gawronski & Bodenhausen, 2006) have affirmed such a possibility, so let us examine it carefully. For instance, consider an individual who *knows* the contents of some stereotype (e.g., that all professors are absent-minded) yet does not believe in it. Does that represent an inconsistency with our claim that subjective knowledge represents a belief? It does not! The confusion here is one between "believing that" and "believing in." Knowing the contents of a stereotype means that one *believes that* such a stereotype exists. For instance, one may believe very strongly *that* the stereotype of women states that women are relational, conflict avoidant, and nurturing, yet one might not personally subscribe to such a stereotype or *believe in it*. Similarly, one may know or *believe* very strongly *that* the ancient Egyptians believed the Earth to be flat, without oneself believing this to be true, etc.

Evidence

A major assumption of the lay epistemic theory is that knowledge is derived from evidence. In other words the individual is assumed to depart from an inference rule of an "if E then C" type in which the antecedent term represents the evidence (E), and the consequent term the conclusion C. Such conclusion can also be thought of as a hypothesis (H) that is supported by the evidence.[1] More formally speaking, the reasoning from evidence to conclusions is syllogistic. It includes a *major premise*, the "if E then C" inference rule, and a *minor premise*, which instantiates the antecedent of the rule E affirming that the evidence in question has been obtained, jointly yielding the conclusion C. For instance, a person might subscribe to the stereotype "if university professor then smart" (constituting a major premise), and infer that an encountered individual Dr. Smith, known to be a university professor (minor premise) is, therefore, smart (the conclusion). A special category of evidence concerns other people's opinions. In particular, if these are revered by an individual—hence constituting "epistemic authorities" for that person—their views may carry particular weight for her or him and occasionally override other types of evidence. This lends the epistemic process a distinctly social flavour and highlights the centrality of social reality concerns (Hardin & Higgins, 1996) to human epistemic endeavors.

Terminating the epistemic sequence

It is generally agreed among philosophers of knowledge that the sequence of hypothesis generation and testing (whether in science or in common sense) has no unique or objective point of termination. In principle, one could continue constructing further and further hypotheses and proceed to test them interminably without ever crystallizing firm knowledge on any topic. Of course, such epistemic "obsession" would be highly dysfunctional and paralyzing. Indeed, most of the time people are quite capable of forming judgments based on available evidence and of self-regulating adaptively on the basis of those judgments. An important mechanism allowing this to happen has to do with a motivational variable referred to as the need for cognitive closure (Kruglanski, 2004). Two types of the need for closure have been distinguished, referred to respectively as the needs for nonspecific and specific closure.

The need for nonspecific closure denotes a desire for a firm answer to a question; any firm answer as compared to confusion and ambiguity. The need for a specific closure denotes a specific, desirable, answer to a question, e.g., an esteem-enhancing answer, an optimistic answer, and so on. Each of these needs is assumed to vary in degree and to lie on a continuum ranging from a low to a high motivational magnitude. Thus, one may desire nonspecific closure strongly, mildly, or not at all, actually craving to avoid it. Similarly, one may desire to reach a particular conclusion (or specific closure) with varying degrees of strength. Finally, both types of need determine the length of the epistemic sequence of hypothesis generation and testing. The higher the need for nonspecific closure the shorter the sequence and the stronger the tendency to "seize and freeze" on accessible, closure-affording, evidence. The higher the need for a specific closure, the stronger the tendency to terminate the sequence when the available evidence appears to yield the desired conclusion, or to keep the sequence going until such conclusion seems implied by the evidence.

Explorations in lay epistemics

Over the last three decades, research in the lay epistemic framework has taken place within three separate paradigms, centered respectively on (1) the *need for cognitive closure*, (2) the *unimodel* of social judgment, and (3) the concept of *epistemic authority*. We describe these in turn and show how they interface in addressing functionally interdependent facets of human epistemic behavior.

Need for closure research: The "why" of epistemic behavior

The intrapersonal level

The most extensive research program to date inspired by the lay epistemic framework concerned the need for nonspecific cognitive closure. It addresses the underlying motivation of knowledge formation, addressing the "why" aspect of human epistemics. The magnitude of the need for closure was assumed to be determined by the perceived benefits of closure, and by the costs of lacking closure. For instance, the need for closure was assumed to be elevated where action was required because the launching of intelligible action requires prior closure. Additionally, the need for closure was assumed to be elevated in circumstances where the possession of closure would obviate costly or laborious information processing, as may occur under time pressure, in the presence of ambient noise, or when a person is fatigued or intoxicated (see Kruglanski, 2004, for a review). When the need for closure is elevated, the absence of closure is aversive and stressful.

In a recent pair of studies Roets and van Hiel (2008) found that in a decision-making context (i.e., where closure was required) high (but not low) NFCC scoring individuals had increased systolic blood pressure and heart rate as well as a rise in self-reported feelings of distress (Study 1). Moreover, as long as no conclusive solution was obtained, high (but not low) NFCC individuals showed a progressive increase of arousal assessed via a galvanic skin response. In addition to the transient situational determinants of the need for closure, this motivation was also assumed to represent a dimension of individual differences and a scale was constructed to assess it (Webster & Kruglanski, 1994). By now this scale has been translated into numerous languages and has been shown to converge in its results with situational manipulations of the need for closure;[2] an improved version of the scale was recently published by Roets and van Hiel (2007). These results pertained to phenomena on intrapersonal, interpersonal, group, and intergroup levels of analysis. In the present chapter we address them briefly. More extensive recent reviews are given in Kruglanski and Webster (1996), Kruglanski (2004), and in Kruglanski, Pierro, Mannetti, and De Grada (2006c).

Seizing and freezing phenomena. As noted earlier, a heightened need for cognitive closure induces in individuals the tendency to "seize" on early, closure-affording evidence and "freeze" on the judgments (beliefs) it suggests. These tendencies were studied in reference to several classic phenomena in social cognition and perception.

For instance, Kruglanski and Freund (1983) presented participants with information about a target person's past behaviors in a work context. Participants were then asked to make a judgment about how successful the target would be at a new job. The information about the target included both positive and negative information, with the order of this information varied such that some participants saw the negative information first while others saw the positive information first. Need for closure was manipulated via time pressure by giving some participants a 3-minute limit to make their judgments (after listening to the information), with a stopwatch in sight reminding them of the time constraint. In the low time pressure condition, participants were told they would have an unlimited time to complete the judgments.

It was predicted that need for closure would exert a stronger primacy effect when participants were in a high (vs. low) accountability condition. To manipulate accountability, some participants were told that they would have to explain their predictions to others and that their judgment would be compared to objective standards. In the low accountability condition participants were told that they would not be able to find out how other people judged the target or how the target actually performed at the new job.

As predicted, participants' judgments of the target person were based more on the early appearing information when under time pressure (vs. no time pressure). As shown in Figure 1, the difference between the high as compared to the low time pressure conditions was significantly greater when accountability was high (vs. low). These results demonstrate the ability of need for closure to induce the tendency to "seize" and freeze" on early information. The primacy effect of need for closure was subsequently replicated in a number of further studies (Ford & Kruglanski, 1995; Freund, Kruglanski, & Shpitzazjzen, 1985; Richter & Kruglanski, 1998; Webster, Richter, & Kruglanski, 1996).

In an intriguing demonstration of need for closure's impact on the use of contextually activated information, Pierro and Kruglanski (in press) conducted a study on the influence of need for closure on the *transference effect* in social judgment. The Freudian concept of transference refers to the process by which a psychotherapeutic patient superimposes onto the therapist her or his childhood fantasies with regard to a significant childhood figure (typically a parent). However, Andersen and her colleagues (e.g., Andersen & Cole, 1990, Andersen, Glassman, Chen, & Cole, 1995) showed that the transference effect could be part and parcel of normal sociocognitive functioning in which a significant other's schema is

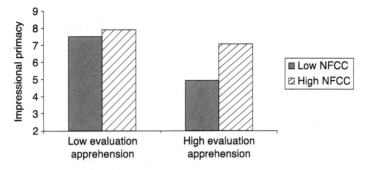

Figure 1 The effect of need for closure (NFCC, operationalized in this study via time pressure) and evaluation apprehension on impressional primacy (Kruglanski & Freund, 1983).

mistakenly applied to a new target that resembles the significant other in some respects. In a first session of Pierro and Kruglanski's (in press) experiment participants completed the revised 14-item need for closure scale (Pierro & Kruglanski, 2005) and were asked to visualize and describe a significant other. In a second session participants were presented with information about a target person with whom they expected to interact. The target person was either described in similar terms as their significant other, or was depicted as dissimilar from that person. After having studied this information, participants were presented with a recognition test of their memory for the target. Items about the target person that were not presented in the description were included in the recognition test. The degree of transference was operationally defined as the proportion of statements falsely recognized as having been included in the description of the target person that were consistent with the representation of the significant other provided in the first session. As shown in Figure 2, the results indicated that participants high on the need for closure exhibited a more pronounced transference effect, as indicated by higher false alarm rates, in the similar (vs. dissimilar) condition than did participants low on the need for closure.

Other studies found evidence that need for closure, whether induced situationally or measured via a trait scale, augments the effects of prevalent stereotypes on judgments about persons (Dijksterhuis, Van Knippenberg, Kruglanski, & Schaper, 1996; Jamieson & Zanna, 1989; Kruglanski & Freund, 1983). A stereotype represents a knowledge structure affording quick judgments about members of a stereotyped "category." That need for closure augments the tendency to utilize stereotype-based evidence in impression formation therefore supports the notion that this need induces the "seizing" and freezing" tendencies assumed by the lay epistemic theory.

The interpersonal level

Beyond its effects on intrapersonal phenomena in the domain of social judgment, need for closure was shown to exert a variety of interpersonal phenomena in

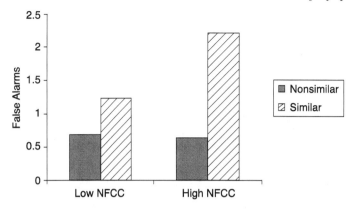

Figure 2 The effect of target similarity and need for closure (NFCC) on false alarm rate (Pierro & Kruglanski, in press).

realms of linguistic expression, communication and persuasion, empathy, and negotiation behavior.

Linguistic expression. Several studies looked at need for closure effects on language abstractness in interpersonal communications. Abstract language indicates a *permanence* of judgments across situations, and hence a greater stability of closure. For instance, characterizing an individual's behavior in a given situation as reflecting this person's aggressiveness (an abstract depiction) implies that he or she may be expected to behave aggressively in other contexts as well. By contrast, depicting the same behavior as a "push" (that is, concretely) carries fewer trans-situational implications. Accordingly, it is possible to predict that individuals under high (vs. low) need for closure would generally tend to employ abstract terms in their communications. Consistent with this prediction, Boudreau, Baron, and Oliver (1992) found that participants, when communicating their impressions to a knowledgeable and potentially critical other (assumed to induce a fear of invalidity and lower the need for closure), tended less to describe a target in abstract trait terms than did participants communicating their impressions to a recipient assumed to have little knowledge on the communication topic.

Using Semin and Fiedler's (1991) linguistic category paradigm, Rubini and Kruglanski (1997) found that participants under high (vs. low) need for closure (manipulated via noise *or* measured via the need for closure scale) tended to frame their questions in more abstract terms, inviting reciprocal abstractness from the respondents. That, in turn, contributed to the creation of greater interpersonal distance between the interlocutors, lessening their liking for each other. Webster, Kruglanski, and Pattison (1997) explored need for closure effects on the "linguistic intergroup bias (LIB)." The LIB reflects the tendency to describe negative in-group behaviors in concrete terms and positive out-group behaviors in concrete terms (suggesting their specificity), and to describe positive in-group behaviors and negative out-group behaviors in abstract terms (suggesting their generality). Consider how need for closure may impact these phenomena. On the one hand, need for closure should induce a general tendency toward abstraction because of the desire of high need for closure individuals for stable knowledge that transcends the specific situation. However, abstract judgments about positive out-group and negative in-group behaviors should run counter to the tendency for individuals with high need for closure to display in-group favoritism (insofar as the in-group is typically the provider of stable knowledge). These two tendencies work *in concert* as far as judgment of positive in-group and negative out-group behaviors are concerned, and are *in conflict* (hence possibly cancelling each other out) as far as negative in-group and positive out-group behaviors are concerned. As shown in Figure 3, Webster et al. (1997) found that high (vs. low) need for closure participants exposed to positive in-group or negative out-group behaviors described such behaviors more abstractly. However, high and low need for closure participants did not differ on the abstractness of their descriptions of negative in-group or positive out-group behaviors.

Persuasion. Research by Kruglanski, Webster, and Klem (1993) explored the conditions under which need for closure may increase or decrease the susceptibility to persuasion. To do this, participants were presented with information about a legal case, and allowed time to process the information and then to talk with a partner (fellow "juror") in order to reach a verdict in the case. When participants were given complete information about the case, including legal analysis suggesting the appropriate verdict, individuals high (vs. low) on the need for closure were less likely to be persuaded by their fellow juror (who argued for the opposite verdict). However, when high need for closure individuals were given incomplete information lacking the legal analysis, they were more likely to be persuaded by their fellow

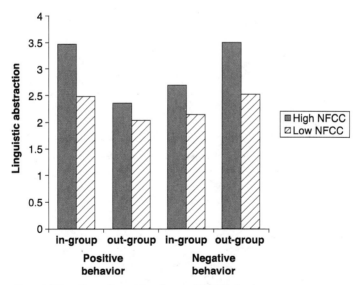

Figure 3 The effect of need for closure (NFCC), in-group versus out-group status, and type of behavior on abstractness of description (Webster et al., 1997).

juror than their low need for closure counterparts. In short, individuals high (vs. low) on the need for closure tend to resist persuasion attempts when they have formed a crystallized opinion about a topic, but tend to change their attitudes when presented with persuasive appeals when they lack an opinion about the topic.

Empathy. Webster-Nelson, Klein, and Irvin (2003) found that, because high need for closure individuals tend to "freeze" on their own perspective, they are less able to empathize with their interaction partners, especially when those are dissimilar from themselves. In their study the need for closure was manipulated via an induction of mental fatigue. Using a dispositional measure of the need for closure, Schteynberg, Gelfand, Imai, Mayer, and Bell (2008) found that high (vs. low) scorers were less sensitive to injustice done to their team-mate by the experimenter (perceived the experimenter as less unfair). In a referential task paradigm, Richter and Kruglanski (1999) found that individuals with high (vs. low) dispositional need for closure tended less to implement an effective "audience design." They tended less to "tune" their messages to their interlocutors' unique attributes; as a consequence their communications were less effectively decoded by their recipients.

Negotiation behavior. To test the effect of need for closure in the domain of negotiation behavior, De Dreu, Koole, and Oldersma (1999) measured participants' dispositional need for closure and then (after a 30-minute delay) had them engage in a task in which they operated as sellers and interacted with presumed buyers (actually simulated by computer-programmed responses). The participant's (seller's) task was to negotiate the terms of the sale, including delivery time, price, and form of payment. Each of these was associated with rewards for the participant in the form of chances in a lottery such that greater profit for the seller was associated with higher chances of winning. Participants engaged in six rounds of negotiations, beginning with the buyer. The buyers' responses were preprogrammed to remain at a moderate level, while conceding slightly at each round. To manipulate the focal point to which participants might adjust their negotiations, they were either told that previous participants had received 11,000 points (high focal point), 3000 points (low focal point), or simply that the range of possible points was from 0 to 14,000 points (no focal point).

Three dependent measures were assessed. First, prior to the start of the negotiations participants were asked to indicate the minimum amount they would be willing to accept in the negotiation. Second, participants' concessions in the task were determined by the decrease in the amount of points participants demanded from the first to the last rounds of negotiation (with greater numbers indicating a larger concession). After the six trials (in which most participants did not reach an agreement), participants completed a self-report measure of the extent to which they thought systematically during the task.

As shown in Figure 4, individuals with high (vs. low) dispositional need for closure tended more to adhere to anchor values. That is, they determined the minimal profits they themselves would accept according to the alleged profits attained by others in the task. When no focal point was provided, high versus low

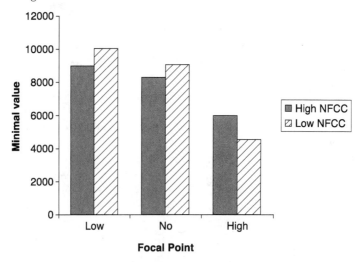

Figure 4 The effect of need for closure (NFCC) and focal point on the minimal value found acceptable in a negotiation (De Dreu et al., 1999).

need for closure participants did not differ in the minimal value they expressed the willingness to accept. In addition, high (vs. low) need for closure participants made smaller concessions to their negotiation partners and engaged in less systematic information processing.

In another study on negotiation, De Dreu and Koole (1997) lowered participants' need for closure via accountability instructions (Tetlock, 1992) or by increasing the costs of invalid judgments (Kruglanski & Freund, 1983). These manipulations lowered participants' tendency to use the *"consensus implies correctness"* heuristic, as well as their tendency to behave competitively and to reach an impasse when a majority suggested a competitive strategy.

The foregoing findings exemplify need for closure effects on a variety of intrapersonal and interpersonal variables (for an extensive review see Kruglanski, 2004). Extensive research also examined the effects of the closure motivation on groups, resulting in a phenomenon of *group centrism* described next.

Group centrism. Some people are more group oriented than others, and most people are more group oriented in some situations than in other situations. Kruglanski et al. (2006c) defined the concept of "group centrism" by the degree to which individuals strive to enhance the "groupness" of their collectivity. Groupness, in turn, has been defined by a firm, consensually supported, "shared reality" (Hardin & Higgins, 1996) unperturbed by dissents and disagreements. While reality sharing has been regarded as the defining essence of groupness (e.g., Bar-Tal, 1990, 2000), its attainment may be facilitated by several aspects of group interaction enhanced by the need for closure. At the initial phases of group formation, this can involve members' attempts to arrive at a speedy consensus, by exerting uniformity pressures on each other (De Grada, Kruglanski, Mannetti, & Pierro, 1999).

To further test the influence of need for closure on the group decision-making process, Pierro, Mannetti, De Grada, Livi, and Kruglanski (2003) engaged participants in a group task 2 months after participants' need for closure had been assessed. Participants were divided into groups based on their need for closure scores, with some groups containing high need for closure individuals and others individuals low on need for closure. Each group was composed of four individuals, each role-playing a manager in a corporation. The group's goal was to determine which of the company's employees should be given a cash award for their work performance. Each "manager" represented a candidate nominated by this "manager's" department. The dependent measures included the asymmetry of speaking time (seizing and holding the floor), perceptions of each participant's influence over the group, and each member's style assessed on the laissez faire/autocratic dimension.

The results indicated that groups composed of high (but not of low) need for closure members displayed the emergence of an autocratic group structure wherein influence emanates from a centralized authority, enhancing the likelihood of commonly shared opinions. As shown in Figure 5, in groups composed of high need for closure persons, some members more than others disproportionately controlled the group discussion by "seizing" the discussion floor and continuing to talk when others attempted to interrupt. Furthermore, in high (but not low) need for closure groups, members' level of autocratic style (as assessed by independent judges) was positively correlated with their control of the discussion floor. Finally, individuals' floor control was positively correlated with their influence on the group (as indexed by self-report and by assessment of independent observers). This research supports the notion that groups composed of high need for closure members are more likely to form autocratic structures, in which a single person or a restricted number of individuals serve as foci of influence, that shape the groups' commonly shared realities.

The laboratory findings just described are consistent with Gelfand's (2008) cross-cultural research carried out in 35 countries across the globe in which she finds a significant relationship between the country's degree of autocracy and

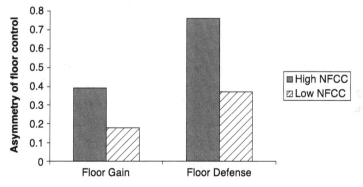

Figure 5 The effect of need for closure (NFCC) on asymmetry of floor control during group decision making (Pierro et al., 2003).

situational constraint, in turn related to inhabitants' need for closure. Although these results may reflect the notion that high need for closure individuals tend to construct autocratic societies, they may also mean that life in tight, autocratic, societies tends to engender members with a high need for closure. These two possible tendencies are not necessarily incompatible. Their existence and interrelation could be profitably probed in further research.

In addition to influencing group structure, intensified quest for uniformity under heightened need for closure tends to lead to an intolerance of diversity (Kruglanski, Shah, Pierro, & Mannetti, 2002; Shah, Kruglanski, & Thompson, 1998). Diversity is a feature that may impede the arrival at consensus, thereby reducing the group's ability to reach closure. In this vein, heightened need for closure, through the implementation of time pressure and ambient noise, has been shown to lead to a rejection of opinion deviates in a working group (Kruglanski & Webster, 1991). Elevated need for closure was also found to foster favoritism toward one's in-group, in direct proportion to its degree of homogeneity and opinion uniformity. Finally, need for closure was found to foster out-group derogation (Kruglanski et al., 2002; Shah et al., 1998), which degree was *inversely* related to the out-group's homogeneity and opinion uniformity (Kruglanski et al., 2002). These findings are consistent with the notion that high need for closure individuals are attracted to groups (whether in-groups or out-groups) that promise to offer firm shared realities to their members, affording stable cognitive closure.

The quest for stable shared reality on the part of individuals with high need for closure should express itself in conservatism and the upholding of group norms and traditions. Indeed, both political conservatism (Jost, Glaser, Kruglanski, & Sulloway, 2003a, 2003b) and the tendency to maintain stable group norms across generational cycles (Livi, 2003) were found to be related to a heightened need for closure. Chirumbolo (2002), and van Hiel, Pandelaere, and Duriez (2004) found that the relation between need for closure and conservatism was mediated by general political attitudes, notably Right Wing Authoritarianism, and Social Dominance Orientation. Roets and van Hiel (2006) found additionally that these relationships reflected both the "freezing" and the "seizing" tendencies induced by the NFCC, the latter being specifically assessed via the Decisiveness facet of the NFCC scale. Chirumbolo and Leone (2008) also found in two election studies (the 2004 European elections and the 2005 Italian Regional elections) that need for closure was linearly (and positively) related to voting along the left-right continuum. Finally, Chirumbolo, Areni, and Sensales (2004) found that Italian students high (vs. low) on the need for closure were more nationalistic, religious, exhibited a preference for right-wing political parties, reported anti-immigrant attitudes, scored lower on pluralism and multiculturalism, and preferred autocratic leadership and a centralized form of political power.

Kosic, Kruglanski, Pierro, and Mannetti (2004) found evidence that need for closure augments loyalty to one's in-group and instils a reluctance to abandon it and "defect" to alternative collectivities. Such loyalty persists to the extent that one's in-group is salient in the individuals' social environment. If, however, an alternative group's views became overridingly salient, high need for closure may in fact prompt members to switch groups. In this vein, Croat and Polish immigrants to Italy who were high (vs. low) on need for closure tended to assimilate less to the Italian culture (i.e., they maintained loyalty to their culture of origin) if their social environment at entry consisted of their co-ethnics. However, if it consisted of members of the host culture (i.e., of Italians), high (vs. low) need for closure immigrants tended more to "defect" and assimilate to the Italian culture.

Need for closure may also influence the attitudes of members of existing groups toward potential newcomers into their midst. We have already reported Chirumbolo et al.'s (2004) finding as to the anti-immigration attitudes of high (vs. low) need for closure Italians. More recently, Dechesne, Schultz, Kruglanski, Orehek, and Fishman (2008) investigated whether individuals high on the need for closure would prefer groups with impermeable (vs. permeable) boundaries. Dutch undergraduate students first completed the need for closure scale, and subsequently read a news article highlighting either the permeability or the impermeability of their college's boundaries. Participants in the impermeable condition read a passage stating that "the choice of one's university is virtually irreversible" whereas participants in the permeable condition read a passage depicting the choice of one's university as reversible. As shown in Figure 6, participants high (vs. low) on the need for closure expressed greater identification with impermeable (vs) permeable group boundaries that do not allow much traffic in and out of the group. The same pattern of results was found for liking of the group. Dechesne et al. (2008) also found that American students with high (vs. low) need for closure had more negative attitudes toward immigration into the US.

Conclusions. In summary, a great deal of research attests to the considerable role that the need for cognitive closure plays in intrapersonal, interpersonal, and group phenomena. Basically these have to do with the importance of knowledge construction processes in human affairs: At the individual level these processes affect the formation of social judgments, attitudes, and impressions. At the interpersonal

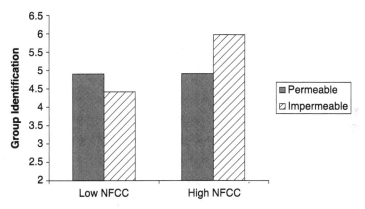

Figure 6 The effect of group permeability and need for closure (NFCC) on in-group identification (Dechesne et al., 2008).

level they enter into communication and persuasion, empathy, and negotiation behavior, and at the group level into the formation of consensus and the forging of stable social realities for the members. In all these domains, and on all these levels of analysis, the need for closure has been shown to constitute a variable with implications for major classes of social psychological phenomena.

Essentially, the need for closure paradigm addresses the *motivational* underpinnings of knowledge formation, the "why" of epistemic behavior, affecting the extent of information processing en route to a judgment, and the tendency to "seize and freeze" on judgment affording information. By contrast, the unimodel paradigm considered next "zooms in" on the *informational* aspect of the epistemic process and investigates the "how" of the epistemic process, illuminating the way in which given information exerts impact on individuals' judgments (Erb et al., 2003; Kruglanski & Thompson, 1999a, 1999b; Kruglanski et al., 2006b, 2007).

The unimodel of human judgment: The "how" of epistemic behavior

The function of rule following in lay epistemics

A basic aspect of the lay epistemic theory concerns the role of evidence in knowledge formation. As noted earlier, the lay epistemic theory assumes that all knowledge derives from evidence, broadly conceived. In other words, to construct new knowledge, or to form a new judgment the individual is assumed to use an inference rule of an "if–then" type, whereby if a given evidence E obtains, the conclusion C follows (or the hypothesis H is supported).

Although the foregoing depiction of inference as a case of syllogistic reasoning may seem deliberative, conscious, and explicit, it need be none of these. An identical mechanism may underlie processes typically considered as associative or "mechanistic." Consider the phenomenon of classical conditioning. Although it has been viewed as prototypic of associative learning, compelling evidence exists (Holyoak, Koh, & Nisbett, 1989; Rescorla, 1985; Rescorla & Holland, 1982; Rescorla & Wagner, 1972) that it is fundamentally rule based.

Thus, based on an extensive review of pertinent conditioning studies, Holyoak and colleagues (1989, p. 320) concluded that:

> representations of the environment take the form of . . . [if–then] rules that compose mental models . . . the rat's knowledge about the relation between tones and shocks might be informally represented by a rule such as "if a tone sounds in the chamber then a shock will occur, so stop other activities and crouch."

From this perspective (Holyoak et al., 1989, p. 320):

> Rules drive the system's behavior by means of a recognize–act cycle. On each cycle the conditions of rules are matched against representations of active

declarative information, which we ... term *messages*; rules with conditions that are satisfied by current messages become candidates for execution. For example, if a message representing the recent occurrence of a tone is active, the conditions of the above rule will be matched and the actions it specifies may be taken.

Note the affinity of this conception to the basic syllogistic sequence: The "rule" assumed by Holyoak and colleagues (1989) is analogous to the major premise, and the "message" that "matches the rule" is analogous to the minor premise, i.e., instantiation of the antecedent term in the major premise, warranting the inference of the consequent term.

Whereas the work reviewed by Holyoak et al. (1989) concerned the phenomena of classical conditioning, a recent integration of evaluative conditioning phenomena attests that it too is "propositional"; that is, rule-following (Mitchell, De Houwer, & Lovibond, in press). In evaluative conditioning a neutral CS (e.g., a book) is presented concomitantly with an affectively laden UCS (e.g., a smiling, or a pouting face); subsequently, it is found that the CS acquired the affective valence of the UCS. Although evaluative conditioning differs in a number of important respects from classical conditioning (Baeyens, Crombez, Van den Bergh, & Eelen, 1988; Walther, Nagengast, & Trasselli, 2005) the rule-following nature of the conditioning process appears common to both. As Mitchell et al. (in press) put it in reference to evaluative conditioning "... associative learning results, ... in humans ... not from the automatic formation of links, but from the operation of controlled reasoning processes" (p. 6) in which "The process of reasoning about the relationship between events produces ... declarative, propositional knowledge about those events ..." (p. 14), hence "[conditional, if–then] ... links that specify how the two events are related" (p. 15, parentheses added).

It is noteworthy that the rules involved in conditioning may be applied in given informational contexts with considerable ease and alacrity. The notion that "automatic" phenomena in the domain of (motor or cognitive) skill acquisition involve a routinization of "if–then" sequences has been central to Anderson's (1983) ACT* model that Smith (1984, 1989; Smith & Branscombe, 1988; Smith, Branscombe, & Bormann, 1988) extended to the realm of social judgment. That research has demonstrated that social judgments represent a special case of procedural learning based on practice that strengthens the "if–then" components resulting in increased efficiency (or "automaticity").

Awareness

Efficiency implies, in turn, a lowered need to commit attentional resources to the carrying out of social judgments. In William James' (1890, p. 496) felicitous phrasing "consciousness deserts all processes when it can no longer be of use." According to his parsimony principle of consciousness, routinization removes the need for conscious control of the process, rendering awareness of the process superfluous. In a related vein, Logan (1992) suggested that automatization of certain skills effects a shift of attention to higher organizational levels.

It is in this sense, then, that some judgmental phenomena, mediated by well-routinized "if–then" rules, may take place outside conscious awareness. Helmholtz (1910/2000) discussed the notion of unconscious *inference* in the realm of perception. More recently, social cognitive work on spontaneous trait inferences (Newman & Uleman, 1989; Uleman, 1987) suggests that lawful (i.e., rule-following) inferences presumably can occur without explicit inferential intentions, and without conscious awareness of making an inference. "The spontaneous trait inference that John is 'clumsy' on the basis of the information that he stepped on Stephanie's foot while dancing" (Newman & Uleman, 1989, p. 156), surely requires the inference rule "if stepping on a dancing partner's foot, then clumsy" or some variant thereof: A person who did not subscribe to that premise would be unlikely to reach that particular conclusion.

Unconscious inferences are also exemplified by Schwarz and Clore's (1996) "feelings as information" model. A mood state may be mistakenly attributed to a given cause. For instance, a positive mood engendered by pleasant weather may be treated as a basis for an inference of a general life satisfaction (Schwarz & Clore, 1983, Schwarz, Servay, & Kumpf, 1985) based on an "if–then" rule linking one's feeling state with general satisfaction. As Schwarz and Clore (1996, p. 437) summarized it ". . . reliance on . . . experiences [for various inferences] generally does not involve conscious attribution."

Thus a variety of evidence and theoretical considerations converge on the notion that judgments (whether assessed directly or through their behavioral manifestations) are rule based and, in this sense, derived from "evidence". To make a judgment is to go beyond the "information given" (Bartlett, 1932; Bruner, 1973), by using it as testimony for a conclusion in accordance with an "if–then" statement to which the individual subscribes. Such implicational structure appears to characterize explicit human inferences (Anderson, 1983), implicit conclusion drawing (Schwarz & Clore, 1996), conditioning responses in animal learning studies (Holyoak et al., 1989; Rescorla & Wagner, 1972), and perceptual judgments of everyday objects (Gregory, 1997; Pizlo, 2001; Rock, 1983). The elementary "if–then" form appears essential to all such inferences, whether conscious or nonconscious, instantaneous or delayed, innate or learned. It is a fundamental building block from which all epistemic edifices are constructed.[3]

In describing the knowledge (or judgment) formation process as syllogistic, we do not mean to suggest that individuals necessarily engage in explicit syllogistic reasoning (e.g., Newell & Simon, 1972). Nor do we mean to imply that individuals are familiar with the intricacies of formal logic—a proposition belied by over 30 years of work on the Wason (1966) problem among others. For instance, people might incorrectly treat an *implicational* "If A then B" relation as an *equivalence* relation, "Only if A then B," suggesting that also "if B then A" (which was not originally intended). We also accept that often people may be better able to recognize the "correct" implicational properties of concrete statements in familiar domains rather than those of abstract, unfamiliar statements (Evans, 1989). None of it is inconsistent with the notion that persons generally reason from subjectively relevant rules of implicational "if–then" format (see also Abelson, 1968; Mischel & Shoda, 1995).

Parametric determinants of informational impact

Given the syllogistic structure of knowledge formation from evidence to conclusion, it is possible now to analyze the conditions under which the information given in a specific context would affect the individual's judgments. As noted earlier, a syllogism includes a major premise and a minor premise that jointly yield a conclusion. In this sense, the "information given" is the minor premise, which affirms the antecedent condition of a pre-existing inference rule serving as a major premise and mediating the road from evidence to conclusion. Accordingly, in order that a given piece of information exerted judgmental impact the individual should subscribe to the major premise linking a given antecedent condition and a given consequent in an "if X then Y" fashion. Subscribing to an inference rule is a matter of degree reflecting the strength of belief in the conditional association linking a given X with a given Y. The continuum of belief strength defines the *parameter of subjective relevance* of information X to conclusion Y.

However, a general subscription to an inference rule merely defines an *availability* of such rule in a person's memory (Higgins, 1996). In addition, the rule needs to be momentarily *accessible* to a person, or to be activated from memory. In turn, rule activation may be more or less difficult depending on its prior history of activation, i.e., its frequency and recency of activation (Higgins, 1996). The difficulty issue also arises in reference to an individual's ability to recognize that a given, situationally present, piece of information *matches* an inference rule and in this sense constitutes a minor premise that jointly with a major premise is capable of yielding a conclusion. Specifically, the information may be less or more salient in a given context, constituting a weaker or stronger signal against the background of irrelevant noise. In addition, the information may be presented in a more or less lengthy format and to be less or more difficult to decipher. All these may determine the difficulty of recognizing that the information given is relevant to a requisite judgment, or represents a minor premise in the appropriate syllogism. The *difficulty of the inference task* (including the activation of the major premise from memory, and recognition that the information given represents the minor premise), defines another parameter that affects the degree to which the information given would impact the judgment rendered. Specifically, the greater the difficulty of the inference task, the greater should be the amount of cognitive and motivational resources needed to perform it.

As the foregoing discussion suggests, it is useful to distinguish conceptually between *potential relevance* of X to Y reflecting the degree to which the "If X then Y" inferential rule has been generally learned and believed in, and *contextual* or *perceived relevance* reflecting the degree to which X is recognized as relevant to Y in a given situation. Beyond degree of belief, perceived relevance is affected by accessibility of the rule, difficulty of identifying the X and individual's motivational and cognitive resources available for overcoming the difficulty.

Resource availability as a determinant of informational impact. The relationship between the availability of processing resources and the ability to handle demanding inferential tasks has implications for the kinds of information that would affect judgments in different circumstances: Under conditions of limited processing resources, the easier-to-process information is likely to be utilized and to affect judgments to a greater extent than the difficult-to-process information. However, under conditions of ample processing resources, the difficult-to-process information would be utilized more *if* it appears to be more relevant to the judgmental task than the easy-to-process information. The foregoing assumptions afforded a reconceptualization of a considerable body of research findings formerly interpreted from a dual mode perspective on social judgment (see Chaiken & Trope, 1999).

It is important to disavow here any implication that the presence or absence of cognitive resources is systematically related to the quality of cognitive inference performance. Thus we assume that highly routinized and accessible rules (major premises) can be processed with minimal resources when matched with the appropriate situational information (minor premises). Furthermore, we intend no implication that the presence of resources would lead individuals to rely on objectively "better" rules or even on subjectively "better" (more relevant) rules. All we are asserting is that, in the absence of resources, individuals would rely more on easy-to-process information, whereas in the presence of ample resources they would also entertain the use of more difficult information. These notions are illustrated in research reviewed below.

Persuasion research. A pervasive finding in persuasion research has been that "peripheral" or "heuristic" cues exert judgmental impact (i.e., effect change in recipients' attitudes or opinions) under conditions of low processing resources (e.g., where recipients' interest in the task is low, when they are cognitively busy or distracted, when their need for cognition is low, etc.). By contrast, "message arguments" typically exerted their effects under high processing resources (e.g., high interest in the task, or ample cognitive capacity). However, in reviews of these studies (Erb et al., 2003; Kruglanski, Pierro, Mannetti, Erb, & Chun, 2007; Kruglanski & Thompson, 1999a, 1999b; Kruglanski, Thompson, & Spiegel, 1999; Pierro, Mannetti, Erb, Spiegel, & Kruglanski, 2005) it became apparent that often in persuasion research the type of the information (i.e., "peripheral" or "heuristic" cues versus message arguments) was confounded with task demands. Because the message arguments were typically lengthier, more complex, and placed later in the informational sequence, their processing may have imposed higher processing demands than the processing of "cues" that were invariably brief, simple, and presented upfront. When these confoundings were experimentally removed, the previously found differences between conditions under which the "cues" versus the "message arguments" (or vice versa) exerted their persuasive effects were eliminated (Erb et al., 2003; Kruglanski et al., 2007; Kruglanski & Thompson, 1999a; Pierro et al., 2005).

One of the most important contributions of the dual-process models was the finding that when persuasion occurred as the result of "central" or "systematic" information processing, defined as *message* or *issue processing*, the resulting attitude change was more persistent over time and was more strongly related to subsequent behaviors. However this research always presented source information *briefly and upfront*, with message arguments coming later and being presented in a *lengthier and more complex* format. This research design led to the conclusion that persuasion as a result of "central" or "systematic" processing of message arguments led to greater attitude persistence and a stronger attitude–behavior link. According to the unimodel framework, however, source information and message arguments serve the same role as evidence in forming judgments. Therefore any persuasion as a result of extensive processing of information, including source information, should lead to attitude persistence and behavior consistent with the attitude.

To test this notion, Pierro, Mannetti, Orehek, and Kruglanski (2008) presented participants with either brief (50 words) or lengthy (full-page) source information. The source, an education consultant, was described as either expert (a full professor of cognitive psychology at a prestigious university specializing in curriculum development) or inexpert (a professor at a low-prestige technical institute studying the psychology of tourism). Participants then read a passage written by the source arguing for the adoption of a new policy that would require participation in psychology experiments for students. Student participants were told either that this policy would be implemented soon (high involvement) or that it would be implemented following their graduation (low involvement). Immediately after reading the persuasive message, only when the source information was lengthy (but not brief) were participants in the high-involvement condition more in favor of the policy when it was presented by an expert (vs. inexpert) source. However, only when the source information was short (but not lengthy) were participants in the low-involvement condition more in favor of the policy when it was presented by an expert (vs. inexpert) source. This result replicates prior findings by Kruglanski and colleagues (for recent review, see Kruglanski et al., 2007).

Despite the fact that the short source information did have immediate persuasive effect under low involvement, this effect did not persist as much as did the effect of lengthy source information under high involvement. Specifically, participants in the high-involvement condition who received lengthy (vs. short) source information displayed greater attitude persistence and intentions to participate in experiments 3 weeks later. Finally, Figure 7 shows that participants in the high-involvement condition and who received lengthy (vs. brief) source information were more likely to engage in attitude-consistent behaviors by participating in an experiment they had been invited to attend in the expert (but not an inexpert) source condition. No such differences were found for participants in the low-involvement condition with an expert source, or the high-involvement condition with an inexpert source. This behavior occurred a full month after participants had received the persuasive appeal, suggesting that attitude change as a result of extensively processed *source information* (often considered peripheral and heuristic) can result in persistent attitudes and a strong attitude–behavior link.

The persistence of attitude change following extensive processing of source information suggests that it is the extent of information processing rather than the type of information (source vs. message argument) that determines the stability of attitude change. Presumably, extensive processing of evidence warranting the adoption of a given attitude (i.e., source information or message argument) creates many linkages between the attitude concept and information stored in memory.

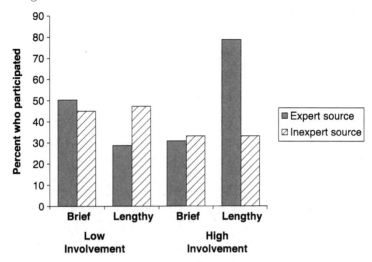

Figure 7 The effect of issue involvement, source expertise, and length of source information on participation behavior (Pierro et al., 2008).

These linkages may later facilitate retrieval of the attitude, rendering it readily activated and highly accessible, hence increasing its potential to guide behavior (Fazio, 1990).

Dispositional attributions. A major question posed by attribution researchers concerned the process whereby a given behavior performed by an actor is causally ascribed to the situational context, or to the actor's disposition. In this vein, Trope and Alfieri (1997) found that ambiguous behavior tends to be disambiguated by assimilation to the context in which it is taking place. For instance, an ambiguous facial expression is likely to be perceived as sad if the context was sad as well (e.g., a funeral), and as happy if the context was happy (e.g., a party). However, once the behavior had been identified, and the question of its causal origin was pondered, the context plays a subtractive (rather than an assimilative) role in determining the behavior's attribution. Specifically, the role of the context is subtracted to determine the role of the actor's disposition in producing the behavior. For instance, if the context was sad, an individual's sad expression would not be attributed to the actor's dispositional sadness because other persons in the same situation would probably be sad as well.

Of present interest, Trope and Alfieri (1997) found that the assimilative process of behavior identification was independent of cognitive load, whereas the subtractive process of dispositional attribution was undermined by load. These investigators also found that invalidating the information on which the behavior identification process was based, by stating that the actor was unaware of the potential situational demands on their behavior, did not alter these identifications, whereas invalidating that same information did alter the dispositional judgments. Two alternative explanations may account for these results: (1) that the two processes are qualitatively distinct, (2) that for some reason the behavior identification task in Trope and Alfieri's (1997) work was less demanding than the dispositional attribution task.

Consistent with the latter interpretation, Trope and Gaunt (2000) discovered that when demands associated with the dispositional attribution task were lowered (e.g., by increasing the salience of the information given), the subtraction of context from dispositional attributions was no longer affected by load. Furthermore, Chun, Spiegel, and Kruglanski (2002) found that when the behavior identification task was made more difficult (e.g., by decreasing the salience of the information given) it was also undermined by load. Under those conditions, too, invalidating the information on which the behavioral identifications were based did alter these identifications. These findings are consistent with the present notion that, when a given inferential task (e.g., of "behavior identification" or of "dispositional attribution") is sufficiently demanding, it is exigent of cognitive resources and can be undermined by load.

Base-rate neglect. Earlier, we suggested that the judgmental impact of information depends on individuals appreciating its (subjective) relevance to the question at stake, and that such appreciation, in turn, depends on the relation between inferential task demands and processing resources. Jointly, these notions are capable of casting a new light on the problem of base-rate neglect, and on conditions under which statistical versus "heuristic" information may impact individuals' judgments.

In the original demonstrations of base-rate neglect (Kahneman & Tversky, 1973) the base-rate information was typically presented briefly, via a single sentence, and upfront. By contrast, the individuating ("representativeness") information was presented subsequently via a relatively lengthy vignette. If one assumes that participants in such studies had sufficient motivation and cognitive capacity to process the entire informational "package" with which they were presented, they might have been challenged to fully process the later, lengthier, and hence more demanding vignette information and to have given it considerable weight in the ultimate judgment. This is analogous to the finding in persuasion studies that the lengthier, later-appearing, message argument information but not the brief, upfront-appearing, "cue" information, has impact under ample processing resources (e.g., of high processing motivation and cognitive capacity). If the above is true, we should be able to "move" base-rate neglect around by reversing the relative length and ordinal position in the informational sequence of the base-rate and the individuating ("representativeness") information. A series of studies by Chun and Kruglanski (2006) attempted just that.

In our first study we replicated the typical lawyer–engineer paradigm (Kahneman & Tversky, 1973) in one condition by presenting brief and upfront base-rate information followed by lengthier individuating information. In another condition we reversed these relations by presenting brief individuating information first followed by lengthier and more complex base-rate information. To make the information complex and lengthy, the overall base-rate of lawyers was decomposed into base-rates of various sub-categories. For example, rather than being told that engineers made up 70% of the population and lawyers made up 30% of the population, participants were told that the population consisted of 14% electrical engineers,

6% chemical engineers, 9% divorce lawyers, 4% nuclear engineers, 10% civil engineers, 11% criminal lawyers, 12% sound engineers, 8% genetic engineers, 10% trade lawyers, and 16% mechanical engineers. As predicted, the former condition replicated the typical finding of base-rate neglect, whereas the latter condition revealed considerable base-rate utilization.

A subsequent study added a manipulation of cognitive load in which participants rehearsed a nine-digit number while reading the information. As shown in Figure 8, the former results were now replicated in the low load condition, but were reversed in the high load condition. Under high cognitive load, when the base-rate information was presently briefly upfront, participants judged the likelihood of Dan being an engineer to be greater in the 70% engineer condition as compared to the 30% engineer condition. However, there was no significant difference between the two engineer conditions in the low cognitive load condition. This shows a use of the base-rate information while under load if the base-rates are easy to process. In contrast, when the base-rate information was lengthy and presented at the end, participants under load did not judge the likelihood of Dan being an engineer differently in the 70% as compared to the 30% condition. However, participants not under load did judge the likelihood of Dan being an engineer as significantly higher in the 70% condition as compared to the 30% condition. This demonstrates the use of base-rates when participants are not under load when the base-rates are difficult to process. Regardless of information type, under load the brief upfront information was utilized more than the lengthy subsequent information, whereas in the absence of load, the lengthy and subsequent information was utilized more.

To summarize then, evidence across domains (i.e., of persuasion, attribution, and judgment under uncertainty) supports the hypothesis that the higher the demands imposed by the inferential task at hand, the greater must be the processing resources if the information given is to exert judgmental impact commensurate with its potential relevance.

Relative relevance, task demands, and processing resources. Often the different types of information presented to research participants have (inadvertently) differed in their subjective relevance to these persons. For instance, in the domain of persuasion Pierro, Mannetti, Kruglanski, and Sleeth-Keppler (2004) carried out an extensive content analysis of experimental materials in persuasion studies to conclude that, typically, the "cues" presented to participants were judged as less relevant to the judgmental (attitudinal) topic than were the "message arguments". Recall that in much persuasion research the "cues" but not the "message arguments" exerted judgmental impact under low processing resources, whereas the "message arguments" did so under high processing resources. From the present perspective, it is possible to generalize these findings in terms of the following derivations:

(a) Given ample processing resources, the *more relevant* information (e.g., the "message arguments" in much persuasion research) would have a greater judgmental impact than the *less relevant* information; however (b) given limited processing resources (relative to the task demands) the *easier to process* information

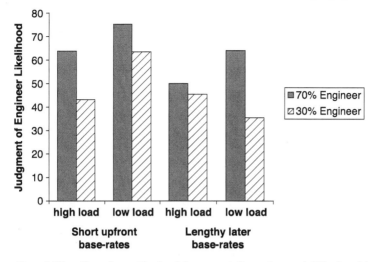

Figure 8 The effect of cognitive load, base-rate information, and difficulty of base-rate processing on likelihood estimation judgments (Chun & Kruglanski, 2006).

(of above-threshold relevance) would have a greater judgmental impact than the *more difficult to process* information.

Pierro and colleagues (2004) tested these notions in three experimental studies based on the same research design in which (1) the relevance sequence (early information less relevant than subsequent information, or vice versa) and (2) processing motivation (high, low) were manipulated orthogonally. However, the studies differed in contents of the information given. In the first study, both the early and the later information consisted of message arguments; in the second study both consisted of heuristic information (namely, pertinent to the "consensus heuristic") and in the third study, contrary to the typical sequence in persuasion research, the early information consisted of message arguments and the later information, of heuristic cues (again regarding consensus).

All three experiments yielded the same general result: When the later, and hence the more difficult to process, information was more subjectively relevant to the judgmental topic than the early information, it exerted judgmental (persuasive impact) only under high motivation conditions but not under low motivation conditions. By contrast, the early, less relevant information exerted its effect only under low motivation but not under high motivation. A very different pattern obtained where the early information was more relevant than the latter information. Here the impact of the early information invariably overrode that of the later information: Under low processing motivation this may have been so because the earlier information was easier to process than the later information, and under high processing motivation—because the early information was in fact more relevant than the later information.

Metacognitive inferences: Ease versus content of retrieval. In recent years social psychologists became increasingly interested in the problem of metacognitive inferences (for reviews see Jost, Kruglanski, & Nelson, 1998; Petty, Brinol, Tormala, & Wegener, 2007). One of the most researched metacognitive phenomena of social psychological interest has been the "ease of retrieval" effect in self-perception. The fascination with this phenomenon goes back to Tversky and Kahneman's (1973) classic work on the availability heuristic pertaining to the "ease with which instances or associations come to mind" (p. 208). In a well-known follow-up on Tversky and Kahneman's work, Schwarz et al. (1991) attempted to disentangle the experience of "ease" from the number of instances recovered because of the felt ease. For instance, in one of the Schwarz et al. (1991) studies participants were asked to retrieve either 6 or 12 instances of behaving assertively. Presumably it is easier to retrieve a few instances of a given behavior than many instances. Hence, if ease of retrieval is responsible for the availability effect, participants should perceive themselves as more assertive after recalling 6 instances of assertive behavior than after recalling 12 such instances. That is precisely what Schwarz et al. (1991) found, suggesting that the metacognitive experience of ease or fluency can serve as an important determinant of social judgments.

Following this seminal research, a variety of further studies sought to identify the boundary conditions for the ease of retrieval effect and to pinpoint the circumstances under which alternative sources of information (such as the content versus amount of retrieved information) would have a stronger judgmental effect than ease of retrieval (for reviews see Petty et al., 2007; Schwarz, 2004). Although a number of such boundary conditions were empirically identified, work on this topic stopped short of providing general theoretical understanding of circumstances under which a given information source (rather than its alternatives) would affect judgments. The unimodel affords such understanding. From its perspective, any contextually given information may affect judgments if it fits (as a minor premise) an inference rule (a major premise) to which an individual subscribes.

Support for this possibility was recently obtained in several experimental studies by Igou, Fishbach, and Kruglanski (2008). Specifically, this work demonstrated that the degree to which ease of retrieval versus the amount of instances retrieved affect social judgments depends on (1) the perceived validity of the inference rule linking *ease* of retrieval or the amount of instances retrieved to the corresponding trait, (2) saliency of the information concerning ease or amount of instances, and (3) accessibility of the ease = trait, and the amount = trait rules. For example, participants in one study were asked to rate the friendliness of targets based on the information provided. They were told that three people had been asked to recall instances in which they had been friendly. The information regarding the ease of retrieving relevant information, the amount of information retrieved, and the content of the retrieved information was manipulated. One target person ostensibly found recalling friendly behaviors to be either "easy" or "difficult," another either listed "many" or "only a few" behaviors, and the third recalled behaviors that were either "very friendly" or "only somewhat friendly." Participants rated the target person as friendlier in cases in which the target found it easy to recall behaviors, recalled many behaviors, or were very friendly. However, these differences were more pronounced (and were statistically significant only) when the critical pieces of information were underlined in the text, making the relevant piece of information salient.

Conclusions. Growing evidence from a variety of domains (persuasion, attribution, judgment under uncertainty, person perception) supports the unimodel's derivations that the subjective relevance of information determines its impact on judgments, that the appreciation of subjective relevance depends on the relation between task demands and (cognitive and motivational) resources, and that as a function of resources information may affect judgments either in accordance with its relative relevance or with its relative ease of processing.

Focusing on the concept of "evidence" highlighted by lay epistemic theory affords an integration of a large set of dual-process models of social judgments that assumed binary, qualitatively distinct, modes of processing. Such integration is achieved by highlighting the critical importance of several judgmental parameters in determining the impact of the information given on individuals' judgments and impressions, and by separating (both conceptually and empirically) the values of such parameters (e.g., information's degree of subjective relevance, or experienced difficulty of processing) from informational contents with which they were often confounded in prior research (for a more extensive discussion see Kruglanski et al., 2007).

Epistemic authority: The "who" of epistemic behavior

According to lay epistemic theory the construct of evidence functions in the same way (i.e., syllogistically) irrespective of the specific contents of evidence. This doesn't mean, however, that all types of evidence have equal status. Different individuals may hold different assumptions about the conditional (if–then) relations between conceptual categories; hence they may differ in what to them constitutes compelling evidence for a given proposition. For an expert car mechanic an unusual noise emanating from the engine may compellingly signal a problem with the carburettor, whereas for a mechanically inexperienced individual this particular noise may have little informative value. In general, people's "evidential" assumptions in specific domains may vary widely depending on their background knowledge. Because people's concerns typically extend beyond their domains of expertise they may often rely on other people as knowledge providers. Thus a broad category of evidence refers to other people's opinions and is denoted by lay epistemic theory's construct of *epistemic authority* (Kruglanski, 1989; Kruglanski et al., 2005), that is, to a source to whom an individual turns to obtain knowledge on various topics (Kruglanski, 1989). In other words, individuals may subscribe to general "if X then Y" rules in which the antecedent X denotes a given epistemic authority, e.g., of an expert ("If Expert says so then it is Correct"), the group ("If the Group believes so, then it is Correct"), or the self ("If I believe so, then it is Correct").

The concept of "epistemic authority" is akin to the notion of *source credibility* (encompassing a combination of perceived expertise and trustworthiness) and it addresses the extent to which an individual is prepared to rely on a source's information and to accept it as evidence for the veracity of the source's pronouncements. The ascribed epistemic authority of various sources in the individuals' social environments may vary and the authority of a given source may vary across domains as well as across individuals' life-span developmental phases.

The features that identify a source as an epistemic authority can be *general*, having to do with seniority (for example, of an elder), a role (for example, of a priest, a leader, or a teacher), level of education (for example, a PhD), appearance in print (for example, in a book or a newspaper), or *specific*, as in assigning epistemic authority to a particular person, or a particular newspaper (say, the *New York Times*).

Furthermore, a source may exert influence in numerous life domains, serving as a *generalized epistemic authority*; alternatively, it may influence only a specific area (for example, cardiology, statistics, or auto mechanics) where it is thought to possess valid knowledge. In the former role we may find priests, therapists, or parents, whereas in the latter role we may find specialists in certain well-defined fields. Individuals may differ widely in their reliance on various epistemic authorities and in their extent of such reliance across domains. Some people may accept the judgment of a source (a rabbi, a priest, a psychiatrist, or a teacher) in any life domain; others may consult a source with regard to matters related to its specific domain of competence, and to consult other sources in alternative life domains.

Source characteristics (such as expertise) were often implied to offer somewhat inferior counsel as to correct judgments, and were treated as suboptimal heuristics used only when one's processing resources were depleted and when one's "sufficiency threshold" of required confidence was low (Chaiken, Liberman, & Eagly, 1989). In contrast, according to the present theory epistemic authority of some sources (e.g., a religious prophet, a parent, a political leader, or the printed word) might be extremely powerful, often to the point of overriding other types of information and exerting a determinative influence on individuals' judgments and corresponding behaviors. Furthermore, whereas in prior treatments of source credibility effects, the discussion centered on sources *external* to the self (cf. Chaiken et al., 1989; Hovland, Janis, & Kelley, 1953; Kruglanski & Thompson, 1999a, 1999b; Petty & Cacioppo, 1986), the present theory considers the *self* as a particularly important target of epistemic authority assignments.

Research summarized in the paper by Kruglanski et al. (2005) has revealed (1) developmental trends involving a decline in authority assigned to the primary caregivers, coupled with an increase in epistemic authority attributed to the *self*, and involving an increase in differentiation and specificity of epistemic authorities across domains; (2) stable individual differences in epistemic authority effects; (3) a hierarchical structure and operation of epistemic authorities; (4) the relative role of the self and external sources as perceived epistemic authorities.

Developmental trends

Raviv, Bar-Tal, Raviv, and Houminer (1990) assessed children's attribution of epistemic authority to their *mothers, fathers, teachers*, and *friends*. They investigated kindergarten children (4–5 years old), first graders (6–7 years old), and third graders (8–9 years old). Several significant trends appeared in these data, yielding the following pattern of interest: during childhood (i.e., during the ages 4–10), (a) the perception of parents as epistemic authorities remains relatively stable, with decreases in a few knowledge areas, (b) the perception of the teacher as an epistemic authority remains stable with an increase in the area of science, (c) the perceived epistemic authority of friends increases in the social domain.

Raviv et al. (1990) also found that across age groups the perception of teachers and friends varied more as a function of knowledge areas than the perception of parents. The children selected teachers and friends as epistemic authorities in certain knowledge areas only, whereas the parents tended to be perceived as overall authorities across domains, possibly as a function of continued material dependence on the parents inducing a motivation to view them as all-powerful and knowledgeable.

Individual differences in the distribution of epistemic authority assignments across sources

Individuals differ systematically in their distributional profiles of epistemic authority across sources: these differences, in turn, affect individuals' search for, and use of, information. Bar (1983) devised a Hierarchy of Epistemic Authorities Test designed to investigate the epistemic authority assigned by Israeli college students to various sources. This test revealed intriguing gender differences in epistemic authority assignments. In domains prototypically classified as masculine (such as work and finances) women viewed their *peer group* as a more dominant epistemic authority than did men, whereas in domains prototypically classified as feminine (social life, interpersonal relations, children's education) men endowed their *peer group* with greater epistemic authority than did women. Possibly then, where one's own epistemic authority is low (as may be the case for men in the feminine domains, and for women in masculine domains) one's reference group gains in epistemic authoritativeness as compared with domains where one's self-ascribed epistemic authority is high.

The hierarchical organization of epistemic authorities. In Bar's (1983) research individuals' epistemic authorities predicted these people's behavior in an "information-purchasing" task: Participants were willing to pay greater amounts of (hypothetical) money for information from their highest (domain-specific) authority than for information from lower epistemic authorities. This and other findings suggest the hierarchic organization of epistemic authorities. Bar (1983, 1999) found that individuals turn first to information provided by sources whom they regard as highest in epistemic authority, that they process such information more extensively, that they derive from it greater confidence, and that they tend more to act in accordance with its perceived implications.

Bar (1999, Study 2) also inquired whether epistemic authority effects might not represent the workings of heuristic cues relied upon only in the absence of sufficient processing resources. To that end, Bar superimposed on her product choice procedure orthogonal manipulations of time pressure (high versus low) and evaluation apprehension (high versus low). Contrary to the suboptimal heuristics hypothesis the foregoing effects held across variations in time pressure and evaluation apprehension: Regardless of the presence/absence of time pressure and/or of evaluation apprehension participants (1) tended to first open the window on a PC pertaining to their dominant (versus non-dominant) epistemic authority, (2) were more confident in their decisions if those were based on the recommendations of a dominant (vs. a non-dominant) epistemic authority, and (3) tended to spend more time on information contained in a "window" belonging to their dominant (vs. non-dominant) epistemic authority. These results argue against the notion that epistemic authority functions merely as a "peripheral" or "heuristic" cue that affords low confidence and is used only when individuals' processing resources or motivational engagement are low.

Effects of self-ascribed epistemic authority: External information search under need for closure. A unique aspect of the epistemic authority construct is that it treats identically the *self* and *external sources* of information. Indeed, several recent studies looked at informational effects as a function of the self-ascribed epistemic authority. In one such study, Pierro and Mannetti (2004, cited in Kruglanski et al., 2005) measured the strength of individuals' self-ascribed epistemic authority in the highly specialized domain of cell phones. To that end, they constructed a 13-item scale including questions such as "I truly have considerable knowledge about different types of cell phones," "I can say a great many things about technical specs of different cell phones," "I can offer people useful advice regarding the purchase of a cell phone." Pierro and Mannetti (2004) also assessed their participants' dispositional need for cognitive closure. The main dependent variable of interest was participants' readiness to search for information from external sources in case they entertained the purchase of a cell phone. It was found that the higher the individuals' *self-ascribed epistemic authority* in a domain, the less external information they purported to seek.

Of greater interest, the tendency to seek external information was moderated by the need for cognitive closure. For individuals with low self-ascribed epistemic authority, the higher their need for closure, the stronger their tendency to engage in an external information search. For individuals with high self-ascribed epistemic authority, the higher their need for closure, the lower their tendency to engage in an external search, and presumably the higher their tendency to rely on their own experience and experts. In other words, under the pressure for cognitive closure individuals are forced to choose, and to discriminate more acutely between their various epistemic authorities in selecting the source they trust the most.

Self-ascribed epistemic authority and learning from experience. Among the most interesting implications of the epistemic authority construct are those concerning *learning from experience*. The concept of "experience" has long been privileged in psychological theory. The use of experiential learning in training and education has been inspired by John Dewey's (1916, 1958) instructional philosophy, Carl Rogers' (1951, 1967) person-centered approach to therapy, and humanistic psychology more generally (e.g., Shafer, 1978). In social psychology, Fazio and Zanna (1981) suggested that attitudes acquired via direct experience with the attitude object are the strongest, and most tightly related to behavior. Yet these authors also hinted at the possibility of *moderators* that qualify the power of experience in shaping attitudes. As they put it (Fazio & Zanna, 1981, p. 184):

> An attitude formed by indirect means could conceivably also be held with extreme confidence, and, hence, be more predictive of behavior than a direct experience attitude. For example, a child's attitude toward members of a given ethnic or racial group may be held with great confidence, even though formed indirectly because of his or her parents' extreme credibility.

This quote suggests that experience *may not* constitute a superior base of knowledge under all conditions. Yet Fazio and Zanna (1981) stop short of identifying the conditions under which direct experience will be less capable of shaping attitudes. The concept of self-ascribed epistemic authority may be helpful in this regard.

From this perspective, whether or not an individual would treat her or his personal experience as a reliable knowledge base may depend on this person's self-ascribed capability to draw reliable conclusions from the experience, or on her or his self-ascribed epistemic authority in a domain. In the absence of such authority a person may fail to draw confident knowledge from the experience. An individual may speak English all her or his life without deriving the principles of English grammar from this experience; she or he may drink a wide range of wines over the years without forming notions about the different varietals or vintages; or play tennis on a weekly basis without forming notions about the proper strokes, strategies, and tactics of this game.

Our analysis suggests that the extent to which individuals tend to draw confident conclusions from any type of information is related to their assignment of authority to the information source. When the information consists of one's own experience, the source simply is oneself. In these circumstances, the higher one's self-ascribed epistemic authority, the more readily one may trust one's own interpretation of information, and the more one might be able to "benefit" from the experience. However, when the information is interpreted by an external communicator (e.g., a teacher or a parent), the individual's tendency to accept the interpretation may partially depend on the perceived gap in epistemic authority between the source and the self. When the authority imputed to the source is considerably higher than that imputed to the self, the source's pronouncements are likely to be attended to closely and/or be assigned considerable weight. However, when the assigned authorities are more nearly equal, the source's statements might not be taken as seriously because of a sense that there is little the source could contribute over and above one's own ability to process the information.

In other words, a "reverence effect" may be expected whereby pronouncements by an external source will have greater impact on persons whose perceived *authority gap* between themselves and the source is large rather than small. In a study designed to investigate these notions, Ellis and Kruglanski (1992) assessed their participants' self-ascribed epistemic authority in mathematics via a questionnaire specifically designed for this purpose. Participants also responded to the numerical aptitude test (Cattell & Epstein, 1975) to serve as a control measure for their actual maths ability, and they filled out a post-experimental questionnaire designed to assess their perceptions of their own and the instructor's epistemic authority in mathematics.

The mathematical learning task employed in this research consisted of multiplication problems in which some numbers were replaced by letters. The participants' task was to substitute the numbers for the letters. These substitutions were carried out in accordance with five arithmetic rules that participants needed to learn in the course of the experiment. Participants were randomly assigned to one of three experimental conditions: In the *experiential* condition they were given self-instruction booklets with exercises related to the five arithmetic rules. In the *instructional principles* condition the experimenter was introduced as a PhD in mathematics, and he explicitly articulated the relevant mathematical principles. In the intermediate, *instructional-examples*, condition the instructor solved the problems on the board *and* stated the arithmetic principle underlying each solution.

Following these procedures, participants took a performance test on the principles they had just been taught. Participants in the two instructional conditions were additionally asked to estimate the gap in ability between themselves and the instructor. The results of this research indicated that method of instruction significantly interacted with participants' self-ascribed epistemic authority (SAEA). The results are shown in Figure 9. Controlling for participants' actual mathematical ability, in the *experiential* condition participants with a high SAEA did significantly better than participants with a low SAEA. In the *instructional principles* condition the low SAEA participants tended to do better than their high SAEA counterparts, and in the intermediate, *instructional-examples* condition the high and low SAEA participants did not differ in their performance.

In the two instructional conditions participants with a high SAEA perceived the gap between their own and the instructor's ability as significantly lower than did participants with a low SAEA. Of greater interest, in both instructional conditions

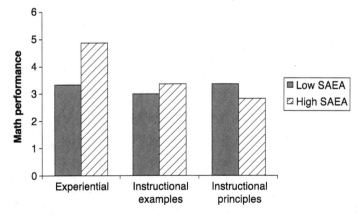

Figure 9 The effect of self-ascribed epistemic authority (SAEA) and instructional condition on maths performance (Ellis & Kruglanski, 1992).

participants who perceived a large gap between themselves and the instructor did better in both instructional conditions than participants who perceived a smaller gap. A large gap indicates that the source's relative epistemic authority (compared to one's own) is considerable. This may turn the recipient into a "true believer," enhancing her or his readiness to accept the source's conclusions.

These findings identify an important boundary condition on the efficacy of experience as a mediator of learning. It appears that in order to be able to learn from experience individuals need to believe in their ability to draw inferences from the experience; that is, possess high self-ascribed epistemic authority in a domain. It is of particular interest that self-ascribed epistemic authority is empirically distinct from actual ability in a domain. In the study described here the correlation between the two, though significant, was relatively low ($r = .36$), and the interaction between SAEA and method of instruction remained significant, even after controlling for actual mathematical ability. Finally, it is of interest that in the instructional learning conditions participants whose perceived gap between their own and the instructor's ability was large (vs. small) did significantly better at the mathematical learning task, attesting to a "reverence effect" whereby the impact of an external source is greater if its authority is high relative to one's own perceived authority.

Summary. Although according to lay epistemic theory all evidence functions in the same (syllogistic) manner, the evidence category subsumed under the notion of epistemic authority is special in a number of respects. It represents the fundamental notion that human knowledge is socially constructed and that it is heavily influenced by the opinions of significant others whose judgments one holds in high regard. It also touches on the *developmental aspect* of knowledge construction, the liberation of one's knowledge formation processes from reliance on a limited number of primary care givers, the evolution of epistemic self-reliance, and the diversification of one's array of information sources in accordance with their perceived domains of expertise. The concept of epistemic authority also acknowledges that individuals (as well as groups) may exhibit relatively stable differences in their hierarchy of epistemic authorities, which determines who they will turn to for information and advice, and on whose recommendations they will act. Finally, this concept suggests that individuals' tendency to independently process domain-specific information on a topic may be a function of a *gap* between their own self-ascribed epistemic authority and the perceived authority of a given communication source.

Integrating the why, how, and who of lay epistemics

The three research programs inspired by the lay epistemic theory illuminate distinct aspects of knowledge formation. The need for closure program focused on the *motivational underpinnings* of the process. The unimodel program addressed the mechanism of justifying (or "proving") one's judgments and conclusions via the appropriate *evidence* and the psychological process that permits the information given to become such evidence. Finally, the epistemic authority program addressed the essential *metacognitive, developmental,* and *differential* aspects of knowledge formation that determine how individuals function in their informational ecologies to form their opinions and attitudes.

It is of interest to consider how the three categories of process embodied by the foregoing research programs interface, and what implications follow from their possible interrelations. The need for closure (representing the "why" of epistemic behavior) represents a desire for firm knowledge. In turn, firm knowledge requires a firm inferential basis; that is, availability in memory of firmly believed-in rules or major premises to which situationally present information may be fitted, functioning as minor premises (representing the "how" of epistemic behavior). It follows that, under high need for closure, individuals may be more likely *to form* such rules, as well as have a chronically accessible variety of general, "all-purpose" rules (or "heuristics") that they can use across a broad spectrum of situations.

Consistent with this logic, Dechesne and Wigboldus (2008) recently discovered that individuals high in need for closure are especially prone to form rules or notice systematic patterns even when not explicitly instructed to do so. Participants in the experiment were instructed to use designated keys on the keyboard to indicate as quickly and accurately as possible whether an A or a B appeared on a computer screen. The experiment consisted of 280 trials. Importantly, the As and the Bs appeared in a fixed order of ABBABAB. Awareness of this pattern, and its use as a rule, facilitates responding to upcoming stimuli. A reduction in response latencies over time can thus be interpreted as a manifestation of a stronger tendency to form and use inferential rules to respond to situational demands. To the extent that high (vs. low) need for closure fosters the motivation to form and use rules, a more pronounced reduction of response latencies over time was expected to occur among high (vs. low) need for closure participants. That is precisely what was found. As shown in Figure 10, downward trends in response latencies significantly covaried with the need for closure, such that higher need for closure was associated with a more pronounced trend in the downward direction. Admittedly, the Dechesne and Wigboldus (2008) results could be due to motivated attention to the stimuli, rather than the tendency to form rules as such. Further studies (currently under way) are needed to explore in a more comprehensive manner the hypothesized rule-forming proclivity of high need for closure individuals.

It also seems plausible that high (vs. low) need for closure individuals should subscribe to beliefs about general, all-purpose, epistemic authorities. A unique such authority is one's own self. Consistent with this notion, high (vs. low) need for closure individuals have been consistently reporting higher confidence in their judgments, possibly reflecting a high self-ascribed epistemic authority, attesting to reliance on the "I am generally right" or "If it is my judgment, then it is correct" heuristic (Kruglanski, 2004). Moreover, considerable evidence reviewed earlier attests to group-centric tendencies under heightened need for closure (Kruglanski et al., 2006). A major aspect of group centrism is the quest for consensus, or the "group is right" heuristic; that is, "if my group believes it, then it is correct" heuristic. There is also evidence that individuals under high need for closure prefer an autocratic or hierarchical decision-making structure, possibly reflecting the bestowal of epistemic

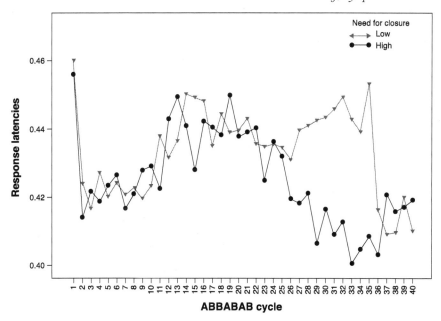

Figure 10 The effect of ABBABAB cycle and need for closure on response latencies (Dechesne & Wigboldus, 2008).

authority on anointed experts, or operation of the "experts are correct" heuristic ("if expert, then correct"). In this sense the heightened confidence, the group-centric tendencies, and the autocratic orientations observed under high need for closure may all represent a reliance on broad, "all-purpose" rules affording a general inferential base for knowledge formation. Finally, as the findings of Pierro and Mannetti (2004) suggest, under a heightened need for closure individuals may sharpen their discrimination between various epistemic authorities and come to rely more fully on their *dominant* epistemic authority, occupying the top of their epistemic hierarchy.

In short, the three research programs based on the lay epistemic theory interlock in significant ways. Because knowledge is based on evidence, and evidence reflects an operation of "if–then" inferential rules, individuals who are particularly motivated to have stable knowledge (i.e., those with an elevated need for closure) may quickly construct such rules from contingency information. Because general inferential heuristics may afford quick formation of knowledge across diverse content domains, individuals with a high need for closure may be particularly prone to bestow domain-general epistemic authority on various agents including themselves.

Understanding these interrelated epistemic processes and their representation in real-world circumstances where knowledge formation may assume heightened psychological importance promises to offer new insights into a variety of social problems besetting contemporary societies. For instance, it would be of considerable interest to consider how uncertainty promoted by economic and political turmoil may elevate whole populations' need for cognitive closure, and how such need, in turn, might lead to group centrism and derogation of (and readiness to engage in violence against) out-groups, as well as fostering the readiness to embrace fundamentalist, closure-affording, ideologies and epistemic authorities. In our own work we have found that exposure of participants to an uncertainty-evoking event, recall of the 9/11 attack on the Twin Towers in New York, elevated individuals' need for cognitive closure, and that need for closure increased participants' tendencies toward in-group favoritism, and out-group derogation, as well as the positive evaluation of decisive and consistent ("staying on course") leaders and negative evaluation of open-minded and flexible ("flip flopper") ones (Orehek et al., 2007). Applying the theory of lay epistemics to major real-world phenomena constitutes an exciting challenge for future generations of research on knowledge formation processes, with significant contribution potential to policy in broad domains of endeavor.

Notes

1 For Popper (1959) the process of hypothesis testing is represented by the premise If H then E, which implies that one can only falsify a hypothesis via a logical modus tollens (if E is false then we can conclude that H must be false), but not verify it as we are suggesting. According to our analysis, however, the knower may depart from the assumption that *if and only if* hypothesis H were true evidence E would be observed. The *if and only if* framing implies that not only if H then E is true, but also if E then H is true. This way one could logically derive the hypothesis from the evidence in a modus ponens fashion, whereby E (the evidence is observed) therefore H (the hypothesis is supported). Of course, the *if and only if* assumption may need to be modified on the basis of subsequent information which would cast doubt on the originally derived conclusion that H was proven or supported. For instance, if an alternative hypothesis H_1 were posed and the need to distinguish it from the original H arose, one would formulate an inference rule whereby *if and only if* H but not H_1 were true then E_1 would obtain, etc.

2 In a recent paper, Roets, van Hiel, Cornelis, and Soetens (2008) argued that in addition to exerting a direct motivational effect similar to that of dispositional NFCC, situational manipulations of need for closure (via time pressure or noise) exert an effect on cognitive capacity as well as manifesting in deteriorated task performance.

3 That the general implicational *if–then* structure represents the gist of inference is a mainstay of most major depictions of this process in the philosophy of science and of knowledge literatures. Consider the venerated Hempel–Openheim (1948) scheme of scientific explanation, known as the deductive nomological (D-N) framework. According to this model, a scientific explanation contains two major elements: an *explanandum*, a sentence "describing the phenomenon to be explained" and an *explanans*, "the class of sentences that account for the phenomenon" (Hempel & Oppenheim, 1948, reprinted in Hempel, 1965, p. 247). For the explanans to successfully explain the explanandum, "the explanandum must be a logical consequence of the explanans" and "the sentences constituting the explanans must be true" (Hempel, 1965, p. 248). That is, any proper explanation takes the form of a sound deductive argument in which the explanandum follows as a conclusion from the premises in the explanans. For instance, the sentence "All gases expand when heated under constant pressure," or "If something is a gas, then it expands when heated under constant pressure," constitutes a major premise that in conjunction with the appropriate minor premise— that is, information that "some particular substance is a gas that has been heated under constant pressure"—affords the inference that this substance will expand, or an explanation of why it did expand.

References

Abelson, R. P. (1968). Psychological implication. In R. P. Abelson, E. Aronson, W. J. McGuire, T. M. Newcomb, M. J. Rosenberg, & R. H. Tannenbaum (Eds.), *Theories of cognitive consistency: A sourcebook* (pp. 112–139). Chicago: Rand McNally.

Andersen, S. M., & Cole, S. W. (1990). "Do I know you?" The role of significant others in general social perception. *Journal of Personality and Social Psychology, 59*, 384–399.

Andersen, S. M., Glassman, N. S., Chen, S., & Cole, S. W. (1995). Transference in social perception: The role of chronic accessibility in significant-other representations. *Journal of Personality and Social Psychology, 69*, 41–57.

Anderson, J. R. (1983). *The structure of cognition*. Cambridge, MA: Harvard University Press.

Baeyens, F., Crombez, G., Van den Bergh, O., & Eelen, P. (1988). Once in contact always in contact: Evaluative conditioning is resistant to extinction. *Advances in Behaviour Research and Therapy, 10*, 179–199.

Bar, R. (1983). *Hierarchy of Epistemic Authority Test*. Unpublished Master's thesis, Tel Aviv University.

Bar, R. (1999). *The impact of epistemic needs and authorities on judgment and decision making*. Unpublished doctoral dissertation, Tel Aviv University.

Bar-Tal, D. (1990). *Group beliefs: A conception for analyzing group structure, processes, and behavior*. New York: Springer-Verlag.

Bar-Tal, D. (2000). *Shared beliefs in a society: A social psychological analysis*. Thousand Oaks, CA: Sage Publications, Inc.

Bartlett, F. C. (1932). *Remembering: A study in experimental and social psychology*. New York: Cambridge University Press.

Boudreau, L. A., Baron, R. M., & Oliver, P. V. (1992). Effects of expected communication target expertise and timing of set on trait use in person description. *Journal of Personality and Social Psychology, 18*, 447–451.

Brewer, M. B. (1988). A dual process model of impression formation. In T. K. Srull & R. S. Wyer (Eds.), *Advances in social cognition* (Vol. 1, pp. 1–36). Hillsdale, NJ: Lawrence Erlbaum Associates Inc.

Bruner, J. S. (1973). *Beyond the information given: Studies in the psychology of knowing*. Oxford, UK: Norton.

Cattell, R. B., & Epstein, A. R. (1975). *Comprehensive ability battery*. Champaign, IL: Institute for Personality and Ability Testing.

Chaiken, S., Liberman, A., & Eagly, A. H. (1989). Heuristic and systematic information processing within and beyond the persuasion context. In J. S. Uleman & J. A. Bargh (Eds.), *Unintended thought*. New York: Guilford Press.

Chaiken, S., & Trope, Y. (1999). *Dual process theories in social psychology*. New York: Guilford Press.

Chirumbolo, A. (2002). The relationship between need for cognitive closure and political orientation: The mediating role of authoritarianism. *Personality and Individual Differences, 32*, 603–610.

Chirumbolo, A., Areni, A., & Sensales, G. (2004). Need for closure and politics: Voting, political attitudes and attributional style. *International Journal of Psychology, 39*, 245–253.

Chirumbolo, A., & Leone, L. (2008). Individual differences in need for closure and voting behaviour. *Personality and Individual Differences, 44*, 1279–1288.

Chun, W. Y., & Kruglanski, A. W. (2006). The role of task demands and processing resources in the use of base-rate and individuating information. *Journal of Personality and Social Psychology, 91*, 205–217.

Chun, W. Y., Spiegel, S., & Kruglanski, A. W. (2002). Assimilative behavior identification can also be resource dependent: A unimodel perspective on personal-attribution phases. *Journal of Personality and Social Psychology, 83*, 542–555.

Dechesne, M., Schultz, J. M., Kruglanski, A. W., Orehek, E., & Fishman, S. (2008). *A psychology of borders: Need for closure and the allure of group impermeability*. Unpublished manuscript, University of Maryland, MD, USA.

Dechesne, M., & Wigboldus, D. (2008). Unpublished data. University of Nijmegen, The Netherlands.

De Dreu, C. K. V., & Koole, S. L. (1997). *Motivated use of heuristics in negotiation*. Unpublished raw data.

De Dreu, C. K. W., Koole, S. L., & Oldersma, F. L. (1999). On the seizing and freezing of negotiator inferences: Need for cognitive closure moderates the use of heuristics in negotiation. *Personality and Social Psychology Bulletin, 25*, 348–362.

De Grada, E., Kruglanski, A. W., Mannetti, L., & Pierro, A. (1999). Motivated cognition and group interaction: Need for closure affects the contents and processes of collective negotiations. *Journal of Experimental Social Psychology, 35*, 346–365.

Dewey, J. (1916). *Democracy and education*. New York: Free Press.

Dewey, J. (1958). *Experience and nature*. New York: Collier Macmillan.

Dijksterhuis, A. P., Van Knippenberg, A. D., Kruglanski, A. W., & Schaper, C. (1996). Motivated social cognition: Need for closure effects on memory and judgment. *Journal of Experimental Social Psychology, 32*, 254–270.

Ellis, S., & Kruglanski, A. W. (1992). Self as epistemic authority: Effects on experiential and instructional learning. *Social Cognition, 10*, 357–375.

Erb, H. P., Kruglanski, A. W., Chun, W. Y., Pierro, A., Mannetti, L., & Spiegel, S. (2003). Searching for commonalities in human judgment: The parametric unimodel and its dual mode alternatives. In W. Stroebe & M. Hewstone (Eds.), *European review of social psychology* (Vol. 14, pp. 1–47). Hove, UK: Psychology Press.

Evans, J. St. B. T. (1989). *Bias in human reasoning: Causes and consequences*. Hove, UK: Lawrence Erlbaum Associates Ltd.

Fazio, R. H. (1990). Multiple processes by which attitudes guide behavior: The MODE model as an integrative framework. In M. P. Zanna (Ed.), *Advances in experimental social psychology* (Vol. 23, pp. 75–109). New York: Academic Press.

Fazio, R. H., & Zanna, M. P. (1981). Direct experience and attitude–behavior consistency. In L. Berkowitz (Ed.), *Advances in experimental social psychology*. (Vol. 14, pp. 161–203). New York: Academic Press.

Fiske, S. T., & Neuberg, S. L. (1990). A continuum model of impression formation, from category-based to individuating processes: Influences of information and motivation on attention and interpretation. In M. P. Zanna (Ed.), *Advances in experimental social psychology* (Vol. 23, pp. 1–74). New York: Academic Press.

Ford, T. E., & Kruglanski, A. W. (1995). Effects of epistemic motivations on the use of accessible constructs in social judgments. *Personality and Social Psychology Bulletin, 21*, 950–962.

Freud, A. (1965). *Normality and pathology in childhood: Assessments of development*. New York: International Universities Press.

Freund, T., Kruglanski, A., & Schpitzajzen, A. (1985). The freezing and unfreezing of impressional primacy: Effects of the need for structure and the fear of invalidity. *Personality and Social Psychology Bulletin, 11*, 479–487.

Gawronski, B., & Bodenhausen, G. V. (2006). Associative and propositional processes in evaluation: An integrative review of implicit and explicit attitude change. *Psychological Bulletin, 132*, 692–731.

Gelfand, M. (2008). *Situated culture: A multilevel analysis of situational constraint across 35 nations.* Paper presented at the Social Psychology Winter Conference, Park City, Utah.

Gregory, R. L. (1997). *Eye and brain: The psychology of seeing* (5th ed.). Princeton, NJ: Princeton University Press.

Hardin, C. D., & Higgins, E. T. (1996). Shared reality: How social verification makes the subjective objective. In R. M. Sorrentino & E. T. Higgins (Eds.), *Handbook of motivation and cognition* (Vol. 3, pp. 28–84). New York: Guilford Press.

Helmholtz, H. v. (1910/2000). *Helmholtz's treatise on physiological optics.* Bristol, UK: Thoemmes Press.

Hempel, C. (1965). *Aspects of scientific explanation and other essays in the philosophy of science.* New York: Free Press.

Hempel, C., & Oppenheim, P. (1948). Studies in the logic of explanation. *Philosophy of Science, 15,* 135–175. [Reprinted in Hempel (1965), pp. 245–290.]

Higgins, E. T. (1996). Knowledge activation: Accessibility, applicability and salience. In E. T. Higgins & A. W. Kruglanski (Eds.), *Social psychology: Handbook of basic principles.* (pp. 133–168). New York: Guilford Press.

Hilton, D. (2007). Causal explanation: From social perception to knowledge-based causal attribution. In A. W. Kruglanski & E. T. Higgins (Eds.), *Social psychology: A handbook of basic principles* (Vol. 2). New York: Guilford Press.

Holyoak, K. J., Kohl, K., & Nisbett, R. E. (1989). A theory of conditioned reasoning: Inductive learning within rule-based hierarchies. *Psychological Review, 96,* 315–340.

Hovland, C. I., Janis, I. L., & Kelley, H. H. (1953). *Communication and persuasion.* Newhaven, CT: Yale University Press.

Igou, E. R., Fishbach, A., & Kruglanski, A. W. (2008). *An epistemic analysis of retrieval effects on judgment.* Unpublished manuscript, Tilburg University.

James, W. (1890). *The principles of psychology.* New York: Henry Colt & Co.

Jamieson, D. W., & Zanna, M. P. (1989). Need for structure in attitude formation and expression. In A. R. Pratkanis, S. J. Breckler, & A. G. Greenwald (Eds.), *Attitude structure and function.* Hillsdale, NJ: Lawrence Erlbaum Associates Inc.

Jost, J. T., Glaser, J., Kruglanski, A. W., & Sullaway, F. J. (2003a). Political conservatism as motivated social cognition. *Psychological Bulletin, 129,* 339–375.

Jost, J. T., Glaser, J., Kruglanski, A. W., & Sullaway, F. J. (2003b). Exceptions that prove the rule: Using a theory of motivated social cognition to account for ideological incongruities and political anomalies. *Psychological Bulletin, 129,* 383–393.

Jost, J. T., Kruglanski, A. W., & Nelson, T. T. O. (1998). Social metacognition: An expansionist review. *Personality and Social Psychology Review, 2,* 137–154.

Kahneman, D. (2003). A perspective on judgment and choice: Mapping bounded rationality. *American Psychologist, 58,* 697–720.

Kahneman, D., & Tversky, A. (1973). On the psychology of prediction. *Psychological Review, 80,* 237–251.

Kosic, A., Kruglanski, A. W., Pierro, A., & Mannetti, L. (2004). Social cognition of immigrants' acculturation: Effects of the need for closure and the reference group at entry. *Journal of Personality and Social Psychology, 86,* 796–813.

Kruglanski, A. (1980). Lay epistemologic process and contents: Another look at attribution theory. *Psychological Review, 87,* 70–87.

Kruglanski, A., & Freund, T. (1983). The freezing and un-freezing of lay-inferences: Effects on impressional primacy, ethnic stereotyping and numerical anchoring. *Journal of Experimental Social Psychology, 19,* 448–468.

Kruglanski, A. W. (1989). *Lay epistemics and human knowledge: Cognitive and motivational bases.* New York: Plenum.

Kruglanski, A. W. (2004). *The psychology of closed mindedness*. New York: Psychology Press.

Kruglanski, A. W., Erb, H. P., Pierro, A., Mannetti, L., & Chun. W. Y. (2006a). On parametric continuities in the world of binary either ors [target article]. *Psychological Inquiry, 17*, 153–165.

Kruglanski, A. W., & Orehek, E. (2007). Partitioning the domain of social inference: Dual mode and systems models and their alternatives. *Annual Review of Psychology, 58*, 291–316.

Kruglanski, A. W., Pierro, A., Mannetti, L., & De Grada, E. (2006b). Groups as epistemic providers: Need for closure and the unfolding of group-centrism. *Psychological Review, 113*, 84–100.

Kruglanski, A. W., Pierro, A., Mannetti, L., Erb, H. P., & Chun, W. Y. (2007). On the parameters of social judgment. In M. P. Zanna (Ed.), *Advances in experimental social psychology* (Vol. 39, pp. 255–296). New York: Academic Press.

Kruglanski, A. W., Raviv, A., Bar-Tal, D., Raviv, A., Sharvit, K., Ellis, S., et al. (2005). Says who? Epistemic authority effects in social judgment. In M. P. Zanna (Ed.), *Advances in experimental social psychology* (Vol. 37, pp. 345–392). New York: Academic Press.

Kruglanski, A. W., Shah, J. Y., Pierro, A., & Mannetti, L. (2002). When similarity breeds content: Need for closure and the allure of homogeneous and self-resembling groups. *Journal of Personality and Social Psychology, 83*, 648–662.

Kruglanski, A. W., & Thomson, E. P. (1999a). Persuasion by a single route: A view from the unimodel. *Psychological Inquiry, 10*, 83–109.

Kruglanski, A. W., & Thomson, E. P. (1999b). The illusory second mode or, the cue is the message. *Psychological Inquiry, 10*, 182–193.

Kruglanski, A. W., Thomson, E. P., & Spiegel, S. (1999). Separate or equal?: Bimodal notions of persuasion and a single process "unimodel". In S. Chaiken & Y. Trope (Eds.), *Dual-process theories in social psychology* (pp. 293–313). New York: Guilford Press.

Kruglanski, A. W., & Webster, D. M. (1991). Group members' reactions to opinion deviates and conformists at varying degrees of proximity to decision deadline and of environmental noise. *Journal of Personality and Social Psychology, 61*, 212–225.

Kruglanski, A. W., & Webster, D. M. (1996). Motivated closing of the mind: "Seizing" and "freezing". *Psychological Review, 103*, 263–283.

Kruglanski, A. W., Webster, D. M., & Klem, A. (1993). Motivated resistance and openness to persuasion in the presence or absence of prior information. *Journal of Personality and Social Psychology, 65*, 861–876.

Livi, S. (2003). *Il bisogno di chiusura cognitiva e la transmissione delle norme nei piccoli gruppi.* [The need for cognitive closure and norm transmission in small groups.] Unpublished doctoral dissertation, University of Rome "La Sapienza", Italy.

Logan, G. D. (1992). Attention and preattention in theories of automaticity. *American Journal of Psychology, 105*, 317–339.

Maio, G. R., & Haddock, G. G. (2007). Attitude change. In A. W. Kruglanski & E. T. Higgins (Eds.), *Social psychology: Handbook of basic principles* (2nd ed., pp. 565–586). New York: Guilford Press.

Mischel, W., & Shoda, Y. (1995). A cognitive-affective system theory of personality: Reconceptualizing situations, dispositions, dynamics, and invariance in personality structure. *Psychological Review, 102*, 246–268.

Mitchell, C. J., De Houwer, J., & Lovibond, P. F. (in press). The propositional nature of human associative learning. *Behavioural and Brain Sciences*.

Newell, A., & Simon, H. A. (1972). *Human problem solving*. Englewood Cliffs, NJ: Prentice Hall.

Newman, L. S., & Uleman, J. S. (1989). Spontaneous trait inference. In J. S. Uleman & J. A. Bargh (Eds.), *Unintended thought*. New York: Guilford Press.

Orehek, E., Fishman, S., Dechesne, M., Doosje, B., Kruglanski, A. W., Cole, A. P. et al. (2007). *Certainty quest and the social response to terrorism*. Unpublished manuscript. University of Maryland.

Petty, R. E., & Cacioppo, J. T. (1986). The elaboration likelihood model of persuasion. In L. Berkowitz (Ed.), *Advances in experimental social psychology* (Vol. 19, pp. 123–205). San Diego, CA: Academic Press.

Petty, R. E., Brinol, P., Tormala, Z. L., & Wegener, D. T. (2007). The role of metacognition in social judgment. In A. Kruglanski & E. T. Higgins (Eds.), *Social psychology: A handbook of basic principles*. New York: Guilford Press.

Petty, R. E., & Wegener, D. T. (1999). The elaboration likelihood model: Current status and controversies. In S. Chaiken & Y. Trope (Eds.), *Dual-process models in social psychology*. New York: Guilford Press.

Pierro, A., & Kruglanski, A. W. (2005). *Revised Need for Cognitive Closure Scale*. Unpublished manuscript. Università di Roma, "La Sapienza", Italy.

Pierro, A. & Kruglanski, A. W. (in press). "Seizing and freezing" on a significant-person schema: Need for closure and the transference effect in social judgment. *Personality and Social Psychology Bulletin*.

Pierro, A., & Mannetti, L. (2004). *Motivated consumer search behavior: The effects of epistemic authority*. Unpublished manuscript. University of Rome "La Sapienza", Italy.

Pierro, A., Mannetti, L., De Grada, E., Livi, S., & Kruglanski A. W. (2003). Autocracy bias in groups under need for closure. *Personality and Social Psychology Bulletin*, *29*, 405–417.

Pierro, A., Mannetti, L., Erb, H. P., Spiegel, S., & Kruglanski, A. W. (2005). Informational length and order of presentation as determinants of persuasion. *Journal of Experimental Social Psychology*, *41*, 458–469.

Pierro, A., Mannetti, L., Kruglanski, A. W., & Sleeth-Keppler, D. (2004). Relevance override: On the reduced impact of "cues" under high motivation conditions of persuasion studies. *Journal of Personality and Social Psychology*, *86*, 251–264.

Pierro, A., Mannetti, L., Orehek, E., & Kruglanski, A. W. (2008). *Persistence of attitude change and attitude–behavior correspondence based on extensive processing of source information*. Unpublished manuscript. University of Rome, "La Sapienza", Italy.

Pizlo, Z. (2001). Perception viewed as an inverse problem. *Vision Research*, *41*, 3145–3161.

Popper, K. R. (1959). *The logic of scientific discovery*. New York: Basic Books.

Raviv, A., Bar-Tal, D., Raviv, A., & Houminer, D. (1990). Development in children's perception of epistemic authorities. *British Journal of Developmental Psychology*, *8*, 157–169.

Rescorla, R. A. (1985). Conditioned inhibition and facilitation. In R. R. Miller & N. E. Spear (Eds.), *Information processing in animals: Conditioned inhibition* (pp. 299–326). Hillsdale, NJ: Lawrence Erlbaum Associates Inc.

Rescorla, R. A., & Holland, P. C. (1982). Behavioral studies of social learning in animals. *Annual Review of Psychology*, *33*, 265–308.

Rescorla, R. A., & Wagner, A. R. (1972). A theory of Pavlovian conditioning: Variations in the effectiveness of reinforcement and nonreinforcement. In A. H. Black & W. F. Prokasy (Eds.), *Classical conditioning II: Current research and theory* (pp. 64–99). New York: Appleton-Century-Crofts.

Richter, L., & Kruglanski, A. W. (1998). Seizing on the latest: Motivationally driven recency effects in impression formation. *Journal of Experimental Social Psychology*, *13*, 279–301.

Richter, L., & Kruglanski, A. W. (1999). Motivated search for common ground: Need for closure effects on audience design in interpersonal communication. *Personality and Social Psychology Bulletin*, *25*, 1101–1114.

Rock, I. (1983). *The logic of perception*. Cambridge, MA: MIT Press.

Roets, A., & van Hiel, A. (2006). Need for closure relations with authoritarianism, conservative beliefs and racism: The impact of urgency and permanence tendencies. *Psychologica Belgica*, *46*, 235–252.

Roets, A., & van Hiel, A. (2007). Separating ability from need: Clarifying the dimensional structure of the Need for Closure Scale. *Personality and Social Psychology Bulletin*, *33*, 266–280.

Roets, A., & van Hiel, A. (2008). Why some hate to dilly-dally and others do not: The arousal-invoking capacity of decision-making for low and high scoring need for closure individuals. *Social Cognition*, *26*, 259–272.

Roets, A., van Hiel, A., Cornelis, I., & Soetens, B. (2008). Determinants of task performance and invested effort: A need for closure by relative cognitive capacity interaction analysis. *Personality and Social Psychology Bulletin*, *34*, 779–792.

Rogers, C. R. (1951). *Client-centred therapy: Its current practice, implications, and theory*. Oxford, UK: Houghton Mifflin.

Rogers, C. R. (1967). *The therapeutic relationship and its impact: A study of psychotherapy with schizophrenics*. Oxford, UK: Wisconsin Press.

Rubini, M., & Kruglanski, A. W. (1997). Brief encounters ending in estrangement: Motivated language-use and interpersonal rapport. *Journal of Personality and Social Psychology*, *12*, 1047–1060.

Schteynberg, G., Gelfand, M., Imai, L., Mayer, D., & Bell, C. (2008). [*Unpublished data.*] University of Maryland, College Park, USA.

Schwarz, N. (2004). Metacognitive experiences in consumer judgment and decision making. *Journal of Consumer Psychology*, *14*, 332–348.

Schwarz, N., Bless, H., Strack, F., Klumpp, G., Rittenauer-Schatka, H., & Simons, A. (1991). Ease of retrieval as information: Another look at the availability heuristic. *Journal of Personality and Social Psychology*, *61*, 195–202.

Schwarz, N., & Clore, G. L. (1983). Mood, misattribution, and judgments of well-being: Informative and directive functions of affective states. *Journal of Personality and Social Psychology*, *45*, 513–523.

Schwarz, N., & Clore, G. L. (1996). Feelings and phenomenal experiences. In E. T. Higgins & A. W. Kruglanski (Eds.), *Social psychology: Handbook of basic principles* (pp. 433–465). New York: Guilford Press.

Schwarz, N., Servay, W., & Kumpf, M. (1985). Attribution of arousal as a mediator of the effectiveness of fear-arousing communications. *Journal of Applied Social Psychology*, *15*, 178–188.

Semin, G. R., & Fiedler, K. (1991). The linguistic category model, its bases, applications and range. In W. Stroebe & M. Hewstone (Eds.), *European review of social psychology* (Vol. 2, pp. 1–30). London: Wiley.

Shafer, J. B. P. (1978). *Humanistic psychology*. Englewood Cliffs, NJ: Prentice Hall.

Shah, J. Y., Kruglanski, A. W., & Thompson, E. P. (1998). Membership has its (epistemic) rewards: Need for closure effects on in-group bias. *Journal of Personality and Social Psychology*, *75*, 383–393.

Smith, E. R. (1984). Model of social inference processes. *Psychological Review*, *91*, 392–413.

Smith, E. R. (1989). Procedural efficiency: General and specific components and effects on social judgment. *Journal of Experimental Social Psychology*, *25*, 500–523.

Smith, E. R., & Branscombe, N. R. (1988). Category accessibility as implicit memory. *Journal of Experimental Social Psychology, 24*, 490–504.

Smith, E. R., Branscombe, N. R., & Bormann, C. (1988). Generality of the effects of practice on social judgment tasks. *Journal of Personality and Social Psychology, 54*, 385–395.

Tetlock, P. E. (1992). The impact of accountability on judgment and choice: Toward a social contingency model. In M. P. Zanna (Ed.), *Advances in experimental social psychology* (Vol. 25, pp. 331–376). San Diego, CA: Academic Press.

Trope, Y., & Alfieri, T. (1997). Effortfulness and flexibility of dispositional judgment processes. *Journal of Personality and Social Psychology, 73*, 662–674.

Trope, Y., & Gaunt, R. (2000). Processing alternative explanations of behavior: Correction of integration? *Journal of Personality and Social Psychology, 79*, 344–354.

Tversky, A., & Kahneman, D. (1973). Availability: A heuristic for judging frequency and probability. *Cognitive Psychology, 5*(2), 207–232.

Uleman, J. S. (1987). Consciousness and control: The case of spontaneous trait inferences. *Personality and Social Psychology Bulletin, 13*, 337–354.

Van Hiel, A., Pandelaere, M., & Duriez, B. (2004). The impact of need for closure on conservative beliefs and racism: Differential mediation by authoritarian submission and authoritarian dominance. *Personality and Social Psychology Bulletin, 30*, 824–837.

Walther, E., Nagengast, B., & Trasselli, C. (2005). Evaluative conditioning in social psychology: Facts and speculations. *Cognition and Emotion, 19*, 175–196.

Wason, P. C. (1966). Reasoning. In B. M. Foss (Ed.), *New horizons in psychology* (pp. 113–135). Harmondsworth, UK: Penguin.

Webster, D. M., & Kruglanski, A. W. (1994). Individual differences in need for cognitive closure. *Journal of Personality and Social Psychology, 67*, 1049–1062.

Webster, D. M., Kruglanski, A. W., & Pattison, D. A. (1997). Motivated language use in intergroup contexts: Need for closure effects on the linguistic intergroup bias. *Journal of Personality and Social Psychology, 72*, 1122–1131.

Webster, D. M., Richter, L., & Kruglanski, A. W. (1996). On leaping to conclusions when feeling tired: Mental fatigue effects on impressional primacy. *Journal of Experimental Social Psychology, 32*, 181–195.

Webster-Nelson, D., Klein, C. T., & Irvin, J. E. (2003). Motivational antecedents of empathy: Inhibiting effects of fatigue. *Basic and Applied Social Psychology, 25*, 37–50.

3 Motivated closing of the mind

"Seizing" and "freezing"

Arie W. Kruglanski, University of Maryland
Donna M. Webster, University of Florida

The construction of new knowledge is a pervasive human pursuit for both individuals and collectives. From relatively simple activities such as crossing a busy road to highly complex endeavors such as launching a space shuttle, new knowledge is indispensable for secure decisions and reasoned actions. The knowledge-construction process is often involved and intricate. It draws on background notions activated from memory and local information from the immediate context. It entails the extensive testing of hypotheses and the piecing of isolated cognitive bits into coherent wholes. It integrates inchoate sensations with articulate thoughts, detects meaningful signals in seas of ambient noise, and more.

Two aspects of knowledge construction are of present interest: its motivated nature and its social character. That knowledge construction has a motivational base should come as no particular surprise. The host of effortful activities it comprises pose considerable demands on resource allocation; hence, it may well require motivation to get under way. Specifically, individuals may desire knowledge on some topics and not others, and they may delimit their constructive endeavors to those particular domains. But what kind of a motivational variable is the "desire for knowledge"? At least two answers readily suggest themselves: Knowledge could be desired because it conveys welcome news in regard to a given concern or because it conveys any definite news (whether welcome or unwelcome) in instances in which such information is required for some purpose. For instance, a mother may desire to know that her child did well on the Scholastic Aptitude Test (SAT) so that she may send her or him to a selective college, whereas the college admissions officer may desire to simply know how well or poorly the child did so that he or she may make the appropriate admission decision. The former type of desire has been referred to as the need for a specific closure, and the latter has been referred to as the need for a nonspecific closure. The need for a specific closure implies the desirability of a particular answer to a question (e.g., that one's child did well on the SAT), whereas the need for a nonspecific closure implies the desirability of any answer as long as it is definite (Kruglanski, 1989, 1990a, 1990b). Various needs for specific closure have received considerable emphasis in the social cognition literature (e.g., for reviews, see Kruglanski, in press; Kunda, 1990). The need for nonspecific closure has attracted much less attention. A major purpose of this chapter is to redress this imbalance by focusing on the latter type of desire.

In addition to its motivated nature, the knowledge-construction process is suffused with social significance. First, various social entities (other persons, groups, or social categories) are often the objects of knowledge-construction endeavors. In other words, constructive efforts are frequently meant to yield socially relevant knowledge. Furthermore, other people may often supply the informational means whereby constructive ends are attained. They may provide social comparison information (Festinger, 1954) or feedback pertinent to self-verification or self-enhancement motives (Swann, 1990). They may supply consensus information in instances in which consensus is desired, confirm one's favorite hypotheses, or bear witness to one's efficacy and control. Of course, people might impede rather than facilitate the attainment of desired knowledge and be occasionally the bearers of "bad news." Even then, however, they remain motivationally relevant to one's epistemic purposes as potential sources of pertinent information. An important objective of this chapter is, therefore, to flesh out the social psychological significance of knowledge-construction processes, particularly as these processes relate to the need for (nonspecific) closure.

In what follows, we present theory and research elucidating the nature of this need, its antecedent conditions, and its consequences. Essentially, we hope to demonstrate that the need for closure exerts a broad range of effects on the knowledge-construction process and hence, indirectly, on a wide range of related social psychological phenomena at the intrapersonal, interpersonal, and group levels of analysis.

The need for closure

The need for cognitive closure refers to individuals' desire for a firm answer to a question and an aversion toward ambiguity. As used here, the term *need* is meant to denote a motivated tendency or proclivity rather than a tissue deficit (for a similar usage, see Cacioppo & Petty, 1982). We assume that the need for cognitive closure is akin to a person's goal (Pervin, 1989). As such, it may prompt activities aimed at the attainment of closure, bias the individual's choices and preferences toward closure-bound pursuits, and induce negative affect when closure is threatened or undermined and positive affect when it is facilitated or attained.

A motivational continuum in regard to closure

We assume that the motivation toward closure varies along a continuum anchored at one end with a strong need for closure and at the other end with a strong need to avoid closure. Closure, in other words, may not be desired universally. Although in some circumstances people may strive to attain it, in other situations they may actively avoid it or exhibit little preference for it over ambiguity. Individuals at the need for closure end of the continuum may display considerable cognitive impatience or impulsivity: They may "leap" to judgment on the basis of inconclusive evidence and exhibit rigidity of thought and reluctance to entertain views different from their own. At the opposite end of the continuum, denoting a high need to avoid closure, people may savor uncertainty and be reluctant to commit to a definite opinion. In those circumstances, individuals may suspend judgment and be quick to engender alternatives to any emergent view.

Effects of the motivation for closure are assumed to be monotonic along the continuum. By this assumption, the motivational effects should be directionally similar for any pair of points on the continuum: A higher (vs. lower) degree of the need for closure should effect a higher or lower degree of some phenomenon, irrespective of the points' specific locations. Thus, comparing low and high need for closure conditions should yield effects directionally similar to those involved in comparing high and low need to avoid closure conditions. Evidence reviewed in subsequent sections consistently supports this assumption.

Antecedents of the motivation toward closure

What conditions may induce a given motivation toward closure? According to the present analysis, these may be conditions that highlight the perceived benefits or desirability of closure or of the absence of closure (see also Kruglanski, in press). For instance, a potential benefit of closure may be the ability to act or decide in time for meeting an important deadline. Thus, the need for closure should be heightened under time pressure. An alternative benefit of closure is removal of the necessity for further information processing; if so, need for closure should be heightened under conditions that render processing difficult, laborious, or aversive. Some such conditions (e.g., environmental noise) may reside in the exogenous context of processing, whereas others (e.g., tedium and dullness of a cognitive task) may relate to endogenous aspects of processing (Kruglanski, 1975). Yet other conditions may stem from the perceiver's organismic state. For instance, people may find processing particularly arduous when in a state of fatigue. Accordingly, need for closure should be heightened under noise, when the task is unpleasant or dull, or when the individual is fatigued. It should also be heightened when closure is valued by significant others, because possessing closure may promise to earn their esteem and appreciation. Finally, it should be heightened, simply, when judgment on some topic is required (as compared with cases in which the individual feels free to remain opinionless).

The need for closure may be lowered and that to avoid closure heightened by conditions that highlight the costs of closure and the benefits of openness. In some situations, closure costs may be made salient by "fear of invalidity," or a gnawing concern about a costly judgmental mistake (e.g., when the perceiver is "outcome dependent" on the target; cf. Fiske & Neuberg, 1990). Under these conditions, people may desire to suspend judgment or avoid premature closure. This may seem to imply that validity concerns are necessarily at odds with those of closure. Obviously, however, no one would consciously adopt a closure she or he judged invalid. In fact, the very notion of subjective knowledge connotes the joint sense of closure and validity. To know, for example, that Washington, D.C., is the capital of the United States is at once to have closure on the topic and to believe it to be true. This logic notwithstanding, psychological concerns for closure and validity may arise fairly independently of each other; more important, they may pull information processing in diametrically opposed directions.

When closure concerns loom large, for example, individuals may perform closure-promoting activities without sacrificing their sense of validity. They may generate fewer competing hypotheses or suppress attention to information inconsistent with their hypotheses. Both processes may promote a sense of valid closure uncontested by alternative interpretations or inconsistent evidence. By contrast, when validity concerns are salient, people may engage in a thorough and extensive information search and generate multiple alternative interpretations to account for known facts. To wit, they may process information in exactly the opposite manner to that observed under a heightened need for closure. In fact, when validity represents the overriding concern, individuals may be motivated to postpone closure and, in extreme cases, to avoid it altogether. This is not inevitable, however: If a particular closure appears valid beyond the shadow of a doubt (e.g., because of the impeccable credibility of its source), the fear of invalidity may increase the tendency to embrace it rather than prompting its avoidance or postponement. Thus, closure avoidance should be conceptually distinguished from the fear of invalidity. Although closure avoidance may be often induced by such fear, this may not hold invariably.

The need to avoid (or postpone) closure may arise for alternative reasons, such as when the judgmental task is intrinsically enjoyable and interesting (relative to possible alternative pursuits) and closure threatens to terminate this pleasant activity. Finally, as noted earlier, individuals may exhibit stable personal differences in the degree to which they value closure. Such differences may spring from various sources, such as cultural norms (Hofstede, 1980) or personal socialization histories that place a premium on confidence and "know-how." Accordingly, we have recently developed a measure of individual differences in need for closure and established its reliability and validity (Webster & Kruglanski, 1994).

A major upshot of the foregoing analysis is that the need for closure may be operationally defined in a broad variety of ways. If our theory is correct, such diverse operationalizations should prove functionally equivalent in regard to theoretically relevant phenomena. Specific evidence for such an equivalence is examined subsequently.

Consequences of the need for closure: The urgency and permanence tendencies

The motivation toward cognitive closure may affect the way individuals process information en route to the formation, alteration, or dissolution of knowledge. Because such processes are typically embedded in social-interaction contexts, they may significantly affect the way a person thinks about, feels about, acts toward, and even talks about others.

What form might such effects assume? We posit two general tendencies that need for closure may instill: the *urgency tendency* and the *permanence tendency*. The urgency tendency refers to the inclination to "seize" on closure quickly. People under a heightened need for closure may perceive that they desire closure immediately. Any further postponement of closure is experienced as bothersome, and the individual's overriding sense is that he or she simply cannot wait.

The permanence tendency refers to the desire to perpetuate closure, giving rise to the dual inclination (a) to preserve, or "freeze" on, past knowledge and (b) to safeguard future knowledge. Individuals under a heightened need for closure may thus desire an enduring closure and, in extreme cases, abhor losing closure ever again. The urgency and permanence notions both rest on the assumption that people under a heightened need for closure experience its absence as aversive. They may, therefore, wish to terminate this unpleasant state quickly (the urgency tendency) and keep it from recurring (the permanence tendency).

The abstract tendencies toward urgency and permanence may translate into a variety of concrete social psychological phenomena. Specifically, people under a heightened need for closure may seize on information appearing early in a sequence and freeze on it, becoming impervious to subsequent data. Such seizing and freezing trends may affect information processing and, indirectly, the multiple social psychological phenomena information processing may mediate.

Extent of information processing

Because of the tendency to seize on early information and immediately freeze, people under a heightened need for closure may process less information before committing to a judgment and generate fewer competing hypotheses to account for the available data. Paradoxically, they may feel more assured of those judgments, even though they are less grounded in thorough exploration. Specifically, the fewer competing hypotheses a person might entertain, the more confidence he or she may have in those hypotheses (Kelley, 1971) simply because fewer alternatives to a given judgment may appear plausible, enhancing the individual's confidence in those that are.

Cue utilization

A straightforward implication of our seizing and freezing postulate is that people under a heightened need for closure should base their judgments predominantly on early or preexisting cues rather than on later information. As a concrete implication, people under a high (vs. low) need for closure should often exhibit stronger primacy effects in impression formation (Asch, 1946). Furthermore, individuals under a heightened need for closure should rely more on stereotypes than on case-specific or individuating information simply because stereotypes represent preexisting knowledge structures, ready to be used momentarily, whereas individuating information may require extensive further processing. The tendency, based on need for closure, to overutilize early cues implies a disposition to keep one's estimates close to initial anchors rather than correct them in light of subsequent evidence (Tversky & Kahneman, 1974). A similar tendency induced by a heightened need for closure may augment the assimilation of judgments to semantic primes (Higgins, Rholes, & Jones, 1977). The rationale for these predictions is straightforward: Anchors as well as primes define initial bases for a judgment and should be seized and frozen on under a heightened need for closure.

The quest for epistemic permanence: Consensus and consistency strivings

Once a person under a heightened need for closure has managed to formulate a belief and freeze on it, he or she may tend to preserve it for future reference. This is what our permanence notion implies. Such a tendency may manifest itself in a preference for consensual opinions that are unlikely to be challenged and potentially undermined by significant others. As a corollary, people high in need for closure should prefer to associate with similar-minded others, feel positively disposed toward group members who facilitate consensus, and feel negatively disposed toward dissenters or opinion deviates who jeopardize consensus.

Beyond the consensus bias, permanence strivings might induce a bias toward consistency, expressed as a preference for general knowledge applicable across situations over situationally restricted knowledge. Among other things, such a preference may manifest itself in the way people use language in social contexts. Specifically, they may exhibit, under a heightened need for closure, an increased tendency to use trait terms or abstract category labels in describing others, simply because these terms and labels connote transsituational stability (e.g., to say someone is intelligent or friendly means she or he would behave intelligently or in a friendly manner across numerous specific instances).

Separating seizing from freezing: The point of belief crystallization

According to the present theory, a demarcation point separating seizing phenomena from those of freezing is the juncture during which a belief crystallizes and turns from hesitant conjecture to a subjectively firm "fact." Before that point, it should be possible to observe pure seizing, manifest, for example, in quickened pace and enhanced volume of the informational search under a heightened need for closure. As an additional implication, seizing should dispose people to be relatively open to persuasion attempts because such attempts promise to furnish the coveted closure. Subsequent to crystallization, by contrast, it should be possible to witness freezing manifest as a reluctance to continue information processing or a resistance to persuasive arguments aimed at undermining one's current closure and effecting cognitive change. The notion that the predecision action phase is characterized by cognitive openness (the deliberation mind-set) and that the postdecision phase is characterized by narrow restrictiveness (the implementation mind-set) was stressed also by Gollwitzer (1990).

In summary, our theory (a) views the need for closure as a desire for confident knowledge, (b) suggests that motivation toward closure varies along a continuum from a strong need for closure to a strong need to avoid closure, (c) views the need for closure both as an individual-differences variable and as a situationally inducible state prompted by the perceived benefits or costs of lacking closure, and (d) implies that need for closure may affect how an individual thinks, feels, acts toward, and speaks about socially significant others. The empirical evidence for the present theory is reviewed in subsequent sections of this chapter. First, however, we consider its conceptual predecessors and examine its relation to those earlier notions. We ultimately argue that, commonalities with alternative formulations notwithstanding, the need for closure construct is unique and fundamentally different from previous relevant notions in its essence, antecedent conditions, and consequences.

Historical precursors of the need for closure concept

Variability in individuals' tendency toward closed-mindedness or open-mindedness has been addressed in several prior discussions in the personality and social psychology literature. Freud (1923) linked openness to new experiences to the trait of basic trust rooted in successful passage through the oral period. By contrast, closed-mindedness was assumed to reflect a basic distrust rooted in an oral fixation. In its extreme form, such distrust was presumed to foster a paranoid delusional system totally closed off from reality and hence impervious to any informational or logical challenges to its integrity. Frenkel-Brunswik (1949) and Eysenck (1954) used the term *intolerance of ambiguity* to refer to perceptual-cognitive rigidity and emotional ambivalence (Adorno, Frenkel-Brunswik, Levinson, & Sanford, 1950); Rokeach (1960) investigated the phenomenon of closed-mindedness, referring to the impact of belief systems on attitudes toward new information. Kagan (1972) posited that uncertainty resolution is a primary determinant of behavior, and Sorrentino carried out substantial research on "certainty" and "uncertainty" orientations, respectively referring to the degree to which a person "likes to stick to familiar events and traditional beliefs" (Sorrentino & Short, 1986, p. 400) or "attempts to integrate new events or beliefs into already existing belief systems" (Sorrentino & Short, 1986, p. 399).

Need for closure shares some commonality with those earlier notions, but it is also unique in major respects. The primary commonality resides in the fact that those notions too refer to individuals' prejudiced disposition and their tendency to eschew new ideas or experiences. Unlike the need for closure construct, however, the earlier concepts were mostly psychodynamic, referred to personality typologies, were linked to particular contents of beliefs, were often conceived of as cognitive rather than motivational, and often emphasized the deleterious consequences of avoidance of uncertainty or the quest for certainty.

Psychodynamic character

Work by Adorno et al. (1950) was strongly committed to a psychoanalytic view of prejudiced individuals. According to this analysis, such people are characterized by a unique syndrome of correlated and dynamically interactive factors, including conventionalism, authoritarian submission, authoritarian aggression, anti-intraception, superstition and stereotypy, power and toughness, destructiveness and cynicism, projectivity, and sexual preoccupation (e.g., see Adorno et al., 1950, p. 228). Each of those variables is assumed to reflect unique aspects of one's psychosexual development. For instance, the conventional pattern reflects a lack of a firm superego so that the individual is "under the sway of its external representatives" (Adorno et al., 1950, p. 753). Authoritarian aggression and submission are thought to reflect a:

> specific resolution of the Oedipus complex [in which] love for the mother comes under a severe taboo. The resulting hatred against the father is then transformed by reaction-formation into love. The transformation of hatred into love, never succeeds completely . . . part of the preceding aggressiveness is . . . turned into masochism, while another part is left over as sadism, which seeks an outlet in those with whom the subject does not identify himself: ultimately the outgroup. (Adorno et al., 1950, p. 759)

Although critical of Adorno et al.'s (1950) confusion of authoritarianism with its specific manifestation in fascism, Rokeach (1960) maintained, nonetheless, a strong psychodynamic orientation in his analysis of closed and open minds. As he expressed it, "The closed system is nothing more than the total network of psychoanalytic defense mechanisms organized together to form a cognitive system and designed to shield a vulnerable mind" (Rokeach, 1960, p. 70). In more recent work, Sorrentino (Sorrentino & Short, 1986) carried on the psychoanalytic tradition by depicting the closed-minded, certainty-oriented individual as someone who "probably did not make it through the oral and anal stages of development successfully, thus developing a basic mistrust in the world, a dependence on authority, and a low sense of autonomy in an unfamiliar environment" (p. 400).

By contrast to the foregoing formulations, the present theoretical analysis makes no psychoanalytic commitments. Instead, the need for closure is assumed to have diverse potential antecedents. Although early developmental anxieties may not be discounted, they are not considered the exclusive antecedents of this motivation. As noted earlier, for instance, different cultures may vary in the extent to which they value judgmental confidence and clarity (Hofstede, 1980). Through cultural learning and socialization, then, individuals may internalize those values and come to regard their realization as a matter of personal objective. Such individuals may be high in need for closure for cultural reasons. Finally, the psychodynamic emphasis is closely linked with an implication of pathology and dysfunctionality whereby closed-minded individuals are assumed to grossly distort reality in their need to avoid uncertainties. Need for closure theory carries no such implication. According to this conception, people under a high need for closure may be correct in their judgment if the initial cue they seized and froze on was correct. To the contrary, people with a high need to avoid closure may commit errors if they too readily "unfroze" correct judgments and diluted them through excessive openness to misleading or irrelevant information.

Personality versus situation

Furthermore, the present theory highlights especially the potential situational determinants of the need for closure. The very notion of situational antecedents contrasts sharply with previous formulations of closed-mindedness and open-mindedness in terms of personality typologies. Because these formulations are imbued with psychoanalytic meanings, they are rather incompatible with a situational analysis: The psychodynamic processes they assume are typically described at a macro level of analysis; they relate to protracted developmental phases (the oral or anal period, for example) taking years to unfold. It is unlikely that they may find functionally equivalent counterparts in microlevel situational factors of incomparably briefer duration. Precisely such functional equivalence, however, is asserted by the present analysis, whereby need for closure is determined by perceived benefits or costs of closed or open states as influenced by situational, cultural, or personality factors.

Cognitive style versus motive

Whereas the need for closure is a distinctly motivational construct, previous psychological analyses depicted closed-mindedness and open-mindedness in terms of cognitive style or structure. Sorrentino and Short (1986), for example, explicitly disavowed a motivational interpretation of the uncertainty orientation and described it "as a cognitive rather than a motivational variable" (p. 382) better thought of as "cold" rather than "hot" (p. 392). Similarly, Rokeach (1960) viewed closed-mindedness and open-mindedness as properties of belief–disbelief systems and stressed the predominantly cognitive character of his theory (e.g., p. 399).

Content specificity

By contrast, the theory of the authoritarian personality (Adorno et al., 1950) does depict rigidity as motivated, specifically by ego defenses against aggressive impulses toward authority figures. However, psychodynamic defenses may lend rigidity to specific relevant belief contents related, for example, to admiration of the powerful, or the in-group, and disdain for the powerless, or the out-group. Even though such rigidity may generalize to other domains as well (Frenkel-Brunswik, 1949, 1951), these processes are secondary and derivative from rigidity in a circumscribed domain of conflicted content areas. Rokeach's (1960) work on dogmatism also incorporated significant content elements. For example, the closed belief system was considered to involve the assumption that "the world one lives in is . . . threatening" or that "authority is absolute . . . and people are to be accepted or rejected according to their agreement or disagreement with such authority" (p. 56). Similarly, the open belief system was presumed to hold that "the world one lives in . . . is a friendly one" and that "authority is not absolute . . . and people are not to be evaluated (if they are to be evaluated at all) according to their agreement or disagreement with such authority" (Rokeach, 1960, p. 56). By contrast to the content specificity in the preceding formulations, need for closure theory eschews commitment to particular belief contents and posits that the desire for closure may manifest itself equally in regard to diverse types of belief.

Unilaterality of emphasis

Previous relevant formulations often stressed unilaterally the tendency to eschew uncertainty or seek certainty. Uncertainty eschewal was central to Adorno et al.'s (1950) formulation and its emphasis on the defensive function of cognitive rigidity. Accordingly, Adorno et al. focused on the negative valence of ambiguity, stressing its avoidance or intolerance. A unilateral emphasis on uncertainty reduction also characterized Kagan's (1972) formulation that viewed such reduction as a primary motive for behavior. Similarly, Sorrentino and Short (1986) viewed orientation toward "clarity about self or the environment" (p. 382) as primary for both certainty-oriented and uncertainty-oriented individuals.

Even though they may differ in emphasis on the approach of certainty or avoidance of uncertainty aspect, all of the preceding analyses underscore the same trend toward increased certainty or decreased uncertainty. Need for closure theory, on the other hand, suggests that the trend may be reversed under some conditions and that people may actually approach uncertainty if its perceived benefits and the perceived costs of certainty outweigh the perceived costs of uncertainty and the benefits of certainty.

Empirical relations of need for closure with related constructs

The foregoing discussion suggests that although need for closure may share a degree of commonality with alternative constructs relevant to closed-mindedness and open-mindedness, it differs from those alternative concepts in important respects. Empirically, this should result in low to moderate correlations between the need for closure and related concepts. Extant evidence is consistent with this supposition. In psychometric work on the Need for Closure Scale, Webster and Kruglanski (1994) reported correlations of .26 between need for closure and the F scale assessing authoritarianism (Sanford, Adorno, Frenkel-Brunswik, & Levinson, 1950), .29 between need for closure and intolerance of ambiguity (Frenkel-Brunswik, 1949), and .28 between need for closure and dogmatism (Rokeach, 1960).

Intelligence and need for closure

Because individuals high in need for closure often limit their information-processing activities, this may suggest a negative relationship between intelligence and need for closure. On the other hand, need for closure may sometimes promote extensive information processing in instances in which closure is lacking. Theoretically, then, the relationship between need for closure and intelligence is not readily apparent. Empirically, this relation is nonsignificant ($r = -.17$).

Further connections and distinctions: Need for cognition, central–systematic processing, and peripheral–heuristic processing

The need for cognition refers to the extent to which one "engages in and enjoys thinking" (Cacioppo & Petty, 1982, p. 1). In other words, for people high in this need, the activity of thinking as such is the desired end. By contrast, for those high in need for closure, the desired end is cognitive closure. Although having closure obviates the necessity to think further about an issue, one may refrain from thinking without necessarily attaining closure. Thus, although some negative relation between the need for cognition and the need for closure should be expected, it should not be very strong. The empirical correlation between the two constructs is, in fact, low and negative ($r = -.28$; Webster & Kruglanski, 1994).

Need for cognition is one among several variables assumed to effect a processing shift from the reliance on peripheral cues to a thorough consideration of central informational contents (Petty & Cacioppo, 1986). A somewhat similar distinction has been drawn between the processing of information heuristically and systematically (Chaiken, Lieberman, & Eagly, 1989). The question, therefore, is how need for closure theory relates to the peripheral–heuristic versus central–systematic distinctions. The answer is that although our theory shares some common ground with those alternative conceptions, it differs in important respects. The commonality resides in the fact that need for closure theory also posits conditions under which people process information briefly and superficially and others wherein they do so thoroughly and methodically. Unlike the alternative formulations, however, need for closure theory does not postulate two qualitatively different modes of information processing. Rather, it regards the difference between brief and thorough processing as a matter of extent. Furthermore, whereas both the peripheral–central and the heuristic–systematic models may view some of the information-processing costs (produced, for example, by ambient noise, fatigue, or time pressure) as depleting the individual's cognitive capacity, the present analysis stresses their motivating potential in arousing the need for closure. A detailed consideration of the capacity versus motivation issue is undertaken at a later juncture.

Openness to experience

Finally, the present distinction between closed-mindedness and open-mindedness is shared by the Openness factor of the big five (McCrae & Costa, 1985). The specific areas to which one might be open or closed include fantasy, aesthetics, feelings, actions, ideas, and values (Costa & McCrae, 1992; McCrae, 1993–1994). As in the present conception, then, the closed and open dimension is seen as relevant to a broad range of domains rather than being restricted to specific contents. Also, both conceptions highlight the possibility of motivated openness, in counterdistinction to alternative notions stressing the ubiquitous quest for certainty. Again, however, openness to experience is essentially an individual-differences dimension to which situational considerations seem rather foreign. Furthermore, the openness to experience construct depicts a general psychological syndrome (manifest, for example, in artistic creativity, susceptibility to hypnosis, rich fantasy lives, and unconventional attitudes) rather than the effects of a specific motivation. The motivational part of the syndrome includes need for change, sensation seeking, and intellectual understanding, which are rather different from need for closure per se. For instance, according to our conception, a person under a need for closure can exhibit openness to information (i.e., seizing) in the precrystallization phase of judgment formation. Such a possibility does not seem relevant to the openness construct.

In summary, then, the present need for closure theory seems both conceptually and empirically distinct from relevant alternative formulations. It appears to be more general than historical treatments of open-mindedness and closed-mindedness and less committed to specific antecedents (e.g., of psychosexual origins), cognitive contents (e.g., assumptions about authority), or approach-avoidance trends (e.g., toward certainty and away from uncertainty). It also constitutes a distinctly motivational theory that highlights the effects of its key variable on the extent of processing rather than on shifts from one qualitative processing mode to another. Those unique properties of the need for closure construct yield a variety of predictions not readily derivable from previous formulations. We turn now to the empirical evidence for those predictions.

Empirical evidence

Seizing and freezing effects

Earlier we posited two general tendencies that need for closure may instigate: the urgency tendency of seizing on judgmentally relevant cues and the permanence tendency of freezing on judgments the cues imply. Operating jointly, the seizing and freezing sequence may produce a broad range of judgmental effects observable under a heightened need for closure.

Extent of information processing

At a minimum, the seizing and freezing mechanism implies a reduced extent of information processing under a heightened need for closure. The speeded-up reliance on early cues implied by seizing and the truncation of further exploration due to freezing suggest that individuals under a high (vs. low) need for closure should consider less evidence before forming a judgment. In an experiment relevant to this proposition, Mayseless and Kruglanski (1987, Study 2) had participants perform a tachistoscopic recognition task of identifying barely visible digits on a screen. As a means of arousing the need for closure, participants were told that forming unambiguous, clear-cut opinions is positively correlated with high mental concentration and intelligence. This manipulation was designed to enhance the perceived value (or benefit) of closure and, hence, to increase the need for closure. Note that stating that unambiguous or clear-cut opinions are valuable does not, in itself, demand briefer information processing. To the contrary, it seems more reasonable to assume that the arrival at clarity and the dispelling of ambiguity would require, if anything, more rather than less extensive processing. The present seizing and freezing notion implies the opposite, of course.

As a means of inducing the need to avoid closure, participants were given accuracy instructions and promised extra experimental credit for correctly identifying 9 of 10 digits. A neutral control condition was also included in which no motivational induction took place. Participants were allowed to operate the tachistoscope an unlimited number of times. As predicted, their extent of informational search (number of times they operated the tachistoscope) was lowest in the need for closure condition, intermediate in the control condition, and highest in the need to avoid closure condition.

Hypothesis generation

In addition to a reduced extent of processing "external" stimulus information, the seizing and freezing notions imply that, under heightened need for closure, there will be a parallel reduction in "internal" hypothesis generation. Presumably, those two processes are intimately linked: Examination of external information may suggest new, internally formed hypotheses, the testing of which may require, in turn, further processing of external information. Need for closure effects on hypothesis generation were specifically addressed in another experiment conducted by Mayseless and Kruglanski (1987, Study 3). Participants were shown enlarged photographs of parts of common objects (e.g., a comb, a toothbrush, and a nail). These photos were taken from unusual angles, masking the objects' actual nature. On each trial, participants were urged to list the maximal number of hypotheses concerning an object's identity and ultimately chose the identity most likely to be correct. As in the study mentioned earlier (Mayseless & Kruglanski, 1987, Study 2), need for closure was induced by informing participants that clear-cut opinions relate to mental concentration and intelligence. Again, this, in and of itself, should not artificially "demand" a curtailment of hypothesis generation. Rather, an emphasis on clarity and intelligence may demand increased hypothesis generation, contrary to the present prediction.

To induce the need to avoid closure, the instructions noted a correlation between the desirable mental qualities and correct visual recognition. As in the previous study, a neutral control condition devoid of a motivational induction was included. The results showed, as predicted, that participants in the need to avoid closure condition generated the largest number of hypotheses, followed by participants in the control condition; participants in the need for closure condition produced the fewest hypotheses.

Subjective confidence

An interesting corollary to the notion that individuals under a high (vs. low) need for closure generate fewer hypotheses is that they will be quicker to attain high judgmental confidence. This implication follows from Kelley's (1971) discounting principle, whereby reduction in the number of alternative hypotheses should boost an individual's confidence in each hypothesis. Relevant to this prediction, in the tachistoscopic recognition study conducted by Mayseless and Kruglanski (1987, Study 2), participants' confidence in their initial hypotheses and the magnitude of confidence shifts (upward or downward) occasioned by each successive stimulus presentation were significantly lower in the need to avoid closure condition than in the need for closure condition, with the control condition falling in the middle.

Elevated confidence of participants under heightened need for closure has been replicated in several studies using widely divergent methods, such as ambient noise (Kruglanski & Webster, 1991; Kruglanski, Webster, & Klem, 1993), dullness of the task (Webster, 1993), and time pressure (Kruglanski & Webster, 1991), of inducing this motivation. Identical results were obtained when need for closure was assessed via our individual-differences measure (Webster & Kruglanski, 1994) rather than manipulated situationally.

Elevated confidence under a heightened need for closure is striking against the backdrop of reduced information processing under those very circumstances. This finding is incongruous with the common presumption that attainment of secure views requires more rather than less extensive processing, and it defines an "unfounded confidence" paradox under a heightened need for closure.

Seeking diagnostic or prototypical information

Restriction of hypothesis generation under a heightened need for closure (Mayseless & Kruglanski, 1987, Study 3) should, finally, affect not only the amount of information sought by hypothesis-testing participants but also the type of information sought. Specifically, under high need for closure, participants may seek prototypical information about a category, whereas, under high need to avoid closure, they might instead seek diagnostic information (Trope & Bassok, 1983) capable of discriminating among different categories. Consider an interviewer testing the focal hypothesis that an interviewee is a painter. Under a high need for closure, this individual may refrain from generating specific competing alternatives to this hypothesis and search for information capable of demarcating it from the diffuse nonpainter hypothesis. Such information may pertain to features prototypical of painters (e.g., "bohemian" life-style or artistic ability). The case may be very different, however, if the individual's need to avoid closure was aroused. This might motivate her or him to be sensitive to possible specific alternatives to the hypothesis, such as that the interviewee is an architect. If so, the interviewer might specifically seek information diagnostic in regard to the painter–architect pair: Artistic ability is presumably shared by painters and architects alike and hence is nondiagnostic, whereas bohemian life-style is diagnostic because it may principally characterize painters but not architects. In research designed to investigate these possibilities (Kruglanski & Mayseless, 1988), we asked participants to evaluate whether a target belonged to a given professional category, subtly hinting at a competing alternative possibility. As expected, individuals under a high need for closure, manipulated through implied time pressure, sought more prototypical information than diagnostic information, whereas those under need to avoid closure, manipulated through instilled fear of invalidity, sought more diagnostic information capable of differentiating between the competing alternatives.

Early-cue utilization

Perhaps the broadest implication of the seizing and freezing mechanism is that under a high (vs. low) need for closure, individuals tend to base their final judgments on early cues. Because of the urgency tendency, such cues should be quickly utilized to form an initial judgment (seizing), and, because of the permanence tendency, such a judgment should tend to stay fixed (freezing) rather than be altered in light of subsequent evidence. This fundamental process may underlie a diverse array of phenomena that, at first glance, might appear unrelated.

Impressional-primacy effects. An obvious such phenomenon is the impressional "primacy effect" (Asch, 1946; Luchins, 1957), that is, the tendency to base impressions of a social target more on information presented early versus late in a sequence. If primacy effects are an instance of the seizing and freezing process, they should be appropriately magnified under high need for closure and attenuated under high need to avoid closure. This prediction has received support in several studies differing in the ways in which needs for closure or closure avoidance were operationalized. Specifically, need for closure has been variously operationalized in terms of scores on the Need for Closure Scale (Webster & Kruglanski, 1994), time pressure (Freund, Kruglanski, & Schpitzajzen, 1985; Heaton & Kruglanski, 1991; Kruglanski & Freund, 1983), instructions to form an overall evaluative judgment of the target (vs. separately evaluating each of his or her characteristics; Freund et al., 1985), and degree of mental fatigue (Webster, Richter, & Kruglanski, 1995). Need to avoid closure has been operationalized in terms of evaluation apprehension (Freund et al., 1985; Kruglanski & Freund, 1983) or potential costs to the evaluation target (in the case of a participant's mistake; Freund et al., 1985). As predicted, in all of these studies, the magnitude of primacy effects varied positively with need for closure and negatively with need to avoid closure.

Note, however, that in the research described thus far, it was relatively easy for participants to downplay the late appearing evidence if motivated to do so. It is quite possible that if the late evidence is particularly compelling and participants high in need for closure are pressured to seriously consider it, they may change their mind more abruptly and completely than those low in need for closure, manifesting a recency effect. In dynamic systems terms (Vallacher & Nowak, in press), need for closure could serve as a "control parameter," effecting quick gravitation to "attractors" representing conclusions implied by the early and late appearing evidence.

Anchoring effects. A different instance of early-cue utilization may underlie the "anchoring" effect discovered by Tversky and Kahneman (1974). Consider a probability-estimation task (cf. Bar-Hillel, 1973) in which participants assess the probability of compound conjunctive or disjunctive events. Participants typically use the probability of the simple constituent events as an anchor and then adjust. When the adjustment is insufficient, they should therefore overestimate the probability of conjunctive events (calculation of which involves the multiplication of fractions) and underestimate the probability of disjunctive events (calculation of which involves the addition of fractions). If anchoring represents a special case of cue utilization, it should be appropriately affected by the need for closure. Consistent with this notion, participants' tendency to overestimate the likelihood of conjunctive events and underestimate that of disjunctive events increased under need for closure manipulated via time pressure and decreased under need to avoid closure manipulated by evaluation apprehension (Kruglanski & Freund, 1983, Study 2).

The correspondence bias. The correspondence bias in person perception (Jones, 1979) is among the most persistently studied phenomena in social cognition (see discussion by Trope & Higgins, 1993). It is, therefore, of considerable interest that it too may represent a special case of early-cue utilization and be appropriately influenced by the need for closure. The correspondence bias refers to a perceiver tendency to overascribe actors' behavior to personal inclinations, even in the presence of situational pressures that in and of themselves should be capable of eliciting the behavior. In an original demonstration of this phenomenon, Jones and Harris (1967) presented participants with essays allegedly written by a person given either a free choice or no choice in the matter of doing so. In both cases, that is, even when the writer was denied choice, participants assumed that his or her attitude was largely congruent with the essay content.

Different theorists (Gilbert, Pelham, & Krull, 1988; Jones, 1979; Quattrone, 1982) have implied that the underlying mechanism for the correspondence bias could involve the anchoring and insufficient adjustment process discussed earlier. Thus, when participants come to judge the writer's attitude, the most salient evidence is the very behavior that took place. Often, the earliest hypothesis this suggests is that the behavior faithfully mirrored the writer's attitude. This attitude-correspondence hypothesis may pop to mind spontaneously or "automatically" and serve as an initial anchor to be subsequently adjusted via a "controlled" cognitive process during which further relevant evidence (e.g., concerning pertinent situational constraints) is considered.

Such controlled adjustment, however, may require substantial cognitive effort. For instance, Gilbert et al. (1988) found that when perceivers were cognitively busy, the correspondence bias was enhanced. This may mean that the increased effort required by the adjustment process was more than the participants were willing to put out, which suggests that motivational considerations may indeed enter into the correspondence bias. Research by Tetlock (e.g., 1985) supports this possibility. He found that such bias was markedly reduced when participants were made to feel accountable for their judgments. Presumably, manipulation of accountability motivated participants to process information in a more discriminating manner, affording a more adequate adjustment of the initial bias.

The preceding findings are consistent with the notion that, as with the primacy or anchoring effect, the correspondence bias represents an over-utilization of early cues. If so, the correspondence bias too should be appropriately affected by the need for closure. In a recent set of studies, Webster (1993) tested this proposition, manipulating the need for closure via task attractiveness. Her underlying assumption was that when an activity is attractive or intrinsically motivated (e.g., Deci & Ryan, 1985; Higgins & Trope, 1990; Kruglanski, 1975), this should induce the motivation to extensively explore it (Berlyne, 1960) and, hence, to avoid premature closure. By contrast, when an activity is extrinsically motivated, the motivation may be to reach closure quickly so as to reach the exogenous reward without delay.

An attitude-attribution task was used in which a target made a speech critical of student-exchange programs under free-choice or no-choice conditions. As a means of portraying this task as unattractive, the task participants expected to perform subsequently (the watching of comedy videos) promised to be particularly attractive. This was assumed to render relatively unappealing or subjectively costly the current, duller task and hence to elevate the need for closure.

As a means of portraying the same task as attractive, the subsequent task promised to be particularly unattractive (watching a video of a statistics lecture). This was assumed to render the current task subjectively appealing and hence to lower the need for closure. Finally, in a third, control condition, the subsequent task was portrayed as largely similar to the current one (also involving attitude attributions), lending it intermediate appeal. Manipulation checks confirmed that the experimental manipulations produced the corresponding differences in need for cognitive closure. Most important, the correspondence bias in the no-choice condition was affected by the need for closure in the predicted manner: Substantial correspondence bias was already present in the control condition (replicating prior research), and such bias was significantly enhanced in the unattractive task condition and completely eliminated in the attractive task condition.

The same pattern of results was obtained in Webster's second study, in which need for closure was assessed via the Need for Closure Scale (Webster & Kruglanski, 1994). Finally, when the initial cues implied a situational rather than a personal attribution, the results of the previous two studies were completely reversed. The tendency to overascribe the essay to the writer's attitude was reduced under a high need for closure (manipulated via task attractiveness) and enhanced under a low need for closure, both as compared with the control condition. This last finding is particularly significant because it demonstrates that need for closure effects are content free and depend on the order in which cues are received rather than on their specific substance (e.g., implying a personal or a situational attribution).

Stereotypic judgments. From a social psychological perspective, some particularly interesting sources of early cues are previously formed stereotypes, prejudices or attitudes readily accessible in memory. Such preexisting knowledge structures may preempt the use of case-specific (or individuating) information in the forming of social judgments. The present seizing and freezing mechanism suggests that such preemption should be particularly likely under a heightened need for closure, simply because extensive processing of case-specific information may substantially postpone closure. In an early demonstration of those effects, Kruglanski and Freund (1983, Study 3) found that ethnic stereotypes of Ashkenazi and Sephardi Jews influenced grade assignments for a literary composition more in conditions likely to elevate the graders' need for closure (time pressure, lack of accountability, or both) than in conditions likely to reduce it (accountability and no time pressure). Time pressure also increased the degree to which preexisting prejudice against women in management versus individuating information about specific applicants' qualifications tended to affect discrimination toward female versus male candidates (Jamieson & Zanna, 1989).

Construct accessibility effects. A key assumption in predicting more pronounced judgmental influence of stereotypes under a high (vs. low) need for closure is that such stereotypes are highly accessible in memory. Such accessible guides to judgment should be seized and frozen on under a heightened need for closure. A direct test of this assumption was recently carried out by Ford and Kruglanski (1995), who used a priming paradigm developed by Higgins et al. (1977). In the context of an allegedly unrelated memory experiment, participants were primed by either the negatively valenced adjective *reckless* or the positively valenced adjective *adventurous*. They were subsequently presented a passage about Donald that was ambiguous with respect to the adventurous–reckless pair. Participants' task was to characterize Donald using a single word. In this situation, participants high in dispositional need for closure (Webster & Kruglanski, 1994) exhibited stronger assimilation of judgment to prime than participants low in this need. That is, participants high (vs. low) in need for closure tended more to characterize Donald in terms suggesting recklessness in the negative prime condition and adventurousness in the positive prime condition. An independently executed study by Thompson, Roman, Moscovitz, Chaiken, and Bargh (1994), using a different method of priming (the scrambled sentence technique) and of assessing need for closure (Neuberg & Newsom's, 1993, Personal Need for Structure Scale), yielded the same results. Participants high in need for structure–closure exhibited greater assimilation of their judgments to primed constructs than participants low in this need. Finally, both Ford and Kruglanski (1995) and Thompson et al. (1994) succeeded in significantly reducing the assimilation-to-prime effect under accuracy instructions (i.e., in conditions likely to reduce participants' need for closure).

Isolating the urgency and permanence effects

Whereas the seizing and freezing research described earlier examined the joint workings of the urgency and permanence tendencies, further studies have aimed at separating their effects. In the next section, we examine work pertaining to permanence phenomena as such, followed by research on the boundary conditions for urgency versus permanence effects.

Consensus and consistency biases

As already noted, the permanence tendency involves the desire to maintain closure over time. The freezing phenomenon represents one manifestation of such a desire: Once closure has been attained, confronting it with new information might risk its subsequent dissolution. Freezing may be understood as an attempt to forestall this possibility. However, the permanence tendency may manifest itself in other ways as well, specifically in a bias toward consensual judgments unlikely to be contested by significant others. Furthermore, it may promote a preference for abstract judgments connoting transsituational consistency, and in this sense permanence, of knowledge.

Consensus

An indication that need for closure may enhance the desire for consensus appeared in a pair of studies conducted by Kruglanski et al. (1993). In this research, the participant acted as a juror whose task was to discuss a legal case with another juror. Half of the participants received prior information allowing them to form a fairly confident opinion about the case. The remaining participants received no prior information, forestalling secure opinion formation. The need for closure was either manipulated via noise produced by a computer printer (Kruglanski et al., 1993, Study 2) or assessed via the Need for Closure Scale (Study 3). In both cases, participants under a high need for closure professed greater desire to agree with the other juror (i.e., to attain consensus) than did participants under a low need for closure. Of even greater interest, the specific manner in which participants tended to deal with their desire for consensus varied as a function of the informational conditions: When presence of an information base led participants to crystallize a prior opinion, they professed a preference for an easily persuadable partner. Presumably, such a partner could be readily won over to the participant's side, affording consensus via what Festinger (1950) called the "change other" strategy. By contrast, when absence of an informational base kept participants from crystallizing a prior opinion, they professed a significant preference for a persuasive partner. Presumably, such a partner could readily convince the participant to adopt a given view, hence forging consensus by what Festinger (1950) called the "change self" strategy. These findings, too, emerged regardless of whether need for closure was operationalized via ambient noise or scores on the Need for Closure Scale.

Rejection of opinion deviates

When both the "change other" and "change self" strategies fail, however, there may exist a third possible way of attaining consensus in a group. It consists of "rejecting the deviate" and thus achieving consensus in a group by excluding the dissenters (Festinger, 1950; Schachter, 1951). If the permanence tendency fosters a quest for consensus and if, under the appropriate conditions, this encourages the rejection of deviates, heightening group members' need for closure should yield evidence of enhanced "rejectionism." This prediction was investigated in a series of experiments by Kruglanski and Webster (1991).

In their first study, need for closure was operationally defined via time pressure or temporal proximity of attitude assessment to the group-decision deadline. Our assumption has been that when the deadline is relatively remote, group members' predominant concern might be to safeguard the quality of their decision. This may induce a need to avoid premature closure and increase the tolerance for ambiguity induced by dissenting views. With the deadline approaching, however, the implied time pressure may induce an overriding need for closure. This may reduce group members' tolerance for dissent and increase their tendency to reject the deviates.

In a field experiment designed to test those ideas (Kruglanski & Webster, 1991, Study 1), groups of Tel Aviv (boy and girl) scouts were presented with a decision of choosing a location for their annual "working camp" of 2 weeks' duration. Two choices of kibbutz settlements were presented. One was an affluent, centrally located kibbutz (Naan) amply endowed with such accoutrements as swimming pools, tennis courts, and color TVs. The other choice was a fledgling borderline kibbutz (Ktora) in the Judean desert lacking at the time even such basic amenities as in-house bathrooms.

Despite what to some might appear the obvious choice, the idealistically inspired scouts predominantly preferred the rugged, little settlement over its lush alternative. This fact was well known to the investigators and was treated as the group's consensual opinion. To introduce our deviancy manipulation, we asked one member in each group (known to occupy a median sociometric standing) to argue for either the consensual choice (the conformist role) or the unpopular alternative (the deviant role) and to do so either early on in the deliberation process or late, near the putative deadline.

Actually, there existed three experimental conditions related to the timing of opinion expression. In the *objectively early* condition, the confederate announced her or his (conforming or deviant) opinion near the commencement of discussion. In the *objectively late* condition, he or she did so near the expected deadline. In the *subjectively early* condition, she or he did so at the same actual time as in the objectively late condition; because the deadline was appropriately postponed, however, the participant believed that he or she had as much discussion time remaining as did others in the subjectively early condition.

The available evidence confirmed that participants' need for closure was proportionate to the discussion time they believed they had at their disposal. Specifically, participants' differentiation between attractiveness of the two choice alternatives was significantly lower in the early conditions (objective as well as subjective) than in the (objectively) late condition. This suggests that participants were more open-minded to both alternatives when they perceived little (vs. a great deal of) time pressure to make up their mind. Those findings were paralleled by expressed confidence in the attractiveness ratings, which was significantly higher at the late versus the early (objective and subjective) points. Both findings support the notion that time pressure, induced by perceived proximity of the deadline, contributed in the expected manner to need for closure arousal.

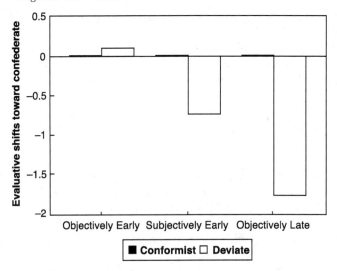

Figure 1 Evaluations of the conformist and the deviate at different degrees of proximity to the group-decision deadline.

The main dependent variable of interest was an evaluative shift toward the confederate in the deviant and conformist roles. Results are depicted in Figure 1. As can be seen, the evaluative shifts toward the conformist were negligible and did not appreciably vary as a function of timing. The shifts toward the deviant exhibited a strikingly different pattern. They were progressively more negative as the expected deadline drew near.

We (Kruglanski & Webster, 1991, Study 2) conceptually replicated this experiment, manipulating need for closure via ambient noise. Groups of University of Maryland students were instructed to discuss to consensus compulsory drug testing for campus athletes. Students were preselected to be in favor of such testing. Two members of each group were confederates, whose behavior during the discussion was systematically varied as function of our experimental manipulations. One confederate enacted a conformist's role and expressed opinions consistent with the expected consensus (i.e., in favor of drug testing). The other confederate enacted a deviant's role and expressed opinions at odds with the expected consensus (arguing against drug testing). As a means of controlling for possible effects due to the confederates' personalities, the conformist and deviant roles were rotated across the experimental sessions.

As in the Kruglanski et al. (1993) research described earlier, the noise was produced via a computer printer. We assumed that in a noisy environment, information processing would be more laborious, and hence subjectively costly, and that this would heighten participants' need for closure, leading to greater rejection of the deviate.

If participants in the noise (vs. no-noise) condition experience a higher need for closure, they may experience greater subjective confidence in their opinion.

This turned out to be the case, although the difference was statistically borderline ($p < .13$). Of greater interest, the deviant was evaluated more negatively ($p < .001$) under noise than under no noise (see Table 1). Although the conformist was evaluated somewhat more positively under noise (vs. no noise), this difference was not significant.

To examine the possible alternative interpretation that derogation of the deviant under noise stemmed from the irritability that noise might have induced rather than the need for closure, we replicated our experiment (Kruglanski & Webster, 1991, Study 3) with a single exception. Participants in one condition were provided with an alternative way of safeguarding collective closure: the possibility of formally excluding the deviant from decision making. Specifically, participants in this condition were allowed to form a decision by majority rather than by consensus. To see whether the noise manipulation induced differences in the need for closure, we looked again at participants' expressed confidence in their opinion. As expected, the confidence ratings were significantly higher ($p < .015$) under noise than under no noise. Of greater interest, the only condition in which the deviant was downgraded was the noise–consensus cell (see Table 2). Thus, it appears that noise-induced irritability may not have accounted for derogation of the deviant. The deviant would have been upsetting enough to foster rejection only when he or she may have undermined the other members' sense of closure by constituting a dissenting voice in a significant reference group.

Table 1 Mean evaluations of the deviate and the conformist as a function of environmental noise

Confederate's opinion	Noise	No noise
Deviant	8.12	14.87
Conformist	15.75	14.68

Note: Adapted from "Group members' reactions to opinion deviates and conformists at varying degrees of proximity to decision deadline and of environmental noise," by A. W. Kruglanski and D. M. Webster, 1991, *Journal of Personality and Social Psychology, 61*, p. 219. Copyright 1991 by the American Psychological Association.

Table 2 Mean evaluations of the deviate and the conformist as a function of environmental noise and group-decision rule

Confederate's opinion	Consensus rule Noise	Consensus rule No noise	Majority rule Noise	Majority rule No noise
Deviant	11.87	21.07	18.67	20.00
Conformist	20.75	22.36	20.58	20.50

Note: Adapted from "Group members' reactions to opinion deviates and conformists at varying degrees of proximity to decision deadline and of environmental noise," by A. W. Kruglanski and D. M. Webster, 1991, *Journal of Personality and Social Psychology, 61*, p. 221. Copyright 1991 by the American Psychological Association.

Additional evidence that rejection is not merely the consequence of noise-related irritability is the finding, described subsequently, that the conformist might be actually evaluated more positively under noise (vs. no noise). The reason this may not have been apparent in the research described thus far is that, in those experiments, the conformist merely reiterated the normative opinion, and hence her or his statements may have lacked saliency. As a means of overcoming this problem, in our last study (Kruglanski & Webster, 1991, Study 4), the conformist was made to assume a leader's role (including initiation of conversations with the deviate and issuing of repeated reminders to the group of the consensus objective). In this study, too, participants under noise (vs. no noise) reported higher judgmental confidence ($p < .01$). More important, whereas the deviant continued to be downgraded more ($p < .0001$) under noise (vs. no noise), the conformist was actually applauded more ($p < .01$) in this condition. Taken as a body, then, the reviewed findings support the notion that need for closure increases participants' desire for consensus and that this may lead to derogating those who hinder consensus and countenancing those who facilitate it.

Need for closure-based permanence seeking and linguistic abstraction biases

If need for closure induces the tendency to seek permanent knowledge and avoid the recurrence of ambiguity, such a need should also foster bias toward general, transsituationally stable knowledge. Accordingly, people under a heightened need for closure should prefer abstract descriptions and category labels over concrete (and hence situationally specific) ones.

Global attributions for failure

Consistent with this reasoning, Mikulincer, Yinon, and Kabili (1991) found, in one study, that "need for structure" assessed via a questionnaire (Naccarato, Thompson, & Parker, 1986), a notion highly akin to the need for closure, was positively correlated with stable and global self-attributions for failure assessed by the Attributional Style Questionnaire (Seligman, Abramson, Semmel, & von Baeyer, 1979). By contrast, an individual-differences measure of the "fear of invalidity" (Naccarato et al., 1986), assumed to often foster a need to avoid closure, was associated with the tendency to make specific (vs. global) attributions for failure.

In a second study conducted by Mikulincer et al. (1991), failure was induced experimentally via unsolvable problems. Here, too, participants who reported a high need for structure and a low fear of invalidity attributed failure on the problems to more global causes than did other types of participants. Furthermore, failure impaired subsequent performance on a different task for participants high in need for structure but not for those low in need for structure. Finally, in their third experiment, Mikulincer et al. (1991) varied the need for structure experimentally. Specifically, this need was induced by leading participants to believe that the research examined their ability to create "firm beliefs." Fear of invalidity was induced by telling participants that the purpose of the research was to examine their ability to make "correct judgments" about their performance. It was found that participants exposed to failure feedback exhibited performance deficits on a subsequent, unrelated task in the need for structure condition but not in the fear of invalidity condition. These results were interpreted to mean that need for structure–closure induces a globalized belief about one's low abilities that may translate, in turn, into subsequent performance deficits.

Use of trait labels in communication

Whereas Mikulincer et al. (1991) referred to globality of beliefs about the self, a recent experiment by Boudreau, Baron, and Oliver (1992) pertained to the tendency to use global trait labels in descriptions of others. Specifically, Boudreau et al. (1992) found that an expectation to communicate impressions of a target to an expert (a clinical psychology graduate student) suppressed the proportion of traits used by college students in their person descriptions. By contrast, an expectation to communicate to a fifth grader increased the proportion of trait labels in such descriptions. Boudreau et al. interpreted these results in terms of an increased fear of invalidity (and hence lowered need for closure) when confrontation with an expert is expected and an increased need for structure–closure when a confrontation with "inferiors" (presumably less capable of drawing definite conclusions about the target on their own) is expected.

Need for closure and the linguistic intergroup bias

Maass and her colleagues demonstrated, in a series of studies (for a review, see Maass & Arcuri, 1992), that positive in-group and negative out-group behaviors are often described in relatively abstract terms, implying that such behaviors are associated with constant characteristics of the actor. By contrast, negative in-group and positive out-group behaviors tend to be described in relatively concrete terms, restricting the behaviors to the specific situation and affording little generalization. These phenomena have been collectively referred to as the linguistic intergroup bias. Research aimed at uncovering the underlying mechanism of the linguistic intergroup bias has obtained evidence for expectancy-based as well as motivational explanations. According to the expectancy explanation, the general stereotype of the in-group is positive and that of the out-group is negative. Thus, positive behaviors of the in-group and negative behaviors of the out-group are consistent with the abstract stereotype and, hence, could be assimilated thereto. By contrast, negative in-group and positive out-group behaviors are inconsistent with the corresponding stereotypes. Instead, they tend to be viewed as unique and described in their own, concrete terms.

The motivational explanation has been phrased in terms of in-group protection. As Maass and Arcuri (in press) put it:

> Assuming that concrete descriptions dissociate the actor from the act, whereas abstract descriptions imply that the behavior reflects a stable and enduring

property of the actor, one may argue that the linguistic intergroup bias helps to portray the ingroup in a favorable light while derogating the outgroup.

According to the present analysis, the need for closure may constitute another motivational factor with consequences for the linguistic abstraction level at which in-group and out-group behaviors are described. Of even greater interest, those consequences may constitute a joint function of strivings for transsituational consistency and consensus that the permanence tendency based on need for closure may foster. As noted earlier, strivings for transsituational consistency should increase the abstraction level of linguistic descriptions. This tendency should apply across the board (i.e., for positive and negative behaviors of in-groups as well as out-groups). On the other hand, the permanence tendency should also enhance the striving for in-group consensus and lend the in-group particular attractiveness as a source of motivational gratification (i.e., of consensus strivings). This may increase the motivation for in-group protectiveness.

Consider how inclinations toward abstraction and in-group protectiveness may interact. With respect to positive in-group behaviors and negative out-group behaviors, those inclinations should work in concert and converge on the same outcome: enhanced abstraction level of the linguistic descriptions. However, in the case of negative in-group behaviors and positive out-group behaviors, those inclinations should clash: The in-group protectiveness tendency should effect a reduced abstraction level, whereas the abstraction tendency should effect an increased abstraction level. In short, it is possible to predict that individuals with a high (vs. low) need for closure will adopt a higher level of linguistic abstraction when describing positive behaviors of in-group members and negative behaviors of out-group members. The differences due to need for closure should be reduced if not completely eliminated for negative behaviors of in-group members and positive behaviors of out-group members. These notions were examined in a recent study by Webster, Kruglanski, and Pattison (1995, Study 1).

In this research, the in-group versus out-group status of a given person was operationally defined in terms of a controversial issue, endorsement of the pro-choice or pro-life stand on abortion. At the beginning of the semester, students in an introductory psychology course at the University of Florida filled out, as part of a "mass testing" procedure, several personality measures, including the Need for Closure Scale (Webster & Kruglanski, 1994). Individuals with scores in the upper 25% of the distribution were labeled the high need for closure group, and those in the lower 25% of the distribution were labeled the low need for closure group.

The experimental sessions commenced several weeks later. The study was introduced as an investigation of impression formation. Participants were asked to fill out a questionnaire in which they provided general information about their attitudes on various issues. Embedded in this questionnaire was an item concerning the respondent's stand on abortion ("I consider myself pro-choice/pro-life"). In addition, participants were asked to provide, to the best of their ability, transcripts of two conversations during which they persuaded another person of something.

This information, in a condensed form, was presumably to be handed to another participant as a basis for impression formation about the information provider.

The participant also was asked to form an impression of another target (called Pat) on the basis of similar materials. The two conversations Pat had allegedly provided were used to manipulate the valence of the target's behavior. A positive behavior referred to an instance in which Pat selflessly persuaded a peer to accept monetary assistance, and a negative behavior referred to an instance in which Pat persuaded a friend to cheat. Participants also learned of Pat's stance on the pro-choice–pro-life issue. After reviewing the information, participants were asked to describe, in their own words, Pat's behavior relevant to the two conversations. This constituted the main dependent variable of the research.

The design of the experiment was a 2 × 2 × 2 factorial; dispositional need for closure (high vs. low) and target's group status (in-group vs. out-group) were between-subjects variables, and target behavior (positive vs. negative) was a within-subject variable. Participants' descriptions of Pat's behaviors were analyzed via a method developed by Semin and Fiedler (1988) in which a distinction is drawn among four levels of abstraction in interpersonal terms. The most concrete terms are descriptive action verbs (e.g., "A hits B") providing objective descriptions of specific, observable events. Next in level of abstraction are interpretive action verbs that refer to larger classes of behavior (e.g., "A hurts B"), although they clearly refer to a specific behavioral instance. Even more abstract are state verbs (e.g., "A hates B") depicting enduring psychological states that apply beyond specific situations, even though they maintain a reference to a specific person (B in this case). Finally, the most abstract terms are adjectives (e.g., "A is aggressive") in that they generalize beyond a specific situation, object, or behavior.

For each phrase in the participant's descriptions, language abstraction was coded by two raters (the interrater agreement level was .89). The abstraction score was computed by a simple monotonic scheme involving the numbers 1, 2, 3, and 4 to weigh the frequency of the four respective linguistic categories. Thus, descriptive action verbs were given the weight of 1; interpretive action verbs, 2; state verbs, 3; and adjectives, 4. The resulting score was akin to an ordinal scale indicating the degree of abstractness involved in language use.

Appropriate manipulation checks indicated that participants high versus low in the dispositional need for closure exhibited the expected differences on our state-like indicators of this motivation. Thus, those high in the dispositional need for closure expressed greater confidence in their impressions of Pat than those low in the dispositional need for closure; also, they reported that forming an impression of Pat required less thought and that the impression formation task was easier. A composite index of these state-like manifestations of the need for closure yielded the expected effect of our individual-differences measure of this motivation ($p < .01$). In other words, high scorers on the Need for Closure Scale manifested, in the specific experimental situation, a response pattern assumed to be indicative of an "acute" need for closure state. The in-group–out-group manipulation also appeared to work; participants perceived the in-group target as more similar to themselves than the out-group target ($p < .04$). The critical abstraction data are

Table 3 Language abstractness as a function of need for closure, in-group–out-group status, and behavior valence

	Behavior valence			
	Positive		Negative	
Need for closure	In-group	Out-group	In-group	Out-group
High	3.46$_a$	2.37$_b$	2.72$_b$	3.49$_a$
Low	2.49$_b$	2.04$_b$	2.13$_b$	2.51$_b$

Note: The higher the figure, the higher the level of abstraction. Means with different subscripts differ significantly at $p < .05$. Adapted from *Motivated language use in intergroup contexts: Need for closure effects on the linguistic intergroup bias*, by D. M. Webster, A. W. Kruglanski, and D. S. Pattison, 1995, Experiment 1, p. 32, unpublished manuscript, University of Florida.

displayed in Table.3. An analysis of variance performed on these results yielded a significant main effect of the need for closure variable ($p < .01$) qualified by a significant ($p < .05$) three-way interaction among need for closure, target's group status, and behavior positivity.

Specifically, participants high (vs. low) in need for closure generally adapted a higher abstraction level ($p < .0001$) in their descriptions. However, as predicted, this difference was significant only for positive behaviors of the in-group member ($p < .05$) and negative behaviors of the out-group member ($p < .05$). The difference was much reduced and nonsignificant for negative behaviors of the in-group member and positive behaviors of the out-group member.

The foregoing data pattern is consistent with our hypothesis that the permanence tendency induced by a heightened need for closure produces both a general inclination toward linguistic abstraction and a more specific inclination toward in-group protectionism. Those inclinations may work in concert for positive behaviors of the in-group and negative behaviors of the out-group, leading to a pronounced difference in the abstraction level adopted by participants high versus low in need for closure. The same inclinations may be in conflict, however, for negative behaviors of the in-group and positive behaviors of the out-group, reducing the difference in abstraction level adopted by participants high versus low in need for closure with respect to those behavioral categories.

In an additional experiment, we (Webster, Kruglanski, & Pattison, 1995, Study 2) used an identical task and procedure but operationalized need for closure via ambient noise. Appropriate manipulation checks indeed attested that noise heightened the need for closure in the expected ways. Participants in the noisy condition, in comparison with those in the quiet condition, reported higher confidence in their judgments and reported that the task required less thought and was easier. A composite index based on those items yielded a significant main effect of noise ($p < .05$). The target's in-group versus out-group status also produced the expected differences in that participants perceived the out-group target as less similar to themselves than the in-group target ($p < .01$). The linguistic abstraction data are summarized in Table 4.

Table 4 Linguistic abstractness as a function of behavior valence, target group membership, and environmental noise

	Positive behavior							Negative behavior						
	In-group member			Out-group member				In-group member			Out-group member			
Environment	Abstraction level	s	n	Abstraction level	s	n		Abstraction level	s	n	Abstraction level	s	n
Noisy	3.521a	.743	16	2.654b	.661	13		2.493b	.940	16	3.526a	.775	13
Quiet	2.700b	.798	13	2.462b	.794	15		2.322b	.876	13	2.600b	.784	15

Note. The higher the figure, the higher the level of linguistic abstraction. Means with different subscripts differ significantly at $p < .05$. s = linguistic abstraction index (adapted from Semin and Fiedler, 1988). Adapted from *Motivated language use in intergroup contexts: Need for closure effects on the linguistic intergroup bias,* by D. M. Webster, A. W. Kruglanski, and D. S. Pattison, 1995, Experiment 2, p. 33, unpublished manuscript, University of Florida.

As predicted, participants under noise adopted a generally higher abstraction level in their descriptions than participants in the quiet environment. This difference was significant only for positive behaviors of the in-group member and negative behaviors of the out-group member ($p < .01$ in both cases). The abstraction-level difference proved nonsignificant for negative behaviors of the in-group member and positive behaviors of the out-group member, however. These data closely replicated those of the previous study in which need for closure was operationalized as an individual-differences variable rather than manipulated via noise.

Boundary conditions of urgency versus permanence effects

Research described thus far addressed the joint operation of the urgency and permanence tendencies (reflected in the seizing and freezing phenomena) and the separate effects of the permanence tendency promoting strivings for consensus and consistency. It is of interest to consider now the separate effects of the urgency tendency and, more important perhaps, the boundary conditions separating its applicability domain from that of the permanence tendency. In other words, the question is, When are need for closure effects mediated by the urgency tendency, and when are they mediated by the permanence tendency? As noted earlier, we assume that a relevant boundary condition here is the moment of belief crystallization, that is, the juncture during which an opinion is solidified. Heightened need for closure during the precrystallization phase should intensify seizing: At that knowledge-formation stage, high need for closure signifies a discrepancy between actual and desired states (of lacking closure on the one hand and wanting it on the other). This state of affairs should potentiate urgent seizing geared to remove the discrepancy. After crystallization, however, a heightened need for closure should intensify freezing. At that stage, the need for closure is gratified, and hence there is no discrepancy between actual and desired states. The higher the need for closure, the more psychologically important such gratification and the stronger the tendency to perpetuate it or lend it permanence via freezing.

Interactive effects of need for closure and initial confidence on social information seeking

One way in which the precrystallization and postcrystallization periods may be differentiated from each other is in terms of judgmental confidence: Before crystallization, individuals' confidence in a judgment should be relatively low, whereas, after crystallization, it should be higher by comparison. Furthermore, seizing may be distinguished from freezing by the intensity and extent of the informational search. During the seizing phase, the individual may search for information rather energetically and voluminously. By contrast, during the freezing phase, she or he may be reluctant to consider new information and, if at all, do so sparingly and hesitantly.

Those notions were tested in two experiments by Kruglanski, Peri, and Zakai (1991). Participants were presented with five series of drawings. All series contained either two or four standard drawings on a given topic (a man, woman, or tree), each drawn by a different person, and a criterion drawing on a different topic (invariably a house) drawn by one of the individuals who had prepared the standard drawings. Participants' task was to identify, for each series, the particular standard drawing of the person responsible for the criterion drawing. The time allotted was 3 min. Participants stated their interim judgment after 1 min and, during the remaining 2 min, were allowed to engage in an information search concerning alleged other participants' responses. This was accomplished by having participants turn over some (or all) of the standard drawings, which bore on their backs the percentages of previous participants choosing them as the correct answers.

Initial confidence was manipulated via the number of choice alternatives presented to participants. In the high confidence condition, participants chose between two standard drawings; in the low confidence condition, they chose from among four drawings. Appropriate checks verified that this confidence manipulation had the intended effect.

The two studies differed in how they manipulated the need for closure. Our pilot research suggested that the novel experimental task was somewhat confusing to participants, introducing a relatively high base level of the need for closure. Rather than attempting to further elevate it via experimental manipulations, we therefore decided to lower it instead in some conditions. In one study, we did so by providing participants with clear criteria for assessing the drawings' similarity (the drawing's size and location on the page, its linear quality, its degree of elaboration, and the presence–absence of a depth dimension). In the second study, we did so via a fear of invalidity induction whereby mistaken judgments were to be punished by a loss of points.

Two aspects of the information search were of interest: (a) the alacrity with which participants commenced and (b) its overall extent, that is, the number of drawings participants turned over. If low confidence typifies the precrystallization phase and high confidence typifies the postcrystallization phase, and if, moreover, the need for closure produces seizing in the former phase and freezing in the latter, need for closure should exert opposite effects on the dependent variables at the two confidence levels. In the low confidence condition, high versus low need for closure should induce seizing manifest in a relatively hurried commencement of the informational search and its relatively ample extent. By contrast, in the high confidence condition, high versus low need for closure should induce freezing manifest via relatively retarded commencement and sparse extent of the informational search. As Table 5 indicates, that is exactly what happened. Thus, initial confidence may constitute a boundary condition separating the urgency tendency underlying seizing from the permanence tendency underlying freezing.

Motivated reactions to persuasion in the presence or absence of prior information

The dramatically disparate effects of need for closure on information processing in the precrystallization versus postcrystallization phases should have intriguing implications for the persuasion process: In the precrystallization phase, heightened

Table 5 Mean numbers of drawings turned over and latency of turning over the first drawing

	Confidence level			
	High		Low	
Need for closure	Mean no. of drawings turned over	Latency of turning over first drawing	Mean no. of drawings turned over	Latency of turning over first drawing
Experiment 1				
High	2.62	65.11	3.60	39.79
Low	3.94	37.01	3.00	47.84
Experiment 2				
High	2.60	60.39	3.52	33.67
Low	4.37	19.47	2.82	49.01

Note: From "Interactive effects of need for closure and initial confidence on social information seeking," by A. W. Kruglanski, N. Peri, and D. Zakai, 1991, *Social Cognition, 9*, pp. 136 and 137. Copyright 1991 by Guilford Publications, Inc. Adapted with permission.

need for closure may enhance individuals' tendency to accept persuasion, whereas, in the postcrystallization phase, it may enhance their tendency to resist persuasion. Specifically, the discrepancy under a heightened need for closure between actual and desired states before crystallization should induce the tendency to urgently remove it. A persuasive communication offers a means of doing so; hence, it should be quickly accepted. By contrast, in the postcrystallization phase, an absence of discrepancy between the desire for closure and its possession should induce the tendency to maintain this pleasing state in relative permanence. This should induce a resistance to persuasion because it requires at least a temporary unfreezing of one's mind.

These notions were examined in the research by Kruglanski et al. (1993, Studies 2 and 3) referred to earlier. Dyads were formed consisting of a naïve participant and a confederate. The experiment was portrayed as a psychological investigation of legal juries. A participant and a confederate were presented with the essentials of a legal case (a civil suit against an airline company by a lumber company). For half of the participants, the materials included a "legal analysis" affording the formation of a definite opinion favoring the defendant or the plaintiff. The remaining participants received no such analysis, and hence they lacked an informational base for a confident opinion.

The presence or absence of an opinion base was crossed orthogonally with need for closure, manipulated via environmental noise produced by a rackety computer printer. Participants read the case materials, recorded their opinion (or hunch) concerning the appropriate verdict, and confronted a confederate who argued for the opposite verdict. The results supported our theoretical analysis. In the absence of the legal analysis assumed to prevent the development of a confident opinion (representing the precrystallization phase), participants evinced greater persuadability under noise than under no noise. Specifically, they tended more to change their

Table 6 Mean prediscussion to postdiscussion verdict shifts and time spent in discussion as a function of environmental noise and informational base

Informational base	Noise		No noise	
	Verdict shift	Time spent in discussion (min)	Verdict shift	Time spent in discussion (min)
Present	1.48	6.99	3.04	6.25
Absent	4.64	3.89	3.23	5.67

Note: The higher the figures, the greater the shifts from initial to final verdict. Adapted from "Motivated resistance and openness to persuasion in the presence or absence of prior information," by A. W. Kruglanski, D. M. Webster, and A. Klem, 1993, *Journal of Personality and Social Psychology*, 65, p. 866. Copyright 1993 by the American Psychological Association.

prediscussion verdicts and spent less time arguing with the confederate in the noisy versus the quiet condition. Precisely the opposite happened when participants were given the legal analysis affording a crystallized opinion. In this condition, participants under noise (vs. no noise) evinced less persuadability. They shifted less in their verdicts and spent more time arguing with the confederate. The relevant data are summarized in Table 6.

This experiment was conceptually replicated with scores on the Need for Closure Scale as a way of operationalizing need for closure. The same data pattern was reproduced: Participants high (vs. low) in need for closure, as assessed by our scale, were more readily persuaded in instances in which absence of prior information presumably prevented them from crystallizing an opinion and were less readily persuaded in instances in which prior information made such crystallization possible (see Table 7).

The "fight rather than switch" paradox

Note that, in both of our studies, freezing on a prior opinion under a heightened need for closure led to considerable arguing with a different-minded person. Such

Table 7 Mean prediscussion to postdiscussion verdict shifts and time spent in discussion as a function of dispositional need for closure and informational base

Informational base	Dispositional need for closure			
	High		Low	
	Verdict shift	Time spent in discussion (min)	Verdict shift	Time spent in discussion (min)
Present	1.50	7.32	3.46	5.60
Absent	4.10	4.20	2.30	6.47

Note: The higher the figures, the greater the shifts from initial to final verdict. Adapted from "Motivated resistance and openness to persuasion in the presence or absence of prior information," by A. W. Kruglanski, D. M. Webster, and A. Klem, 1993, *Journal of Personality and Social Psychology*, 65, p. 870. Copyright 1993 by the American Psychological Association.

a tendency to "fight rather than switch" under a heightened need for closure could be paradoxical and potentially dysfunctional from the individual's own perspective. For instance, an individual who craves closure so as not to expend energy on laborious information processing (e.g., under noise) ends up expending considerable energy, in fact, on heated argument. Apparently, then, even though the goal of closure may have originally evolved on the basis of rational (energy saving) considerations, once in place it may acquire functional autonomy from those incipient considerations and prompt activities that may, ironically, defeat them.

General discussion

Theoretical convergence

If knowledge construction constitutes a pervasive cognitive activity typically occurring in social contexts, an epistemic motivation of key relevance to such activity should have significant consequences for diverse aspects and domains of social cognition. We have outlined a conceptual framework in which the need for (nonspecific) cognitive closure is identified as one such epistemic motivation and reviewed empirical evidence converging on a broad range of social-cognitive phenomena affected by that need.

We have defined need for closure as a desire for definite knowledge on some issue and the eschewal of confusion and ambiguity. It is assumed to represent a relatively stable dimension of individual differences as well as a situationally inducible state influenced by perceived benefits of closure (or costs of lacking it). Finally, need for closure is presumed to exert its effects via two general tendencies: the urgency tendency, reflecting the inclination to attain closure as quickly as possible, and the permanence tendency, reflecting the tendency to maintain it for as long as possible.

Jointly, the urgency and permanence tendencies may produce the inclinations to seize and then freeze on early judgmental cues. A seizing and freezing sequence under heightened need for closure may (a) reduce the extent of information processing and hypothesis generation (Mayseless & Kruglanski, 1987); (b) elevate judgmental confidence (e.g., Kruglanski & Webster, 1991; Kruglanski et al., 1993; Mayseless & Kruglanski, 1987; Webster & Kruglanski, 1994); (c) focus the information search on prototypical rather than diagnostic evidence (Kruglanski & Mayseless, 1988); (d) effect the use of early cues giving rise to impressional primacy, anchoring effects, or stereotypic judgments (Freund et al., 1985; Heaton & Kruglanski, 1991; Jamieson & Zanna, 1989; Kruglanski & Freund, 1983; Webster & Kruglanski, 1994); (e) induce the tendency to exhibit correspondence or overattribution biases (Webster, 1993); and (f) increase the tendency to assimilate judgments to primed constructs (Ford & Kruglanski, 1995; Thompson et al., 1994).

Beyond the promotion of epistemic freezing, the permanence tendency under a heightened need for closure may effect a preference for consensual knowledge unlikely to be challenged by significant others and a preference for consistent knowledge generalizable across specific situations. The greater predilection for consensus under high (vs. low) need for closure has been shown to be manifest in (a) an increased preference for a persuadable partner by participants who are high (vs. low) in need for closure and who have a prior opinion base, (b) an increased preference for a persuasive partner by participants who are high (vs. low) in need for closure and who do not have a prior opinion base (Kruglanski, Webster, & Klem, 1993), (c) rejection of opinion deviates, and (d) countenance accorded to salient conformists (Kruglanski & Webster, 1991).

The greater predilection for transsituational consistency in knowledge exhibited by participants under high (vs. low) need for closure has been shown to be manifest in the tendency to (a) ascribe failures to global (vs. specific) self-characteristics (Mikulincer et al., 1991), (b) communicate social knowledge using abstract trait labels (Boudreau et al., 1992), and (c) use abstract linguistic descriptions (Webster, Kruglanski, & Pattison, 1995) in reference to positive in-group behaviors and negative out-group behaviors, consistent with the linguistic intergroup bias (Maass & Arcuri, 1992). Also as predicted, these differences in abstraction were largely absent in reference to positive out-group and negative in-group behaviors. In accordance with the theory, the quest for in-group consensus due to the permanence tendency may inspire stronger in-group favoritism and protectionism under a heightened need for closure. This may instill the inclination to concretize (and hence situationally restrict) negative in-group behaviors and positive out-group behaviors, contrary to the general preference for abstraction associated with permanence strivings under a heightened need for closure.

A significant boundary condition separating the effects of seizing from those of freezing has been hypothesized to reside at the point of belief crystallization. Before that juncture, need for closure is assumed to augment seizing; subsequent to that juncture, it is assumed to enhance freezing. Consistent with these notions, participants under a high (vs. low) need for closure have been shown to exhibit shorter latencies of information seeking and more ample information seeking when their initial confidence in a hypothesis is low (assumed to represent a precrystallization seizing) and longer latencies and sparser information seeking when their initial confidence is high (assumed to represent postcrystallization freezing; Kruglanski et al., 1991). Similarly, participants under a high need for closure have been shown to be more accepting of persuasion in conditions preventing the formation of a confident opinion (representing precrystallization seizing) and more resistant to persuasion in conditions affording the formation of an opinion (representing postcrystallization freezing; Kruglanski et al., 1993).

Methodological convergence

If, as the present theory maintains, need for closure is generally aroused by the perceived benefits of closure or costs of lacking closure, the same effects should obtain across a broad variety of conditions, the only common element of which relates to such benefits or costs. The data reviewed earlier provide ample support for this supposition. Specifically, similar, theoretically predicted effects emerged under such seemingly disparate conditions as those created by time pressure, ambient noise, mental fatigue, a request (vs. no request) for judgment, and exposure to a dull activity. All such conditions may render closure beneficial, and hence they should all induce the motivation to attain it.

Furthermore, many of these effects were replicated by means of an individual-differences measure of need for closure (Webster & Kruglanski, 1994), consistent with the notion that need for closure both is situationally malleable and represents a stable personality trait. Finally, whenever they were used, manipulations designed to lower the need for closure or arouse the need to avoid closure (specifically, accountability, evaluation apprehension, or accuracy instructions) had the exact opposite effects to instructions designed to elevate the need for closure (e.g., time pressure and noise). This supports the monotonicity assumption mentioned earlier, whereby motivational effects are directionally similar across different loci on the need for closure continuum. These results also support the very conception of a continuum as such in that manipulations assumed to heighten the need for closure (noise, mental fatigue, time pressure, and boredom) consistently produced the opposite effects to those assumed to heighten the need to avoid closure (evaluation apprehension, accuracy, and accountability instructions). In summary, then, the multiple operationalism adopted in the research reviewed here supports the theoretical assumptions concerning the nature of the need for closure and its instigating conditions.

Need for closure as a scientific construct: Its reality status, evidential support, and heuristic value

Any introduction of a novel scientific construct demands a careful critical scrutiny: Is it sufficiently distinct from previous notions? Is it "real"? Is evidence for it open to plausible alternative interpretations? What advantages does it offer anyway? Does it afford new insights (i.e., Does it have a heuristic value?)? Does it point to previously neglected commonalities (i.e., Does it have an integrative value?)? The distinctiveness issue has been confronted at an earlier juncture; we have concluded that, as a concept, need for closure contains several unique features that set it apart from previous formulations. It is distinctly motivational, content free, and, by and large, more general than its predecessors. The issues of reality, alternative interpretations, and heuristic and integrative values are considered next.

Is it real?

The need for closure variable admittedly constitutes a "hypothetical construct" knowable only indirectly via its effects. To state that a concept is hypothetical does not mean, however, that it is unreal. As Kurt Lewin (1947) remarked in reference to the "group" notion, a scientific construct is real if its effects are real. Moreover, hypothetical constructs are the rule in science rather than the exception: *Schema, associative network, dissonance,* and *electron,* among others, are examples of hypothetical constructs whose utility may not be doubted. Commenting on this issue (in the heyday of positivism in psychology), MacCorquodale and Meehl (1948, p. 105) noted that if one objected to constructs "on the ground that they refer to unobservables or are 'hypothetical' ... a large and useful amount of modern science would have to be abandoned."

Alternative interpretations: the issue of overinclusiveness

A different question altogether is whether the real (i.e., empirically observed) effects obtained in the research described here are ascribable to the need for closure or readily explicable by competing alternative interpretations. In this connection, the very breadth of the need for closure construct raises the specter of overinclusiveness. Because, by assumption, need for closure is arousable by a wide range of seemingly unrelated conditions (representing the heterogeneous benefits of closure or costs of lacking it), one may wonder whether it does not constitute, in fact, a post hoc explanation invoked to account for any degradation of cognitive performance. A quick reflection suggests that this is not the case. Thus, it is easy to think of conditions that reduce the extent of information processing (e.g., lack of expertise), affect the magnitude of primacy effects (e.g., manipulating attention to early vs. late appearing information; Anderson, 1965), or affect the recall of stimulus information before the forming of an impression (Anderson & Hubert, 1963) yet seem largely unrelated to the need for closure construct. Broad though it may be, this construct is apparently not all that encompassing.

Superfluity

A question may be raised as to whether the putative effects of the need for closure may not be explicable, alternatively, by the various situational demands used to operationalize it. Such a state of affairs would render the construct redundant and superfluous. For instance, if it seems "intuitively obvious" that time pressure and fatigue augment the use of simplistic cues, little would be gained by additionally invoking the need for closure in this context. A moment's reflection, however, suggests that need for closure theory has definite advantages over the mere assertion of an empirical relation between situational demands and cue-utilization phenomena. Even if that relation, as such, was intuitively obvious, its underlying mechanisms might not be. Two alternative hypotheses, involving, respectively, cognitive capacity and motivation, immediately spring to mind in this connection. The first hypothesis states that situational demands may deplete individuals' cognitive resources and impel them to resort to simple cues. The second hypothesis suggests that demands may render the processing of information costly, motivating individuals to simplify the activity and hence save energy and effort. The present theory highlights the latter possibility in particular, and the relationship between that possibility and the depletion of capacity alternative is addressed next.

Motivation versus capacity depletion

To understand how situational demands introduced in our experiments may have affected participants' relative[1] cognitive capacity and information-processing motivation, one must consider possible ways in which these constructs interrelate. We assume that, as far as formation of judgments is concerned, relative capacity and motivation are multiplicatively interrelated. That is, at least some degrees of capacity and motivation are required for judgmental activity to occur. Setting either at zero will undermine it, and no amount of increment in the remaining one may compensate for the deficit. Above the zero level, however, the two variables may exhibit a compensatory relation. Reduction in capacity may be offset by an increment in motivation, and vice versa. According to this model, our situational-demand manipulations did not exhaust capacity completely (or set it to zero level). Specifically, our accountability and accuracy instructions clearly and consistently attenuated the effects of such situational demands as time pressure, mental fatigue, and noise (e.g., Kruglanski & Freund, 1983; Webster, Richter, & Kruglanski, 1995). It appears, then, that when sufficiently motivated, participants are perfectly capable of overcoming the effects of various situational constraints on information processing, at least at the magnitudes at which these constraints are typically manipulated in social psychology experiments.

Note that the multiplicative relation between capacity and motivation allows for two separate possibilities: one in which the two are independent of each other and one in which they are causally related. According to the independence assumption, capacity reduction as such (e.g., resulting from organismic energy depletion or situational demands) has no motivational consequences whatsoever, even though it may be compensated for by motivational increments. This is analogous to the case in which deflation of bicycle tires may be compensated for by enhanced pedaling effort even though it does not cause it.

According to the causality assumption, on the other hand, depletion of relative cognitive capacity does induce a motivation to expend less effort on the requisite judgment. This motivation translates into the need for cognitive closure (Kruglanski, in press), that is, the desire for confidence and clarity, obviating the need for further processing. Our analysis assumes, in fact, that the various effects of our situational-demand manipulations, for example, were due not to capacity reduction as such but to a motivational state it may have engendered. What evidence is there for this contention?

Note that the various situational demands introduced in the present research had a variety of motivational consequences. Specifically, they systematically affected our research participants' preferences and affective reactions to social stimuli. As mentioned already, in research by Kruglanski et al. (1993), participants with firm opinions on a topic, when placed in a noisy environment, expressed a stronger preference for nonpersuasive, nondominant discussion partners unlikely to challenge their preexisting closure. However, participants lacking a firm opinion expressed a greater preference under noise (vs. no noise) for persuasive and self-assured partners presumably capable of supplying quick closure.

Heightened need for closure should lead to a more negative evaluation of opinion deviates whose dissenting views threaten to undermine closure. Indeed, in research conducted by Kruglanski and Webster (1991), group members under time pressure (vs. no pressure) or environmental noise (vs. no noise) tended more to reject the opinion deviates and extol the conformists (or "opinion leaders") whose actions were seen to facilitate consensus.

Note that, as such, the capacity-restriction concept seems incapable of explaining such patterns of interpersonal preferences or evaluations. The notion of cognitive capacity is devoid of specific implications in regard to affective, evaluative, or preferential reactions. On the other hand, a motivational state readily implies preferences and affective expressions (or evaluations) contingent on whether a given state of affairs is perceived to advance the motivational end or undermine it. Thus, the clear motivational effects of situational demands are inconsistent with the independence assumption whereby those demands exert purely cognitive effects (albeit capable of compensation by motivational increments).

Similarly inconsistent with the independence assumption is the pervasive finding that individuals exposed to situational demands exhibit higher judgmental confidence than their nonexposed counterparts. The independence assumption seems to require just the contrary, specifically that a reduction of capacity without an independent compensatory increase in motivation should effect a decline rather than a rise in confidence. Yet one finds, time and time again, that research participants' confidence is at its highest, in fact, when their relative cognitive capacity is reduced (e.g., by noise or fatigue) without introduction of a compensatory motivation (e.g., Kruglanski et al., 1993; Webster, 1993; Webster, Kruglanski, & Pattison, 1995).

Admittedly, situational demands may impair cognitive capacity and induce a motivational state without the two being necessarily related. Thus, it is possible, in principle, that the observed cognitive or judgmental effects of our various manipulations stemmed from capacity restrictions rather than constituting the indirect derivatives of the induced motivation. Some evidence against this possibility was obtained in recent studies (Kruglanski et al., 1993; Webster, 1993) in which the effects of specific situational demands (e.g., noise) were rendered nonsignificant once the motivation for closure was statistically controlled (Baron & Kenny, 1986), suggesting that those effects were in fact mediated by (rather than independent of) the need for closure. These findings speak most directly in support of the cause–effect model of the capacity–motivation relation and against the independence alternative.

Finally, recall that most effects of the situational demands were replicated by means of our individual-differences measure of the need for closure. Most of the items in that scale (26 of 42) have clear motivational flavor (e.g., terms such as "I like," "enjoy," "hate," "dislike," or "prefer"). It is highly unlikely that scores on this measure are readily susceptible to an alternative interpretation in terms of capacity restrictions. Thus, all things considered, it appears that the need for closure theory offers the most comprehensive and parsimonious account of the entire set of present data, including the effects of situational demands and information-processing constraints manipulated in some of our studies.

Heuristic value

The foregoing discussion suggests that even for relatively straightforward effects such as those of situational demands on the use of simple cues, need for closure theory yields valuable, novel insights. In addition, however, this theory affords the identification of phenomena that, far from appearing obvious or straightforward, may seem complex, surprising, or even paradoxical. For instance, it suggests that the same conditions that increase openness to persuasion in some circumstances may decrease it in other circumstances (Kruglanski et al., 1993), that the same conditions that augment the search for information in some contexts retard it in different contexts (Kruglanski et al., 1991), and that the same situational stresses that foster disapproval and rejection of a deviate may elicit approbation and acceptance of a conformist (Kruglanski & Webster, 1991). Moreover, need for closure theory implies complex linkages between situational demands, for example, and level of linguistic abstraction (Webster, Kruglanski, & Pattison, 1995) rather unanticipated by known alternative perspectives. Also, it identifies intriguing paradoxes like those of unfounded confidence (higher confidence level despite more restricted information processing) and energy-consuming "fighting rather than switching," despite conditions favoring energy conservation. It is highly unlikely that these phenomena would be accessed through extant alternative formulations, attesting to the considerable heuristic value of the present analysis.

Integrative value

The present theory and research highlight the considerable integrative advantages for social psychology of focusing on the fundamental epistemic process whereby judgments or opinions are formed (Kruglanski, 1980, 1989, 1990a). Numerous social psychological phenomena appear to be mediated by such a process in which the need for cognitive closure plays a pivotal part. Indeed, the work reviewed here attests to the relevance of need for closure to such diverse phenomena as primacy effects in impression formation, correspondence biases in causal attribution, stereotyping, groups' reactions to deviates, and the use of language in intergroup contexts.

The need for closure should be just as relevant to numerous other phenomena, unexamined as yet from the present perspective. To mention a few prominent examples, need for closure should enhance the bothersomeness of cognitive inconsistency (that undermines cognitive closure) and hence elevate the magnitude of cognitive dissonance (Festinger, 1957) or balance strivings (Heider, 1958; for a discussion, see Kruglanski & Klar, 1987). Similarly, need for closure should augment the tendency of beliefs to persevere (Ross, Lepper, & Hubbard, 1975), increase the confirmation bias in hypothesis testing (Klayman & Ha, 1987), and enhance the false consensus effect (Ross, Greene, & House, 1977) and the tendency toward self-verification (Swann & Read, 1981). These apparent links among previously unconnected phenomena offer a synthesis of a fragmented social psychological domain (cf. Vallacher & Nowak, in press) under the aegis of a unified epistemic paradigm.

In conclusion, the theory and research described here suggest that need for cognitive closure represents a useful construct of wide applicability to social psychology. Because of the ubiquitous circumstances of its arousal and its widely ramifying consequences, its continued study promises considerable new insights of both theoretical and real-world significance.

Note

1 The notion of relative cognitive capacity intends to capture the functional commonality shared by situational demand manipulations (time pressure and noise) and momentary decreases in the perceiver's mental powers (e.g., resulting from fatigue or alcoholic intoxication). Both types of manipulation represent a reduction of cognitive capacity in relation to task requirements: Situational demands induce it by increasing task requirements, and mental power decreases, by lowering the perceiver's capabilities.

References

Adorno, T. W., Frenkel-Brunswik, E., Levinson, D. J., & Sanford, R. N. (1950). *The authoritarian personality*. New York: Harper & Brothers.

Anderson, N. H. (1965). Primacy effects in personality impression formation using a generalized order effect paradigm. *Journal of Personality and Social Psychology, 2*, 1–9.

Anderson, N. H., & Hubert, S. (1963). Effects of concomitant verbal recall on order effects in personality impression formation. *Journal of Verbal Learning and Verbal Behavior, 2*, 379–391.

Asch, S. E. (1946). Forming impressions of personality. *Journal of Abnormal and Social Psychology, 41*, 258–290.

Bar-Hillel, M. (1973). On the subjective probability of compound events. *Organizational Behavior and Human Performance, 9*, 396–406.

Baron, R. M., & Kenny, D. A. (1986). The moderator-mediator variable distinction in social psychological research: Conceptual, strategic and statistical considerations. *Journal of Personality and Social Psychology, 51*, 1173–1182.

Berlyne, D. E. (1960). *Conflict, arousal and curiosity*. New York: McGraw-Hill.

Boudreau, L. A., Baron, R., & Oliver, P. V. (1992). Effects of expected communication target expertise and timing of set on trait use in person description. *Personality and Social Psychology Bulletin, 18*, 447–452.

Cacioppo, J. T., & Petty, R. E. (1982). The need for cognition. *Journal of Personality and Social Psychology, 42*, 116–131.

Chaiken, S., Lieberman, A., & Eagly, A. H. (1989). Heuristic and systematic information processing within and beyond the persuasion context. In J. S. Uleman & J. A. Bargh (Eds.), *Unintended thought: Limits of awareness, intention and control* (pp. 212–252). New York: Guilford Press.

Costa, P. T., Jr., & McCrae, R. R. (1992). *Revised NEO Personality Inventory (NEO-PI-R) and NEO Five-Factor Inventory (NEO-FFI) professional manual*. Odessa, FL: Psychological Assessment Resources.

Deci, E. L., & Ryan, R. M. (1985). *Intrinsic motivation and self-determination in human behavior*. New York: Plenum.

Eysenck, H. J. (1954). *The psychology of politics*. New York: Praeger.

Festinger, L. (1950). Informal social communication. *Psychological Review, 57*, 271–282.

Festinger, L. (1954). A theory of social comparison processes. *Human Relations, 7*, 117–140.

Festinger, L. (1957). *A theory of cognitive dissonance*. Stanford, CA: Stanford University Press.

Fiske, S. T., & Neuberg, S. L. (1990). A continuum of impression formation, from category-based to individuating processes: Influences of information and motivation on attention and interpretation. In M. P. Zanna (Ed.), *Advances in experimental social psychology* (Vol. 23, pp. 1–74). New York: Academic Press.

Ford, T. E., & Kruglanski, A. W. (1995). Effects of epistemic motivations on the use of accessible constructs in social judgment. *Personality and Social Psychology Bulletin, 21*, 950–962.

Frenkel-Brunswik, E. (1949). Intolerance of ambiguity as emotional and perceptual personality variable. *Journal of Personality, 18*, 108–143.

Frenkel-Brunswik, E. (1951). Personality theory and perception. In R. R. Blake & G. V. Ramsey (Eds.), *Perception: An approach to personality* (pp. 226–275). New York: Ronald Press.

Freud, S. (1923). The ego and the id. In J. Strachey (Ed. and Trans.), *Standard edition of the complete psychological works of Sigmund Freud* (pp. 171–225). London: Hogarth Press.

Freund, T., Kruglanski, A. W., & Schpitzajsen, A. (1985). The freezing and unfreezing of impressional primacy: Effects of the need for structure and the fear of invalidity. *Personality and Social Psychology Bulletin, 11*, 479–487.

Gilbert, D. T., Pelham, B. W., & Krull, D. S. (1988). On cognitive busyness: When person perceivers meet persons perceived. *Journal of Personality and Social Psychology, 54*, 733–740.

Gollwitzer, P. M. (1990). Action phases and mind-sets. In E. T. Higgins & R. M. Sorrentino (Eds.), *Handbook of motivation and cognition: Foundations of social behavior* (Vol. 2, pp. 53–92). New York: Guilford Press.

Heaton, A., & Kruglanski, A. W. (1991). Person perception by introverts and extraverts under time pressure: Need for closure effects. *Personality and Social Psychology Bulletin, 17*, 161–165.

Heider, F. (1958). *The psychology of interpersonal relations*. New York: Wiley.

Higgins, E. T., Rholes, W. S., & Jones, C. R. (1977). Category accessibility and impression formation. *Journal of Experimental Social Psychology, 13*, 141–154.

Higgins, E. T., & Trope, Y. (1990). Activity engagement theory: Implications of multiply identifiable input for intrinsic motivation. In E. T. Higgins & R. M. Sorrentino (Eds.), *Handbook of motivation and cognition: Foundations of social behavior* (Vol. 2, pp. 229–264). New York: Guilford Press.

Hofstede, G. (1980). *Culture's consequences: International differences in work-related values*. Beverly Hills, CA: Sage.

Jamieson, D. W., & Zanna, M. P. (1989). Need for structure in attitude formation and expression. In A. Pratkanis, S. Breckler, & A. G. Greenwald (Eds.), *Attitude structure and function* (pp. 46–68). Hillsdale, NJ: Erlbaum.

Jones, E. E. (1979). The rocky road from acts to dispositions. *American Psychologist, 34*, 107–117.

Jones, E. E., & Harris, V. A. (1967). The attribution of attitudes. *Journal of Experimental Social Psychology, 3*, 1–24.

Kagan, J. (1972). Motives and development. *Journal of Personality and Social Psychology, 22*, 51–66.

Kelley, H. H. (1971). Attribution in social interaction. In E. E. Jones, D. E. Kanause, H. H. Kelley, R. E. Nisbett, S. Valins, & B. Weiner (Eds.), *Attribution: Perceiving the causes of behavior* (pp. 1–26). Morristown, NJ: General Learning Press.

Klayman, J., & Ha, Y.-W. (1987). Confirmation, disconfirmation, and information in hypothesis testing. *Psychological Review, 94*, 211–228.

Kruglanski, A. W. (1975). The endogenous-exogenous partition in attribution theory. *Psychological Review, 82*, 387–406.

Kruglanski, A. W. (1980). Lay epistemo-logic—process and contents: Another look at attribution theory. *Psychological Review, 87*, 70–87.

Kruglanski, A. W. (1989). *Lay epistemics and human knowledge: Cognitive and motivational bases*. New York: Plenum.

Kruglanski, A. W. (1990a). Lay epistemic theory in social-cognitive psychology. *Psychological Inquiry, 1*, 181–197.

Kruglanski, A. W. (1990b). Motivations for judging and knowing: Implications for causal attribution. In E. T. Higgins & R. M. Sorrentino (Eds.), *Handbook of motivation and cognition: Foundations of social behavior* (Vol. 2, pp. 333–368). New York: Guilford Press.

Kruglanski, A. W. (in press). Motivated social cognition: Principles of the interface. In E. T. Higgins & A. W. Kruglanski (Eds.), *Social psychology: A handbook of basic principles*. New York: Guilford Press.

Kruglanski, A. W., & Freund, T. (1983). The freezing and un-freezing of lay-inferences: Effects on impressional primacy, ethnic stereotyping and numerical anchoring. *Journal of Experimental Social Psychology, 19*, 448–468.

Kruglanski, A. W., & Klar, Y. (1987). A view from a bridge: Synthesizing the consistency and attribution paradigms from the lay-epistemic perspective. *European Journal of Social Psychology, 17*, 211–241.

Kruglanski, A. W., & Mayseless, O. (1988). Contextual effects in hypothesis testing: The role of competing alternatives and epistemic motivations. *Social Cognition, 6*, 1–21.

Kruglanski, A. W., Peri, N., & Zakai, D. (1991). Interactive effects of need for closure and initial confidence on social information seeking. *Social Cognition, 9*, 127–148.

Kruglanski, A. W., & Webster, D. M. (1991). Group members' reactions to opinion deviates and conformists at varying degrees of proximity to decision deadline and of environmental noise. *Journal of Personality and Social Psychology, 61*, 212–225.

Kruglanski, A. W., Webster, D. M., & Klem, A. (1993). Motivated resistance and openness to persuasion in the presence or absence of prior information. *Journal of Personality and Social Psychology, 65*, 861–876.

Kunda, Z. (1990). The case for motivated reasoning. *Psychological Bulletin, 108*, 480–498.

Lewin, K. (1947). Frontiers in group dynamics. *Human Relations, 1*, 5–41.

Luchins, A. S. (1957). Primacy-recency in impression formation. In C. I. Hovland (Ed.), *The order of presentation in persuasion* (pp. 33–61). New Haven, CT: Yale University Press.

Maass, A., & Arcuri, L. (1992). The role of language in the persistence of stereotypes. In G. Semin & K. Fiedler (Eds.), *Language, interaction and social cognition* (pp. 129–143). Newbury Park, CA: Sage.

Maass, A., & Arcuri, L. (in press). Language and stereotyping. In N. Macrae, M. Hewstone, & C. Stangor (Eds.), *The foundations of stereotypes and stereotyping*. New York: Guilford Press.

MacCorquodale, K., & Meehl, P. E. (1948). On a distinction between hypothetical constructs and intervening variables. *Psychological Review, 55*, 95–107.

Mayseless, O., & Kruglanski, A. W. (1987). What makes you so sure? Effects of epistemic motivations on judgmental confidence. *Organizational Behavior and Human Decision Processes, 39*, 162–183.

McCrae, R. R. (1993–1994). Openness to experience as a basic dimension of personality. *Imagination, Cognition and Personality, 13*, 39–55.

McCrae, R. R., & Costa, P. T., Jr. (1985). Openness to experience. In R. Hogan & W. H. Jones (Eds.), *Perspectives in personality* (pp. 145–172). Greenwich, CT: JAI Press.

Mikulincer, M., Yinon, A., & Kabili, D. (1991). Epistemic needs and learned helplessness. *European Journal of Personality, 5*, 249–258.

Naccarato, M. F., Thompson, M. M., & Parker, K. (1986). *Update on the development of the need for structure and fear of invalidity scales*. Unpublished manuscript.

Neuberg, S. L., & Newsom, J. (1993). Individual differences in chronic motivation to simplify: Personal need for structure and social-cognitive processing. *Journal of Personality and Social Psychology, 65*, 113–131.

Pervin, L. A. (Ed.). (1989). *Goal concepts in personality and social psychology*. Hillsdale, NJ: Erlbaum.

Petty, R. E., & Cacioppo, J. T. (1986). The elaboration likelihood model of persuasion. In L. Berkowitz (Ed.), *Advances in experimental social psychology* (Vol. 19, pp. 123–205). New York: Academic Press.

Quattrone, G. A. (1982). Overattribution and unit formation: When behavior engulfs the person. *Journal of Personality and Social Psychology, 42*, 593–607.

Rokeach, M. (1960). *The open and closed mind*. New York: Basic Books.

Ross, L., Greene, D., & House, P. (1977). The "false consensus effect": An egocentric bias in social perception and attribution processes. *Journal of Experimental Social Psychology, 13*, 279–301.

Ross, L., Lepper, M. R., & Hubbard, M. (1975). Perseverance in self-perception and social perception: Biased attribution processes in the debriefing paradigm. *Journal of Personality and Social Psychology, 35*, 880–892.

Sanford, R. N., Adorno, E., Frenkel-Brunswik, E., & Levinson, D. J. (1950). The measurement of implicit antidemocratic trends. In E. Adorno, E. Frenkel-Brunswick, D. J. Levinson, & R. N. Sanford (Eds.), *The authoritarian personality* (pp. 222–279). New York: Harper & Row.

Schachter, S. (1951). Deviation, rejection and communication. *Journal of Abnormal and Social Psychology, 46*, 190–207.

Seligman, M. E. P., Abramson, L. Y., Semmel, A., & von Baeyer, C. (1979). Depressive attributional style. *Journal of Abnormal Psychology, 88*, 242–247.

Semin, G. R., & Fiedler, K. (1988). The cognitive functions of linguistic categories in describing persons: Social cognition and language. *Journal of Personality and Social Psychology, 54*, 558–568.

Sorrentino, R. M., & Short, J. C. (1986). Uncertainty orientation, motivation and cognition. In R. M. Sorrentino & E. T. Higgins (Eds.), *Handbook of motivation and cognition: Foundations of social behavior* (pp. 379–403). New York: Guilford Press.

Swann, W. B., Jr. (1990). To be known or to be adored? The interplay of self-enhancement and self-verification. In E. T. Higgins & R. M. Sorrentino (Eds.), *Handbook of motivation and cognition: Foundations of social behavior* (Vol. 2, pp. 408–448). New York: Guilford Press.

Swann, W. B., & Read, S. J. (1981). Self-verification processes: How we sustain our self-conceptions. *Journal of Experimental Social Psychology, 17*, 351–372.

Tetlock, P. E. (1985). Accountability: A social check on the fundamental attribution error. *Social Psychology Quarterly, 48*, 227–236.

Thompson, E. P., Roman, R. J., Moscovitz, G. B., Chaiken, S., & Bargh, J. A. (1994). Accuracy motivation attenuates covert priming: The systematic reprocessing of social information. *Journal of Personality and Social Psychology, 66*, 474–489.

Trope, Y., & Bassok, M. (1983). Information gathering strategies in hypothesis testing. *Journal of Experimental Social Psychology, 19*, 560–576.

Trope, Y., & Higgins, E. T. (1993). The "what," "when" and "how" of dispositional inference: New answers and new questions. *Personality and Social Psychology Bulletin, 19*, 493–500.

Tversky, A., & Kahneman, D. (1974). Judgment under uncertainty: Heuristics and biases. *Science, 185*, 1124–1131.

Vallacher, R. R., & Nowak, A. (in press). The emergence of dynamical social psychology. *Psychological Inquiry*.

Webster, D. M. (1993). Motivated augmentation and reduction of the overattribution bias. *Journal of Personality and Social Psychology, 65*, 261–271.

Webster, D. M., & Kruglanski, A. W. (1994). Individual differences in need for cognitive closure. *Journal of Personality and Social Psychology, 67*, 1049–1062.

Webster, D. M., Kruglanski, A. W., & Pattison, D. S. (1995). *Motivated language use in intergroup contexts: Need for closure effects on the linguistic intergroup bias.* Unpublished manuscript, University of Florida, Gainesville.

Webster, D. M., Richter, L., & Kruglanski, A. W. (1995). *On leaping to conclusions when feeling tired: Mental fatigue effects on impressional primacy.* Unpublished manuscript, University of Maryland, College Park.

4 Intuitive and deliberate judgments are based on common principles

Arie W. Kruglanski, University of Maryland
Gerd Gigerenzer, Max Planck Institute
For Human Development

At times, people's judgments seem intuitive: They come to mind quickly and effortlessly, seemingly popping out of nowhere, without much conscious awareness of their origins or of the manner of their formation. Other judgments seem deliberate: They arise from a lengthy and painstaking thought process that is transparent and accessible to awareness. These two types of judgments have been treated separately in the cognitive sciences, with analytic philosophy, economics, and decision theory focused on deliberate, reflective decisions and psychoanalysis and social psychology dealing also with intuitive, spontaneous behavior. Following this division of labor among disciplines, psychologists have proposed that the mind is similarly divided. Over the last 3 decades, a considerable number of models have been premised on the assumption that judgments can be formed via two qualitatively distinct processes or systems.[1] Such dual-systems models characterized intuitive and deliberate judgments in terms of several, presumably aligned, aspects: Intuitive judgments have been assumed to be associative, quick, unconscious, effortless, heuristic, and error-prone. Deliberative judgments have been assumed to be rule based, slow, conscious, effortful, analytic, and rational. The claims for the existence of two separate systems (or processes)[2] of judgment were buttressed by a variety of empirical findings interpreted in support of the dualistic distinction (for reviews see Evans, 2008; Kruglanski & Orehek, 2007).

Though the dualistic paradigm has enjoyed considerable popularity in social cognition, judgment, and decision-making domains (e.g., Chaiken & Trope, 1999; Epstein, Lipson, Holstein, & Huh, 1992; Kahneman, 2003; Sloman, 1996; Strack & Deutsch, 2004), it has not gone unchallenged (e.g., Gigerenzer, 2009; Gigerenzer & Regier, 1996; Kruglanski, Erb, Pierro, Mannetti, & Chun, 2006; Osman, 2004). Recently, Keren and Schul (2009) offered a particularly detailed and incisive critique of the dual-systems theories. They noted that contrary to the dualistic premises, (a) dimensions assumed to distinguish the two systems (e.g., judgmental speed, ease, or resource-dependence) are continuous rather than dichotomous,[3] (b) these dimensions are unaligned rather than aligned,[4] and (c) the dimensions fail the isolability requirement that the putative separate systems of judgment operate independently of each other.

Intuitive and deliberate judgments 105

In concluding their critique, Keren and Schul (2009, p. 546) urged judgment and decision-making researchers to explore "the natural complement of dual-systems theories, namely, a unimodel." Accordingly, in the present note, we sketch a unified theory of judgment intended as a general alternative to the dualistic paradigm. This theory represents a convergence of our separate research programs and their potential integration: Kruglanski's unimodel work is complemented by Gigerenzer's work on heuristics (their function, origins, and ecological rationality); the latter is extended by the unimodel's emphasis on individual and situational differences in motivation and cognitive resources as these interact with judgmental task demands. Our theory is unified in its focus on features that different instances of judgment share. These common features include cues, processing by rules, selection of a rule, and (perceived) ecological rationality of rules.

As a preview of what is to come, we first outline our framework and discuss its properties, including questions of rule selection and ecological rationality. We show how the present approach affords an alternative interpretation of findings adduced in support of the dual-system and dual-process models and how it enables novel predictions, corroborated in specific studies.

A sketch for a unified theory of judgment

1. Judgments called intuitive and deliberative are both based on rules. These rules can be of the optimizing or satisficing (heuristic) kind. Moreover, intuitive and deliberative judgments need not be based on different rules: The very same rules can underlie both.
2. There exists a rule selection problem for both intuitive and deliberative judgments. How do individuals select a rule from their adaptive toolbox for a given problem? We argue that there are (at least) four factors involved: The task itself and individual memory constrain the set of applicable rules, whereas individual processing potential and (perceived) ecological rationality of the rule, given the task, guide the final selection from that set.
3. When two or more rules have nearly equal ecological rationality, rule conflict may occur. In such cases, proper application of a given rule may suffer interference from other competing rules.
4. Rules are based on core cognitive capacities, such as recognition memory. Individual differences in these capacities, trait or state, influence the speed and the accuracy with which a rule is executed. Moreover, the same factors also impact the selection of rules for a given task. Thus, there is no general relation between the type of rule and its difficulty of application. Rules typically characterized as intuitive (e.g., heuristics based on learned stereotypes) may be easy or difficult to apply, depending on their degree of routinization and their momentary accessibility, so may rules considered deliberative (e.g., rules of logic or mathematics).
5. There is a reciprocal relation between the difficulty of rule application and individuals' processing potential: The greater such difficulty, the more processing potential is needed for application. Consequently, when processing potential is

limited, only easy-to-apply rules will mediate judgments. In contrast, when processing potential is high, both easy and difficult rules will be considered and selected in accordance with their (perceived) ecological rationality.
6. The accuracy of both deliberate and intuitive judgments depends on the ecological rationality of the rule for the given class of problems. Accordingly, more complex rules are not necessarily more accurate than simpler ones, nor are statistical rules necessarily more accurate than heuristic rules.

In the subsequent sections, we examine the various features of our proposed framework in some detail.

Intuitive and deliberative judgments are rule based

The rule concept

By rules, we mean inferential devices for categorization, estimation, paired comparisons, and other judgmental tasks that go beyond the information given. The rule concept denotes an if–then relation of the type *if (cues) then (judgment)*. The rule-based manufacture of judgments can be thought of as syllogistic. The rule itself constitutes the major premise. Rule instantiation can be thought of as the minor premise; it affords the application of the preexisting rule to a specific judgmental context. The if–then relation between cue and judgment can be probabilistic (McGuire, 1960; Wyer, 1970). In other words, the rule might affirm that if cue, or given combination of cues (X), appears then judgment (Y) is indicated with a given probability.

Some rules constitute explicit algorithms that are consciously applied; others constitute implicit, unconsciously applied associations; and yet others have been described as retrieval based (Logan, 1988; Rickard, Sin-Heng, & Pashler, 2008) or instance based (Medin & Ross, 1989), and so on. We recognize that all these mechanisms differ in numerous ways. Yet for our purpose of depicting the essential process of judgment, what matters is the conditional, if–then link generally embodied by such devices.

Our suggestion that judgments are rule based is not unique. Other authors, across diverse domains of psychology and cognitive science, have been making similar proposals (for a review see, e.g., Hahn & Chater, 1998). Rule following has been assumed to play a key role in linguistic behavior (e.g., Chomsky, 1986), animal learning (e.g., Rescorla & Holland, 1982), and perceptual phenomena (e.g., Rock, 1983), among others. Examples from the latter two domains illustrate the ubiquity of rule-based judgments.

Perceptual inferences

Hardly anything can be considered more intuitive or automatic than the visual illusions to which the human eye falls prey. Yet, students of perception have compellingly argued that these are based on (hardwired) propositional rules that our brain uses. Consider Figure 1. The dots on its left appear concave; they recede

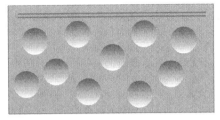 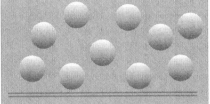

Figure 1 Unconscious inferences by a simple heuristic: convex and concave perceptions as function of shading.

into the surface and away from the observer. In contrast, the dots on the right of the figure seem convex; they appear to bulge and extend toward the observer. Intriguingly, these appearances reverse when the page is turned upside down. Now, the previously concave dots appear convex and vice versa. What explains these effects? The visual illusion appears to be based on an inferential rule that bets on two properties of the environments (Kleffner & Ramachandran, 1992).

The brain assumes a three-dimensional world and uses the shaded parts of the dots to guess in what direction of the third dimension they extend. To make a good guess, the brain assumes that:

1. Light comes from above (in relation to retinal coordinates).
2. There is only one source of light.

These two structures describe human (and mammalian) history, when the sun and the moon were the only sources of light, and only one operated at a time. The brain exploits these assumed structures by using a simple rule of thumb: If the shade is in the upper part then the dots recede into the surface; if the shade is in the lower part then the dots project up from the surface.

This visual illusion illustrates that unconscious, fast, and effortless intuitive processes can follow rules, specifically heuristic rules. It also illustrates that the rationality of the rule is ecological; that is, it resides in the match between rule and environment. If there is a three-dimensional world with the two properties described, the rule leads to good inferences; however, if this is not the case, as in the two-dimensional picture in Figure 1, the rule leads to a visual illusion. Systematic errors that are due to a reasonable bet on the environment but that fail due to specific, unexpected circumstances are "good" errors. Our point is that good errors are characteristic of every intelligent system (Gigerenzer, 2005). Intelligence means to take risks and to make bets or, to use a phrase of Jerome Bruner (1973), to go beyond the information given.

The idea that even the most basic perceptual judgments are rule based receives support from research in psychophysics (Pizlo, 2001). Whereas Fechner (1860/1966) posited that the percept is a result of a causal chain of events emanating from the object, subsequent approaches provided evidence that the percept involves an *unconscious* inference (Helmholtz, 1910/2000) from an associated bundle of sensations. An approach recently developed within the computer vision community treats perception as the solution of an inverse[5] problem that depends critically on innate constraints, or rules, for interpreting proximal stimuli (e.g., the retinal images). According to this view "perception is about *inferring* [emphasis added] the properties of the distal stimulus X given the proximal stimulus Y" (Pizlo, 2001, p. 3146). Finally, in a recent *Annual Review of Psychology* article, the investigators treated object perception as a visual inference problem and proposed that "the visual system resolves ambiguity through built in knowledge of . . . how retinal images are formed and uses this knowledge to automatically and unconsciously *infer* [emphasis added] the properties of objects" (Kersten, Mamoassian, & Yuille, 2004, p. 273).

Associative processes

Investigators in domains of classical and evaluative conditioning have agreed that rules play a key role in these patently associative processes. This notion was originally advanced by Edward Tolman (1932) in his sign learning theory of classical conditioning, a paradigmatic example of associative learning. In Tolman's theory, the conditioning procedure sets up an expectancy that a given sign or cue will be followed by some event (or significate). Such expectancy has been thought to represent a conditional rule of the if–then variety. Contemporary theorists of classical conditioning concur in that conclusion (Holyoak, Koh, & Nisbett, 1989; Rescorla, 1985; Rescorla & Wagner, 1972). The same assessment was reached with regard to evaluative conditioning, which consists of associating a valenced unconditioned stimulus (say, a smiling face) with a neutral conditioned stimulus (say, a neutral face). "We find clear support for the role of propositional process in learning. In stark contrast, little unambiguous support is found for an automatic link formation mechanism" (Mitchell, DeHouwer, & Lovibond, 2009, p. 185).

Rule following or rule conforming?

An important distinction in cognitive science has been between rule following, and rule conforming behavior (Chomsky, 1986; Hahn & Chater, 1998; Marcus, Brinkman, Clahsen, Wiese, & Pinker, 1995). Phenomena describable by rules need not reflect rule following, in that the latter, but not necessarily the former, involves mental representation of the input and output classes and of the conditional relation between them. For instance, an apple falling to the ground displays a rule-describable behavior characterized by Newton's laws, yet the apple obviously does not possess a mental representation of laws of any kind. In contrast, authentic rule following is exhibited by the behavior of an individual who decides to get out of bed on the sound of her alarm clock. In this case, the person has mental representation of the alarm, and its significance: Simply, she or he is following a rule whereby *if the alarm sounds, it is time to get up.*

Our conception of judgment formation clearly refers to rule following rather than to rule conforming.[6] Unlike the rigid nature of rule conforming, rule following can be flexible and varied. Depending on their current degree of accessibility (Higgins, 1996), rules can be primed or activated from memory (D. G. Smith, Standing, & deMan, 1992). Rules are potentially malleable; they can be learned and unlearned; they can be forgotten and retrieved. None of these characteristics applies to rule conforming, in which the entity in question behaves as a passive object at the mercy of external forces whose specific characteristics it neither registers nor recognizes.

We assume that the formation of both intuitive and deliberative judgments reflects rule following. Indeed, we suggest that examples of specific deliberative and intuitive judgments juxtaposed in the dual-systems literature often involved the operation of different rules (i.e., rules of different contents). Judgments characterized as deliberative have been often linked to statistical or logical rules (e.g., Kahneman, 2003; Kahneman & Tversky, 1973). Judgments classified as intuitive have been linked to different rules, for example, stereotypic rules about characteristics of different professions (e.g., lawyers and engineers); rules related to source characteristics, such as expertise; rules related to the ease with which instances of a category come to mind; and rules based on the fluency experience. For instance, Kahneman (2003, p. 699) classified as intuitive the various heuristics that people use (e.g., the representativeness heuristic or the availability heuristic). Yet heuristics have been generally defined as rules of thumb, displaying a propositional structure. In fact, Kahneman (2003, p. 699) himself asserted that the extensional (i.e., analytic) and prototypical (i.e., representativeness based, or intuitive) judgments are "governed by characteristically different logical *rules* [emphasis added]," suggesting that both judgmental processes are rule based. In this vein, too, Osman (2004, p. 1001) concluded from studies on tutoring aimed to increase people's use of the conjunction rule (when such rule was deemed appropriate) that such increases "occur when participants supplement one type of *rule-based* [emphasis added] reasoning . . . for another."

Intuitive and deliberative judgments can be based on the same rules

Inferential rules come in a wide variety of contents and can be stated at different levels of generality. A key distinction is between optimizing and satisficing (heuristic) rules. Bayes' rule and the maximization of expected utility are examples of optimizing rules, whereas Table 1 gives 10 examples of heuristic rules (see Gigerenzer & Brighton, 2009). Unlike Bayes' rule, a heuristic is a rule that ignores part of the information and does not attempt to calculate the maximum or minimum of a function. Optimizing rules, such as Bayes' rule and Neyman-Pearson decision theory (also known as signal detection theory) have been proposed for both intuitive and deliberative judgments (Gigerenzer & Murray, 1987). Similarly, each of the ten heuristics in Table 1 can underlie both intuitive and deliberate judgments, when deliberate denotes judgments rendered with forethought and cognitive effort. Thus, intuitive judgments not only are based on rules but also can be based on the very same rules as deliberate judgments.

Consider first the recognition heuristic that can be highly successful if there is a correlation between recognition and criterion in the environment. Based on Adaptive Control of Thought–Rational theory (ACT-R; Anderson, 1983), the

Table 1 Ten heuristics that are likely in the adaptive toolbox of humans

Heuristic	Definition
Recognition heuristic: Goldstein & Gigerenzer (2002)	If one of two alternatives is recognized, infer that it has the higher value on the criterion.
Fluency heuristic: Jacoby & Dallas (1981); Schooler & Hertwig (2005)	If both alternatives are recognized but one is recognized faster, infer that it has the higher value on the criterion.
Take-the-best: Gigerenzer & Goldstein (1996)	To infer which of two alternatives has the higher value, (a) search through cues in order of validity, (b) stop search as soon as a cue discriminates, and (c) choose the alternative this cue favors.
Tallying: Unit-weight linear model, Dawes, 1979	To estimate a criterion, do not estimate weights, but simply count the number of positive cues.
Satisficing: Simon (1955); Todd & Miller (1999)	Search through alternatives, and choose the first one that exceeds your aspiration level.
$1/N$; equality heuristic: DeMiguel et al. (2009)	Allocate resources equally to each of N alternatives.
Default heuristic: Johnson & Goldstein (2003); Pichert & Katsikopoulos (2008)	If there is a default, do nothing.
Tit-for-tat: Axelrod (1984)	Cooperate first, and then imitate your partner's last behavior.
Imitate the majority: Boyd & Richerson (2005)	Consider the majority of people in your peer group, and imitate their behavior.
Imitate the successful: Boyd & Richerson (2005)	Consider the most successful person, and imitate his or her behavior.

Note: Each heuristic can underlie both intuitive and deliberate judgments.

recognition process is described by if–then rules, and the recognition heuristic is another rule that exploits this process (Schooler & Hertwig, 2005). The process of recognition is clearly not a deliberate one, and reliance on the recognition heuristic is often also not deliberate, but both reaction time and functional magnetic resonance imaging studies suggest that it could be a default setting of the brain (Pachur & Hertwig, 2006; Volz et al., 2006). Yet, the same heuristic can also be used deliberately, for instance, as a strategy for investing in stocks suggested by analyst Peter Lynch and tested by Ortmann, Gigerenzer, Borges, and Goldstein (2008) or as a strategy for predicting the outcomes of sports events. In this vein, deliberate reliance on mere name recognition could predict the winners of the 128 Wimbledon Gentleman Singles matches as well as or better than relying on official statistics such as the Association of Tennis Professionals (ATP) rankings and as good as or better than the seeding of the Wimbledon experts (Scheibehenne & Bröder, 2007; Serwe & Frings, 2006). These results demonstrate that heuristics need not be linked to automatic, intuitive processing or to error-prone judgments. More information about this is provided later.

The same argument can be made for each of the other heuristics, to different degrees. The fluency heuristic may represent the case in which it is rather rare that people rely deliberately on what came first to mind, but such cases may exist, for instance, when a person requesting advice for a choice between A and B is impressed by how quickly the responder answered A and takes this speed as clear evidence for A. The take-the-best heuristic is relied on both intuitively (Bröder, 2003; Rieskamp & Otto, 2006) and deliberately when designing decision systems without trade-offs. Deliberate use may occur for reasons of simplicity and transparency, which in turn increases safety and a feeling of justice. For instance, the contest rules of the International Federation of Football Associations rely on the take-the-best heuristic to decide which teams in a group can move ahead. The cues are ordered (total points, difference in number of goals, etc.), and decisions are made sequentially, without trade-offs. The same type of rule governs right-of-way in traffic (police officer's hand signs, traffic light, traffic sign, etc.), to which people apply it purposely to increase safety (Gigerenzer, 2007).

Tallying is relied on both intuitively, typically only by a small proportion of people (e.g., Bröder, 2003), and deliberately, in designing unit-weighted scoring systems for IQ tests and in democratic elections systems in which every voter has the same vote. The equality heuristic, or $1/N$, has been used to describe how parents intuitively allocate their love, time, and attention to their children (Hertwig, Davis, & Sulloway, 2002) and share windfall money in the ultimatum game (Takezawa, Gummerum, & Keller, 2006) and how professional and lay investors deliberately try to diversify and reduce risk (DeMiguel, Garlappi, & Uppal, 2009). A person who relies on the default heuristic ignores all information concerning an issue, such as organ donation, and just follows the legal default, which appears to be the major factor in the strikingly different rates of potential organ donors between countries (Johnson & Goldstein, 2003). Finally, imitation rules are known to be relied on automatically, as research on children testifies (Tomasello, 2000), and thoughtfully and purposefully, as in educational training in which children are instructed to copy, from drawing letters to skills in sports (Boyd & Richerson, 2005).

In summary, we argue that intuitive and deliberative judgments are both based on rules and can even be based on exactly the same rules. The important questions for research are what are these heuristics, when are they applied, and in which situations are they successful?

Where do rules come from?

Rules and the appropriate situations for their use can be acquired through personal experience, social development, and acculturation. This applies to both intuitive and deliberate judgments. We assume that every rule exploits core capacities and that the specific capacities determine the set of rules a species or an individual can execute in a reliable way.

Evolved core capacities

We use the term core capacity to designate an ability for which a species has the potential, enabled by its genes, although the individual typically needs to exercise this potential in order to express and master it. One example is long-term memory, which the human genome enables, but which the individual can master to various levels of competence, as illustrated by the stunning ability to recite long poems and sagas in oral traditions compared with the relative loss of this capacity in modern societies.

To execute a rule properly, an organism needs specific evolved capacities. This holds for rules in animals and humans alike (Hutchinson & Gigerenzer, 2005). Because humans and animals have common ancestry and related sensory and motor processes, they share common core capacities, which are exploited by common rules. For instance, ball players of various sorts (e.g., a baseball outfielder, or a cricket player) rely on simple rules to catch a ball. The simplest is the gaze heuristic, which works if the fly ball is high up in the air: Fix your gaze on the ball, start running, and adjust the running speed so that the angle of gaze remains constant (see Gigerenzer, 2007). This heuristic ignores all the information necessary for computing the trajectory of the ball. The same heuristic is applied by various animal species to catch a prey. In pursuit and predation, bats, birds, and dragonflies maintain a constant optical angle between themselves and their prey, as do dogs when catching a Frisbee (Shaffer, Krauchunas, Eddy, & McBeath, 2004). Among the core capacities needed for this heuristic is the ability to track visually moving objects against a noisy background, an ability no robot has today as well as a human being or a dog.

The same evolved capacity is needed when the rule is used in (what has been described as) an intuitive way or a deliberate way. For instance, sailors are taught to rely on the gaze heuristic deliberately when they fear that another boat is on a collision course: Fixate your eye on the other boat, and if the optical angle remains constant, change course because otherwise a collision will occur. Similarly, whether one of the heuristics in Table 1 is used consciously or unconsciously, the core capacities needed appear to be exactly the same. These include recall memory, recognition memory, and the ability to imitate the behavior of others.

Rule acquisition

Experience. Personal experience constitutes an important source of rule acquisition. Individuals learn to associate specific cues with specific states of affairs so that when a cue is registered, the state of affairs is inferred. For instance, a child may learn that snow is cold (*if snow then cold*), that water is wet, and that disobeying one's parents results in punishment. In conditioning work, the conditional link between the stimulus (the cue) and the response (the criterial judgment) may be established through a pairing of the stimulus and the response, followed by a reinforcement (in the instrumental learning paradigm) of the conditioned stimulus and the unconditioned stimulus (in the classical learning paradigm; Holyoak et al., 1989), and so on.

Social development. Kruglanski et al. (2005) described how in the course of social development the child acquires rules that link given social sources with given types of knowledge, bestowing on them epistemic authority. Initially the child tends to ascribe epistemic authority to adult caretakers, primarily the parents, in all domains of activity exemplifying the *if parent (says so) then it is correct* rule. This is gradually replaced by distinctions among domains and ascription of differential epistemic authority to different sources (teachers, peers, one's self).

Source rules. Source rules bestowing epistemic authority on given agents may lend them the powers to instruct and enable them to act as teachers and tutors. In this vein, Osman (2004, pp. 997–998) reviewed tutoring studies in which participants' logical thinking in Wason's (1968) selection task improved considerably as a result of their being taught the pertinent logical rules. According to Osman (2004, p. 998), "large improvements in performance are the result of clarifying the task requirements," that is, getting participants to attend to the correct cues and to apply the appropriate rules in relevant task contexts.

Acculturation. Numerous inference rules are learned via socialization into a given culture (Chiu & Hong, 2006). For instance, stereotypes (e.g., related to gender, race, age, ethnic group or profession) are rules concerning properties implied by given category memberships. Beliefs that an engineer is likely to be interested in mechanical toys and mathematical puzzles or that a lawyer is articulate and well dressed (both cited in studies of the representativeness heuristic) are acquired through immersion in the specific shared reality of one's group that subscribes to these notions. Schooling and academic training impart to the students a variety of rules concerning the properties of things and the implications of concepts, including the rules of statistics and other formal disciplines. Thus, the same processes of rule acquisition pertain to rules depicted as intuitive and those depicted as deliberative.

Routinization of rules: Deliberation becomes intuitive

It has been long known that automatic phenomena involve a routinization of if–then sequences. A novice piano player may be engaged in a highly controlled, attention-demanding activity that following the "rules" of music requires, yet the accomplished concert pianist may follow those same rules without much conscious awareness. The notion that social judgments represent a special case of procedural learning (Anderson, 1983), based on practice that strengthens the if–then connections, has been generally accepted in the social cognition literature (cf. Bargh, 1996; Neal, Wood, & Quinn, 2006; E. R. Smith & Branscombe, 1988).

Music and sports are examples of how skills are learned in a deliberate fashion but at some point become intuitive; that is, attention is no longer directed to the movements and people cannot explain how they do what they do. As a consequence of this transition, when experienced golf players were instructed to pay attention to the sequence of movements in their swing, their performance decreased, although the same intervention increased the accuracy of novices (Beilock, Bertenthal, McCoy, & Carr, 2004; Beilock, Carr, MacMahon, & Starkes, 2002).

Similarly, the judgments of experienced handball players were better when they had no time to think than when they could inspect a game scene for 45 seconds (Johnson & Raab, 2003). In general, many, but not all, skills are learned deliberately and then become intuitive or turn into gut feelings. There are, however, exceptions when a skill is learned by observation rather than by instruction, and the nature of the skill, the cues and rules, are never represented in language (Gigerenzer, 2007). The transition from deliberate to intuitive rules is a valuable process given that attention is a scarce resource. In the words of Alfred North Whitehead (cited in Egidi & Marengo, 2004, p. 335):

> It is a profoundly erroneous truism, repeated by all copy-books and by eminent people when they are making speeches, that we should cultivate the habit of thinking of what we are doing. The precise opposite is the case. Civilization advances by extending the number of operations which we can perform without thinking about them.

Some principles of rule selection

Consideration set of rules

Unlike the hardwired rules that mediate perceptual inferences, rules that mediate higher cognitive judgments are typically selected from a rule set in the individual's adaptive toolbox (Gigerenzer & Selten, 2001). We propose that such selection follows a two-step process: First, the task and individual memory constrain the set of applicable rules, resulting in a consideration set; and second, difficulty of instantiation, individual processing potential, and (perceived) ecological rationality of the rule guide the final choice of a rule from that set.

Task type constrains the consideration set of rules. Because rules are specialized, not every rule can be included in the choice set for a given task. For instance, if an individual faces a two-alternative choice task, the first four heuristics in Table 1 are in the choice set; the others cannot be applied (assuming there are no other individuals present to imitate). A mathematical task may constrain the set of rules differently for a seasoned mathematician and a novice, so may a chess problem for a master and an amateur player, and so on.

Memory constraints on the consideration set of rules. To be represented in the consideration set, a rule (or major premise of the syllogism) needs to be accessed from memory, which can be facilitated by priming (Higgins, 1996). Too, the input to the rule (the minor premise) may need memory input (Marewski & Schooler, 2010). For instance, consider again the first four rules in Table 1. If one alternative is recognized and the other not then the recognition heuristic is in the choice set, but the others are not. If both are recognized then the recognition heuristic is no longer applicable, but the other three are. If no additional information about cue values in this situation is obtained then the fluency heuristic remains in the choice set, whereas if such cue knowledge is obtained then experimental evidence suggests that take-the-best and tallying are preferred over the fluency heuristic.

It is important that immediate memory constraints are not absolute; what comes immediately to mind can be expanded by an intensive memory search. In other words, although some rules may be difficult to access or retrieved from memory in a given situation, they might still be accessed through an effortful attempt. Such an attempt might be enabled if the individual possessed sufficient processing potential, as elaborated subsequently.

Rule selection

If the consideration set includes more than one rule, a selection step is required, in which a given rule is chosen as a means for reaching judgment. The first factor affecting this step is difficulty of instantiating the rule in a specific context. Just as accessing a rule (the syllogism's major premise) from memory may be more or less difficult, so may be instantiating it in given conditions, that is, recognizing the rule-matching cue (the minor premise) in given circumstances. Contributing to such difficulty is noisiness of the judgmental environment and faintness of the cue, that is, a low signal to noise ratio. Again, overcoming the difficulty requires that the individual possess sufficient processing potential, which concept is discussed next.

Processing potential. Two aspects of processing potential are attentional capacity and processing motivation (e.g., Petty & Cacioppo, 1986; Tetlock, 1985). Individuals' attentional capacity may be taxed by cognitive load or busyness with other matters. Ability to focus attention may also depend on circadian rhythm (Kruglanski & Pierro, 2008), degree of mental fatigue (Webster, Richter, & Kruglanski, 1996), or alcoholic intoxication (Steele & Josephs, 1990). Processing motivation is often a function of the importance individuals assign to the judgmental task, their issue involvement (Petty & Cacioppo, 1986), and the magnitude of their accuracy, or accountability, goals in given circumstances (Tetlock, 1985). In addition, processing motivation is determined by individuals' stable motivational proclivities, such as their need for cognition (Cacioppo & Petty, 1982) or need for cognitive closure (Kruglanski, 2004; Kruglanski, Pierro, Mannetti, & DeGrada, 2006; Kruglanski & Webster, 1996).

An individual whose attentional capacity is depleted or whose processing motivation is low might be disinclined to conduct an extensive memory search or to invest extensive efforts in attempts to instantiate the rule, when this is difficult. Moreover, in such conditions, the individual may be loath to apply rules whose implementation requires laborious computational analyses. Consequently, individuals whose capacity or motivation are low may base their judgments on relatively simple inferential rules rather than on complex ones or may be less able to carefully assess the ecological rationality of a rule, that is, to properly estimate its validity in a given environment.

For instance, Petty, Wells, and Brock (1976) demonstrated that under capacity-depleting conditions, individuals were less sensitive to the quality of message arguments that tended to be relatively lengthy and complex and, hence, difficult to process. Consequently, under limited resource conditions, easy to use heuristics were used to a greater extent than more complex inferential rules. In this vein, Mata, Schooler, and Rieskamp (2007) reasoned that due to age-related decline in cognitive abilities, older adults more than younger ones would tend to use simple heuristics rather than more cognitively demanding strategies. Consistent with this hypothesis, Mata et al. (2007) found that older (vs. younger) adults instructed to infer which of two diamonds was more expensive tended to use the frugal take-the-best heuristic (Gigerenzer & Goldstein, 1996) or the take-two heuristic (Dieckman & Rieskamp, 2007) more and tended to use the more laborious weighted additive rule less. It was also found that the higher the magnitude of individuals' accuracy motivation, or their need for cognition, the greater their readiness to apply complex rules and to digest compound information (Kruglanski & Thompson, 1999a, 1999b; Petty & Cacioppo, 1986). By contrast, the higher the magnitude of their need for closure, the lesser their readiness to do so and the greater their tendency to rely on simple judgmental heuristics (Pierro, Mannetti, Erb, Spiegel, & Kruglanski, 2005).

Whereas the use of simple, easy to process heuristics may be more likely under low resource conditions, the selection and use of complex, laborious to apply, rules may be more likely under high resource conditions—but only in situations in which they are more subjectively valid, or high in perceived ecological rationality. More information about this is provided later.

Ecological rationality. Besides processing capacity and motivation, an important factor in the selection of a rule is the (perceived) ecological rationality of a rule for a given task. The study of ecological rationality asks which rule will lead to a better outcome (e.g., higher accuracy) in a given task environment. This requires studying the match between rules and structures of environments. For instance, the redundancy and variability of cue weights in the environment can guide the choice between take-the-best and tallying heuristics (Table 1). Redundancy is defined as the correlation between cues, and variability measures the distribution of the weights of cues. If redundancy and variability are high, one can expect that take-the-best will be more accurate than tallying; if both are low, the opposite follows (Hogarth & Karelaia, 2007). There is evidence for adaptive strategy selection (for an early review, see Payne, Bettman, & Johnson, 1993). Dieckmann and Rieskamp (2007) showed that in environments with high redundancy, take-the-best is as accurate as and more frugal than naïve Bayes (a strategy that integrates all cues) and then experimentally demonstrated that in high-redundancy environments, take-the-best predicted participants' judgments best, whereas in low-redundancy environments, compensatory strategies predicted best, indicating adaptive strategy selection. Rieskamp and Otto (2006) showed that in an environment with high variability of cue validities, judgments consistent with take-the-best increased over experimental trials from 28% to 71%, whereas in an environment with low variability, they decreased to 12%. Bröder (2003) reported similar selection of take-the-best dependent on the variability or cue validities. Strategy selection theory (Rieskamp & Otto, 2006) provides a quantitative model that can be understood as a reinforcement theory in which the unit of reinforcement is not a behavior but a rule or a heuristic.

This model allows predictions about the probability that a person selects one rule from a set of rules based on its perceived ecological rationality.

Rule conflict

At times, two or more rules may appear of nearly equal ecological rationality, creating a psychological situation of rule conflict. In such circumstances, judgment yielded by a given rule may differ from judgment yielded by another rule. For instance, in Asch's (1946) classic study, epistemic authority accorded to one's vision (i.e., the rule *if my vision suggests it, it is probably correct*) may be contradicted by the consensus heuristic (i.e., the rule *if the consensus supports it, it is probably correct*). Typically, rule conflict is resolved in favor of the stronger of the competing rules, that is, the rule with greatest perceived ecological rationality. This may produce implicit biases and rule violations, that is, improper application of a given rule because of interference from other incompatible rules.

In summary, to understand both deliberate and intuitive judgments, we need a theory of rule selection. Here, we identified a two-phase selection process involving (a) formation of the rules' choice set considered by the individual and (b) selection of a rule from the set allowing for the possibility of rule conflict.

Selected empirical evidence

If it is to serve as an alternative to existing dual-systems models, the present framework not only should specify models of heuristic rules and of rule selection but also ought (a) to be able to reinterpret findings cited in their support and (b) to afford novel, empirically verifiable insights. To demonstrate our general approach, we discuss here selected evidence in each of these categories.

Reinterpretations

Belief biases. A major implication of our rule-following framework is the possibility of rule conflict, mentioned earlier. Such conflict offers a plausible reinterpretation of the phenomenon of belief bias (Evans, 2008), viewed as a major source of support for the dual-systems notion. Belief bias is said to exist when individuals' prior beliefs interfere with the proper logical derivations of conclusions from premises. For instance, in the study by Evans, Barston, and Pollard (1983) participants were presented with the (major) premise, "No addictive things are inexpensive," and the (minor) premise, "Some cigarettes are inexpensive." Evidence for a belief bias was inferred from the finding that 71% of the participants thought that these premises warranted the conclusion, "Some addictive things are not cigarettes," which does not logically follow.

The notion that beliefs in given states of affairs can interfere with the application of specific rules is readily explicable in terms of the concept of rule conflict. Simply, the real world belief that some addictive things are not cigarettes may have been previously deduced in a rulelike fashion from the appropriate evidence, for example, from one's general familiarity with the class of addictive things that includes noncigarettes (e.g. "If there exists an addictive substance that is not a cigarette then some addictive things are noncigarettes"; "cocaine is an addictive substance that is not a cigarette," therefore "some addictive things are non-cigarettes"), undermining the proper deduction from the experimentally given premises (that "Some cigarettes are not addictive").

Our framework additionally suggests that in a clash between a focal rule (represented by the logical task given to participants by the experimenter) and a conclusion yielded by a prior rule (the so called biasing belief), interference from the latter will be reduced if the focal rule was well practiced or routinized and, hence, high in perceived ecological rationality. This derivation is consistent with the findings that (a) tutoring of research participants in various rules, for example, the conjunction rule, or the rule involved in Wason's (1968) selection task, considerably improves correct deductions from those rules (Osman, 2004, p. 998, p. 1001) and that (b) rules couched in participants' everyday experience, hence characterized by considerable ecological rationality, are applied more logically or consistently than are abstract rules detached from participants' familiar realities (Evans, 2008). Similarly, there is evidence that firmly held beliefs, understood here as beliefs deduced from ecologically rational rules, exert a particularly pronounced belief bias (Evans, 2008, p. 264). In the same vein, Reyna (2004) found that experts, that is, individuals with schemas (or rules) held with supreme confidence or a sense of ecological rationality, are more likely to apply those rules, which can lead to bias and error in novel judgmental situations.

Sloman's (1996) S-criterion. The phenomenon of rule conflict may also underlie Sloman's (1996) simultaneity, or S-criterion, for determining a systems separateness. Specifically, "A reasoning problem satisfies *Criterion S* if it causes people to believe two contradictory responses" (Sloman, 1996, p. 11). Consider Sloman's example of the statement that the "whale is a mammal." Whales are commonly perceived to resemble fish more than typical mammals, like dogs or cats. In this case, a person may need to deal with two contradictory beliefs, one derived from whales' outward similarity to fish and the other based on scholastic knowledge whereby whales are considered mammals. But as with Evans's (2008) evidence for belief bias, what we have here are two conflicting rules implying different conclusions. One rule is based on similarity, or the representativeness heuristic; namely, if X looks like a fish, swims like a fish, and lives like a fish then X is a fish. The other rule is derivable from alternative premises, for instance, known features of the mammal category, say breastfeeding of offspring, or from the epistemic authority of the source, namely, if a biologist claims that X (e.g., that whales are mammals) then indeed X. Thus, the simultaneity phenomenon need not attest to system separateness and is instead explicable in terms of the notion of rule conflict, discussed earlier.

Novel insights

In what follows, we discuss three classes of novel findings afforded by our unitary framework and incompatible with implications of the dual-systems models. These concern evidence that (a) instantiation difficulty determines the amount of processing potential that a rule requires for it to be selected for use, (b) higher processing potential is not aligned with selecting more complex rules, and (c) less processing can lead to more accurate judgments. We consider these in turn.

Instantiation difficulty determines the amount of processing potential a rule requires

Typically, dual-systems and dual-process models have implied that heuristic rules are selected when the individuals' processing potential is low, whereas extensional rules (e.g., statistical or logical rules) are used when the individuals' processing potential is high. However, the present analysis suggests that the amount of processing potential required for selecting a given rule depends on the difficulty of rule instantiation in given informational ecologies. Take the expertise heuristic, *if expert then correct*. In much persuasion research (for reviews see Erb et al., 2003; Kruglanski and Thompson, 1999a, 1999b) the instantiation of this rule was easy to accomplish because the expertise information was conveyed via a single line of text. Under those conditions, the expertise rule was used predominantly under conditions of low processing potential. However, in several studies (Kruglanski & Thompson, 1999a, 1999b, Kruglanski, Erb, at al., 2006; Kruglanski, Pierro, et al., 2006) instantiation of the expertise rule was made difficult by presenting the expertise information in the form of a lengthy curriculum vitae from which (low or high) expertise could be effortfully gleaned. Under those conditions, use of the expertise heuristic occurred predominantly in the presence of ample processing resources.

In a similar vein, Chun and Kruglanski (2006) showed in a series of experiments that use of the base rate rule might require either low processing potential or high processing potential, depending on its instantiation difficulty. When the base rate information was given in an easy to use form, that is, simply and succinctly, the base rate rule was used (base rate neglect was minimized) under low processing potential (e.g., in the presence of cognitive load). However, when such information was made difficult to glean (as the overall base rates had to be concatenated from several subsamples), the base rate rule was used only in the presence of ample processing potential. These findings lead one to question prior suggestions that rules referred to as intuitive (i.e., heuristic rules) are used under low processing potential, whereas rules referred to as deliberative tend to be used under high processing potential. After all, any rule can be made more or less difficult to instantiate or retrieve from memory and, hence, be more or less exigent of processing potential. The very same rule can be made easy to apply, in which case its use would resemble intuitive judgment or be more difficult to apply, resembling deliberative judgment.

Higher processing potential is not aligned with selecting more complex rules

Beside instantiation difficulty, a major factor in rule selection is the rule's (perceived) ecological rationality. Considerations of such rationality additionally invalidate the alignment of simple rules with low processing potential and complex rules with high processing potential. Specifically, our analysis suggests that to the extent that a rule (whether simple or complex) is difficult to retrieve or instantiate, it will not be selected and used under insufficient processing potential. Crucially, however, the obverse of this relation does not hold. That is, more complex rules will not be necessarily selected under high processing potential. Instead, under high potential, considerations of ecological rationality will prevail, and the individual will be able to select the most ecologically rational rule currently available.

In support of these notions, Pierro, Mannetti, Kruglanski, and Sleeth-Keppler (2004) showed that under limited processing potential, the easy to process rule is selected even if a more ecologically rational rule is potentially available. By contrast, under ample processing potential, the most ecologically rational rule is selected, regardless of whether it is easy or difficult to process. These findings imply that under ample processing potential the individual is able to engender an extensive set of rules to choose from and is able to select the most rational rule from the set. In contrast, under limited processing potential, the individuals' rule sets might exclude from consideration the most ecologically rational rule if it is difficult to process.

Consistent with the foregoing analysis are findings that individuals classified as take-the-best users for tasks in which this heuristic is most ecologically rational showed higher IQs than did those who were classified as relying on more complex, compensatory rules, suggesting that cognitive capacity as measured by IQ "is not consumed by strategy execution but rather by strategy selection" (Bröder & Newell, 2008, p. 209). Further evidence for the hypothesis that under ample resource conditions individuals use the most ecologically rational (rather than complex) rules derives from a series of studies by Cokely, Parpart, and Schooler (2009).

Less effort can lead to higher accuracy

A major question about judgments concerns their accuracy. This is hardly surprising as accuracy is a valuable asset to possess. Beyond the intrinsic value of having a grasp on reality, accuracy affords predictability that may help individuals cope with their social and physical environments. For that reason, psychological researchers and theorists have expended considerable efforts to identify judgmental procedures that increase accuracy and those that may undermine it. In most analyses, simple heuristics have been depicted as suboptimal rules of thumb: Though often yielding reasonable estimates, they were considered inferior, by and large, to normative procedures (but see Evans, 2008). Accordingly, they have been often equated with judgmental biases giving rise to the ubiquitous heuristics and biases label. In this vein, Tversky (1972, p. 98) asserted that the heuristic of elimination-by-aspects "cannot be defended as a rational procedure of choice." Similarly, Keeney and Raiffa (1993, pp. 77–78) stated that the use of (lexicographic) heuristics "is more widely adopted in practice than it deserves to be [and] will rarely pass a test of reasonableness."

Related to the notion that heuristics constitute suboptimal shortcuts to normative calculations is the pervasive view that more information is better for accuracy.

Rudolph Carnap (1947) proposed the principle of total evidence, suggesting the advisability of using all the available evidence in estimating a probability. In many theories of cognition (e.g., the Bayesian model, or prospect theory), it is similarly assumed that all pieces of information are, or should be, integrated in the final judgment (Gigerenzer & Brighton, 2009). McArthur and Baron's (1983) suggestion that active perceivers are typically more accurate than passive perceivers could be interpreted in terms of the greater amounts of information that active exploration may afford. Too, these authors' notion of sins of omission refers to cases in which the perceiver misses part of what is afforded because of attentional selectivity or because the stimulus array is impoverished. Again then, errors are traced to limited information search.

One of the first types of evidence for less-can-be-more came for the tallying heuristic (Table 1). This simple rule, reminiscent of the use of tally sticks for counting and traceable back some 30,000 years, has probably survived for a very good reason. Following the pioneering work of Dawes (1979; Dawes & Corrigan, 1974), Czerlinski, Gigerenzer, and Goldstein (1999) compared the tallying heuristic with multiple linear regression in 20 studies. Tallying ignores all cue weights, whereas multiple regression estimates the optimal beta weights. The authors found that averaged across all studies, tallying nevertheless achieved a higher predictive accuracy than did multiple regression. This does not mean that tallying will outperform multiple regression in all circumstances. The challenge for researchers is to delineate the tasks, or informational ecologies (Fiedler, 2007), under which each of these inferential rules produces the more accurate predictions (see Einhorn & Hogarth, 1975).

Similar less-is-more effects have been found for several other rules. A most striking discovery was that take-the-best—which relies on only one reason and ignores the rest—can predict more accurately than linear multiple regression models and tallying (Czerlinski et al., 1999). Subsequently it was found that relying on one good reason often also resulted in more accurate predictions than complex nonlinear methods, including a three-layer feedforward connectionist network trained with the backpropagation algorithm, exemplar-based models (nearest-neighbor classifier), classification and regression trees (CART), and Quinlan's decision-tree induction algorithm C4.5 (Brighton, 2006; Chater, Oaksford, Nakisa, & Redington, 2003; Gigerenzer & Brighton, 2009). These results put heuristics on par with standard statistical models of rational cognition. This is not to say that relying on one good reason is always better, but it raises the question, in what tasks is relying on one good reason better than relying on all reasons? A formal answer has been found with the bias-variance dilemma (Gigerenzer & Brighton, 2009).

The notion that simple rules can yield accurate inferences in appropriate ecologies has been highlighted by various theories of social cognition and perception (Funder, 1987; McArthur & Baron, 1983; Swann, 1984). The ecological approach emphasizes that in their natural environments humans and animals generally draw accurate inferences, when accuracy is defined in pragmatist terms as that which works (James, 1907, 1909). Less-is-more effects are of primary importance for the argument that heuristics are not aligned with error-prone judgments, and complex statistical rules are not aligned with rational judgments. These alignments miss the ecological nature of judgment and run the risk of misinterpreting the adaptive use of less effortful rules as signs of limited capacities or even irrationality.

Conclusion

In this chapter, we presented a number of convergent arguments and empirical evidence for a unified theoretical approach that explains both intuitive and deliberate judgments as rule based, as opposed to the dual-systems approach of qualitatively different processes. Moreover, using a sample of heuristic rules (Table 1), we provided empirical evidence that the same rules can underlie both intuitive and deliberate judgments. Because there can be more than one rule, any theory of judgment needs to address the rule selection problem, which is hidden in dual-process accounts because the processes are not well specified. We proposed a two-step selection process, in which the task and the contents of memory constrain the choice set of rules an individual can consider, and processing potential and (perceived) ecological rationality determine the final selection of a rule.

Although the specific features of our theoretical framework need to be elaborated, one thing seems clear. The conceptual and empirical difficulties entailed by the partition between intuitive and deliberate judgments, and their alignment with multiple similar dichotomies have impeded a deeper examination of the psychology of judgment. It is time to move beyond imprecise dualisms and toward specific models of the judgmental process. These include models of heuristic inference rules, their building blocks, and their adaptations to task environments that humans confront. This chapter takes a step in that direction.

Notes

1 A distinction is sometimes drawn between dual-process and dual-system formulations (e.g., Gawronski & Bodenhausen, 2006; Kruglanski & Orehek, 2007). The dual-process formulations were typically domain specific (e.g., pertaining to the domain of persuasion or attribution), whereas the dual-system models were more general and assumed to apply across domains. Also, the dual-process formulations were information focused; they typically coordinated the proposed dual processes to two separate information classes (e.g., peripheral cues vs. message arguments, social categories vs. personality attributes). The dual-systems models typically purported to be process-focused and were somewhat less concerned with informational inputs. The terms dual modes and dual routes have also been used, and these various terms have also been treated interchangeably by some authors (for discussion see Keren & Schul, 2009). All dualistic models, however, regardless of type, draw a qualitative distinction between judgment formation that is accomplished easily and quickly and one that is slow, extensive, and arduous.
2 However, the Strack and Deutsch (2004) reflective–impulsive model does align both systematic and heuristic reasoning with processes in the reflective system and juxtaposes these to associative processes in the impulsive system.
3 Indeed, even if the dual-systems/dual-process model offered a weaker version of their position and assumed the (obviously) continuous nature of such characteristics, they would still need to define meaningful cutoff points on the relevant continua, a task never seriously undertaken.

4 Moreover, even if meaningful cut-offs were defined, assuming six dichotomies, one would end up with a $2^6 = 64$ cell matrix of which only two cells (those representing the conjunction of all six dichotomies) had entries. Again, this logical implication of the alignment assumption has never been considered seriously or tested empirically.
5 Inverse in the sense that the proximal stimulus (e.g., the retinal image) originally produced by the distal stimulus is now used to decode such stimulus, going backward as it were.
6 In cognitive science, a debate has ensued on whether human reasoning is based on rules or similarities (between specific instances of experienced events). Hahn and Chater (1998) have offered a comprehensive analysis of arguments on both sides of this issue, suggesting, "Possibly, these two classes are too broad to allow an overall empirical assessment" (p. 199). These authors also argued that the ample evidence adduced for the rule conception could be alternatively interpreted in terms of the similarity conception and vice versa. It is not our intention to enter here into this intricate debate. Nonetheless, it is noteworthy that both similarity and rule-based notions assume a mental representation of stimuli by the judging individual; hence, both fall outside the purview of mere rule conforming phenomena (Hahn & Chater, 1998). Furthermore, both imply a mentally represented input to output function. In that sense then, both assume a conditional if–then relation between input and output representations. Similarity determination, for instance, has entailments. A given degree of perceived similarity is informative; it goes beyond the information given and brings forth certain implications. Whereas the rule versus similarity debate is not presently resolvable, we find the rule-based formulation to be based on considerable data, as well as consistent with common experience and broadly plausible. Consequently, we adopt it in our analysis and explore its implications.

References

Anderson, J. R. (1983). *The structure of cognition*. Cambridge, MA: Harvard University Press.
Asch, S. (1946). Forming impressions of personality. *Journal of Abnormal and Social Psychology*, *41*, 258–290.
Axelrod, R. (1984). *The evolution of cooperation*. New York, NY: Basic Books.
Bargh, J. A. (1996). Automaticity in social psychology. In E. T. Higgins & A. W. Kruglanski (Eds.), *Social psychology: Handbook of basic principles* (pp. 169–183). New York, NY: Guilford Press.
Beilock, S. L., Bertenthal, B. I., McCoy, A. M., & Carr, T. H. (2004). Haste does not always make waste: Expertise, direction of attention, and speed versus accuracy in performing sensorimotor skills. *Psychonomic Bulletin & Review*, *11*, 373–379.
Beilock, S. L., Carr, T. H., MacMahon, C., & Starkes, J. L. (2002). When paying attention becomes counterproductive: Impact of divided versus skill-focused attention on novice and experienced performance of sensorimotor skills. *Journal of Experimental Psychology: Applied*, *8*, 6–16.
Boyd, R., & Richerson, P. J. (2005). *The origin and evolution of cultures*. New York, NY: Oxford University Press.
Brighton, H. (2006). Robust inference with simple cognitive models. In C. Lebiere & R. Wray (Eds.), *AAAI spring symposium: Cognitive science principles meet AI-hard problems* (pp. 17–22). Menlo Park, CA: American Association for Artificial Intelligence.
Bröder, A. (2003). Decision making with the "adaptive toolbox": Influence of environmental structure, intelligence, and working memory load. *Journal of Experimental Psychology: Learning, Memory, and Cognition*, *29*, 611–625.
Bröder, A., & Newell, B. R. (2008). Challenging some common beliefs: Empirical work within the adaptive toolbox metaphor. *Judgment and Decision Making*, *3*, 205–214.

Bruner, J. S. (1973). *Beyond the information given: Studies on the psychology of knowing*. Oxford, England: W. W. Norton.
Cacioppo, J. T., & Petty, R. E. (1982). The need for cognition. *Journal of Personality and Social Psychology, 42*, 116–131.
Carnap, R. (1947). *Meaning and necessity*. Chicago, IL: University of Chicago Press.
Chaiken, S., & Trope, Y. (1999). *Dual-process theories in social psychology*. New York, NY: Guilford Press.
Chater, N., Oaksford, M., Nakisa, R., & Redington, M. (2003). Fast, frugal and rational: How rational norms explain behavior. *Organizational Behavior and Human Decision Processes, 90*, 63–86.
Chiu, C.-Y., & Hong, Y. (2006). *Social psychology of culture*. New York, NY: Psychology Press.
Chomsky, N. (1986). *Knowledge of language: Its nature, origin, and use*. Westport, CT: Prager.
Chun, W. Y., & Kruglanski, A. W. (2006). The role of task demands and processing resources in the use of base rate and individuating information. *Journal of Personality and Social Psychology, 91*, 205–217.
Cokely, E. T., Parpart, P., & Schooler, L. J. (2009). There is no "the" heuristic system: Paradoxical effects of fluency, aging, and cognitive reflection. Unpublished manuscript.
Czerlinski, J., Gigerenzer, G., & Goldstein, D. G. (1999). How good are simple heuristics? In G. Gigerenzer, P. M. Todd, & the ABC Research Group, *Simple heuristics that make us smart* (pp. 97–118). New York, NY: Oxford University Press.
Dawes, R. H. (1979). The robust beauty of improper linear models in decision making. *American Psychologist, 34*, 571–582.
Dawes, R. H., & Corrigan, B. (1974). Linear models in decision making. *Psychological Bulletin, 81*, 95–106.
DeMiguel, V., Garlappi, L., & Uppal, R. (2009). Optimal versus naive diversification: How inefficient is the 1/N portfolio strategy? *Review of Financial Studies, 22*, 1915–1953.
Dieckmann, A., & Rieskamp, J. (2007). The influence of information redundancy on probabilistic inferences. *Memory & Cognition, 35*, 1801–1813.
Egidi, M., & Marengo, L. (2004). Near-decomposability, organization, and evolution: Some notes on Herbert Simon's contribution. In M. Augier & J. J. March (Eds.), *Models of a man: Essays in memory of Herbert A. Simon* (pp. 335–350). Cambridge, MA: MIT Press.
Einhorn, H. J., & Hogarth, R. M. (1975). Unit weighting schemes for decision making. *Organizational Behavior and Human Performance, 13*, 171–192.
Epstein, S., Lipson, A., Holstein, C., & Huh, E. (1992). Irrational reactions to negative outcomes: Evidence for two conceptual systems. *Journal of Personality and Social Psychology, 38*, 889–906.
Erb, H.-P., Kruglanski, A. W., Chun, W. Y., Pierro, A., Mannetti, L., & Spiegel, S. (2003). Searching for commonalities in human judgment: The parametric unimodel and its dual mode alternatives. *European Review of Social Psychology, 14*, 1–47.
Evans, J. St. B. T. (2008). Dual-processing accounts of reasoning, judgment, and social cognition. *Annual Review of Psychology, 59*, 255–278.
Evans, J. St. B. T., Barston, J. L., & Pollard, P. (1983). On the conflict between logic and belief in syllogistic reasoning. *Memory & Cognition, 11*, 295–306.
Fechner, G. T. (1966). *Elements of psychophysics*. New York, NY: Holt, Reinhart, & Winston. (Original work published 1860)
Fiedler, K. (2007). Informational ecology and the explanation of social cognition and behavior. In A. W. Kruglanski & E. T. Higgins (2007). *Social psychology: A handbook of basic principles* (2nd ed., pp. 176–200). New York, NY: Guilford Press.

Funder, D. C. (1987). Errors and mistakes: Evaluating the accuracy of social judgment. *Psychological Bulletin, 101*, 75–90.

Gawronski, B., & Bodenhausen, G. V. (2006). Associative and propositional processes in evaluation: An integrative review of implicit and explicit attitude change. *Psychological Bulletin, 132*, 692–731.

Gigerenzer, G. (2005). I think; therefore, I err. *Social Research, 72*, 195–218.

Gigerenzer, G. (2007). *Gut feelings: The intelligence of the unconscious.* New York, NY: Viking.

Gigerenzer, G. (2009). Surrogates for theory. *APS Observer, 22*(2), 21–23.

Gigerenzer, G., & Brighton, H. (2009). Homo heuristicus: Why biased minds make better inferences. *Topics in Cognitive Science, 1*, 107–143.

Gigerenzer, G., & Goldstein, D. G. (1996). Reasoning the fast and frugal way: Models of bounded rationality. *Psychological Review, 103*, 650–669.

Gigerenzer, G., & Murray, D. J. (1987). *Cognition as intuitive statistics.* Hillsdale, NJ: Erlbaum.

Gigerenzer, G., & Regier, T. (1996). How do we tell an association from a rule? Comment on Sloman (1996). *Psychological Bulletin, 119*, 23–26.

Gigerenzer, G., & Selten, R. (Eds.). (2001). *Bounded rationality: The adaptive toolbox.* Cambridge, MA: MIT Press.

Goldstein, D. G., & Gigerenzer, G. (2002). Models of ecological rationality: The recognition heuristic. *Psychological Review, 109*, 75–90.

Hahn, U., & Chater, N. (1998). Similarity and rules: Distinct? Exhaustive? Empirically distinguishable? *Cognition, 65*, 197–230.

Helmholtz, J. A. (2000). *Treatise on physiological optics.* New York, NY: Dover. (Original work published 1910)

Hertwig, R., Davis, J. R., & Sulloway, F. J. (2002). Parental investment: How an equity motive can produce inequality. *Psychological Bulletin, 128*, 728–745.

Higgins, E. T. (1996). Knowledge activation: Accessibility, applicability and salience. In E. T. Higgins & A. W. Kruglanski (1996). *Social psychology: A handbook of basic processes* (pp. 133–168). New York, NY: Guilford.

Hogarth, R. M., & Karelaia, N. (2007). Heuristic and linear models of judgment: Matching rules and environments. *Psychological Review, 114*, 733–758.

Holyoak, K. J., Kohl, K., & Nisbett, R. E. (1989). A theory of conditioned reasoning: Inductive learning within rule-based hierarchies. *Psychological Review, 96*, 315–340.

Hutchinson, J. M. C., & Gigerenzer, G. (2005). Simple heuristics and rules of thumb: Where psychologists and behavioural biologists might meet. *Behavioural Processes, 69*, 97–124.

Jacoby, L. L., & Dallas, M. (1981). On the relationship between autobiographical memory and perceptual learning. *Journal of Experimental Psychology: General, 110*, 306–340.

James, W. (1907). *Pragmatism.* Cambridge, MA: Harvard University Press.

James, W. (1909). *The meaning of truth.* Cambridge, MA: Harvard University Press.

Johnson, E. L., & Goldstein, D. G. (2003). Do defaults save lives? *Science, 302*, 1338–1339.

Johnson, J. G., & Raab, M. (2003). Take the first: Option generation and resulting choices. *Organizational Behavior and Human Decision Processes, 91*, 215–229.

Kahneman, D. (2003). A perspective on judgment and choice: Mapping bounded rationality. *American Psychologist, 58*, 697–720.

Kahneman, D., & Tversky, A. (1973). On the psychology of prediction. *Psychological Review, 80*, 237–251.

Keeney, R. L., & Raiffa, H. (1993). *Decisions with multiple objectives-preferences and value tradeoffs.* New York, NY: Cambridge University Press.

Keren, G., & Schul, Y. (2009). Two is not always better than one: A critical evaluation of two-system theories. *Perspectives on Psychological Science, 4*, 500–533.

Kersten, D., Mammassian, P., & Yuille, A. (2004). Object perception as Bayesian inference. *Annual Review of Psychology, 55*, 271–304.

Kleffner, D. A., & Ramachandran, V. S. (1992). On the perception of shape from shading. *Perception & Psychophysics, 52*, 18–36.

Kruglanski, A. W. (2004). *The psychology of closed mindedness.* New York, NY: Psychology Press.

Kruglanski, A. W., Erb, H. P., Pierro, A., Mannetti, L., & Chun. W. Y. (2006). On parametric continuities in the world of binary either ors. *Psychological Inquiry 17*, 153–165.

Kruglanski, A. W., & Orehek, E. (2007). Partitioning the domain of human inference: Dual mode and system models and their alternatives. *Annual Review of Psychology, 8*, 291–316.

Kruglanski, A. W., & Pierro, A. (2008). Night and day, you are the one: On circadian mismatches and the transference effect in social perception. *Psychological Science, 19*, 296–301.

Kruglanski, A. W., Pierro, A., Mannetti, L., & De Grada, E. (2006). Groups as epistemic providers: Need for closure and the unfolding of group centrism. *Psychological Review, 113*, 84–100.

Kruglanski, A. W., Raviv, A., Bar-Tal, D., Sharvit, K., Ellis, S., Bar, R., Pierro, A., & Mannetti, L. (2005). Says who? Epistemic authority effects in social judgment. In M. P. Zanna (Ed.), *Advances in experimental social psychology* (Vol. 37, pp. 346–392). San Diego, CA: Academic Press.

Kruglanski, A. W., & Thomson, E. P. (1999a). The illusory second mode or, the cue is the message. *Psychological Inquiry, 10*, 182–193.

Kruglanski, A. W., & Thomson, E. P. (1999b). Persuasion by a single route: A view from the unimodel. *Psychological Inquiry, 10*, 83–109.

Kruglanski, A. W., & Webster, D. M. (1996). Motivated closing of the mind: "Seizing" and "freezing." *Psychological Review, 103*, 263–283.

Logan, G. D. (1988). Toward an instance theory of automatization. *Psychological Review, 95*, 492–527.

Marcus, G., Brinkmann, U., Clahsen, H., Wiese, R., & Pinker, S. (1995). German inflection: The exception that proves the rule. *Cognitive Psychology, 29*, 189–256.

Marewski, J. N., & Schooler, L. J. (2010). *How memory aids strategy selection.* Manuscript submitted for publication.

Mata, R., Schooler, L., & Rieskamp, J. (2007). The aging decision maker: Cognitive aging and the adaptive selection of decision strategies. *Psychology and Aging, 22*, 796–810.

McArthur, L. Z., & Baron, R. M. (1983). Toward an ecological theory of social perception. *Psychological Review, 90*, 215–238.

McGuire, W. J. (1960). A syllogistic analysis of cognitive relationships. In C. I. Hovland & M. J. Rosenberg (Eds.), *Attitude organization and change: An analysis of consistency among attitude components* (pp. 65–111). New Haven, CT: Yale University Press.

Medin, D. L., & Ross, B. H. (1989). The specific character of abstract thought: Categorization, problem solving, and induction. In R. J. Sternberg (Ed.), *Advances in the psychology of human intelligence* (Vol. 5, pp. 189–223). Hillsdale, NJ: Erlbaum.

Mitchell, C. J., DeHouwer, J., & Lovibond, P. F. (2009). The propositional nature of human associative learning. *Behavioral & Brain Science, 32*, 183–198.

Neal, D. T., Wood, W., & Quinn, J. M. (2006). Habits: A repeat performance. *Current Directions in Psychological Science, 16*, 198–202.

Ortmann, A., Gigerenzer, G., Borges, B., & Goldstein, D. G. (2008). The recognition heuristic: A fast and frugal way to investment choice? In C. R. Plott & V. L. Smith (Eds.), *Handbook of experimental economics results* (Vol. 1, No. 28, pp. 993–1003). Amsterdam, Holland: North-Holland.

Osman, B. (2004), Quality assessment, verification, and validation of modeling and simulation applications. *Proceedings of the 2004 Winter Simulation Conference*, 122–129.

Pachur, T., & Hertwig. (2006). On the psychology of the recognition heuristic: Retrieval primacy as a key determinant of its use. *Journal of Experimental Psychology, Learning, Memory, and Cognition, 32*, 983–1002.

Payne, J. W., Bettman, J. R., & Johnson, E. J. (1993). *The adaptive decision maker*. New York, NY: Cambridge University Press.

Petty, R. E., & Caccioppo, J. T. (1986). The elaboration likelihood model of persuasion. In L. Berkowitz (Ed.), *Advances in experimental social psychology* (Vol. 19, pp. 123–205). San Diego, CA: Academic Press.

Petty, R. E., Wells, G. L., & Brock, T. C. (1976). Distraction can enhance or reduce yielding to propaganda: Thought disruption versus effort justification. *Journal of Personality and Social Psychology, 34*, 874–884.

Pichert, D., & Katsikopoulos, K. V. (2008). Green defaults: Information presentation and pro-environmental behavior. *Journal of Environmental Psychology, 28*, 63–73.

Pierro, A., Mannetti, L., Erb, H. P., Spiegel, S., & Kruglanski, A. W. (2005). Informational length and order of presentation as determinants of persuasion. *Journal of Experimental Social Psychology, 41*, 458–469.

Pierro, A., Mannetti, L., Kruglanski, A. W., & Sleeth-Keppler, D. (2004). Relevance override: On the reduced impact of "cues" under high motivation conditions of persuasion studies. *Journal of Personality and Social Psychology, 86*, 251–264.

Pizlo, Z. (2001). Perception viewed as an inverse problem. *Vision Research, 41*, 3145–3161.

Rescorla, R. A. (1985). Conditioned inhibition and facilitation. In R. R. Miller & N. E. Spear (Eds.), *Information processing as animals: Conditioned inhibition* (pp. 299–326). Hillsdale, NJ: Erlbaum.

Rescorla, R. A., & Holland, P. C. (1982). Behavioral studies of associative learning in animals. *Annual Review of Psychology, 33*, 265–308.

Rescorla, R. A., & Wagner, A. R. (1972). A theory of Pavlovian conditioning: Variations in the effectiveness of reinforcement and nonreinforcement. In A. H. Black & W. F. Procasy (Eds.), *Classical conditioning II: Current theory and research* (pp. 64–99). New York, NY: Appleton Century Croft.

Reyna, V. (2004). How people make decisions that involve risk: A dual-processes approach. *Current Directions in Psychological Science, 13*, 60–66.

Rickard, T. C., Sin-Heng, J., & Pashler, H. (2008). Spacing and the transition from calculation to retrieval. *Psychological Bulletin and Review, 15*, 656–661.

Rieskamp, J., & Otto, P. E. (2006). SSL: A theory of how people learn to select strategies. *Journal of Experimental Psychology: General, 135*, 207–236.

Rock, I. (1983). *The logic of perception*. Cambridge, MA: MIT Press.

Scheibehenne, B., & Bröder, A. (2007). Predicting Wimbledon 2005 tennis results by mere player name recognition. *International Journal of Forecasting, 3*, 415–426.

Schooler, L., & Hertwig, R. (2005). How forgetting aids heuristic inference. *Psychological Review, 112*, 610–628.

Serwe, S., & Frings, C. (2006). Who will win Wimbledon? The recognition heuristic in predicting sports events. *Journal of Behavioral Decision Making, 19*, 321–332.

Shaffer, D. M., Krauchunas, S. M., Eddy, M., & McBeath, M. K. (2004). How dogs navigate to catch Frisbees. *Psychological Science, 15*, 437–441.

Sloman, S. A. (1996). The empirical case for two systems of reasoning. *Psychological Bulletin, 119*, 3–22.

Smith, D. G., Standing, L., & deMan, A. (1992). Verbal memory elicited by ambient odor. *Perceptual Motor Skills, 72,* 339–343.

Smith, E. R., & Branscombe, N. R. (1988). Category accessibility as implicit memory. *Journal of Experimental Social Psychology, 24,* 490–504.

Steele, C. M., & Josephs, R. A. (1990). Alcohol myopia: Its prized and dangerous effects. *American Psychologist, 45,* 921–933.

Strack, F., & Deutsch, R. (2004). Reflective and impulsive determinants of social behavior. *Personality and Social Psychology Review, 8,* 220–247.

Swann, W. B. (1984). Quest for accuracy in person perception: A matter of pragmatics. *Psychological Review, 91,* 457–477.

Takezawa, M., Gummerum, M., & Keller, M. (2006). A stage for the rational tail of the emotional dog: Roles of moral reasoning in group decision making. *Journal of Economic Psychology, 27,* 117–139.

Tetlock, P. E. (1985). Accountability: A social check on the fundamental attribution error. *Social Psychology Quarterly, 48,* 227–236.

Todd, P. M., & Miller, G. F. (1999). From pride and prejudice to persuasion: Realistic heuristics for mate search. In G. Gigerenzer, P. M. Todd, & the ABC Research Group (Eds.), *Simple heuristics that make us smart* (pp. 287–308). New York, NY: Oxford University Press.

Tolman, E. C. (1932). *Purposive behavior in animals and men.* New York, NY: Appleton Century Crofts.

Tomasello, M. (2000). *The cultural origins of human cognition.* Cambridge, MA: Harvard University Press.

Tversky, A. (1972). Elimination by aspects: A theory of choice. *Psychological Review, 79,* 281–299.

Volz, K. G., Schooler, L. J., Schubotz, R. I., Raab, M., Gigerenzer, G., & von Cramon, D. Y. (2006). Why you think Milan is larger than Modena: Neural correlates of the recognition heuristic. *Journal of Cognitive Neuroscience, 18,* 1924–1936.

Wason, P. C. (1968). Reasoning about a rule. *Quarterly Journal of Experimental Psychology, 20,* 273–281.

Webster, D. M., Richter, L., & Kruglanski, A. W. (1996). On leaping to conclusions when feeling tired: Mental fatigue effects on impression formation. *Journal of Experimental Social Psychology, 32,* 181–195.

Wyer, R. S. Jr. (1970). Quantitative prediction of opinion and belief change: A further test of the subjective probability model. *Journal of Personality and Social Psychology, 16,* 559–570.

5 Political conservatism as motivated social cognition

John T. Jost, Stanford University
Jack Glaser and Frank J. Sulloway, University of California
Arie W. Kruglanski, University of Maryland

> Conservatism is a demanding mistress and is giving me a migraine.
> George F. Will, *Bunts*

For more than half a century, psychologists have been tracking the hypothesis that different psychological motives and tendencies underlie ideological differences between the political left and the right. The practice of singling out political conservatives for special study began with Adorno, Frenkel-Brunswik, Levinson, and Sanford's (1950) landmark study of authoritarianism and the fascist potential in personality. An asymmetrical focus on right-wing authoritarianism (RWA) was criticized heavily on theoretical and methodological grounds (e.g., Christie, 1954; Eysenck, 1954; Rokeach, 1960; Shils, 1954), but it has withstood the relentless tests of time and empirical scrutiny (e.g., Altemeyer, 1981, 1988, 1996, 1998; Billig, 1984; Brown, 1965; Christie, 1991; Elms, 1969; Sidanius, 1985; W. F. Stone, 1980; W. F. Stone, Lederer, & Christie, 1993; Tetlock, 1984; Wilson, 1973c). A voluminous literature, which we review here, facilitates the comparison of cognitive styles and motivational needs of political conservatives with those of moderates, liberals, radicals, and left-wingers. In addition to classic and contemporary approaches to authoritarianism, we cover less obvious sources of theory and research on individual differences associated with dogmatism and intolerance of ambiguity, uncertainty avoidance, need for cognitive closure, and social dominance orientation (SDO) insofar as each of these psychological variables contributes to a deeper and more nuanced understanding of political conservatism.

The study of authoritarianism and other personality theories of political attitudes is often dismissed a priori as an illegitimate, value-laden attempt to correlate general psychological profiles with specific ideological beliefs (e.g., Durrheim, 1997; J. L. Martin, 2001; Ray, 1988). The psychological study of ideological conservatism is one that invites controversy (e.g., Redding, 2001; Sears, 1994; Sidanius, Pratto, & Bobo, 1996; Sniderman & Tetlock, 1986; Tetlock, 1994; Tetlock & Mitchell, 1993), but this circumstance does not mean that researchers should avoid it. Our view is that it is a legitimate empirical issue whether there are demonstrable links between a clearly defined set of psychological needs, motives, and properties and the adoption of politically conservative attitudes. The measurement of individual differences is an excellent starting point for understanding the psychological basis of political ideology, but we argue that approaching political conservatism exclusively from the standpoint of personality theory is a mistake. The hypothesis that people adopt conservative ideologies in an effort to satisfy various social-cognitive motives requires a novel theoretical perspective that overcomes two crucial limitations of traditional research on the psychology of conservatism.

First, too many measures of individual differences have conflated psychological and political variables in an attempt to measure a construct that is really a hybrid of the two. Wilson (1973c), for instance, offered an amalgamated definition of conservatism as "resistance to change and the tendency to prefer safe, traditional and conventional forms of institutions and behaviour" (p. 4). However, Wilson and Patterson's (1968) Conservatism Scale (C-Scale)—which is the psychological instrument that has been most widely used to measure conservatism—combines nonpolitical stimuli that are meant to elicit general attitudes concerning uncertainty avoidance (e.g., modern art, jazz music, horoscopes) and stimuli that have explicitly political referents (e.g., death penalty, legalized abortion, socialism, religion). The fact that such a seemingly heterogeneous scale would exhibit reasonable psychometric properties with respect to reliability and validity suggests that Wilson and his colleagues were accurately perceiving a link between general epistemic motivations and conservative ideology (see also Bagley, Wilson, & Boshier, 1970; Wilson, 1973a). Nevertheless, theoretical and empirical efforts are generally hampered by the failure to distinguish clearly between psychological and ideological variables (Sniderman & Tetlock, 1986).

Second, treating political conservatism solely as an individual-difference variable neglects growing evidence that situational factors influence the experience and expression of conservatism (e.g., Crowe & Higgins, 1997; Greenberg et al., 1990; Jost, Kruglanski, & Simon, 1999; Kruglanski & Webster, 1991; Sales & Friend, 1973; Sulloway, 1996, 2001). If classic personality theories are correct in positing that character rigidity and motivational threat are related to the holding of conservative attitudes, then system instability and other threatening circumstances should also increase conservative tendencies in the population as a whole (e.g., Fromm, 1941; McCann, 1997; Reich, 1946/1970; Sales, 1972, 1973; Sanford, 1966). In an effort to stimulate innovative approaches to the study of situations as well as dispositions that foster ideological conservatism, we cast a wide net in reviewing theories of motivated social cognition that are not conventionally regarded as political in nature, including theories of lay epistemics, regulatory focus, and terror management. Thus, we argue that tendencies toward political conservatism are influenced by a multiplicity of social-cognitive motives.

Overview

We propose that a motivated social-cognitive approach offers the greatest potential for unifying relatively diverse theories and findings related to the psychological basis of political conservatism—that is, theories and findings that link social and cognitive motives to the contents of specific political attitudes. Specifically, we distill key insights from theories of personality and individual differences, theories of epistemic and existential needs, and sociopolitical theories of ideology as individual and collective rationalizations. Following this eclectic review of theoretical perspectives, we examine the balance of evidence for and against several variants of the hypothesis that people embrace political conservatism (at least in part) because it serves to reduce fear, anxiety, and uncertainty; to avoid change, disruption, and ambiguity; and to explain, order, and justify inequality among groups and individuals. Treating political conservatism as a special case of motivated social cognition (a) goes beyond traditional individual-difference approaches; (b) maintains a clear distinction between psychological motives and political outcomes and helps to explain relations between the two; (c) highlights situational as well as dispositional variables that relate to conservatism; (d) takes into account a wider variety of epistemic, existential, and ideologically defensive motivations than has been considered previously; and (e) provides an integrative framework for understanding how these motives work together to reduce and manage fear and uncertainty.

The motivated social-cognitive perspective

To set the stage, we use the term *motivated social cognition* to refer to a number of assumptions about the relationship between people's beliefs and their motivational underpinnings (e.g., Bruner, 1957; Duckitt, 2001; Dunning, 1999; Fiske & Taylor, 1991; Greenwald, 1980; Hastorf & Cantril, 1954; Higgins, 1998; Kruglanski, 1996; Kunda, 1990; Rokeach, 1960). In the post-Freudian world, the ancient dichotomy between reason and passion is blurred, and nearly everyone is aware of the possibility that people are capable of believing what they want to believe, at least within certain limits. Our first assumption, too, is that conservative ideologies—like virtually all other belief systems—are adopted in part because they satisfy some psychological needs. This does not mean that conservatism is pathological or that conservative beliefs are necessarily false, irrational, or unprincipled. From the present perspective, most human beliefs are subjectively rational in the sense of being deduced from a set of premises to which believers subscribe (Kruglanski, 1999; Kruglanski & Thompson, 1999a, 1999b), and they are also at least partially responsive to reality constraints (Kunda, 1990). In this sense, any given person's conservatism may well be principled in that it is related logically or psychologically to other observations, values, beliefs, and premises. At the same time, adherence to principles and syllogistic reasoning do not occur in a motivational vacuum but rather in the context of a variety of virtually inescapable personal and social motivations (e.g., Hastorf & Cantril, 1954; Kunda, 1990; Lord, Ross, & Lepper, 1979) that are not necessarily consciously accessible (e.g., Kruglanski, 1996, 1999). Thus, political attitudes may well be principled (e.g., Sniderman, Piazza, Tetlock, & Kendrick, 1991; Sniderman & Tetlock, 1986) and motivationally fueled at the same time.

General theoretical assumptions

We find it useful to distinguish between *directional* and *nondirectional motives* involved in belief formation. Directional motives reflect the desire to reach a specific conclusion, such as that the self is worthy or valuable (e.g., Dunning, 1999; Greenwald, 1980; Kunda, 1990), that Republican leaders are benevolent and moral (e.g., Lind, 1996), that the economy will improve, or that one's position of privilege will be preserved (Sears & Funk, 1991; Sidanius, 1984). By contrast, nondirectional motives, such as the "need to know" (Rokeach, 1960), the need for nonspecific closure (Kruglanski & Webster, 1996), the fear of invalidity (Kruglanski & Freund, 1983), and the need for cognition (Cacioppo & Petty, 1982) reflect the desire to arrive at a belief or understanding, independent of its content. Both directional and nondirectional motives are assumed to affect belief formation by determining the extent of information processing (Ditto & Lopez, 1992), bringing about selective exposure to information (Frey, 1986) and affecting other modes of processing available information (Kruglanski, 1996). The possibility that we consider in this chapter is that a kind of matching process takes place whereby people adopt ideological belief systems (such as conservatism, RWA, and SDO) that are most likely to satisfy their psychological needs and motives (such as needs for order, structure, and closure and the avoidance of uncertainty or threat).[1]

A theoretical assumption we make is that the same motives may underlie different beliefs and that different motives may underlie the same belief. The need for self-enhancement, for example, could lead one to praise or to criticize another person, by preserving a concept of self that is either generous or superior, respectively. Similarly, the belief that a friend, spouse, or family member is praiseworthy could arise not only from self-enhancement but also from needs for impression management, cognitive consistency, and accuracy. In the context of political conservatism, this means that (a) a temporary motive (such as the need for cognitive closure or prevention focus or terror management) could lead one to express liberal as well as conservative beliefs, depending on one's chronically accessible ideology (Greenberg, Simon, Pyszczynski, Solomon, & Chatel, 1992; Jost et al., 1999; Liberman, Idson, Camacho, & Higgins, 1999), and (b) some people might adopt conservative beliefs out of a desire for certainty, whereas others adopt the same beliefs because of a threat to self-esteem or an ideological threat to the system.

From our theoretical perspective, motivational and informational influences on belief formation are not at all incompatible. On the contrary, in most cases they are both necessary, and they work together in any instance of belief formation, although their functions in the belief formation process are very different. Information serves as evidence that provides the basis for forming beliefs at either a conscious or unconscious level. Some of this evidence is derived from source expertise (Kruglanski & Thompson, 1999a, 1999b; McGuire, 1985) and "referent informational influence" (Turner, 1991), and these factors help to explain why parents and other authority figures are effective at socializing children to hold specific political beliefs (e.g., Altemeyer, 1981, 1988, 1996; Rohan & Zanna, 1998; Sears, 1983). Other information is contained in messages (or arguments) rather than sources (Kruglanski & Thompson, 1999b), and this information may be more readily assimilated when it is perceived as providing support for prior beliefs (e.g., Hastorf & Cantril, 1954; Lord et al., 1979). Thus, information often plays a rationalizing or legitimizing role in the construction and preservation of ideological belief systems.

Whether specific beliefs may be considered objectively true or false has little (or nothing) to do with the subjective reasons for believing. Arriving at desired conclusions may be considered epistemologically valid only if the evidence supports those conclusions. Motives to maintain security or resolve uncertainty or to avoid threat or prevent negative outcomes might lead one to adopt beliefs that are, for example, socially or economically conservative, but the degree to which these beliefs are rational or correct must be assessed independently of the motivations that drive them (Kruglanski, 1989). Thus, it does not follow from our motivated social-cognitive analysis that politically conservative beliefs (or any other beliefs) are false simply because they are motivated by epistemic, existential, and ideological concerns.

A motivated social-cognitive approach is one that emphasizes the interface between cognitive and motivational properties of the individual as they impact fundamental social psychological phenomena (e.g., Bruner, 1957; Dunning, 1999; Fiske & Taylor, 1991; Greenwald, 1980; Higgins, 1998; Kruglanski, 1996; Kunda, 1990). It may be distinguished from several other psychological approaches. For instance, our approach departs from the assumptions of "cold cognitive" approaches to attitudes and social judgment, which discount motivational constructs as explanations, favoring instead information-processing limitations and mechanisms as determinants of social judgments (e.g., Hamilton & Rose, 1980; D. T. Miller & Ross, 1975; Srull & Wyer, 1979). "Hot cognitive" approaches highlight the pervasive role that affect and motivation play in attention, memory, judgment, decision making, and human reasoning, as well as highlighting the cognitive, goal-directed aspects of most motivational phenomena (e.g., Bargh & Gollwitzer, 1994; Kruglanski, 1996). Ideology is perhaps the quintessential example of hot cognition, in that people are highly motivated to perceive the world in ways that satisfy their needs, values, and prior epistemic commitments (Abelson, 1995).

Distinguishing motivated social cognition from other theories of conservatism

With regard to other theories of conservatism, a motivated social-cognitive perspective may be distinguished from (a) a stable individual-differences approach; (b) a pure instrumental or self-interest theory of conservatism; and (c) theories of modeling, imitation, or simple reinforcement. Although we suggest in this review that there may be individual differences associated with political conservatism (such as authoritarianism, intolerance of ambiguity, need for cognitive closure), we also argue that there should be considerable situational variation in expressions of conservative tendencies. Thus, we are influenced by personality theories of conservatism, but we find them most useful for identifying needs and motivations that may be temporarily as well as chronically accessible. This opens the door to situationalist, social psychological theorizing and research on the manifestations of political conservatism.

Past research and theory on conservatism in sociology, economics, and political science has often assumed that people adopt conservative ideologies out of self-interest (see Sears & Funk, 1991). This account fits well with data indicating increased conservatism among upper-class elites (e.g., Centers, 1949; Sidanius & Ekehammar, 1979). Although we grant that self-interest is one among many motives that are capable of influencing political attitudes and behavior, our review requires a reexamination of this issue. Specifically, many of the theories we integrate suggest that motives to overcome fear, threat, and uncertainty may be associated with increased conservatism, and some of these motives should be more pronounced among members of disadvantaged and low-status groups. As a result, the disadvantaged might embrace right-wing ideologies under some circumstances to reduce fear, anxiety, dissonance, uncertainty, or instability (e.g., Jost, Pelham, Sheldon, & Sullivan, 2003; Lane, 1962; Nias, 1973), whereas the advantaged might gravitate toward conservatism for reasons of self-interest or social dominance (e.g., Centers, 1949; Sidanius & Ekehammar, 1979; Sidanius & Pratto, 1999).

A motivated social cognitive perspective also defies relatively straightforward theories of imitation and social learning, which assume that people are conservative because their parents (or other agents of influence) modeled conservative attitudes or behaviors. Correlations between the political attitudes of parents and their offspring generally attain statistical significance, but they leave the majority of variance unexplained (e.g., Altemeyer, 1988; Sears, 1983; Sidanius & Ekehammar, 1979; Sulloway, 1996). We do not deny that personality goals, rational self-interest, and social learning are important factors that drive conservatism, but our perspective stresses that politically conservative orientations are multiply determined by a wide variety of factors that vary personally and situationally. We argue that conservatism as a belief system is a function of many different kinds of variables, but that a matching relationship holds between certain kinds of psychological motives and specific ideological outcomes. Thus, the general assumptions of our motivated social-cognitive perspective may be applied usefully to the analysis of any coherent belief system (irrespective of content), but the specific array of epistemic, existential, and ideological motives that we review here uniquely characterizes political conservatism as a system of interrelated beliefs.

The ideology of conservatism

The ideology of conservatism has long served as subject matter for historians (e.g., Diamond, 1995; Kolko, 1963), journalists (e.g., Lind, 1996; I. F. Stone, 1989), political scientists (e.g., Carmines & Berkman, 1994; Conover & Feldman, 1981; Huntington, 1957; McClosky & Zaller, 1984), sociologists (e.g., Anderson, Zelditch, Takagi, & Whiteside, 1965; Danigelis & Cutler, 1991; Lo & Schwartz, 1998; Mannheim, 1927/1986, 1936; A. S. Miller, 1994), and philosophers (e.g., Eagleton, 1991; Habermas, 1989; Rorty, 1989). Our goal in this chapter is to summon the unique analytical powers drawn from a variety of psychological theories of motivated social cognition to shed light on the anatomy of conservatism. Following Abric (2001), we argue that political conservatism, like many other complex social representations, has both a stable definitional *core* and a set of more malleable, historically changing *peripheral* associations (what Huntington, 1957, referred to as *secondary issues*). It is the ideological core of political conservatism (more than its peripheral aspects) that we hypothesize to be linked to specific social, cognitive, and motivational needs.[2]

Conceptual definitions

Core aspects of conservative ideology. Dictionary definitions of conservatism stress "the disposition and tendency to preserve what is established; opposition to change" (Neilson, 1958, p. 568) and "the disposition in politics to maintain the existing order" (Morris, 1976, p. 312). Traditionalism and hostility to social innovation were central to Mannheim's (1927/1986) sociological analysis of conservatism. Rossiter (1968), too, defined *situational conservatism* in the *International Encyclopedia of the Social Sciences* as "an attitude of opposition to disruptive change in the social, economic, legal, religious, political, or cultural order" (p. 291).[3] He added, "The distinguishing mark of this conservatism, as indeed it is of any brand of conservatism, is the *fear of change* [italics added], which becomes transformed in the political arena into the fear of radicalism" (p. 291). Consistent with this notion, Conover and Feldman (1981) found that the primary basis for self-definitions of liberals and conservatives has to do with acceptance of, versus resistance to, change (see also Huntington, 1957). This dimension of conservatism is captured especially well by Wilson and Patterson's (1968) C-Scale and by Altemeyer's (1996, 1998) RWA Scale.

A second core issue concerns preferences for inequality. As Giddens (1998), following Bobbio (1996), wrote, "One major criterion continually reappears in distinguishing left from right: *attitudes toward equality* [italics added]. The left favours greater equality, while the right sees society as inevitably hierarchical" (p. 40). This characterization is consistent with many historical and political definitions of conservative and right-wing ideology (Muller, 2001), and it is also reflected in several scales used to measure conservatism (Knight, 1999). Specifically, measures of political–economic conservatism (Sidanius & Ekehammar, 1979), SDO (Pratto, Sidanius, Stallworth, & Malle, 1994), and economic system justification (Jost & Thompson, 2000) all focus on attitudes toward equality.

Relations between resistance to change and acceptance of inequality. Although we believe that the two core dimensions of political conservatism—resistance to change and acceptance of inequality—are often related to one another, they are obviously distinguishable. Vivid counterexamples come to mind in which the two dimensions are negatively related to one another. For instance, there is the "conservative paradox" of right-wing revolutionaries, such as Hitler or Mussolini or Pinochet, who seem to advocate social change in the direction of decreased egalitarianism. In at least some of these cases, what appears to be a desire for change is really "an imaginatively transfigured conception of the past with which to criticize the present" (Muller, 2001, p. 2625). There are also cases of left-wing ideologues who, once they are in power, steadfastly resist change, allegedly in the name of egalitarianism, such as Stalin or Khrushchev or Castro (see J. Martin, Scully, & Levitt, 1990). It is reasonable to suggest that some of these historical figures may be considered politically conservative, at least in the context of the systems they defended.[4]

In any case, we are not denying that liberals can be rigid defenders of the status quo or that conservatives can support change. We assume that historical and cultural variation in political systems affects both the meaning of conservatism and the strength of empirical associations between the psychological and ideological variables we investigate. To take one fairly obvious example, it seems likely that many left-wingers in totalitarian communist regimes would exhibit mental rigidity and other psychological characteristics that are often thought to be associated with right-wingers in other contexts. To be sure, social scientists in the West have undersampled these populations in developing and assessing their theories.

Despite dramatic exceptions, the two core aspects of conservatism are generally psychologically related to one another for most of the people most of the time (Muller, 2001). In part, this is because of the historical fact that traditional social arrangements have generally been more hierarchical and less egalitarian compared with nontraditional arrangements. Therefore, to resist change in general has often meant resisting increased efforts at egalitarianism; conversely, to preserve the status quo has typically entailed entrusting the present and future to the same authorities who have controlled the past. Accordingly, several common measures of political conservatism include items gauging both resistance to change and endorsement of inequality (see Knight, 1999; Sidanius, 1978, 1985; Wilson, 1973c). As most Western societies have passed through the various major revolutions and reform movements that have characterized the period since the Middle Ages, the strength of the connection between resistance to change and opposition to equality has weakened (see also Sulloway, 1996). In a hypothetical world of complete equality, it is quite plausible that the two dimensions would be uncorrelated and that conservatives would fear changes that would reduce equality.

These observations underscore the importance of investigating our hypotheses in as many different national and cultural contexts as possible, including cultures in which the status quo is relatively egalitarian and/or left-wing. Examples involving socialist or communist countries make clear that resistance to change and antiegalitarianism are independent constructs in principle, even if they tend to be (imperfectly) correlated in most cases. Such political contexts offer the best opportunities to determine whether our specific epistemic, existential, and ideological motives are associated with allegiance to the status quo (whether left-wing or right-wing) or whether they are associated with right-wing attitudes in particular. Unfortunately, little or no empirical data are available from the major communist or formerly communist countries such as China, Russia, and Cuba. Nevertheless, we have made a special effort to seek out and incorporate results obtained in 12 different countries, including those with historical influences of socialism or communism, including Sweden (Sidanius, 1978, 1985), Poland (Golec, 2001), East Germany (Fay & Frese, 2000), West Germany (Kemmelmeier, 1997), Italy (Chirumbolo, 2002), England (Kirton, 1978; Kohn, 1974; Nias, 1973; Rokeach, 1960; Smithers & Lobley, 1978; Tetlock, 1984), Canada (Altemeyer, 1998), and Israel (Fibert & Ressler, 1998; Florian, Mikulincer, & Hirschberger, 2001). As we reveal below, the empirical results from these countries are not generally different from those obtained in other national contexts.

Peripheral aspects of conservative ideology. Historically, conservatism as an ideological belief system has embodied many things, including the desire for order and stability, preference for gradual rather than revolutionary change (if any), adherence to preexisting social norms, idealization of authority figures, punishment of deviants, and endorsement of social and economic inequality (e.g., Eckhardt, 1991; Eysenck & Wilson, 1978; Kerlinger, 1984; Lentz, 1939; Mannheim, 1927/1986; McClosky & Zaller, 1984; Sidanius et al., 1996; W. F. Stone & Schaffner, 1988; Tomkins, 1963; Wilson, 1973c). Some of these preferences are directly related to the core aspects of ideology, whereas others are not. The fact that conservatism stands for so many different goals and affects so many areas of life means that people who are motivated to uphold conservative ideals are sometimes faced with perplexing dilemmas. The degree of complexity involved in the ideological label of conservatism not only gives George F. Will (1998) a migraine from time to time, as the opening quotation of this article suggests, but it also makes the concept of conservatism a particularly difficult one to define and to study with the methods of social science (Muller, 2001). Matters are made even more complicated by the fact that historical and cultural factors change the manifestations of conservatism. For instance, conservatism in the United States during the 1960s entailed support for the Vietnam War and opposition to civil rights, whereas conservatism in the 1990s had more to do with being tough on crime and supporting traditional moral and religious values (A. S. Miller, 1994). In post-fascist Europe, conservatives have emphasized their opposition to communism, economic redistribution, and the growth of the welfare state (Muller, 2001). But even in the context of historical and cultural variation, there is some utility in identifying major social and psychological factors that are associated with core values of ideological conservatism, as Mannheim (1927/1986) and many others have argued.[5]

Operational definitions

The biggest conceptual challenge we faced in reviewing the research literature was in clearly distinguishing between psychological independent variables and political dependent variables. Many available measures of conservatism confound the two types of variables, making it difficult to assess the hypothesis that a given set of psychological motives is associated with right-wing political attitudes. The dependent variables we have selected for review (a) are intended as measures of social and political attitudes rather than general psychological tendencies that are content free, (b) tap right-wing or politically conservative attitudes rather than extreme ideological opinions in general, (c) reflect methodological diversity to increase generalizability of meta-analytic results, and (d) correspond relatively well to core and, to a lesser extent, peripheral aspects of conservative ideology, as outlined above. Applying these criteria, we were able to identify studies using 88 different samples that used direct measures of political identification, conservative ideological opinion, resistance to social and political change, and/or preference for social and economic inequality. The methodological properties of several of these scales were reviewed by Knight (1999) as measures of right-wing conservatism (as contrasted with liberalism, radicalism, and left-wing ideology).

Measures stressing resistance to change. Consistent with our conceptual definition of political conservatism, many of the studies in our review used measures that emphasized the dimension of resistance to change. Wilson and Patterson's (1968) C-Scale and Altemeyer's (1988, 1996, 1998) RWA Scale address several core and peripheral aspects of conservative ideology, but the primary focus of each is on resistance to change. The C-Scale measures the favorability of attitudes toward each of 50 items, including some that pertain to social change (mixed marriage, Sabbath observance, the theory of evolution, modern art, royalty) others that pertain to maintaining inequality (White superiority, socialism, women judges, apartheid), and still others that are peripheral (at best) to the core meaning of political conservatism (birth control, suicide, jazz music, divorce). At least three of Wilson's (1973a, p. 51) seven major dimensions of conservatism directly measure attitudes toward stability versus change (preference for conventional attitudes and institutions, religious dogmatism, resistance to scientific progress), so it is probably best thought of as a conservatism scale that stresses resistance to social and political change.

Although the construct of authoritarianism was originally used by Adorno et al. (1950) to deal primarily with attitudes toward minority groups (and therefore attitudes about social inequality), Altemeyer's (1998) RWA Scale largely emphasizes resistance to change. Items include the following: "Authorities such as parents and our national leaders generally turn out to be right about things, and the radicals and protestors are almost always wrong"; "Some young people get rebellious ideas, but as they get older they ought to become more mature and forget such things"; and "Some of the worst people in our country nowadays are those who do not respect our flag, our leaders, and the normal way things are supposed to be done." Thus, the RWA Scale largely measures ideological commitment to tradition, authority, and social convention against threats of change, protest, and political rebellion (Altemeyer, 1981, 1988, 1996, 1998).

One or both of these two instruments (the C-Scale or the RWA Scale) was administered to 31 (or 35%) of the 88 samples included in our review. An additional 3 samples received conceptually related measures of authoritarianism versus rebelliousness (Kohn, 1974), conservatism–radicalism (Smithers & Lobley, 1978), and authoritarian conservatism (Fay & Frese, 2000), bringing the total to 39% of the samples.

Measures stressing acceptance of inequality. A number of additional instruments used to measure right-wing political ideology (the Fascism Scale [F-Scale], the SDO Scale, the Economic System Justification Scale, and measures of general and economic conservatism) focus as much or more on attitudes toward inequality than on resistance to change. (Of course, in most societies, some degree of inequality is the status quo.) The F-Scale, for instance, measures right-wing derogation of low-status minority groups (Adorno et al., 1950), and the SDO Scale measures group-based dominance and generalized opposition to inequality (see Jost & Thompson, 2000;

Sidanius & Pratto, 1999). Jost and Thompson's (2000) Economic System Justification Scale and Golec's (2001) Economic Conservatism Scale both tap the belief that large differences in income are legitimate and necessary for society. Sidanius's (1978, 1985) General Conservatism Scale includes attitude referents focusing on acceptance versus rejection of a number of changes relating to the degree of inequality in society (increased taxation of the rich, increased aid to the poor, greater equality in salaries, a female president of the United States, racial equality). These scales were administered to 26 (or 30%) of the samples included in our review.

Measures stressing political identification and issue-based conservatism. Some studies we review measured self-reported political orientation directly (Chirumbolo, 2002; Fibert & Ressler, 1998; Golec, 2001; Jost et al., 1999; Kemmelmeier, 1997; Tetlock, 1984), and others measured conservative voting records (Gruenfeld, 1995; McCann, 1997; Tetlock, 1983; Tetlock, Bernzweig, & Gallant, 1985). Still others addressed specific issues that are related to the periphery but not necessarily to the core of political conservatism, including attitudes and behavioral decisions related to the death penalty, severity of punishment for criminals, funding for the police department, and conversion to authoritarian churches (Florian et al., 2001; Jost et al., 1999; Rosenblatt, Greenberg, Solomon, Pyszczynski, & Lyon, 1989; Sales, 1972, 1973). The Political–Economic Conservatism Scale used by Rokeach (1960) and Sidanius (1978) tapped attitudes toward the specific issue of government control of industry, labor, and capitalism. In total, these measures were administered to 37 (or 42%) of the samples in our review.

Theories relating to the psychology of conservatism

The most general form of the hypothesis that we investigate here is that there are observable empirical regularities that link specific psychological motives and processes (as independent variables) to particular ideological or political contents (as dependent variables). Many different theoretical accounts of conservatism have stressed the motivational underpinnings of conservative thought, but they have identified different needs as critical. Our review brings these diverse accounts together for the first time and integrates them. Specific variables that have been hypothesized to predict conservatism include fear and aggression (Adorno et al., 1950; Altemeyer, 1998), intolerance of ambiguity (Fibert & Ressler, 1998; Frenkel-Brunswik, 1949), rule following and negative affect (Tomkins, 1963, 1965), uncertainty avoidance (Sorrentino & Roney, 1986; Wilson, 1973b), need for cognitive closure (Kruglanski & Webster, 1996), personal need for structure (Altemeyer, 1998; Schaller, Boyd, Yohannes, & O'Brien, 1995; Smith & Gordon, 1998), need for prevention-oriented regulatory focus (Higgins, 1997; Liberman et al., 1999), anxiety arising from mortality salience (Greenberg et al., 1990, 1992), group-based dominance (Pratto et al., 1994; Sidanius & Pratto, 1999), and system justification tendencies (Jost & Banaji, 1994; Jost, Burgess, & Mosso, 2001). In what follows, we summarize major theoretical perspectives and use them to generate a comprehensive list of motives that are potential predictors of political conservatism. We first describe the theories and then, because many of them postulate similar motives, we review the cumulative evidence for and against each of the motives all at once.

We review several major theories that may be used to illustrate linkages between motivational and cognitive processes and social and political contents. These theories may be classified into three major categories: (a) theories of personality and individual differences, (b) theories stressing the satisfaction of epistemic and existential needs, and (c) sociopolitical theories regarding the rationalization of social systems. Taken individually, no single theory provides an adequate conceptualization of conservatism in all of its forms. By unifying these diverse theoretical perspectives, it becomes clearer that conservatism results from the intersection of social, cognitive, and motivational factors.

Personality and individual-difference theories of conservatism

The tradition of research on the personality correlates of political conservatives began with Adorno et al. (1950) and has thrived right up until the present day (e.g., Altemeyer, 1998; W. F. Stone et al., 1993). Although personality theories do not explicitly regard political conservatism to be a special case of motivated social cognition, the insights and findings garnered from these perspectives are consistent with the message we present, mainly because such theories have stressed the motivated character of personality and individual differences. Our hope is that by combining the insights gained from these personality theories with the experimental methods favored by researchers of motivated social cognition, future work will be in a better position to directly investigate the motivated and dynamic aspects of political conservatism.

The theory of RWA

As intellectual descendants of the Frankfurt School, the authors of *The Authoritarian Personality* (Adorno et al., 1950) sought to integrate Marxist theories of ideology and social structure with Freudian theories of motivation and personality development to explain the rise of fascism throughout Europe in the 1930s and 1940s. Specifically, they proposed that harsh parenting styles brought on by economic hardship led entire generations to repress hostility toward authority figures and to replace it with an exaggerated deference and idealization of authority and tendencies to blame societal scapegoats and punish deviants (see also Reich, 1946/1970). The theory of authoritarianism holds that fear and aggressiveness resulting from parental punitiveness motivate individuals to seek predictability and control in their environments. Authoritarian attitudes, which may be elicited by situational threats, combine an anxious veneration of authority and convention with a vindictiveness toward subordinates and deviants (Altemeyer, 1998; Fromm, 1941; Peterson, Doty, & Winter, 1993; W. F. Stone et al., 1993). Authoritarianism is often taken to be synonymous with conservatism, but Wilson, theorizing that conservatism is the general factor underlying all social attitudes (Wilson, 1973b; Wilson & Patterson,

1968), contended that authoritarianism is but one manifestation of the more general factor of conservatism (Wilson, 1968).

An exhaustive effort to update theory and research on authoritarianism and to respond to various conceptual, methodological, and statistical objections has been undertaken by Altemeyer (1981, 1988, 1996, 1998). Altemeyer's (1981) model presents a more methodologically sophisticated and statistically robust approach to measuring and conceptualizing authoritarianism, distinguishing it from various response sets associated with acquiescence, and he rejects orthodox Freudian interpretations of the syndrome. Altemeyer's (1981) RWA is characterized by (a) "a high degree of submission to the authorities who are perceived to be established and legitimate"; (b) "a general aggressiveness, directed against various persons, which is perceived to be sanctioned by established authorities"; and (c) "a high degree of adherence to the social conventions which are perceived to be endorsed by society" (p. 148). This reconceptualization, which combines resistance to change and endorsement of inequality, is consistent with two newly emerging theories, social dominance theory (Pratto et al., 1994; Sidanius & Pratto, 1999) and system justification theory (Jost & Banaji, 1994; Jost et al., 2003), both of which are discussed below.

Scores on the RWA Scale have been found to predict a broad range of attitudes and behaviors related to social, economic, and political conservatism as defined in the general culture at the time. For instance, the scale has correlated reliably with political party affiliation; reactions to Watergate; pro-capitalist attitudes; severity of jury sentencing decisions; punishment of deviants; racial prejudice; homophobia; religious orthodoxy; victim blaming; and acceptance of covert governmental activities such as illegal bugging, political harassment, denial of the right to assemble, and illegal drug raids (Altemeyer, 1981, 1988, 1996, 1998). Peterson et al. (1993) reported correlational evidence linking authoritarianism to a wide variety of conservative attitudes, including opposition to environmentalism, abortion rights, diversity on university campuses, and services for AIDS patients and homeless people. Ray (1973), in questioning the discriminant validity of RWA, reported a correlation of .81 between the RWA Scale and his own conservatism scale. Altemeyer (1996, 1998, p. 53) summarized the results of several studies of the attitudes of Canadian and U.S. legislators in which he found strong differences in RWA between conservative politicians and others and concluded that:

> High RWA lawmakers also score higher in prejudice, and wish they could pass laws limiting the freedom of speech, freedom of the press, the right of assembly, and other freedoms guaranteed in the Bill of Rights. They want to impose strict limitations on abortion, they favor capital punishment, and they oppose tougher gun control laws. Finally, politicians answer the RWA Scale with such extraordinary levels of internal consistency, it appears the scale provides our most powerful measure of the liberal-conservative dimension in politics.

Thus, a relatively strong relation has been established between RWA and political conservatism among political elites as well as the masses.

Altemeyer's (1998) work is also important in identifying the two main directions in which extremely conservative and authoritarian attitudes may lead. First, they may lead to an actively hostile or dominant approach to dealing with socially sanctioned scapegoats and devalued out-groups, which is also the primary focus of social dominance theory (Sidanius & Pratto, 1999; Whitley, 1999). Second, RWA may lead to a more passively submissive or deferential posture toward authorities, which would make its subscribers ideal candidates to follow the next Hitler or Mussolini (Altemeyer, 1998; Fromm, 1941; Reich, 1946/1970). Thus, extreme right-wing attitudes "lock" people into a "dominance-submissive authoritarian embrace" (Altemeyer, 1998, p. 47), and the specific manifestation of these attitudes presumably depends on the social and historical context and the motivations that are elicited from these contexts.

Intolerance of ambiguity

Frenkel-Brunswik's work on intolerance of ambiguity was closely related to research on the authoritarian personality, but it was distinctive with regard to methodology and content. In an abstract published in 1948, she reported a study of ethnic prejudice involving the attitudes of adults and children (9 to 14 years old). Frenkel-Brunswik (1948, p. 268) argued that intolerance of ambiguity constituted a general personality variable that related positively to prejudice as well as to more general social and cognitive variables. As she put it, individuals who are intolerant of ambiguity:

> are significantly more often given to dichotomous conceptions of the sex roles, of the parent-child relationship, and of interpersonal relationships in general. They are less permissive and lean toward rigid categorization of cultural norms. Power–weakness, cleanliness–dirtiness, morality–immorality, conformance–divergence are the dimensions through which people are seen. . . . There is sensitivity against qualified as contrasted with unqualified statements and against perceptual ambiguity; a disinclination to think in terms of probability; a comparative inability to abandon mental sets in intellectual tasks, such as in solving mathematical problems, after they have lost their appropriateness. Relations to home discipline and to the ensuing attitude towards authority will likewise be demonstrated quantitatively.

Frenkel-Brunswik (1949, 1951) developed further the theory of ambiguity intolerance and elaborated the antecedent conditions of this psychological disposition and its manifold consequences. At the time, ambiguity intolerance was viewed in Freudian terms as stemming from an underlying emotional conflict involving feelings of hostility directed at one's parents combined with idealization tendencies. Although stable individual differences in the intolerance of ambiguity have been observed across many generations of researchers and participants, theoretical explanations have changed somewhat. Anticipating current perspectives on uncertainty avoidance (Hofstede, 2001; Sorrentino & Roney, 2000; Wilson, 1973b),

Budner (1962), for example, defined intolerance of ambiguity as "the tendency to perceive ambiguous situations as sources of threat" (p. 29).

Intolerance of ambiguity, by increasing cognitive and motivational tendencies to seek certainty, is hypothesized to lead people to cling to the familiar, to arrive at premature conclusions, and to impose simplistic clichés and stereotypes. In a review of research on ambiguity intolerance, Furnham and Ribchester (1995, p. 180) provided the following list of consequences of this tendency:

> Resistance to reversal of apparent fluctuating stimuli, the early selection and maintenance of one solution in a perceptually ambiguous situation, inability to allow for the possibility of good and bad traits in the same person, acceptance of attitude statements representing a rigid, black-white view of life, seeking for certainty, a rigid dichotomizing into fixed categories, premature closure, and remaining closed to familiar characteristics of stimuli.

Thus, theories of intolerance of ambiguity combine psychodynamic antecedents with a wide range of perceptual, cognitive, motivational, social, and political consequences. Arguably, it is this richness that accounts for the persistence of interest in this concept over the 50 years since its introduction.

Mental rigidity, dogmatism, and closed-mindedness

One of the persistent criticisms of Adorno et al.'s (1950) work on authoritarianism and the F-Scale designed to measure fascistic potential was that it neglected authoritarianism among left-wingers (e.g., Shils, 1954). In part to address this concern, Rokeach (1960) developed a scale of dogmatism that was meant to provide a more balanced measure of authoritarianism. The scale contained items tapping *double think*, which was defined as susceptibility to logically contradictory beliefs and denial of contradictions in one's belief system, as well as a narrow future orientation and a strong orientation toward authority. Rokeach (1960, p. 67) argued that dogmatism is indicative of closed-mindedness, which he contrasted with open-mindedness:

> All belief-disbelief systems serve two powerful and conflicting sets of motives at the same time: the need for a cognitive framework to know and to understand and the need to ward off threatening aspects of reality. To the extent that the cognitive need to know is predominant and the need to ward off threat is absent, open systems should result. . . . But as the need to ward off threat becomes stronger, the cognitive need to know should become weaker, resulting in more closed belief systems.

Thus, Rokeach's theory, like some of its predecessors, combines elements of epistemic and existential motivation in seeking to explain social and political attitudes. In another passage, he argued further that, "if the closed or dogmatic mind is extremely resistant to change, it may be so not only because it allays anxiety but also because it satisfies the *need to know*" (Rokeach, 1960, p. 68). Rokeach's theory also seeks to combine cognitive and motivational needs in explaining ideological rigidity. Its influence clearly extends to contemporary research on the role of cognitive sophistication and integrative complexity in political ideology (e.g., Sidanius, 1985, 1988; Tetlock, 1983, 1984).

The theory of ideo-affective polarity

Several commentators (Abelson & Prentice, 1989; Alexander, 1995; Milburn, 1991; W. F. Stone, 1986; W. F. Stone & Schaffner, 1988; Thomas, 1976) have noted that Silvan Tomkins's (1963, 1965, 1987, 1995) theory of ideological polarity is one of the most fascinating accounts of the origins and implications of left-wing and right-wing thinking, but it is lamentably underresearched. It is a distinctive theory because it explicitly stresses the role of affect and motivation in ideology and because it assumes that ideological predilections permeate nearly every domain of a person's life, including one's attitudes toward the arts, music, science, philosophy, and so on, so that "if one knows what an individual believes about the nature of literature, one would also know what he would believe about the nature of mathematics" (Tomkins, 1995, p. 117).

According to polarity theory, there exist generalized orientations (or *ideo-affective postures*) toward the world that may be regarded as belonging either to the ideological left or to the right, and they are associated with liberty and humanism in the first case and rule following and normative concerns in the second. Those who resonate with left-wing ideologies believe that people are basically good and that the purpose of society is to facilitate human growth and experience. By contrast, those who resonate with right-wing ideologies believe that people are essentially bad and that the function of society is to set rules and limits to prevent irresponsible behavior. On these issues, Tomkins's (1963, 1965, 1987, 1995) theory bears more than a passing resemblance to the theory of authoritarianism (e.g., Adorno et al., 1950).

These ideological orientations are multiply determined, according to the theory, but it is clear that one's preferences are developed early in childhood emotional life; this occurs through the acquisition of *personal scripts*, a term that refers to affectively charged memories of social situations involving the self and important others (Carlson & Brincka, 1987; Tomkins, 1987). For example, childhood experiences arising from a parental focus on the child and his or her inner self are expected to reinforce feelings of excitement, joy, surprise, distress, and shame, in turn leading the child to gravitate toward the humanistic orientation, or left-wing perspective. In contrast, more structured, punitive parenting engenders emotions such as anger and contempt, which reflect the normative orientation, or right-wing perspective (Loye, 1977; W. F. Stone, 1986; Tomkins, 1963, 1965).

Most of the empirical research relevant to the theory of ideological polarity has used a 59-item Polarity Scale developed by Tomkins (1964/1988) and updated by W. F. Stone and Schaffner (1988). Items tapping the right-wing or normative orientation include the following: "Children should be taught to obey what is right even though they may not always feel like it" and "If I break the law I should be punished for the good of society." Scores on the Polarity Scale have been found to predict reactions to presidential assassinations (Tomkins, 1995); preferences for individualistic versus sociotropic values (Carlson & Levy, 1970; de St. Aubin, 1996); attitudes toward war and peace (Eckhardt & Alcock, 1970); assumptions concerning human nature, religiosity, and political orientation (de St. Aubin, 1996; Elms, 1969); and a number of other affective responses (see W. F. Stone, 1980). The theory is groundbreaking not only in its attempt to identify affective and motivational bases of conservatism (related to anger, contempt, and the desire for punitiveness) but also in its suggestion that a disproportionate number of conservatives are driven by a motivation to establish and follow rules and norms in a wide variety of domains inside and outside of politics.

A dynamic theory of conservatism as uncertainty avoidance

Consistent with Tomkins's (1963, 1965) and others' emphases on affective bases of ideology and with the research on intolerance of ambiguity, Wilson (1973b) proposed a dynamic theory that treats conservatism as the product of (partially unconscious) motives and needs having to do with fear and anxiety. The central tenet of the theory is that "the common basis for all the various components of the conservative attitude syndrome is a *generalized susceptibility to experiencing threat or anxiety in the face of uncertainty*" (Wilson, 1973b, p. 259). According to this perspective, conservatism is multiply determined by what Wilson (1973b) labeled *genetic* factors, such as anxiety proneness, stimulus aversion, low intelligence, and physical unattractiveness, as well as by *environmental* factors such as parental coldness, punitiveness, rigidity, inconsistency, low social class, and low self-esteem.

Wilson (1973b) hypothesized a great many different sources of threat or uncertainty, including death, anarchy, foreigners, dissent, complexity, novelty, ambiguity, and social change. Conservative attitudinal responses to these sources of uncertainty include superstition, religious dogmatism, ethnocentrism, militarism, authoritarianism, punitiveness, conventionality, and rigid morality. Despite a few recent exceptions (e.g., Fay & Frese, 2000; McAllister & Anderson, 1991), the theoretical account of conservatism as a motivated response to environmental uncertainty has been largely lost in the field of political psychology since the publication of a volume edited by Wilson (1973c) on that topic. Although Wilson's emphasis was clearly on individual differences arising from genetic and environmental influences, his theory targeted the reduction of uncertainty and threat as motives for political conservatism. Our approach to political conservatism as motivated social cognition seeks to resurrect these fruitful notions and to expand and elaborate on the ways in which conservative systems of thought are adopted to meet the epistemic and existential needs of individuals, groups, and social systems.

Epistemic and existential need theories

Although the three theories of cognitive–motivational processes reviewed here involve recognition (and even assessment) of individual differences—much as theories of personality assume epistemic and existential needs—neither individual differences nor their developmental roots are accorded central research attention in these frameworks. Rather, these theories, which are like Wilson's (1973b) theory of uncertainty avoidance in other respects, place particular emphasis on the mutually constitutive role of cognitive and motivational processes in determining conservative response tendencies. We turn now to a summary of theories of lay epistemics, regulatory focus, and terror management.

Lay epistemic theory

In an effort to unify cognitive and motivational accounts of behavior, Kruglanski (1989) developed a theory of lay epistemics whereby knowledge and beliefs are arrived at through a process of motivated informational search. Knowledge acquisition, according to this theory, follows a two-step epistemic process of hypothesis generation and testing (Popper, 1959). Informational factors include the availability and accessibility of various knowledge structures that the individual may use to construct the relevant hypotheses and their testable implications. Often, such constructive processes can be quite labor intensive and effortful. They may require considerable mental resources, including cognitive capacity and epistemic motivation. A central motivational construct in the theory of lay epistemics is the need for cognitive closure, which refers to the expedient desire for any firm belief on a given topic, as opposed to confusion and uncertainty.

A variety of factors may arouse the need for closure. These have to do with the perceived benefits and costs of possessing (or lacking) closure and may vary as a function of the person, the immediate situation, and the culture (see also Hofstede, 2001). For example, the benefits of possessing cognitive closure include the potential affordance of predictability and the guidance of action. Consistent with the notion that situations lead people to seek out nonspecific closure, Dittes (1961) found that failure-induced threat caused research participants to reach "impulsive closure" on an ambiguous task. More generally, the need for cognitive closure should be elevated in any situation in which the importance of action looms large, as under time pressure (e.g., Jost et al., 1999; Kruglanski & Freund, 1983; Shah, Kruglanski, & Thompson, 1998), ambient noise (Kruglanski & Webster, 1996), mental fatigue (D. M. Webster, Richter, & Kruglanski, 1996), or alcohol intoxication (D. M. Webster, 1994), because such states render sustained information processing to be subjectively costly.

Building on research devoted to uncertainty orientation (e.g., Sorrentino & Roney, 1986, 2000) and the personal need for structure (e.g., Schaller et al., 1995), D. M. Webster and Kruglanski (1994) developed and validated an individual-difference measure of the need for cognitive closure, the Need for Closure Scale (NFCS). This 42-item scale comprises five factors or subscales, respectively described as (a) preference for order and structure, (b) emotional discomfort associated with ambiguity, (c) impatience and impulsivity with regard to decision making, (d) desire for security and predictability, (e) closed-mindedness. Some illustrative items of this scale are "I think that having clear rules and order at work is essential for success"; "I'd rather know bad news than stay in a state of uncertainty"; "I usually make important decisions quickly and confidently"; "I don't like to go into a situation without knowing what I can expect from it"; and "I do not usually consult many different opinions before forming my own view."

Whether evoked situationally or measured as a stable personality dimension, the need for closure has been found to produce the same consequences. Specifically, it fosters the tendency to *seize* on information that affords closure and to *freeze* on closure once it has been attained. The need for closure, whether varied situationally or measured dispositionally, has been associated with tendencies to engage in social stereotyping (Kruglanski & Freund, 1983), to succumb to primacy effects in impression formation (Kruglanski & Freund, 1983; D. M. Webster & Kruglanski, 1994), to exhibit correspondence bias in attitude attribution (D. M. Webster, 1993), to resist persuasive influence (Kruglanski, Webster, & Klem, 1993), and to reject opinion deviates (Kruglanski & Webster, 1991). If the theory of lay epistemics is correct, there are situational and dispositional factors that may encourage a general cognitive–motivational orientation toward the social world that is either open and exploratory or closed and immutable (Kruglanski & Webster, 1996).

To understand the hypothesized relation between need for closure and political conservatism (see also Golec, 2001; Jost et al., 1999), it is important to draw a distinction between the process of resisting change in general and the specific contents of and/or direction of the change. On one hand, the need for closure suggests a perpetuation of the reigning ideology, whatever its contents. Thus, increasing the need for closure among people whose accessible ideological positions are conservative would result in a stronger relation between need for closure and conservatism. Likewise, increasing the need for closure among people whose accessible ideological positions are liberal would result in a strengthened relation between need for closure and liberalism. In this sense, the lay epistemic theory supports the contention that rigidity of ideological attitudes may be associated with different ideological contents and is not necessarily restricted to right-wing conservatism (Rokeach, 1960).

On the other hand, persons with a high (vs. low) need for closure are hardly indifferent to ideological contents. Specifically, contents that promise or support epistemic stability, clarity, order, and uniformity should be preferred by high-need-for-closure persons over contents that promise their epistemic opposites (i.e., instability, ambiguity, chaos, and diversity). In this sense, a need for closure that is impartial or nonspecific (i.e., content free) becomes partial or specific with regard to contents that are explicitly related to closure (Kruglanski, 1989). To the extent that there is a match between the need for closure and certain politically conservative attitudinal contents, then conservative attitudes should be generally preferred by people who have a high need for closure (Jost et al., 1999).

Regulatory focus theory

Higgins (1997, 1998) proposed a regulatory focus theory that is pertinent to the psychology of conservatism. This theory distinguishes between two categories of desired goals, namely those related to advancement, growth, and aspirations (ideals) and those related to safety, security, and responsibilities (oughts). Distinct regulatory systems are presumed to address these two classes of goals. The promotion system reflects individuals' self-regulation in relation to their hopes and aspirations (ideals), and it gratifies nurturance needs. The goal of the promotion system is accomplishment. By contrast, the prevention system reflects self-regulation in relation to one's duties and obligations (oughts), and the goal of this system is safety. According to this theory, a parenting history of protection focusing on the avoidance of negative outcomes combined with the exercise of punishment as a disciplinary tool produces a strong prevention focus as a stable individual orientation. A parenting style of encouraging accomplishments by focusing on achieving positive outcomes and withdrawing love as a form of discipline produces a strong promotion focus as a stable individual orientation.

It is also plausible that an emphasis on prevention (vs. promotion) induces a heightened need for cognitive closure as one consequence of the craving for a secure and comprehensible reality. Like the theory of lay epistemics, regulatory focus theory leaves open the possibility of anchoring disproportionately on left-wing ideas (to the extent that a leftist ideology constitutes the status quo), but at the same time, the theory suggests a general preference by prevention-oriented, versus promotion-oriented, individuals for conservative over liberal ideologies, all else being equal. Finally, like the theory of lay epistemics, regulatory focus theory allows for situational as well as personality factors to drive the inclination toward conservatism.

Regulatory focus, then, has fairly obvious implications for individuals' attitudes toward stability and change, and perhaps even for left- versus right-wing preferences. Specifically, the promotion goals of accomplishment and advancement should naturally introduce a preference for change over stability, insofar as advancement requires change. The prevention goals of safety and security, on the other hand, should favor stability over change, to the extent that stability entails predictability and hence psychological security and control. In signal-detection terms, a promotion focus is concerned with obtaining hits and avoiding *misses*, whereas a prevention focus is concerned with obtaining *correct rejections* and avoiding *false alarms*. Any change has the potential benefit of providing an opportunity for advancement and accomplishment (a hit) but has the potential cost of introducing an error of commission. Because such an error is of relatively low concern to persons with a promotion focus, they should be relatively open to change. By contrast, stability has the potential benefit of safety and security (a correct rejection) but has the potential cost of introducing an error of omission, which is of lesser concern to individuals with a prevention focus who, therefore, should be resistant to change. To the extent that political conservatism is motivated, at least in part, by the desire for security and stability and the avoidance of threat and change, situations inducing a prevention-oriented regulatory focus might also induce a conservative shift in the general population.

Terror management theory

A novel theoretical perspective suggests that conservative thoughts and behaviors may arise from motivations to make sense of the world and cope with existential crises inherent in the human experience. Terror management theory (Greenberg, Pyszczynski, & Solomon, 1986; Greenberg et al., 1990; Rosenblatt et al., 1989) posits that cultures and their attendant worldviews serve to buffer anxiety (and prevent terror) arising from the thoughts humans invariably have about their own mortality. According to terror management theory, which builds on the work of Ernest Becker (1973) and others, the denial of death is so prevalent that cultural institutions evolve as a way of coping with existential anxiety and human mortality. In this context, it is also worth noting that Wilson (1973d) listed fear of death as one of the threatening factors that might be associated with political conservatism.

Terror management theory holds that cultural worldviews or systems of meaning (e.g., religion) provide people with the means to transcend death, if only symbolically. The cornerstone of this position is that awareness of mortality, when combined with an instinct for self-preservation, creates in humans the capacity to be virtually paralyzed with fear (Arndt, Greenberg, Solomon, Pyszczynski, & Simon, 1997). Fear of death, in turn, engenders a defense of one's cultural worldview. Consequently, the theory predicts that if the salience of one's mortality is raised, the worldview will be more heavily endorsed to buffer the resulting anxiety (Greenberg et al., 1990; Rosenblatt et al., 1989). Under conditions of heightened mortality salience, defense and justification of the worldview should be intensified, thereby decreasing tolerance of opposing views and social, cultural, and political alternatives.

The relevance of terror management theory to the psychology of conservatism should be apparent. When confronted with thoughts of their own mortality (Greenberg et al., 1990; Rosenblatt et al., 1989), people appear to behave more conservatively by shunning and even punishing outsiders and those who threaten the status of cherished worldviews. This perspective is especially consistent with the notion of conservatism as motivated social cognition; terror management theory holds that social intolerance is the consequence of worldview-enhancing cognitions motivated by the need to buffer anxiety-inducing thoughts. It should be noted, however, that Greenberg et al. (1992) argued against a necessary relation between mortality salience and political conservatism. Acknowledging that most of the demonstrated effects of mortality salience have had a politically conservative or intolerant flavor, they nevertheless claimed that thoughts about death lead only to a defense of dominant values and that such values could be liberal or even, paradoxically, tolerant.

Ideological theories of individual and collective rationalization

The theories we review next differ somewhat from the cognitive–motivational process frameworks considered above. Whereas the cognitive–motivational theories focus on the individual and treat conservatism and related phenomena more or less exclusively as manifestations of epistemic and existential mechanisms, sociopolitical theories focus on the societal system and the ideological (as well as psychological) functions that political conservatism might fulfill. Theories of social dominance and system justification are useful not only for expanding the range of motives under consideration but also for clarifying the nature of the connection between political conservatism and racism, sexism, and ethnocentric intolerance (e.g., Altemeyer, 1998; Bahr & Chadwick, 1974; Jost & Banaji, 1994; Jost et al., 2001; Mercer & Cairns, 1981; Pratto, 1999; Sidanius et al., 1996; Whitley, 1999).

Social dominance theory

Unlike theories that seek to explain conservatism with reference to affective differences arising from parenting styles or childhood socialization, social dominance theory emphasizes evolutionary and societal factors as determinants of politically conservative (or "hierarchy-enhancing") orientations. According to social dominance theory, human societies strive to minimize group conflict by developing ideological belief systems that justify the hegemony of some groups over others (Pratto, 1999; Pratto et al., 1994; Sidanius, 1993; Sidanius & Pratto, 1999; Sidanius et al., 1996). This is achieved through the promulgation of various "legitimizing myths" such as the following: (a) "paternalistic myths," which assert that dominant groups are needed to lead and take care of subordinate groups, who are incapable of leading and taking care of themselves; (b) "reciprocal myths," which claim that a symbiotic relationship exists between dominant and subordinate groups and that both groups help each other; and (c) "sacred myths," which allege that positions of dominance and subordination are determined by God or some other divine right (see Sidanius, 1993, pp. 207–209). Ideological devices such as these are inherently conservative in content because they seek to preserve existing hierarchies of status, power, and wealth and to prevent qualitative social change (e.g., Sidanius & Pratto, 1999).

Social dominance theory holds that attitudes pertaining to social dominance are determined jointly by biology and socialization and that there are important individual differences among people with regard to SDO (e.g., Pratto et al., 1994; Sidanius & Pratto, 1999). Items from the SDO Scale tap agreement or disagreement with statements such as the following: "Some people are just more worthy than others"; "It is not a problem if some people have more of a chance in life"; and "This country would be better off if we cared less about how equal all people are." Thus, the SDO Scale measures individual differences with respect to the motivated tendency to preserve the dominance of high-status groups such as men (rather than women), Whites (rather than Blacks and other ethnic minorities), and upper-class elites (rather than the working class). Jost and Thompson (2000) demonstrated that the SDO Scale is composed of two correlated factors or subscales, namely the desire for group-based dominance and opposition to equality. Although social dominance motives are said to be universal (e.g., Sidanius & Pratto, 1993), their strength differs considerably across groups and individuals (e.g., Jost & Thompson, 2000; Pratto, 1999; Pratto et al., 1994).

Correlations between SDO scores and those of conventional measures of political and economic conservatism average approximately .30 in a variety of national and cultural contexts (Altemeyer, 1998; Pratto, 1999; Pratto et al., 1994; Sidanius et al., 1996; Whitley & Lee, 2000). Scores on the scale have been found also to correlate reliably with identification with the Republican party, nationalism, cultural elitism, anti-Black racism, sexism, RWA, and the belief in a just world (Altemeyer, 1998; Pratto et al., 1994). The scale predicts policy attitudes that are supportive of "law and order," military spending, and capital punishment, as well as attitudes that are unsupportive of women's rights, racial equality, affirmative action, gay and lesbian rights, and environmental action (see Jost & Thompson, 2000; Pratto et al., 1994). It is of theoretical interest that, in addition to the notion of legitimizing the status quo, social dominance theory also implies the notion that increasing the degree of hierarchy or group dominance is a motivationally appealing ideological goal at least under some circumstances, such as when one belongs to a high-status group (Altemeyer, 1998; Pratto, 1999; Sidanius & Pratto, 1999).

In a very useful discussion, Altemeyer (1998) distinguished between the motivational bases of RWA and SDO. He argued that RWA best accounts for passive deference or submission to authoritarian or fascist leaders—including the tendency to "trust unworthy people who tell them what they want to hear" (Altemeyer, 1998, p. 87), whereas SDO best accounts for more active attempts to punish or humiliate derogated out-group members, that is, the desire to "become the alpha animal" (Altemeyer, 1998, p. 87). Altemeyer (1998, p. 75) compared the two motivational types as follows:

> Right-wing authoritarians, who do *not* score high on [personal power, meanness, and dominance], seem to be highly prejudiced mainly because they were raised to travel in tight, ethnocentric circles; and they fear that authority and conventions are crumbling so quickly that civilization will collapse and they will be eaten in the resulting jungle. In contrast, High SDO's *already* see life as "dog eat dog" and— compared with most people—are determined to do the eating.

The point is that RWA and SDO—which correlate only modestly at about .20 (Altemeyer, 1998, p. 87; Sidanius & Pratto, 1999, p. 74; Whitley, 1999, p. 129)— may be motivated by somewhat different concerns, but they are both highly motivated ideologies. Together, they account for both halves of the "dominance-submissive authoritarian embrace" (Altemeyer, 1998, p. 47), and they predict more than half of the statistical variance in prejudice and ethnocentrism. One can therefore infer that the most inexorable right-wingers are those who are motivated simultaneously by fear and aggression.

System justification theory

We have shown above that most traditional personality theories about the functions of conservative ideology, especially theories of authoritarianism, dogmatism, and anxiety reduction, stress ego-defensive or ego-justifying aspects of conservatism, that is, the satisfaction of individual needs for security, obedience, and projection (e.g., Adorno et al., 1950; Altemeyer, 1981, 1988; Rokeach, 1960; Wilson, 1973c). Although ego-justifying motives constitute an important part of the appeal of conservatism, there are also group-justifying and system-justifying motives that are satisfied in a particularly efficient manner by right-wing ideologies (Jost & Banaji, 1994; Jost & Thompson, 2000). Social dominance theory, for example, stresses the emergence of conservative legitimizing myths as group-justifying attempts to rationalize the interests of dominant or high-status group members (Sidanius & Pratto, 1999). System justification theory focuses on the motivated tendency for people to do cognitive and ideological work on behalf of the social system, thereby perpetuating the status quo and preserving inequality (e.g., Jost, 1995; Jost & Banaji, 1994).

One of the central goals of system justification theory is to understand how and why people rationalize the existing social system, especially when their support appears to conflict with other important motives to maintain or enhance self-esteem and to maintain or enhance group standing (e.g., Jost & Banaji, 1994; Jost & Burgess, 2000; Jost & Thompson, 2000). The theory draws partially on Marxian and feminist theories of dominant ideology and on sociological theories of legitimization to explain the acceptance of conservative ideas and practices (Jost, 1995; Jost et al., 2001). It also draws on ideas from cognitive dissonance theory (Festinger, 1957) and just world theory (Lerner, 1980) to argue that people are motivated to perceive existing social arrangements as fair, legitimate, justifiable, and rational, and perhaps even natural and inevitable.

The theory of system justification is especially well suited to address relatively puzzling cases of conservatism and right-wing allegiance among members of low-status groups, such as women and members of the working class (e.g., Lane, 1962; Lipset, 1960/1981; Stacey & Green, 1971). To the extent that nearly everyone is motivated (at least to some extent) to explain and justify the status quo in such a way that it is perceived as fair and legitimate, political conservatism should cut across social classes (e.g., Jost & Banaji, 1994; Kluegel & Smith, 1986). This is consistent with the analysis of Rossiter (1968), who observed, "Situational conservatism is not confined to the well-placed and well-to-do. Persons at all levels of being and possessing may lament change in the status quo" (p. 291).

The strongest form of the system justification hypothesis, which draws also on the logic of cognitive dissonance theory, is that under certain circumstances members of disadvantaged groups would be even more likely than members of advantaged groups to support the status quo (see Jost et al., 2003). If there is indeed a motivation to justify the system to reduce ideological dissonance and defend against threats to the system's legitimacy, then it may be that those who suffer the most because of the system are also those who would have the most to explain, justify, and rationalize. One way to minimize dissonance would be to redouble one's commitment and support for the system, much as hazed initiates pledge increased loyalty to the fraternity that hazes them (e.g., Aronson & Mills, 1959) and, presumably, to the fraternity system in general.

An additional hypothesis that may be derived from system justification theory is that people should be motivated to defend the existing social system against threats to the stability or legitimacy of the system. If there is a defensive motivation associated with system justification, then it should be more pronounced under circumstances that threaten the status quo. This is a possibility that was suggested by early accounts of authoritarianism (e.g., Adorno et al., 1950; Fromm, 1941; Reich, 1946/1970; Sanford, 1966), but situational threats have received much less attention in recent years in comparison with the measurement of individual differences (but see Sales, 1972, 1973). Thus, we hypothesized that situations of crisis or instability in society will, generally speaking, precipitate conservative, system-justifying shifts to the political right, but only as long as the crisis situation falls short of toppling the existing regime and establishing a new status quo for people to justify and rationalize.

A theoretical integration of epistemic, existential, and ideological motives

Although we maintain distinctions among specific hypotheses for the purposes of assessing cumulative empirical evidence for and against each, one of the virtues of our motivated social-cognitive perspective is that it helps to integrate seemingly unrelated motives and tendencies. Specifically, we argue that a number of different epistemic motives (dogmatism; intolerance of ambiguity; cognitive complexity; closed-mindedness; uncertainty avoidance; needs for order, structure, and closure), existential motives (self-esteem, terror management, fear, threat, anger, and pessimism), and ideological motives (self-interest, group dominance, and system justification) are all related to the expression of political conservatism. Now we draw on the perspective of motivated social cognition to advance the integrative argument that epistemic, existential, and ideological motives are themselves interrelated.

Theoretical and empirical considerations lead us to conclude that virtually all of the above motives originate in psychological attempts to manage uncertainty and fear. These, in turn, are inherently related to the two core aspects of conservative thought mentioned earlier—resistance to change and the endorsement of inequality. The management of uncertainty is served by resistance to change insofar as change (by its very nature) upsets existing realities and is fraught with epistemic insecurity. Fear may be both a cause and a consequence of endorsing inequality; it breeds and justifies competition, dominance struggles, and sometimes, violent strife. Epistemic motives, by definition, govern the ways in which people seek to acquire beliefs that are certain and that help to navigate social and physical worlds that are threateningly ambiguous, complex, novel, and chaotic. Thus, epistemic needs affect the style and manner by which individuals seek to overcome uncertainty and the fear of the unknown (e.g., Kruglanski, 1989; Rokeach, 1960; Sorrentino & Roney, 2000; Wilson, 1973c).[6]

Existential motives, too, involve a desire for certainty and security that is associated with resisting rather than fostering change. Empirical work demonstrates that uncertainty-related threats and mortality salience have similar and compatible effects on social and political attitudes, suggesting that epistemic and existential motives are in fact highly interrelated (e.g., Dechesne, Janssen, & van Knippenberg, 2000; McGregor, Zanna, Holmes, & Spencer, 2001). Epistemic commitments, it seems, help to resolve existential conflicts, and existential motives affect the search for knowledge and meaning. Insofar as knowledge and meaning are derived from extant cultural arrangements and conventionally accepted definitions of reality, the terror arising from the possibility of one's own demise may induce resistance to change (Greenberg, Porteus, Simon, & Pyszczynski, 1995; Greenberg et al., 1990).

Ideological beliefs, it has often been noted, help to reduce uncertainty and mitigate feelings of threat and worthlessness (e.g., Abelson, 1995; Adorno et al., 1950; Altemeyer, 1998; Kluegel & Smith, 1986; Lane, 1962; Rokeach, 1960; Sanford, 1966; Tomkins, 1963, 1965; Wilson, 1973c). That is, people embrace ideological belief systems at least in part because they inspire conviction and purpose. Even more specifically, it has been argued that needs for system justification arise from the motivated desire to reduce uncertainty (Hogg & Mullin, 1999), and the belief in a just world has been linked to epistemic needs to increase prediction and control and to existential needs to maintain self-esteem and provide meaning and a sense of security (e.g., Kluegel & Smith, 1986; Lerner, 1980). Authoritarianism has long been associated with rigid and dogmatic thinking styles (e.g., Altemeyer, 1998; Frenkel-Brunswik, 1948, 1949; Rokeach, 1960) and with a variety of internal and external threats (e.g., Adorno et al., 1950; McGregor et al., 2001; Sales, 1972, 1973). One of the most consistent and enduring targets of right-wing criticism has been immigration, which is often experienced as frightening, confusing, and potentially threatening to the status quo. Describing the increase in right-wing popularity in Europe following the terrorist attacks on New York and Washington of September 11, 2001, Cowell (2002) wrote that "the right appears to be benefiting from a deep-seated fear that Western Europe—cozy and prosperous—is the target of a wave of chaotic immigration" from Africa and the Middle East.

Fear, aggression, threat, and pessimism, we propose, may be reciprocally related to the endorsement of inequality. Insofar as inequality seems intrinsically linked to the struggle for dominance (Sidanius & Pratto, 1999), its engagement may exact a price in the form of fear, anxiety, and suspiciousness. Fear, in turn, may be (temporarily) allayed by admitting the reality of threat and preparing to address it by single-mindedly confronting one's foes (real or imaginary) and hence embracing inequality as a social necessity.[7]

In summary, then, we argue that fear and uncertainty are centrally linked to the core convictions of political conservatives to resist change and justify inequality, especially to the extent that the status quo breeds inequality. Whereas a plethora of motives (discussed earlier) might prompt individuals to embrace a specific form of conservative ideology, the core aspects of conservatism seem especially appealing to people who are situationally or dispositionally prone to experience fear or to find uncertainty aversive. Thus, a motivated social-cognitive perspective allows for the theoretical integration of a large number of variables that are relevant to overcoming fear and uncertainty in an effort to provide a coherent, though incomplete, psychological portrait of political conservatives.

Evidence linking epistemic, existential, and ideological motives to political conservatism

We have reviewed several theories of individual differences, epistemic and existential needs, and individual and collective rationalization to arrive at eight specific hypotheses concerning the motivated social-cognitive bases of political conservatism. In what follows, we consider evidence for and against the hypotheses that political conservatism is significantly associated with (1) mental rigidity and closed-mindedness, including (a) increased dogmatism and intolerance of ambiguity, (b) decreased cognitive complexity, (c) decreased openness to experience, (d) uncertainty avoidance, (e) personal needs for order and structure, and (f) need for cognitive closure; (2) lowered self-esteem; (3) fear, anger, and aggression; (4) pessimism, disgust, and contempt; (5) loss prevention; (6) fear of death; (7) threat arising from social and economic deprivation; and (8) threat to the stability of the social system. We have argued that these motives are in fact related to one another psychologically, and our motivated social-cognitive perspective helps to integrate them. We now offer an integrative, meta-analytic review of research on epistemic, existential, and ideological bases of conservatism.

The data for our review come from 38 journal articles, 1 monograph, 7 chapters from books or annual volumes, and 2 conference papers involving 88 different samples studied between 1958 and 2002. Some of the original data are derived from archival sources, including speeches and interviews given by politicians and opinions and verdicts rendered by judges, whereas others are taken from experimental, field, or survey studies. The total number of research participants and individual cases is 22,818 (see Table 1). The data come from 12 different countries, with 59 of the samples (or 67% of the total) coming from the United States. The remaining samples were studied in England ($n = 8$), New Zealand (4), Australia (3), Poland (3), Sweden (2), Germany (2), Scotland (2), Israel (2), Italy (1), Canada (1), and South Africa (1). Sixty percent of the samples are exclusively composed of college or university student populations, but they account for only 37% of the total number of research participants included in our review. The remaining samples include family members, high school students, student teachers, adult extension students, nonstudent adults, professionals, politicians, judges, political activists, and religious ministers. Only one of our hypotheses (concerning system instability) was assessed exclusively with samples from the United States, and only one other hypothesis (concerning self-esteem) was assessed exclusively with student samples (including one sample of adult education students).

Epistemic motives

By far the most convincing research on left–right differences pertains to epistemic motives associated with mental rigidity and closed-mindedness. The notion that political conservatives are less flexible in their thinking than others originated with

Table 1 Characteristics of samples and participants used in meta-analysis

Characteristic	No. of samples	No. of cases/participants
Country of sample		
Australia	3	1,042
Canada	1	354
England	8	1,330
Germany	2	571
Israel	2	279
Italy	1	178
New Zealand	4	998
Poland	3	368
Scotland	2	58
South Africa	1	233
Sweden	2	326
United States	59	17,081
Total	88	22,818
Type of sample		
Exclusively undergraduates	53	8,522
Not exclusively undergraduates	35	14,296
Total	88	22,818

work on authoritarianism (Adorno et al., 1950), intolerance of ambiguity (Frenkel-Brunswik, 1949), and dogmatism (Rokeach, 1960), and it also played a defining role in Wilson (1973c) and colleagues' conception of conservatism as uncertainty avoidance. Christie (1954) reported significant negative correlations ranging from −.20 to −.48 between IQ and scores on the F-Scale, but researchers since then have focused on differences in cognitive style rather than ability. Research on cognitive sophistication and integrative complexity provides the soundest basis for evaluating claims linking epistemic motivation to political ideology (e.g., Gruenfeld, 1995; Sidanius, 1985, 1988; Tetlock, 1983, 1984). Recent work on personal need for structure (Schaller et al., 1995) and the need for cognitive closure (D. M. Webster & Kruglanski, 1994) helps to complete the picture.

Dogmatism

A long-standing controversy within the psychological study of ideology has to do with whether intolerance, closed-mindedness, and cognitive simplicity are associated more with right-wing attitudes than with left-wing attitudes (e.g., Eysenck, 1954; Eysenck & Wilson, 1978; Sidanius, 1985, 1988; Tetlock, 1983, 1984; Wilson, 1973c). An early and persistent criticism of the work on authoritarianism, for example, has been that, in its zeal to identify right-wing dogmatism, it has failed to diagnose the dogmatism of the left (e.g., Rokeach, 1960; Shils, 1954). Over the years, there have been numerous backers of both the rigidity-of-the-right hypothesis (e.g., Altemeyer, 1981; Christie, 1956) and the more symmetrical extremist-as-ideologue hypothesis (e.g., Ray, 1973; Shils, 1954). W. F. Stone (1980) concluded that there was virtually no evidence for the syndrome of left-wing authoritarianism and that rigidity and closed-mindedness were consistently associated more with conservative thinking styles than with their alternatives. This position has been echoed by Altemeyer (1981, 1998) and Billig (1984), among others.

This is not to say that there is no such thing as leftist extremism or dogmatism (see Barker, 1963), but even when researchers have identified an increase in dogmatism among leftists in comparison with moderates, the highest dogmatism scores are still obtained for conservatives. Rokeach's (1956) Dogmatism Scale, which has been widely used in the psychological literature, contains such ideologically neutral items as the following: "A man who does not believe in some great cause has not really lived"; "Of all the different philosophies which exist in this world there is probably only one which is correct"; and "To compromise with our political opponents is dangerous because it usually leads to the betrayal of our own side." Because the items measure general epistemic attitudes rather than specific political opinions, dogmatism is included in our review as a psychological variable predicting political contents rather than as a political dependent variable.

Even though it is measured in an ideologically neutral way, dogmatism has been found to correlate consistently with authoritarianism, political–economic conservatism, and the holding of right-wing opinions (Barker, 1963; Christie, 1991; Elms, 1969; Pettigrew, 1958; Rokeach, 1960; Smithers & Lobley, 1978; Stacey & Green, 1971). Thus, more support exists for the rigidity-of-the-right hypothesis than for its alternatives. In commenting on Shils's (1954) critique, Altemeyer (1998, p.71) concluded:

> I have yet to find a single "socialist/Communist type" who scores highly (in absolute terms) on the [Left-Wing Authoritarianism] Scale. Shils may have been right about his era, but the "authoritarian on the left" has been as scarce as hens' teeth in my samples.

Evidence suggests that dogmatism has been no more useful than the construct of authoritarianism for identifying rigidity of the left (see Table 2), but this has not deterred researchers from considering the possibility. Following Rokeach's (1960) lead, numerous investigators have brought a variety of methods and theories to bear on the general question of whether political conservatives are more closed-minded (i.e., mentally rigid, intolerant of ambiguity, complexity, etc.) than are liberals, moderates, and others.

Intolerance of ambiguity

Research on ambiguity tolerance waxed and waned from the early 1950s to the late 1970s, using a wide range of measurement techniques (e.g., Block & Block, 1950; Budner, 1962; Eysenck, 1954; Feather, 1969, Sidanius, 1978, 1985). Frenkel-Brunswik (1949) assessed ambiguity tolerance using case study material obtained in interviews. Block and Block (1950) measured tolerance of ambiguity by the number of trials a participant took to establish an individual perceptual norm in

Table 2 Correlations between dogmatism–intolerance of ambiguity and political conservatism

Psychological variable	Political variable	Pearson's r	Cohen's d	Source	Sample characteristic
Dogmatism	F-Scale (fascism)	.82***	2.87	Pettigrew (1958)	49 female University of North Carolina undergraduates
		.56**	1.35	Rokeach (1960)[a]	13 members of the student Communist Society, University College, England
	Political–economic conservatism	.13*	0.26	Rokeach (1960)	202 Michigan State University undergraduates
		.11	0.22	Rokeach (1960)	207 New York University and Brooklyn College undergraduates
		.20**	0.41	Rokeach (1960)	153 Michigan State University undergraduates
		.28***	0.58	Rokeach (1960)	186 Michigan State University undergraduates
	Authoritarianism–rebelliousness	.48***	1.09	Kohn (1974)	62 University of Reading undergraduates, England
	Conservatism–radicalism	.20***[b]	0.41	Smithers & Lobley (1978)	295 University of Bradford undergraduates, England
	C-Scale	.58***	1.42	A.C. Webster & Stewart (1973)	93 Protestant ministers, New Zealand
	C-Scale (short form)	.44***	0.98	Kirton (1978), Sample 1	286 adults, England
		.47***	1.06	Kirton (1978), Sample 2	276 adults, England
Category specificity	F-Scale (fascism)	−.03	−0.06	Pettigrew (1958)	49 female University of North Carolina undergraduates
Inflexibility	C-Scale (short form)	.59***	1.46	Kirton (1978), Sample 1	286 adults, England
		.54***	1.28	Kirton (1978), Sample 2	276 adults, England

Psychological variable	Political variable	Pearson's r	Cohen's d	Source	Sample characteristic
Intolerance of ambiguity	C-Scale (short form)	.59***	1.46	Kirton (1978), Sample 1	286 adults, England
			1.46	Kirton (1978), Sample 2	276 adults, England
	Authoritarianism–rebelliousness	.67***	1.81	Kohn (1974)	62 University of Reading undergraduates, England
	General Conservatism Scale	.27***	0.56	Sidanius (1978)	192 high school students, Stockholm, Sweden
	Political–economic conservatism	.06	0.12	Sidanius (1978)	192 high school students, Stockholm, Sweden (same sample)
	Right-wing political orientation	.41***[c]	0.89	Fibert & Ressler (1998)	159 second-year students, Ben-Gurion University, Israel
Mean effect size		.37***	0.82		Total (unique) N^a = 2,173
Weighted mean effect size		.34***	0.73		
95% confidence interval		.30, .37			

Note. F-Scale = Fascism Scale; C-Scale = Conservatism Scale.

[a] Rokeach (1960, pp. 83, 121) reported correlations between dogmatism and the F-Scale ranging from .54 to .77 for multiple large samples drawn from England, New York, and Ohio. However, the samples could not be matched to correlation coefficients based on his report. [b] Pearson's *r* was derived from the originally reported *F* statistic, $F(1, 292) = 12.50$, $p < .001$. [c] Pearson's *r* was derived from the originally reported *F* statistic, $F(1, 158) = 31.52$, $p < .001$. [d] When multiple tests were computed on the same sample, the sample was counted only once in the calculation of total (unique) *N*; mean effect sizes (weighted and nonweighted), and overall significance levels. Multiple effect sizes drawn from the same sample were averaged prior to inclusion in calculations of overall average effect sizes.

* $p < .10$. ** $p < .05$. *** $p < .001$. (All tests two-tailed, converted from one-tailed tests when necessary.)

the autokinetic paradigm. A number of questionnaire measures of ambiguity tolerance were devised (see Furnham & Ribchester, 1995, for a review), the first being Walk's A Scale, reproduced by O'Connor (1952). Similar tests were developed by Eysenck (1954) and Budner (1962), among others.

As hypothesized by Frenkel-Brunswik (1948), intolerance of ambiguity has been found to correlate positively with ethnocentrism (O'Connor, 1952) and authoritarianism (e.g., Kenny & Ginsberg, 1958; Pawlicki & Almquist, 1973). At least a few studies, which are summarized in Table 2, provide support for the notion that intolerance of ambiguity is associated with political conservatism (e.g., Kirton, 1978; Kohn, 1974; Sidanius, 1978). A study of Israeli university students by Fibert and Ressler (1998) found that intolerance of ambiguity scores were indeed significantly higher among moderate and extreme right-wing students compared with moderate and extreme left-wing students. The notion that conservatism is associated with intolerance of ambiguity is consistent with a great many theories, and it is implicit in ideological theories of integrative complexity. It may also provide a psychological context for understanding statements such as this one made by George W. Bush at an international conference of world leaders in Italy: "I know what I believe and I believe what I believe is right" (Sanger, 2001).[8] Our review suggests that there is a relatively strong connection between dogmatism and intolerance of ambiguity, on the one hand, and various measures of political conservatism, on the other. The weighted mean effect size (r), aggregated across 20 tests of the hypothesis conducted in five different countries involving more than 2,000 participants (see Table 2), was .34 ($p < .0001$).[9]

Integrative complexity

There is by now a relatively large and methodologically sophisticated body of work that addresses left-wing and right-wing differences in cognitive complexity (e.g., Gruenfeld, 1995; Sidanius, 1984, 1985, 1988; Tetlock, 1983, 1984). Content-analytic techniques have been developed to measure integrative complexity, which refers to the extent of differentiation among multiple perspectives or dimensions and the higher order integration or synthesis of these differentiated components (e.g., Tetlock, 1983, 1984). Whereas prior research assessing dogmatism and rigidity among different ideological groups primarily made use of respondents drawn from the population as a whole, Tetlock's (1983, 1984; Tetlock et al., 1985) work on integrative complexity has focused on thinking styles among political elites.

In an inventive series of studies, Tetlock (1983, 1984) and his collaborators (Tetlock et al., 1985) analyzed archival data drawn from speeches and interviews with political elites. The results are often taken as evidence for Shils's (1954) contention that ideologues of the extreme left and extreme right are more dogmatic and closed-minded than political centrists, and some of the findings (e.g., Tetlock, 1984) do suggest that extreme leftists show less cognitive complexity than moderate leftists. At the same time, however, there is a clear indication in Tetlock's data that conservative ideologues are generally less integratively complex than their liberal or moderate counterparts (see Table 3). For example, a study of U.S. senatorial

Table 3 Correlations between integrative complexity and political conservatism

Psychological variable	Political variable	Pearson's r	Cohen's d	Source	Sample characteristic
Integrative complexity	Conservative voting record	−.44***[a]	−0.98	Tetlock (1983)	Speeches from 45 Senators, USA
	Conservative political party and orientation	−.30***	−0.63	Tetlock (1984)	Interviews with 87 members of the House of Commons, England
	Conservative voting record and orientation	−.61*****[b]	−1.54	Tetlock et al. (1984), Sample 1	Speeches from 35 Senators, 82nd Congress, USA
		−.38**[c]	−0.82		Speeches from 35 Senators, 83rd Congress, USA (same sample)
		−.45***[d]	−1.01	Tetlock et al. (1984), Sample 2	Speeches from 45 Senators, 94th Congress, USA
		−.46;***[e]	−1.04		Speeches from 45 Senators, 96th Congress, USA (same sample)
		.00[f]	0.00		Speeches from 45 Senators, 97th Congress, USA (same sample)
	Conservative voting record (civil liberties)	−.47**	−1.06	Tetlock et al. (1985)	Opinions from 23 Supreme Court justices, USA
	Conservative voting record (economic issues)	−.48**	−1.09	Tetlock et al. (1985)	Opinions from 23 Supreme Court justices, USA (same sample)
	Conservative voting record and orientation	.19[g]	0.39	Gruenfeld (1995), Sample 1	16 Supreme Court justices, USA
		.13[h]	0.26	Gruenfeld (1995), Sample 2	32 Supreme Court opinions, USA
		.00[i]	0.00	Gruenfeld (1995), Sample 3	24 Supreme Court cases, USA
Cognitive flexibility					
Measure 1	General Conservatism Scale	−.19**	−0.39	Sidanius (1985)	134 high school students, Stockholm, Sweden
Measure 2		−.16*	−0.32	Sidanius (1985)	134 high school students, Stockholm, Sweden (same sample)
Measure 3		−.11	−0.22	Sidanius (1985)	134 high school students, Stockholm, Sweden (same sample)

(continued)

Table 3 Correlations between integrative complexity and political conservatism *(continued)*

Psychological variable	Political variable	Pearson's r	Cohen's d	Source	Sample characteristic
Cognitive complexity					
Measure 1		−.11	−0.22	Sidanius (1985)	134 high school students, Stockholm, Sweden (same sample)
Measure 2		−.01	−0.02	Sidanius (1985)	134 high school students, Stockholm, Sweden (same sample)
Ordination	C-Scale	−.23**[i]	−0.47	Hinze et al. (1997)	84 University of North Texas undergraduates
Functionally independent constructs		.00[k]	0.00	Hinze et al. (1997)	84 University of North Texas undergraduates (same sample)
Attributional complexity	RWA Scale	−.17***	−0.35	Altemeyer (1998)	354 University of Manitoba undergraduates, Canada
	SDO Scale	−.19****	−0.39	Altemeyer (1998)	354 University of Manitoba undergraduates, Canada (same sample)
Mean effect size		−.20****	−0.43		Total (unique) N[u] = 879
Weighted mean effect size		−.20****	−0.41		
95% confidence interval		−.13, −.26			

Note. C-Scale = Conservatism Scale; RWA = Right-Wing Authoritarianism; SDO = Social Dominance Orientation.

[a] A partial r was derived from the originally reported beta statistic, $\beta = .35$, $t(39) = 3.02$, according to the formula: $\sqrt{t^2/(t^2 + df)}$. [b] Pearson's r was derived from the mean (Fisherized) effect size of two originally reported F statistics, one for the difference between liberals and conservatives, $F(1, 32) = 15.24$, $p < .001$, and one for the difference between moderates and conservatives, $F(1, 32) = 23.37$, $p < .001$, and one for the difference between moderates and conservatives, $F(1, 32) = 10.70, p < .01$. [c] Pearson's r was derived from the mean (Fisherized) effect size of two originally reported F statistics, one for the difference between liberals and conservatives, $F(1, 32) = 2.13$, $p < .25$, and one for the difference between moderates and conservatives, $F(1, 32) = 10.70, p < .01$. [d] Pearson's r was derived from the mean (Fisherized) effect size of two originally reported F statistics, one for the difference between liberals and conservatives, $F(1, 84) = 12.70$, $p < .001$. [e] Pearson's r was derived from the mean (Fisherized) effect size of two originally reported F statistics, $F(1, 84) = 23.61$, $p < .01$. [f] Tetlock et al. (1984) reported that "No significant differences existed among ideological groups in this Congress" (p. 934), so we made the conservative assumption that $r = 0$. [g] Gruenfeld (1995) reported that $F < 1.00$ for the difference between liberals ($M = 1.64$) and conservatives ($M = 1.76$), so we calculated Pearson's r on the assumption that $F = 0.50$. [h] Gruenfeld (1995) reported that $F < 1.00$ for the difference between liberals ($M = 1.38$) and conservatives ($M = 1.56$), so we calculated Pearson's r on the assumption that $F = 0$. [j] Pearson's r was derived from the originally reported F statistic, $F(1, 82) = 4.59$, $p = .035$. [k] Pearson's r was derived from the originally reported F statistic, $F(1, 82) = 0.007$, $p = .935$. The precise r would have been .01, but the direction of the effect was not specified by Hinze et al. (1997). When multiple tests were computed on the same sample, the sample was counted only once in the calculation of total (unique) N, mean effect sizes (weighted and nonweighted), and overall significance levels. Multiple effect sizes drawn from the same sample were averaged prior to inclusion in calculations of overall average effect sizes.

* $p < .10$. ** $p < .05$. *** $p < .01$. **** $p < .001$. (All tests two-tailed, converted when necessary.)

speeches in 1975 and 1976 indicates that politicians whose voting records were classified as either liberal or moderate showed significantly more integrative complexity than did politicians with conservative voting records, even after controlling for political party affiliation (Tetlock, 1983). These results were replicated almost exactly in a study of U.S. Supreme Court justices by Tetlock et al. (1985). In neither of these studies were liberals found to be significantly less (or more) complex in their thinking than were moderates. Gruenfeld (1995), however, failed to replicate Tetlock's (1983, 1984) results after controlling for majority versus minority opinion status; she obtained no significant differences between liberals and conservatives on integrative complexity.

Additional evidence does suggest that an overall main effect relationship holds between cognitive complexity and political conservatism. Tetlock's (1984) study of members of the British House of Commons revealed a moderate negative correlation between integrative complexity and ideological conservatism ($r = -.30, p < .01$). He found that the most integratively complex politicians were moderate socialists, who scored significantly higher on complexity than extreme socialists, moderate conservatives, and extreme conservatives. Tetlock, Hannum, and Micheletti (1984) compared the speeches of liberals and conservatives in five separate U.S. congressional sessions. They found that liberals and moderates scored significantly higher than conservatives on integrative complexity in all three Democratic-controlled Congresses. Of the two examinations by Tetlock et al. (1984) of Republican-controlled Congresses, one revealed no differences among liberals, conservatives, and moderates, and the other indicated that moderates exhibited significantly greater complexity than conservatives, whereas liberals did not differ from the other two groups. The authors concluded that their findings "lend indirect support to the rigidity-of-the-right hypothesis" and that a "general trait interpretation of integrative complexity appears to apply more readily to conservatives than to liberals and moderates" (p. 987).

Sidanius (1984, 1985, 1988) proposed context theory as an alternative to the notions that cognitive sophistication is lower among right-wing proponents or among extremist ideologues of either side (see also Sidanius & Lau, 1989). Briefly, his argument was that the relation between cognitive complexity and conservatism should depend on which specific subdimension of conservatism one is dealing with and the psychological function that is related to that subdimension. With regard to political–economic conservatism, Sidanius (1985) hypothesized that because of greater political interest and commitment, extremists of the right and left would "display *greater* [italics added] cognitive complexity, flexibility, and tolerance of ambiguity than political 'moderates'" (p. 638). By contrast, with regard to conservative social attitudes concerning issues of race and immigration, Sidanius (1985) predicted (and found) that cognitive complexity would be negatively and monotonically related to conservatism. Other evidence in support of context theory includes findings from the United States and Sweden that right- and left-wing extremists (on political and economic issues) are more likely than moderates to express political interest and to engage in active information search (Sidanius, 1984), to exhibit cognitive complexity (Sidanius, 1985, 1988), and to report high levels of self-confidence and willingness to deviate from social convention (Sidanius, 1988). It is important to note, however, that at least two studies (Sidanius, 1978, 1985) yield greater support for the notion that cognitive flexibility decreases in a linear fashion with increasing general conservatism than they did for any curvilinear prediction. Unfortunately, the studies listed in Table 3 do not provide sufficient statistical information to allow a meta-analytic test for the presence of a quadratic trend in the overall data. However, inspection of the means reported in these studies strongly suggests that the overall trend is linear rather than curvilinear, with liberals exhibiting the highest levels of integrative complexity and flexibility. Overall, we obtained a weighted mean effect size (*r*) of −.20 *(p* < .0001) for 21 tests of the relation between integrative complexity and political conservatism, assessed in four different national contexts (see Table 3).

Openness to experience

Wilson's (1973b) psychological theory of conservatism assumes, among many other things, that conservatives are less inclined to seek out strong external stimulation in the form of other people as well as in the form of nonsocial stimuli. He interpreted findings indicating that conservatives score lower on measures of extraversion as consistent with this formulation (Wilson, 1973b, p. 262). Somewhat more direct evidence was provided by Kish (1973), who found that conservatives scored lower than others on measures of general sensation seeking (see Table 4). Joe, Jones, and Ryder (1977) obtained a correlation of −.38 between scores on an Experience Inventory Scale (including subscales of Aesthetic Sensitivity, Openness to Theoretical or Hypothetical Ideas, Indulgence in Fantasy, and Openness to Unconventional Views of Reality) and scores on Wilson and Patterson's (1968) C-Scale. A follow-up study by Joe et al. revealed that conservatives were also less likely than nonconservatives to volunteer for psychology experiments that required openness to experience (i.e., experiments on aesthetic interest, fantasy production, and sexual behavior) but not for experiments on decision making and humor. These findings are consistent with other research indicating that conservatives are less likely than others to value broad-mindedness, imagination, and "having an exciting life" (Feather, 1979, 1984).

One of Costa and MacRae's (1985) Big Five dimensions of personality addresses openness to experience. Pratto et al. (1994) found that openness to experience was correlated with low scores on the SDO Scale in at least one of their samples ($r = -.28$, $p < .01$). Jost and Thompson (2000) administered the Big Five inventory along with the Economic System Justification Scale to a sample of 393 students at the University of Maryland at College Park, and they found that system justification was associated with lower levels of openness to experience ($r = -.19$, $p < .001$). Peterson and Lane (2001), too, found that openness to experience was negatively correlated with RWA scores in a sample of college students that they followed for 4 years. Correlational results from 21 tests conducted in the United States and Australia (see Table 4) provide consistent evidence that people who hold politically conservative attitudes are generally less open to new and stimulating experiences (weighted mean $r = -.32$, $p < .0001$).

Table 4 Correlations between openness to experience and political conservatism

Psychological variable	Political variable	Pearson's r	Cohen's d	Source	Sample characteristic
General Sensation Seeking	F-Scale	−.45**[a]	−1.01	Kish & Donnenwerth (1972)	42 adult extension students, USA
General Sensation Seeking (short form)	C-Scale	−.33***	−0.70	Kish (1973), Sample 1	186 undergraduates, USA
General Sensation Seeking	C-Scale	−.54***	−1.28	Kish (1973), Sample 2	51 adult extension social work students, USA
		−.48**	−1.09	Glasgow & Cartier (1985)	42 University of Nevada-Reno undergraduates
Experience Inventory		−.38***	−0.82	Joe et al. (1977), Sample 1	124 undergraduates, USA
Willingness to volunteer for experiments requiring open-mindedness		−.15:+.[b]	−0.30	Joe et al. (1977), Sample 2	205 undergraduates, USA
Valuing broad-mindedness		−.39,***	−0.85	Feather (1979), Sample 1	558 family members (14 years and older), Adelaide, Australia
		−.43***	−0.95	Feather (1979), Sample 2	358 Flinders University undergraduates and their family members (14 years and older), Australia
		−.34***	−0.72	Feather (1984)	124 Flinders University students, Australia
Valuing imaginativeness		−.32***	−0.68	Feather (1979), Sample 1	558 family members (14 years and older), Adelaide, Australia
		−.44***	−0.98	Feather (1979), Sample 2	358 Flinders University undergraduates and their family members (14 years and older), Australia
Valuing an exciting life		−.50***	−1.15	Feather (1984)	124 Flinders University students, Australia
		−.27***	−0.56	Feather (1979), Sample 1	558 family members (14 years and older), Adelaide, Australia

(continued)

Table 4 Correlations between openness to experience and political conservatism (continued)

Psychological variable	Political variable	Pearson's r	Cohen's d	Source	Sample characteristic
Openness to Experience (from the Big Five Personality Inventory)		−.31***	−0.65	Feather (1979), Sample 2	358 Flinders University undergraduates and their family members (14 years and older), Australia
	SDO Scale	−.25**	−0.52	Feather (1984)	126 Flinders University students, Australia
		−.28**	−0.58	Pratto et al. (1994), Sample 9	97 San Jose State University undergraduates
	Economic System Justification Scale	−.19***	−0.39	Jost & Thompson (2000)	393 University of Maryland undergraduates
	RWA Scale	−.36***	−0.77	Peterson et al. (1997), Sample 1	198 University of New Hampshire undergraduates
		−.33***	−0.70	Peterson et al. (1997), Sample 2	157 parents of University of New Hampshire undergraduates
		−.31**	−0.65	Peterson & Lane (2001)	69 first-year University of New Hampshire undergraduates
		−.42***	−0.93	Peterson & Lane (2001)	69 University of New Hampshire senior undergraduates (same sample)
Mean effect size		−.35***	−0.77		Total (unique) N[c] = 2,606
Weighted mean effect size		−.32***	−0.68		
95% confidence interval		−.28, −.35			

Note. F-Scale = Fascism Scale; C-Scale = Conservatism Scale; SDO = Social Dominance Orientation; RWA = Right-Wing Authoritarianism.
[a] A weighted mean r was derived from originally reported correlations for men ($r = -.81$, $n = 13$) and women ($r = -.29$, $n = 29$). [b] Pearson's r was derived from the originally reported F statistic, $F(1, 201) = 4.50$. [c] When multiple tests were computed on the same sample, the sample was counted only once in the calculation of total (unique) N. mean effect sizes (weighted and nonweighted), and overall significance levels. Multiple effect sizes drawn from the same sample were averaged prior to inclusion in calculations of overall average effect sizes.
* $p < .05$. ** $p < .01$. *** $p < .001$. (All tests two-tailed, converted when necessary.)

Uncertainty avoidance

The crux of Wilson's (1973b) theory is that ambiguity and uncertainty are highly threatening to conservatives. Wilson, Ausman, and Mathews (1973) examined the artistic preferences of people who scored high and low on the C-Scale by soliciting evaluative ratings of paintings that had been classified as either simple or complex and either abstract or representational. They found that conservatives exhibited a relatively strong preference for simple rather than complex paintings and a much weaker preference for representational rather than abstract paintings (see Table 5). Similarly, it has been shown that conservatives were more likely to prefer simple poems over complex poems (Gillies & Campbell, 1985) and unambiguous over ambiguous literary texts (McAllister & Anderson, 1991). Similar results have been obtained when preferences for familiar versus unfamiliar stimuli were compared. For instance, Glasgow and Cartier (1985) demonstrated that conservatives were more likely than others to favor familiar over unfamiliar music. Converging results that political conservatives are less tolerant of ambiguity, less open to new experiences, and more avoidant of uncertainty compared with moderates and liberals may provide a psychological context for understanding why congressional Republicans and other prominent conservatives in the United States have sought unilaterally to eliminate public funding for the contemporary arts (Lehrer, 1997).

In a useful effort to apply Wilson's (1973b) theory of conservatism as uncertainty reduction to the workplace, Fay and Frese (2000) used a German translation of an authoritarianism scale to investigate work-related attitudes and openness to organizational and technological innovation. This study has the virtue of distinguishing more clearly between psychological variables (acceptance vs. rejection of innovation) and ideological variables (authoritarianism) than is typically afforded by studies using the C-Scale. Fay and Frese (2000) found that authoritarianism was associated with an unwillingness to change work habits, a rejection of new technology, and relative disinterest in work innovation in an East German context (see Table 5). Atieh, Brief, and Vollrath (1987) found that conservatives were especially likely to value job security over task variety at work. In diverse aesthetic and organizational contexts, then, evidence from three countries suggests that conservatives are generally motivated to eschew ambiguity, novelty, and uncertainty (weighted mean $r = -.27$, $p < .0001$).

Personal needs for order and structure

A number of theories, including theories of authoritarianism, dogmatism, and uncertainty avoidance, imply that conservatives should have heightened motivational needs for order and structure. The research that exists is consistent with these expectations (see Table 6). For example, A. C. Webster and Stewart (1973) obtained a correlation of .24 between the need for order and scores on the C-Scale. Eisenberg-Berg and Mussen (1980) found that politically conservative adolescents were more likely to describe themselves as neat, orderly, and organized than were liberal adolescents. Altemeyer (1998) obtained a moderate correlation of .34 between scores on Schaller et al.'s (1995) Personal Need for Structure Scale and

Table 5 Correlations between uncertainty tolerance and political conservatism

Psychological variable	Political variable	Pearson's r	Cohen's d	Source	Sample characteristic
Preference for complex paintings	C-Scale	−.56***	−1.35	Wilson et al. (1973)	30 adults aged 23–34, USA
Preference for abstract paintings		−.14	−0.28	Wilson et al. (1973)	30 adults aged 23–34, USA (same sample)
Preference for complex poems		−.31*	−0.65	Gillies & Campbell (1985)	34 Glasgow University undergraduates, Scotland
Preference for modern over traditional poems		.04	0.08	Gillies & Campbell (1985)	34 Glasgow University undergraduates, Scotland (same sample)
Preference for unfamiliar music[a]		−.30**	−0.63	Glasgow & Cartier (1985)	42 University of Nevada–Reno undergraduates
Preference for complex music[a]		−.24	−0.49	Glasgow & Cartier (1985)	42 University of Nevada–Reno undergraduates (same sample)
Preference for ambiguous literary texts		−.40*[b]	−0.87	McAllister & Anderson (1991)	24 adults aged 18–46, Scotland
Comfort with job insecurity[a]		−.22***	−0.45	Atieh et al. (1987)	155 graduate and undergraduate students, USA
Preference for task variety		−.16**	−0.32	Atieh et al. (1987)	155 graduate and undergraduate students, USA (same sample)
Readiness to change at work	Authoritarian-conservatism	−.33***	−0.70	Fay & Frese (2000)	478 adults aged 20–67, East Germany
Acceptance of new technology[a]		−.23***	−0.47	Fay & Frese (2000)	478 adults aged 20–67, East Germany (same sample)
Interest in work innovation		−.42***	−0.93	Fay & Frese (2000)	478 adults aged 20–67, East Germany (same sample)
Attempts at innovation		−.21***	−0.43	Fay & Frese (2000)	478 adults aged 20–67, East Germany (same sample)
Mean effect size		−.28***	−0.58		Total (unique) N[c] = 763
Weighted mean effect size		−.27***	−0.57		
95% confidence interval		−.21, −.34			

Note: C-Scale = Conservatism Scale.
[a] Variables have been rephrased from the original source (e.g., "preference for complex" rather than "preference for simple") and coefficient signs reversed accordingly to facilitate comparison with other studies and calculate meaningful mean effect sizes. [b] Pearson's r was derived from the mean of two originally reported Mann–Whitney U statistics, one for the difference in preferences between texts that were high versus low in ambiguity (U = 34.0, p < .05), and one for the difference in preferences between texts that were low versus moderate in ambiguity (U = 32.5, p < .05). [c] When multiple tests were computed on the same sample, the sample was counted only once in the calculation of total (unique) N; mean effect sizes (weighted and nonweighted), and overall significance levels. Multiple effect sizes drawn from the same sample were averaged prior to inclusion in calculations of overall average effect sizes.
* p < .10. ** p < .05. *** p < .01. **** p < .001. (All tests two-tailed, converted when necessary.)

Table 6 Correlations between needs for order, structure, and closure and political conservatism

Psychological variable	Political variable	Pearson's r	Cohen's d	Source	Sample characteristic
Need for order	C-Scale	.24*	0.49	A. C. Webster & Stewart (1973)	93 Protestant ministers, New Zealand
Personal need for structure	RWA Scale	.34***	0.72	Altemeyer (1998)	354 University of Manitoba undergraduates, Canada
	SDO Scale	.06	0.12	Altemeyer (1998)	354 University of Manitoba undergraduates, Canada (same sample)
Need for cognitive closure	F-Scale (authoritarianism)	.27**	0.56	D. M. Webster & Kruglanski (1994)	97 University of Maryland undergraduates
	Right-wing political party and orientation	.29**	0.61	Kemmelmeier (1997)	93 University of Mannheim undergraduates, Germany
	Political orientation	.23**a	0.48	Chirumbolo (2002)	178 undergraduates and working adults, Italy
	F-Scale (authoritarianism)	.46***b	1.04	Chirumbolo (2002)	178 undergraduates and working adults, Italy (same sample)
	Self-reported conservatism	.21***	0.43	Jost et al. (1999), Sample 1	613 University of Maryland undergraduates
	Self-reported conservatism	.26***	0.54	Jost et al. (1999), Sample 2	733 University of Maryland undergraduates
	Support for the death penalty	.47*	1.06	Jost et al. (1999), Sample 3	19 University of California, Santa Barbara, undergraduates
	Religious and nationalist right-wing beliefs	.27**	0.56	Golec (2001), Sample 1	119 adults aged 18–30, Poland
		.31***	0.65	Golec (2001), Sample 2	126 Warsaw School of Advanced Social Psychology students, Poland
		.82***	2.87	Golec (2001), Sample 3	122 student political activists, Poland

(continued)

Table 6 Correlations between needs for order, structure, and closure and political conservatism (continued)

Psychological variable	Political variable	Pearson's r	Cohen's d	Source	Sample characteristic
	Economic right-wing beliefs	−.22*	−0.45	Golec (2001), Sample 1	120 adults aged 18–30, Poland
		−.26**	−0.54	Golec (2001), Sample 2	120 Warsaw School of Advanced Social Psychology students, Poland
	Conservative self-placement (economic issues)	.61***	1.54	Golec (2001), Sample 3	122 student political activists, Poland
		−.13	−0.26	Golec (2001), Sample 1	119 adults aged 18–30, Poland
	Conservative self-placement (social issues)	.72***	2.08	Golec (2001), Sample 3	106 student political activists, Poland
		.07	0.14	Golec (2001), Sample 1	120 adults, aged 18–30, Poland
		.70***	1.96	Golec (2001), Sample 3	109 student political activists, Poland
Mean effect size		.26***	0.64		Total (unique) N[c] = 2,548
Weighted mean effect size			0.54		
95% confidence interval		.22, .29			

Note. C-Scale = Conservatism Scale; RWA = Right-Wing Authoritarianism; SDO = Social Dominance Orientation; F-Scale = Fascism Scale.
[a] A partial r was derived from the originally reported beta statistic, $\beta = .25$, $t(177) = 3.17$, according to the formula $\sqrt{t^2/(t^2 + df)}$. [b] A partial r was derived from the originally reported beta statistic, $\beta = .46$, $t(177) = 6.95$, according to the formula $\sqrt{t^2/(t^2 + df)}$. [c] When multiple tests were computed on the same sample, the sample was counted only once in the calculation of total (unique) N; mean effect sizes (weighted and non-weighted), and overall significance levels. Multiple effect sizes drawn from the same sample were averaged prior to inclusion in calculations of overall average effect sizes.
* $p < .05$. ** $p < .01$. *** $p < .001$. (All tests two-tailed, converted when necessary.)

RWA scores. This evidence is consistent not only with research on dogmatism, intolerance of ambiguity, and uncertainty avoidance but also with the notion that in the realm of political attitudes, authoritarians long for order and structure, advocating such diverse measures as firm parental discipline, comprehensive drug testing, core educational curricula, and quarantines for AIDS patients (Peterson et al., 1993).

Need for cognitive closure

An even more specific account of closed-mindedness exists in studies of impulsive closure and the need for cognitive closure (e.g., Dittes, 1961; D. M. Webster & Kruglanski, 1994) than in studies of dogmatism and intolerance of ambiguity. Here we consider evidence pertaining to the hypothesis that there is a match between content-free epistemic motives to make decisions that are quick, firm, and final and content-laden political attitudes associated with the right wing (see Table 6). In validating their individual-difference scale of the need for closure, the NFCS, D. M. Webster and Kruglanski (1994) obtained a correlation of .27 between NFCS scores and authoritarianism. In two large samples of undergraduate students at the University of Maryland at College Park, Jost et al. (1999) administered batteries of measures that included the NFCS and a single-item measure of self-reported liberalism–conservatism, with several other instruments separating the two. Modest positive correlations were obtained between need for closure and conservatism in each of the samples, $r(613) = .21, p < .001$, and, $r(733) = .26, p < .001$.

A study conducted by Kemmelmeier (1997) in Germany demonstrates further that need-for-closure scores increase in a steady, monotonic fashion as one moves from left-wing to right-wing party membership. Democratic socialists scored lower on the NFCS than did members of the Green Party, who scored lower than members of the Social Democratic Party, who scored lower than members of the Free Democratic Party, who scored lower than members of the right-wing Christian Democratic Party. Results yielded no evidence for the hypothesis that extreme individuals of the left and right would exhibit greater cognitive rigidity (e.g., Shils, 1954) nor for Sidanius's (1984, 1985) suggestion that politically extreme individuals in general would exhibit greater flexibility and sophistication in their thinking. Instead, Kemmelmeier reported a positive monotonic effect of cognitive style on political ideology such that increased needs for cognitive closure were indeed associated with membership in right-wing organizations. These results were replicated in Italy by Chirumbolo (2002).

Jost et al. (1999) hypothesized that people who scored high on the NFCS would be especially likely to support the death penalty, insofar as capital punishment implies a resolution that is unambiguous, permanent, and final. That is, an empirical connection between nonspecific epistemic motives and specific ideological opinions was postulated. An overall correlation of .47 ($p < .05$) was obtained between need for closure and endorsement of capital punishment, with the strongest NFCS subscale predictors of support for capital punishment being Discomfort With Ambiguity ($r = .66, p < .01$) and Preference for Order ($r = .55, p < .02$). Little wonder, then, that advocates of the death penalty, who tend to be politically conservative in general, frequently argue that state-sanctioned executions are beneficial because they allow victims and observers to finally experience "closure."

Research conducted in Poland by Golec (2001) corroborates the independent hypotheses that (a) the need for closure is associated with the preservation of the status quo (whether left-wing or right-wing) and (b) there is a matching tendency for people who are high on the need for closure to prefer right-wing ideologies over left-wing ideologies (perhaps especially when they are relatively high on political expertise). In two studies involving Polish citizens and students of various colleges and universities, Golec (2001) found that NFCS scores were correlated positively with religious and nationalist conservatism, but they were correlated negatively with (pro-capitalist) economic conservatism, presumably because of Poland's traditionally socialist economy (see Table 6). However, when she examined youth affiliates of various political parties (who may be regarded as relatively high in political expertise and involvement), the strongest ever associations between the (ideologically content-free) NFCS and political conservatism were observed. In a study involving 122 research participants, need for closure was strongly correlated with self-placement on scales of social conservatism ($r = .70$) and economic conservatism ($r = .72$), and it was also strongly correlated with beliefs indicating religious and nationalist conservatism ($r = .82$) as well as economic conservatism ($r = .61$). Thus, personal needs for order, structure, and closure appear to be especially well satisfied by right-wing political contents. Aggregating across 20 tests of the hypothesis in six different national contexts, we found stable and reasonably strong support for the notion that these specific epistemic motives are associated with a wide variety of politically conservative attitudes and orientations (weighted mean $r = .26$, $p < .0001$).

Existential motives

Threats to self-esteem

According to theories of authoritarianism and uncertainty avoidance, people should be more likely to embrace political conservatism to the extent that their self-esteem is chronically low or otherwise threatened. Although threats to self-esteem have been shown to evoke impulsive closure (Dittes, 1961), racism (Sidanius, 1988), and out-group derogation (Fein & Spencer, 1997), there is relatively little evidence to date linking threatened self-esteem to political conservatism per se. In arguing that a sense of inferiority leads to a generalized fear of uncertainty leading to conservatism, Wilson (1973b) appears to have relied on a single study by Boshier (1969) in which self-esteem correlated negatively at −.51 with scores on the C-Scale in a sample of continuing education students in New Zealand. One study did find that adolescent conservatives were more likely than liberals to report "worrying about doing something bad" (Eisenberg-Berg & Mussen, 1980, p. 169), but they were also more likely to see themselves as ambitious and successful.

A pair of experimental studies conducted by Sales and Friend (1973) demonstrate that inducing a failure experience can lead people to respond in an increasingly authoritarian manner. Specifically, receiving false feedback that they had performed relatively poorly on an anagram task led people to score higher on a balanced version of the F-Scale (compared with a preexperimental control condition). Conversely, receiving success feedback led people to score lower on authoritarianism. Although the effects were relatively small in magnitude and the results were presented too ambiguously to include in our meta-analysis, these experiments are important because they suggest that situational factors can influence the expression of political conservatism.[10]

In general, however, consistently supportive evidence for the self-esteem hypothesis has been hard to come by (see Table 7). For instance, Altemeyer (1998) found that individual self-esteem was uncorrelated with both RWA and SDO, but that collective self-esteem was weakly and negatively related to SDO. Pratto et al. (1994) reported that self-esteem was significantly and negatively correlated with SDO in three of their nine samples, but correlations varied widely across the nine samples. Our review, which aggregates effect sizes across 17 tests of the hypothesis involving a total of 1,558 university (or adult education) students from three different countries, leads to the conclusion that there is indeed a relationship between self-esteem and political conservatism, but it is relatively weak in magnitude (weighted mean $r = -.09$, $p < .001$), especially in comparison with our other findings.

Despite the lack of large effect sizes, Altemeyer (1998, p. 81) has argued that high authoritarians respond more defensively to ego-threatening situations than do low authoritarians. Specifically, he observed that:

> High RWAs asked for evidence supporting the validity of a self-esteem scale when they thought they had scored highly on it, but did not want to know about the validity of the test when told they had scored poorly on it. They also asked to be told if they looked unprejudiced on the Ethnocentrism scale, but said they did not want to be informed if they scored highly in prejudice.

Thus, conservatives may not have lower self-esteem in general, but the possibility remains that they respond differently than others to potentially ego-threatening situations. A related possibility is that conservative ideologues are not necessarily lower in self-esteem but have less stable self-esteem. These considerations lead us to conclude that more research, especially with nonstudent samples, is needed to determine whether conservatives respond more defensively (or more aggressively) to self-related threats.

Fear, anger, and aggression

Although far more research exists on cognitive differences between conservatives and other people than on emotional differences, it is a persistent claim that conservatives are more likely than others to be motivated by fear, aggression, and contempt (e.g., Adorno et al., 1950; Altemeyer, 1996, 1998; Duckitt, 2001; Krugman, 2002; I. F. Stone, 1989; Tomkins, 1963, 1995). Classic and contemporary theories of authoritarianism similarly stress the possibility that conservatives

Table 7 Correlations between self-esteem and political conservatism

Psychological variable	Political variable	Pearson's r	Cohen's d	Source	Sample characteristic
Self-esteem	C-Scale	-.51***	-1.19	Boshier (1969)	40 adult education students, New Zealand
Self-acceptance		-.13	-0.26	Boshier (1969)	40 adult education students, New Zealand (same sample)
Self/ideal discrepancy		-.30*	-0.63	Boshier (1969)	40 adult education students, New Zealand (same sample)
Ego defensiveness		.15	0.30	Wilson (1973d)	91 California State University undergraduates
Rosenberg Self-Esteem Scale	SDO Scale	-.09	-0.18	Pratto et al. (1994), Sample 1	98 University of California, Berkeley, undergraduates
			-0.37	Pratto et al. (1994), Sample 2	403 San Jose State University undergraduates
		.09	0.18	Pratto et al. (1994), Sample 3a	80 Stanford University undergraduates
		.01	0.02	Pratto et al. (1994), Sample 3b	57 Stanford University undergraduates (subset of Sample 3a)
		.16	0.32	Pratto et al. (1994), Sample 4	90 Stanford University undergraduates
		-.23**	-0.47	Pratto et al. (1994), Sample 5	144 San Jose State University undergraduates
		-.01	-0.02	Pratto et al. (1994), Sample 6	48 Stanford University undergraduates
		-.29**	-0.61	Pratto et al. (1994), Sample 8	115 Stanford University undergraduates
		-.14	-0.28	Pratto et al. (1994), Sample 9	95 San Jose State University undergraduates
	RWA Scale	.01	0.02	Altemeyer (1998)	354 University of Manitoba undergraduates, Canada
	SDO Scale	.07	0.14	Altemeyer (1998)	354 University of Manitoba undergraduates, Canada (same sample)

Psychological variable	Political variable	Pearson's r	Cohen's d	Source	Sample characteristic
Collective self-esteem	RWA Scale	.04	0.08	Altemeyer (1998)	354 University of Manitoba undergraduates, Canada (same sample)
	SDO Scale	−.08	0.16	Altemeyer (1998)	354 University of Manitoba undergraduates, Canada (same sample)
Mean effect size		−.07**	−0.14		Total (unique) $N = 1,558$
Weighted mean effect size		−.09***	−0.17		
95% confidence interval		−.04, −.13			

Note: C-Scale = Conservatism Scale; SDO = Social Dominance Orientation; RWA = Right-Wing Authoritarianism.

[a] When multiple tests were computed on the same sample, the sample was counted only once in the calculation of total (unique) N; mean effect sizes (weighted and nonweighted), and overall significance levels. Multiple effect sizes drawn from the same sample were averaged prior to inclusion in calculations of overall average effect sizes.

* $p < .10$. ** $p < .01$. *** $p < .001$. (All tests two-tailed, converted when necessary.)

are punitive toward societally sanctioned scapegoats because of underlying fear and hostility. As Altemeyer (1998, p. 52) argued:

> First, High RWAs are scared. They see the world as a dangerous place, as society teeters on the brink of self-destruction from evil and violence. This fear appears to *instigate* aggression in them. Second, right-wing authoritarians tend to be highly self-righteous. They think themselves much more moral and upstanding than others—a self-perception considerably aided by self-deception, their religious training, and some very efficient guilt evaporators (such as going to confession). This self-righteousness *disinhibits* their aggressive impulses and releases them to act out their fear-induced hostilities.

Consistent with the notion that conservatives perceive the world as generally threatening, Altemeyer (1998) reported a relatively strong correlation of .49 between the perception of a dangerous world and RWA in a sample of 354 students from the University of Manitoba, Canada. Duckitt (2001) replicated this finding with several samples in New Zealand and South Africa, and he has also obtained weaker (but still significant) correlations between the perception of a dangerous world and SDO. To the extent that conservatives are more generally fearful than others, one might expect that they would also exhibit higher levels of neuroticism, but this does not generally seem to be the case (see Table 8). However, an inventive research program on the dream lives of liberals and conservatives in the United States found that Republicans reported three times as many nightmares as did Democrats (Bulkeley, 2001). This work, although speculative, suggests that fear, danger, threat, and aggression may figure more prominently in the unconscious motivations of conservatives than liberals.

A clever pair of experimental studies conducted by Lavine, Polichak, and Lodge (1999) supports the utility of a motivated social-cognitive perspective on political conservatism. Hypothesizing that right-wing authoritarians would be chronically sensitive to fear-related stimuli, these researchers used response latency measures to gauge high and low authoritarians' automatic vigilance for words that were pretested to be either high or low in threat and danger. In the first study, Lavine and colleagues found that, compared with low authoritarians, high authoritarians responded faster in a lexical decision task to nonpolitical but threatening stimuli (e.g., cancer, snake, mugger) but not to nonthreatening stimuli (e.g., telescope, tree, canteen). In a second study, research participants were primed with words that could be interpreted as threat-related or not (e.g., *arms*) and then exposed to target words that either completed (*weapons*) or failed to complete (*legs*) the threatening prime–target association. Results indicated that high authoritarians responded marginally more quickly than low authoritarians to threatening word pairs but not to nonthreatening word pairs (see Table 8). If, as it seems, conservatives are more susceptible to fear, it may help to explain why military defense spending and support for national security receive much stronger backing from conservative than liberal political leaders in the United States and elsewhere. Overall, our review of research conducted in five different countries and involving 22 tests of

Table 8 Correlations between fear of threat or loss and political conservatism

Psychological variable	Political variable	Pearson's r	Cohen's d	Source	Sample characteristic
Feeling that life is changing for the worse	C-Scale	.22***	0.45	Nias (1973)	214 adults, England
Neuroticism	C-Scale	.08	0.16	Nias (1973)	214 adults, England (same sample)
		.03	0.06	Wilson (1973d)	97 student teachers aged 18–34, England
	SDO Scale	−.02	−0.04	Pratto et al. (1994), Sample 7	224 Stanford University undergraduates
		.13	0.26	Pratto et al. (1994), Sample 9	97 San Jose State University undergraduates
		−.08	−0.16	Pratto et al. (1994), Sample 11	100 Stanford University undergraduates
		.21**	0.43	Pratto et al. (1994), Sample 12	139 Stanford University undergraduates
	Economic System Justification Scale	−.02	−0.04	Jost & Thompson (2000)	395 University of Maryland undergraduates
	RWA Scale	.15**	0.30	Peterson et al. (1997), Sample 1	198 University of New Hampshire undergraduates
		−.09	−0.18	Peterson et al. (1997), Sample 2	157 parents of University of New Hampshire undergraduates
		.20*	0.41	Peterson & Lane (2001)	69 University of New Hampshire senior undergraduates
Perception of a dangerous world	RWA Scale	.49,****	1.12	Altemeyer (1998)	354 University of Manitoba undergraduates, Canada
		.45****	1.01	Duckitt (2001), Sample 2	484 Auckland University students, New Zealand
		.54****	1.28	Duckitt (2001), Sample 3	381 Auckland University students, New Zealand
		.45****	1.01	Duckitt (2001), Sample 4	233 White Afrikaans students, South Africa
	SDO Scale	.00	0.00	Altemeyer (1998)	354 University of Manitoba undergraduates, Canada
		.15****	0.30	Duckitt (2001), Sample 2	484 Auckland University students, New Zealand
		.21****	0.43	Duckitt (2001), Sample 3	381 Auckland University students, New Zealand
		.29****	0.61	Duckitt (2001), Sample 4	233 White Afrikaans students, South Africa

(continued)

Table 8 Correlations between fear of threat or loss and political conservatism (continued)

Psychological variable	Political variable	Pearson's r	Cohen's d	Source	Sample characteristic
Response latency to danger-related words	RWA Scale	.26**[a]	0.54	Lavine, Polichak, & Lodge (1999), Sample 1	94 State University of New York at Stony Brook undergraduates
Primed response facilitation to threat-related words	RWA Scale	.17*[b]	0.35	Lavine, Polichak, & Lodge (1999), Sample 2	91 State University of New York at Stony Brook undergraduates
Persuasive impact of threatening messages	RWA Scale	.30**[c]	0.63	Lavine, Burgess, et al. (1999)	44 voting-eligible undergraduates, University of Minnesota
Mean effect size		.16****	0.33		Total (unique) N[d] = 3,371
Weighted mean effect size		.18****	0.38		
95% confidence interval		.15, .22			

Note. C-Scale = Conservatism Scale; SDO = Social Dominance Orientation; RWA = Right-Wing Authoritarianism.
[a] Pearson's r was derived from the originally reported t statistic, $t(56) = 1.98$, $p < .05$. Degrees of freedom are discrepant from the sample size reported in the table because the t test involved a tertile split of the sample. [b] Pearson's r was derived from the originally reported t statistic, $t(52) = 1.28$, $p < .10$. Degrees of freedom are discrepant from the sample size reported in the table because the t test involved a tertile split of the sample. [c] Pearson's r was derived from the originally reported t statistic, $t(42) = 2.03$, $p < .05$. [d] When multiple tests were computed on the same sample, the sample was counted only once in the calculation of total (unique) N mean effect sizes (weighted and nonweighted), and overall significance levels. Multiple effect sizes drawn from the same sample were averaged prior to inclusion in calculations of overall average effect sizes.
* $p < .10$. ** $p < .05$. *** $p < .01$. **** $p < .001$. (All tests two-tailed, converted when necessary.)

the hypothesis suggests that fear and threat are indeed related to political conservatism (weighted mean $r = .18$, $p < .0001$). The correlation is substantially higher if one omits the studies in which neuroticism was used as the measure of fear and threat (weighted mean $r = .30$, $p < .0001$).

Pessimism, disgust, and contempt

George F. Will (1998) joked that his "gloomy temperament received its conservative warp from early and prolonged exposure to the Chicago Cubs" (p. 21), a baseball team that has not won the pennant since 1945. Pessimism, he argued, is an essential characteristic of the conservative temperament: "Conservatives know the world is a dark and forbidding place where most new knowledge is false, most improvements are for the worse" (Will, 1998, p. 21). Psychologists, too, have pondered differences between the left and right in terms of optimism–pessimism and other affective dimensions.

Tomkins (1963, 1965, 1987, 1995), for instance, proposed that left-wingers and right-wingers would resonate with different emotional experiences and that right-wingers would gravitate toward fear, anger, pessimism, disgust, and contempt. Consistent with Tomkins's theory, a study of political imagination conducted by Carlson and Brincka (1987) demonstrated that people projected different emotions onto Republican and Democratic political candidates. Specifically, people associated conservative leaders with expressions of anger, contempt, and excitement, and they associated liberal leaders with shame, distress, and joy. However, these findings may have had more to do with political stereotypes than with actual affective differences between liberals and conservatives.

In a study of emotional reactions to welfare recipients, Williams (1984) found that people who were classified as conservatives on the basis of scores on Tomkins's (1964/1988) Polarity Scale expressed greater disgust and less sympathy than did their liberal counterparts. A study of high school students also indicated that political conservatives were less likely than liberals to describe themselves as "sympathetic," and conservative boys (but not girls) were less likely to describe themselves as "loving," "tender," and "mellow" (Eisenberg-Berg & Mussen, 1980). In general, however, affective differences between the left and right are understudied relative to cognitive differences.

To explain hypothesized or observed correlations between political conservatism and fear, anger, and other negative emotions, psychologists have typically (or stereotypically) pointed the finger at parenting styles and practices. The argument that parental punitiveness produces children who grow up to hold right-wing attitudes is an assumption that is shared by theories of authoritarianism (Adorno et al., 1950; Altemeyer, 1988), ideo-affective polarity (Tomkins, 1963, 1965, 1995), uncertainty avoidance (Wilson 1973b), and regulatory focus (Rohan & Zanna, 1998). Good research linking parental behavior to the political attitudes of their children is scant and insufficient (but see Peterson, Smirles, & Wentworth, 1997) for the obvious reason that it would require 20 or 30 years of continuous snooping to do it comprehensively. There are clear methodological shortcomings associated with retrospective self-report techniques and reliance on childhood memories, and even under the best of circumstances, there are limitations to drawing causal conclusions on the basis of correlational evidence. Nevertheless, Altemeyer (1988) reported weak positive correlations between individuals' recall of parental anger and punishment strategies, on the one hand, and current RWA scores, on the other. Altemeyer (1998) found that correlations between parents' RWA scores and those of their children are more substantial, hovering around .40, with neither parent being more influential than the other (p. 85).

In an elaboration of Higgins's regulatory focus theory, Rohan and Zanna (1998) argued that right-wing parents are more likely to be demanding and punitive in stressing instrumental concerns to have good manners and to be neat and clean, whereas egalitarian parents are more likely to use warmth in stressing values relating to being considerate of others. These differences in parenting styles may help to explain why right-wing parents are apparently less close to their children in comparison with more egalitarian parents (Rohan & Zanna, 1998; Sidanius & Ekehammar, 1979). Regulatory focus theorists argue that conservatives prioritize conformity, tradition, and security and that they are likely to be driven by ought guides (Rohan & Zanna, 1998) and the desire to prevent negative outcomes (Crowe & Higgins, 1997). It is noteworthy that ought discrepancies (i.e., prevention-focus failures) have been related to anxiety and resentment anger (Strauman & Higgins, 1988), and these are largely the same emotional states that have been associated with political conservatism in other research programs (e.g., Altemeyer, 1998; Carlson & Levy, 1970; Sales, 1972, 1973; Tomkins, 1963, 1965). Nevertheless, more research is needed before concluding that (a) political conservatives are more pessimistic or contemptuous than others, and (b) their negative emotions stem from experiences with parental aggression.

Fear and prevention of loss

The notion that political conservatives would be more sensitive than others to the threat of loss is inherent in theories of authoritarianism (e.g., Adorno et al., 1950; Altemeyer, 1998) and fear of uncertainty (Wilson, 1973b), and it is highly consistent with regulatory focus theory as well (e.g., Crowe & Higgins, 1997; Liberman et al., 1999). To the extent that conservatives are especially sensitive to the possibilities of loss—one reason why they wish to preserve the status quo—it follows that they should be generally more motivated by negatively framed outcomes (potential losses) than by positively framed outcomes (potential gains). This is consistent also with Tomkins's (1963, 1965, 1987, 1995) theory of ideo-affective polarity insofar as pessimism is characteristic of right-wing personalities and optimism is characteristic of left-wing personalities.

At least one study indicates that authoritarians are indeed more responsive to threatening or negatively framed persuasive messages than to positively framed messages. Five days before the 1996 U.S. presidential election, Lavine et al. (1999) presented high and low authoritarians—as classified on the basis of a short form of Altemeyer's (1998) RWA Scale—with persuasive arguments that stressed either the potential rewards of voting (e.g., "a way to express and live in accordance with important values") or the potential costs of not voting (e.g., "not voting allows others to take away your right to express your values"). This team of researchers found that high authoritarians were moved significantly more by threatening messages than by reward messages, whereas low authoritarians were marginally more influenced by the reward message than the threat message. Furthermore, these persuasive effects were found to carry over into behavioral intentions and actual voting behaviors.

Research on regulatory focus theory suggests that framing events in terms of potential losses rather than gains leads people to adopt cognitively conservative, as opposed to innovative, orientations (Crowe & Higgins, 1997; Liberman et al., 1999). For instance, Crowe and Higgins (1997) used framing manipulations (by stressing losses rather than gains) to evoke a prevention (vs. promotion) focus, which was found to be associated with relatively low cognitive complexity, high mental rigidity, a narrowing of decision-making alternatives, and conservative and repetitive response styles, as well as with inabilities to complete multifaceted tasks and to rebound from failure. Liberman et al. (1999) found that individuals in a prevention focus, whether assessed as an individual-difference dimension or induced situationally through framing manipulations, were less inclined to switch to a new, substitute task and more likely to return to an old, interrupted task. Furthermore, individuals in a prevention focus, but not those in a promotion focus, exhibited the "endowment effect," which captures the reluctance to exchange previously acquired objects for others of equal or better value. In general, research indicates that a prevention orientation, which focuses on potential threats and losses, does facilitate cognitive conservatism, but the extension to politically conservative attitudinal contents has yet to be demonstrated conclusively. Future research would do well to address this lacuna.

Fear of death

A relatively straightforward implication of theories of uncertainty avoidance (Wilson, 1973b) and especially theories of terror management (Greenberg et al., 1990, 1992) is that the salience of one's own mortality should increase ideological defensiveness in general and perhaps ideological conservatism in particular. High-profile terrorist attacks such as those of September 11, 2001, might simultaneously increase the cognitive accessibility of death and the appeal of political conservatism. Consistent with this notion is the correlation of .54 between scores on a Fear of Death Scale and scores on the C-Scale obtained by Wilson (1973d; see Table 9). The most thorough, programmatic research to assess the effects of mortality salience on social and political attitudes has been carried out by Greenberg, Pyszczynski, Solomon, and their associates. By leading experimental research participants to anticipate the cognitive and affective experience of death (e.g., Rosenblatt et al., 1989), they have demonstrated that mortality salience leads people to defend culturally valued norms and practices to a stronger degree (Greenberg et al., 1990, 1995) and to distance themselves from, and even to derogate, out-group members

Table 9 Correlations between mortality salience and political conservatism

Psychological variable	Political variable	Pearson's r	Cohen's d	Source	Sample characteristic
Fear of death	General Conservatism Scale	.54***	1.28	Nash (1972, cited in Wilson, 1973d)	74 California State University undergraduates
Mortality salience	Bond-setting for prostitutes	.44*[a]	0.97	Rosenblatt et al. (1989), Sample 1	22 municipal court judges, USA
		.40**[b]	0.87	Rosenblatt et al. (1989), Sample 2	78 undergraduates, USA
		.65***[c]	1.71	Rosenblatt et al. (1989), Sample 3	32 undergraduates, USA
		.77***[d]	2.41	Rosenblatt et al. (1989), Sample 4	83 undergraduates, USA
		.45*[e]	1.01	Rosenblatt et al. (1989), Sample 5	36 undergraduates, USA
		.56**[f]	1.35	Rosenblatt et al. (1989), Sample 6	34 undergraduates, USA
	Severity of punishment for criminals	.23*[g]	0.46	Florian et al. (2001)	120 undergraduates from Bar-Ilan University, Israel
Mean effect size		.52***	1.26		Total (unique) $N = 479$
Weighted mean effect size		.50***	1.20		
95% confidence interval		.43, .57			

Note: [a] Pearson's r was derived from the originally reported F statistic, $F(1, 20) = 4.70, p < .05$. [b] Pearson's r was derived from the originally reported F statistic, $F(1, 47) = 8.77, p < .003$. [c] Pearson's r was derived from the originally reported F statistic, $F(1, 31) = 23.12, p < .0001$. [d] Pearson's r was derived from the originally reported F statistic, $F(1, 79) = 116.54, p < .0001$. [e] Pearson's r was derived from the originally reported t statistic, $t(34) = 2.94, p < .01$. [f] Pearson's r was derived from the originally reported F statistic, $F(1, 32) = 14.98, p < .0005$. [g] Pearson's r was derived from the originally reported F statistic, $F(1, 116) = 6.23, p < .05$.
* $p < .05$. ** $p < .01$. *** $p < .001$. (All tests two-tailed, converted when necessary.)

to a greater extent (Harmon-Jones, Greenberg, Solomon, & Simon, 1996; McGregor et al., 2001). In addition, the fear of death has been linked to system-justifying forms of stereotyping and enhanced liking for stereotype-consistent women and minority group members (Schimel et al., 1999).

Mortality salience has also been shown to evoke greater punitiveness, and even aggression, toward those who violate cultural values. In one especially memorable study with relevance for political conservatism (Rosenblatt et al., 1989), municipal judges were found to set significantly higher bond assessments for prostitutes following a mortality salience manipulation (M = $455) as compared with a control condition (M = $50). Although much more research is needed on a wider set of political variables, it is conceivable that political conservatives' heightened affinities for tradition, law and order, and strict forms of parental and legal punishment (including the death penalty) are partially related to feelings of fear and threat, including fear and threat arising from chronic (or situational) mortality salience. Although we found only eight relatively clear-cut tests of the mortality salience–political conservatism hypothesis (see Table 9), and seven of these tests involved reactions to criminals, the mean-weighted effect size was very strong (r = .50, p < .0001).

In addition to a general main effect trend for mortality salience to lead people to embrace attitudes and behaviors that are generally associated with conservative and right-wing ideological positions (e.g., Adorno et al., 1950; Altemeyer, 1998; Peterson et al., 1993), there is some evidence in the terror management literature that political ideology and mortality salience interact with one another. A study by Greenberg et al. (1990, Study 2), for instance, found that mortality salience led high authoritarians to derogate someone who was dissimilar to them, but it did not have this effect on low authoritarians. In another study by Greenberg et al. (1992, Study 1), mortality salience enhanced political intolerance among conservatives, but it enhanced political tolerance among liberals, presumably because tolerance is an important attribute of the cultural worldview for the latter but not the former group. As with theories of epistemic motivation and regulatory focus, we argue that needs for terror management are broad enough to be satisfied by a wide variety of attitudinal contents (see also Dechesne et al., 2000), but there seems to be a better match between the contents of politically conservative attitudes and the general underlying motive than is the case with liberal or moderate attitudes.

Threat to the stability of the social system

Although most contemporary research on authoritarianism addresses individual differences in social and political attitudes, the notion that system-level threats (as well as threats to one's self-concept) increase authoritarianism is part of the original theory (e.g., Adorno et al., 1950; Fromm, 1941; Reich, 1946/1970; Sanford, 1966). For example, Reich (1946/1970, p. 13) observed that as the German economy fell precipitously between 1929 and 1932, the number of votes for the Nazi party rose from 800,000 to 17 million. History suggests that people do not always move to the political right under conditions of crisis; in the United States, the same economic depression resulted in a significant left-wing movement led by

Franklin D. Roosevelt. Nevertheless, the possibility remains that a threat to the stability of the social system, such as that felt in the aftermath of September 11, 2001, may increase right-wing conservatism, at least under certain circumstances.[11] This possibility is suggested by the theory of uncertainty avoidance (Wilson, 1973b) and by the theory of system justification, which hypothesizes that (a) there is an ideological motivation to defend the existing social system against instability, threat, and attack, and (b) this motivation is stronger among proponents of right-wing than of left-wing ideology (Jost et al., 2001).

There is by now substantial archival research suggesting that during times of societal crisis, people are more likely to turn to authoritarian leaders and institutions for security, stability, and structure (e.g., Doty, Peterson, & Winter, 1991; McCann, 1997; Peterson et al., 1993; Rickert, 1998; Sales, 1972, 1973). Sales (1972), for instance, found that during periods of severe economic threat (the depression years of 1930–1939), people were more likely to join authoritarian churches, such as Southern Baptist and Seventh Day Adventist, and less likely to join nonauthoritarian churches, such as Northern Baptist and Episcopalian, compared with periods of relative prosperity (1920–1930). Similarly, years of heavy unemployment in Seattle, Washington (1961, 1964, 1969, and 1970), were accompanied by higher than usual conversion rates there for an authoritarian church—Roman Catholic—and lower than usual conversion rates for a nonauthoritarian church—United Presbyterian—whereas relatively good economic years in Seattle (1962, 1965, and 1966) coincided with lower than usual conversion rates for the Roman Catholic Church and higher than usual conversion rates for the United Presbyterian Church.[12]

Sales (1973) reviewed disparate evidence in support of the general hypothesis that poor economic conditions in society are associated with social and cultural trends that emphasize authoritarian themes of power, toughness, cynicism, superstition, submission, and aggression. For instance, he provided evidence that literary and popular culture themes during the 1930s were significantly more conservative and authoritarian than during the 1920s. He also found that budgets in Pittsburgh, Pennsylvania, and New York City allocated more money to their police departments relative to their fire departments in the 1930s than in the 1920s despite the fact that crime fell during this time period. Doty et al. (1991) failed to replicate these differences in budgetary priorities when comparing a different, high-threat period in the United States (1978–1982) with a low-threat period (1983–1987). However, when they investigated reelection bids for highly liberal and conservative incumbents in the U.S. House of Representatives, they found that conservatives lost 2.4 percentage points and liberals gained 7.8 percentage points from the high-threat to the low-threat period. This supported the threat-conservatism hypothesis (see Table 10).

McCann (1997) recruited history professors to rate all of the U.S. presidential election years between 1788 and 1992 on the degree to which the social, economic, and political circumstances of that period were "threatening to the American established order." Results indicated that during system-threatening times, presidential candidates who were rated as high on power motivation, forcefulness, and strength were elected by larger margins of victory than during nonthreatening

Table 10 Correlations between system instability and political conservatism

Psychological variable	Political variable	Pearson's r	Cohen's d	Source	Sample characteristic
Economic threat	Conversion to authoritarian churches	.49***[a]	1.12	Sales (1972)	6,887 adults joining four churches between 1920–1939, USA
	Conversion to nonauthoritarian churches	−.44**[a,b]	−0.98	Sales (1972)	3,601 adults joining four churches between 1920–1939, USA
	City budget for police vs. fire departments	.51*[c]	1.19	Sales (1973), Study 1	Annual Pittsburgh city budget for 20 years (1920–1939)
		.77***[d]	2.41	Sales (1973), Study 1	Annual New York city budget for 20 years (1920–1939)
Societal threat (late 1960s)	City budget for police vs. fire departments	.92***[e]	4.69	Sales (1973), Study 2	State and local budget expenditures (1967–1969 vs. 1959–1964), USA
		.78*[f]	2.49	Sales (1973), Study 2	City government expenditures (1967–1969 vs. 1959–1964), USA
	Victory margins for conservative vs. liberal incumbents	.29*[g]	0.61	Doty et al. (1991)[h]	60 incumbent candidates, House of Representatives, USA
Social, economic, and political threat	Power, forcefulness, and strength of winning presidential candidate	.40*[i]	0.87	McCann (1997)	33 winning presidential candidates (1824–1964), USA
	Presidential strength—conservatism	.49**[j]	1.12	McCann (1997)	33 winning presidential candidates (1824–1964), USA (same sample)
Mean effect size		.64***	1.81		Total (unique) N[k] = 10,639 (approximate, includes people and years)
Weighted mean effect size		.47***	1.08		
95% confidence interval		.46, .49			

Note. [a] Correlations are unweighted means aggregated across several different churches. [b] The sign on this correlation has been reversed in the calculation of mean effect sizes so that it is theoretically meaningful. Positive correlations reflect a positive relation between threat and conservatism. [c] Pearson's r was derived from the originally reported F statistic, $F(1, 18) = 6.18, p < .05$. [d] Pearson's r was derived from the originally reported F statistic, $F(1, 18) = 26.47, p < .001$. [e] Pearson's r was derived from the originally reported F statistic, $F(1, 7) = 37.17, p < .001$. [f] Pearson's r was derived from the originally reported F statistic, $F(1, 7) = 10.64, p < .025$. [g] Pearson's r was derived from the originally reported t statistic, $t(58) = 2.33, p < .05$. [h] Doty et al. (1991) also attempted to replicate Sales's (1973) analyses regarding police and fire department budgets, but reported only that there was no trend with a categorical analysis (without providing significance levels). They did, however, report a −.72 year-by-year correlation with their threat index, but express concerns about the validity of such an analytic approach. [i] Pearson's r was derived from the originally reported F statistic, $F(1, 29) = 5.66, p < .05$. [j] Pearson's r was derived from the originally reported F statistic, $F(1, 29) = 9.13, p < .01$. [k] When multiple tests were computed on the same sample, the sample was counted only once in the calculation of total (unique) N mean effect sizes (weighted and nonweighted), and overall significance levels. Multiple effect sizes drawn from the same sample were averaged prior to inclusion in calculations of overall average effect sizes.
* $p < .05$. ** $p < .01$. *** $p < .001$. (All tests two-tailed, converted when necessary.)

times. For nine tests of the hypothesis, all conducted with data from the United States but from different historical time periods, we found reasonably strong support for the notion that threats to the stability of the social system increase politically conservative choices, decisions, and judgments (weighted mean $r = .47$, $p < .0001$). As Huntington (1957) wrote, "When the foundations of society are threatened, the conservative ideology reminds men of the necessity of some institutions and desirability of the existing ones" (pp. 460–461).

Summary

Our review of the evidence indicates that there is consistent and relatively strong support for the general hypothesis that a specific set of social-cognitive motives are significantly related to political conservatism. Almost all of our specific hypotheses were corroborated. Effect sizes with absolute values of weighted mean rs ranging from .18 to .27 were obtained for variables of uncertainty avoidance; integrative complexity; needs for order, structure, and closure; and fear of threat in general. Stronger effect sizes were observed for dogmatism, intolerance of ambiguity, openness to experience, mortality salience, and system instability (with weighted mean rs ranging from .32 to .50). On the basis of this evidence, we conclude that a set of interrelated epistemic, existential, and ideological motives successfully predict the holding of politically conservative attitudes. As illustrated in Figure 1, how people

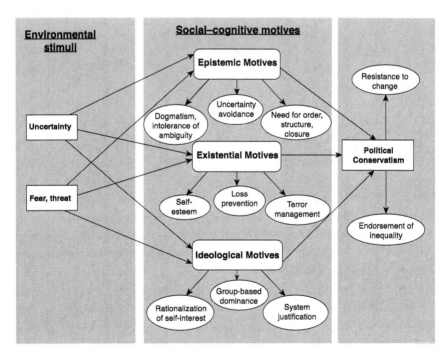

Figure 1 An integrative model of political conservatism as motivated social cognition.

respond to threatening environmental stimuli, such as fear and uncertainty, plays a significant role in the development and expression of political beliefs concerning resistance to change, inequality, and other core aspects of conservative ideology.

Concluding remarks

We have argued that several specific motives relating to the management of fear and uncertainty are associated with the ideology of political conservatism. Our analysis in terms of motivated social cognition helps both to integrate seemingly unrelated hypotheses derived from the literature on personality and individual differences and social psychology and to expand on these hypotheses to further understand the role of situational factors in the vicissitudes of conservatism. By reviewing the results from many different studies aggregated across various behavioral domains and contexts, we found that a moderate to strong relationship does exist between an interrelated set of epistemic, existential, and ideological motives and the expression of political conservatism. In concluding, we consider issues that are deserving of future empirical attention and summarize what we have learned by viewing political conservatism through a motivated social-cognitive lens.

A plea for future research

One of the most promising implications of treating political conservatism as a specific manifestation of motivated social cognition is a theoretical and practical focus on situational determinants. This is because explanations in social cognition tend to emphasize the temporary accessibility of certain attitudes, beliefs, goals, and motives and their perceived applicability to the immediate situation (e.g., Bargh & Gollwitzer, 1994; Higgins, 1996; Kruglanski, 1989). We have reviewed existing evidence concerning the effects of situationally induced threats on conservative political outcomes, but much more of interest remains to be done. Our hope is that, by underscoring the cognitive–motivational bases of political conservatism, future research will at long last address a wider range of social situations and conditions that give rise and momentum to conservative attitudes, thoughts, behaviors, and even social movements.

Although the evidence concerning the effects of threat on conservative ideology is highly instructive, other situational predictors of conservative attitudes and responses are still relatively understudied in the psychology of conservatism. Because conservatism often takes the form of a social movement that is shared by large groups of people in particular historical periods (e.g., Diamond, 1995; Habermas, 1989; Kolko, 1963; Lyons & Berlet, 1996), it may be thought of as a social norm that emerges under certain social and political circumstances. Our review indicates that too many psychological accounts of conservatism in the past have treated it solely as a dispositional orientation and not as a situational reaction, although it is true that the disposition is often hypothesized to develop in response to certain social and family situations in childhood (e.g., Adorno et al., 1950; Altemeyer, 1981, 1988; Sears, 1983; Sulloway, 1996; Tomkins, 1995). For the sake of understanding the nature of ideology, we hope future studies are as successful at documenting the temporary accessibility of right-wing attitudes as studies of individual differences have been at documenting the chronic accessibility of such orientations and their correlates.

Consistent with these goals, we note that there is a strong need to go beyond purely correlational research designs, which limited the validity of the earlier personality research on authoritarianism, dogmatism, and the origins of political ideology and contributed to its eventual obscurity (see W. F. Stone et al., 1993). Thus far, the strongest experimental evidence bearing on the possibility of manipulating conservative tendencies probably comes from the mortality salience paradigm used by terror management theorists. Priming thoughts of death has been shown to increase intolerance, out-group derogation, punitive aggression, veneration of authority figures, and system justification (Florian et al., 2001; Greenberg et al., 1990, 1995; McGregor et al., 2001; Rosenblatt et al., 1989; Schimel et al., 1999; van den Bos & Miedema, 2000). Other archival and experimental evidence suggests that social and economic threats increase authoritarian and right-wing responding (e.g., Doty et al., 1991; Jost, 1996; McCann, 1997; Reich, 1946/1970; Sales, 1972, 1973; Sales & Friend, 1973). Experimental paradigms developed in studies of the need for cognitive closure, prevention versus promotion regulatory focus, and system justification are also highly promising candidates for use in future research on situational variation in conservatism. The next generation of researchers should also strive, whenever possible, to include more direct measures of epistemic, existential, and ideological motives.

All of the motives we have reviewed are theoretically related to one or both of two core dimensions of conservative thought, namely, resistance to change and support for inequality. The quest for certainty and ideological stability, we have argued, is linked to the goal of resisting social and political change (e.g., Wilson, 1973c). Motives pertaining to fear and threat, by comparison, are more likely to be associated with ideological support for inequality, insofar as it justifies the striving for security and dominance in social hierarchies (e.g., Sidanius & Pratto, 1999). These are theoretical points that await direct empirical confrontation, especially as regards the direction of causality. Do psychological motives cause the adoption of specific ideological beliefs concerning resistance to change and support for inequality, or do these ideological commitments carry with them psychological consequences, or both? Our review has presented consistent correlational evidence linking the psychological and the political, and our integrated theoretical framework has identified plausible interpretations of these data, but direct causal investigations are needed in the future to substantiate the particulars of our theoretical perspective.

Finally, it is also important that subsequent research reflect a wide range of political ideologies and broadly representative samples so that it does not merely address the ideological life of college students (see Sears, 1986; Whitley & Lee, 2000). On one hand, political ideology probably has greater consistency and meaning for college-educated respondents; on the other, the ideological contents of political conservatism (and its opposites) may be different in a predominantly liberal environment such as a college campus compared with other contexts. Such locations may prove useful in future studies of social and cognitive motives associated with political liberalism, which we would also encourage. Although we have made a special effort to include nonstudent samples in our review, two-thirds of the studies we reviewed were conducted with university students. The use of nonrepresentative samples stymied research progress on the authoritarian personality for many years (e.g., Hyman & Sheatsley, 1954) until it was revived by Altemeyer (1981, 1988, 1996, 1998). It is essential that contemporary researchers of political conservatism do not make the same mistake.

The trend to investigate ideological opinions and right-wing tendencies in a wide variety of national contexts is one that we hope continues (e.g., Fay & Frese, 2000; Fibert & Ressler, 1998; Golec, 2001; Hamilton, Sanders, & McKearney, 1995; Jost et al., 2001; Kemmelmeier, 1997; Mercer & Cairns, 1981; Sidanius, 1984, 1985; Sidanius & Ekehammar, 1979). We reviewed research conducted in 12 different countries: the United States, Canada, England, Scotland, Sweden, Italy, Germany, Poland, Israel, Australia, New Zealand, and South Africa. Thus, the conclusions we have reached possess a considerable degree of cultural generalizability. Nevertheless, future research—especially if conducted in traditionally socialist or communist societies in which adherence to the status quo is unconfounded with right-wing ideological orientation—would add significantly to knowledge about political conservatism as motivated social cognition. Our conviction is that important and groundbreaking advances await any researcher who is willing and able to conduct causal, experimental studies on the personal and situational determinants of conservative ideological responses in research samples that are representative and culturally diverse. We hope this chapter serves as a stimulus for renewed, methodologically sophisticated attention to the psychological bases of political conservatism.

What have we learned?

Understanding the psychological underpinnings of conservatism has for centuries posed a challenge for historians, philosophers, and social scientists. By now, hundreds of empirical investigations have been carried out worldwide, and at least three types of theories have been offered to explicate the psychological bases of conservative and right-wing ideologies. Our contribution here has been to review and summarize this work and to integrate it within the ambitious and broad framework of motivated social cognition (see Figure 1). In doing so, we have drawn a number of conclusions, which should be made explicit in order to better understand the various ways in which political conservatism may be thought of as a form of motivated social cognition.

An important conclusion that follows from our analysis is that political attitudes and beliefs possess a strong motivational basis (e.g., Duckitt, 2001; Dunning, 1999; Fiske & Taylor, 1991; Kruglanski, 1996; Kunda, 1990). Conservative ideologies, like virtually all other belief systems, are adopted in part because they satisfy various psychological needs. To say that ideological belief systems have a strong motivational basis is not to say that they are unprincipled, unwarranted, or unresponsive to reason or evidence. Although the (partial) causes of ideological beliefs may be motivational, the reasons (and rationalizations) whereby individuals justify those beliefs to themselves and others are assessed according to informational criteria (Kruglanski, 1989, 1999).

Many different theoretical accounts of conservatism over the past 50 years have stressed motivational underpinnings, but they have identified different needs as critical. Our review brings these diverse accounts together for the first time. Variables significantly associated with conservatism, we now know, include fear and aggression (Adorno et al., 1950; Altemeyer, 1998; Lavine et al., 1999), dogmatism and intolerance of ambiguity (Fibert & Ressler, 1998; Frenkel-Brunswik, 1948; Rokeach, 1960; Sidanius, 1978), uncertainty avoidance (McGregor et al., 2001; Sorrentino & Roney, 1986; Wilson, 1973b), need for cognitive closure (Golec, 2001; Jost et al., 1999; Kemmelmeier, 1997; Kruglanski & Webster, 1996), personal need for structure (Altemeyer, 1998; Schaller et al., 1995; Smith & Gordon, 1998), terror management (Dechesne et al., 2000; Greenberg et al., 1990, 1992; Wilson, 1973d), group-based dominance (Pratto et al., 1994; Sidanius, 1993; Sidanius & Pratto, 1999), and system justification (Jost & Banaji, 1994; Jost et al., 2001; Jost & Thompson, 2000). From our perspective, these psychological factors are capable of contributing to the adoption of conservative ideological contents, either independently or in combination.

The socially constructed nature of human belief systems (see Jost & Kruglanski, 2002) makes it unlikely that a complete explanation of conservative ideology could ever be provided in terms of a single motivational syndrome. Ideologies, like other social representations, may be thought of as possessing a core and a periphery (Abric, 2001), and each may be fueled by separate motivational concerns. The most that can be expected of a general psychological analysis is for it to partially explain the core of political conservatism because the peripheral aspects are by definition highly protean and driven by historically changing, local contexts.

We regard political conservatism as an ideological belief system that is significantly (but not completely) related to motivational concerns having to do with the psychological management of uncertainty and fear. Specifically, the avoidance of uncertainty (and the striving for certainty) may be particularly tied to one core dimension of conservative thought, resistance to change (Wilson, 1973c). Similarly, concerns with fear and threat may be linked to the second core dimension of conservatism, endorsement of inequality (Sidanius & Pratto, 1999). Although resistance to change and support for inequality are conceptually distinguishable, we have argued that they are psychologically interrelated, in part because motives pertaining to uncertainty and threat are interrelated (e.g., Dechesne et al., 2000; McGregor et al., 2001; van den Bos & Miedema, 2000).

In conclusion, our comprehensive review integrates several decades of research having to do with the psychological bases of political conservatism. Most of what is known about the psychology of conservatism fits exceedingly well with theories of motivated social cognition. The integrative framework developed here has implications for resolving historically controversial issues, and we have argued that it has great generative potential for guiding future work on the subject of conservatism. By attending to the multiple, potentially reinforcing influences of epistemic, existential, and ideological motivations involved in political conservatism, we hope that future research strengthens understanding of belief systems in general. It should also shed light on the nature of relations between the micro and the macro, that is, on the reciprocal dynamics between the needs of individual and group actors on one hand and the complex characteristics of social and political systems, institutions, and organizations on the other.

Notes

1 Rokeach (1960) advanced a similar argument concerning the match between cognitive structure and ideological content:

> We thus see in the case of fascism that ideological content and structure support each other. There is no incompatibility between them and thus psychological conflict is not engendered or guilt feelings aroused. For this reason, authoritarian ideological structures may be psychologically more reconcilable—more easily "attachable"—to ideologies that are antidemocratic than to those that are democratic in content. If a person's underlying motivations are served by forming a closed belief system, then it is more than likely that his motivations can also be served by embracing an ideology that is blatantly anti-equalitarian. If this is so, it would account for the somewhat greater affinity we have observed between authoritarian belief structure and conservatism than between the same belief structure and liberalism. (p. 127)

2 Social scientists have debated for years whether political ideology exists at all as a coherent, internally consistent system of beliefs in the minds of individuals (e.g., Converse, 1964; Judd, Krosnick, & Milburn, 1981; Kerlinger, 1984; McGuire, 1985). Granting that ideologies—like other attitudes—possess a high degree of malleability, we argue that it is still worthwhile to consider the psychological characteristics of conservative thought. Specifically, we propose that one might distinguish between a relatively stable ideological core of conservatism comprised of resistance to change and acceptance of inequality (e.g., Giddens, 1998; Huntington, 1957; Mannheim, 1927/1986; Rossiter, 1968) and more ideologically peripheral issues (such as school busing or gun control) that are likely to vary considerably in their ideological relevance across time. Because the conservative core may be grounded in powerful and relatively stable individual needs, it may persist as a deep personality structure, the surface manifestations of which might change with the tides of social and political debate.

3 In the most recent edition of the *International Encyclopedia of the Social Sciences*, Muller's (2001) definition of conservatism similarly stresses resistance to change (as well as belief in the legitimacy of inequality). He observed: "For conservatives, the historical survival of an institution or practice—be it marriage, monarchy, or the market—creates a *prima facie* case that it has served some need" (p. 2625). That is, what conservatives share is a tendency to rationalize existing institutions, especially those that maintain hierarchical authority.

4 The clearest example seems to be Stalin, who secretly admired Hitler and identified with several right-wing causes (including anti-Semitism). In the Soviet context, Stalin was almost certainly to the right of his political rivals, most notably Trotsky. In terms of his psychological makeup as well, Stalin appears to have had much in common with right-wing extremists (see, e.g., Birt, 1993; Bullock, 1993; Robins & Post, 1997).

5 Our motivated social-cognitive perspective also recognizes that people might occasionally adopt conservative ideologies for reasons having little if anything to do

with either acceptance of change or support for inequality. For instance, they may be motivated by (conscious or unconscious) attempts to secure the approval of conservative parents, acceptance by conservative peers, or the trust of conservative superiors. In addition, people may be drawn (e.g., by perceived self-interest) to accept peripheral elements of a conservative ideology (e.g., related to such issues as racial integration, school busing, or taxation) and eventually accept other elements of the ideology because of their association with likeminded others who share their position on local issues and also endorse core conservative positions (related to resistance to change and acceptance of inequality).

6 As suggested by an anonymous reviewer, it is also possible that conservatives do not fear uncertainty per se but rather are especially concerned with minimizing future negative outcomes. In this sense, it may be that a pessimistic, risk-averse prevention orientation characterizes conservatives' thinking about uncertain outcomes, which may explain why they would, for example, adopt a worst case scenario perspective with regard to military foreign policy.

7 Although the attainment of certainty and defense against threat represent conceptually distinguishable concerns, there is a sense in which certainty is also served by inequality in the epistemic domain, namely by revering epistemic authorities (Ellis & Kruglanski, 1992), whose pronouncements may afford a quick sense of certainty.

8 On another occasion, President Bush informed a British reporter: "Look, my job isn't to try to nuance . . . My job is to tell people what I think" (Sanger, 2002).

9 In all cases, mean rs and weighted mean rs are based on Fisher's z conversions, following procedures recommended by Rosenthal (1991). Effect sizes have been weighted by $n - 3$, as recommended by Rosenthal (1991). Confidence intervals for weighted mean rs were calculated using the formula recommended by Cooper (1998, p. 140).

10 In a dissertation study conducted by Jost (1996), Yale University undergraduate students were randomly assigned to experimental conditions in which they were led to believe that alumni from their university were either more or less socioeconomically successful than alumni from a comparison school (see also Jost & Burgess, 2000). This manipulation was intended to evoke feelings of low social status rather than low self-esteem (and no measures of self-esteem were taken), but the findings were very similar to those obtained by Sales and Friend (1973). Jost (1996) found that Yale students who were assigned to the low socioeconomic success condition exhibited significantly higher scores on Altemeyer's (1981) RWA Scale than did students assigned to the high socioeconomic success condition, $r(133) = .17$, $p < .05$. That is, a situational manipulation of low perceived socioeconomic status was found to increase authoritarianism, and this effect was not attributable to differences in education or other variables.

11 In the aftermath of the attacks of September 11, 2001, the *New York Times* has reported significant increases in right-wing populism in the following countries, among others: Belgium, Holland, France, Switzerland, Norway, Denmark, and Portugal (Cowell, 2002; Gordon, 2002; Judt, 2002; Krugman, 2002). Conservative or right-wing parties were already on the rise in Italy, Austria, and the United States.

12 We see this research as generally supporting John Lennon's (1970) famous observation that "God is a concept by which we measure our pain" (track 10), insofar as people embrace different religious conceptions as a function of the degree of adversity and threat they experience.

References

References marked with an asterisk indicate studies included in the meta-analysis.

Abelson, R. P. (1995). Attitude extremity. In R. E. Petty & J. A. Krosnick (Eds.), *Attitude strength: Antecedents and consequences* (pp. 25–41). Mahwah, NJ: Erlbaum.

Abelson, R. P., & Prentice, D. A. (1989). Beliefs as possessions: A functional perspective. In A. R. Pratkanis, S. J. Breckler, & A. G. Greenwald (Eds.), *Attitude structure and function* (pp. 361–381). Hillsdale, NJ: Erlbaum.

Abric, J. C. (2001). A structural approach to social representations. In K. Deaux & G. Philogéne (Eds.), *Representations of the social* (pp. 42–47). Oxford: Blackwell.

Adorno, T. W., Frenkel-Brunswik, E., Levinson, D. J., & Sanford, R. N. (1950). *The authoritarian personality*. New York: Harper.

Alexander, I. E. (1995). Ideology as part of the Tomkins legacy. In E. V. Demos (Ed.), *Exploring affect: The selected writings of Silvan S. Tomkins* (pp. 101–167). Cambridge, England: Cambridge University Press.

Altemeyer, R. A. (1981). *Right-wing authoritarianism*. Winnipeg, Manitoba, Canada: University of Manitoba Press.

Altemeyer, R. A. (1988). *Enemies of freedom: Understanding right-wing authoritarianism*. San Francisco: Jossey-Bass.

Altemeyer, R. A. (1996). *The authoritarian specter*. Cambridge, MA: Harvard University Press.

*Altemeyer, R. A. (1998). The other "authoritarian personality." In M. P. Zanna (Ed.), *Advances in experimental social psychology* (Vol. 30, pp. 47–91). New York: Academic Press.

Anderson, B., Zelditch, M., Jr., Takagi, P., & Whiteside, D. (1965). On conservative attitudes. *Acta Sociologica, 8*, 189–203.

Arndt, J., Greenberg, J., Solomon, S., Pyszczynski, T., & Simon, L. (1997). Suppression, accessibility of death-related thoughts, and cultural world-view defense: Exploring the psychodynamics of worldview defense. *Journal of Personality and Social Psychology, 73*, 5–18.

Aronson, E., & Mills, J. (1959). The effect of severity of initiation on liking for a group. *Journal of Abnormal and Social Psychology, 59*, 177–181.

*Atieh, J. M., Brief, A. P., & Vollrath, D. A. (1987). The Protestant work ethic conservatism paradox: Beliefs and values in work and life. *Personality and Individual Differences, 8*, 577–580.

Bagley, C., Wilson, G. D., & Boshier, R. (1970). The Conservatism Scale: A factor structure comparison of English, Dutch, and New Zealand samples. *Journal of Social Psychology, 81*, 267–268.

Bahr, H. M., & Chadwick, B. A. (1974). Conservatism, racial intolerance, and attitudes toward racial assimilation among Whites and American Indians. *Journal of Social Psychology, 94*, 45–56.

Bargh, J. A., & Gollwitzer, P. M. (1994). Environmental control of goal-directed action: Automatic and strategic contingencies between situations and behavior. In W. Spaulding (Ed.), *Nebraska Symposium on Motivation: Vol. 41. Integrative views of motivation, cognition, and emotion* (pp. 71–124). Lincoln: University of Nebraska Press.

Barker, E. N. (1963). Authoritarianism of the political right, center, and left. *Journal of Social Issues, 19*, 63–74.

Becker, E. (1973). *The denial of death*. New York: Free Press.

Billig, M. (1984). Political ideology: Social psychological aspects. In H. Tajfel (Ed.), *The social dimension* (Vol. 2, pp. 446–470). Cambridge, England: Cambridge University Press.

Birt, R. (1993). Personality and foreign policy: The case of Stalin. *Political Psychology, 14*, 607–625.

Block, J., & Block, J. (1950). Intolerance of ambiguity and ethnocentrism. *Journal of Personality, 19*, 303–311.

Bobbio, N. (1996). *Left and right*. Cambridge, England: Polity Press.

*Boshier, R. (1969). The relationship between self-concept and conservatism. *Journal of Social Psychology, 33*, 139–141.

Brown, R. (1965). *Social psychology*. New York: Free Press.

Bruner, J. S. (1957). On perceptual readiness. *Psychological Review, 64*, 123–152.

Budner, S. (1962). Intolerance of ambiguity as a personality variable. *Journal of Personality, 30*, 29–59.

Bulkeley, K. (2001, July). *Dreams and politics*. Paper presented at the annual meeting of the Association for the Study of Dreams, Santa Cruz, CA.

Bullock, A. (1993). *Hitler and Stalin: Parallel lives*. New York: Vintage Books.

Cacioppo, J. T., & Petty, R. E. (1982). The need for cognition. *Journal of Personality and Social Psychology, 42*, 116–131.

Carlson, R., & Brincka, J. (1987). Studies in script theory: III. Ideology and political imagination. *Political Psychology, 8*, 563–574.

Carlson, R., & Levy, N. (1970). Self, values, and affects: Derivations from Tomkins' polarity theory. *Journal of Personality and Social Psychology, 16*, 338–345.

Carmines, E. G., & Berkman, M. (1994). Ethos, ideology, and partisanship: Exploring the paradox of conservative Democrats. *Political Behavior, 16*, 203–218.

Centers, R. (1949). *The psychology of social classes*. Princeton, NJ: Princeton University Press.

*Chirumbolo, A. (2002). The relationship between need for cognitive closure and political orientation: The mediating role of authoritarianism. *Personality and Individual Differences, 32*, 603–610.

Christie, R. (1954). Authoritarianism re-examined. In R. Christie & M. Jahoda (Eds.), *Studies in the scope and method of "The Authoritarian Personality"* (pp. 123–196). Glencoe, IL: Free Press.

Christie, R. (1956). Eysenck's treatment of the personality of communists. *Psychological Bulletin, 53*, 411–430.

Christie, R. (1991). Authoritarianism and related constructs. In J. P. Robinson, P. R. Shaver, & L. S. Wrightsman (Eds.), *Measures of personality and social psychological attitudes* (pp. 501–571). San Diego, CA: Academic Press.

Conover, P. J., & Feldman, S. (1981). The origins and meaning of liberal/conservative self-identification. *American Journal of Political Science, 25*, 617–645.

Converse, P. E. (1964). The nature of belief systems in mass publics. In D. Apter (Ed.), *Ideology and discontent*. New York: Free Press.

Cooper, H. (1998). *Synthesizing research* (3rd ed.). Thousand Oaks, CA: Sage.

Costa, P. T., & MacRae, R. R. (1985). *The NEO Personality Inventory Manual*. Odessa, FL: Psychological Assessment Resources.

Cowell, A. (2002, May 18). Europe "is rubbing its eyes" at the ascent of the right. *The New York Times*, p. A3.

Crowe, E., & Higgins, E. T. (1997). Regulatory focus and strategic inclinations: Promotion and prevention in decision-making. *Organizational Behavior and Human Decision Processes, 69*, 117–132.

Danigelis, N. L., & Cutler, S. J. (1991). Cohort trends in attitudes about law and order: Who's leading the conservative wave? *Public Opinion Quarterly, 55*, 24–49.

Dechesne, M., Janssen, J., & van Knippenberg, A. (2000). Derogation and distancing as terror management strategies: The moderating role of need for closure and permeability of group boundaries. *Journal of Personality and Social Psychology, 79*, 923–932.

de St. Aubin, E. (1996). Personal ideology polarity: Its emotional foundation and its manifestation in individual value systems, religiosity, political orientation, and assumptions concerning human nature. *Journal of Personality and Social Psychology, 71*, 152–165.

Diamond, S. (1995). *Roads to dominion: Right-wing movements and political power in the United States.* New York: Guilford Press.

Dittes, J. E. (1961). Impulsive closure as a reaction to failure-induced threat. *Journal of Abnormal and Social Psychology, 63,* 562–569.

Ditto, P. H., & Lopez, D. F. (1992). Motivated skepticism: Use of differential decision criteria for preferred and nonpreferred conclusions. *Journal of Personality and Social Psychology, 63,* 568–584.

*Doty, R. M., Peterson, B. E., & Winter, D. G. (1991). Threat and authoritarianism in the United States, 1978–1987. *Journal of Personality and Social Psychology, 61,* 629–640.

*Duckitt, J. (2001). A dual-process cognitive-motivational theory of ideology and prejudice. *Advances in Experimental Social Psychology, 33,* 41–113.

Dunning, D. (1999). A newer look: Motivated social cognition and the schematic representation of social concepts. *Psychological Inquiry, 10,* 1–11.

Durrheim, K. (1997). Theoretical conundrum: The politics and science of theorizing authoritarian cognition. *Political Psychology, 18,* 625–656.

Eagleton, T. (1991). *Ideology: An introduction.* New York: Verso.

Eckhardt, W. (1991). Authoritarianism. *Political Psychology, 12,* 97–121.

Eckhardt, W., & Alcock, N. Z. (1970). Ideology and personality in war/ peace attitudes. *Journal of Social Psychology, 81,* 105–116.

Eisenberg-Berg, N., & Mussen, P. (1980). Personality correlates of sociopolitical liberalism and conservatism in adolescents. *Journal of Genetic Psychology, 137,* 165–177.

Ellis, S., & Kruglanski, A. W. (1992). Self as epistemic authority: Effects on experiential and instructional learning. *Social Cognition, 10,* 357–375.

Elms, A. C. (1969). Psychological factors in right-wing extremism. In R. A. Schoenberger (Ed.), *The American right wing* (pp. 143–163). New York: Holt, Rinehart, & Winston.

Eysenck, H. J. (1954). *The psychology of politics.* London: Routledge & Kegan Paul.

Eysenck, H. J., & Wilson, G. D. (Eds.). (1978). *The psychological basis of ideology.* Lancaster, England: MTP Press.

*Fay, D., & Frese, M. (2000). Conservatives' approach to work: Less prepared for future work demands? *Journal of Applied Social Psychology, 30,* 171–195.

Feather, N. T. (1969). Preference for information in relation to consistency, novelty, intolerance of ambiguity and dogmatism. *Australian Journal of Psychology, 31,* 235–249.

*Feather, N. T. (1979). Value correlates of conservatism. *Journal of Personality and Social Psychology, 37,* 1617–1630.

*Feather, N. T. (1984). Protestant ethic, conservatism, and values. *Journal of Personality and Social Psychology, 46,* 1132–1141.

Fein, S., & Spencer, S. J. (1997). Prejudice as self-image maintenance: Affirming the self through negative evaluations of others. *Journal of Personality and Social Psychology, 73,* 31–44.

Festinger, L. (1957). *A theory of cognitive dissonance.* Evanston, IL: Row, Peterson.

*Fibert, Z., & Ressler, W. H. (1998). Intolerance of ambiguity and political orientation among Israeli university students. *Journal of Social Psychology, 138,* 33–40.

Fiske, S. T., & Taylor, S. E. (1991). *Social cognition* (2nd ed.). New York: McGraw Hill.

*Florian, V., Mikulincer, M., & Hirschberger, G. (2001). An existentialist view on mortality salience effects: Personal hardiness, death-thought accessibility, and cultural worldview defenses. *British Journal of Social Psychology, 40,* 437–453.

Frenkel-Brunswik, E. (1948). Tolerance toward ambiguity as a personality variable [Abstract]. *American Psychologist, 3,* 268.

Frenkel-Brunswik, E. (1949). Intolerance of ambiguity as an emotional perceptual personality variable. *Journal of Personality, 18,* 108–143.

Frenkel-Brunswik, E. (1951). Personality theory and perception. In R. Blake and G. Ramsey (Eds.), *Perception: An approach to personality* (pp. 356–419). New York: Oxford University Press.

Frey, D. (1986). Selective exposure to information: A review of recent research. In L. Berkowitz (Ed.), *Advances in experimental social psychology* (Vol. 19, pp. 41–80). New York: Academic Press.

Fromm, E. (1941). *Escape from freedom*. New York: Holt, Rinehart, & Winston.

Furnham, A., & Ribchester, T. (1995). Tolerance of ambiguity: A review of the concept, its measurement and applications. *Current Psychology: Developmental, Learning, Personality, Social, 14*, 179–200.

Giddens, A. (1998). *The third way: The renewal of social democracy*. Cambridge, England: Polity Press.

*Gillies, J., & Campbell, S. (1985). Conservatism and poetry preferences. *British Journal of Social Psychology, 24*, 223–227.

*Glasgow, M. R., & Cartier, A. M. (1985). Conservatism, sensation-seeking, and music preferences. *Personality and Individual Differences, 6*, 393–395.

*Golec, A. (2001, July). *Need for cognitive closure and political conservatism: Studies on the nature of the relationship*. Paper presented at the annual meeting of the International Society of Political Psychology, Cuernavaca, Mexico.

Gordon, P. H. (2002, April 23). The jolt in a victory on the right. *The New York Times*, p. A23.

Greenberg, J., Porteus, J., Simon, L., & Pyszczynski, T. (1995). Evidence of a terror management function of cultural icons: The effects of mortality salience on the inappropriate use of cherished cultural symbols. *Personality and Social Psychology Bulletin, 21*, 1221–1228.

Greenberg, J., Pyszczynski, T., & Solomon, S. (1986). The causes and consequences of the need for self-esteem: A terror management theory. In R. F. Baumeister (Ed.), *Public self and private self* (pp. 189–207). New York: Springer-Verlag.

Greenberg, J., Pyszczynski, T., Solomon, S., Rosenblatt, A., Veeder, M., Kirkland, S., & Lyon, D. (1990). Evidence for terror management theory: II. The effects of mortality salience on reactions to those who threaten or bolster the cultural worldview. *Journal of Personality and Social Psychology, 58*, 308–318.

Greenberg, J., Simon, L., Pyszczynski, T., Solomon, S., & Chatel, D. (1992). Terror management and tolerance: Does mortality salience always intensify negative reactions to others who threaten one's world-view? *Journal of Personality and Social Psychology, 63*, 212–220.

Greenwald, A. G. (1980). The totalitarian ego: Fabrication and revision of personal history. *American Psychologist, 35*, 603–618.

*Gruenfeld, D. H. (1995). Status, ideology, and integrative ideology on the U.S. Supreme Court: Rethinking the politics of political decision making. *Journal of Personality and Social Psychology, 68*, 5–20.

Habermas, J. (1989). *The new conservatism: Cultural criticism and the historians' debate* (S. W. Nicholsen, Trans.). Cambridge, MA: MIT Press.

Hamilton, D. L., & Rose, T. L. (1980). Illusory correlation and the maintenance of stereotypic beliefs. *Journal of Personality and Social Psychology, 39*, 832–845.

Hamilton, V. L., Sanders, J., & McKearney, S. J. (1995). Orientations toward authority in an authoritarian state: Moscow in 1990. *Personality and Social Psychology Bulletin, 21*, 356–365.

Harmon-Jones, E., Greenberg, J., Solomon, S., & Simon, L. (1996). The effects of mortality salience on intergroup discrimination between minimal groups. *European Journal of Social Psychology, 26*, 677–681.

Hastorf, A. H., & Cantril, H. (1954). They saw a game: A case study. *Journal of Abnormal and Social Psychology, 49*, 129–134.

Higgins, E. T. (1996). Knowledge activation: Accessibility, applicability, and salience. In E. T. Higgins & A. W. Kruglanski (Eds.), *Social psychology: Handbook of basic principles* (pp. 133–168). New York: Guilford Press.

Higgins, E. T. (1997). Beyond pleasure and pain. *American Psychologist, 52*, 1280–1300.

Higgins, E. T. (1998). Promotion and prevention: Regulatory focus as a motivational principle. *Advances in Experimental Social Psychology, 30*, 1–45.

*Hinze, T., Doster, J., & Joe, V. C. (1997). The relationship of conservatism and cognitive-complexity. *Personality and Individual Differences, 22*, 297–298.

Hofstede, G. H. (2001). *Culture's consequences: Comparing values, behaviors, institutions, and organizations across nations* (2nd ed.). Thousand Oaks, CA: Sage.

Hogg, M. A., & Mullin, B.-A. (1999). Joining groups to reduce uncertainty: Subjective uncertainty reduction and group identification. In D. Abrams & M. A. Hogg (Eds.), *Social identity and social cognition* (pp. 249–279). Oxford: Blackwell.

Huntington, S. (1957). Conservatism as an ideology. *American Political Science Review, 51*, 454–473.

Hyman, H. H., & Sheatsley, P. B. (1954). "The Authoritarian Personality": A methodological critique. In R. Christie & M. Jahoda (Eds.), *Studies in the scope and method of "The Authoritarian Personality"* (pp. 50–122). Glencoe, IL: Free Press.

*Joe, V. C., Jones, R. N., & Ryder, S. (1977). Conservatism, openness to experience and sample bias. *Journal of Personality Assessment, 41*, 527–531.

Jost, J. T. (1995). Negative illusions: Conceptual clarification and psychological evidence concerning false consciousness. *Political Psychology, 16*, 397–424.

Jost, J. T. (1996). Ingroup and outgroup favoritism among groups differing in socioeconomic success: Effects of perceived legitimacy and justification processes (Doctoral dissertation, Yale University, 1996). *Dissertation Abstracts International, 57*, 763B.

Jost, J. T., & Banaji, M. R. (1994). The role of stereotyping in system-justification and the production of false consciousness. *British Journal of Social Psychology, 33*, 1–27.

Jost, J. T., & Burgess, D. (2000). Attitudinal ambivalence and the conflict between group and system justification motives in low status groups. *Personality and Social Psychology Bulletin, 26*, 293–305.

Jost, J. T., Burgess, D., & Mosso, C. (2001). Conflicts of legitimation among self, group, and system: The integrative potential of system justification theory. In J. T. Jost & B. Major (Eds.), *The psychology of legitimacy: Emerging perspectives on ideology, justice, and intergroup relations* (pp. 363–388). New York: Cambridge University Press.

Jost, J. T., & Kruglanski, A. W. (2002). The estrangement of social constructionism and experimental social psychology: History of the rift and prospects for reconciliation. *Personality and Social Psychology Review, 6*, 168–187.

*Jost, J. T., Kruglanski, A. W., & Simon, L. (1999). Effects of epistemic motivation on conservatism, intolerance, and other system justifying attitudes. In L. Thompson, D. M. Messick, & J. M. Levine (Eds.), *Shared cognition in organizations: The management of knowledge* (pp. 91–116). Mahwah, NJ: Erlbaum.

Jost, J. T., Pelham, B. W., Sheldon, O., & Sullivan, B. (2003). Social inequality and the reduction of ideological dissonance on behalf of the system: Evidence of enhanced system justification among the disadvantaged. *European Journal of Social Psychology, 33*, 13–36.

*Jost, J. T., & Thompson, E. P. (2000). Group-based dominance and opposition to equality as independent predictors of self-esteem, ethnocentrism, and social policy attitudes among African Americans and European Americans. *Journal of Experimental Social Psychology, 36,* 209–232.

Judd, C. M., Krosnick, J. A., & Milburn, M. A. (1981). Political involvement in attitude structure in the general public. *American Sociological Review, 46,* 660–669.

Judt, T. (2002, April 28). America's restive partners [Electronic version]. *The New York Times* (Late edition final), Section 4, p. 15.

*Kemmelmeier, M. (1997). Need for closure and political orientation among German university students. *Journal of Social Psychology, 137,* 787–789.

Kenny, D. T., & Ginsberg, R. (1958). The specificity of intolerance of ambiguity measures. *Journal of Abnormal and Social Psychology, 56,* 300–304.

Kerlinger, F. M. (1984). Social attitude statement and referent scales. (pp. 118–342). *Liberalism and conservatism: The nature and structure of social attitudes.* Hillsdale, NJ: Erlbaum.

*Kirton, M. J. (1978). Wilson and Patterson's Conservatism Scale: A shortened alternative form. *British Journal of Social and Clinical Psychology, 17,* 319–323.

*Kish, G. B. (1973). Stimulus-seeking and conservatism. In G. D. Wilson (Ed.), *The psychology of conservatism* (pp. 197–207). London: Academic Press.

*Kish, G. B., & Donnenwerth, G. V. (1972). Sex differences in the correlates of stimulus seeking. *Journal of Consulting and Clinical Psychology, 38,* 42–49.

Kluegel, J. R., & Smith, E. R. (1986). *Beliefs about inequality: Americans' views of what is and what ought to be.* New York: Aldine De Gruyter.

Knight, K. (1999). Liberalism and conservatism. In J. P. Robinson, P. R. Shaver, & L. S. Wrightsman (Eds.), *Measures of political attitudes* (pp. 59–158). San Diego, CA: Academic Press.

*Kohn, P. M. (1974). Authoritarianism, rebelliousness, and their correlates among British undergraduates. *British Journal of Social and Clinical Psychology, 13,* 245–255.

Kolko, G. (1963). *The triumph of conservatism: A re-interpretation of American history, 1900–1916.* New York: Free Press of Glencoe.

Kruglanski, A. W. (1989). *Lay epistemics and human knowledge: Cognitive and motivational basis.* New York: Plenum.

Kruglanski, A. W. (1996). Motivated social cognition: Principles of the interface. In E. T. Higgins & A. W. Kruglanski (Eds.), *Social psychology: Handbook of basic principles.* New York: Guilford Press.

Kruglanski, A. W. (1999). Motivation, cognition, and reality: Three memos for the next generation of research. *Psychological Inquiry, 10,* 54–58.

Kruglanski, A. W., & Freund, T. (1983). The freezing and unfreezing of lay inferences: Effects of impressional primacy, ethnic stereotyping, and numerical anchoring. *Journal of Experimental Social Psychology, 19,* 448–468.

Kruglanski, A. W., & Thompson, E. P. (1999a). The illusory second mode or, the cue is the message. *Psychological Inquiry, 10,* 182–193.

Kruglanski, A. W., & Thompson, E. P. (1999b). Persuasion by a single route: A view from the unimodel. *Psychological Inquiry, 10,* 83–109.

Kruglanski, A. W., & Webster, D. M. (1991). Group members' reactions to opinion deviates and conformists at varying degrees of proximity to decision deadline and of environmental noise. *Journal of Personality and Social Psychology, 61,* 215–225.

Kruglanski, A. W., & Webster, D. M. (1996). Motivated closing of the mind: "Seizing" and "freezing." *Psychological Review, 103,* 263–283.

Kruglanski, A. W., Webster, D. M., & Klem, A. (1993). Motivated resistance and openness to persuasion in the presence or absence of prior information. *Journal of Personality and Social Psychology, 65,* 861–876.

Krugman, P. (2002, April 23). The angry people. *The New York Times*, p. A23.
Kunda, Z. (1990). The case for motivated reasoning. *Psychological Bulletin, 108*, 480–498.
Lane, R. E. (1962). The fear of equality. In R. E. Lane (Ed.), *Political ideology: Why the American common man believes what he does* (pp. 57–81). New York: Free Press.
*Lavine, H., Burgess, D., Snyder, M., Transue, J., Sullivan, J. L., Haney, B., & Wagner, S. H. (1999). Threat, authoritarianism, and voting: An investigation of personality and persuasion. *Personality and Social Psychology Bulletin, 25*, 337–347.
*Lavine, H., Polichak, J., & Lodge, M. (1999, September). *Authoritarianism and threat: A response latency analysis*. Paper presented at the annual meeting of the American Political Science Association, Atlanta, GA.
Lehrer, J. (1997, July 23). The arts: A congress divided [Television broadcast]. *News hour*. New York and Washington, DC: Public Broadcasting Service. (Transcript available from www.pbs.org/newshour/bb/entertainment/july-dec97/nea_7-23.html)
Lennon, J. (1970). God. On *Plastic Ono band* [Record]. London: Northern Songs.
Lentz, T. F. (1939). Personage admiration and other correlates of conservatism-radicalism. *Journal of Social Psychology, 10*, 81–93.
Lerner, M. J. (1980). *The belief in a just world: A fundamental delusion*. New York: Plenum Press.
Liberman, N., Idson, L. C., Camacho, C. J., & Higgins, E. T. (1999). Promotion and prevention choices between stability and change. *Journal of Personality and Social Psychology, 77*, 1135–1145.
Lind, M. (1996). *Up from conservatism: Why the right is wrong for America*. New York: Free Press.
Lipset, S. M. (1981). Working-class authoritarianism. In S. M. Lipset (Ed.), *Political man: The social bases of politics* (pp. 87–126). Baltimore: Johns Hopkins University Press. (Original work published 1960)
Lo, C. Y. H., & Schwartz, M. (Eds.). (1998). *Social policy and the conservative agenda*. Oxford, England: Blackwell.
Lord, C. G., Ross, L., & Lepper, M. R. (1979). Biased assimilation and attitude polarization: The effects of prior theories on subsequently considered evidence. *Journal of Personality and Social Psychology*, 37, 2098–2109.
Loye, D. (1977). *The leadership passion*. San Francisco: Jossey-Bass.
Lyons, M., & Berlet, C. (1996). *Too close for comfort: Right-wing populism, scapegoating, and Fascist potentials in U.S. politics*. Boston: South End Press.
Mannheim, K. (1936). *Ideology and utopia*. New York: Harcourt, Brace.
Mannheim, K. (1986). *Conservatism: A contribution to the sociology of knowledge* (D. Kettler, V. Meja, & N. Stehr, Trans.). New York: Routledge & Kegan Paul. (Original work published 1927)
Martin, J., Scully, M., & Levitt, B. (1990). Injustice and the legitimation of revolution: Damning the past, excusing the present, and neglecting the future. *Journal of Personality and Social Psychology, 59*, 281–290.
Martin, J. L. (2001). The Authoritarian Personality, 50 years later: What lessons are there for political psychology? *Political Psychology, 22*, 1–26.
*McAllister, P., & Anderson, A. (1991). Conservatism and the comprehension of implausible texts. *European Journal of Social Psychology, 21*, 147–164.
*McCann, S. J. H. (1997). Threatening times, "strong" presidential popular vote winners, and the victory margin, 1824–1964. *Journal of Personality and Social Psychology, 73*, 160–170.
McClosky, H., & Zaller, J. (1984). *The American ethos*. Cambridge, MA: Harvard University Press.

McGregor, I., Zanna, M. P., Holmes, J. G., & Spencer, S. J. (2001). Compensatory conviction in the face of personal uncertainty: Going to extremes and being oneself. *Journal of Personality and Social Psychology, 80,* 472–488.

McGuire, W. J. (1985). Attitudes and attitude change. In G. Lindzey & E. Aronson (Eds.), *Handbook of social psychology* (pp. 233–346). New York: Random House.

Mercer, W. G., & Cairns, E. (1981). Conservatism and its relationship to general and specific ethnocentrism in Northern Ireland. *British Journal of Social Psychology, 20,* 13–16.

Milburn, M. A. (1991). *Persuasion and politics: The social psychology of public opinion.* Pacific Grove, CA: Brooks-Cole/Wadsworth.

Miller, A. S. (1994). Dynamic indicators of self-perceived conservatism. *Sociological Quarterly, 35,* 175–182.

Miller, D. T., & Ross, M. (1975). Self-serving biases in the attribution of causality: Fact or fiction? *Psychological Bulletin, 82,* 213–225.

Morris, W. (Ed.). (1976). *The American heritage dictionary of the English language* (New college ed.). Boston: Houghton Mifflin.

Muller, J. Z. (2001). Conservatism: Historical aspects. In N. J. Smelser & P. B. Baltes (Eds.), *International encyclopedia of the social and behavioral sciences* (pp. 2624–2628). Amsterdam: Elsevier.

Neilson, W. A. (Ed.). (1958). *Webster's new international dictionary of the English language* (2nd ed., unabridged). New York: Merriam.

*Nias, D. K. B. (1973). Attitudes to the common market: A case study in conservatism. In G. D. Wilson (Ed.), *The psychology of conservatism* (pp. 239–255). New York: Academic Press.

O'Connor, P. (1952). Ethnocentrism, "intolerance of ambiguity," and abstract reasoning ability. *Journal of Abnormal and Social Psychology, 47,* 526–530.

Pawlicki, R. E., & Almquist, C. (1973). Authoritarianism, locus of control, and tolerance of ambiguity as reflected in membership and nonmembership in a women's liberation group. *Psychological Reports, 32,* 1331–1337.

Peterson, B. E., Doty, R. M., & Winter, D. G. (1993). Authoritarianism and attitudes toward contemporary social issues. *Personality and Social Psychology Bulletin, 19,* 174–184.

*Peterson, B. E., & Lane, M. D. (2001). Implications of authoritarianism for young adulthood: Longitudinal analysis of college experiences and future goals. *Personality and Social Psychology Bulletin, 27,* 678–690.

*Peterson, B. E., Smirles, K. A., & Wentworth, P. A. (1997). Generativity and authoritarianism implications for personality, political involvement, and parenting. *Journal of Personality and Social Psychology, 72,* 1202–1216.

*Pettigrew, T. F. (1958). The measurement and correlates of category width as a cognitive variable. *Journal of Personality, 26,* 532–544.

Popper, K. R. (1959). *The logic of scientific discovery.* New York: Harper.

Pratto, F. (1999). The puzzle of continuing group inequality: Piecing together psychological, social, and cultural forces in social dominance theory. *Advances in Experimental Social Psychology, 31,* 191–263.

*Pratto, F., Sidanius, J., Stallworth, L. M., & Malle, B. F. (1994). Social dominance orientation: A personality variable predicting social and political attitudes. *Journal of Personality and Social Psychology, 67,* 741–763.

Ray, J. J. (1973). Conservatism, authoritarianism, and related variables: A review and empirical study. In G. D. Wilson (Ed.), *The psychology of conservatism* (pp. 17–35). New York: Academic Press.

Ray, J. J. (1988). Cognitive style as a predictor of authoritarianism, conservatism, and racism: A fantasy in many movements. *Political Psychology, 9*, 303–308.

Redding, R. E. (2001). Sociopolitical diversity in psychology: The case for pluralism. *American Psychologist, 56*, 205–215.

Reich, W. (1970). *The mass psychology of fascism* (V. R. Carfagno, Trans.). New York: Farrar, Straus, & Giroux. (Original work published 1946)

Rickert, E. J. (1998). Authoritarianism and economic threat: Implications for political behavior. *Political Psychology, 19*, 707–720.

Robins, R. S., & Post, J. M. (1997). *Political paranoia: The psychopolitics of hatred*. New Haven, CT: Yale University Press.

Rohan, M. J., & Zanna, M. P. (1998). The "products of socialization": A discussion of self-regulatory strategies and value systems. In J. M. Darley & J. Cooper (Eds.), *Attribution and social interaction: The legacy of Edward E. Jones*. Washington, DC: American Psychological Association.

Rokeach, M. (1956). Political and religious dogmatism: An alternative to the authoritarian personality. *Psychological Monographs, 70*(18, Whole No. 425), 43.

*Rokeach, M. (1960). *The open and closed mind*. New York: Basic Books.

Rorty, R. (1989). *Contingency, irony, and solidarity*. Cambridge, England: Cambridge University Press.

*Rosenblatt, A., Greenberg, J., Solomon, S., Pyszczynski, T., & Lyon, D. (1989). Evidence for terror management theory: I. The effects of mortality salience on reactions to those who violate or uphold cultural values. *Journal of Personality and Social Psychology, 57*, 681–690.

Rosenthal, R. (1991). *Meta-analytic procedures for social research* (2nd ed.). Thousand Oaks, CA: Sage.

Rossiter, C. (1968). Conservatism. In D. Sills (Ed.), *International encyclopedia of the social sciences* (pp. 290–295). New York: Macmillan & Free Press.

*Sales, S. M. (1972). Economic threat as a determinant of conversion rates in authoritarian and nonauthoritarian churches. *Journal of Personality and Social Psychology, 23*, 420–428.

*Sales, S. M. (1973). Threat as a factor in authoritarianism: An analysis of archival data. *Journal of Personality and Social Psychology, 28*, 44–57.

Sales, S. M., & Friend, K. E. (1973). Success and failure as determinants of level of authoritarianism. *Behavioral Science, 18*, 163–172.

Sanford, N. (1966). *Self and society: Social change and individual development*. New York: Atherton Press.

Sanger, D. E. (2001, July 25). On world stage, America's president wins mixed reviews. *The New York Times*, p. A1.

Sanger, D. E. (2002, April 8). Mideast turmoil: Assessment. *The New York Times*, p. A6.

Schaller, M., Boyd, C., Yohannes, J., & O'Brien, N. (1995). The prejudiced personality revisited: Personal need for structure and formation of erroneous group stereotypes. *Journal of Personality and Social Psychology, 68*, 544–555.

Schimel, J., Simon, L., Greenberg, J., Pyszczynski, T., Solomon, S., Waxmonsky, J., & Arndt, J. (1999). Stereotypes and terror management: Evidence that mortality salience enhances stereotypic thinking and preferences. *Journal of Personality and Social Psychology, 77*, 905–926.

Sears, D. O. (1983). The persistence of early political predispositions: The roles of attitude object and life stage. In L. Wheeler & P. Shaver (Eds.), *Review of personality and social psychology* (Vol. 4, pp. 79–116). Beverly Hills, CA: Sage.

Sears, D. O. (1986). College sophomores in the laboratory: Influence of a narrow data base on social psychology's view of human nature. *Journal of Personality and Social Psychology, 51,* 515–530.

Sears, D. O. (1994). Ideological bias in political psychology: The view from scientific hell. *Political Psychology, 15,* 547–556.

Sears, D. O., & Funk, C. L. (1991). The role of self-interest in social and political attitudes. *Advances in Experimental Social Psychology, 24,* 1–85.

Shah, J. Y., Kruglanski, A. W., & Thompson, E. P. (1998). Membership has its (epistemic) rewards: Need for closure effects on in-group bias. *Journal of Personality and Social Psychology, 75,* 383–393.

Shils, E. A. (1954). Authoritarianism: "Right" and "left." In R. Christie & M. Jahoda (Eds.), *Studies in the scope and method of "The Authoritarian Personality"* (pp. 24–49). Glencoe, IL: Free Press.

*Sidanius, J. (1978). Intolerance of ambiguity and socio-politico ideology: A multidimensional analysis. *European Journal of Social Psychology, 8,* 215–235.

Sidanius, J. (1984). Political interest, political information search, and ideological homogeneity as a function of sociopolitical ideology: A tale of three theories. *Human Relations, 37,* 811–828.

*Sidanius, J. (1985). Cognitive functioning and sociopolitical ideology revisited. *Political Psychology, 6,* 637–661.

Sidanius, J. (1988). Political sophistication and political deviance: A structural equation examination of context theory. *Journal of Personality and Social Psychology, 55,* 37–51.

Sidanius, J. (1993). The psychology of group conflict and the dynamics of oppression: A social dominance perspective. In S. Iyengar & W. J. McGuire (Eds.), *Explorations in political psychology* (pp. 183–219). Durham, NC: Duke University Press.

Sidanius, J., & Ekehammar, B. (1979). Political socialization: A multivariate analysis of Swedish political attitude and preference data. *European Journal of Social Psychology, 9,* 265–279.

Sidanius, J., & Lau, R. R. (1989). Political sophistication and political deviance: A matter of context. *Political Psychology, 10,* 85–109.

Sidanius, J., & Pratto, F. (1993). The inevitability of oppression and the dynamics of social dominance. In P. Sniderman, P. E. Tetlock, & E. G. Carmines (Eds.), *Prejudice, politics, and the American dilemma* (pp. 173–211). Stanford, CA: Stanford University Press.

Sidanius, J., & Pratto, F. (1999). *Social dominance: An intergroup theory of social hierarchy and oppression.* New York: Cambridge University Press.

Sidanius, J., Pratto, F., & Bobo, L. (1996). Racism, conservatism, affirmative action, and intellectual sophistication: A matter of principled conservatism or group dominance? *Journal of Personality and Social Psychology, 70,* 476–490.

Smith, M. R., & Gordon, R. A. (1998). Personal need for structure and attitudes toward homosexuality. *Journal of Social Psychology, 138,* 83–87.

*Smithers, A. G., & Lobley, D. M. (1978). Dogmatism, social attitudes and personality. *British Journal of Social and Clinical Psychology, 17,* 135–142.

Sniderman, P. M., Piazza, T., Tetlock, P. E., & Kendrick, A. (1991). The new racism. *American Journal of Political Science, 35,* 423–645.

Sniderman, P. M., & Tetlock, P. E. (1986). Symbolic racism: Problems of motive attribution in political analysis. *Journal of Social Issues, 42,* 129–150.

Sorrentino, R. M., & Roney, C. J. R. (1986). Uncertainty orientation, achievement-related motivation, and task diagnosticity as determinants of task performance. *Social Cognition, 4,* 420–436.

Sorrentino, R. M., & Roney, C. J. R. (2000). *The uncertain mind: Individual differences in facing the unknown*. Philadelphia: Psychology Press/Taylor & Francis.

Srull, T. K., & Wyer, R. S. (1979). The role of category accessibility in the interpretation of information about persons: Some determinants and implications. *Journal of Personality and Social Psychology, 37*, 1660–1672.

Stacey, B. G., & Green, R. T. (1971). Working-class conservatism: A review and an empirical study. *British Journal of Social and Clinical Psychology, 10*, 10–26.

Stone, I. F. (1989). *In a time of torment (1961–1967)*. Boston: Little, Brown.

Stone, W. F. (1980). The myth of left-wing authoritarianism. *Political Psychology, 2*, 3–19.

Stone, W. F. (1986). Personality and ideology: Empirical support for Tomkins' polarity theory. *Political Psychology, 7*, 689–708.

Stone, W. F., Lederer, G., & Christie, R. (Eds.). (1993). *Strength and weakness: The Authoritarian Personality today*. New York: Springer-Verlag.

Stone, W. F., & Schaffner, P. E. (1988). *The psychology of politics*. New York: Springer-Verlag.

Strauman, T. J., & Higgins, E. T. (1988). Self-discrepancies as predictors of vulnerability to distinct syndromes of chronic emotional distress. *Journal of Personality, 56*, 685–707.

Sulloway, F. J. (1996). *Born to rebel: Birth order, family dynamics, and creative lives*. New York: Pantheon.

Sulloway, F. J. (2001). Birth order, sibling competition, and human behavior. In H. R. Holcomb III (Ed.), *Conceptual challenges in evolutionary psychology: Innovative research strategies* (pp. 39–83). Dordrecht, the Netherlands: Kluwer Academic.

*Tetlock, P. E. (1983). Cognitive style and political ideology. *Journal of Personality and Social Psychology, 45*, 118–126.

*Tetlock, P. E. (1984). Cognitive style and political belief systems in the British House of Commons. *Journal of Personality and Social Psychology, 46*, 365–375.

Tetlock, P. E. (1994). Political psychology or politicized psychology: Is the road to scientific hell paved with good moral intentions? *Political Psychology, 15*, 509–529.

*Tetlock, P. E., Bernzweig, J., & Gallant, J. L. (1985). Supreme Court decision making: Cognitive style as a predictor of ideological consistency of voting. *Journal of Personality and Social Psychology, 48*, 1227–1239.

*Tetlock, P. E., Hannum, K. A., & Micheletti, P. M. (1984). Stability and change in the complexity of senatorial debate: Testing the cognitive versus rhetorical style hypotheses. *Journal of Personality and Social Psychology, 46*, 979–990.

Tetlock, P. E., & Mitchell, G. (1993). Liberal and conservative approaches to justice: Conflicting psychological portraits. In B. A. Mellers & J. Baron (Eds.), *Psychological perspectives on justice* (pp. 234–255). Cambridge, England: Cambridge University Press.

Thomas, D. B. (1976). Exploring the personality-ideology interface: Q-sort of Tomkins' polarity theory. *Experimental Study of Politics, 5*, 47–87.

Tomkins, S. S. (1963). Left and right: A basic dimension of ideology and personality. In R. W. White (Ed.), *The study of lives* (pp. 388–411). Chicago: Atherton.

Tomkins, S. S. (1965). Affect and the psychology of knowledge. In S. S. Tomkins & C. E. Izard (Eds.), *Affect, cognition, and personality: Empirical studies* (pp. 72–97). New York: Springer.

Tomkins, S. S. (1987). Script theory. In J. Aronoff & A. I. Rubin (Eds.), *The emergence of personality* (pp. 147–216). New York: Springer.

Tomkins, S. S. (1988). *Polarity Scale*. In W. F. Stone & P. E. Schaffner (Eds.), *The psychology of politics* (pp. 292–298). New York: Springer-Verlag. (Original, unpublished work developed 1964)

Tomkins, S. S. (1995). Ideology and affect. In E. V. Demos (Ed.), *Exploring affect: The selected writings of Silvan S. Tomkins* (pp. 109–167). New York: University of Cambridge Press.

Turner, J. C. (1991). *Social influence*. Buckingham, England: Open University Press.
van den Bos, K., & Miedema, J. (2000). Toward understanding why fairness matters: The influence of mortality salience on reactions to procedural fairness. *Journal of Personality and Social Psychology, 79*, 355–366.
*Webster, A. C., & Stewart, R. A. C. (1973). Theological conservatism. In G. D. Wilson (Ed.), *The psychology of conservatism* (pp. 129–147). London: Academic Press.
Webster, D. M. (1993). Motivated augmentation and reduction of the overattribution bias. *Journal of Personality and Social Psychology, 65*, 261–271.
Webster, D. M. (1994). *Groups under the influence: Need for closure effects on the use of shared and unique information*. Unpublished doctoral dissertation, University of Maryland at College Park.
*Webster, D. M., & Kruglanski, A. W. (1994). Individual differences in need for cognitive closure. *Journal of Personality and Social Psychology, 67*, 1049–1062.
Webster, D. M., Richter, L., & Kruglanski, A. W. (1996). On leaping to conclusions when feeling tired: Mental fatigue effects on impressional primacy. *Journal of Experimental Social Psychology, 32*, 181–195.
Whitley, B. E., Jr. (1999). Right-wing authoritarianism, social dominance orientation, and prejudice. *Journal of Personality and Social Psychology, 77*, 126–134.
Whitley, B. E., Jr., & Lee, S. E. (2000). The relationship of authoritarianism and related constructs to attitudes toward homosexuality. *Journal of Applied Social Psychology, 30*, 144–170.
Will, G. F. (1998). *Bunts*. New York: Scribner.
Williams, S. (1984). Left–right ideological differences in blaming victims. *Political Psychology, 5*, 573–581.
Wilson, G. D. (1968). Authoritarianism or conservatism? *Papers in Psychology, 2*, 58.
Wilson, G. D. (1973a). Development and evaluation of the C-Scale. In G. D. Wilson (Ed.), *The psychology of conservatism* (pp. 49–69). London: Academic Press.
Wilson, G. D. (1973b). A dynamic theory of conservatism. In G. D. Wilson (Ed.), *The psychology of conservatism* (pp. 257–265). London: Academic Press.
Wilson, G. D. (Ed.). (1973c). *The psychology of conservatism*. London: Academic Press.
*Wilson, G. D. (1973d). The temperamental basis of attitudes. In G. D. Wilson (Ed.), *The psychology of conservatism* (pp. 187–196). London: Academic Press.
*Wilson, G. D., Ausman, J., & Mathews, T. R. (1973). Conservatism and art preferences. *Journal of Personality and Social Psychology, 25*, 286–288.
Wilson, G. D., & Patterson, J. R. (1968). A new measure of conservatism. *British Journal of Social and Clinical Psychology, 8*, 264–269.

Part II
How people want

6 A theory of goal systems

Arie W. Kruglanski, University of Maryland
James Y. Shah, University of Wisconsin
*Ayelet Fishbach, Ron Friedman, Woo Young Chun,
and David Sleeth-Keppler*, University of Maryland

The theory outlined in the present chapter adopts a cognitive approach to motivation. We describe a research program premised on the notion that the cognitive treatment affords conceptual and methodological advantages enabling new insights into problems of motivated action, self-regulation and self-control. We begin by placing our work in the broader historical context of social psychological theorizing about motivation and cognition. We then present our theoretical notions and trace their implications for a variety of psychological issues including activity experience, goal commitment, choice, and substitution. The gist of this chapter describes our empirical research concerning a broad range of phenomena informed by the goal-systemic analysis.

Motivation versus cognition, or motivation as cognition

Motivation versus cognition: the "separatist program." Social psychological theories have often treated motivation as *separate* from cognition, and have often approached it in a somewhat *static* manner. The separatism of the "motivation *versus* cognition" approach was manifest in several major formulations and debates. Thus, for example, the dissonance versus self-perception debate (Bem, 1972) pitted against each other motivational (i.e., dissonance) versus cognitive (i.e., self-perception) explanations of attitude change phenomena. A similar subsequent controversy pertained to the question of whether a motivational explanation of biased causal attributions in terms of ego-defensive tendencies (cf. Kelley, 1972) is valid, given the alternative possibility of a purely cognitive explanation (Miller & Ross, 1975).

The separatism of the "motivation *versus* cognition" approach assigned distinct functions to motivational and cognitive variables. This is apparent in major social psychological notions of persuasion, judgment or impression formation. For instance, in the popular dual-mode theories of persuasion (Petty & Cacioppo, 1986; Chaiken & Chen, 1999) the degree of processing motivation acts as an important *selector* of persuasive mode: High processing motivation (operationalized, e.g., via high personal involvement in an issue) is associated with extensive processing of message arguments, whereas low processing motivation is associated with brief processing of "peripheral" or heuristic cues. In the alternative "unimodel" of persuasion too (Kruglanski & Thompson, 1999a, b; Kruglanski, Thompson, &

Spiegel, 1999; Kruglanski, Erb, Spiegel, & Pierro, 2001) motivation determines the extent of processing any kind of information (i.e., one associated with message arguments *or* with peripheral/heuristic cues).

The "static" approach. Beyond its *separation* from cognition, motivation has been often treated *statically* in social psychological research. Social psychologists typically assumed that due to chronic or momentary causes individuals have either high or low degree of some motivation, such as the need for closure (Kruglanski & Webster, 1996; Webster & Kruglanski, 1998), the need for cognition (Cacioppo & Petty, 1982), or "learning" or "performance" goals (Dweck, 1999) that systematically impacts various relevant phenomena. Whereas the change instigated by a given motivational state could be considered dynamic, the motivational state itself was treated statically, that is, as fixed at a given magnitude. To say that it was static is not to imply that social psychologists' traditional approach to motivation was inappropriate. Quite the contrary, it yielded a rich crop of important findings about the effects of motivational variables on judgment, action, and performance (see e.g., Kruglanski, 1996a for a review).

Motivation as cognition: depicting dynamism. Nonetheless, a static depiction does miss something important about motivation, namely its *malleability* and *dynamism*: Our wishes, interests, and desires are rarely so steadfast or constant. Often, they fluctuate from one moment to the next as we succumb to an assortment of distractions, temptations, and digressions. Rather than relentlessly keeping to the task at hand we often daydream, ruminate, run to the fridge or check our email, and our shifting moods and emotional states often track our changing motivational conditions. An insight into such motivational dynamics may be gained if we abandon the separateness assumption of the "motivation versus cognition" program, and adopt the "motivation as cognition" approach instead. The "motivation as cognition" paradigm is naturally fitted to handle dynamism because in cognitive systems dynamism is the "name of the game." Our cognitive activity hardly ever stops, not even in our sleep. Our associations are in a constant flux, and our thoughts "ignite" each other in rapid succession. Many of these thoughts are motivational in nature; they represent our goals, the means to pursue them, or discrepancies from goal attainment.

The present story belongs, therefore, in the "motivation as cognition" paradigm. Its topic is the behavior of goal systems, defined as the mental representations of motivational networks composed of interconnected goals and means. Different goal systems may be activated at the same time through environmental priming (cf. Bargh & Barndollar, 1996) and they may compete with each other for mental resources. We assume that motivational phenomena are a joint function of cognitive principles (that goal systems share with other cognitive systems) as they are applied to uniquely motivational contents, that is, to goals and to means. Put differently, the cognitive properties of goal systems set the constraints within which the motivational properties may express themselves. In the sections below, we first discuss the cognitive and the motivational properties of goal systems. We then describe empirical research on a wide array of goal-systemic phenomena determined jointly by both sets of properties.

Cognitive properties of goal systems

Two categories of cognitive properties play a major role in the behavior of goal systems: these are their *structural* and their *allocational* properties. The structural properties of goal systems stem from their cognitive-interconnectedness, and the allocational properties—from the attentional resource-limitation that characterizes all deliberative cognitive functioning.

Structural properties of goal systems

Interconnectedness: Its form and its strength. Goal systems consist of mentally represented networks wherein goals may be cognitively associated to their corresponding means of attainment and to alternative goals as well. Beyond cognitive linkage to their corresponding goals, means may be associated with other means. Mental representations of motivational constructs (i.e., goals and means) may include facilitative as well as inhibitory links. Typically, facilitative links may exist between *vertically* connected elements, that is, between goals and their corresponding means. Inhibitory links may exist primarily between *lateral* elements, that is, between competing goals or competing means. A possible goal system is depicted in Figure 1. As shown, a superordinate goal is cognitively connected to its various sub-goals or way-stations en route to that goal, in turn connected to their own means of attainment. Lateral interconnections within a goal system also are represented, including interconnections between different sub-goals and between various attainment means to those particular sub-goals.

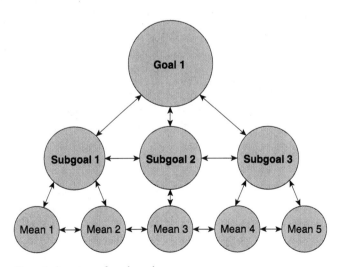

Figure 1 A system of goals and means.

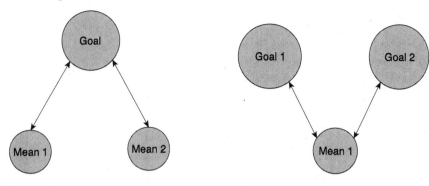

Figure 2 Equifinality configuration.   *Figure 3* Multifinality configuration.

Interconnections have two major aspects of interest, their *form* and their *strength*. Concerning form, interconnected goal systems may exhibit different "architectures" or come in different configurations: the number of means attached to a given goal may vary and so may the number of goals attached to a given mean. The number of means linked to a given goal defines the *equifinality* set encapsulated in the slogan of "all roads lead to Rome" (see Figure 2). Size of the equifinality set determines the amount of available *choice* between the means and the range of *substitutability* of one means for another if pursuit of the latter was thwarted or resulted in failure.

The number of goals linked to a given means defines the *multifinality set* encapsulated in the notion of "many birds with one stone" (see Figure 3). As we shall see later, size of the multifinality set may partially affect the perceived value, or the motivational "bang for the buck," a given means may afford.

The second structural aspect of goal systems refers to interconnection *strength* between the units. Strength is not independent of form because it is positively related to *uniqueness* of the interconnections. The presence of additional means associated with a goal and/or of additional goals associated with a means should dilute the strength of activating the goal by the means or vice versa. Thus, the *lower* the number of means connected to a given goal (i.e., the *smaller* the equifinality set) or the *lower* the number of goals connected to a given means (i.e., the smaller the multifinality set), the stronger the cognitive association strength between a given means and the goal. This is analogous to the classic "fan effect" discussed by John Anderson (1974, 1983) wherein the greater the number of specific facts linked to a general mental construct, the less likely it is that any particular fact will be retrieved or recalled upon the presentation of the construct. Relations between uniqueness and association strength are represented in Figures 4 and 5.

Uniqueness of association is only one among several determinants of association strength. Another determinant is repeated pairing of elements with one another, i.e., a mean with a given goal, a goal with another goal, or of a means with another means. A mental representation of an association could derive also from pronouncements of a trusted "epistemic authority" (Kruglanski, 1989; Elis & Kruglanski, 1992). A mother could teach her child that the way to produce

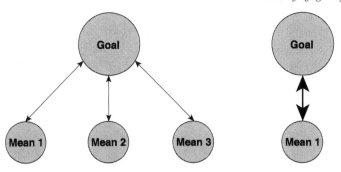

Figure 4 Uniqueness and strength of goal-means association.

water is to turn the faucet, and this could establish an immediate association between the goal (of producing water) and the means (of faucet-turning), etc.

Transfer of properties within a goal system. Association strength is important because it affects the facility of *traffic* between the units. This affords the *transfer* of various motivational properties from one unit to another. The units may activate each other (Anderson, 1983; Neely, 1977; Rumelhart & Ortony, 1977) but activation is not the only property that spreads. Other properties too may flow along the links. Metaphorically then, these links resemble cognitive *railroad tracks* enabling the transportation of different psychological properties across the units. Besides spreading activation, one could have a transfer of *commitment*, or of specific *affective qualities* from goals to means (or vice versa) in proportion to the strength of their association.

Subconscious impact. Depending partly on their strength of activation, some cognitive elements may enter conscious awareness while others might not. Nonetheless, the latter too may impact subsequent activities and reactions (Draine & Greenwald, 1998). In goal systems theory, we distinguish between currently pursued *focal goals* of which goal status one is explicitly aware and *background goals* whose presence need not be consciously registered. For example, one might assume that all one is doing is pursuing a casual conversation with a friend whereas in fact one is also

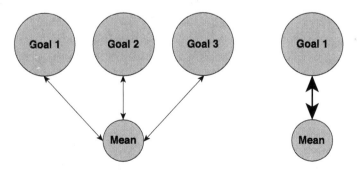

Figure 5 Uniqueness and strength of mean-goal association.

(subconsciously) self-enhancing or impression-managing. Or, one may feel that one's choice of one's marital partner is driven by her/his intelligence and warmth unaware that she/he also reminds one of one's mother or father and that this is an important cause of the partner's appeal.

An intriguing methodological implication of the notion of subconscious impact is that goals can be subliminally primed. Pioneering work of Bargh and his colleagues (e.g., Bargh & Barndollar, 1996) supports the existence of implicit goal priming as does our own work, reviewed subsequently (see also Draine & Greenwald, 1998).

Contextual dependence. We know that human cognitions are subject to *contextual framing* effects and goal systems should be no exception. From that perspective, goal systems are hardly invariant or fixed. All to the contrary, they are highly flexible and context-dependent, in that their shape and form may vary in accordance with situational framing effects. As noted earlier, a pronouncement by a trusted source or "epistemic authority" (cf. Kruglanski, 1989; Elis & Kruglanski, 1992) may set up, alter, or eliminate cognitive-connections between goal-systemic elements. Additionally, the activation of some such elements may occur in some contexts only but not others. This means for example that a different set of means to the same goal (i.e., a different equifinality set) may be envisaged by the same individual in different contexts; as a consequence she or he may select different means to the same goal in those varying circumstances. As shown in Figure 6, in context 1, mean x to goal A may be preferred over its alternatives s, t, and u, whereas in context 2 mean y to the same goal may be preferred over x, s, and t; consequently, x will be chosen in the first context but not in the second.

Moreover, the *substitutability* relations between various means may be context-specific. In one context, means x and y may be seen as connected to the same goal A which would render them mutually substitutable, whereas in another context x and y may be seen as connected to different goals which would render them non-substitutable. These relations are graphically depicted in Figure 7.

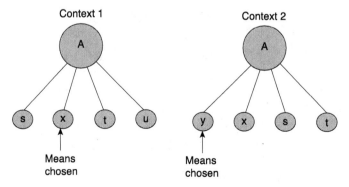

Figure 6 Choice of means is context-dependent.

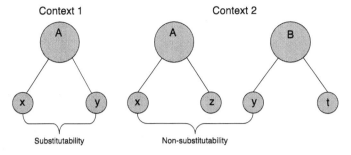

Figure 7 Mean substitutability is context-dependent.

The allocational properties of goal systems

The fundamental *allocational* property of goal systems rests on the assumption of *limited mental resources*. From that perspective, the allocation of cognitive resources constitutes a "constant sum" game, so that the more resources are accorded to a given portion of one's mental field the less mental resources are left for the remaining portions. We are assuming that, typically, goal pursuit is resource-dependent. If so, the greater the investment of resources in pursuit of a given goal or in the implementation of a given mean the less resources should be available for alternative goals or means. One implication of this is that currently active goals may *pull resources* away from each other. This may interfere with progress toward each of these goals, and impede their attainment. Similarly, alternative means to the same goal may compete with each other for mental resources and imply the need to exercise choice among them (so that at least the mean chosen may receive the required resources). Finally, one might envisage a resource-competition between a goal and its associated mean as well. Excessive concentration on a goal while pursuing the means, that is a failure to effect a full transition from a mind-set of "deliberation" to that of "implementation" (cf. Gollwitzer, 1996) might represent a counterproductive rumination or an exaggerated "assessment" orientation that undermines effective "locomotion" toward one's goals (cf. Kruglanski, Thompson, Higgins, Shah, Atash, & Pierro, 2000). Thus, in addition to the structural properties of goal systems, their allocational properties too may place important constraints on adaptive self-regulation.

Motivational properties of goal systems

Neither the structural nor the allocational properties of goal systems are unique: They characterize all cognitive systems not just goal systems. Cognitive psychologists have typically assumed, for example, that the organization of concepts in memory consists of inter-linked nodes which may vary in strength of association to one another (cf. Anderson, 1973; 1984). Similarly, the doctrine of limited mental resources is a mainstay in much cognitive theorizing (cf. Kahneman, 1973) and is hardly of special pertinence to goal systems. What makes goal systems unique is their composition of motivationally relevant entities, that is, of goals and of means. Both are endowed with special properties that do not pertain to alternative cognitive systems. We will briefly discuss what some major such properties might consist of.

Goal striving. To a considerable extent, human action is goal-driven (cf. Gollwitzer & Bargh, 1996). It represents the striving to attain specific desirable objectives. Goal striving is typically exigent of resources, and it may result in *success* or in *failure* (to reach the desired end). Successful attainment of one's objective generally engenders *positive affect* of pleasure or satisfaction, whereas failure to attain one's goals engenders *negative affect* of displeasure and disappointment. Specific types of goals may lend unique shades of positive or negative affect as function of their attainment or non-attainment. In this vein, Higgins (1997) distinguished between *promotion goals* whose attainment engenders feelings of happiness and pride—and non-attainment, feelings of sadness and dejection—and *prevention goals* whose attainment gives rise to feelings of calm and relaxation where non-attainment gives rise to ones of tension and agitation.

Goal commitment. By goal commitment we mean the degree to which an individual is determined to pursue a goal. Goal commitment is assumed to vary as a function of subjective utility determined by a multiplicative function (c.f., Atkinson, 1954) of the value assigned to the goal and its expectancy of attainment (S.U. = f (E × V). In other words, there will be no commitment to a goal if:

(1) its subjective expectancy of attainment was nil no matter how high its subjective value (e.g., one wouldn't commit to the goal of possessing the Mona Lisa painting, no matter how great its perceived artistic value);
(2) its value was nil, no matter how high the expectancy of attainment (e.g., one may refrain from committing to the goal of purchasing a new vacuum cleaner even if the expectancy of being able to do so was complete, simply because one's old vacuum cleaner was perfectly OK, and hence the value of the new acquisition was nil).

Recent evidence implies that with respect to some goals at least, namely sacred duties and obligations, their high magnitude may dampen the *weight* of the expectancy factor in the multiplicative formula, such that the expectancy matters less and less the greater the magnitude of the duty or obligation (cf. Shah & Higgins, 1997). Also, some individuals, e.g., inveterate "locomotors" (Kruglanski et al., 2000) may be so inclined to engage in sheer movement toward goals that they may commit to goals primarily on the basis of attainment expectancy (assuring progress and movement) and give relatively little weight to value. Finally, in some domains, such as achievement, *magnitude* of the value component may depend on that of the expectancy component such that the lower the expectancy of attainment (the harder the task) the greater the value of success (cf. Atkinson, 1954). We assume then, that goal commitment is a multiplicative function of value and expectancy but the way these are combined or weighted may depend on specific goals and/or individuals.

Goal commitment may express itself in persistence of goal strivings, as well as in emotional reactivity to successful or unsuccessful strivings. Thus, a goal to which one is strongly (vs. less strongly) committed would elicit greater magnitude of positive affect upon attainment and greater magnitude of negative affect upon attainment failure.

Means choice and substitution. Subjective utility considerations may also drive the choice of appropriate means. All else being equal, at a given goal value the mean most likely to be chosen is that which promises the greatest *expectancy* of attainment. However, all else need not be equal, at least not in all circumstances. Beside the focal goal the individual may be consciously pursuing, there may exist other, background goals that he or she strives to attain, often without conscious awareness. For instance, the individual may be fatigued and because of that opt for a mean that promises goal attainment with a minimal expenditure of effort. Alternatively, he or she may be in a hurry and hence opt for a means that may seem to be the quickest way of reaching the goal. In yet other instances, she or he may wish to impress an audience, and hence may opt for the most "impressive" or "dramatic" means that promises to attain such an effect. Such choices may sacrifice the expectancy of goal attainment for multifinality considerations, that is, for the potentiality of a given mean gratifying goals over and above the currently focal objective. The trading of expectancy for multifinality need not sacrifice subjective utility, however. For multifinality increases the value component of the equation and hence might often compensate for a potential loss of expectancy.

As noted earlier, a strong commitment to a goal may express itself in persistent efforts toward goal attainment. Such efforts may often include the coping with failure to attain the goal or to advance toward the goal. Coping, in turn, may include a "means-shift" (Kruglanski & Jaffe, 1988), that is, the *substitution* of a new mean for one that has failed to bring about the desired result. Substitution may involve a selection from a previously represented means-constellation, or it may require the generation of new means, and hence the mental construction of novel goal-systemic relations.

Whereas the generation of appropriate means may advance goal pursuit, rival alternative goals may undermine it by introducing *goal conflict* (cf. Lewin, 1935; Miller, 1944). Adaptive coping would require the management or resolution of such a conflict so that subjective utility is maximized and that a goal pursuit most likely to accomplish it is carried out.

Joint workings of cognitive and motivational principles in self-regulation

We are assuming that the various motivational phenomena just discussed (e.g., goal commitment, means choice and substitution, the management of goal conflict) function within the structural and allocational *constraints* inherent in goal systems' cognitive nature. In other words, whereas motivational phenomena have their own endogenous determinants (related to considerations of expectancy and value described earlier) they are also determined by the (exogenous) cognitive conditions of a given goal system that affect the nature and values of these endogenous factors. In that sense, self-regulation is enabled by a joint operation of cognitive and motivational principles that *interactively* impact goal-driven action. This general notion affords new insights into numerous self-regulatory phenomena addressed in the following sections.

Goal systems theory: A summary

It is well to take stock at this point and to summarize the fundamental postulates of goal systems theory. It assumes that:

(1) Goal systems are characterized by two types of properties: *cognitive* and *motivational*.
(2) Goal systems' cognitive properties are (a) structural, and (b) allocational. A major structural property of goal systems is interconnectedness, characterized by the form and strength of links between goals and means within a given system. A major allocational property of goal systems resides in the restricted nature of mental resources to be distributed in a "constant sum" fashion among various goal-systemic elements.
(3) Goal systems' motivational properties comprise (a) the principle of subjective utility that determines goal commitment and mean-choice. Furthermore, (b) goal striving is accompanied by affective feedback engendered in response to success and failure outcomes, and (c) is characterized by persistence of pursuit, including means substitution and the management of goal conflict.
(4) The various motivational properties of goal systems are constrained, hence partially determined, by their cognitive properties. The research described in the following sections illustrates this general notion with a wide variety of phenomena. In accordance with the theory's breadth, the goals we investigated ranged from narrow task-goals to life-long objectives. Our research methods too were correspondingly varied. We often used "micro-cognitive" priming techniques to tap the momentary activation potentials within goal systems, but we also relied on structured questionnaires to explore the chronic representations of such systems and we used a variety of cognitive, behavioral, and outcome-related measures to investigate diverse goal-systemic effects.

Empirical explorations of goal systems

The goal-systemic research described below falls into two broad categories, related respectively to (1) the strength as well as the type (facilitative and inhibitory) of associative links between goal-systemic elements, and (2) their configurational patterns. We discuss them in turn.

Associative links between goal-systemic elements

(1) Associative connections between goals and means. Our empirical work often involved the application of cognitive methods (related to goal systems' cognitive properties) to a variety of motivational phenomena (related to goal systems' motivational essence). Thus, in much of our research we assessed the degree of association between goal-systemic elements. Our methodology was based on priming one such element, say a goal or a mean, and measuring the extent to which this activates another element, e.g., another mean or goal. We used either supraliminal or subliminal priming (our participants did not consciously realize that a prime had been presented) and we typically measured consequent construct activation via a lexical decision task. Using these methods we investigated first whether the degree to which related goals and means (that is, elements within the same goal system) are associated is stronger than the degree to which unrelated goals and means (that do not belong within the same goal system) are.

Participants responded to a computer program by listing three different attributes it was their goal to possess and one positive attribute they were *not* currently trying to possess. They also listed one activity they could perform to attain each of the four attributes. We regarded these as means to those particular goals. After completing the initial procedure, the computer prompted the participants to list all the activities they could think of that would help them attain each of the attributes. Finally, participants completed a lexical decision procedure in which they were asked to determine whether a word was an attribute or an activity. The four attributes listed by the participant and the first attainment means listed for each attribute were randomly included in the presented set of prime and target words. The links between attributes and means could be assessed then, by examining reaction times when the *attribute* or *goal* was the prime for the *means*. The reaction times to the means when primed with the corresponding goal that participants were currently pursuing were significantly faster than when the prime was a non-goal control. The difference between the goal and control primes disappeared, however, when the goal was one that participants were not currently pursuing. This latter finding argues against an alternative explanation of our results in terms of a mere semantic association between related goal and mean words in the general language. It appears, instead, that the dynamic interrelation of goals and means within the same goal system contributes to their cognitive association over and above their possible semantic affinity. These findings are shown in Figure 8.

(2) Uniqueness of linkage and associative strength. Data from the same study support the assumption that the strength of association between goal-systemic elements is positively related to their uniqueness. Recall that following the listing of a single activity that would help them attain the goal, participants listed all such activities they could think of. We found that the *lower* the number of activities participants listed, that is, the greater the uniqueness of the goal-means connections, the faster the lexical decision times to the first activity listed after being primed with the corresponding goal, that is, the stronger the degree to which the goal cognitively activated that particular mean. These data are displayed in Figure 9.

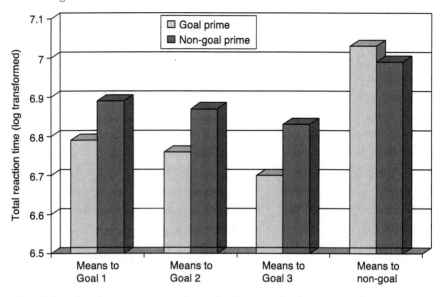

Figure 8 Reaction times to means under goal and non-goal priming.

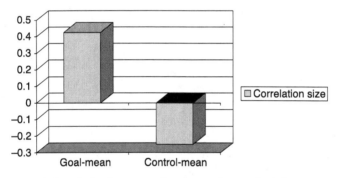

Figure 9 Correlation between uniqueness and strength of the goal-mean association.

(3) Transfer of commitment from goals to means. The fact that goals and means are cognitively associated, and that the strength of their association is positively related to its uniqueness is neither particularly surprising nor particularly "motivational" (cf. Anderson, 1974; 1983). These features, however, form the necessary basis for the transfer of motivational properties from the goal to the means; a much more interesting and motivationally relevant phenomenon. A means strongly associated with a goal may immediately bring the goal to mind, evoking feelings and attitudes associated with that goal while thinking about or engaging in the means. In an early study designed to investigate this issue, participants generated a goal and listed either one or two means, i.e., activities designed to attain that goal. Participants were then asked to indicate how committed they were to engaging in the activity.

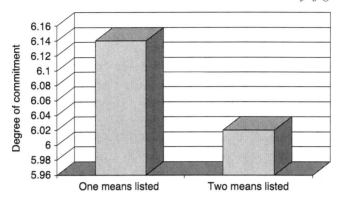

Figure 10 Degree of commitment as function of means uniqueness.

We found that participants rated themselves as more committed to the activity when it was the only means listed (thus the strength of its association with the goal was high) versus when it was one of the two activities listed, which lowers uniqueness, hence, proportionately, association strength. Assuming that the degree of commitment to the goal is relatively high, this is consistent with the notion that the transfer of commitment from the goal to the means is greater the stronger their association (see Figure 10).

Correspondence between commitment to goal and to means. The foregoing study *assumed* that participants' commitment to the goal was relatively high, but it did not assess it. Ideally, one would expect *a direct correspondence* between commitment to the goal and to the means. In our next study we collected data pertinent to this issue by explicitly assessing goal as well as means commitment. Participants, University of Maryland students, listed a goal they were striving to attain, and then 1, 2, or 6 activities they were engaged in toward attaining that goal (e.g., one participant listed "becoming a broadcaster" as a goal and "taking an editing class" as an activity). Goal commitment was assessed before the listing of means, through ratings of (1) goal importance, (2) likelihood of attainment, (3) amount of invested efforts, and (4) plans to attain the goal in the near future. Next, depending on the experimental condition, participants listed activities they may work on, or are already working on, in order to attain the goal. Finally, commitment to the first activity listed was assessed through ratings of (1) its perceived importance, (2) likelihood of its pursuit, (3) investment of efforts in it, (4) its pursuit in the present, (5) frequency of engagement in it, and (6) perceived interest in it. All ratings were made on 7-point scales. As predicted, we found that correlations between commitment to the goal and commitment to the first activity listed was highest ($r=.43$, $p<.05$) in the one-activity condition where the uniqueness (and hence presumably the strength) of the association was the highest; it was substantially lower ($r=.24$) in the *two-activities* condition; and it was lowest in the six-activities condition ($r=.08$) where uniqueness also was lowest, consistent with the notion that commitment-transfer varies as function of the degree of association between the goal and its means (see Figure 11).

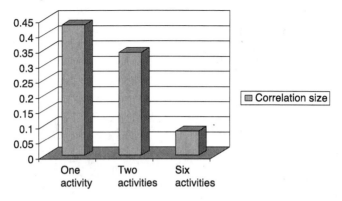

Figure 11 Correlation between commitment to goal and to first activity listed as function of number of activities.

Direct measurement of the degree of association. In the studies so far, we have *inferred* the degree of association strength from the number of means to a goal participants listed. In our next study we used a direct measure of association strength by assessing the degree to which the goal primes its corresponding means. Participants in this study provided two attributes it was their goal to possess, and listed one activity they believed could help them attain each attribute. They were then subliminally primed with the goals (or control words) and performed a lexical decision task with the activities (i.e., the means) as targets. Then they rated the emotions they felt when thinking about possessing the attribute, and the emotions they felt when engaging in the activity. Specifically, participants were asked to indicate how agitated, dejected, happy, and relaxed they felt regarding each goal and activity and they provided their answers on a 5-point scale ranging from 0 (not at all) to 4 (a great deal). Separate emotion-totals for each goal and activity were created after first reverse-scoring the negatively valenced emotion items. As illustrated in Figure 12, our analyses indicated that the correlation between the emotional magnitude of a participant's goal (e.g., a goal of "becoming educated") and the emotional magnitude of a corresponding means (e.g., a means of "studying") depended on strength of the goal-means association. We found that the correlation between the emotional significance of a goal and the emotional significance of a means was significantly greater the stronger the degree to which the goal primed its corresponding means.

Transfer of affective-quality from goals to social means. Beyond the magnitude of commitment and of affect, the degree of the goal-means association may determine the transfer of unique affective qualities between the two. In a study designed to investigate this possibility, participants listed either an "ought" goal defined by Higgins (1987) as a *duty or an obligation*, or an "ideal" goal defined as a *hope or an aspiration*. Higgins' (1987, 1997) research suggests that the attainment of "ought" goals gives rise to "prevention-type" affect, expressed in such emotions as *relief, calm,* and *relaxation*. By contrast, the attainment of "ideal" goals gives rise to "promotion-type" affect expressed in such emotions as *happiness, pride,* or *enjoyment*.

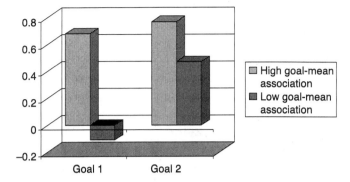

Figure 12 Correlations between emotional commitment to two goals and their associated means.

Participants then listed three acquaintances whom they believed were related to attainment of the goal (i.e., to constitute "social means" to the goal in question). We assumed that the order in which the acquaintances were listed reflected the strength of their association to the goal (for a similar methodology see Higgins, King, & Mavin, 1982). Participants rated their expected emotions following goal attainment using three items related to ideal-type affect (namely, *happy, proud, enjoy*) and three items related to ought-type affect (namely, *relieved, calm, relaxed*). They used the same items to rate their feelings toward each acquaintance. We found that the affective qualities associated with ideal or ought goals were transferred to individuals related to these goals' attainment and that the degree of transfer was proportionate to the order in which these persons were listed. Thus, for an ideal-type goal, ideal-type affect felt with respect to the first person listed was more pronounced than ideal-type affect felt with regard to the second person listed, which in turn was more pronounced than the ideal-type affect felt with respect to the third person listed. Similarly, for the ought-type goal, the corresponding (goal-type) affect was stronger with respect to the first two persons listed than with respect to the third person listed. No significant relation existed between the strength of *ideal-type* affect and the listing order of acquaintances when the goal was of an *ought type*, nor between the strength of an ought-type affect and listing order when the goal was of an *ideal type*. This data-pattern, shown in Figure 13, supports the notion of transfer of specific affective qualities from the goal to the associated means as function of their degree of association.

In summary, the degree of cognitive association between a goal and a mean seems to determine the degree of transfer between the two of (1) the degree of commitment, as well as (2) the quantity, and (3) the quality of affect. These findings have intriguing implications for the topic of intrinsic motivation (for recent discussions, see Shah & Kruglanski, 2000; Sansone & Harackiewicz 2000): When an activity is strongly associated with a goal (and its attainment), it might "mesh," or form a "unit-relation" with it (Heider, 1958); that is, be experienced as an *end in itself*, or as intrinsically motivated. That is perhaps why various goal properties

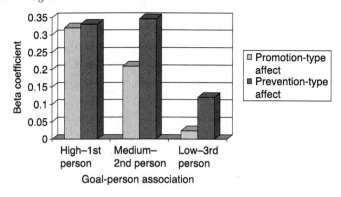

Figure 13 Correlation between goal-related and activity-related affect.

(such as goal commitment) "spill over," and come to characterize such intrinsically motivated activities. This suggests, for example, that:

(i) intrinsic motivation could be conceptualized as lying on a continuum (determined by the association strength of a goal and an activity), rather than representing a qualitative dichotomy as has been typically surmised (cf. Deci and Ryan, 1985; Kruglanski, 1975);
(ii) rather than reserving the notion of intrinsic motivation for specific types of goals, such as those of autonomy, competence or relatedness (cf. Deci and Ryan, 1985) any goal and any relevant activity could be structurally tied together (or associated) to produce intrinsic motivation; and
(iii) depending on the specific characteristics of the goal, different intrinsically motivated activities to whom those characteristics are transferred would be experienced differently. Thus, whereas all intrinsically motivated activities might give rise to positive affect, the *specific type* of positive affect might vary as function of the goal (e.g., whether it constitutes an "ideal" or an "ought") to which the activity is intrinsic.

The present 'transfer' notion is reminiscent of the goal-gradient phenomenon enunciated by Clark Hull (1932, pp. 25–26). According to Hull's goal-gradient hypothesis, "the goal reaction gets conditioned the most strongly to the stimuli preceding it, and other reactions of the behavior sequence get conditioned to their stimuli progressively weaker as they are more remote (in time or space) from the goal reaction."

The animal-learning theorist that he was, Hull conceived of the goal-gradient principle in terms of time and space that separate the animal from the goal. The present transfer principle is broader in nature and linked to the strength cognitive associations between means and ends, that transcend temporal and spatial considerations. Thus, merely thinking of a strongly associated means (e.g., of studying, working out at the gym, or going out on a date) may call to mind the respective goals of these activities (good grades, a fit body, the admiration of one's partner) and the attendant feelings and cognitions linked with their attainment.

(4) Goal-systemic phenomena and the determinants of subjective utility: Goal-means association and goal commitment. The structural property of *association strength* and the motivational property of *attainment expectancy* afford jointly the prediction that the degree to which a goal is associated with a mean should be positively related to goal commitment. The reason is that mean-accessibility may increase the perceived expectancy of goal attainment and hence increase the subjective utility of the goal's pursuit determined by the expectancy and value formula. The foregoing hypothesis corresponds to common experience wherein the excitement about a goal pursuit is augmented by the sense of "know how" regarding goal accomplishment, and hence an expectancy of success that may cement goal commitment. Consider the difference between a goal such as 'shopping' to which the means (e.g., visiting the neighborhood mall) jumps immediately to mind, versus writing a theoretical paper to which the means (i.e., the relevant ideas) are not as readily discerned. As common experience attests, it is relatively easier to commit to shopping than to writing and the latter pursuit may require a considerably greater amount of self-discipline to stay on track.

In a study designed to investigate these notions, participants generated their goals and corresponding means. They then completed a subliminal priming task on a computer. In one condition designed to experimentally strengthen the goal-means association, participants completed repeated trials presenting goals as primes and means as targets. In another condition, participants completed trials wherein control words were the primes and means were the targets. We found that commitment to the goal was higher in the experimental (vs. the control) condition where the association between goals and means was systematically strengthened (see Figure 14).

That commitment to a goal is increased when the mean to that goal is apparent is indirectly supported by the "mental contrasting" work of Oetingen (2000, Oetingen, Pak, & Schnetter, 2001). She finds that where focusing on a desired state is followed by contrasting it with the actual state (a comparison likely to instigate a means-generation activity), commitment to the goal is markedly more contingent

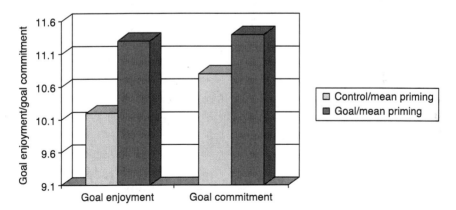

Figure 14 Effects of manipulated goal-means association.

on the *expectancy* of goal attainment as compared to a situation where focusing on the actual state is followed by thinking about the desired state, or to a situation of focusing on the desired state exclusively. These results may indicate that the mental-contrasting procedure instigates a means-generation attempt that may or may not succeed. When it does succeed, the means is particularly accessible (having just been generated), hence increasing commitment. When it does not succeed, however, not only is the means accessibility low, but one is meta-cognitively aware of the difficulty of altering this state of affairs which may additionally depress commitment.

Inter-goal association undermines goal commitment. Whereas association between a goal and a mean may increase goal commitment, association between a goal and competing goals may undermine commitment because the latter may pull resources away from the focal goal, lowering attainment expectancy, subjective utility, and hence commitment. Suppose that John associates the goal of preparing for the exams with the goal of flirting with Ann, a fellow graduate student with whom he often studies. Such association between competing goals may undermine John's expectancy of doing well, and his overall commitment to studying.

Indeed, we found in several studies that the degree to which a goal primed other goals (either supraliminally or subliminally) was inversely correlated with various measures of commitment, including direct ratings of commitment, reported progress toward the goal, and the magnitude of positive and negative affect proportionate to participants' perceived discrepancies from their goals (see Figure 15). We also found that this relation was moderated by the degree to which the alternative goals were seen as facilitatively related to the focal goal (i.e., the degree to which they partially served as *means* to the goal in question). This overall data-pattern is consistent with the notion that goal commitment is related negatively to a goal's association with its rival alternatives and, is related positively to its association with its attainment means.

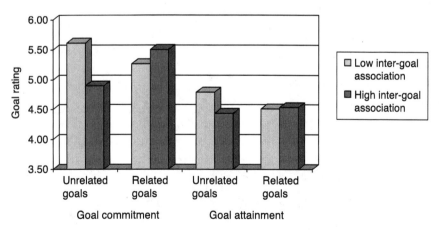

Figure 15 Goal-commitment and goal-attainment as a function of inter-goal association and goals-facilitative relations.

Priming alternative goals undermines goal commitment. The correlational nature of the foregoing findings is mute as to the direction of causality. It is indeed possible that the activation of alternative goals may pull resources away from the focal goal, and hence undermine goal commitment. It is also possible, however, that goals to which one is committed *actively inhibit* their alternatives. The notion that mental resources are limited, and that they are, therefore, allocated among the various goal-systemic elements, suggests that both causal directions may obtain in fact, and our data bear this out. Indeed, we found in several studies (Shah & Kruglanski, in press) that priming participants with an alternative goal undermines their commitment to the focal goal, hampers progress toward that goal, hinders the development of effective means for goal pursuit, and dampens participants' emotional responses to positive and negative feedback about their striving efforts. As in our correlational research above, we found also that the apparent pulling-away of resources by a goal's rival alternatives is attenuated as function of the degree to which these are perceived as facilitatively related to attainment of the focal goal.

In one of the studies designed to test these notions, participants expected to perform two consecutive tasks the first of which consisted of an anagram solution. While working on the anagram task (constituting their "focal" goal at that point), participants were subliminally primed with the second task they expected to perform (that operationally defined the "alternative" goal), or were primed with a control-phrase. We assessed commitment to the focal goal through persistence on the first task, performance success, and extent of affective reactivity to success and failure feedback. As shown in Figure 16, these measures of commitment showed substantial decline in the alternative goal priming (versus control) condition. Consistent with our previous findings, such decline too was substantially attenuated where the alternative goal was seen as facilitatively related to the focal goal, that is, where it partially served as *means* to that goal's attainment.

In another series of studies (Shah, Friedman, & Kruglanski, in press) we found that activation of a given focal goal results in an inhibition of alternative goals as reflected in the slowing down of lexical decision times to such goals, and that the

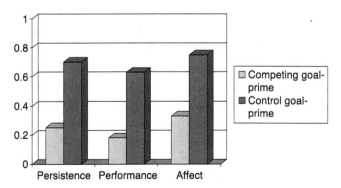

Figure 16 Activation of competing goals undermines commitment to focal goal.

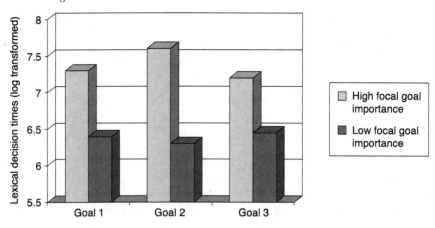

Figure 17 Lexical decision-times to alternative goals when primed with high or low importance focal goals.

magnitude of such inhibition is positively related to participants' commitment to the focal goal. The magnitude of this inhibitory effect was reduced where the alternative goals were seen as facilitatively related to the focal goal. The data from one of the relevant studies are summarized in Figure 17. In that experiment, participants *listed three attributes it was their goal to possess*. They then engaged in a lexical decision task in which the goals (or control words) served as primes and on other trials, as targets. As can be seen, we found that when a goal (versus a control word) served as a prime, this increased the lexical decision times to the alternative goals (versus control words) attesting to their inhibition. This effect was proportionate to participants' commitment to the priming goal (or its perceived importance). Though not represented in the figure, we also found that the inhibition of alternative goals was significantly reduced as function of the degree to which the alternative goals were seen as related *facilitatively* to the focal goals.

Thus, in conformance with the resource-limitation aspect of goal systems, we find evidence both for *the pulling-away of resources* by accessible goal alternatives and for the *shielding* against such a pull by an active inhibition of those alternatives.

Inter-goal associations and self-control: the dynamics of overcoming temptations. The foregoing notion of goal shielding has a distinctly functionalist flavor. It suggests that individuals tend to shield their commitment to important goals against a "goal pull" by attractive alternatives. But what about focal goals that are momentarily alluring yet are relatively detrimental in the "grander" scheme of things, constituting "temptations" that undermine the accomplishment of higher priority goals. In the interest of effective self-regulation, temptations might alert one to the danger by activating (rather than inhibiting) the high importance goals with which they are in conflict. We recently carried out several studies to investigate this possibility.

In one of our studies, participants, University of Maryland students, entered on a computer an important goal they were currently pursuing. They entered predominantly goals related to *academic success, relationships, appearance,* and *religion.* Participants then entered a temptation with regard to the goal they listed which we defined for them as "something you would like to do but ought not to, if you want to attain the goal." For instance, for a goal of "study" participants entered such temptation as to "party," or for a goal of "keeping one's girlfriend" a temptation such as to "watch porno films." Participants then entered two unrelated goals and two unrelated temptations to serve as controls. Then in a lexical decision task we subliminally *primed* them with the relevant (or irrelevant) temptation using the relevant goal as a target, or with the relevant (or irrelevant) goal using the relevant temptation as target. As shown in Figure 18, we found that temptations activated their overarching goals, whereas the overarching goals significantly inhibited temptations.

This study suggests that the facilitative/inhibitory relations between temptations and goals can occur outside awareness exhibiting one of the properties of automaticity (Bargh, 1996): As the primes were presented subliminally and were not consciously recognized by participants, they were unlikely to evoke a deliberate cognitive process. In our next study, we proceeded to probe another aspect of automaticity: its efficiency or relative independence of attentional resources.

In that research we made use of the fact that a large proportion of University of Maryland students listed religious objectives among important life goals (e.g., to "go to heaven" or "not to sin"). We, therefore, used "sin"-related words such as "drugs," "temptation," "premarital," and "sex" as temptations and religion-related words such as "prayer," "Bible," "religion," and "God" as goals. Both served as primes and alternatively as targets in a lexical decision task. We also used irrelevant goals and temptations as controls (in both the prime and the target roles). Approximately half the participants were placed under cognitive load implemented by instruction to memorize a 9-digit number and to reproduce it at the end of the study. The

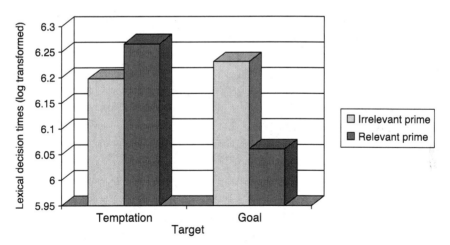

Figure 18 Lexical decision times to temptations and overarching goal-targets primed by relevant versus irrelevant goals versus temptations.

results, summarized in Figure 19, indicated that even though the load had an overall effect of slowing down reaction times, it did not affect the inhibitory/facilitative relations between temptations and goals. Specifically, in replication of our previous study, temptation words (such as "sin") facilitated lexical decision times to goal words (like "religion") whereas goal words slowed down the reaction times to temptations. It begins to appear then that effective self-control may entail the overlearning (to the point of automaticity) of activation and inhibition patterns wherein temptations alert one to higher priority life goals with which they conflict, and the higher importance goals tend to banish temptations out of people's minds.

Our next study went beyond "mere cognition" in testing the behavioral implications of activating goals by temptations. We hypothesized that in the presence of a temptation people would tend to activate their higher priority goal that, in turn, will help them overcome the temptation. Participants in this study were women (University of Maryland undergraduates) known to have weight-loss as a goal. They were randomly assigned to one of three rooms. One room designed to directly prime the goal of "dieting" contained various "diet-related" magazines (namely about beauty, health, and fitness) strewn around the table. The second room contained instead various objects designed to prime tasty, yet fattening, food temptations such as chocolate bars and cookies, as well as a copy of the *Chocolatier* magazine, replete with appealing, and "mouth-watering" illustrations of highly caloric deserts. The third, control, room contained various geographic magazines about US natural attractions.

In each of the separate rooms, participants individually engaged in a lexical decision task including the word "diet" as the critical target. We found that both the "diet" prime, and the food temptation prime activated "diet" to an equal extent and significantly more so than did the control prime. Finally, participants

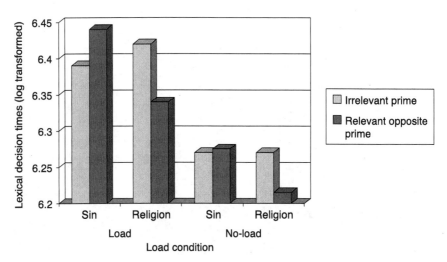

Figure 19 Lexical decision times to "sin" versus "religion" targets after subliminal priming by "religion" versus "sin" opposite primes.

were offered a choice between a Twix bar and an apple as an ostensible gift for taking part in the experiment. We found that in both the "diet" and in the "food temptation" prime conditions, the majority of participants selected the apple as a gift whereas in the control prime condition the majority of the participants selected the Twix bar. It appears then, that for these dieting participants, a tempting stimulus in the form of fattening delicacies was as effective as a direct dieting reminder not only in activating the dieting goal but actually in pursuing it behaviorally. Data relevant to these notions are summarized in Figures 20 and 21.

Our temptation studies thus far are optimistic in their implications, suggesting that temptations activate the "larger" goals they are in conflict with, which, in their turn, tend to inhibit temptations. But as we know too well, at least some of the people some of the time do succumb to temptations, often with dire consequences

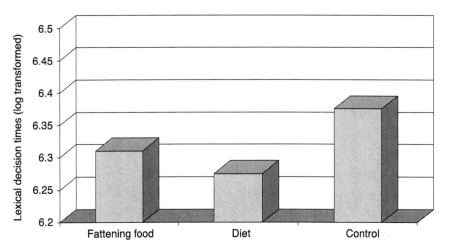

Figure 20 Lexical decision times to the "diet" target in presence of "fattening food," "diet-related," or irrelevant primes.

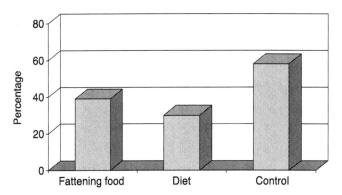

Figure 21 Percentage of participants choosing a Twix bar over an apple as function of "fattening food," "diet," and irrelevant priming.

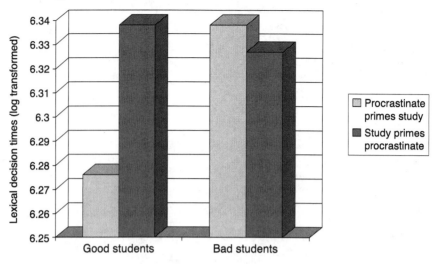

Figure 22 Lexical decision times for "study"-related targets for "good" versus "bad" students.

for their mental and physical health, and with considerable costs to the society at large (e.g., in domains of substance-abuse, safe sex, or domestic violence). We thus proceeded to investigate whether people who are by and large unsuccessful self-regulators exhibit different cognitive relations between their goals and their temptations than do successful self-regulators. Our participants in this study were University of Maryland undergraduates who, by their own admission, were successful or unsuccessful in their academic pursuits. They performed a lexical decision task after first being exposed to a subliminal prime. On some of the trials, the primes were words related to the temptation to avoid studying such as "television," "procrastinate," "phone," and "internet," and target words were related to the goal of studying, for example, "study," "grades," "homework," and "graduate." On other trials the foregoing study words, were the primes and the temptation words were the targets. As shown in Figure 22, we found that for successful students temptation words activated study words to a much greater extent (the lexical decision times were faster) than for unsuccessful students, whereas for the unsuccessful students the study words activated temptation words to a greater extent than for the successful students. These results imply the possibility that successful self-regulation involves the acquisition of "automatic" activation and inhibition patterns enhancing one's ability to focus one's attention on high-priority objectives and shift it away from low-priority objectives, particularly if they conflict with the former and hinder their pursuit.

This concludes our discussion of associative links of facilitative and inhibitory nature among goal-systemic units. We now turn to consider the configurational aspects of goal systems and their implications for various self-regulatory phenomena.

Configurational patterns of goal-systemic linkages

Multifinality as a determinant of choice. As noted earlier, the *equifinal* configuration wherein several means are connected to the same goal poses the problem of *choice* among the means. How may such choice be accomplished? The notion of subjective utility suggests that the mean to be chosen might often be the one that promises to deliver the highest *value* or the utmost "bang" for the psychological "buck." Often, this could be a means that in addition to the focal goal promises to attain additional goals as well, that is, a means characterized by maximal *multifinality*. Indeed, several lines of recent evidence attest to the important role that multifinality plays in means' preference.

In one study we asked University of Maryland students to list two important attributes they could attain by studying. They listed, among others, such attributes as becoming "educated," "successful," or "powerful." Participants were also asked to assess the degree to which these attributes represented distinct goals. Controlling for their subjective value, we found that the degree to which of these attributes were judged to represent *dissimilar* goals was positively related to participants' commitment to studying, suggesting that commitment was strongest when studying was linked to different goals, hence exhibiting the property of multifinality.

In a different study, we presented participants with the opportunity to play a hypothetical lottery in which they had a chance to win a pair of prize packages. As schematically represented in Figure 23, the total content of these packages was identical but in one condition the prizes were distributed in such a way so as to strongly invoke two separate goals. In that condition, one of the prize packages consisted entirely of items related to *fitness*, and the other of items related entirely to *entertainment*. In another condition, each package contained a mix of fitness and entertainment items, so that the separateness of the two goals was less salient. Instead, a general "better living" goal might have been invoked in this condition.

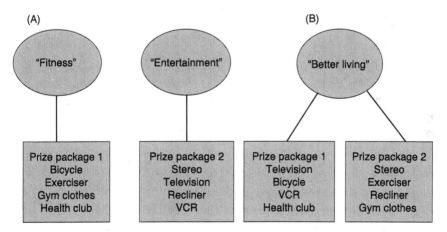

Figure 23 Packaging of same prizes to suggest two (A) versus one (B) goals.

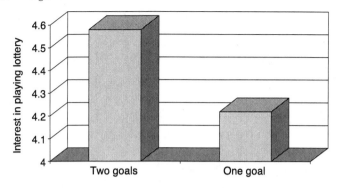

Figure 24 Interest in playing a lottery serving one goal versus two goals.

We found that participants were significantly more interested in playing the lottery where two separate goals seemed clearly invoked, consistent with the notion that multifinality (the "two birds with one stone" notion) may be an important determinant of preferences (see Figure 24).

Multifinality in unconscious choice. A fascinating feature of human choice is that it may often be driven by unconscious considerations. Besides pursuit of the focal goal, the multifinal choice may often be driven by a variety of "background" goals of which the chooser may not be consciously aware. In a classic study by Nisbett and Wilson (1977) passersby at a department store chose among four different nightgowns of a similar quality, or among four identical pairs of nylon stockings. A strong position-effect was found, such that the rightmost object in the array was heavily over-chosen. The central highlight of this research was that the participants seemed entirely unaware of having exhibited the position-effect and in that sense their choices may have been unconsciously driven. Still, the question may be asked, *why* did these choices exhibit a rightmost skew to begin with? A possible answer is implied by the present notion of multifinality. In these terms, participants in the Nisbett and Wilson (1977) studies may have had two goals in mind (see Figure 25): (1) making a reasonable choice (this was their "focal" goal that would have been equally gratified by any object in the array), and (2) reaching quick closure after the entire array had been examined (this may have constituted a "background goal" of which participants have been consciously aware). Assuming that participants examined the array from left to right, both goals were satisfied by the rightmost object in the array, which was therefore more multifinal than its alternatives. Indeed, participants ended up overchoosing that particular object by a large margin, as already noted.

To test this analysis, we recently replicated the Nisbett and Wilson (1977) study with slight variations. In our experiment, the focal goal was kept constant, but the background goal was varied. Specifically, University of Maryland students chose among four pairs of identical athletic socks the one that seemed to them of the best quality. In one condition, participants were placed under time-pressure to

A theory of goal systems 233

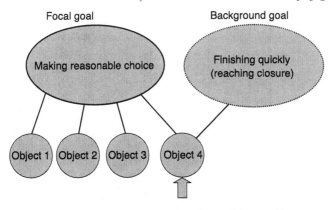

Figure 25 A multifinality interpretation of the Nisbett and Wilson (1977) finding of a right-position preference.

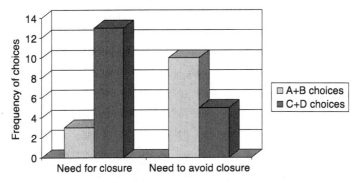

Figure 26 Frequency of choices as function of need for closure.

increase the need for closure (Kruglanski & Webster, 1996; Webster & Kruglanski, 1998). No time-pressure was applied in the second condition, where in addition participants were given accuracy instructions to reduce their need for closure. If our analysis is correct, we should replicate the rightmost preferences in the need for closure condition, but not in the need to avoid closure condition. As shown in Figure 26 that is exactly what happened. As in the Nisbett and Wilson (1977) experiments, participants seemed wholly unaware of being affected by time-pressure or accuracy instructions. Instead, they justified their choices entirely in terms of the socks' quality. Thus, some of the reasons they gave were that "stitching looked the best" in the pair chosen, that "the material was thicker in padding," that the "socks appeared more durable," etc. suggesting that the need for closure and the need to avoid closure constituted "background goals" in this situation, operating outside of participants' awareness.

Of course, need for closure is merely one among many possible background goals a person can commit to. To test the generality of the multifinality principle in another study, we varied a different background goal: a desire to identify or disidentify with one's group. In this research we took advantage of two recent events of considerable significance for the College Park campus; one positive, the other negative. The positive event was inclusion of the UMD basketball team in the group of finalists (the "final four") in an important inter-collegiate tournament (the NCAA tournament). The negative event was an outbreak of vandalism in College Park in the aftermath of the loss to Duke at that very tournament. The two events occurred in close temporal proximity, and our research took place a week after the latter of the two (i.e., the vandalism) took place. Our participants, all University of Maryland students, were asked to recall either one or the other event and to report their feelings about it. Not surprisingly, participants reported "feeling proud" in the "final four" condition suggesting a goal of identifying with their university. And they reported "feeling ashamed" in the vandalism condition, suggesting a goal of disidentifying with the university.

In an ostensibly separate "mini-experiment" participants chose which of two batches of material is more durable. In fact, both were batches of the same material, only one was colored red representing one of the UMD colors (which are red, black, and yellow), whereas the other was colored purple, constituting a control color. As shown in Figure 27, in the "final four" condition, participants rated the material with the UMD color (i.e., red) as more durable than the control color (purple). By contrast, in the "vandalism" condition, participants rated the purple-colored (control) as more durable than the UMD color.

As in our prior study, participants exhibited no awareness that their choices might have anything to do with color of the swatches or their relation to their university. In a post-experimental interview, the reasons they gave for their selection were based entirely on the perceived quality of the fabric, e.g., its "thickness," "apparent strength," or "stiffness," indicating that participants were not cognizant of the multifinal nature of their choice, nor of the background goals that might have affected it.

Number of active goals and size of the equifinality set. Obviously, the greater the number of goals active at a given time, the greater the degree of multifinality a means could

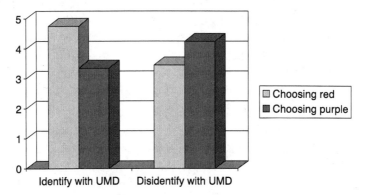

Figure 27 Ratings of durability of materials as function of identification with the University of Maryland.

possibly attain. Granting the additional assumption that the *difficulty* of identifying a means is proportionate to its multifinality (it may be harder to locate a means that gratifies many goals versus only a few), it follows that the greater the number of currently active goals the more difficult it should be to find an appropriately multifinal means, and as a consequence, the fewer such means to a given focal goal would be identified. For instance, if one's sole goal was to find *something to eat* there exists a virtually endless range of possibilities to choose from (including different fruits and vegetables, fish and meats, dairy products, a variety of sweets, etc.). However, if in addition to the *eating* goal one also wished to maintain a *slim figure*, and look out for one's *health*, the range of possibilities should become much narrower, shrinking to a relatively limited list of "health" or "diet" foods.

More generally then, the presence of alternative goals should restrict the size of the *equifinality set*, or the number of substitutable means to a given focal goal. We investigated this notion in a number of studies. In the first of these, participants listed *one goal* they had for themselves. They did so either on a clean survey form or one that had been previously filled out (presumably by another participant) and partially erased. In this "partially filled-out" survey, instead of one goal the fictitious participant listed five goals known (on the basis of a pilot study) to be quite common among university students. These were: "exercising," "health," "good grades," "love," and "taking care of Mom" goals. Participants were then asked to write down all the possible activities that could help them achieve the goal they themselves had listed. As shown in Figure 28, participants listed substantially more activities when no alternative goals were present, supporting the hypothesized relation between one's mental awareness of alternative goals and the equifinality set of means one tends to generate with respect to the focal goal.

To control for the competing hypothesis of *mere distraction* by alternative items, in the next study we asked participants to list one goal they were currently pursuing, and then list another 3 of their personal goals, or 3 presumed goals of the president of the United States. This study also compared the thinking about *current* versus *future* goals. In one condition, participants listed their (or the president's) current goal(s) and in another condition, goals they would likely have a year hence. We

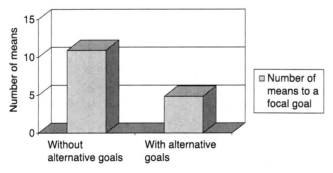

Figure 28 Number of means to a focal goal as function of the presence of goal-alternatives.

assumed that in thinking about a present goal participants would already have at the back of their minds alternative pressing objectives; this should constrain the number of activities listed with respect to the focal goal. However, when thinking about a future goal, alternative goals might be less likely to weigh in one's considerations. Thus, we expected that in the single-goal condition, participants would list more activities (or means) with respect to future versus current goals. This effect should be reduced in the three-goals condition because explicitly listing the alternative goals would allow them to exercise their constraints in both the future and the present condition. Our data, shown in Figure 29, are consistent with these assumptions. First off, in the *current-goals* condition alternative personal goals (but not the president's goals) reduced significantly the equifinality set-size of means to the focal goal. Furthermore, in the *single-goal* condition more activities were listed in the future versus the present condition. This effect was significantly reduced in the *alternative goals* condition.

Whereas in our research so far we explicitly manipulated the presence of alternative goals, an interesting question is what "natural" condition may foster their appearance or disappearance, and hence affect the equifinality set-size to the focal goal? As the research described earlier indicates, commitment to a focal goal may represent one such condition. Commitment to a focal goal may effect the inhibition of the alternative goals especially if the latter were seen as less important in the overall scheme of things (thus, representing "temptations") than the focal goal. In terms of our initial example, under intense hunger, presumably increasing one's commitment to the goal of eating, the alternative goals of maintaining a slim figure, low cholesterol, or healthy diet, may be appreciably suppressed or inhibited. Under these conditions, the range of foods one might consider, i.e., the means to satisfy one's hunger, might be considerably larger than might be the case if one's hunger was only moderate.

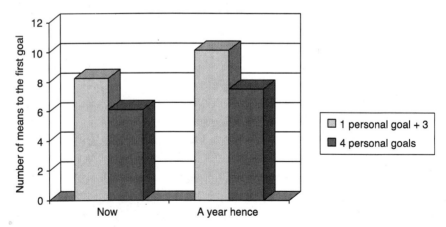

Figure 29 Number of means generated for the first goal listed as a function of the alternative goals listed.

In addition, the alternative goals may be momentarily primed within the context of a given goal pursuit. This, in turn, should reduce the equifinality set-size with regard to the focal goal. These possibilities should be probed in future research. But for now let us consider an important possible *consequence* of equifinality set-size—the possibility of substituting one means for another following a failure to advance toward one's chosen goal.

Substitution phenomena. In a remark attributed to Thomas Edison, he alluded to the substitution issue by stating that he had never failed, only found 10,000 ways that didn't work! Generally speaking, substitution (of tasks, medications, diets, exercise-regimens, or symptoms, for example) constitutes a response to thwarting one's progress toward a goal by choosing an alternate route to the same objective. Such thwarting may result from *failure* of an original attempt, its *interruption*, or *elimination* of the routine means of moving toward a given end. The problem of *substitution* is fundamental to social and personality psychology, as witnessed by the attention it received from classic motivational theorists such as Freud (1923/1961) and Lewin (1935).

From a goal-systemic perspective, substitutability of means depends on an equifinality configuration linking them to the same objective. Both choice and substitution relate to equifinality, yet they address opposite aspects of this configuration: The problem of *choice* refers to how the means *differ* (e.g., which is more *multifinal*, or promises to deliver a greater value than the others) so that a satisfactory choice among them would be possible. By contrast, *substitution* refers to how the activities are the *same*, so that they could replace one another. An interesting aspect of this analysis is that, as noted earlier, goal-systemic configurations are malleable and subject to contextual framing effects; accordingly, substitutability too should be context-dependent.

In a study designed to investigate this issue, we framed two instances of the same activity (of anagram solution) as relating either to the *same* promotion or prevention goal or to *different* goals wherein one instance of the activity was linked to a "prevention," and the other, to a "promotion" goal (Higgins, 1998) in a counterbalanced fashion. Following the procedure devised by Shah, Higgins, and Friedman (1998) participants were led to believe that, in order to motivate them to try their hardest they would receive either 1 or 2 extra credit points depending on whether they found 80% of all the possible solutions to the anagrams or not. This contingency, however, was framed to either represent the opportunity for a reward (a promotion concern) or the opportunity to avoid punishment (a *prevention* concern). In the promotion-frame condition participants were told that they would receive 1 extra credit point for their participation but that if they found 80% of all the possible words, they would get an additional point. In the prevention-frame condition, participants were told they would receive 2 extra credit points for their participation but if they failed to find 80% of all the possible solutions they would lose one of their extra credit points. Participants then completed two different anagram tasks (each with its own promotion or prevention contingency).

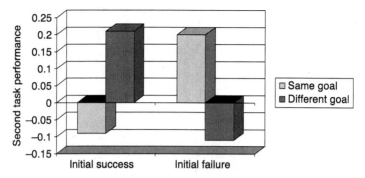

Figure 30 The effect of goal-commonality and success/failure on second task-performance.

As shown in Figure 30, we found that failure at the first task *increased* performance on the second task if both had the same regulatory focus framing but not if they had a different regulatory focus framing. Assuming that successful performance reflects an investment of efforts in an activity, these results suggest that when two tasks are framed as connected to the same goal, failure on one increases efforts invested in the other—attesting to substitution. We also found that success at the first task *decreased* performance on the second when it had the same (vs. different) regulatory focus framing, attesting that substitution was no longer pertinent when the objective was attained via the first attempted route.

Substitutability in modes of self-esteem enhancement. A goal-systemic analysis helps to shed light on some seemingly incompatible findings about the substitutability issue in modes of self-esteem enhancement. Specifically, work of Steele and Lui (1983) and of Tesser, Martin and Cornell (1996) suggested that various psychological phenomena such as dissonance-reduction, self-affirmation, and self-esteem maintenance are mutually substitutable. Presumably, that is so because the high-level goal of self-esteem restoration is of paramount importance for the participants, and dissonance-reduction, self-affirmation, and esteem-maintenance activities constitute functionally equivalent means to reaching that particular goal.

However, Stone, Wiegand, Cooper, and Aronson (1997) demonstrated that when dissonance is aroused by a hypocrisy manipulation, participants prefer to reduce dissonance directly despite a ready availability of a self-affirmatory activity, suggesting that the direct and indirect modes of self-esteem restoration aren't, after all, fully substitutable for each other, contrary to former claims.

Goal systems theory offers a resolution to this seeming dilemma. Specifically, we assume that a dissonance manipulation, implemented by inducing the individual to behave in a hypocritical manner, activates not only the abstract goal of *self-esteem restoration* but also the sub-goal of proving one is *not a hypocrite*. Our multifinality-notion suggests that the direct goal of dissonance-reduction should be preferred in this case (if one had one's "rathers") over self-affirmation, just as found by Stone et al. (1996). A graphic representation of these relations is shown in Figure 31.

A theory of goal systems 239

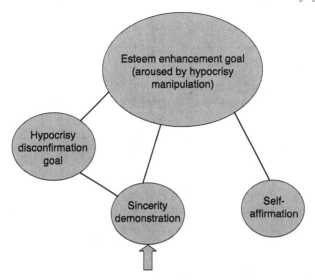

Figure 31 Preference for sincerity demonstration over self-affirmation in a hypocrisy manipulations study.

Note, however, that according to the goal-systemic analysis dissonance-reduction or hypocrisy are *nonunique* as far as multifinal choices are concerned. As shown in Figure 32, raising concerns about another cherished value, say, about one's courage should result in a preference for a direct affirmation of that value, i.e., affirmation of one's valor over alternative ways of self-esteem restoration, say through the affirmation of sincerity, or the denial of hypocrisy.

Finally, if one's self-esteem was undermined in a yet different way (e.g., via an athletic failure) hypocrisy denial and self-affirmation might be fully substitutable with no particular preference between them being manifest (see Figure 33), simply

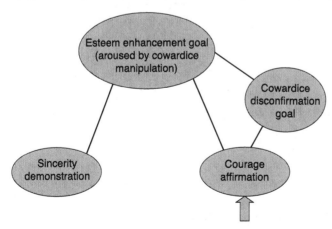

Figure 32 Preference for courage-affirmation over sincerity demonstration in a (hypothetical) cowardice-manipulation study.

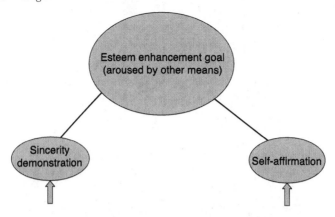

Figure 33 Full substitutability of self-affirmation and sincerity demonstration when esteem-enhancement goal is aroused by other means.

because in this case neither is more multifinal than the other. In short, the answer to the question of whether hypocrisy denial and self-affirmation are fully substitutable is that *it all depends*. What it depends on is the *context* and more specifically, the goal system that is mentally set-up for participants in a given situation.

Social psychological implications of goal-systemic effects

An essential property of goal systems theory is its breadth and, content-free nature. It is that feature which renders the theory applicable to numerous domains of social psychological phenomena. More specifically, other persons may figure in our goal-systemic framework in three possible roles:

(1) They may serve as *primes* that activate various goal-systemic elements (e.g., colleagues at a scientific convention may activate one's goals of productivity and achievement as well as one's perceived discrepancies from those objectives giving rise to feelings of anxiety or dejection (cf. Higgins, 1997);
(2) They may function as social *means* to goal attainment in that their assistance, special skills, or services rendered may advance one toward one's chosen objectives (e.g., one's collaborators may serve as means to getting one's work done, one's family members may serve as means to goals of intimacy and affection, and so on);
(3) They may function as *ends* in themselves, e.g., their love, affection, and respect may represent goals that one strives to attain via various means (hard work, impression management, reciprocal affection, etc.).

Interpersonal implications of goal systems

Others as social primes. In a recent study relevant to the social priming notion, participants (University of Wisconsin students) were asked to name their mother

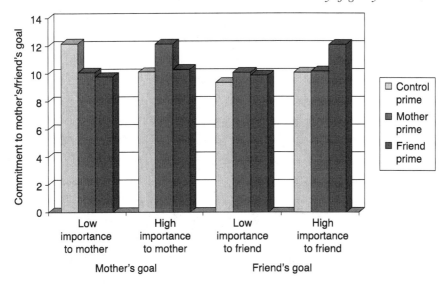

Figure 34 Commitment to goals as a function of social primes.

and a close friend and to indicate a goal each of these significant others had for them. After completing a series of filler questionnaires, participants reported how committed they were to pursuing the goals they had listed previously during the upcoming week. While being asked these questions, participants were subliminally primed with the name of either their friend, their mother, or a control word.

As shown in Figure 34, participants were significantly more likely to express commitment to a goal when first primed with the specific person-construct to whom the goal was associated. Moreover, this effect varied as a function of the importance of these goals to the specific others. Thus, the more strongly a participant's mother desired that the goal in question be pursued, the greater the extent to which her subliminal "presence" increased a participant's commitment to that goal.

A second study examined participants' actual pursuit of an anagram task-goal as a function of whether they were primed with the name of a significant other who would want them to do well on that goal, a significant other who would rather have them do something else instead, or a control prime irrelevant to the task. This experiment required participants to complete an alleged measure of "verbal fluency," which turned out to involve the finding of anagram solutions. Before completing the task, participants were told that they would perform a lexical decision task meant to assess how quickly they recognized words generally because this skill could affect their anagram performance and therefore needed to be controlled for. This lexical decision task was meant to assess whether priming participants with the name of a significant other who either wanted them to do well or wanted them to "do something else instead" affected the accessibility of the task-goal relative to a control condition (as seen in speed of participants' responses to goal-related words). Indeed, subliminally priming participants with the name of

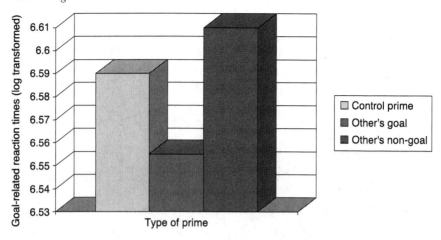

Figure 35 Goal-related reaction times as a function of social primes.

a significant other who wanted them to perform well increased the accessibility of goal-related items whereas priming participants with a significant other who wanted them to do something else instead seemed to inhibit the accessibility of goal-related items relative to the baseline-control condition, as seen in Figure 35.

Do these changes in goal accessibility actually influence how participants pursue a given task-goal? As shown in Figure 36, participants persisted significantly longer and found significantly more solutions when they had been primed with the name of the significant other who had wanted them to do well. Moreover, participants primed with the name of a significant other who had wanted them to do something else instead persisted significantly less and found significantly fewer solutions than participants in the baseline condition. Additional analyses revealed that changes in task-persistence and performance were mediated by changes in goal accessibility. These results attest to the role of significant others as "primes" the mere thought

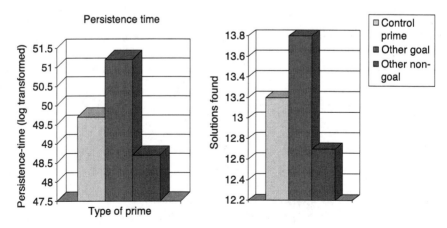

Figure 36 Persistence time and solutions found as a function of a social prime.

of whom may activate the individual's appropriate goal systems that, in turn, may affect subsequent actions and performances.

Others as means. But beyond representing *primes* for various goals, other people may often constitute important *means* to goal attainment. For instance, they may constitute social mirrors that reflect one's various attributes, or provide comparison standards for assessing one's social standing and/or progress toward desired objectives. Other persons may also provide actual assistance in one's attempts to attain various goals such as "education," "wealth," "prestige," or "attractive appearance," the achievement of which is virtually unthinkable without someone's helping hand (e.g., a teacher's, a business partner's, a political ally's, or a cosmetician's). In the interpersonal realm, one's friends may be conceived of as "means" of gratifying sundry goals as those of "being loved," "receiving emotional support," "having a good time," "sharing one's experiences," "expressing one's views," "receiving intellectual stimulation," etc.

Indeed, different individuals as well as entire cultures may differ in their "goal-systemic" conceptions of interpersonal relations. Consider the quintessential notion of "friendship," certainly a key term in the realm of human contacts. Some friendship-notions may be *multifinal* requiring of a friend to fulfill a large variety of functions in diverse domains (e.g., intellectual, instrumental, emotional, and social). Other friendship-notions may be "unifinal," a friend being defined as someone who gratifies any objective at all. A person subscribing to the latter conception might have separate friends for different realms of activity. Thus, one might have a "tennis friend," a "family friend," a "conversational friend," "a friend for cultural pursuits," "a helpful friend," etc. It seems plausible that such divergent conceptions of friendship would have intriguing consequences for the way one's friendship relations may unfold. For instance, persons subscribing to a multifinal (versus a unifinal) definition of friendship may have fewer friends simply because multifinal means (that is, ones which satisfy multiple constraints) may be more difficult to procure than unifinal means. Such difficulty of procurement may have intriguing, additional consequences as well. Thus, individuals with a multifinal (vs. a unifinal) conception of friendship may be more committed to their friends, exert greater efforts in maintaining friendships, sustain their friendship for longer time periods, find it more difficult to replace one's friends (e.g., upon moving to a different location), and end up with friends that are more similar to each other (insofar as each friend has similar relevance to a wider range of dimensions). We recently carried out an investigation that looked into the consequences of subscribing to a multifinal versus a unifinal conception of friendship, and examined them both *within* and *between* two different cultures, namely the US and Germany. This particular comparison was prompted by Kurt Lewin's (1935) informal observation that these two cultures approach friendship very differently, and that the Americans have quicker "surface accessibility" than the Germans yet their friendship ends up being less "deep" in some sense than that of the Germans. As Lewin (p. 20) put it:

> Compared with Germans, Americans seem to make quicker progress toward friendly relations early in the acquaintance process and with many more

persons. Yet this development often stops at a certain point and the quickly acquired friends will, after years of relatively close relations, say good bye as easily as after a few weeks of acquaintance.

We wondered, therefore, if Lewin's insight might not reflect differences in the degree to which Germans subscribe to a more multifinal conception of friendship than do the Americans, and whether such *cross-cultural* differences, should they exist, may not be echoed by similar differences in friendship pattern *within* each culture. Our cultural samples consisted of university students. The German sample consisted of undergraduates at the University of Chemnitz (in Eastern Germany) and the US sample, of undergraduates at the University of Maryland. We presented our participants with a multifinal and a unifinal definition of friendship and asked them to indicate the extent to which they subscribed to each. Specifically, participants read the following two definitions of friendship:

(A) Some people consider people as friends even though they are involved in few or only one aspect of their life. For example, they consider as friends people that make possible/facilitate one activity, interest, or need;

(B) Some people consider as friends people that are involved in many aspects of their life. For example, they consider as friends people that make possible/facilitate many of their current activities, interests and needs.

Participants were then asked to indicate to what extent their personal friendship-choices reflected definition A versus B by circling a number on a 7-point scale. Subsequently, participants answered a series of questions relating to their current close friendships, specifically: (a) how many close friends they have, (b) how similar to each other they perceived their friends to be, (c) how difficult it would be for them to find new friends should they need to relocate, (d) how much maintenance their friendships required, (e) how long it normally took them to acquire good friends. We also asked participants to rate (f) the importance to them of friendship as compared to other aspects of their lives, (g) the importance of having many friends, and (h) the frequency of having terminated past friendships due to a conflict in a relationship.

The results revealed strong associations between participants' adherence to a multifinal (vs. unifinal) definition of friendship and several significant aspects of their friendship-patterns. For *both* the German and the US samples, participants high on the multifinality dimension reported having significantly fewer friends, perceived it as more difficult to find new friends if they had to relocate, perceived their friends as being more similar to each other, presumably because of their relevance to the same set of multiple goals, perceived themselves as exerting greater efforts toward the maintenance of friendships, perceived themselves as more committed to their friends, and as more likely to terminate their friendship due to conflicts, presumably owing to a greater number of potential areas of friction in a multifinal versus unifinal relation (see Table 1).

Table 1 Zero order correlations between friendship multifinality and aspects of the friendship relation (combined German and U.S. samples)

Number of friends	Friends perceived similarity	Difficulty of making friends	Efforts to maintain friendship	Commitment to friends	Friendship termination
−20**	.13*	.26***	.15*	.31***	.25***

Note: Friendship multifinality
* p < .05   ** p < .01   *** p < .001.

Of particular interest, our findings confirmed Lewin's hunch as to the differences in friendship-patterns between Germans and Americans, and were consistent with our hunch as to its relation to differences in friendship-multifinality. As shown in Figure 37, the Germans subscribed to a more multifinal definition of friendship on average than did the Americans. They also reported having fewer friends, reported exerting greater efforts in friendship-maintenance, reported greater commitment to their friends (as indexed by perceived difficulty of replacing their friends), rated the overall importance of friendship as higher, and the importance of having *many* friends as lower.

Others as ends in themselves. Finally, specific others could constitute important social goals that is, significant social-ends of one's personal strivings. One may strive to attain the affection, love, or respect of a particular other (e.g., one's parent, a potential romantic partner, or one's boss). One may want to possess, control, or dominate a particular other, and so on. It seems plausible to assume then that one's relations with that other person could importantly depend on the specific goal which she or he may represent. As with other goals, the commitment to such social goals may be enhanced by the accessibility of their attainment means, and undermined by the

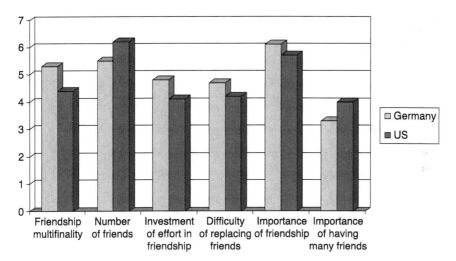

Figure 37 Differences in friendship patterns between German and US samples.

accessibility of alternative goals in the same environment. Finally, the goals that the other represents may enter into intriguing relations with the individual's alternative goals. For instance, the goal of intimacy and familial closeness may seem in conflict with one's career goals. If the latter goals loomed larger and seemed more subjectively important in an overall scheme of things, affectionate relations with one's family members might come to be treated as a "temptation" to be overcome, rather than as a legitimate and independent concern to be addressed. If that were the case, the sight of one's wife or children, for example, might activate one's career concerns and the attendant tensions and anxieties these often instigate. This may consequently inhibit the goal of closeness and intimacy and undermine the quality of one's familial relations more generally. These intriguing possibilities are speculative at the moment, yet they seem worthy of a further, more thorough, examination.

Conclusion

Søren Kierkegaard (1986), the Danish existential philosopher, argued in a celebrated work that "purity of heart is to will one thing." As common experience instructs us, however, willing "one thing only" is no simple matter. Instead, we typically experience numerous wants, obligations, and desires that impinge upon us if not exactly at the same moment, at least very close together temporally speaking. One motivational thought leads to another, and soon we find ourselves in a swirl of musings about things we need to do, would like to do, or failed to do. Ironically, as in social psychology and Western culture more generally, *motivation* is often juxtaposed to *cognition* (or "passion" to "reason"), our motivational states are so labile and dynamic precisely because they are carried by a stream of associations that incessantly flow through our minds and—whether consciously or not—affect our experiences, our feelings, and our actions.

The theory in the preceding pages is meant to tap such dynamic complexity of motivational states. To that end we defined the concept of goal systems as a mental representation of cognitively interwoven constructs whose contents consist of "goals" and "means." We have assumed that the functioning of goal systems is guided jointly by two classes of properties: cognitive and motivational. Understanding it may furnish important insights into a broad variety of phenomena of traditional interest to personality and social psychologists. Among others these are:

(1) Activity experience and intrinsic motivation both presently conceptualized in terms of the transfer of psychological properties (such as the degree of commitment, magnitude of emotional investment, and the quality of affect) from goals to means as function of their degree of association.
(2) Effective self-regulation consisting in:

   (a) the (over)learnt *inhibition* of rival alternative goals particularly to the extent that their attainment is deemed less important in an overall scheme of things than progress toward one's focal objective;
   (b) the (over)learnt *activation* of superordinate alternatives upon confrontation with conflicting, lower-order "temptations."

(3) Generation of equifinal means to a focal goal as inverse function of the activation-level of alternative goals, and the phenomena of *choice* (including subconscious choice), and *substitution* that the equifinality-constellation affords.
(4) A variety of social psychological phenomena with goal-systemic underpinnings, including cases where other people constitute:

  (a) primes that activate individuals' goal-systemic elements,
  (b) social means to a variety of goals, and
  (c) ends, or goals, in and of themselves.

The empirical data described above are consistent with numerous aspects of our goal systems theory. Admittedly, however, this work constitutes merely a beginning. Additional conceptual and empirical efforts will be needed to fully explore the possibilities inherent in a goal-systemic perspective on self-regulatory phenomena. To mention one example, on the conceptual level it should be important to address and elaborate the distinction between competing goals, versus negative means, that is, "hindrances" or "barriers" to goal attainment (Lewin, 1935; Oetingen, 2000). Both may interfere with pursuit of a given focal goal, yet they may do so via different mechanisms.

On the empirical level, a wide variety of problems in the three-fold interface between cognition, motivation, and action await a goal-systemic probing, which implications could cast novel light on numerous social psychological phenomena analyzable from the means-goals perspective.

Finally, on the practical level, goal systems analysis may enable important insights into a wide range of major problems in living. For instance, *goal commitment*, one of our central variables, is pertinent to the ability to form close relationships, or to succeed in one's chosen profession. Understanding the dynamics of commitment may improve our ability to foster commitment to realistic goals, and to reduce (or inhibit) commitment to unattainable or unrealistic pursuits. A clearer understanding of *activity experience* may enhance our ability to improve people's quality of life and increase our attempts to foster adaptive patterns of coping with stress or psychological trauma (e.g., bereavement, or major illness). Understanding the cognitive dynamics of overcoming temptations may increase our ability to promote adaptive self-control, and hence improve overall life-satisfaction. Goal-systemic insights into the processes of choice may increase our ability to promote adaptive choices in the social and the professional realms, etc.

References

Anderson, J. R. (1974). Retrieval of propositional information from long-term memory. *Cognitive Psychology, 6*, 451–474.

Anderson, J. R. (1983). *The architecture of cognition.* Cambridge, MA: Harvard University Press.

Anderson, J. R. (1984). Spreading activation. In J. R. Anderson & S.M. Kosslyn (Eds.), *Essays on Learning and Memory.* San Francisco, CA: Freeman.

Bargh, J. A. (1996). Automaticity in social psychology. In E. T. Higgins & A. W. Kruglanski (Eds.), *Social psychology: Handbook of basic principles* (pp. 169–183). New York, NY: Guilford.

Bargh, J. A., & Barndollar, K. (1996). Automaticity in action: The unconscious as repository of chronic goals and motives. In P. M. Gollwitzer & J. A. Bargh (Eds.), *The psychology of action* (pp. 457–481). New York: Guilford.

Bem, D. J. (1972). Self-perception theory. In L. Berkowitz (Ed.), *Advances in experimental social psychology* (Vol. 6, pp. 1–62). New York: Academic Press.

Cacioppo, J. T., & Petty, R. E. (1982). The need for cognition. *Journal of Personality and Social Psychology, 42*, 116–132.

Chartrand, T. L., & Bargh, J. A. (1996). Automatic activation of impression formation and memorization goals: Nonconscious goal priming reproduces effects of explicit task instructions. *Journal of Personality and Social Psychology, 71*, 464–478.

Chen, S., & Chaiken, S. (1999). The heuristic-systematic model in its broader context. In S. Chaiken & Y. Trope (Eds.). (1999). *Dual-process theories in social psychology*. (pp. 73–96). New York, NY, US: The Guilford Press.

Deci, E. L. & Ryan, R. M. (1985). *Intrinsic motivation and self-determination in human behavior.* New York: Plenum.

Draine, S. C., & Greenwald, A. G. (1998). Replicable unconscious semantic priming. *Journal of Experimental Psychology: General, 127*, 286–303.

Dweck, C. S. (1999). *Self-theories: Their role in motivation, personality, and development.* Philadelphia, PA: Psychology Press.

Elis, S., & Kruglanski, A. W. (1992). Self as epistemic authority: Effects on experiential and instructional learning. *Social Cognition, 10*, 357–375.

Freud, S. (1961). The ego and the id. In J. Strachey (Ed. And Trans.). *The standard edition of the complete psychological works of Sigmund Freud* (Vol. 19, pp. 3–66). London: Hogarth Press. (Original work published in 1923.)

Freud, S. (1923) *The Ego and the Id. S.E. 19:* 1–66.

Gollwitzer, P.M. (1996). The volitional benefits of planning. In: P. M. Gollwitzer & J. A. Bargh (Eds.). *The psychology of action* (pp. 287–312). New York: Guilford Press.

Gollwitzer, P. M., & Bargh, J. A. (Eds.). (1996). *The psychology of action: Linking cognition and motivation to behavior.* New York: Guilford.

Heider, F. (1958). *The psychology of interpersonal relations.* New York: Wiley.

Higgins, E. T. (1997). Beyond pleasure and pain. *American Psychologist, 52*, 1280–1300.

Higgins, E. T. (1987). Self-discrepancy: A theory relating self and affect. *Psychological Review, 94*, 319–340.

Higgins, E. T., King, G. A., & Mavin, G. H. (1982). Individual construct accessibility and subjective impressions and recall. *Journal of Personality and Social Psychology, 43*, 35–47.

Hull, C. L. (1932). The goal-gradient hypothesis and maze learning. *Psychological Review, 39*, 25–43.

Kelley, H. H. (1972). Causal schemata and the attribution process. In E. E. Jones et al. (Eds.) *Attribution: Perceiving the causes of behavior* (pp. 151–174). Morristown, NJ: General Learning Press.

Kierkegaard, S. (1886). *Purity of heart is to will one thing.* (translation into English by D. Steere, 1938, 3rd ed., 1956). New York: Harper and Row.

Kruglanski, A. W., Erb, H. P., Pierro, A., & Spiegel, S. (2001). A parametric unimodel of human judgment: A fanfare to the common thinker. In L. G. Aspinwall & U. M. Staudinger (Eds.), *A psychology of human strengths: Perspectives on an emerging field.* Washington, D.C.: APA Press.

Kruglanski, A. W., Thompson, E. P., Higgins, E. T., Atash N. N., Pierro, A., Shah, J. Y., & Spiegel, S. (2000) To "do the right thing" or to "just do it": Locomotion and assessment as distinct self-regulatory imperatives. *Journal of Personality and Social Psychology, 79,* 793–815.

Kruglanski, A. W., & Thompson, E. P. (1999a). Persuasion by a single route: A view from the unimodel. *Psychological Inquiry, 10*(2), 83–110.

Kruglanski, A. W., & Thompson, E. P. (1999b). The illusory second mode, or the cue is the message. *Psychological Inquiry, 10*(2), 182–193.

Kruglanski, A. W., & Webster, D. M. (1996). Motivated closing of the mind: "Seizing" and "freezing". *Psychological Review, 103,* 263–283.

Kruglanski, A. W. (1996a). Motivated social cognition: principles of the interface. In E. T. Higgins & A. W. Kruglanski (Eds.), *Social psychology: Handbook of basic principles* (pp. 493–520). New York, NY: Guilford.

Kruglanski, A. W. (1989). *Lay epistemics and human knowledge: Cognitive and motivational bases.* New York: Plenum.

Kruglanski, A., & Jaffe, Y. (1988). Curing by Knowing: The epistemic approach to cognitive therapy. In L. Abramson (Ed.), *Social cognition and clinical psychology.* New York: The Guilford Press.

Kruglanski, A. (1975). The endogenous-exogenous partition in attribution theory. *Psychological Review, 82*(3), 87–406.

Lewin, K. (1935). *A dynamic theory of personality.* New York: McGraw Hill.

Miller, N. E. (1944). Experimental studies of conflict. In J. McV. Hunt (Ed.) *Personality and behavior disorders* (Vol. 1, pp. 431–465). New York: Ronald Press.

Miller, D. T., & Ross, M. (1975). Self-serving biases in the attribution of causality: Fact or fiction? *Psychological Bulletin, 82,* 213–225.

Neely, J.H. (1977). Semantic priming and retrieval from lexical memory: Roles of inhibitionless spreading activation and limited-category attention. *Journal of Experimental Psychology: General, 106,* 226–254.

Nisbett, R. E., & Wilson, T. D. (1977). Telling more than we can know: Verbal reports on mental processes. *Psychological Review, 87,* 231–259.

Oetingen, G. (2000). Expectancy effects on behavior depend on self-regulatory thought. *Social Cognition, 18,* 101–129.

Oetingen, G., Pak, H. and Schnetter, K. (2001). Self-regulation of goal setting: Turning free fantasies about the future into binding goals. *Journal of Personality and Social Psychology, 80,* 736–753.

Petty, R. E., & Cacioppo, J. T. (1986). The elaboration likelihood model of persuasion. In L. Berkowitz (Ed.), *Advances in experimental social psychology* (Vol. 19, pp. 123–205). New York: Academic Press.

Sansone, D. & Harackiewicz, J. M. (2000) (Eds.) *Intrinsic and extrinsic motivation: The search for optimal motivation and performance.* New York: Academic Press.

Shah, J. Y., & Kruglanski, A. W. (in press). Priming against your will: How goal pursuit is affected by accessible alternatives. *Journal of Experimental Social Psychology.*

Shah, J. Y., Friedman, R. S. & Kruglanski, A. W. (in press). Forgetting all else: On the antecedents and consequences of goal shielding. *Journal of Personality and Social Psychology.*

Shah. J. Y. & Kruglanski, A. W. (2000). The structure and substance of intrinsic motivation. In Sansone, C. and Harackiewicz, J. M. (Eds.) *Intrinsic and extrinsic motivation: The search for optimal motivation and performance.* New York: Academic Press.

Steele, C. M., & Lui, T. J. (1983). Dissonance processes as self-affirmation. *Journal of Personality and Social Psychology, 45,* 5–19.

Stone, J., Wiegand, A. W., Cooper, J., & Aronson, E. (1997). When exemplification fails: Hypocrisy and the motive for self-integrity. *Journal of Personality and Social Psychology, 72*, 54–65.

Tesser, A., Martin, L. L., & Cornell, D. P. (1996). On the substitutability of self-protective mechanisms. In P. M. Gollwitzer & J. A. Bargh (Eds.), *The psychology of action: Linking cognition and motivation to behavior* (pp. 48–68). New York: Guilford Press.

Webster, D. M. and Kruglanski, A. W. (1998). Cognitive and social consequences of the motivation for closure. *The European Review of Social Psychology*.

Part III
How people act

7 The rocky road from attitudes to behaviors

Charting the goal systemic course of actions

Arie W. Kruglanski, University of Maryland
Katarzyna Jasko, Jagiellonian University
Marina Chernikova, Maxim Milyavsky, and Maxim Babush, University of Maryland
Conrad Baldner and Antonio Pierro, University of Rome "La Sapienza"

Gordon Allport's (1935) oft-cited statement that "the concept of attitude . . . is the most distinctive and indispensable concept in contemporary American social psychology" (p. 798) has reverberated in the proliferation of attitude research over the years. Indeed, the scientific study of attitudes has been the most popular and voluminous topic of research in all of social psychology (for reviews see, e.g., Ajzen & Fishbein, 1975; Albarracin, Johnson, & Zanna, 2005; Eagly & Chaiken, 1993; Krosnick & Petty, 1995; McGuire, 1968; Petty & Wegener, 1998, among others). A search for the term "attitude" on PSYCInfo yields a staggering 390,308 results, as compared with the results for terms such as "cognition" (132,490 results), "motivation" (124,454 results), and "decision" (155,889 results).

Arguably, the immense popularity of the attitude construct owes in part to the fact that attitudes were assumed to predict behavior. Allport (1929) viewed "an attitude (as) a disposition to act" (p. 221, parentheses added). Other authors, too, emphasized the presumptive link between attitudes and behavior. Thus, Cohen (1960) stated that "attitudes are always seen as precursors of behavior, as determinants of how a person will actually behave in his daily affairs" (pp. 137–138). Similarly, Petty and Wegener (1998) affirmed that "attitudes (are) important because of the fundamental role that individuals' attitudes . . . play in the critical choices people make regarding their own health and security as well as those of their families, friends and nations" (p. 3230). If psychology's overarching "goal is the prediction and control of behavior" (Watson, 1913, p. 158), it follows that the attitude-behavior link is of crucial importance, hence understanding it poses a significant challenge for psychological science.

Accordingly, substantial work in social psychology was devoted to questions about the kinds of attitudes that promote behavior and the conditions that facilitate the attitude-behavior link (e.g., Ajzen, 1985, 2012, 2014; Ajzen & Fishbein,

1980; Fabrigar, Petty, Smith, & Crites, 2006; Fazio, 1990, 1995; Fishbein & Ajzen, 1975; Krosnick & Petty, 1995; Regan & Fazio, 1977; Sivacek & Crano, 1982, among others).

The search for moderators of the attitude-behavior relation was likely sparked by early accumulation of findings that not all attitudes actually prompt behavior. Well known in this regard is Wicker's (1969) review, which found "little evidence to support the postulated existence of stable, underlying attitudes within the individual which influence both his verbal expressions and his actions" (p. 75). Wicker concluded, somewhat pessimistically, that "it is considerably more likely that attitudes will be unrelated or only slightly related to overt behaviors than that attitudes will be closely related to actions" (p. 65) and he challenged researchers to look for "factors . . . which are consistently *better predictors* of overt behavior than attitudes" (Wicker, 1969, p. 75, italics added).

The gauntlet thrown down by Wicker (1969) was heartily picked up by social psychologists; however, rather than relinquishing the concept of attitudes as predictors of behavior and seeking "better predictors" elsewhere, investigators proceeded to elaborate influential conceptual frameworks and to generate empirical findings concerning moderating conditions required for the attitude-behavior relationship to be manifest.

Roughly, much of the work on the attitude-behavior relation was carried out under two major research programs centered on the notions of (a) *attitude strength*, and (b) *behavior focus*, respectively. The attitude strength program (see Krosnick & Petty, 1995, for a comprehensive review) adopts the premise that only sufficiently strong attitudes drive behavior, where attitude strength is attested by indices such as accessibility, extremity, confidence, and elaborative basis, among others. The behavior focus program (Ajzen, 1985, 2012, 2014; Ajzen & Fishbein, 1980; Fishbein & Ajzen, 1975) maintains that general object attitudes are unlikely to be related to behavior (a notion they discuss under their *compatibility principle*, Fishbein & Ajzen, 2010, pp. 258–259), and that behavioral prediction is better accomplished from attitudes toward the behavior itself.

Both research programs are reviewed and extensively discussed in this chapter. First, however, we present a novel perspective on the attitude-behavior relation anchored in the psychology of goals. Broadly, we propose that attitudes toward objects, even if strong, or toward behavior, even if highly positive, are insufficient in and of themselves to incite action.[1] Instead, human behavior is driven by *goals*. The latter notion seems to be common knowledge in fact. People pervasively respond to the question of *why* they performed a past behavior, or why they intend to perform a future behavior by pointing to a state of affairs (a goal) that their behavior was or is meant to achieve (cf. Gollwitzer, 1999). Why does one run every evening? To be fit (defining fitness as the goal). Why does one study till the wee hours of the morning? To pass an exam.

To say that behavior is goal driven is not meant to suggest that attitudes are *irrelevant* to behavior. To be sure, attitudes are involved in the enactment of behavior by contributing to *goal formation*. However, object attitudes alone do not produce goals. For behavior to occur, a conjunction of several things of uncertain likelihood must take place, a perfect storm of sorts.

In a gist, attitudes toward objects contribute to the evaluative part of goals: An attitude (*liking*)[2] for an object that one does not presently possess must translate into a desire for it or a "want" of sufficient magnitude (Berridge, 2004; Kruglanski, Chernikova, Rosenzweig, & Köpetz, 2014) and then be conjoined to a perceived attainability (i.e., reasonable expectancy) of obtaining the object of one's desire; beyond a certain threshold the desirability-attainability compound transforms into a *goal* whose attainment may be enabled by a behavioral *means*. Even this might not suffice for behavior to take place, however, for a goal might be overridden by other, more pressing objectives activated in the situation.[3] A goal must dominate those alternative concerns for behavior in its service to take place. In a sense then, the goal construct is the proverbial "elephant in the room," the missing link whose explicit recognition promises to cast a new light upon the attitude-behavior enigma.

Our analysis is much indebted to prior theories and empirical findings on the attitude-behavior consistency, and it integrates them with recent work on the psychology of goals (e.g., Bargh & Ferguson, 2000; Fishbach & Ferguson, 2007; Kruglanski, 1996; Kruglanski et al., 2002, 2012, 2014; Morsella, Bargh, & Gollwitzer, 2009). In essence, we flesh out from a goal theoretic perspective what may have been only implicit in our predecessors' ideas. However, the proposed explication is not a mere rehash of existing concepts; instead, it identifies exceptions to prior formulations and reveals phenomena that have been heretofore obscured.

To foreshadow what is to come, we begin by presenting our conceptual perspective on the attitude-behavior relation. We then review major prior analyses of this relation and reinterpret them in goal theoretic terms. A closing discussion draws the implications of our analysis for conceptual and empirical matters concerning the concept of attitudes and its ultimate relevance to behavior.

A goal-systemic analysis of the attitude-behavior relation

Defining the "attitude concept"

Although various definitions of the term attitude have been offered,[4] the one that has stuck and has managed to command wide consensus views attitude as a positive or negative *evaluation* of some object (e.g., Ajzen & Fishbein, 1975; Bem, 1970; Cacioppo, Harkins, & Petty, 1981; Eagly & Chaiken, 1993; Fazio, 2007; Petty, Wegener, & Fabrigar, 1997; Thurstone, 1931). In what follows, therefore, we too adopt this widely accepted view of attitudes as evaluations.

We also are assuming that an attitude thus defined is essentially a cognitive construct with several distinctive properties often discussed under the common rubric of *attitude strength* (Krosnick & Petty, 1995): An attitude is a *judgment* that a given object or state of affairs falls somewhere on the continuum between *good* and *bad*, or *likable* versus *unlikable*. It is possible also to conceptualize attitudes as located on two separate continua: one of goodness, the other of badness (Armitage & Conner, 2000). The specific location on the continuum (or continua) defines the property of *attitude extremity* (Krosnick & Petty, 1995). As a cognitive construct, too, one's *degree of confidence* in an attitude (or evaluation) may vary depending on the kind of evidence one has for the attitudinal belief in question. For instance if one's own epistemic authority in a given domain (Kruglanski et al., 2005) was high, one could infer one's attitude from one's own experiences or gut feelings toward the entity in question (Fazio & Zanna, 1978). If evaluations of an object on separate goodness and badness dimensions were disparate (e.g., the object was judged as highly positive but also as highly negative) one could speak of attitude ambivalence (Armitage & Conner, 2000). Too, as cognitive constructs attitudes may vary in their accessibility, that is, in the readiness to which object evaluations (or liking for the object) come to mind upon exposure to the object (Fazio, 1990; Higgins, 1996).

Properties of the "goal" concept

We view the goal concept as a cognitive construct, a mental representation whose contents are of motivational significance (Kruglanski, 1996, p. 599). These contents define a goal as "a desirable[5] future state of affairs one intends to attain through action" (Kruglanski, 1996, p. 600). This dynamic definition pertains to goals of all types and levels of importance or of generality. It describes such grand life objectives as getting an advanced degree or becoming a concert violinist, and also such minute goals as crossing a busy street, picking an hors d'oeuvre from a tray, or avoiding a conversation with a stranger. In all these cases, a desirable state perceived as attainable (a coveted academic or artistic attainment, a safe arrival at a desired location, consumption of a tasty snack, preserving one's privacy) fosters action aimed at its attainment. Beyond its dynamic contents, a goal's cognitive properties as a mental representation render it subject to the same processes and principles that govern all cognitive constructs, including the processes of inference, knowledge activation, and unconscious impact as discussed subsequently.

Desirability and attainability. As already noted, for something to be adopted as a goal it must be recognized as *desirable* as well as *attainable* given one's resources. In other words, to adopt a given goal one needs to *infer* from appropriate evidence that the state of affairs in question is sufficiently desirable and attainable.

The desirability (related to value) and attainability (related to expectancy) components of goals are immanent in major theoretical analyses of motivation. Atkinson (1964) for instance noted that "the strength of the tendency to act in a certain way depends upon the strength of expectancy that the act will be followed by a given consequence (or goal) and the value of that consequence (or goal) to the individual" (p. 274). More recently, Shah and Higgins (1997) stated that "an increase in either attainment expectancy (i.e., attainability) or *attainment value* (i.e., desirability) produces an increase in goal commitment" (p. 447). Similarly, Forster, Liberman, and Friedman (2007) argued that goal priming effects (reflecting goal magnitude) are proportional to the product of the goal's expectancy and its value (desirability) and described empirical evidence supportive of this notion.

Empirical Study 1: Lay perceptions of the goal concept. Notions of desirability and attainability are presupposed also by lay conceptions of the goal concept. We asked 104 American adult participants on Mechanical Turk to evaluate a scenario generated by a computer program designed to write stories. The scenario described the following situation:

> Taylor is a freshman in college. He recently learned about a 1-year scholarship at his college. The winner of the scholarship receives *$0/$10,000*. Each applicant has a *0%/25%* chance of winning the scholarship.

In a between-participants design, each of our subjects viewed one of the four versions of this vignette, and responded to the questions: (a) Would it make sense for Taylor to set a goal to get this scholarship? (yes/no); and (b) Would it be rational for Taylor to set a goal to get this scholarship? (yes/no).

Results of this study are clear (see Figure 1). Almost all participants responded that it would not be rational, and would not make sense, for the protagonist to set a goal in the *zero desirability/zero attainability*, *zero desirability/high attainability*, and *high desirability/zero attainability* conditions. In contrast, almost all participants in the *high desirability/high attainability* condition answered that it would be rational, and would make sense, for the protagonist to set a goal in these circumstances. A X^2 test comparing whether the four conditions were different from results that could be expected by chance was highly significant ($p < .001$). These findings, presented in Figure 1, attest that lay participants view some degree of desirability and some (above zero) degree attainability as essential to goal setting.

Accessibility. As cognitive structures, goals vary in their (momentary or chronic) accessibility (Higgins, 1996) and can be activated or primed by relevant environmental stimuli such as its semantic associates (Bargh & Ferguson, 2000; Fishbach & Ferguson, 2007; Morsella et al., 2009) or their means of attainment (Shah &

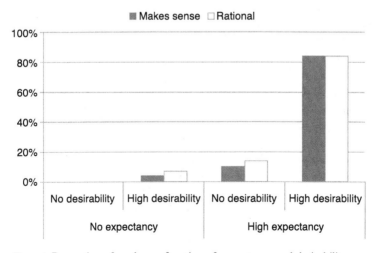

Figure 1 Perception of goals as a function of expectancy and desirability.

Kruglanski, 2003). It has been generally assumed, that for it to drive behavior, a previously formed goal needs to be activated (i.e., to be either chronically or momentarily accessible). We assume, for example, that activating individuals' liking toward objects via the *measurement* of attitude accessibility (as described in Fazio, 1990) may lead to quick goal formation, for instance where the objects' perceived attainability was high and no competing and more dominant goals were active in the situation.

Unconscious impact. Decades of recent research have yielded consistent evidence that activated goals can drive behavior below the level of actors' conscious awareness. Indeed, studies show that unconsciously activated goals can lead to the same cognitive and behavioral outcomes as conscious goals (Bargh, Gollwitzer, Lee-Chai, Barndollar, & Trötschel, 2001; Chartrand & Bargh, 1996). For example, Bargh et al. (2001) found in a classic study that subliminally priming people with a goal to cooperate led them to cooperate more in a resource-management game; moreover, this effect was not mediated by consciously reported intentions (for similar findings, see Hassin, Bargh, & Zimerman, 2009; Kleiman & Hassin, 2011; Milyavsky, Hassin, & Schul, 2012).

Evidence that goal priming studies actually activate goals rather than semantic concepts or attitudes derives from research (Bargh et al., 2001) indicating that priming of a goal (e.g., achievement) unlike semantic priming (e.g., priming of a trait "achiever") *intensifies rather than decays with time*, which is the case for mere concepts or attitudes (Kunda, Davies, Adams, & Spencer, 2002). In addition, Bargh et al. (2001) showed that people who were subliminally primed (vs. not primed) with an automatic goal to achieve exhibited *greater task persistence in the face of obstacles*, and *higher resumption* after distraction—features uniquely characteristic of goal-driven activities (e.g., Lewin, 1935; Tolman, 1932).

In summary, we are assuming that behavior in general is goal driven, and that this pertains both to deliberative behaviors whose identification and choice may require considerable energy, and to spontaneous behaviors that follow automatically from goal activation. For instance, one might sit closer to or further from another person because one *wanted* (and had the *goal*, however implicit) to initiate contact with that individual, or avoid contact as the case may be. Such a goal would be constructed on the basis of relative attitude (e.g., for contact vs. no contact) with that person, but only where alternative links in the attitude to behavior chain were also present. Thus, attitude toward contact would not determine behavioral distancing where distancing was not seen as an attainable option (as in a tightly packed metro train), nor where an alternative dominant goal (e.g., cooperation with that person) was activated. In what follows, we discuss in greater detail the several links that mediate the attitude to behavior relation.

The "rocky road" model of attitude-behavior relations

On liking and wanting

Liking is not wanting. As noted earlier, attitude refers to positive evaluation or "liking" of an object or a state. Liking for an object is neither a sufficient nor a necessary condition for wanting it. It is not sufficient because, for instance, *one may like what one possesses already* in which case liking for that object may not produce wanting. Moreover, liking for something in the absolute is not a *necessary* condition for wanting it, because one may *prefer an undesirable state* (that one generally dislikes) over an *even less undesirable state* (the lesser evil as it were). For instance, a person may strive to leave one's homeland and immigrate to a foreign country even though one may not like in particular being there, yet staying behind might be dangerous for oneself and one's family. As elaborated subsequently, it is relative liking for the one state versus another that induces wanting, which then may translate into goal formation.

A similar argument was made by Bagozzi (1992, p. 184) in an early article. As he aptly noted:

> In and of themselves, evaluative appraisals such as those found in attitudes do not imply motivational commitments. In contrast, the existence of a desire, in the presence of a belief that one can act, is a sufficient motivator to activate an intention and does not require a positive evaluation. A person can want or desire to do something even though it is unappealing, unpleasant, or in some other way evaluated negatively (e.g., Fred wants to go to his father's funeral although he is distressed at the prospect of doing so). Likewise, one can want or desire not to do something even though it is evaluated positively (e.g., Gail desires not to exercise today although she regards favorably the consequences of doing so). Of course, desires often coincide with evaluations, but it is important to recognize that these reactions are unique responses with potentially different antecedents and consequences.

Finally, Berridge (2004, p. 195) recently proposed in the same vein that:

> "Liking" by itself is simply a triggered affective state—there is no object of desire or incentive target, and no motivation for reward. It is the process of incentive salience attribution [wanting] that makes a specific associated stimulus or action the object of desire, and that tags a specific behavior as the rewarded response.

Furthermore: "'Liking' without 'wanting' can be produced, and so can 'wanting' without 'liking'" (Berridge, 2004, p. 194). For instance, manipulation of the mesolimbic dopamine systems was shown to change *wanting* for a reward without changing *liking* for it. Unlike liking, wanting is particularly influenced by dopamine neurotransmission; dopamine manipulations in the nucleus accumbens have been shown to change wanting the reward without having an effect on liking for it (Berridge & Robinson, 2003). Accordingly, Berridge (2004, p. 194) noted:

> "Liking" without "wanting" happens after brain manipulations that cause mesolimbic dopamine neurotransmission to be suppressed. For example, disruption of mesolimbic dopamine systems . . . dramatically reduces "wanting"

to eat a tasty reward, but does not reduce affective facial expressions of "liking" for the same reward.

Wanting as relative liking. To be sure, liking is not irrelevant to wanting. In fact, research by Aarts, Custers, and colleagues (Aarts, Custers, & Holland, 2007; Custers & Aarts, 2005, 2007) demonstrated that associating positive or negative affect with states such as "socializing" contributed to them becoming goals (i.e., conditions that one *wants* to attain or avoid) that drive behavior. However, how does liking translate into wanting? We discuss this issue next.

Specifically, "wanting" refers to greater (*approach*) or lesser (*avoidance*) liking for a possible *future state* relative to the *current state*. That is, wanting appears when the anticipated assessment (like or dislike) for the future state is either more or less positive than that of the current state. Simply put, wanting arises from a *discrepancy* between liking for the present versus the future state. The motivating properties of discrepancy are highlighted in major psychological theories of motivation (cf., Carver & Scheier, 1982, 1998; Custers & Aarts, 2005, 2007; Higgins, 1987; Miller, Galanter, & Pribram, 1960; Oettingen, Pak, & Schnetter, 2001; Wiener, 1948).

The discrepancy concept is also immanent in the lay understanding of desire, and is pervasively represented in everyday parlance. Questions like "Would you *like* some coffee," "Would you *like* to play tennis," are tantamount to asking "Do you *want* coffee?" Do you *want* [to play] tennis?" They inquire into one's desire for those future states (having coffee, playing tennis) and imply a possible *discrepancy* between liking for them versus liking of their absence.[6]

We finally assume that a discrepancy in liking between a present and a future state needs to reach above a certain threshold of magnitude to translate into wanting. Minute discrepancies in liking, say, slightly lesser liking for sleeping in versus exercising at the gym may not necessarily result in positively wanting to do the latter.

Empirical Study 2: Bridging a discrepancy removes a desire. If discrepancy (beyond a certain magnitude) induces a desire, eliminating the discrepancy should remove the desire. Generically, the latter case represents satiation (e.g., Karsten, 1928) a state in which the gap is bridged between what one desired and what one had already; thus, eliminating wanting while keeping liking intact.

To demonstrate this phenomenon empirically, we administered surveys to two groups of participants ($N = 53$), university students at a major state university: those who were about to eat lunch at the student union, and those who had just eaten lunch. We asked participants to name the main food item they were about to eat (or had just eaten), how much they wanted it, and how much they liked it.[7] We found that although participants' liking remained stable, as reflected in similar ratings both before ($M = 5.96$) and after eating ($M = 5.49$; $p > .95$), participants' wanting was significantly higher before eating ($M = 5.51$) than after eating ($M = 4.73$; interaction $p = .01$; see Figure 2). In other words, removing the discrepancy between the dislike of hunger and the enjoyment of (liking for) its satisfaction, removed the desire for food while leaving intact the attitude toward (liking for) the food.

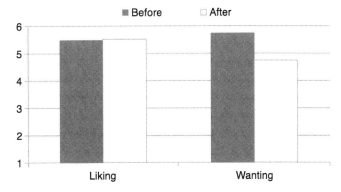

Figure 2 Liking and wanting of the meal.

Two types of discrepancy. Two separate types of motivating discrepancy may be distinguished, namely those related to *promotion* and of *prevention* orientations (Higgins, 2012). In the case of promotion, the probability of wanting, p(W), varies as a function of the degree to which one's relative liking for some *future* state of affairs L_F exceeds that of one's liking for the *present* state L_P. In the case of prevention, p(W) varies as a function of the degree to which the present state L_P is liked better than some impending[8] future state L_F. In Higgins' (2012) theory, prevention also describes the case where the present state represents a negative (i.e., disliked) departure from some, better liked, status quo. For instance, dissonance theorists (e.g., Aronson, 1968; Festinger, 1957) depict a situation where the performance of counterattitudinal behavior creates a disliked state of dissonance and introduces the goal of dissonance reduction, which in turn is served by the means of attitude change.

Stated formally, let *Relative Promotive Liking* (RL_{PROM}) ~ $f(L_F > L_P)$, and let *Relative Preventive Liking* (RL_{PREV}) ~ $f(L_P > L_F)$, then probabilities of promotive Wanting, $p(W_{PROM})$, and of preventive Wanting, $p(W_{PREV})$, respectively, could be expressed simply as

$$p(W_{PROM}) \sim (RL_{PROM}) \qquad (1)$$
$$p(W_{PREV}) \sim (RL_{PREV}) \qquad (2)$$

Of interest too, even though the promotion and prevention *wants* differ in regard to the valence of their desired states (i.e., 1 and 0, respectively), their motivational salience appears to be similar. In support of that notion, Reynolds and Berridge (2008) demonstrated that desired and fearful environments evoke similar brain activity in the nucleus accumbens.

Wanting, goal setting, and acting. Major motivational theories imply that an existing discrepancy suffices to engender behavior aimed at its removal (e.g., Carver & Scheier, 1982, 1998; Miller et al., 1960; Powers, 1973; Wiener, 1948). In this vein, Carver and Scheier (2011) discuss a "discrepancy-reducing feedback loop ... (*whereby*) if there is a discrepancy between the (present and an intended state), the discrepancy is countered by subsequent action" (p. 4, parentheses added).

We assume, however, that *wanting* in and of itself is not tantamount to *goal setting*, hence it may not necessarily engender a goal-driven action. One may want the weather to be nice during one's vacation, wish the stock market to be bullish, or desire that a parent's operation will turn out well, without any of these defining one's goal. As noted earlier, apart from *desirability* of appreciable enough magnitude, the object of one's desire must possess *attainability* through one's actions (Kruglanski, 1996; Kruglanski et al., 2014). Attainability through one's actions contributes to *expectancy* that one can reach the desired state and a sufficiently high expectancy may result in goal formation (Oettingen et al., 2001). On the other hand, a lack of perceived attainability through one's own activities may result in the delegation of goal attainment to other sources. Relevant to this point is research by Kay, Gaucher, Napier, Callan, and Laurin (2008) showing that in the absence of perceived control over outcomes, that is, of goals' attainability via one's own actions, individuals tended to "outsource" the fulfillment of their wants to an external agency such as God or the government.

Granting sufficient degrees of desirability and attainability, a goal may be formulated (Kruglanski et al., 2014) but even that need not result in the initiation of (goal-driven) behavior. First, as already noted, a goal needs to be accessed or activated from memory at a given moment (Bargh, 1990; Bargh et al., 2001; Fishbach & Ferguson, 2007; Stroebe, van Koningsbruggen, Papies, & Aarts, 2013). A dormant goal that is not of current concern is unlikely to promote action (Eitam & Higgins, 2010). Second, a goal needs to be sufficiently *dominant* in a given context, so that it is not overridden by other, more pressing concerns. Thus, we assume that goals differ in their importance to the individual and in case of goal conflict the more important goal takes precedence over the less important one. A person on the way to a job interview might fail to show up at the designated venue on learning that his or her spouse fell ill, that her or his house caught fire, or that her or his child went missing. One's goals may be ordered according to their hierarchy of importance to the individual (Kenrick, Griskevicius, Neuberg, & Schaller, 2010; Kruglanski & Köpetz, 2010). For instance, evolutionary (deep) goals such as survival or safety may normally trump self-presentation, as when one drops the hot dish from the oven while bringing it to the dinner guests. It is also true, however, that in some circumstances a generally less important goal may assert its dominance over a generally more important goal. For instance, whereas normally *survival* may take precedence over assertion of one's *social identity*, when one's group is severely humiliated the individual may be prepared to risk life and limb to redress the harm (Kruglanski, Bélanger, et al., 2013; Pyszczynski, Sullivan, & Greenberg, 2015).

In other words, where a relative liking (RL) for a given state of affairs is situationally activated, a want may be created that overrides other, less salient, concerns. In this vein, Custers and Aarts (2005, 2007) demonstrated that priming affect (and hence RL) associated with a given condition increases the *dominance* of the correspondent *goal*, prompting relevant goal-driven behaviors. Similarly, Pessiglione et al. (2007) found that participants exerted greater behavioral effort with a subliminal pound versus penny reward cue on a given trial. Additionally, Shah, Friedman, and Kruglanski (2002) showed that situationally induced commitment to a focal goal (that renders it dominant) fosters "forgetting all else," that is, induces the inhibition of other contemporaneous objectives (see also Huang & Bargh, 2014).

Means choice. Finally, even if a goal were dominant in a given situation this does not mean that a *specific* goal-relevant behavior would be necessarily pursued. A behavior constitutes a *means to a goal*, and there might exist other accessible means that might be preferred by an actor in given circumstances. This raises the question of criteria whereby a means to a goal is selected. Given that an individual was able to carry out the activity that the means entails, two essential criteria determine means selection, namely those of (a) *instrumentality* and (b) *supplementarity*. The instrumentality criterion refers to the principle that a means is selected as a positive function of its perceived likelihood (behavioral expectancy) of goal attainment (e.g., Labroo & Kim, 2009). The supplementarity criterion refers to the principle that, all else being equal, a means that promises to confer additional value beyond the specific focal goal, would be selected over one that confers lesser supplementary value. Evidence for the supplementarity principle comes from research on multifinality (for review of relevant findings see Kruglanski, Köpetz et al., 2013) demonstrating that a means that uniquely serves several different objectives is preferred over means that serves fewer objectives. A special case of supplementarity arises where the behavior that serves an ulterior end is additionally an end in itself. For instance, one may view tennis as a means to the goal of fitness but also enjoy tennis for its own sake, and so forth.

In a gist, then, attitudes seem to be quite remote from specific behaviors, and in order for them to produce behavior several "bridges" must be crossed. First, the attitude, or relative liking needs to engender wanting. Second, the wanting (desirability) needs to be conjoined to expected *attainability*, that is, the sense that one would be able to fulfill one's desire through one's actions. Lacking attainability, a want alone would not produce behavior. Third, the desirability or attainability compound would need to be of a sufficient magnitude to produce goal commitment. Fourth, the goal would need to be currently activated; fifth, that goal would need to be dominant in the situation rather than being overridden by alternative objectives. Sixth, for a given *behavior* to be carried out in specific circumstances it would need to be chosen as the preferred means to the goal, resulting in the formation of a specific *implementation intention* (Gollwitzer, 1999). These notions are schematically represented in Figure 3 that depicts *"a centralized self-regulatory function that coordinates multiple goal pursuit"* (Fishbach, 2014, p. 143).

In this depiction, attitudes constitute components of the *Relative Liking* terms, whether of the promotive or preventive variety (i.e., RL_{PROM} and RL_{PREV}). Beyond some threshold of magnitude, these translate into the Want (W) ingredients of several currently active goals, each of which incorporates in addition the essential, *attainability*, components (A). The goals are processed and compared via the central self-regulatory function, and as a result, a given goal is accorded dominance, becoming the *focal goal* in the situation. That goal may be associated with several behavioral means of which the most appropriate (i.e., the most apparently effective, parsimonious, or multifinal) is selected for implementation.[9] As with goal

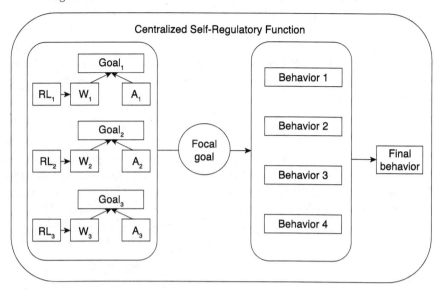

Figure 3 Centralized self-regulatory function.

selection, means selection and the formation of implementation intentions (Gollwitzer, 1999) are carried out via a central self-regulatory process whose extent may depend on the individual's mental resources.

According to the present theory then, the presence of attitude-behavior consistency in a given domain is contingent on the fulfillment of several critical conditions. Specifically, a chain of events needs to occur, each link of which is necessary for the attitude in question to prompt a specific behavior. To state it formally, the conditional probability of a specific behavior (b_x) given an attitude L (toward an object or a state of affairs), $p(b_x/RL)$ can be expressed as function of the concatenation of several conditional probabilities, namely (a) the probability of *wanting* given the attitude or *liking* in question $p(W/RL)$, (b) the probability of goal *formation* given a state of *wanting*, $p(G/W)$, (c) the probability of the specific goal being *focal* (dominant) given the *set of currently active goals*, $p(G_F/G_{set})$, and (d) the probability of the specific behavior (b_x) being selected as a means to the focal goal out of the *set of currently accessible means* to that end, $p(b_x/M_{set})$. These relations are expressed in Equation 3.

$$p(b_x/RL) \sim f\,[p(W/RL) \times p(G/W) \times p(G_F/G_{set}) \times p(b_x/M_{set})] \qquad (3)$$

Addressing the attitude-behavior issue: A tale of two approaches

In the sections that follow we examine the two major research paradigms on attitude-behavior consistency and consider their relation to the present model. As noted earlier, these are the (a) *attitude strength*, and (b) *behavior focus* research programs.

The first of these approaches explores the thesis that attitudes relate to behavior as function of their (variously defined) *strength* (cf. Krosnick & Petty, 1995). The second submits that *general attitudes toward objects* are unlikely to relate to behavior, and that a more effective strategy is to focus on attitudes toward the *behavior* itself (Ajzen, 1985, 2012; Ajzen & Fishbein, 1975; Fishbein & Ajzen, 2010).

As will be seen, both approaches differ in several major respects from the present theoretical perspective. For one, they continue to highlight the attitude construct as a major predictor of behavior. In contrast, we assign that role to goals and to perceived goal-means relations. Second, both traditional paradigms focus on attitudes *in the absolute*, that is, on liking for the object as such or liking for the behavior in itself; in contrast our model emphasizes the notion of *relative liking* and views the discrepancy between present and future states as crucial. Third, the traditional approaches neglect the *chain of contingencies* that span the chasm between an attitude and a behavior. In contrast, the present "Rocky Road" model views the sequence of contingent transformations from attitudes to wants, to goals, and ultimately to behavioral means as fundamental to understanding how human behavior unfolds.

The attitude strength paradigm

Following Converse's (1970) oft-cited observation that some voters' responses to attitude scales are unstable (reflecting the so-called "nonattitudes"), a great deal of research was devoted to the concept of *attitude strength* and the idea that only sufficiently strong attitudes drive behavior. Attitude strength, defined as "the extent to which attitudes manifest the qualities of durability and impactfulness," is an umbrella term encompassing a panoply of constructs (Krosnick & Petty, 1995, p. 3). The main strength-related constructs to have received empirical attention are *attitude extremity, direct experience, accessibility, certainty, ambivalence, importance, knowledge, intensity, interest, latitudes of rejection and noncommitment, and affective-cognitive consistency* (Krosnick, Boninger, Chuang, Berent, & Carnot, 1993; Krosnick & Petty, 1995). Considerable research has supported the claims that these indices of attitude strength are positively related to behavior. Examples include studies on attitude accessibility (Fazio, Chen, McDonel, & Sherman, 1982; Fazio, Powell, & Williams, 1989; Fazio & Williams, 1986), certainty (Davidson, Yantis, Norwood, & Montano, 1985; Sample & Warland, 1973), extremity (Fazio & Zanna, 1978; Petersen & Dutton, 1975), direct experience (Fazio & Zanna, 1978; Schlegel & DiTecco, 1982), affective-cognitive consistency (Norman, 1975; Schlegel & DiTecco, 1982), knowledge (Davidson et al., 1985; Fabrigar et al., 2006; Kallgren & Wood, 1986), latitudes of noncommitment (Sherif, Kelly, Rodgers, Sarup, & Tittler, 1973), importance (Farc & Sagarin, 2009; Jaccard & Becker, 1985; Schuman & Presser, 1981), vested interest (Sivacek & Crano, 1982), and ambivalence (Armitage & Conner, 2000; DeMarree et al., 2014).

From the present perspective, measures of attitude strength are *qualifiers* of the basic *liking* concept. That is, one's liking may be based on direct experience, and may be more or less accessible, extreme, confident, and so forth. The stronger the liking in some sense (of a hoped-for future state, or dislike of an impending future state relative to the present state) the greater the RL_{PROM} or RL_{PREV} and thus the more intense the desire (Want) to approach the future state or avoid it as the case may be.

The important point is, however, that no matter how strong the attitude in any of the above senses, it would fail to drive behavior if any of the terms of Equation 3 above went missing. According to the present model, then, though attitude strength at some above-threshold magnitude is *necessary* to engender wanting, it is *insufficient* for that purpose if not discrepant enough from liking for the present state—and even more so if, for instance, the future state was deemed unattainable, or the goal based on the wanting was overridden by another objective.

Indeed, a close inspection of each of the many attitude strength studies demonstrating its relation to behavior inevitably reveals unarticulated goals lurking in the background. Without those goals, and their situational dominance over other possible concerns the behavior in question is highly unlikely to have taken place. Let us consider some examples.

Attitudes based on direct experience. Fazio and colleagues (e.g., Fazio et al., 1982; Fazio, Zanna, & Cooper, 1978; Regan & Fazio, 1977) identified *direct personal experience* with an object as an important moderator of the attitude-behavior consistency. Indeed, experimental evidence gathered by the authors suggests that individuals who acquired their attitudes through direct experience with the attitude objects behave (toward those objects) more consistently with those attitudes than persons whose experience with the objects was indirect.

For example, in a study by Regan and Fazio (1977), participants were given five pages of puzzle problems and asked to work through them (in the direct experience condition) or were presented with the same puzzles without having to complete them (in the indirect experience condition). Afterward, participants' attitudes toward the puzzle problems were measured, and they were given an opportunity to work on any problems they wished in a 15-minute "free-play" session (where the behavioral measure was taken). Regan and Fazio (1977) found that participants who formed attitudes toward the puzzles through direct experience behaved more consistently with their attitudes (i.e., spent more time playing with the puzzles they had evaluated positively, and less time with ones they evaluated less positively) compared with participants who formed their attitudes through indirect experience.

From the present perspective, it is likely that in the Regan and Fazio (1977) study, and other research of this type, participants' attitudes toward the attitude objects were indeed stronger (e.g., more intense or stable)[10] and that this contributed to a greater sense of *wanting* to engage or to avoid engaging with the objects in question. Moreover, participants' sense of *attainability* of success may well have differed in the direct and indirect experience conditions affecting *goal formation*. Finally, in the free-play period of this study, *working on some problem* appears to have been the overriding goal in the situation whose pursuit was enabled by the available puzzles, hence promoting engagement. According to the present analysis, if any of these additional elements was missing, for example, if participants were tired of (or satiated with) puzzle solving, or if a different, more important goal was introduced into the situation, direct experience would be unlikely to promote behavior in those circumstances.

In brief then, a confident, stable attitude (one that might derive from direct experience) defines a *liking* component that often (though not invariably) may result in a desire (wanting); in turn, wanting might give rise to goal formation and the goal could drive a perceived behavioral means to its attainment. In that sense, direct experience could be indeed relevant to the attitude-behavior relationship. As we have seen, however, beyond liking, however strong or stable, several additional conditions would need to be met; a number of further "ducks" would need to be "in a row" (i.e., wanting, goal formation, means selection) for an experience-based attitude to actually eventuate in a behavior.

Accessibility. Fazio's early work on direct experience (Fazio et al., 1978, 1982; Regan & Fazio, 1977) evolved into a more elaborate framework, namely the MODE model that accords a major role to the construct of *attitude accessibility* (alluded to already in the authors' earlier work, cf., Fazio et al., 1982). The MODE model focuses on a distinction between two general classes of attitude to behavior processes—*spontaneous* versus *deliberative*—and considers *motivation* and *opportunity* as the major determinants of which of the two is likely to operate.

In the *spontaneous* process, attitudes are automatically activated from memory upon the individual's encounter with the attitude objects. The attitude influences how the object is construed—either directly (i.e., affecting the object's immediate appraisal) or indirectly (as when it biases perceptions of the object's particular qualities). In contrast, the deliberative process is characterized by weighing the costs and benefits of a particular action. The deliberative process is effortful and an individual must be motivated to engage in it as well as to have the opportunity (i.e., the time and the resources) to do so. Fazio (1990) characterizes the spontaneous process as relatively "theory driven" or top-down, in that the behavior is assumed to follow from activated (attitudinal) constructs. By contrast, the deliberative process is assumed to be "data driven" in that the behavior is assumed to be determined by a relatively laborious consideration of situationally present features.

In general, the MODE model treats motivation and opportunity as conditions necessary to counteract the "mindless" influence of automatically activated attitudes. In this vein, Fazio and Olson (2014) suggest that an "individual must be motivated to engage in the effortful analysis" (p. 3), that is, to actively deliberate about how to behave rather than allowing for automatically activated attitudes to guide behavior. They further state that:

> One might be motivated to gauge the appropriateness, or even counter the influence, of an automatically activated attitude. That motivation might stem from an enhanced desire for accuracy ... a sense of accountability ... a concern with social desirability ... or ... motivations to control prejudiced reactions.

From the present perspective, both the spontaneous and the deliberative cases are governed by the same attitude to behavior process elaborated herein (see

Equation 3). One difference between them is that in the spontaneous case, previously formed attitudes are activated from memory whereas in the deliberative case attitudes are constructed from an elaborative consideration of relevant information (i.e., concerning costs and benefits of given states of affairs). Another difference between them is that production of "spontaneous," or "automatic" behavior does not require much cognitive capacity or energetic resources whereas production of deliberative behavior does require these (cf. Kruglanski et al., 2012). More important, from the present perspective, however, regardless of whether activated from memory or constructed de nouveau, or whether requiring considerable or meager resources, the relative liking or disliking of objects or states must morph into *wanting* and wanting must morph into goal formation before it may impel behavior.

Early evidence that automatically accessible behaviors *can* drive behavior comes from research by Fazio et al. (1989). In this study, the authors first asked participants to rate their liking toward 100 products and measured their response latencies. Then they presented participants with a subset of ten products and allowed them to choose five of them as gifts. Their findings showed that latencies of liking scores predicted whether a product would be chosen as well as the order in which it was chosen. In other words, for positive liking scores the faster the liking responses were toward a product, the more likely the participants were to choose it; for negative liking scores, the opposite was the case—the faster the (dis)liking responses, the less likely the participants were to choose the product in question.

Again, accessibility of liking may attest to strength of attitudes toward the products and relative liking (to having the product vs. lacking it) should well translate into a degree of *wanting* the products in question. Furthermore, *attainability* of those products was well-nigh assured by the experimental procedures setting the conditions for wanting to evolve into goal formation. Finally, as no alternative goals appeared paramount in this experimental context, the goal-driven behavior (choice of the more-liked products) was fairly certain to appear. Had the products been made unattainable, however, or had the liking-wanting link been severed (e.g., by satiation) accessible attitudes should be less likely to predict behavior.

Empirical Study 3: Attainability moderates accessibility effects on attitude-behavior relations. We carried out an empirical study to test the idea that accessibility effects on attitude-behavior relations are moderated by the degree to which the actor's goal is *attainable* through the behavior.

Ninety-four students of "La Sapienza" University of Rome (65.9% female, mean age = 23.5, SD = 4.63) took part in the study. Participants completed all tasks on a computer with Inquisit version 3. Data from four participants who made inconsistent responses were not included in the analyses. Note that when data from these participants were included in the analyses, results did not change.

Attitude accessibility and valence. Participants were presented with names of 16 film genres (e.g., thriller, drama, action, etc.) and were instructed to indicate whether they liked or disliked the genre. Reaction time (RT) was measured; in the analyses a logarithmic transformation was applied to this data. This represented the measure of *attitude accessibility*; lower RTs indicated *higher* accessibility. Participants were then presented with the names of the same genres and were asked to indicate their liking on a 1–7 scale; this represented the measure of *attitude valence*.

Desirability and attainability. Participants were then presented with a series of math problems; these problems were pretested to ensure that they were aversive, but not overwhelmingly aversive. Participants were then presented with a series of two randomly ordered statements that tapped their preferred choice between watching a relatively popular film genre (Thriller), or to continue solving math problems. Participants indicated their preference for each choice on a scale of 1–7. The manipulated likelihood of being assigned to either watch a film or continue solving math problems depended on the experimental condition to which participants were assigned.

In the *high attainability* condition ($n = 30$), participants were presented with the following information: (a) "If you choose to watch a film from the genre Thriller, you will have a *70%* chance of being assigned to watch the video and a *30%* chance of doing more math" (b) "If you choose to do the math task, you have a *100%* chance of being assigned to it."

In the *low attainability* condition ($n = 33$), participants were presented with the following information: (a) "If you choose to watch a film from the genre Thriller, you will have a *30%* chance of being assigned to watch the video and a *70%* chance of doing more math" (b) "If you choose to do the math task, you have a *100%* chance of being assigned to it."

In the third condition (*control*; $n = 31$), participants were presented with options to watch a film from the Thriller genre, or to continue to solve math problems. Attainability information was not mentioned in this condition.

Results. Data from participants who made inconsistent responses on the attitude accessibility task (i.e., like or dislike of film genres) and the attitude valence task were removed (e.g., if a participant indicated like of a particular genre in the accessibility task, then rated it below the midpoint of the attitude valence task, see Fazio et al., 1989, for a similar procedure). Data from three participants in the low attainability and one participant in the control condition were removed for these reasons.

Preference manipulation check. To assess if participants found thrillers to be preferable to the math task, we assessed the desirability for each across each condition. As expected, mean desirability for thriller was higher (4.57) than mean desirability for math (2.64), $F(1, 87) = 50.28$; $p < .0001$.

Control condition. Data from the control condition ($n = 30$) were used to assess the two-way Accessibility × Valence interaction. This sample did not include data from one participant who made an inconsistent response. Main effect of attitude accessibility and attitude valence and their interaction were entered as predictors in this analysis. Both accessibility and valence attitude variables were standardized

Table 1 Results of the multiple regression analysis in the Control condition

	B	SE	t
Valence	.76	.35	2.19*
Accessibility	−.53	.43	−1.24
Valence × Accessibility	−.90	.37	−2.43*

Note: * p < .05.

and the interaction term was based on the standardized scores. Results from the control condition are presented in Table 1.

Valence and accessibility: Main effects. Only the Valence main effect was significant. Specifically, more positive attitudes toward Thriller were associated with greater preference for this film genre.

Two-way interaction. The Valence × Accessibility interaction was significant and in the expected direction. Simple slope analysis show that the positive effect of attitude valence on preference for Thriller was strongest at *high* accessibility ($b = 1.66$, $t = 3.34$, $p = .002$); preference was highest at high valence and high accessibility. The effect of attitude valence on preference at *low* accessibility was very weak ($b = -.14$, $t = -.27$, $p = .791$; see Figure 4). These findings conceptually replicate the classic Fazio et al. (1989) study.

Experimental condition. To test the attitude Accessibility × Attitude Valence × Attainability interaction, data from the high and low attainability conditions were

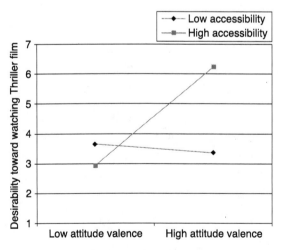

Figure 4 Desirability of watching a thriller film as a function of attitude valence and accessibility (control condition). See the online article for the color version of this figure.

Table 2 Results of the multiple regression analysis in the Experimental condition

	B	SE	t
Valence	.87	.26	3.37**
Accessibility	−.03	.25	−.11
Attainability	−.22	.23	−.95
Valence × Accessibility	−.51	.22	−2.31*
Accessibility × Attainability	−.24	.25	−.95
Valence × Attainability	.66	.26	2.52*
Valence x Accessibility × Attainability	−.60	.22	−2.69-**

Note: * p < .05. ** p < .01.

analyzed jointly ($n = 60$). This sample did not include data from three participants (all in the low attainability condition) who made an inconsistent response. Main effects of Attitude Accessibility (standardized score), Attitude Valence (standardized score), and a contrast code for the Attainability condition (−1 low attainability and 1 high attainability), as well as the two- and three-way interactions between variables were entered as predictors in the analysis. Results from the experimental condition are presented in Table 2.

Attitude valence, accessibility, and attainability: Main effects. Only the main effect for attitude valence was significant in that more positive attitudes were associated with higher desire.

Two-way interactions. The Attitude Valence × Accessibility interaction was significant and in the expected direction; the effect of attitude valence on preference was strongest at high accessibility. The attitude Valence × Attainability was also significant; Valence had a stronger effect on preference in the high Attainability condition.

Three-way interaction. More important, the critical three-way interaction between Valence, Accessibility, and Attainability was significant ($p = .009$). Decomposing this effect, it is found that the two-way Attitude Valence × Accessibility interaction was significant ($b = -1.11$, $t = -3.51$, $p = .0009$) in the *high attainability* condition, but not in the *low attainability* condition ($b = -.08$, $t = -.27$, $p = .787$; see Figures 5 and 6.)

Specifically, simple slope analyses show that in the *high attainability* condition, attitude valence was positively and significantly ($b = 2.63$, $t = 4.33$, $p = .0001$) associated with preference for watching a thriller at *high attitude accessibility*. Preference for thriller was particularly low when valence was low and accessibility high. There was no significant effect of attitude valence, however, under low attitude accessibility ($b = .41$, $t = .98$, $p = .331$).

In summary, these findings support the present analysis whereby accessible attitudes' relation to behavior depends on a goal's attainability by the behavior. In the present study, accessible attitudes were translated into behavioral preferences only where attainability was relatively high and not where it was low.

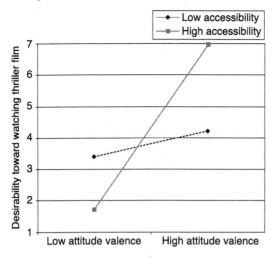

Figure 5 Desirability of watching a thriller film as a function of attitude valence and accessibility (High Attainability condition). See the online article for the color version of this figure.

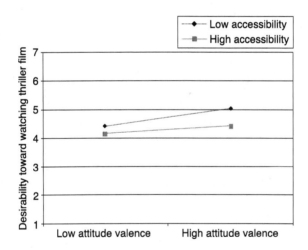

Figure 6 Desirability of watching a thriller film as a function of attitude valence and accessibility (Low Attainability condition). See the online article for the color version of this figure.

Full-fledged MODE model. This was tested in a number of previous studies. Hofmann and Friese (2008), for instance, investigated the effects of dietary constraint and resource capacity, manipulated via alcohol intake, in their joint effect on candy consumption. Whereas dietary restraint was the more important predictor of candy consumption among sober participants, alcohol intake enhanced the relation between prior attitudes toward candy and candy consumption. Similarly, preference for candy bars versus apples (as assessed by a personalized IAT) predicted choice behavior when participants had been made to feel happy, but less so when they were made to feel sad. In the latter condition, participants' beliefs about the attributes of candy bars versus apples proved more influential (Holland, de Vries, Hermsen, & van Knippenberg, 2012). Finally, individual differences in working memory capacity also were shown to play an important role in self-regulation (Hofmann, Gschwendner, Friese, Wiers, & Schmitt, 2008). Essentially, automatic attitudes toward a given temptation more strongly influenced behavior for individuals with lower working memory capacity than for individuals with higher capacity.

From the present theoretical perspective, chronic accessibility[11] of attitudes (i.e., latency of the attitudinal response) toward objects (e.g., candy bars that they did not currently possess) attesting to strength of the attitudes in question could readily translate into a degree of wanting them which, given the assured attainability, might well evolve into goals of obtaining and consuming them upon obtainment. Too, given sufficient cognitive resources, an alternative superordinate goal, for example, of dieting, could be deliberatively activated and thus override the goal of consumption. Of interest, Fishbach, Friedman, and Kruglanski (2003) found that successful self-regulators activate such superordinate goal from memory immediately upon encountering a temptation (e.g., a candy bar for dieters), which mediates their ability to resist the temptation. The latter finding suggests that the self-regulation process can be automatized and liberated from its dependency on resources.

In summary, research cited in support of the MODE model is interpretable within the present framework in which—when combined with perceived attainability—attitudes toward objects may induce desires that contribute to formation of goals that (if dominant), may promote relevant goal-driven behavior. This analysis implies, moreover, that whether automatically activated or retrieved upon a more elaborative consideration, attitudes would not lead to behavior if the relevant attitude objects are not more positively or negatively valued relative to the actor's present states (prompting promotive or preventive *wants*) or if they are unattainable. For instance, an accessible attitude toward candy (e.g., accomplished by attitudinal priming or measured via response latency) may not lead to behavioral choice if one has already eaten enough sweets or if the likelihood of getting it was low (e.g., the candy was displayed in a store window during after-hours).

Importance, certainty, and relevance. Holland, Verplanken, and van Knippenberg (2002) investigated the role of attitude strength, measured by the aspects of *importance, certainty*, and *relevance*, as moderator of the attitude-behavior relationship. They hypothesized, and found, that strong attitudes toward an object (the Greenpeace organization) were more likely to lead to an attitude-related behavior (donating to Greenpeace) than weak attitudes. In the first study session, participants' attitudes toward Greenpeace were assessed, as was the strength of those attitudes. In the second session, participants were paid 10 Dutch guilders and asked whether they wanted to donate some of this money to Greenpeace. It was found that stronger attitudes predicted the amount of donation, whereas weaker attitudes did not. Once again, in this study, attitude strength is likely to have evolved into the desire to donate and, given that the attainability of donation was assured, participants may have formed the goal to donate, which in turn drove their donating behavior. However, regardless of the strength of their attitude toward Greenpeace, participants would not presumably form the goal to donate— and would not subsequently act on that goal—if their expectancy of being able to do so was nonexistent (defining a lack of attainability), for example, or if they had just made a donation and had no more money to spare,[12] or if their prior donation eliminated the discrepancy (hence the Want) between one's positive attitude to Greenpeace, and one's lack of expression of that support.

Alternative attitude strength studies could be similarly interpreted: In all such cases attitude strength did not seem to impact behavior directly but rather to have contributed to a state of wanting that when combined with attainability produced a goal that drove instrumental acts. Because attitudes may ultimately form a part of goals the same aspects of attitude strength, for example, extremity, accessibility, confidence, and so forth, that pertain to attitudes would also characterize goals that are based on the attitudes in question. However, as we have argued throughout, object attitudes alone are not enough and the subsequent links in the chain (depicted in Equation 3) need to be realized for behavior to occur.

Individual differences in attitude-behavior consistency. Closely related to the notion of attitude strength are individual differences in the attitude-behavior relation. The two most often discussed such differences are those of self-monitoring (Snyder, 1983) and self-awareness (Wicklund, 1982). We discuss them briefly in turn.

Self-monitoring. Snyder and his colleagues (cf. Snyder & Kendzierski, 1982; Snyder & Swann, 1976) theorized and found that low monitors whose behavior is guided by internal cues, exhibit substantially greater attitude-behavior covariation than high monitors whose behavior is guided more by situational circumstances. This is likely because low (vs. high) self-monitors' attitudes are more chronically accessible (Higgins, 1996). Consequently, low monitors' attitudes are more likely to be translated into goals and hence drive goal-relevant behavior. Instead, high monitors' goals are more likely to be formed on the basis of situationally primed attitudes giving rise to correspondent goals different from those based on their previously measured attitudes. Consistent with this analysis, Ajzen, Timko, and White (1982) showed that the difference in attitude-behavior consistency between high and low self-monitoring individuals was located in the relation between intentions and behavior. While the attitude-intention relation was similar for both groups, low self-monitors exhibited significantly stronger intention-behavior correlations than did high self-monitors, presumably because the latter had a different goal activated in the situation, prompting a different behavioral intention.

Of particular interest too, Snyder and Kendzierski (1982) found that when the behavior was equally relevant to high and low self-monitors, representing a strong *goal* based on the measured attitudes, the difference between them disappeared in that now the high self-monitors too acted consistently with their attitudes.

Self-awareness. According to Wicklund (1982) individuals high in self-awareness should exhibit greater attitude-behavior consistency than ones low in self-awareness. Specifically (p. 157) highly aware individuals are attuned to their attitudes which has "a motivational consequence: If it is difficult to remove oneself from self-aware condition, then the person can be expected to show increase in consistency." Just as with low self-monitoring, high self-awareness, or high private self-awareness (Froming, Walker, & Lopyan, 1982; Scheier, 1980) represent chronic accessibility of one's attitudes likely to transform into goals that drive behaviors. As Carver and Scheier (1998, p.119) aptly summarized it: "Focusing on the private versus public aspects of the self is nothing more than taking one package of goals as salient, rather than another package of goals. In either case, the goals that are taken up and attended to are the ones that become manifest in actions."

Refocusing on behavior: Ajzen and Fishbein's TRA and TPB models

A unique and highly influential approach to the attitude behavior issue is represented in Fishbein and Ajzen's theories of reasoned action (TRA) and of planned behavior (TPB; e.g., Ajzen, 1985, 2012; Fishbein & Ajzen, 1975, 2010). Their essential argument was two-pronged. (a) First they proposed that *general object attitudes*, of the kind typically addressed by attitude researchers (e.g., Cacioppo et al., 1981; Eagly & Chaiken, 1993; Fazio, 2007; Thurstone, 1931) are in principle unrelated to specific behaviors and hence they should be relinquished as behavioral predictors. (b) Instead, they proposed that focusing on *attitudes toward the behavior* provides a more effective method of behavioral prediction. In what follows, we examine both arguments in greater detail and discuss them from the present theoretical perspective.

On general attitudes and specific behaviors. In most treatments of the attitude concept, its referent was an object, an issue, or a state of affairs. In this vein, Wicker (1969) defined attitudes as "evaluative feelings of pro or con, favorable or unfavorable, with regard to particular objects" (p. 42). Examples of attitude objects included in Wicker's (1969) review range from attitudes toward jobs and minority group members to attitudes toward breastfeeding, public housing, and student cheating. And the issue of attitude-behavior consistency typically referred to the question of whether such attitudes toward objects instigate relevant (approach or avoidance) behaviors toward those objects. Examples of such behaviors include *job performance* and *absences*, as function of attitudes toward the organization, willingness to *provide service* to a minority group member, as function of attitudes toward that group, *applying* for public housing as function of attitudes to public housing, and *cheating* on a self-graded exam, as function of one's attitude toward honesty (Wicker, 1969). In all those instances, the *general attitude* toward the object is clearly conceptually separate from *behavior* toward the object, and the question, again, was whether the former gives rise to the latter.

In a creative break from that tradition, Fishbein and Ajzen (1975, 2010; Ajzen, 1985, 2012) proposed instead to focus on *attitude toward the behavior* as a more reasonable marker of behavior's occurrence. According to Fishbein and Ajzen (2010): "We cannot expect strong relations between general attitudes toward an object and any given behavior directed toward that object" (pp. 258–259). According to the authors then, a general attitude toward an object will predict an *aggregate* of behaviors relevant to the attitude but not any specific behavior (Ajzen, 2012; Fishbein & Ajzen, 2010). Empirical support for that assertion comes from studies by Fishbein and Ajzen (1974) on religious behavior, Weigel and Newman (1976) on environmental behavior, and Werner (1978) on abortion activism, to be discussed later.

Behavior focus. Instead of addressing general object attitudes, Ajzen and Fishbein's (1980; Fishbein & Ajzen, 1975) TRA and Ajzen's (1985) subsequent TPB, center on the construct of *behavioral intention,* assumed to constitute the direct antecedent of actual *behavior.* In turn, behavioral intention is determined by (a) *attitude toward the behavior,* which constitutes the sole attitudinal component in the TPB/TRA models (Ajzen, 2012), (b) *subjective norms,* and (c) *perceived behavioral control.* These factors are themselves determined by underlying behavioral, normative, and control beliefs. According to the TPB then, by measuring attitudes to the behavior, perceived norms, and perceived behavioral control, we should be able to predict intentions to perform a single behavior, which in turn is highly correlated with the behavior's actual occurrence. We elaborate on these concepts in what follows.

Attitude toward the behavior (AB) reflects the degree to which performance of the behavior is positively or negatively valued; such attitude is assumed to vary as function of the sum total of the behavior's believed instrumentalities to different outcomes weighted by their respective desirabilities. For example, attitude toward *running* may depend on one's beliefs in the likelihood that running facilitates (a) cardiac health, (b) weight loss, (c) stress reduction, and so forth; times the subjective desirability (values) of each of these outcomes.

Perceived behavioral control (PBC) refers to people's general expectations regarding the degree to which they are capable of performing a *given behavior,* the extent to which they have the requisite resources and believe they can overcome whatever obstacles they may encounter. Whether these resources and obstacles are internal or external to the person is immaterial (Fishbein & Ajzen, 2010).[13]

PBC is determined by salient control beliefs, which are elicited by asking participants to list the factors they believe would enable them to perform *the behavior* as well as factors that are likely to impede its performance. For instance, in a study on mountain climbing (Ajzen & Driver, 1991), participants listed having good weather, not having proper equipment, living near mountains, lacking skills and knowledge for mountain climbing.

Finally, *subjective norm* (SN) is defined as a perceived social pressure to engage or not engage in a given behavior. It is determined by the total set of accessible normative beliefs concerning the expectations of important others (injunctive norms) and descriptive norms (how important others behave). As can be seen then, all three proposed determinants of behavioral intentions are focused on a specific behavior, including its evaluation or likability (attitude toward the behavior), perceived ability to execute it (i.e., perceived behavioral control), and the degree to which the behavior is normative or not.

Empirical support for the TPB model has been extensive and wide ranging. Its bulk was summarized in several meta-analyses. Some of these were general and cut across broad swathes of different behaviors (Armitage & Conner, 2001; Notani, 1998); others focused on specific behavior-types (e.g., condom use, Al-barracin, Johnson, Fishbein, & Muellerleile, 2001; health behavior, Cooke & French, 2008). In Armitage and Conner's (2001) meta-analysis, for example, the multiple correlation of attitude, subjective norm and perceived behavioral control accounted for 39% of the variance in behavioral intentions. And in a meta-analysis of studies on condom use, correlation of attitudes and norms explained 49% of the variance (Albarracin et al., 2001).

What drives behavioral intentions? A view from a goal-systemic bridge

Ajzen and Fishbein's theories of reasoned action and of planned behavior have been immensely influential[14] and of practical utility in predicting specific behaviors. However, the present conceptual perspective may importantly complement their models by elucidating the psychological processes that must transpire in order that attitudes toward objects and attitudes toward specific behaviors translate into actions.

In essence, we suggest that TPB's behavior focus neglects to explicitly consider that behavior is goal driven.[15] That is, behaviors typically constitute means to goal attainment, and it is goal pursuit that drives behavior in the first place (cf., Huang & Bargh, 2014). It follows that neither attitude toward a behavior, nor subjective norm nor perceived control would predict behavioral intentions *if* the goal served by the behavior was not activated. From the present perspective then, the TPB reverses the natural order of things and puts the (behavioral) "cart" before the "horse" (of goal pursuit). Accordingly, we propose to *reinstate* general object attitudes as important contributors to goal formation, and to *attenuate* the behavior focus of Fishbein and Ajzen's models. In what follows, we examine these notions in greater detail.

Can general object attitudes drive specific behaviors? Consider the relation between a general attitude (A) toward an object and a specific behavior (B) toward it. Assuming that liking or disliking toward an object culminated in a goal to attain or avoid it such goal might be attainable via different behavioral means. This situation is known as one of *equifinality* (Heider, 1958; Kruglanski et al., 2002). If a highly diverse set of means was entertained by the actor, it might be difficult to predict what particular behavior she or he will undertake in the service of the goal, a difficulty seemingly supportive of Ajzen and Fishbein's objection to the use of general attitudes as predictors of behavior. However, note that the difficulty here *is not immanent*, or inevitable in the relation between general object attitudes (transformed into goals) and specific behaviors. Indeed, there can be cases where the goal object is best attained by a specific habitual means (Wood & Neal, 2007).

In those instances, general object attitudes could in fact be highly related to specific behaviors, albeit via mediation of goals based on the attitudes in question. For instance, some individuals' positive attitude toward fitness could translate into their adopting the fitness goal, in turn perceived as best served by swimming. Though, generally speaking, running, weight training, and judo could also be perceived as fitness-related, for the individuals in question they might not be associated with the fitness goal, in which case the relation between individuals' attitude toward fitness and swimming would not be significantly enhanced by an aggregate incorporating also those other behaviors. Moreover, in some cases a positive relation between a fitness attitude and swimming could appear alongside a negative relation between that attitude and running; for example, an individual who feels very positive about fitness could choose to spend all of his or her time swimming, which would leave him or her with hardly any time at all for running. In such a case, the correlation between the attitude and the aggregate containing both swimming and running would be lower than the correlation between the attitude and swimming alone.

Empirical Study 4

General attitudes can drive specific behaviors. To investigate these matters empirically, we recruited 104 MTurkers (43 females).[16]

Attitude. Participants rated their attitude toward "being in shape" on four 11-point scales ranging from –5 to 5, with the endpoints marked "bad–good," "harmful–beneficial," "foolish–wise," and "unpleasant–pleasant." Cronbach's α for the four attitude items was 0.89.

Goal. Participants answered three questions about the extent to which being in shape is their current goal: "Please rate the extent to which being in shape is your current goal," "How likely do you think it is that you will be in shape in the next few months?" and "How important is it to you to be in shape in the next few months?" Participants responded to these items on an 11-point scale ranging from 0 to 10. Cronbach's α for the three goal items was 0.80. The order of the goal and attitude questions was randomized across participants to minimize any potential order effects.

Behaviors. Participants had to indicate how often they performed each of 24 fitness activities (e.g., biking, running, weightlifting) on an 8-point scale ranging from "never" to "daily."

Relations between variables. Our main dependent variable was the frequency of the most often-used behavior for each participant, viewed here as the most preferred means to the goal of fitness. The relevant descriptive statistics and correlations are displayed in Table 3. As may be seen, the correlation between attitudes and goals is highly significant, consistent with our notion that (relative) attitudes constitute

Table 3 Correlations

	Attitude	Goal	Frequency of dominant behavior	Aggregated behavior (sum)
Attitude				
Goal	.58***			
Frequency of the dominant behavior	.27*	.40***		
Aggregated behavior (sum)	.21*	.34**	.53***	
Mean	3.78	6.95	5.70	36.93
SD	1.37	2.17	1.58	8.87

Note: * p < .05. ** p < .01. *** p < .001.

the evaluative component of goals. It is also noteworthy that attitudes are significantly related to each participant's most preferred behavioral means to fitness, although the relation between goals and most preferred behavioral means is stronger (albeit not significantly so). Also of interest, both attitudes and goals are related to (each participant's) aggregate of fitness behavior, with the correlation between goals and aggregates being somewhat higher than the correlation between attitudes and aggregates.

The mediation model. As already noted, our theory suggests that attitudes constitute the evaluative component of goals, which in turn are the drivers of behaviors. This suggests that the relation between attitudes and behaviors should be mediated by goals. We analyzed the mediation model using the PROCESS program (Hayes, 2013). As shown in Figure 7, the total effect of attitude on behavior was significant ($b = 0.31$, $SE = 0.12$, β .27, $p = .010$). Attitude had a significant and positive effect on goal ($b = 0.92$, $SE = 0.14$, $\beta = .58$, $p < .001$). Goal had a positive effect on the most frequent behavior ($b = 0.26$, $SE = 0.09$, $\beta = .36$, $p = .004$). The indirect effect of goal on the most frequent behavior estimated with 20,000 bootstrapped samples was significant ($b = 0.24$, 95% CI [0.10,0.46]). The direct effect of attitude on behavior was not significant ($b = 0.07$, $SE = 0.14$, $\beta = .06$, $p = .613$). The entire model was significant, $F(2, 88) = 8.31$, $p < .001$, $R^2 = .16$. These findings, depicted in Figure 7, are consistent with our theory whereby behavior is driven by goals of which attitudes constitute the evaluative component.

In brief then, adopting the goals-means perspective affords a demarcation between a case where an attitude toward an object is highly related to a specific behavior, and a case where it is not, but is highly related to a behavioral aggregate. The former case obtains where the goal based on the attitude is predominantly served by the *specific behavior*, being the most preferred or habitual means to that objective (Wood & Neal, 2007). In contrast, the latter case obtains where that goal is served often by other equifinal behaviors. An illustration of this demarcation is given in Figure 8. It depicts Goal B that is served by three means, each being equally instrumental to the goal (and so equally often used). In contrast, Goal A is served by three unequally instrumental means. In that latter case, Means 1 is more instrumental (and hence more preferential) than Means 2 and 3.

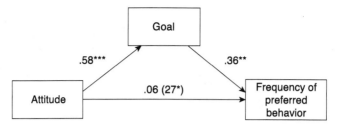

Figure 7 Mediation model of attitudes, goals, and behavior.

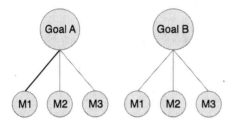

Figure 8 Two cases of goal-means relations. See the online article for the color version of this figure.

The former case—wherein each goal is served by several equal means—typified studies cited in support of the behavioral aggregate hypothesis. Thus, in Fishbein and Ajzen's (1974) study on religious attitudes, researchers gave participants a checklist of 100 religious behaviors, and most participants checked off many such behaviors. Similarly, in Weigel and Newman's (1976) study of environmental attitudes, participants were offered 14 environmentally friendly behaviors and many participants chose more than one of those behaviors. In Werner's (1978) study of abortion activism, participants were given an 83-item checklist of behaviors related to the goal of activism and many participants chose several such means to the goal of activism. We argue that the behavioral aggregate was more closely related to attitudes in these instances because all of the means the participants chose from were equally related to the goal (the example of Goal B in Figure 8). However, in cases in which one means stands out from the rest in terms of its association with the goal (e.g., Goal A in Figure 8), a specific behavior can have a higher correlation with the attitude than does the behavioral aggregate.

To reiterate then, a *general attitude* could be related to a *specific behavior* if the attitude contributed to a dominant goal formation (via the process elaborated earlier) and the goal was habitually served by the behavior in question. More generally then, the goal perspective identifies an important qualification concerning Ajzen and Fishbein's generalization, which categorically denies the possibility of (general) attitude to (specific) behavior relation (cf. the compatibility principle, e.g., Fishbein & Ajzen, 2010, pp. 258–259). However, if *general object attitudes* can be related to specific behaviors (via the mediation of goals to which the attitudes contribute), then the dismissal of general attitudes as predictors of behavior, which motivated the TRA/TPB switch to *attitudes toward the behavior* seems unwarranted. However, let us consider now the constructive aspect of TRA/TPB theorizing that centers on the concept of behavioral intentions.

On the determinants of behavioral intentions. First, it should be clear that the concept of *behavioral intention* in TRA and TPB refers to intention to execute a given *behavior*, and *not* to attain a given *goal*. As Fishbein and Ajzen (2010, p. 39) put it:

> Behavioral intentions are indications of a person's readiness to *perform a behavior*. The readiness to act, represented by an intention, can find expression in such statements as the following: I will engage in the *behavior*, I intend to engage in the *behavior*, I expect to engage in the *behavior*, I plan to engage in the *behavior*, I will try to engage in the *behavior*. (italics added)

In essence, behavioral intention concerns an act that serves as *means* of goal attainment. Furthermore, the concepts of means and goals are clearly distinct at least for the large class of extrinsically motivated behaviors serving ulterior ends distinct from those behaviors (Shah & Kruglanski, 2000).

A staple of the TRA-TPB approach is the notion that behavioral intentions are the antecedents of behavior. According to Ajzen (1991), "the intention to perform a given behavior is 'a central factor in the theory of planned behavior,'" presumably because "the stronger the intention to engage in a behavior, the more likely should be its performance" (p. 181). The latter assertion seems hardly controversial and rather a matter of common sense, however. Systematic research, as well, attests that, especially where the intention is assessed in close proximity to the behavior, its relation to the behavior is strong.[17] None of it seems very surprising. It seems obvious, for instance, that an intention[18] reported moments before the intended behavior should eventuate in the behavior unless something unexpected happened. An individual admitting in line to the box office to her intention "to view a movie" will generally be expected to follow up on her intention, and so too a person reporting an intention of "going for a run" while putting on her running shoes.

The contribution of the Ajzen and Fishbein approach presumably lies not in the presumed *intentions to behaviors* link as such, but rather in their suggested determinants of behavioral intentions, namely attitudes toward the behavior, subjective norms, and perceived behavioral control. Here is where the present analysis diverges from their view. Specifically, we suggest that behavioral intentions are crucially *goal driven*, as the intention to perform a given behavior rests on beliefs that it constitutes a *preferred means* to a currently active goal.

Given the presence of an active goal, out of the class of available means to that goal the *preferred means* might be affected by beliefs about social norms, attitudes to behavior, and perceived behavioral control. But none of these should matter *if an entirely different goal was in place*. For instance, if one likes running (attitude to behavior), most of one's friends applauded running (subjective norm), and one is quite capable of running (perceived behavioral control)—one might well form the behavioral intention to run and implement it too, but only if a relevant goal, say fitness, was activated. Should an entirely different goal be activated, for example, studying for an exam, or preparing a dinner party, attitudes to running, subjective norms about running, and so forth, even if contextually primed, would hardly produce the behavioral intention to run.

Moreover, assuming that a goal assumed to be served by the behavior was indeed activated, it is important to ask what factors determine whether the intention to execute that particular behavior will be formed. As elaborated earlier, we assume that a behavioral intention is formed as function of the behavior's perceived (a) *instrumentality* to goal attainment (Labroo & Kim, 2009; Warshaw & Davis, 1985b), and/or its perceived (b) *supplementarity*, the conferral of added benefits beyond the specific goal's attainment (Kruglanski, Köpetz, et al., 2013).

From that perspective, in cases where they do impact behavioral intentions, "attitude toward the behavior" and "subjective norm" may largely reflect the perceived (by oneself and others) instrumentality/ *supplementarity* of the behavioral means with respect to a *currently* active goal (whereas perceived behavioral control simply reflects one's ability to carry out that behavioral means). In this sense, AB and SN may function as *indirect* indices of instrumentality and supplementarity and there could exist alternative such indices not anticipated by TPB—for instance, *expert opinion* as to what behaviors are instrumental to a current goal, or *motivational biases* that influence perceptions of instrumentality or supplementarity (cf., Bélanger, Kruglanski, Chen, Orehek & Johnson, 2015).[19] These considerations, absent from the TRA and TPB models, follow directly from the assumption that behavior is goal driven, and its choice hinges on its efficacy in regard to goal attainment.

Empirical Study 5

Attitudes toward behavior, perceived instrumentality, and intention formation. We tested the hypothesis that presumed determinants of behavioral intentions identified in the TPB (i.e., attitude to the behavior, subjective norm, and perceived behavioral control) will predict intentions only where the behavior serves as means to an active goal. Consistent with the present theory, we predicted also that in the latter case impact on intentions would be mediated by the perceived *instrumentality* of the behavior to goal attainment. We tested these hypotheses with regard to the behavior of "drinking alcohol when going out."

Forty-seven participants (23 females) took part in this study, which was carried on Amazon's Mechanical Turk on a Friday and Saturday afternoon. Participants rated their *attitude toward the behavior* of "drinking alcohol while going out" on three scales with the endpoints marked "very bad to very good," "very harmful to very beneficial," and "very unpleasant to very pleasant." They also answered the question "How much do you like drinking alcohol when going out?" on a scale ranging from *not at all* to *very much* (Cronbach's β = .89). To measure *subjective norms*, we averaged participants' ratings of agreement with two items (adapted from Fishbein & Ajzen, 2010): "Most people who are important to me approve of me drinking alcohol when going out," and "Most people who are like me drink alcohol when they go out" ($r = .58$). *Perceived behavioral control* was measured with an item "Drinking alcohol when I go out is up to me." *Instrumentality of the behavior* was measured with one item: "How much does alcohol help you have fun when going out?" *Behavioral intention* was measured with one item: "I intend to drink alcohol tonight." Finally, we asked participants whether they had the *goal* of going out to have fun that night on a scale ranging from *definitely not* to *definitely yes*. All items were answered on a 7-point scale.

Results. We tested a moderated mediation model with attitude as a predictor and behavioral intention as the outcome variable. Instrumentality was treated as the mediator and goal was included as a moderator of the instrumentality–behavioral intention path (see Figure 9). We used the PROCESS program for this analysis (Model 14, Hayes, 2013).

The total effect of attitude on intention was significant ($b = .44$, $SE = .18$, $\beta = .34$, $p = .021$). When controlling for attitude toward the behavior, subjective norm and perceived behavioral control had no significant relation to intentions and we excluded them from the final model.[20] Attitude had also a significant and positive effect on perceived instrumentality of the behavior ($b = 1.01$, $SE = 0.17$, $\beta = .67$, $p < .001$). As expected, there was a significant interaction between instrumentality and goal presence ($b = 0.13$, $SE = .05$, $\beta = .28$, $p = .02$). More importantly, the indirect effect of attitude on intention mediated by instrumentality, estimated with 20,000 bootstrapped samples, was significant when the goal was present ($b = 0.52$, 95% CI [0.24, 1.31]) but nonsignificant when the goal was absent ($b = 0.09$, 95% CI [−0.13, 0.35]). Index of moderated mediation was significant (0.13, 95% CI [0.04, 0.34]). The direct effect of attitude after controlling for instrumentality and goal was not significant ($b = 0.31$, $SE = 0.22$, $\beta = .23$, $p = .179$). The entire model was significant, $F(4, 42) = 6.14$, $p < .001$, $R^2 = .37$. Consistent with the present theory then, attitudes toward the behavior predict behavioral intentions only where the behavior serves a current goal, highlighting the centrality of the goal concept to behavior's occurrence.

Prior support for the TRA-TPB models

Indeed, a close review of prior support for the TRA-TPB formulations reveals a clear, albeit unarticulated, presence of active goals to which the behaviors chosen

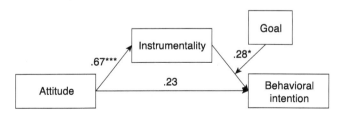

Figure 9 Moderated mediation model of attitude, instrumentality, goal, and behavioral intention.

served as means. To wit, in a widely cited study by Schifter and Ajzen (1985) on weight loss success in college women, the authors were specifically interested only in participants who very likely had the *goal* to lose weight, as attested by the authors' comment that "women who considered themselves overweight were encouraged to participate" in the study (p. 845). More generally, the wording of Schifter and Ajzen's intentions measures was very similar to how one might phrase a goal: The participants were asked to respond to items such as "I will try to *reduce weight* over the next 6 weeks" and "I have decided to lose weight over the next six weeks." These measures are more related to the goal of losing weight in the near future, than to the intention to perform a specific behavior to that end.

Other studies of attitude-behavior relation strongly imply the situational presence of goals that drove the behavior of interest—for instance, Sivacek and Crano (1982) posited that what they termed "vested interest" moderates attitude-behavior consistency. In two studies, they found that the strength of the attitude-behavior relationship varied as a function of individuals' perceived vested interest on the attitude issue, with those who had more vested interest displaying higher attitude-behavior consistency. Specifically, students who felt strongly that they would be affected (either positively or negatively) by the imposition of a university-wide comprehensive exam behaved more consistently with their expressed attitudes toward the exam. Again, it seems highly plausible that for affected students promoting the exam or preventing it (respectively) constituted an important *goal* that drove their behavioral choices.

Attitude toward the behavior as such would matter if the goal(s) to which the behavior was instrumental were present in the situation. For instance, if several of the behavior's consequences (affecting attitude toward the behavior according to TPB) defined situationally present goals, such *multifinal* behavior would be chosen over its less multifinal alternatives (Kruglanski, Köpetz, et al., 2013). In this vein, Fabrigar et al. (2006) suggested that the relevance of an attitude to a particular behavior moderates attitude-behavior consistency. They tested this by giving participants information about two department stores and asking them to choose where they would buy a camera after they had either been given relevant information about the camera department or not. Across three studies, Fabrigar et al. (2006) found that attitudes toward the department stores were more likely to lead to behavior when the attitudes were relevant to the behavior, that is, where the relevant information suggested the camera department to be superior or inferior. Clearly in this case, buying a high-quality camera constituted participants' (hypothetical) *goal* and relevant (vs. irrelevant) information about the camera department pertained to whether a given camera department (vs. its alternative) would be a better (more instrumental) means to that goal. However, general information about the department store (producing an attitude toward the store) pertained to other goals that a purchaser might well have in this situation, concerning customer service, aesthetic experience, and so forth, suggesting that carrying out a purchase in the specific department store may be *multifinal* (Kruglanski, Köpetz, et al., 2013). Therefore, if the camera department was portrayed as superior (for instance) and the attitude toward the department store was positive (i.e., one could expect other concerns to be met in that store) the purchase would be more likely (purchase would be perceived as a more multifinal means) than if the attitude to the department store was negative. However, attitude to the department store should matter little if the camera department was inferior (defining an ineffective means to the focal goal).

Finally, several recent studies have demonstrated that priming manipulations induce behavior only if they create conditions that affect the activation of preexisting goals. Thus, Stroebe et al. (2013) observed that only obese (vs. nonobese) shoppers (for whom weight loss was a likely goal) were influenced by diet/health primes handed out in a recipe flyer, and proceeded to purchase significantly fewer unhealthy snack items. Similarly, Fitzsimons and Bargh (2003) found that priming participants with the word "mom" increased achievement only for those who *wanted* to make their mom proud of them.

In summary, the goal-systemic notions of means-ends relations seem helpful to clarifying the conditions under which (a) a general attitude may or may not bear a substantial relation to a specific behavior, as well as circumstances under which (b) the presumptive determinants of a specific behavioral intention spelled out in the TPB will or will not produce the intention in question. In that sense, the present analysis identifies important limitations to generalizations suggested by the TPB.

General discussion

Beyond random bodily movements and reflex actions, human behavior is purposive or goal driven (cf., Tolman, 1932). This pertains to explicit, highly conscious goals (getting admitted to college, acquiring a home) as well as to implicit, below-the-radar goals induced by subliminal priming—such as goals of cooperation, competition, self-control or achievement (cf. Bargh et al., 2001; Hassin et al., 2009; Kleiman & Hassin, 2011). It pertains to spontaneous or "automatic" behaviors that require little energetic resources, as well as to "deliberative" behaviors whose execution is driven by considerable resources. In all these instances, however different in some respects, behaviors typically constitute means to situationally present goals.

Though attitudes are relevant to goal formation they do not in and of themselves define goals. To address the additional steps that need to take place, the present, goal-systemic, analysis depicts a multiply contingent path (expressed in Equation 3) between attitudes toward objects or states of affairs and behaviors related to those attitudes.

Based on a widely accepted definition of attitudes as evaluative responses akin to liking, we noted first that liking (in an absolute sense) need not be tantamount to wanting (Bagozzi, 1992; Berridge, 2004). Rather, wanting implies a disparity; a discrepancy of a promotive or preventive kind (see Equations 1 and 2), between liking of a present versus a future state. Moreover, in itself wanting (desire) may not produce goal formation (Kruglanski et al., 2014). Rather, perceived attainability should be at an above-threshold level for goal formation to ensue. Furthermore, for a given goal to drive behavior it needs to be dominant in the situation rather than being overridden by other more important objectives (Huang & Bargh, 2014; Shah et al., 2002). Finally, a specific behavioral means needs to be chosen as superior in some sense (e.g., as most instrumental, or most multifinal) to other available means to the same end. In short, for an attitude to eventuate in a specific behavior a chain of events needs to unfold, each constituting a necessary link without which the attitude behavior connection would be severed.

Our analysis builds on prior models and research on attitude-behavior relations and identifies limitations to their applicability. Specifically, we considered from the present theoretical perspective the two major paradigms wherein the attitude behavior relation was studied: (a) the attitude strength paradigm, and (b) the behavioral focus paradigm. In regard to the first paradigm, our theory implies that although strength of an object-attitude at some minimal magnitude seems necessary for relative *liking* (R_L) of future versus present states to transform into *wanting*, attitude strength alone is insufficient to drive behavior. Specifically, wanting must combine with attainability beliefs to foster goal formation, the goal thus formed must be the dominant one in the situation and the behavior must represent a chosen means to that particular goal.

More important, this process is assumed to apply equally to automatically driven, or "spontaneous" behaviors prompted by goal priming (e.g., Bargh et al., 2001) and to behaviors undertaken after a painstaking, "deliberative" consideration of the attitude object's "positive and negative features, (as well as) ... costs and benefits" (Fazio, 1990, p. 89, parentheses added). The latter deliberative process may result in a construction of a new object-attitude that may translate into *wanting* (to attain or avoid it). It is also worth noting that the "choice" aspect of means to the goal may reduce in some cases to just embracing the habitual means that popped up upon goal formation; that might occur if such means was strongly conditioned to the goal and if the actor lacked the motivation or the resources to seek alternative means.

Concerning the *behavior focus* paradigm, the major implication of our analysis is that its dismissal of object attitudes' part in driving behavior was premature. It is such attitudes after all that (in their relative form, R_L) contribute to goal formation, which ultimately results in behavior. Indeed, we have seen that when a given behavior is strongly preferred as means of goal attainment, the relation between the general attitude and the specific behavior can be quite substantial, and it is crucially mediated by goal formation based on the attitude in question (see Figure 7).

Moreover, whereas there can be no doubt that behavioral intentions do drive behavior, we question the proposal of the TRA and TPB models that it is attitude toward the behavior, behavioral norms, and perceived behavioral control that necessarily determine behavioral intentions. According to the present analysis, (a) none of these factors would affect behavioral intentions if the goal to which the behavior was the means was absent, whereas (b) if the goal was present these factors, though relevant, may not be the exclusive or the most important determinants of behavioral intentions. Rather, the behavior's *instrumentality* to the goal and its *supplementarity* (tapping the classic motivational parameters of expectancy and value, respectively) could be the primary determinants of behavioral intentions.

Testability

Our "Rocky Road" model of attitude to behavior relations has numerous testable implications. Two alternative research strategies may be followed in this regard, namely of (a) *subtracting*, or (b) *bypassing* links in the attitude to behavior chain. In that chain the attitude elements (i.e., relative liking) are viewed as distal to behavior, and the wanting and goal elements are viewed as more proximal to behavior. The subtractive strategy rests on the implication that if the proximal elements to which attitudes contributed were missing, the attitude to behavior chain would be severed, and no behavior would follow from mere attitudes. For instance, we predict that an accessible attitude would fail to induce behavior if a reasonable sense of goal attainability was absent. Moreover, even if attainability was present, no attitude-related behavior should follow if a different goal, unrelated to the accessible attitude, was dominant.

Similarly, the determinants of a behavioral intention identified in the TPB (attitudes to the behavior, etc.) should fail to produce the intention (and the correspondent behavior) if the goal was absent to which the behavior in question was a means. Finally, those determinants should fail to engender a behavioral intention if a different behavior was identified as more *instrumental* toward goal attainment (Labroo & Kim, 2009), and/or to bring greater supplementary value, by dint of its *multifinality* (Kruglanski, Köpetz et al., 2013). These varied implications could be profitably probed in future research guided by the present model.

An alternative research strategy rests on *bypassing* the distal elements in the chain and focusing on the proximal ones. Specifically, if measures of the proximal elements were available measures of the distal (constitutive) links would be superfluous and could, therefore, be bypassed in behavioral prediction. For instance, if measures of *wanting* were available, measures of *attitudes* could be dispensed with, because they would have been already encompassed in the wanting measures. Similarly, measures of *goal formation* would obviate measures of *wanting*, because wanting is part and parcel of goal formation. Simply put, effects on behavior of the early links are assumed to be mediated by the subsequent links so once the latter are taken into account, effects of the former would vanish (as in Figure 7 above). These predictions too could be fruitfully explored in future research.[21]

Finally, it is of interest to consider an approach to behavioral prediction based on the goal-systemic perspective. Such an approach would require close attention to the several relevant elements in the attitude to behavior chain as they may be represented in a given context of interest. Specifically, information about the *person* and about the *situation* would be needed. The former would concern the potential actor's general motives in accordance with a broad motivational taxonomy, for example, by Fiske (2003) or Higgins (2012). Information about the situation would concern the motive-relevant goals a given situational context may induce, and the means that the situational constraints may afford. For instance, if an individual was assessed as high on achievement motivation and the situation was deemed to activate an achievement goal, a person may embark on an achievement task if one was available. Moreover, a task believed to be most instrumental to gratifying one's achievement motivation (e.g., one where an immediate feedback was available) might be deemed as preferable over a task less likely to do so (e.g., one with a delayed feedback or absent feedback altogether). In situations where several of the individual's goals were activated, it would be important to determine which one was dominant, and what means would be (subjectively) most likely to promote it.

Where two or more goals of near equal magnitude are activated, a multifinal means might be preferred over a unifinal means relevant to one of those goals exclusively (Kruglanski, Köpetz et al., 2013). Finally, where several equifinal means to a goal seemed available, or in a novel situation where possible means were unfamiliar to the actor, prediction of the behavior would be more uncertain than in a situation where a habitual means to the goal was available (see Figure 8). For instance, some individuals whose goal of *self-enhancement* was situationally activated might pursue it by a habitual means (e.g., by demonstrating a well-practiced skill, or by a careful grooming of one's appearance) whereas other persons may lack a specific self-enhancement habit (cf. Wood & Neal, 2007) and hesitate between different modes of self-enhancement (e.g., whether to appear knowledgeable, sensitive, athletic, or wise). Behavioral prediction may then be more assured in the former versus the latter case.

Coda

All things considered, predicting behaviors from attitudes toward objects or states of affairs is a precarious business fraught with complex contingencies. An attitude (or liking) toward an object is neither a necessary nor a sufficient condition for wanting the object in question; furthermore, wanting in and of itself need not produce goal commitment, which in turn may not drive any given behavior as a means of goal attainment. A more realistic approach to behavioral prediction may require familiarity with the individual's motivational make-up and with the motivationally relevant structure of the situation, including goals that the situation may activate and the means-ends configurations it may evoke.

Notes

1. Other writers made this same point. Specifically, Calder and Ross (1973, p. 7), expressed doubt that "the mere fact that one has an attitude would produce behavior in and of itself." Echoing these writers' sentiment, Fazio (1995, p. 271) expressed reluctance "to ascribe any energizing value to attitudes."
2. By "liking" we mean a positive evaluation rather than merely an affective response.
3. For instance, an individual may abandon the goal of showing up at an important meeting, if the goal of caring for his or her sick child was activated. Again, it is not only the positive attitude toward the child's health but attainability of improving the child's health through one's staying at home that drives the behavior. If the child was in a far distant land, so that one could do little for its benefit, one might have attended the meeting as planned originally.
4. Such as Allport's (1929) notion that "an attitude is a disposition to act," (p. 221) or the tripartite definition of attitude as containing cognitive, affective, and behavioral components (Rosenberg & Hovland, 1960).
5. Beyond a given threshold of desirability (Kruglanski et al., 2014).

6 A special case of this is represented by a discrepancy between one's actual and desired attitude (DeMarree, Wheeler, Briñol, & Petty, 2014). Such a discrepancy may contribute to the formation of a goal to remove the discrepancy by replacing the actual by the desired attitude. In such an instance, the actual attitude is less likely to serve as a basis for goal formation. Indeed, DeMarree et al., 2014 find that where the discrepancy between actual and desired attitudes is large the actual attitude is less likely to predict behavior.

7 The liking measure consisted of an averaged response to five highly correlated questions referring to the main food item participants were about to eat (or had just eaten): (a) *How good is it?* (b) *How tasty is it?* (c) *How beneficial is it?* (d) *How pleasant is it?* (e) *How much do you like it?* Want was measured with the question: *How much do you want to eat it right now?* Answers were recorded with 7-point Likert scales anchored appropriately at the ends.

8 In the case of prevention the negative future state should be perceived as having an above-threshold likelihood of occurring, otherwise no wanting would occur. For instance, one may dislike getting wet, but not want to carry an umbrella unless there is a high threat of rain.

9 Thus, we assume Relative Liking to be a causal antecedent of Wanting; Wanting, and Attainability to be the causal antecedents of goal formation; and goal dominance to be a causal antecedent of behavioral (i.e., means) choice. No order of precedence is assumed to characterize the Want versus Attainability relation, however. That is, an individual might be cognizant of the *attainability* of a given state of affairs either before or after she or he was cognizant of its *desirability*.

10 For example, because participants trusted their own epistemic authority or gut feelings concerning their liking or dislike toward the experienced objects.

11 In that attitude accessibility was measured before the behavioral options were presented.

12 Relevant to this point, Holland et al. (2002) excluded from the analysis members of the Greenpeace organization who did not donate money. These participants ($n = 5$) had a good reason not to donate money, as they already paid membership fees (p. 872). Thus, the authors actually excluded from their study participants who did not have the goal to donate—presumably because including them would change their results.

13 The TPB notion of perceived behavioral control (PBC) is conceptually distinct from the notion of goal attainability. As noted above, PBC refers to one's ability to carry out a *specific behavior*, whereas goal attainability refers to one's general expectancy of being able to accomplish a given goal through one's actions. For instance, attainability may be affected by one's general sense of efficacy (Bandura, 1993) or an incremental mindset (Dweck, 2006) not having to do with a specific behavior.

14 According to Nosek et al.'s (2010) intuitive guide (http://projectimplicit.net/nosek/papers/citations/citedarticles.html) articles with above 3,000 citations count as having "transformational impact." In these terms, three of the Ajzen and Fishbein articles can claim to have exerted transformational impact, notably Fishbein and Ajzen (1975) with 11,300 citations, Ajzen and Fishbein (1980) with 9,824 citations, and Ajzen (1991) with 7,667 citations.

15 Fishbein and Ajzen (2010) do mention the goal concept, in the context of suggesting that behavior is more predictable, and hence more amenable to study, than goal attainment. As they put it "Attainment of a goal depends not only on the person's behavior but also on the other factors over which the person may have little or no control" (p. 57), therefore: "as a general rule, intentions will usually be better predictors of behaviors than of goal attainment" (p. 58). However, our present concern is not whether goals are attained, but rather whether behavior is goal driven and, therefore, predictable from goals active in a situation.

16 We excluded 11 participants from the analyses because they did not perform any activity at all (and therefore had no score on the dependent variable). We also excluded 2 participants from the analyses because they indicated that they performed all 24 physical activities we listed (that is highly unlikely); however, the analyses with and

without those two participants included were nearly identical. Thus, the following analyses refer to 91 participants.
17 Meta-analysis of 47 experimental tests of intention–behavior relations (Webb & Sheeran, 2006) showed that changing participants' intentions had a greater impact on behavior when the time interval between the intention and behavior measures was short (i.e., less than or equal to the median value of 11.5 weeks) as compared with long ($d = 0.46$ vs. 0.23). Other meta-analyses (e.g., Sheeran & Orbell, 1998) have shown the same pattern.
18 Warshaw and Davis (1985a,1985b) draw the distinction between behavioral intentions and behavioral expectations, that is, the expectations that one would execute the behavior and find evidence that the latter (vs. the former) can be the superior predictors of behaviors, for example, where one can foresee that one's intentions to perform a given behavior might change under the circumstances.
19 It is of interest to note in this connection that the multiple correlation of attitude to behavior, subjective norm and perceived behavioral control account for rather low percentage of variance in behavioral intentions (39% in the Armitage & Conner, 2001, analysis and above 36% in Fishbein & Ajzen's, 2010, review). Consistent with the present analysis then, the AB, SN, and PBC measures do not appear to fully tap the determinants of behavioral intentions.
20 It will be noted that in the situation depicted in this study subjective norm was highly correlated with attitude toward the behavior ($r = .85$), suggesting that the attitude reflected an internalized norm, and perceived behavioral control was uniformly high among participants (restricting the range on this variable).
21 It is noteworthy that the present model can be fruitfully applied to all domains of research where the attitude-behavior relations were investigated. Take, for instance, individual differences in attitude-behavior consistency. The findings of such differences presumably reflect the relative stability of individuals' (attitude-derived) goals that drive the consistency. For instance, it is found that low self-monitors tend to act more consistently with their attitudes than do high self-monitors (Snyder, 1983), and it is possible that the attitudes and attitude-derived goals of the former are more stable and chronically accessible than those of the latter. In that instance too, one would predict that if goal formation was rendered impossible (e.g., by eliminating attainability) the attitude behavior consistency for the individuals involved would vanish as well.

References

Aarts, H., Custers, R., & Holland, R. W. (2007). The nonconscious cessation of goal pursuit: When goals and negative affect are coactivated. *Journal of Personality and Social Psychology, 92*, 165–178. http://dx.doi.org/10.1037/0022-3514.92.2.165

Ajzen, I. (1985). From intentions to actions: A theory of planned behavior. In J. Kuhl & J. Beckmann (Eds.), *Action control: From cognition to behavior* (pp. 11–39). Heidelberg, Germany: Springer-Verlag. http://dx.doi.org/10.1007/978-3-642-69746-3_2

Ajzen, I. (1991). The theory of planned behavior. *Organizational Behavior and Human Decision Processes, 50*, 179–211. http://dx.doi.org/10.1016/ 0749-5978(91)90020-T

Ajzen, I. (2012). Attitudes and persuasion. In K. Deaux & M. Snyder (Eds.), *The Oxford handbook of personality and social psychology* (pp. 367–393). New York, NY: Oxford University Press.

Ajzen, I. (2014). The theory of planned behaviour is alive and well, and not ready to retire: A commentary on Sniehotta, Presseau, and Araújo-Soares. *Health Psychology Review*. [Advance online publication.]

Ajzen, I., & Driver, B. L. (1991). Prediction of leisure participation from behavioral, normative, and control beliefs: An application of the theory of planned behavior. *Leisure Sciences, 13*, 185–204. http://dx.doi.org/10.1080/01490409109513137

Ajzen, I., & Fishbein, M. (1975). *Belief, attitude, intention and behavior: An introduction to theory and research*. Reading, MA: Addison-Wesley Publishing Co.

Ajzen, I., & Fishbein, M. (1980). *Understanding attitudes and predicting social behavior*. Eglewood Cliffs, NJ: Prentice Hall.

Ajzen, I., Timko, C., & White, J. B. (1982). Self-monitoring and the attitude–behavior relation. *Journal of Personality and Social Psychology, 42*, 426–435. http://dx.doi.org/10.1037/0022-3514.42.3.426

Albarracín, D., Johnson, B. T., Fishbein, M., & Muellerleile, P. A. (2001). Theories of reasoned action and planned behavior as models of condom use: A meta-analysis. *Psychological Bulletin, 127*, 142–161. http://dx.doi.org/10.1037/0033-2909.127.1.142

Albarracín, D., Johnson, B. T., & Zanna, M. P. (2005). *The handbook of attitudes*. Mahwah, NJ: Erlbaum Publishers.

Allport, G. W. (1929). The composition of political attitudes. *American Journal of Sociology, 35*, 220–238. http://dx.doi.org/10.1086/214980

Allport, G. W. (1935). Attitudes. In C. Murchison (Ed.), *A handbook of social psychology* (pp. 798–844). Worcester, MA: Clark University Press.

Armitage, C. J., & Conner, M. (2000). Attitudinal ambivalence: A test of three key hypotheses. *Personality and Social Psychology Bulletin, 26*, 1421–1432. http://dx.doi.org/10.1177/0146167200263009

Armitage, C. J., & Conner, M. (2001). Efficacy of the theory of planned behaviour: A meta-analytic review. *British Journal of Social Psychology, 40*, 471–499. http://dx.doi.org/10.1348/014466601164939

Aronson, E. (1968). Dissonance theory: Progress and problems. In R. P. Abelson, E. Aronson, W. J. McGuire, T. M. Newcomb, M. J. Rosenberg, & P. H. Tannenbaum (Eds.), *Theories of cognitive consistency: A sourcebook* (pp. 5–27). Chicago, IL: Rand McNally.

Atkinson, J. W. (1964). *An introduction to motivation*. Oxford, England: Van Nostrand.

Bagozzi, R. P. (1992). The self-regulation of attitudes, intentions, and behavior. *Social Psychology Quarterly, 55*, 178–204. http://dx.doi.org/ 10.2307/2786945

Bandura, A. (1993). Perceived self-efficacy in cognitive development and functioning. *Educational Psychologist, 28*, 117–148. http://dx.doi.org/ 10.1207/s15326985ep2802_3

Bargh, J. A. (1990). Goal and intent: Goal-directed thought and behavior are often unintentional. *Psychological Inquiry, 1*, 248–251. http://dx.doi.org/10.1207/s15327965pli0103_14

Bargh, J. A., & Ferguson, M. J. (2000). Beyond behaviorism: On the automaticity of higher mental processes. *Psychological Bulletin, 126*, 925–945.

Bargh, J. A., Gollwitzer, P. M., Lee-Chai, A., Barndollar, K., & Trötschel, R. (2001). The automated will: Nonconscious activation and pursuit of behavioral goals. *Journal of Personality and Social Psychology, 81*, 1014–1027. http://dx.doi.org/10.1037/0022-3514.81.6.1014

Bélanger, J. J., Kruglanski, A. W., Chen, X., Orehek, E., & Johnson, D. J. (2015). When Mona Lisa smiled and love was in the air: On the cognitive energetics of motivated judgments. *Social Cognition, 33*, 104–119. http://dx.doi.org/10.1521/soco.2015.33.2.104

Bem, D. J. (1970). *Beliefs, attitudes, and human affairs*. Oxford, England: Brooks/Cole.

Berridge, K. C. (2004). Motivation concepts in behavioral neuroscience. *Physiology & Behavior, 81*, 179–209. http://dx.doi.org/10.1016/j.physbeh.2004.02.004

Berridge, K. C., & Robinson, T. E. (2003). Parsing reward. *Trends in Neurosciences*, *26*, 507–513. http://dx.doi.org/10.1016/S0166-2236(03)00233-9

Cacioppo, J. T., Harkins, S. G., & Petty, R. E. (1981). The nature of attitudes and cognitive responses and their relationships to behavior. In R. E. Petty, T. M. Ostrom, & T. C. Brock (Eds.), *Cognitive responses in persuasion* (pp. 31–54). Hillsdale, NJ: Erlbaum.

Calder, B. J., & Ross, M. (1973). *Attitudes and behavior*. Morristown, NJ: General Learning Press.

Carver, C. S., & Scheier, M. F. (1982). Control theory: A useful conceptual framework for personality-social, clinical, and health psychology. *Psychological Bulletin*, *92*, 111–135. http://dx.doi.org/10.1037/0033-2909.92.1.111

Carver, C. S., & Scheier, M. F. (1998). *On the self-regulation of behavior*. New York, NY: Cambridge University Press. http://dx.doi.org/10.1017/CBO9781139174794

Carver, C. S., & Scheier, M. F. (2011). Self-regulation of action and affect. In K. D. Vohs & R. F. Baumeister (Eds.), *Handbook of self-regulation: Research, theory, and applications* (2nd ed., pp. 3–21). New York, NY: Guilford Press.

Chartrand, T. L., & Bargh, J. A. (1996). Automatic activation of impression formation and memorization goals: Nonconscious goal priming reproduces effects of explicit task instructions. *Journal of Personality and Social Psychology*, *71*, 464–478. http://dx.doi.org/10.1037/0022-3514.71.3.464

Cogman, B. (Writer), & MacLaren, M. (Director). (2014). Oathkeeper [Television series episode]. In C. Newman, & G. Spence (Producers), *Game of Thrones*. Ireland: HBO.

Cohen, A. R. (1960). Attitudinal consequences of induced discrepancies between cognitions and behavior. *Public Opinion Quarterly*, *24*, 297–318. http://dx.doi.org/10.1086/266950

Converse, P. E. (1970). Attitudes and non-attitudes: Continuation of a dialogue. In E. R. Tufte (Ed.), *The quantitative analysis of social problems* (pp. 168–189). Reading, MA: Addison-Wesley Publishing Co.

Cooke, R., & French, D. P. (2008). How well do the theory of reasoned action and theory of planned behaviour predict intentions and attendance at screening programmes? A meta-analysis. *Psychology & Health*, *23*, 745–765. http://dx.doi.org/10.1080/08870440701544437

Custers, R., & Aarts, H. (2005). Positive affect as implicit motivator: On the nonconscious operation of behavioral goals. *Journal of Personality and Social Psychology*, *89*, 129–142. http://dx.doi.org/10.1037/0022-3514.89.2.129

Custers, R., & Aarts, H. (2007). In search of the nonconscious sources of goal pursuit: Accessibility and positive affective valence of the goal state. *Journal of Experimental Social Psychology*, *43*, 312–318. http://dx.doi.org/10.1016/j.jesp.2006.02.005

Davidson, A. R., Yantis, S., Norwood, M., & Montano, D. E. (1985). Amount of information about the attitude object and attitude-behavior consistency. *Journal of Personality and Social Psychology*, *49*, 1184–1198. http://dx.doi.org/10.1037/0022-3514.49.5.1184

DeMarree, K. G., Wheeler, S. C., Briñol, P., & Petty, R. E. (2014). Wanting other attitudes: Actual-desired attitude discrepancies predict feelings of ambivalence and ambivalence consequences. *Journal of Experimental Social Psychology*, *53*, 5–18. http://dx.doi.org/10.1016/j.jesp.2014.02.001

Dweck, C. (2006). *Mindset: The new psychology of success*. New York, NY: Random House.

Eagly, A. H., & Chaiken, S. (1993). *The psychology of attitudes*. Orlando, FL: Harcourt Brace Jovanovich College Publishers.

Eitam, B., & Higgins, E. T. (2010). Motivation in mental accessibility: Relevance of a representation (ROAR) as a new framework. *Social and Personality Psychology Compass*, *4*, 951–967. http://dx.doi.org/10.1111/j.1751-9004.2010.00309.x

Fabrigar, L. R., Petty, R. E., Smith, S. M., & Crites, S. L., Jr. (2006). Understanding knowledge effects on attitude-behavior consistency: The role of relevance, complexity, and amount of knowledge. *Journal of Personality and Social Psychology, 90*, 556–577. http://dx.doi.org/10.1037/0022-3514.90.4.556

Farc, M. M., & Sagarin, B. J. (2009). Using attitude strength to predict registration and voting behavior in the 2004 US presidential elections. *Basic and Applied Social Psychology, 31*, 160–173. http://dx.doi.org/10.1080/01973530902880498

Fazio, R. H. (1990). Multiple processes by which attitudes guide behavior: The MODE model as an integrative framework. *Advances in Experimental Social Psychology, 23*, 75–109.

Fazio, R. H. (1995). Attitudes as object-evaluation associations: Determinants, consequences, and correlates of attitude accessibility. In R. E. Petty, & J. A. Krosnick (Eds.), *Attitude strength: Antecedents and consequences* (pp. 247–282). Hillsdale, NJ: Erlbaum.

Fazio, R. H. (2007). Attitudes as object-evaluation associations of varying strength. *Social Cognition, 25*, 603–637. http://dx.doi.org/10.1521/soco.2007.25.5.603

Fazio, R. H., Chen, J. M., McDonel, E. C., & Sherman, S. J. (1982). Attitude accessibility, attitude-behavior consistency, and the strength of the object-evaluation association. *Journal of Experimental Social Psychology, 18*, 339–357. http://dx.doi.org/10.1016/0022-1031(82)90058-0

Fazio, R. H., & Olson, M. A. (2014). The MODE model: Attitude–behavior processes as a function of motivation and opportunity. In J. W. Sherman, B. Gawronski, & Y. Trope (Eds.), *Dual-process theories of the social mind* (pp. 155–171). New York, NY: Guilford Press.

Fazio, R. H., Powell, M. C., & Williams, C. J. (1989). The role of attitude accessibility in the attitude-to-behavior process. *Journal of Consumer Research, 16*, 280–288. http://dx.doi.org/10.1086/209214

Fazio, R. H., & Williams, C. J. (1986). Attitude accessibility as a moderator of the attitude-perception and attitude-behavior relations: An investigation of the 1984 presidential election. *Journal of Personality and Social Psychology, 51*, 505–514. http://dx.doi.org/10.1037/0022-3514.51.3.505

Fazio, R. H., & Zanna, M. P. (1978). Attitudinal qualities relating to the strength of the attitude-behavior relationship. *Journal of Experimental Social Psychology, 14*, 398–408. http://dx.doi.org/10.1016/0022-1031(78)90035-5

Fazio, R. H., Zanna, M. P., & Cooper, J. (1978). Direct experience and attitude-behavior consistency: An information processing analysis. *Personality and Social Psychology Bulletin, 4*, 48–51. http://dx.doi.org/10.1177/014616727800400109

Festinger, L. (1957). *A theory of cognitive dissonance.* Stanford, CA: Stanford University Press.

Fishbach, A. (2014). The motivational self is more than the sum of its goals. *Behavioral and Brain Sciences, 37*, 143–144. http://dx.doi.org/10.1017/S0140525X13002021

Fishbach, A., & Ferguson, M. J. (2007). The goal construct in social psychology. In A. W. Kruglanski & E. T. Higgins (Eds.), *Social psychology: Handbook of basic principles* (pp. 490–515). New York, NY: Guilford Press.

Fishbach, A., Friedman, R. S., & Kruglanski, A. W. (2003). Leading us not unto temptation: Momentary allurements elicit overriding goal activation. *Journal of Personality and Social Psychology, 84*, 296–309. http://dx.doi.org/10.1037/0022-3514.84.2.296

Fishbein, M., & Ajzen, I. (1974). Attitudes towards objects as predictors of single and multiple behavioral criteria. *Psychological Review, 81*, 59–74. http://dx.doi.org/10.1037/h0035872

Fishbein, M., & Ajzen, I. (1975). *Belief, attitude, intention, and behavior: An introduction to theory and research.* Reading, MA: Addison-Wesley Publishing Co.

Fishbein, M., & Ajzen, I. (2010). *Predicting and changing behavior: The reasoned action approach.* New York, NY: Psychology Press.

Fiske, S. T. (2003). Five core social motives, plus or minus five. In S. Spencer, S. Fein, M. P. Zanna, & J. M. Olson (Eds.), *Motivated social perception: The Ontario symposium* (Vol. 9, pp. 233–246). Mahwah, NJ: Erlbaum.

Fitzsimons, G. M., & Bargh, J. A. (2003). Thinking of you: Nonconscious pursuit of interpersonal goals associated with relationship partners. *Journal of Personality and Social Psychology, 84,* 148–164. http://dx.doi.org/10.1037/0022-3514.84.1.148

Förster, J., Liberman, N., & Friedman, R. S. (2007). Seven principles of goal activation: A systematic approach to distinguishing goal priming from priming of non-goal constructs. *Personality and Social Psychology Review, 11,* 211–233. http://dx.doi.org/10.1177/1088868307303029

Froming, W. J., Walker, G. R., & Lopyan, K. J. (1982). Public and private self-awareness: When personal attitudes conflict with societal expectations. *Journal of Experimental Social Psychology, 18,* 476–487. http://dx.doi.org/10.1016/0022-1031(82)90067-1

Gollwitzer, P. M. (1999). Implementation intentions: Strong effects of simple plans. *American Psychologist, 54,* 493–503. http://dx.doi.org/10.1037/0003-066X.54.7.493

Hassin, R. R., Bargh, J. A., & Zimerman, S. (2009). Automatic and flexible: The case of non-conscious goal pursuit. *Social Cognition, 27,* 20–36. http://dx.doi.org/10.1521/soco.2009.27.1.20

Hayes, A. F. (2013). *Introduction to mediation, moderation, and conditional process analysis: A regression-based approach.* New York, NY: Guilford Press.

Heider, F. (1958). *The psychology of interpersonal relations.* New York, NY: Wiley. http://dx.doi.org/10.1037/10628-000

Higgins, E. T. (1987). Self-discrepancy: A theory relating self and affect. *Psychological Review, 94,* 319–340. http://dx.doi.org/10.1037/0033-295X.94.3.319

Higgins, E. T. (1996). Knowledge activation: Accessibility, applicability, and salience. In A. W. Kruglanski & E. T. Higgins (Eds.), *Social psychology: Handbook of basic principles* (pp. 133–168). New York, NY: Guilford Press.

Higgins, E. T. (2012). *Beyond pleasure and pain: How motivation works.* New York, NY: Oxford University Press.

Hofmann, W., & Friese, M. (2008). Impulses got the better of me: Alcohol moderates the influence of implicit attitudes toward food cues on eating behavior. *Journal of Abnormal Psychology, 117,* 420–427. http://dx.doi.org/10.1037/0021-843X.117.2.420

Hofmann, W., Gschwendner, T., Friese, M., Wiers, R. W., & Schmitt, M. (2008). Working memory capacity and self-regulatory behavior: Toward an individual differences perspective on behavior determination by automatic versus controlled processes. *Journal of Personality and Social Psychology, 95,* 962–977. http://dx.doi.org/10.1037/a0012705

Holland, R. W., de Vries, M., Hermsen, B., & van Knippenberg, A. (2012). Mood and the attitude–behavior link: The happy act on impulse, the sad think twice. *Social Psychological & Personality Science, 3,* 356–364. http://dx.doi.org/10.1177/1948550611421635

Holland, R. W., Verplanken, B., & van Knippenberg, A. (2002). On the nature of attitude–behavior relations: The strong guide, the weak follow. *European Journal of Social Psychology, 32,* 869–876. http://dx.doi.org/10.1002/ejsp.135

Huang, J. Y., & Bargh, J. A. (2014). The selfish goal: Autonomously operating motivational structures as the proximate cause of human judgment and behavior. *Behavioral and Brain Sciences, 37,* 121–135. http://dx.doi.org/10.1017/S0140525X13000290

Jaccard, J., & Becker, M. A. (1985). Attitudes and behavior: An information integration perspective. *Journal of Experimental Social Psychology*, *21*, 440–465. http://dx.doi.org/10.1016/0022-1031(85)90029-0

Kallgren, C. A., & Wood, W. (1986). Access to attitude-relevant information in memory as a determinant of attitude-behavior consistency. *Journal of Experimental Social Psychology*, *22*, 328–338. http://dx.doi.org/ 10.1016/0022-1031(86)90018-1

Karsten, A. (1928). Untersuchungen zur Handlungs- und Affektpsychologie [Psychological studies of action and affect]. *Psychologische Forschung*, *10*, 142–254. http://dx.doi.org/10.1007/BF00492011

Kay, A. C., Gaucher, D., Napier, J. L., Callan, M. J., & Laurin, K. (2008). God and the government: Testing a compensatory control mechanism for the support of external systems. *Journal of Personality and Social Psychology*, *95*, 18–35. http://dx.doi.org/10.1037/0022-3514.95.1.18

Kenrick, D. T., Griskevicius, V., Neuberg, S. L., & Schaller, M. (2010). Renovating the pyramid of needs contemporary extensions built upon ancient foundations. *Perspectives on Psychological Science*, *5*, 292–314. http://dx.doi.org/10.1177/1745691610369469

Kleiman, T., & Hassin, R. R. (2011). Nonconscious goal conflict. *Journal of Experimental Social Psychology*, *47*, 521–532. http://dx.doi.org/ 10.1016/j.jesp.2011.02.007

Krosnick, J. A., Boninger, D. S., Chuang, Y. C., Berent, M. K., & Carnot, C. G. (1993). Attitude strength: One construct or many related constructs? *Journal of Personality and Social Psychology*, *65*, 1132–1151. http://dx.doi.org/10.1037/0022-3514.65.6.1132

Krosnick, J. A., & Petty, R. E. (1995). Attitude strength: An overview. In R. E. Petty & J. A. Krosnick (Eds.), *Attitude strength: Antecedents and consequences* (pp. 1–24). Mahwah, NJ: Erlbaum.

Kruglanski, A. W. (1996). Goals as knowledge structures. In P. M. Gollwitzer & J. A. Bargh (Eds.), *Linking cognition and motivation to behavior* (pp. 599–618). The psychology of action New York, NY: Guilford Press.

Kruglanski, A. W., Bélanger, J. J., Chen, X., Köpetz, C., Pierro, A., & Mannetti, L. (2012). The energetics of motivated cognition: A force-field analysis. *Psychological Review*, *119*, 1–20. http://dx.doi.org/10.1037/a0025488

Kruglanski, A. W., Bélanger, J. J., Gelfand, M., Gunaratna, R., Hettiarachchi, M., Reinares, F., Orehek, E., Sasota, J., & Sharvit, K. (2013). Terrorism—A (self) love story: Redirecting the significance quest can end violence. *American Psychologist*, *68*, 559–575. http://dx.doi.org/10.1037/a0032615

Kruglanski, A. W., Chernikova, M., Rosenzweig, E., & Köpetz, C. (2014). On motivational readiness. *Psychological Review*, *121*, 367–388. http://dx.doi.org/10.1037/a0037013

Kruglanski, A. W., & Köpetz, C. (2010). Unpacking the self-control dilemma and its modes of resolution. In R. Hassin, K. Ochsner, & Y. Trope (Eds.), *Self-control in society, mind, and brain* (pp. 297–311). Oxford: Oxford University Press. http://dx.doi.org/10.1093/acprof:oso/9780195391381.003.0016

Kruglanski, A. W., Köpetz, C., Bélanger, J. J., Chun, W. Y., Orehek, E., & Fishbach, A. (2013). Features of multifinality. *Personality and Social Psychology Review*, *17*, 22–39. http://dx.doi.org/10.1177/1088868312453087

Kruglanski, A. W., Raviv, A., Bar-Tal, D., Raviv, A., Sharvit, K., Ellis, S., Bar, R., Pierro, A., & Mannetti, L. (2005). Says who? Epistemic authority effects in social judgment. *Advances in Experimental Social Psychology*, *37*, 345–392.

Kruglanski, A. W., Shah, J. Y., Fishbach, A., Friedman, R., Chun, W. Y., & Sleeth-Keppler, D. (2002). A theory of goal-systems. *Advances in Experimental Social Psychology*, *34*, 331–378.

Kunda, Z., Davies, P. G., Adams, B. D., & Spencer, S. J. (2002). The dynamic time course of stereotype activation: Activation, dissipation, and resurrection. *Journal of Personality and Social Psychology, 82*, 283–299. http://dx.doi.org/10.1037/0022-3514.82.3.283

Labroo, A. A., & Kim, S. (2009). The "instrumentality" heuristic: Why metacognitive difficulty is desirable during goal pursuit. *Psychological Science, 20*, 127–134. http://dx.doi.org/10.1111/j.1467-9280.2008.02264.x

Lewin, K. (1935). *A dynamic theory of personality: Selected papers*. New York, NY: McGraw-Hill Book Company, Inc.

McGuire, W. J. (1968). Personality and attitude change: An information-processing theory. In A. G. Greenwald, T. C. Brock, & T. M. Ostrom (Eds.), *Psychological foundations of attitudes* (pp. 171–196). New York, NY: Academic. http://dx.doi.org/10.1016/B978-1-4832-3071-9.50013-1

Miller, G. A., Galanter, E., & Pribram, K. H. (1960). *Plans and the structure of behavior*. New York, NY: Henry Holt & Co. http://dx.doi.org/10.1037/10039-000

Milyavsky, M., Hassin, R. R., & Schul, Y. (2012). Guess what? Implicit motivation boosts the influence of subliminal information on choice. *Consciousness and Cognition, 21*, 1232–1241. http://dx.doi.org/10.1016/j.concog.2012.06.001

Morsella, E., Bargh, J. A., & Gollwitzer, P. M. (Eds.). (2009). *Oxford handbook of human action*. New York, NY: Oxford University Press.

Norman, R. (1975). Affective-cognitive consistency, attitudes, conformity, and behavior. *Journal of Personality and Social Psychology, 32*, 83–91. http://dx.doi.org/10.1037/h0076865

Nosek, B. A., Graham, J., Lindner, N. M., Kesebir, S., Hawkins, C. B., Hahn, C., Schmidt, K., Motyl, M., Joy-Gaba, J., Frazier, R., & Tenney, E. R. (2010). Cumulative and career-stage citation impact of social-personality psychology programs and their members. *Personality and Social Psychology Bulletin, 36*, 1283–1300. http://dx.doi.org/10.1177/0146167210378111

Notani, A. S. (1998). Moderators of perceived behavioral control's predictiveness in the theory of planned behavior: A meta-analysis. *Journal of Consumer Psychology, 7*, 247–271. http://dx.doi.org/10.1207/s15327663jcp0703_02

Oettingen, G., Pak, H., & Schnetter, K. (2001). Self-regulation of goal setting: Turning free fantasies about the future into binding goals. *Journal of Personality and Social Psychology, 80*, 736–753. http://dx.doi.org/10.1037/0022-3514.80.5.736

Pessiglione, M., Schmidt, L., Draganski, B., Kalisch, R., Lau, H., Dolan, R. J., & Frith, C. D. (2007). How the brain translates money into force: A neuroimaging study of subliminal motivation. *Science, 316*, 904–906. http://dx.doi.org/10.1126/science.1140459

Petersen, K. K., & Dutton, J. E. (1975). Centrality, extremity, intensity: Neglected variables in research on attitude-behavior consistency. *Social Forces, 54*, 393–414. http://dx.doi.org/10.1093/sf/54.2.393

Petty, R. E., & Wegener, D. T. (1998). Matching versus mismatching attitude functions: Implications for scrutiny of persuasive messages. *Personality and Social Psychology Bulletin, 24*, 227–240. http://dx.doi.org/10.1177/0146167298243001

Petty, R. E., Wegener, D. T., & Fabrigar, L. R. (1997). Attitudes and attitude change. *Annual Review of Psychology, 48*, 609–647. http://dx.doi.org/10.1146/annurev.psych.48.1.609

Powers, W. T. (1973). *Behavior: The control of perception*. Chicago, IL: Aldine.

Pyszczynski, T., Sullivan, D., & Greenberg, J. (2015). Experimental existential psychology: Living in the shadow of the facts of life. In M. Mikulincer, P. R. Shaver, E. Borgida, & J. A. Bargh (Eds.), *APA handbook of personality and social psychology* (pp. 279–308). Washington, DC: American Psychological Association. http://dx.doi.org/10.1037/14341-009

Regan, D. T., & Fazio, R. (1977). On the consistency between attitudes and behavior: Look to the method of attitude formation. *Journal of Experimental Social Psychology, 13*, 28–45. http://dx.doi.org/10.1016/0022-1031(77)90011-7

Reynolds, S. M., & Berridge, K. C. (2008). Emotional environments retune the valence of appetitive versus fearful functions in nucleus accumbens. *Nature Neuroscience, 11*, 423–425. http://dx.doi.org/10.1038/nn2061

Rosenberg, M. J., & Hovland, C. I. (1960). Cognitive, affective, and behavioral components of attitudes. In M. J. Rosenberg, C. I. Hovland, W. J. McGuire, R. P. Abelson, & J. W. Brehm (Eds.), *Attitude organization and change: An analysis of consistency among attitude components* (pp. 1–14). New Haven, CT: Yale University Press.

Sample, J., & Warland, R. (1973). Attitude and prediction of behavior. *Social Forces, 51*, 292–304. http://dx.doi.org/10.1093/sf/51.3.292

Scheier, M. F. (1980). Effects of public and private self-consciousness on the public expression of personal beliefs. *Journal of Personality and Social Psychology, 39*, 514–521. http://dx.doi.org/10.1037/0022-3514.39.3.514

Schifter, D. E., & Ajzen, I. (1985). Intention, perceived control, and weight loss: An application of the theory of planned behavior. *Journal of Personality and Social Psychology, 49*, 843–851. http://dx.doi.org/ 10.1037/0022-3514.49.3.843

Schlegel, R. P., & DiTecco, D. (1982). Attitudinal structures and the attitude-behavior relation. In M. P. Zanna, E. T. Higgins, & C. P. Herman (Eds.), *Consistency in social behavior: The Ontario Symposium* (Vol. 2, pp. 17–49). Hillsdale, NJ: Erlbaum.

Schuman, H., & Presser, S. (1981). *Questions and answers in attitude surveys: Experiments on question form, wording, and context*. San Diego, CA: Academic Press.

Shah, J. Y., Friedman, R., & Kruglanski, A. W. (2002). Forgetting all else: On the antecedents and consequences of goal shielding. *Journal of Personality and Social Psychology, 83*, 1261–1280. http://dx.doi.org/ 10.1037/0022-3514.83.6.1261

Shah, J., & Higgins, E. T. (1997). Expectancy x value effects: Regulatory focus as determinant of magnitude and direction. *Journal of Personality and Social Psychology, 73*, 447–458. http://dx.doi.org/10.1037/0022-3514.73.3.447

Shah, J. Y., & Kruglanski, A. W. (2000). Aspects of goal networks. In M. Boekaerts, P. R. Pintrich, & M. Zeidner (Eds.), *Handbook of self-regulation* (pp. 85–110). San Diego, CA: Academic Press. http://dx.doi.org/10.1016/B978-012109890-2/50033-0

Shah, J. Y., & Kruglanski, A. W. (2003). When opportunity knocks: Bottom-up priming of goals by means and its effects on self-regulation. *Journal of Personality and Social Psychology, 84*, 1109–1122. http://dx.doi.org/10.1037/0022-3514.84.6.1109

Sheeran, P., & Orbell, S. (1998). Do intentions predict condom use? Meta-analysis and examination of six moderator variables. *British Journal of Social Psychology, 37*, 231–250. http://dx.doi.org/10.1111/j.2044-8309.1998.tb01167.x

Sherif, C. W., Kelly, M., Rodgers, H. L., Jr., Sarup, G., & Tittler, B. I. (1973). Personal involvement, social judgment, and action. *Journal of Personality and Social Psychology, 27*, 311–328. http://dx.doi.org/10.1037/h0034948

Sivacek, J., & Crano, W. D. (1982). Vested interest as a moderator of attitude–behavior consistency. *Journal of Personality and Social Psychology, 43*, 210–221. http://dx.doi.org/10.1037/0022-3514.43.2.210

Snyder, M. (1983). The influence of individuals on situations: Implications for understanding the links between personality and social behavior. *Journal of Personality, 51*, 497–516. http://dx.doi.org/10.1111/j.1467-6494.1983.tb00342.x

Snyder, M., & Kendzierski, D. (1982). Acting on one's attitudes: Procedures for linking attitude and behavior. *Journal of Experimental Social Psychology, 18*, 165–183. http://dx.doi.org/10.1016/0022-1031(82)90048-8

Snyder, M., & Swann, W. B. (1976). When actions reflect attitudes: The politics of impression management. *Journal of Personality and Social Psychology, 34,* 1034–1042. http://dx.doi.org/10.1037/0022-3514.34.5.1034

Stroebe, W., van Koningsbruggen, G. M., Papies, E. K., & Aarts, H. (2013). Why most dieters fail but some succeed: A goal conflict model of eating behavior. *Psychological Review, 120,* 110–138. http://dx.doi.org/10.1037/a0030849

Thurstone, L. L. (1931). The measurement of social attitudes. *The Journal of Abnormal and Social Psychology, 26,* 249–269. http://dx.doi.org/10.1037/h0070363

Tolman, E. C. (1932). *Purposive behavior in animals and men.* Berkeley, CA: University of California Press.

Warshaw, P. R., & Davis, F. D. (1985a). Disentangling behavioral intention and behavioral expectation. *Journal of Experimental Social Psychology, 21,* 213–228. http://dx.doi.org/10.1016/0022-1031(85)90017-4

Warshaw, P. R., & Davis, F. D. (1985b). The accuracy of behavioral intention versus behavioral expectation for predicting behavioral goals. *The Journal of Psychology, 119,* 599–602. http://dx.doi.org/10.1080/00223980.1985.9915469

Watson, J. B. (1913). Psychology as the behaviorist views it. *Psychological Review, 20,* 158–177. http://dx.doi.org/10.1037/h0074428

Webb, T. L., & Sheeran, P. (2006). Does changing behavioral intentions engender behavior change? A meta-analysis of the experimental evidence. *Psychological Bulletin, 132,* 249–268. http://dx.doi.org/10.1037/ 0033-2909.132.2.249

Weigel, R. H., & Newman, L. S. (1976). Increasing attitude-behavior correspondence by broadening the scope of the behavioral measure. *Journal of Personality and Social Psychology, 33,* 793–802. http://dx.doi.org/10.1037/0022-3514.33.6.793

Werner, P. D. (1978). Personality and attitude-activism correspondence. *Journal of Personality and Social Psychology, 36,* 1375–1390. http://dx.doi.org/10.1037/0022-3514.36.12.1375

Wicker, A. W. (1969). Attitudes versus actions: The relationship of verbal and overt behavioral responses to attitude objects. *Journal of Social Issues, 25,* 41–78. http://dx.doi.org/10.1111/j.1540-4560.1969.tb00619.x

Wicklund, R. A. (1982). Self-focused attention and the validity of self-reports. In M. P. Zanna, E. T. Higgins, & C. P. Herman (Eds.), *Consistency in social behavior: The Ontario Symposium* (Vol. 2, pp. 149–172). Hillsdale, NJ: Erlbaum.

Wiener, N. (1948). *Cybernetics: Or control and communication in the animal and the machine.* Cambridge, MA: MIT Press.

Wood, W., & Neal, D. T. (2007). A new look at habits and the habit-goal interface. *Psychological Review, 114,* 843–863. http://dx.doi.org/10.1037/0033-295X.114.4.843

8 To "do the right thing" or to "just do it"

Locomotion and assessment as distinct self-regulatory imperatives

Arie W. Kruglanski, University of Maryland
Erik P. Thompson, Washington University
E. Tory Higgins, Columbia University
M. Nadir Atash, Parsa, Inc.
Antonio Pierro, University of Rome "La Sapienza"
James Y. Shah, University of Wisconsin
Scott Spiegel, University of Maryland

Imagine yourself and your spouse on a holiday eve, at the eleventh hour sally to the local mall to get those missing items on your shopping list. You drive into the parking lot, which brims with hundreds of vehicles, and you look intently for a free spot. By an amazing stroke of luck, a car is about to pull out of a far row. Seizing the moment, you quickly move to fill the space the very millisecond it is vacated. One look at your spouse, however, conveys that all is not well. For, better than a thousand words, your spouse's countenance betrays deep disappointment with your chosen spot. After all, it is quite far from the mall entrance, requiring a considerable hike in chilly weather and under a mountain of packages to boot. Instead of taking it, your spouse would prefer to continue exploring until the perfect spot is found, even if this means cruising through hundreds of occupied spaces. To you, quite frankly, this quest seems frustrating, if not futile. You are simply itching to get on with it, to park the car wherever possible so you can proceed with the shopping task ahead. To be fair and impartial, we leave the saga before finding out whether a perfect spot was ever found. Regardless of whether it was, such differences in viewpoint may not appear to be the stuff of which marital bliss is made. A surprising perspective on this issue is offered in the concluding section of this article. That, however, is not the main point of our story.

Our interest lies instead in the psychological bases of tension between the spouses in the foregoing example. Hardly unique to any specific couple, or even to the interpersonal realm as a whole, such tension may reflect instead the contrasting pull of two basic self-regulatory functions. We call these functions assessment and locomotion (Higgins & Kruglanski, 1995). Assessment constitutes the comparative aspect of self-regulation concerned with critically evaluating entities or states, such as goals or means, in relation to alternatives in order to judge relative quality (i.e., judging the quality of something by considering both its merits and demerits in comparison with an alternative). It is exemplified in our example by one spouse's insistence on finding the perfect parking spot before stopping to shop (i.e., on finding or doing just the "right thing"). Locomotion, in contrast, constitutes the aspect of self-regulation concerned with movement from state to state and with committing the psychological resources that will initiate and maintain goal-related movement in a straightforward and direct manner, without undue distractions or delays. In our initial example, it is represented by the other spouse's impatience to get a move on and, in the felicitous words of the Nike commercial, to "just do it."

Assessment and locomotion together form part and parcel of any self-regulatory activity. According to classic theories (see Carver & Scheier, 1990; Gollwitzer, 1990; Higgins, 1989; Kuhl, 1985; Miller, Galanter, & Pribram, 1960; Mischel, 1974, 1981), self-regulation involves comparing and selecting among alternative desired end-states, comparing and selecting among alternative means to attain the selected desired end-state, and initiating and maintaining movement from some current state toward the desired end-state until the desired end-state is attained. However, assessment in and of itself is not enough. One needs to leap after one has looked, that is, commit the mental and physical resources required to initiate and maintain action that will reduce the discrepancy between one's current state and the desired end-state.

Control theories generally treat the functions of assessment and locomotion as inseparable parts of the whole of self-regulation and, hence, as functionally interdependent. Presumably, from this perspective, the intensity of both should covary with the degree to which a given self-regulatory activity mattered to the individual, and hence they should be positively correlated. In contrast, our present focus is on the degree to which each of these functions receives an independent emphasis. The notion that distinct self-regulatory functions can receive differential emphasis is found in other models as well.

Specifically, the rubicon model of action phases in goal-oriented behavior (see, e.g., Gollwitzer, 1990; Gollwitzer, Heckhausen, & Stellar, 1990; Heckhausen & Gollwitzer, 1987), inspired by Lewin's distinction between goal setting and goal striving (e.g., Lewin, Dembo, Festinger, & Sears, 1944), takes a temporal perspective on the course of action and proposes that different self-regulatory phenomena are associated with each phase. A distinction is made between the *deliberative* function of establishing and committing to fulfilling a preference or wish, which forms a *goal intention*, and the *implemental* function of planning and committing oneself to a particular course of action to fulfill the wish, which forms *behavioral intentions*. Mind-sets can emphasize either the deliberative or implemental functions. It should be noted that locomotion or assessment concerns can play a role in both deliberation and implementation. Indeed, deliberation and implemental processes could vary depending on the extent to which assessment or locomotion is emphasized. When deliberating, for example, one could be concerned with critically comparing alternative goals to select the best one or the right one, or one could be more concerned with completing deliberation promptly in order to move on through implementation to action initiation. The conceptual distinction between deliberative and implemental functions, then, is different from the distinction between assessment and locomotion functions.

The notion that distinct self-regulatory functions can receive differential emphasis is also found in Kuhl's (1985) distinction between action and state orientations. Kuhl (1985) described a fully developed intentional action structure as including a represented relation between a present state and a desired future state and action alternatives that may transform the present state into the future state, as well as the commitment of the actor to perform the intended action under specified situational conditions. When individuals have an action orientation their attention is focused on such a fully developed intentional action structure. In contrast, a state orientation is characterized by perseverating cognitions about some particular state, such as a present state, a past state, or a future state, or even by the absence of any coherent cognition, as in absentmindedness. To the extent that individuals have a state orientation, they are representing only part of the intentional action structure, if that, and in that sense they are absent an action orientation.

The distinction between locomotion and assessment functions does not concern how much of a fully developed intentional action structure is represented. Conceptually, therefore, the distinction between action versus state orientations is quite different from the distinction between locomotion versus assessment functions. The role of commitment in Kuhl's (1985) model does suggest some relation between these distinctions, however. Kuhl (1985) proposed that commitment to taking action is likely to be higher in the action than the state orientation because the latter can fail to represent the relation component that encodes the commitment quality of intention. Actions are expected to be initiated sooner, then, when individuals are in an action versus state orientation (as measured by the Action–Decision subscale of Kuhl's (1985) Action–Control Scale). Because locomotion concerns should increase and assessment concerns decrease, prompt action initiation—action versus state orientation (as measured by the Action–Decision subscale)—would be expected to have a positive association with locomotion and a lower and, if anything, negative association with assessment.

We assume that for various reasons having to do with temperament and socialization, different individuals can develop different degrees of concern for the locomotion and assessment modes. We further assume that the locomotion and assessment modes are relatively orthogonal to each other. After all, the reasons for why an individual may crave movement or progress (i.e., emphasizing locomotion) would seem quite unrelated to reasons for why she or he may develop a concern for standards and for critically evaluating alternatives (i.e., emphasizing assessment). Because of such independence, it is possible for some individuals to be high on both assessment and locomotion, leading to potential conflicts where these tendencies might have opposing action implications, low on both, or high on one and low on the other.

Social psychological characteristics of assessment and locomotion

Our analysis of assessment and locomotion affords the derivation of several specific characteristics that should be associated with each of these self-regulatory dimensions. We briefly describe these in turn.

Focus on self-evaluation

High versus low assessors are assumed to focus on evaluations of their actual self in comparison with alternative standards, including those associated with other people (e.g., you comparing yourself with others; others comparing you with who they want or expect you to be). High (vs. low) locomotors, in contrast, should not be as concerned with self-evaluation.

Affectivity

Because high (vs. low) assessors may perennially evaluate themselves, and because evaluations may evoke varying affective reactions, they should exhibit greater emotional instability than high (vs. low) locomotors. A self-evaluative focus may, moreover, highlight the discrepancies between one's actual self as one state and the desired self as an alternative state (Duval & Wicklund, 1972; Higgins, 1987). As a consequence, high (vs. low) assessors may exhibit more pronounced negative affect and lower optimism and self-esteem. Furthermore, because locomotion or forward movement contributes to a sense of progress, high (vs. low) locomotors may be characterized by a greater degree of positive affect and higher optimism and self-esteem.

Decisiveness

Because of its emphasis on engaging in goal-directed action, a quintessential feature of locomotion is shortened preactional decision processes allowing action to proceed. Therefore, high (vs. low) locomotors should exhibit a greater degree of decisiveness. High (vs. low) assessment, on the other hand, should be inversely related to decisiveness because it inherently involves a more extensive consideration of which goal should be pursued at a given time, or which means to a particular goal may best be selected.

Task orientation

High (vs. low) locomotors should exhibit a stronger task orientation—the tendency to attend to an activity and persist conscientiously until completion. Assessment, on the other hand, is less directly relevant to task orientation. If anything, it should be negatively related to it because high assessors may disrupt smooth task flow by stopping more often to evaluate their selection of means or their choice of goals in the midst of engaging in a particular activity.

Intrinsic motivation and autonomy

High (vs. low) locomotors may exhibit higher levels of intrinsic and autonomous motivation because their propensity to remain "in motion" promotes an increased level of experiential involvement in various tasks (e.g., Csikszentmihalyi, 1975). In contrast, high (vs. low) assessors, concerned as they are with evaluation, may care more about the evaluative consequences of their activities or about how their performance is perceived by others or measures up against external criteria. If high (vs. low) assessors then are more likely to experience activities as means toward ends (goals), then their task motivation may often be relatively extrinsic and nonautonomous (Deci & Ryan, 1991).

Self-regulatory emphasis

A number of further differences between the locomotion and assessment dimensions may relate to the contrasting ways in which individuals high (vs. low) on either locomotion or assessment may carry out self-regulatory activities, such as the following items.

(1) Emphasis on expectancy versus value

High (vs. low) locomotors may pay particular attention to the attainment expectancy of goals, in that attainable goals promise quick movement, whereas unattainable ones signal possible hindrance or thwarting of movement—an obvious anathema to locomotors. In contrast, high (vs. low) assessors may pay particular attention to a goal's value or importance because of their concern with pursuing the right goals, the best goals at a given time, or those goals that will reflect on them most positively if attained.

(2) Means generation and selection

In their attempt to create a large enough selection to afford optimal choice, high (vs. low) assessors may generate a larger number of means per goal. In their impatience to get going, high (vs. low) locomotors may be quick to select a "best" means to a given goal.

(3) Attainment outcomes

Successful completion of most (at least moderately complex) tasks should require a relatively high degree of both the assessment and the locomotion components. Blind locomotion, lacking adequate prior assessment, and paralyzing assessment, lacking translation into action, may equally court failure.

(4) Discrepancy spotting

The assessment construct has a direct implication for individuals' sensitivity to various discrepancies (from standards, alternatives, etc.), high (vs. low) assessors being expected to exhibit a higher such sensitivity. By contrast, the locomotion construct as such has no direct implication for discrepancy spotting. Nonetheless, in circumstances where discrepancy spotting may take away from the opportunity for movement, locomotion and discrepancy spotting may be inversely related. Overall, however, assessment should exhibit a stronger relation to discrepancy spotting than locomotion.

(5) Activity pace

The opposite pattern of relations should be evident in regard to the pace of activities or the speed of task performance. Here, the locomotion construct has a clear and direct implication, high (vs. low) locomotors being expected to exhibit the quicker pace, whereas the assessment construct does not. Nonetheless, in circumstances where assessment activities are compromised by the pace of performance, assessment should bear an inverse relation to pace. Overall, however, locomotion should exhibit a stronger relation to activity pace than assessment.

Research reported in the following pages submits the foregoing theoretical ideas to empirical test. We first describe the scale-construction process of two separate instruments designed to tap the assessment and locomotion orientations. We subsequently report the psychometric properties of the two scales, including their factorial structures and their reliabilities, both computed across numerous replication samples. We then describe research designed to assess the discriminant and convergent validities of our assessment and locomotion scales, including their relations with other instruments designed to measure related and unrelated constructs. The validation phase of our research also includes known group studies and laboratory experiments exploring additional psychological differences postulated to distinguish individuals scoring high (vs. low) on our assessment and locomotion instruments.

Scale construction

Study 1: Developing the locomotion and assessment scales

Our entire process of scale construction was theoretically driven and went through several screening stages. As a first step, the constructs of assessment and locomotion were defined. As noted earlier, assessment was conceptualized as the comparative aspect of self-regulation concerned with critically evaluating entities or states, such as goals and means, in relation to standards and alternatives in order to judge their relative qualities. That definition entails that individuals high on assessment would evaluate themselves and other persons on various dimensions, including the quality of one's own and others' social interactions, various positive and negative characteristics, outcomes and attainments, and so forth. Locomotion, by contrast, was defined as the aspect of self-regulation concerned with movement from state to state, hence, with the initiation and maintenance of goal-directed movement in a straightforward and direct manner, without undue distractions and delays. That definition entails that individuals high on locomotion should be high energy "doers" and "go-getters" who welcome the opportunity to act in relative disregard of the costs and who loathe merely waiting and watching rather than acting.

On the basis of the foregoing characterizations, we proceeded to develop items for the locomotion and assessment scales. We sampled broadly from the conceptual universes assumed to represent the two constructs to generate a pool of opinion statements about the various postulated features of locomotion and assessment. Our assessment items reflected the degree to which respondents were preoccupied with comparisons and evaluations against all kinds of standards and alternatives. Some sample items are "I spend a great deal of time taking inventory of my positive and negative characteristics," "I like evaluating other people's plans," and "I often compare myself with other people." The locomotion items tapped the degree to which respondents felt an urgency to move forward toward their goals and engage in doing. Some sample locomotion items are "When I decide to do something, I can't wait to get started," "I enjoy doing things actively, more than just watching and observing," and "By the time I accomplish a task, I already have the next one in mind." Along these lines, we generated an initial pool of 40 locomotion items and 40 assessment items.

The initial item pool then underwent reviews by two of the present authors (Arie W. Kruglanski and E. Tory Higgins) and several University of Maryland graduate students to whom the concepts of assessment and locomotion were thoroughly explained. Statements judged to be ambiguous, laden with surplus meaning, or lacking in conciseness were revised or eliminated. This reduced our overall pool to 19 locomotion items and 21 assessment items. These were administered to 13 independent samples (shown in Table 1). To obtain samples with sufficient power for appropriate exploratory and confirmatory factor analyses, some related samples were combined to form Aggregate Samples A (Independent Samples 1 and 2), B (Independent Samples 3 and 5), C (Independent Sample 6 only), and D (Independent Samples 9 and 10). The main objective here was to investigate the psychometric structure of the two scales across divergent groups of respondents and at different administration times. To that end, we exploited opportunities for data collection at diverse U.S. locations. An unintended consequence of such methodological opportunism (and the reduced control over the administration of the scales) was an occasional loss of gender information about some of the respondents. By and large, however, our samples afford a relatively complete picture of the scales' essential properties and inspire confidence in their robustness and stability. These samples are described next, followed by our psychometric analyses.

SAMPLE A

This sample consisted of 341 introductory psychology students from the University of Maryland, College Park, and 410 of their counterparts at the University of Arizona. For this sample the locomotion and assessment items were interspersed within the same questionnaire, administered as part of a larger mass testing session in the Spring 1996 semester at both universities. Thus, common to the two

Table 1 Individual samples and scale descriptives for Locomotion and Assessment scales

	Sample	N	M	SD	α	r_{loco}: assm	r with faking	α faking
	Locomotion scale							
1.	UMCP students ($96)	324	4.14	0.71	.82	.12*	.06	.62
2.	UMCP students (paid $97)	192	4.12	0.75	.84	.11	−.11	.72
3.	UMCP students (F96)	453	4.07	0.62	.79	.11*	.12**	.59
4.	UMCP students (lab, F96)	306	4.14	0.66	.80	.10	−.09	.48
5.	UMCP students ($97)	269	4.28	0.68	.83	.10	.20**	.51
6.	UMCP students ($98)	615	4.11	0.68	.79	.13**	.01	.58
7.	UMCP students (lab, $98)	131	4.12	0.71	.81	−.07	.02	.54
8.	U. Arizona students ($96)	387	4.15	0.67	.78	.09	.05	.55
9.	Columbia students ($93)	321	4.13	0.81	.83	.04	.04	.53
10.	Columbia students ($94)	177	4.16	0.81	.84	.10	−.03	.66
11.	Columbia students ($95)	423	4.14	0.85	.85	.07	.08	.49
12.	U.S. Army recruits	146	4.50	0.69	.79	.10	.01	.47
13.	Elite army training program	490	4.14	0.61	.81	.20***	.03	.63
	Assessment scale							
1.	UMCP students ($96)	324	3.98	0.75	.80	−.14**		
2.	UMCP students (paid, $97)	192	4.03	0.71	.79	−.14**		
3.	UMCP students (F96)	453	3.90	0.65	.75	−.07		
4.	UMCP students (lab, F96)	306	3.90	0.69	.77	−.14*		
5.	UMCP students ($97)	269	4.08	0.70	.78	−.11		
6.	UMCP students ($98)	615	4.03	0.72	.78	−.17***		
7.	UMCP students (lab, $98)	131	3.87	0.71	.76	−.22*		
8.	U. Arizona students ($96)	387	3.86	0.73	.78	−.11*		
9.	Columbia students ($93)	321	4.09	0.77	.79	−.08		
10.	Columbia students ($94)	177	4.07	0.70	.75	−.06		
11.	Columbia students ($95)	423	4.01	0.80	.80	−.15**		
12.	U.S. Army recruits	146	3.68	0.63	.60	−.20**		
13.	Elite army combat training	490	3.43	0.45	.57	.03		

Note: The term *lab* indicates students who participated in the experiment in the lab setting of their class and who, in turn, received course credit, loco = locomotion; assm = assessment; UMCP = University of Maryland, College Park; U. = University of; S = Spring; F = Fall; 93 = 1993; 94 = 1994; and so forth.
*$p < .05$. **$p < .01$. ***$p < .001$.

subparts of this sample was the time period during which data were collected. Originally, Sample A counted a total of 751 students. After eliminating data for 51 participants who scored at or above the midpoint on the 6-item Lie Scale index (nearly 7% of the original sample), the resultant N was reduced to 701. No gender data were available on the Arizona sample.

The mean locomotion score was 4.14 ($SD = 0.69$), and the alpha reliability coefficient for the locomotion scale was .80. The mean assessment score was 3.92 ($SD = 0.75$), and the alpha reliability coefficient was .79. Overall, the locomotion mean score was reliably higher than the mean assessment score, $t(700) = 6.28$, $p < .001$. The locomotion and assessment scores were weakly, but reliably, correlated in this particular sample, $r = .11$, $p < .005$. Sex differences were examined for the Maryland subsample. For locomotion, women scored somewhat higher than men ($Ms = 4.24$ and 4.03), $t(322) = 2.64$, $p < .01$. However, for assessment, the sex difference was not reliable ($Ms = 4.05$ and 3.91), $t(322) = 1.61$, $p = .108$.

SAMPLE B

Sample B consisted of introductory psychology students from the University of Maryland, College Park, who completed the locomotion and assessment items dispersed within the same questionnaire in the Fall 1996 and Spring 1997 semesters. Thus, common to the two subparts of this sample was the location at which the research was administered. Originally, this sample consisted of 757 cases. After eliminating 35 cases on the basis of the Lie Scale criterion (3% of the original sample), N was reduced to 722. The resultant sample consisted of 338 men (47%) and 384 women (53%).

The mean locomotion score was 4.14 ($SD = 0.65$), $\alpha = .81$. The mean assessment score was 3.97 ($SD = 0.67$), $\alpha = .76$. Overall, the mean locomotion score in this sample was reliably higher than the mean assessment score, $t(721) = 5.43$, $p < .001$. Locomotion and assessment scores were correlated weakly, but reliably, $r = .13$, $p < .005$. As in Sample A, women scored higher than men on locomotion ($Ms = 4.22$ and 4.06), $t(720) = 3.12$, $p < .005$, whereas the sex difference for assessment was not reliable, $t < 1$.

SAMPLE C

Sample C consisted of introductory psychology students at the University of Maryland, College Park, who completed the locomotion and assessment items (again dispersed within the same questionnaire) in Spring 1998. Originally there were 654 cases. After eliminating 45 cases on the basis of the Lie Scale criterion (4% of the original cases), the resultant N was 609, consisting of 271 men (45%) and 333 women (55%). (Gender information was unavailable for 5 participants.)

The mean locomotion score was 4.12 ($SD = 0.67$), $\alpha = .79$. The mean assessment score was 4.04 ($SD = 0.72$), $\alpha = .78$. Overall, the locomotion mean was reliably higher than the assessment mean, $t(608) = 2.20$, $p < .05$. As in Samples A and B, the locomotion and assessment scores were weakly, but reliably, correlated, $r = .13$, $p < .005$. No reliable sex differences were found in this sample either for locomotion, $t(602) = 1.41$, $p = .16$, or for assessment, $t < 1$.

SAMPLE D

Sample D consisted of Columbia University undergraduates (of various majors) paid to complete the locomotion and assessment measures either in Spring 1993 or in Spring 1994. As in Sample B, common to these two subsamples was the location at which the research was administered. Unlike the other three samples, these students completed the locomotion and assessment scales as separate questionnaires. Originally, there were 531 cases. After eliminating 33 cases on the basis of the Lie Scale criterion (4% of the original cases), the resultant N was 498. Information about gender was unavailable for this sample.

The mean locomotion score was 4.14 (SD = 0.81), α = .84. The mean assessment score was 4.08 (SD = 0.74), α = .77. Overall, locomotion and assessment means did not significantly differ, $t(497)$ = 1.20, p = .23. Finally, in this sample, locomotion and assessment scores were not reliably correlated, r = .06, p = .20.

Exploratory factor analysis

Even though our items were generated and screened in accordance with theoretical considerations, the narrowed item pool we came up with (19 and 21 for locomotion and assessment, respectively) was still deemed excessively large for practical purposes. We thus conducted exploratory factor analyses on our four aggregated samples to afford the choice of the optimal items on the basis of theoretical considerations and recursive psychometric feedback from the data (Muliak, 1987). Replication across diverse samples, rather than a combined omnibus analysis, constituted an important part of our scale development strategy. Its major purpose was to ensure that we did not capitalize on chance or on sample-specific variation.

On the basis of scree plot analyses, a two-factor solution was retained for each scale. As shown in Table 2, for both locomotion and assessment, the second factors were relatively weak, explaining about 10% or less of the variance, and theoretically uninterpretable. We deleted some of the items with high loadings on these factors, and whose specific wording may have been problematic and subject to different interpretations. Thus, the criteria for deletion were theoretical; the exploratory psychometric analysis merely helped to "raise the flag" and occasioned a reconsideration of some of our items.

Table 2 Exploratory factor analysis of Locomotion and Assessment items: Eigenvalue and percentage variance explained for each of the two retained factors

	Eigenvalue		% variance	
Sample	Factor 1	Factor 2	Factor 1	Factor 2
		Locomotion scale		
A	4.37	1.80	23.01	9.52
B	4.58	1.90	24.13	10.03
C	4.30	1.94	23.88	8.79
D	5.36	1.81	28.21	9.52
		Assessment scale		
A	4.82	2.22	21.92	10.13
B	4.54	2.14	20.63	5.51
C	4.73	1.77	22.52	8.44
D	4.93	2.34	22.39	10.63

Note: Sample A combines Individual Samples 1 and 2, and Sample B combines Individual Samples 3 and 5, Sample C is the same as Individual Sample 6, and Sample D combines Individual Samples 9 and 10.

Table 3 Items that make up the Locomotion and Assessment scales

Item

Locomotion items
  1. I don't mind doing things even if they involve extra effort.
  2. I am a "workaholic."
  3. I feel excited just before I am about to reach a goal.
  4. I enjoy actively doing things, more than just watching and observing.
  5. I am a "doer."
  6. When I finish one project, I often wait awhile before getting started on a new one. (reverse-scored)
  7. When I decide to do something, I can't wait to get started.
  8. By the time I accomplish a task, I already have the next one in mind.
  9. I am a "low energy" person. (reverse-scored)
  10. Most of the time my thoughts are occupied with the task I wish to accomplish.
  11. When I get started on something, I usually persevere until I finish it.
  12. I am a "go-getter."

Assessment items
  1. I never evaluate my social interactions with others after they occur. (reverse-scored)
  2. I spend a great deal of time taking inventory of my positive and negative characteristics.
  3. I like evaluating other people's plans.
  4. I often compare myself with other people,
  5. I don't spend much time thinking about ways others could improve themselves. (reverse-scored)
  6. I often critique work done by myself or others.
  7. I often feel that I am being evaluated by others.
  8. I am a critical person.
  9. I am very self-critical and self-conscious about what I am saying.
  10. I often think that other people's choices and decisions are wrong.
  11. I rarely analyze the conversations I have had with others after they occur. (reverse-scored)
  12. When I meet a new person I usually evaluate how well he or she is doing on various dimensions (e.g., looks, achievements, social status, clothes).

Note: In our validation research, the locomotion and assessment items were interspersed in a single questionnaire along with six faking items, not presented as separate sets. This ordering may be obtained by request from the authors.

These procedures resulted in a 12-item assessment scale and a 12-item locomotion scale, whose items were highly relevant theoretically as well as endowed with desirable psychometric properties. The items comprising the two scales are shown in Table 3. For both, respondents indicate the extent to which they endorse each item by responding to a 6-point Likert scale ranging from 1 (*strongly disagree*) to 6 (*strongly agree*).

Study 2: Evaluating the structural validity of the locomotion and assessment scales

The theory behind both the locomotion and the assessment constructs assumes that both are unidimensional. Accordingly, we applied a hierarchical confirmatory factor analysis (HCFA) to test one first-order factor model for each scale. All of the HCFA analyses were conducted using LISREL 8 (Jöreskog & Sörbom, 1993), with the sample covariance matrix as input and maximum likelihood for parameter estimation. Each item was constrained to load on only one factor, and a metric was set for each factor by arbitrarily constraining one loading to unity. Because the chi-square goodness-of-fit is sensitive to sample size and violation of the assumption of multivariate normality, we included five other fit indexes: chi-square (with degree of freedom), the goodness-of-fit index (GFI), the adjusted goodness-of-fit index (AGFI), the comparative fit index (CFI), and root-mean-square residual (RMR). These indexes are recommended by various sources (Bollen, 1989; Muliak, 1987; Tanaka, 1993).

RESULTS

The means and standard deviations for each of the 12 locomotion and 12 assessment items are given in Table 4. These results indicate a considerable consistency in item means and standard deviations across our four data sources.

HIERARCHICAL CONFIRMATORY FACTOR ANALYSIS

Table 5 presents a summary of the fit indexes for each model tested for all four data sources. As can be seen, the fit of the one-factor model for both the locomotion and assessment scales was adequate (i.e., the GFIs were higher than .90, the AGFIs and CFIs were larger than .80, and the RMRs were in the neighborhood of .10).

We used several additional methods to assess the unidimensionality of our scales, including reliability indexes (Green, Lissitz, & Muliak, 1977); interitem correlations and item-scale correlations (Hattie, 1985); principal-components analysis, for which we additionally computed the Lumsden (1961) index (ratio of the first and second eigenvalues—i.e., variance explained by the first principal component relative to variance explained by the second principal component); the Divgi (1980) index (difference between the first and second eigenvalues divided by the second and third eigenvalues); and the Atash (1994) index expressed as:

$$AI = [(r_{kk}/p_1) + (p_2/p_1) + (p_3/p_1)]/3$$

where r_{kk} is the reliability coefficient, p_1 is the proportion of variance explained by the first principal component, p_2 is the proportion of variance explained by the second principal component, and p_3 is the proportion of variance explained by the third principal component.

All these analyses yielded strong evidence for unidimensionality. As shown in Tables 6, 7, and 8, the coefficient alphas for our scales were relatively high (higher than .80 for the locomotion scale and close to .80 for the assessment scale), as were the mean item-item intercorrelations (higher than .20) and mean item-scale correlations.

Table 4 Means (and standard deviations) for Locomotion and Assessment items in Samples A–D

Item	Sample A (n = 702)	Sample B (n = 722)	Sample C (n = 609)	Sample D (n = 498)
		Locomotion scale		
1	4.45 (1.14)	4.40 (1.05)	4.51 (1.14)	4.35 (1.29)
2	2.70 (1.47)	2.68 (1.41)	2.78 (1.44)	3.08 (1.56)
3	5.16 (0.99)	5.21 (0.87)	5.22 (0.92)	4.98 (1.10)
4	4.79 (1.17)	4.91 (1.06)	4.72 (1.21)	4.73 (1.15)
5	4.43 (1.14)	4.40 (1.06)	4.35 (1.15)	4.41 (1.28)
6	3.24 (1.42)	3.19 (1.26)	3.33 (1.10)	3.41 (1.47)
7	4.59 (1.15)	4.62 (1.06)	4.48 (1.28)	4.39 (1.36)
8	3.66 (1.32)	3.62 (1.18)	3.68 (1.38)	3.75 (1.40)
9	4.42 (1.41)	4.48 (1.32)	4.34 (1.21)	4.44 (1.45)
10	4.00 (1.19)	3.98 (1.12)	3.93 (1.19)	3.83 (1.37)
11	4.18 (1.19)	4.11 (1.14)	4.13 (1.41)	4.42 (1.36)
12	4.18 (1.25)	3.13 (1.16)	4.40 (1.23)	4.09 (1.38)
		Assessment scale		
1	4.50 (1.281)	4.71 (1.13)	4.67 (1.27)	5.07 (1.12)
2	3.30 (1.51)	3.37 (1.48)	3.33 (1.57)	3.37 (1.53)
3	3.61 (1.37)	3.63 (1.23)	3.76 (1.33)	3.64 (1.46)
4	4.25 (1.39)	4.19 (1.35)	4.30 (1.36)	4.12 (1.51)
5	3.22 (1.39)	3.20 (1.33)	3.46 (1.41)	3.32 (1.49)
6	4.40 (1.10)	4.41 (1.06)	4.49 (1.01)	4.47 (1.22)
7	4.21 (1.30)	4.33 (1.25)	4.31 (1.26)	4.33 (1.33)
8	3.97 (1.41)	4.13 (1.3)	4.08 (1.39)	4.43 (1.40)
9	4.12 (1.43)	4.21 (1.38)	4.37 (1.37)	4.34 (1.37)
10	3.09 (1.25)	3.03 (1.20)	3.09 (1.23)	3.27 (1.32)
11	4.36 (1.41)	4.48 (1.24)	4.61 (1.31)	4.76 (1.28)
12	3.93 (1.39)	3.93 (1.32)	4.05 (1.37)	3.75 (1.55)

Note: Sample A combines Individual Samples 1 and 2, Sample B combines Individual Samples 3 and 5, Sample C is the same as Individual Sample 6, and Sample D combines Individual Samples 9 and 10.

Table 9 presents the proportion of variance explained by the first principal component (PC), the Lumsden Index, the Divgi Index, and the Atash Index for each of the scales for the four data sources under consideration. Because there is no consensus among researchers as to the criteria to be used for the various indexes, we use stringent standards—values of .30 for the proportion variance, 3.00 for Lumsden Index, and 1.00 for the Atash Index. On the basis of these criteria as well as the previously presented tests, it can be concluded that both the Assessment and Locomotion scales meet the assumptions of unidimensionality.

FURTHER DATA COLLECTION

Because only 7 of the 13 independent samples mentioned earlier were used for the confirmatory factor analyses, we have reported supplementary evidence for scale

Table 5 Model fit for the Locomotion and Assessment scales

Data set	n	X^2	df	X^2 per df	GFI	AGFI	CFI	RMR
Locomotion scale								
Null model								
Sample A	701	2,693.80	136	19.81	.55	.50	.00	.35
Sample B	722	3,252.16	136	23.91	.50	.43	.00	.35
Sample C	609	2,366.98	136	17.40	.55	.50	.00	.34
Sample D	498	2,576.28	136	18.94	.45	.39	.00	.49
One-factor model								
Sample A	701	370.14	54	6.85	.92	.88	.82	.11
Sample B	722	390.90	54	7.24	.91	.87	.83	.09
Sample C	609	326.88	54	6.05	.91	.87	.82	.11
Sample D	498	316.02	54	5.85	.90	.85	.85	.12
Assessment scale								
Null model								
Sample A	701	2,659.79	153	17.38	.55	.50	.00	.36
Sample B	722	2,566.09	153	16.77	.58	.53	.00	.31
Sample C	609	2,245.86	153	14.68	.56	.50	.00	.34
Sample D	498	2,101.34	153	13.73	.54	.49	.00	.40
One-factor model								
Sample A	701	325.00	54	6.02	.93	.89	.83	.11
Sample B	722	304.13	34	5.63	.93	.90	.81	.10
Sample C	609	267.32	55	4.95	.93	.90	.83	.10
Sample D	498	281.72	54	5.22	.91	.87	.78	.13

Note: Sample A combines Individual Samples 1 and 2, Sample B combines Individual Samples 3 and 5, Sample C is the same as Individual Sample 6, and Sample D combines Individual Samples 9 and 10. GFI = goodness-of-fit index; AGFI = adjusted goodness-of-fit index; CFI = comparative fit index, RMR = root-mean-square residual.

Table 6 Coefficient Alpha for Locomotion and Assessment scales in Samples A–D

Sample	Items	Coefficient α
Locomotion scale		
A	12	.82
B	12	.81
C	12	.81
D	12	.86
Assessment scale		
A	12	.79
B	12	.76
C	12	.78
D	12	.77

Note: Sample A combines Individual Samples 1 and 2, Sample B combines Individual Samples 3 and 5, Sample C is the same as Individual Sample 6, and Sample D combines Individual Samples 9 and 10.

Table 7 Mean, lowest, and highest correlation between pairs of scale items in Samples A–D, by scale

		Item-pair correlations		
Sample	Item pairs	M	Lowest	Highest
		Locomotion scale		
A	66	.25	.04	.61
B	66	.26	.01	.64
C	66	.24	.01	.55
D	66	.30	.11	.67
		Assessment scale		
A	66	.24	.08	.54
B	66	.21	.06	.46
C	66	.23	.06	.51
D	66	.22	−.01	.49

Note: Sample A combines Individual Samples 1 and 2, Sample B combines Individual Samples 3 and 5, Sample C is the same as Individual Sample 6, and Sample D combines Individual Samples 9 and 10.

Table 8 Mean, lowest, and highest item-scale total correlations, by scale

		Item-total correlations		
Sample	Items	M	Lowest	Highest
		Locomotion scale		
A	12	.55	.44	.75
B	12	.57	.38	.75
C	12	.55	.38	.72
D	12	.60	.41	.74
		Assessment scale		
A	12	.55	.46	.65
B	12	.53	.42	.62
C	12	.54	.35	.64
D	12	.54	.39	.63

Note: Sample A combines Individual Samples 1 and 2, Sample B combines Individual Samples 3 and 5, Sample C is the same as Individual Sample 6, and Sample D combines Individual Samples 9 and 10.

unidimensionality (Cronbach's alpha) as well as other individual-level sample data of interest in Table 1.

Internal consistency. As can be seen, for the Locomotion Scale, Cronbach's alpha ranged from .78 to .85. Collapsing across the 13 samples, the overall alpha for locomotion was .82. In the omnibus sample ($N = 4,256$), all 12 locomotion items produced item-total correlations greater than .34 (average item-total $r = .47$), and elimination of any one of them reduced the alpha.

For the Assessment Scale, alpha ranged from .57 to .80. Collapsing across the 13 samples, the overall alpha for assessment was .78. In the omnibus sample,

Table 9 Percentage of variance explained by first Principal Component (PC) and the Lumsden (1961), Divgi (1980), and Atash (1994) Indexes, by scale

Sample	First PC	Lumsden	Divgi	Atash
		Index of unidimensionality		
		Locomotion scale		
A	.32	2.98	16.41	1.07
B	.34	3.24	17.52	0.99
C	.31	2.81	15.19	1.10
D	.37	2.54	10.85	0.94
		Assessment scale		
A	.31	3.18	45.84	1.06
B	.28	2.60	93.05	1.13
C	.30	3.05	18.87	1.07
D	.29	2.68	11.06	1.11

Note: The First PC Index can range from 0 to 1. The remaining indexes have a lower boundary of 0, but no absolute upper boundary. Sample A combines Individual Samples 1 and 2, Sample B combines Individual Samples 3 and 5, Sample C is the same as Individual Sample 6, and Sample D combines Individual Samples 9 and 10.

all 12 assessment items produced item-total correlations greater than .28 (average item-total $r = .41$), and elimination of any one of them reduced the alpha. With the exception of the alphas for the Assessment Scale in the two military samples, those obtained for both locomotion and assessment across the many samples indicate levels of internal consistency that are considered good (Nunnaly, 1978).

Temporal stability. Information about the temporal stability of the 12-item Locomotion and Assessment Scales was available from three different undergraduate samples from the University of Maryland, College Park. In each sample, most participants were introductory psychology students who completed the Locomotion and Assessment Scales once in a mass testing session at the beginning of the semester and then again as part of a laboratory session approximately 4–8 weeks later. In the first such sample ($N = 100$), the cross-temporal correlations for the Locomotion and Assessment Scales were .76 and .77, respectively. In a second sample ($N = 72$), the correlations were .74 and .79, respectively. In a third sample ($N = 79$), the correlations were .81 and .57. All of the correlations were significant at $p < .001$. Weighted average correlations were computed across the three samples, using the r to z' transformation and the formula described by McNemar (1969). For locomotion, average $r = .77$; for assessment, average $r = .73$. Thus, participants' responses to both scales appear to be substantially consistent over time.

Study 3: Cross-cultural validation of the scales' structure

We translated the two scales into Italian (appropriately backtranslating them into English), and administered them to a sample of students at the University of

Rome, "La Sapienza." The scales this time were presented in the same 24-item questionnaire with the 12 locomotion items being followed by the 12 assessment items. Our Italian sample consisted of 419 undergraduates, 103 men and 316 women, who participated in the study on a voluntary basis. Their mean age was 21.21 years ($SD = 2.72$).

The mean locomotion score for this sample was 4.54, and the alpha reliability coefficient for the locomotion scale was .73. The mean assessment score was 3.59, and the alpha reliability coefficient for the assessment scale was also .73. The difference between the locomotion and assessment means in this sample was statistically significant, $F(1, 417) = 423.26$, $p < .000$, but there were no significant sex differences among our participants on either locomotion or assessment. Also, the correlation between locomotion and assessment in our sample (.04) was not significantly different from zero.

To analyze the structure of the Italian version of the locomotion and assessment scales, we looked at the degree to which our data could be fitted by one first-order factor model for each scale using LISREL 8 (Jöreskog & Sörbom, 1993). Our results indicated that the fit of the one-factor model for both the locomotion and assessment scales was adequate and highly similar to that obtained with the American samples. The relevant fit indexes for the locomotion and assessment models and the pertinent null models are summarized in Table 10.

Scale validation

Construct validity

Study 4: Known-groups analyses

A version of the known-groups technique was used to assess construct validity. We expected that military personnel, compared with college students, would place a

Table 10 Model fit for the Locomotion and Assessment scales in the Italian sample

Scale/model	n	χ^2	df	χ^2 per df	GFI	AGFI	CFI	RMR
Locomotion								
Null model	419	890.60	66	13.49	.65	.58	–	.20
One-factor model	419	183.48	54	3.40	.93	.89	.84	.07
Assessment								
Null model	419	774.22	66	11.73	.68	.62	–	.19
One-factor model	419	213.18	54	3.95	.92	.88	.78	.07
Locomotion, Assessment, and Big Five								
Null model	419	2,854.11	91	31.36	.48	.40	–	.27
Seven-factor model	419	200.32	56	3.58	.94	.88	.95	.04

Note: Dash indicates that data were not observed for this index. GFI = goodness-of-fit index; AGFI = adjusted goodness-of-fit index; CFI = comparative fit index; RMR = root-mean-square residual.

relatively greater psychological emphasis on action initiation and maintenance than on comparing alternatives and standards. Data from participants in the two military samples were combined into one group, and the data from the 11 college samples were combined into another (see Table 11). Participants' locomotion and assessment scores were then submitted to a mixed-model (Group × Scale) analysis of variance (ANOVA). A main effect for group, $F(1, 4254) = 11.85$, $p < .005$, indicated that collapsing across scale, college students tended to score slightly higher than did the military participants, Ms = 4.06 and 3.98, respectively. The main effect for scale was also reliable, $F(1, 4254) = 856.53$, $p < .001$. Overall, participants tended to score higher on locomotion ($M = 4.19$) than on assessment ($M = 3.91$). Most importantly, the predicted Group × Scale interaction was highly reliable, $F(1, 4254) = 474.92$, $p < .001$. As expected, participants from the military scored higher ($M = 4.50$) than college participants ($M = 4.14$) in locomotion, $t(4254) = 12.16$, $p < .001$. Conversely, military participants scored lower ($M = 3.46$) than college participants ($M = 3.98$) on assessment, $t(4254) = 17.09$, $p < .001$.

Table 11 Correlations of the Locomotion and Assessment scales with other individual difference measures

Scale	Correlation(s)	Weighted average	Sample
Locomotion			
Action–Decision	.35*** to .45***	.42	1, 2, 7
Fear of Invalidity	.26** to .06	−.10	1, 2, 7
Attentional Control	−.43 ***	–	1
Functional Impulsivity	.32***	–	1
Vitality	.46***	–	2
Need for Cognitive Closure	.14* to .26***	.22	1–6
Preference for Order	.22*** to .41***	.33	1–6
Preference for Predictability	−.09 to .13*	.02	1–6
Decisiveness	.28*** to .35***	.30	1–6
Discomfort with Ambiguity	.01 to .12*	.09	1–6
Closed-Mindedness	−.26*** to −.06	−.17	1–6
Self-Esteem (Rosenberg, 1965)	.28*** to .33***	.30	2, 4, 5, 6
Optimism	.38***	–	2
Interaction Anxiety (Leafy, 1983)	−.36***	–	1
Social Anxiety (Fenigstein, Scheier, & Buss, 1975)	−.28***	–	2
Depression (CES–D)	−.18***	–	6
Public Self-Consciousness	.04	–	2
Private Self-Consciousness	.17*	–	2
Need to Evaluate	.21***, .14**	.17	1, 3
Need for Social Comparison	−.04	–	2
Performance Goal Orientation	.24***	–	13
Mastery Goal Orientation	.50***	–	13
Fear of Failure	−.25 ***	–	2

Scale	Correlation(s)	Weighted average	Sample
Achievement Orientation	.45***	–	4
Type A	.56***	–	2
NEO Neuroticism	–.20***	–	6
NEO Extraversion	.38***	–	6
NEO Openness	.05	–	6
NEO Agreeableness	.11**	–	6
NEO Conscientiousness	.56***	–	6
16PF Emotional Stability	.09*	–	13
16PF Extraversion	.17***	–	13
16PF Openness	.04	–	13
16PF Agreeableness	–.03	–	13
16PF Conscientiousness	.25***	–	13
Intrinsic Motivational Orientation	.36***, .47***	.43	2, 4
Extrinsic Motivational Orientation	.36***, .25***	.29	2, 4
Relative Autonomy Index	.38***	–	4
Amotivated	–.24***	–	4
External	.01	–	4
Introjected	.17**	–	4
Identified	.22***	–	4
Intrinsic	.34***	–	4
Social Dominance Orientation	–.08 to –.06	–.07	2, 5, 6
In-group Favoritism	–.05 to .02	.01	3, 6
Conservatism (self-report)	.01 to .14**	.06	1, 2, 3, 6
Age	–.03 to .14*	.06	1–3, 5–7, 13
Gender	.05 to .14**	.09	1–7
Assessment			
Action–Decision	–.42*** to –.18***	–.26	1, 2, 7
Fear of Invalidity	.36*** to .56***	.43	1, 2, 7
Attentional Control	–.18**	–	1
Functional Impulsivity	–.17**	–	1
Vitality	–.17*	–	2
Need for Cognitive Closure	.08 to .20*	.12	1–6
Preference for Order	.07 to .20***	.10	1–6
Preference for Predictability	.11** to .22***	.15	1–6
Decisiveness	–.33*** to –.17	–.24	1–6
Discomfort with Ambiguity	.34*** to .49***	.39	1–6
Closed-Mindedness	–.14* to .03	–.08	1–6
Self-Esteem (Rosenberg, 1965)	–.32*** to –.22**	–.26	2, 4, 5, 6
Optimism	–.21**	–	2
Interaction Anxiety (Leary, 1983)	.25***	–	1
Social Anxiety (Fenigstein et al., 1975)	.30***	–	2
Depression (CES–D)	.28***	–	6
Public Self-Consciousness	.54***	–	2
Private Self-Consciousness	.50***	–	2

(continued)

Table 11 Correlations of the Locomotion and Assessment scales with other individual difference measures *(continued)*

Scale	Correlation(s)	Weighted average	Sample
Need to Evaluate	.19***, .39***	.28	1, 3
Need for Social Comparison	.39***	–	2
Performance Goal Orientation	.41***	–	13
Mastery Goal Orientation	.12*	–	13
Fear of Failure	.24***	–	2
Achievement Orientation	–.01	–	4
Type A	.25***	–	2
Hard Driving	.19**	–	2
Speed/Impatience	.41***	–	2
NEO Neuroticism	.41***	–	6
NEO Extraversion	–.03	–	6
NEO Openness	.16***	–	6
NEO Agreeableness	–.25***	–	6
NEO Conscientiousness	–.04	–	6
16PF Emotional Stability	–.32***	–	13
16PF Extraversion	–.08	–	13
16PF Openness	.16***	–	13
16PF Agreeableness	.08	–	13
16PF Conscientiousness	–.01	–	13
Intrinsic Motivational Orientation	–.07, .01	–.02	2, 4
Extrinsic Motivational Orientation	.40***, .33***	.36	2, 4
Relative Autonomy Index	.02	–	4
Amotivated	.04	–	4
External	.18*	–	4
Introjected	.13*	–	4
Identified	.11	–	4
Intrinsic	.11	–	4
Social Dominance Orientation	.04 to .12*	.08	2, 5, 6
In-group Favoritism	.03 to .16*	.09	3, 6
Conservatism (self-report)	–.11 to .03	–.04	1, 2, 3, 6
Age	–.10 to .01	–.06	1–3, 5–7, 13
Gender	.05 to .14**	.03	1–7

Note: Dash indicates that data were not observed for this index. CES–D = Center for Epidemiological Studies—Depression Scale; 16PF = 16 Personality Factor Questionnaire.
* $p < .05$. ** $p < .01$. *** $p < .001$.

We also examined expected differences as a function of undergraduates' college majors, anticipating that students pursuing such applied, action-oriented majors as business, physical therapy, physical education, kinesiology, and so on would tend to emphasize locomotion more (and assessment less) than students majoring in more analytic areas such as history, physics, and computer science. Locomotion and assessment scores of students from the former constellation of majors (Group 1; $N = 95$) were compared with those of students from the latter group (Group 2; $N = 80$) in a mixed-model (Major Group × Scale) ANOVA. A main effect of scale,

$F(1, 173) = 11.00$, $p < .01$, revealed that students in this sample scored higher on the locomotion index ($M = 4.45$) than on the assessment index ($M = 3.95$). The expected Major Group × Scale interaction also was reliable, $F(1, 173) = 17.41$, $p < .001$. Because the locomotion and assessment indexes were reliably correlated in this sample ($r = .23$, $p < .01$), the interaction was decomposed via two analyses of covariance (ANCOVAs). In each the effect of major group was computed on one index, controlling for the effect of the other index. Although students in Group 1 scored higher in locomotion (adjusted $M = 4.34$) than did students in Group 2 (adjusted $M = 3.96$), $F(1, 172) = 20.14$, $p < .001$, they also scored lower in assessment (adjusted $M = 3.83$) than did students in Group 2 (adjusted $M = 4.09$), $F(1, 172) = 5.57$, $p < .05$. Thus, students whose majors would be expected to emphasize action over analysis indeed scored higher in locomotion and lower in assessment than did students whose majors would be expected to emphasize analysis over action.

Study 5: Convergent-discriminant validity

Correlation between indexes

The correlation between the Locomotion and Assessment Indexes was computed in each of the samples and is displayed in Table 1. This correlation was consistently low and typically slightly positive across the samples, ranging from −.07 to .20. Overall, the correlation between the two indexes was quite small, but it was reliable in the large omnibus sample, $r(4256) = .11$, $p < .001$. The very small amount of overlapping variance (about 1%) is consistent with the proposition that the locomotion and assessment scales are measuring distinct psychological dimensions.

Correlations with socially desirable responding

The samples reported in this chapter were initially trimmed on the basis of participants' responses to a set of six "faking" items embedded among the locomotion and assessment items. These items (e.g., "I have never been late for work or for an appointment") were designed to tap self-promotional or socially desirable tendencies in participants' responding, and they were averaged to form an index. In the pretrimmed omnibus sample ($N = 4528$) a principal-components analysis conducted on the six items produced a single-factor solution ($\alpha = .58$). The average item-total correlation was .31, and elimination of any of the items reduced the alpha coefficient. Across the 13 individual samples, the correlation between locomotion and faking scores ranged from −.11 to .20, with an overall $r = .06$. The correlation between assessment and faking scores ranged from −.22 to .03, with an overall r = −.13. Thus, there was little evidence of a self-promotion bias in participants' responses to the locomotion and assessment items. Trimming the samples for participants scoring over the midpoint on the faking index typically eliminated about 6% of the respondents from each sample.

Correlations with other individual difference measures

We have administered the Locomotion and Assessment Scales to participants completing a variety of other individual difference measures. These have included the Action–Decision Scale (Kuhl, 1985), the Personal Fear of Invalidity Scale (M. M. Thompson, Naccarato, & Parker, 1989), the Attentional Control subscale of the Short Imaginal Processes Inventory (Huba, Aneshensel, & Singer, 1981), the Need for Cognitive Closure Scale (Webster & Kruglanski, 1994), the Life Orientation Test—Revised (Scheier, Carver, & Bridges, 1994), the Self-Consciousness Scale (Fenigstein, Scheier, & Buss, 1975), the Interaction Anxiety Scale (Leary, 1983), the Center for Epidemiological Studies—Depression (CES-D) Scale (Radloff, 1977), the Psychological Vitality Scale (Ryan & Frederick, 1997), the Functional Impulsivity Scale (Dickman, 1990), Rosenberg's (1965) Self-Esteem Scale, the Need to Evaluate Scale (Jarvis & Petty, 1996), the Jenkins Activity Survey (Jenkins, Zyzanski, & Roseman, 1979), the Interpersonal Orientation Scale (Hill, 1987), the Fear of Failure Scale (Herman, 1990), the Achievement Motivation subscale of Jackson's (1974) Personality Research Form, the NEO-Five Factor Inventory (Costa & McCrae, 1992), the Sixteen Personality Factor Questionnaire (Cattell, Cattell, & Cattell, 1993), and the Social Dominance Orientation Scale (Pratto, Sidanius, Stallworth, & Malle, 1994). The correlations between the locomotion and assessment indices and these measures are displayed in Table 11. As indicated there, not all measures were administered in each sample.

Eyeballing the correlations in Table 11, it is apparent that consistent with our definition of the two constructs, locomotion was most strongly associated with a commitment to prompt action (Action–Decision Scale; weighted average $r = .42$, $p < .001$); the ability to stay focused on a task (Attentional Control; $r = .43$, $p < .001$); psychological vitality or energy ($r = .46$, $p < .001$); and measures of achievement striving (or task orientation) such as Type A behavior pattern ($r = .56$, $p < .001$), personality research form (PRF) achievement orientation ($r = .45$, $p < .001$), as well as NEO conscientiousness ($r = .56$, $p < .001$). Consistent with our definition of the assessment construct, assessment scores were most strongly associated with fear of invalidity (weighted average $r = .43$, $p < .001$), discomfort with ambiguity (weighted average $r = .39$, $p < .001$), public and private self-consciousness ($r = .54$, $p < .001$ and $r = .50$, $p < .001$, respectively), need for social comparison ($r = .39$, $p < .001$), and neuroticism ($r = .41$, $p < .001$). Later we discuss more specifically the relations of locomotion and assessment with several psychologically meaningful groupings of variables.

Focus on standards of comparison and evaluation. As discussed earlier, we expected assessment to be more strongly related than locomotion to focus on the self and standards of social comparison. We had no particular reason to suspect that they would relate to such factors in opposite ways. Self-focus was measured with Fenigstein et al.'s (1975) scales of public and private self-consciousness. According to these authors, the former refers to a "general awareness of self as a social object," whereas the latter involves "attending to one's inner thoughts and feelings"

(p. 523). Comparison with standards was measured with the need for social comparison subscale of Hill's (1987) Interpersonal Orientation Scale. In all these cases, we expected assessment versus locomotion to exhibit a stronger relation to the phenomenon being measured.

Consistent with our predictions, assessment was strongly and positively associated with both public ($r = .54$, $p < .001$) and private self-consciousness ($r = .50$, $p < .001$) and with the measure of need for social comparison ($r = .39$, $p < .001$). Locomotion, on the other hand, was quite weakly associated with private self-consciousness ($r = .17$, $p < .05$) and was largely unrelated to public self-consciousness ($r = .04$, ns) and to social comparison motivation ($r = -.04$, ns). In all cases, assessment was more strongly positively associated with these variables than was locomotion, Zs = 7.75, 5.18, and 7.45, all ps < .001, for public and private self-consciousness and need for social comparison, respectively.

The achievement motivation literature distinguishes between *performance goals*, which involve proving one's competence at an activity, and *mastery goals*, which involve the development of proficiency at the activity (Dweck, 1991). Performance goals involve proving that one can meet some tangible standard for success and, especially, proving that one can do well compared with others. Given that assessment is concerned with self-evaluative comparison processes, we expected assessment to be positively related to performance orientation. Mastery goals involve continually learning and making progress. Given that locomotion is concerned with maintaining movement despite obstacles and setbacks, we expected it to be positively related to mastery orientation. Goal orientations were measured with the Goal Orientation Scale (GOS; Button, Mathieu, & Zajac, 1996). This 16-item scale includes items tapping both *performance orientation* (e.g., "I prefer to do things that I can do well rather than things that I do poorly") and *mastery orientation* (e.g., "The opportunity to do challenging work is important to me").

Although locomotion and assessment were both positively correlated with performance and mastery orientations from the GOS (Sample 13 only; see Table 11), locomotion, as predicted, was more strongly associated with mastery orientation ($r = .50$) than with performance orientation ($r = .24$; $Z = 6.71$, $p < .001$), and assessment, as predicted, was more strongly associated with performance orientation ($r = .41$) than with mastery orientation ($r = .12$; $Z = 6.95$, $p < .001$). In addition, performance orientation was more strongly associated with assessment than with locomotion ($Z = 4.21$, $p < .001$), and mastery orientation was more strongly associated with locomotion than with assessment ($Z = 9.44$, $p < .001$). Because mastery and performance orientations were positively correlated in this sample ($r = .30$, $p < .001$), multiple regression analysis was used to gauge the unique relations between these and the locomotion and assessment variables. Mastery orientation, but not performance orientation, was uniquely related to locomotion ($\beta = .47$, $p < .001$; and .05, $p = .21$). Performance orientation, but not mastery orientation, was uniquely related to assessment ($\beta = .40$, $p < .001$; and $-.08$, $p = .10$).

Finally, a propensity for evaluation was measured with Jarvis and Petty's (1996) Need to Evaluate Scale. Although the need to evaluate was positively and reliably associated with both assessment (weighted average $r = .28$, $p < .001$) and locomotion (weighted average $r = .17$, $p < .01$) in the two samples where all those variables were measured, the weighted average correlation was, as expected, reliably stronger for assessment, $Z = 3.23$, $p < .005$.[1]

Measures of positive and negative affect, self-esteem, and outlook. We expected assessment to predict more negative (less positive) affect and lower self-esteem and future outlook, because the comparison processes inherent to assessment would draw attention to discrepancies between actual and desired end-states and discrepancies between self versus others' more positive attributes, and past research has found that such discrepancies are related to a preponderance of negative affect, low self-esteem, and discouragement about the future (Duval & Wicklund, 1972; Higgins, Shah, & Friedman, 1997; Moretti & Higgins, 1990; Pyszczynski & Greenberg, 1987; Ruble, 1983). The locomotion tendency, on the other hand, might show a positive relation to measures of positive affect, self-esteem, and future outlook because positive affect, self-esteem, and optimism can be resources that support persistence at goal-directed activities and, hence, staying on track and advancing toward one's objectives (Aspinwall, 1998; Taylor & Brown, 1988; Trope & Neter, 1994).

An examination of the correlations reported in Table 11 shows that our predictions regarding affect, self-esteem, and outlook were largely supported. Assessment yielded reliably positive correlations with two measures of social anxiety ($rs = .30$ and $.25$, $ps < .001$; see Fenigstein et al., 1975; Leary, 1983) and a measure of depression (Radloff, 1977; $r = .28$, $p < .001$), and reliably negative correlations with self-esteem (weighted average $r = -.26$, $p < .001$) and optimism ($r = -.21$, $p < .01$). In contrast, locomotion yielded the opposite pattern of findings, including small but reliably negative correlations with measures of negative affectivity such as social anxiety ($r = -.28$, $p < .001$) and depression ($r = -.18$, $p < .001$), and significant positive correlations with self-esteem (weighted average $r = .30$, $p < .001$) and optimism ($r = .38$, $p < .001$).

Measures of decisiveness and commitment to action. According to our conceptualization, persons high (vs. low) on locomotion should be decisive and dynamic, whereas persons high (vs. low) on assessment should be preoccupied with the evaluative aspect of self-regulation, which may complicate and extend their decision-making process. We used several instruments to test these notions, specifically, the Decision-Related Action Versus State Orientation subscale of Kuhl's (1985) Action–Control Scale (i.e., the Action–Decision subscale), which measures commitment to prompt action; Thompson et al.'s (1989) Personal Fear of Invalidity Scale, which measures individual differences in indecisiveness associated with evaluation apprehension; Dickman's (1990) Functional Impulsivity Scale, which measures the tendency to spend less time on preactional decision processes than others of equal ability before taking action when to do so is functional; and the Decisiveness subscale of Webster and Kruglanski's (1994) Need for Cognitive Closure (NFCC) Scale, which measures the "decisiveness [of respondents'] judgments and choices" (p. 1050) (e.g., "I usually make important decisions quickly and confidently").

Examination of the correlations in Table 11 confirms our expectations for each of these measures. Specifically, assessment exhibited negative relations with Kuhl's Action–Decision subscale (weighted average $r = -.26$, $p < .001$), with Dickman's Functional Impulsivity Scale ($r = -.17$, $p < .01$), and with Webster and Kruglanski's (1994) Decisiveness scale (weighted average $r = -.24$, $p < .01$) and had a strong positive relation with Thompson et al.'s (1989) Personal Fear of Invalidity Scale (weighted average $r = .43$, $p < .001$). Locomotion, however, exhibited the opposite pattern of relations with these measures, namely, positive correlations with the Action–Decision subscale (weighted average $r = .42$, $p < .001$), with the functional impulsivity scale ($r = .32$, $p < .001$), and with the decisiveness subscale (weighted average $r = .30$, $p < .001$), and a negative, albeit nonsignificant, correlation with the Personal Fear of Invalidity Scale (weighted average $r = -.10$, ns).

Also included among the measures in the study was the Discomfort with Ambiguity subscale of Webster and Kruglanski's (1994) NFCC Scale. To find the right or best alternative, one does not want ambiguity. Assessment, then, should be positively related to discomfort with ambiguity. Given its concern with simply initiating action, locomotion should be less related to discomfort with ambiguity. Consistent with these predictions, assessment was strongly and positively associated with ambiguity discomfort (weighted average $r = .39$, $p < .001$), whereas locomotion was largely unrelated to ambiguity discomfort (weighted average $r = .09$, ns).

Measures of task orientation. We anticipated that locomotion would be positively associated with measures of vitality, task orientation, and a focus on doing. In contrast, the self-evaluative concerns and the negative affects (e.g., anxiety) associated with assessment could undermine vitality, disrupt task focus, and interfere with unswerving concentration on the activity (i.e., the flow). Thus, we expected that whereas locomotion would be strongly and positively associated with measures of vitality, task orientation, and achievement strivings, assessment would be less positively—and possibly even negatively—related to such measures.

Consistent with these expectations, examination of the correlations in Table 11 confirms this pattern for measures of vitality (Ryan & Frederick, 1997; $r = .46$, $p < .001$ for locomotion; $r = .17$, $p < .05$ for assessment), attentional control (Huba et al., 1981; e.g., "I tend to be quite wrapped up and interested in whatever I am doing," "No matter how hard I try to concentrate, thoughts unrelated to my work always creep in" [reverse-scored]; $r = .43$, $p < .001$ for locomotion, $r = -.18$; $p < .01$ for assessment), achievement orientation (Jackson, 1974; e.g., "I enjoy difficult work," "I seldom set standards which are difficult for me to reach" [reverse-scored]; $r = .45$, $p < .001$ for locomotion; $r = -.01$ for assessment), fear of failure (Herman, 1990; e.g., "When I start doing poorly on a task, I feel like giving up," "If given a choice, I have a tendency to select a relatively easy task rather than risk failure"; $r = -.25$, $p < .001$ for locomotion; $r = .24$, $p < .001$ for assessment), and conscientiousness (Costa & McCrae, 1992; e.g., "I'm pretty good about pacing myself so as to get things done on time," "I work hard to accomplish my goals"; $r = .56$, $p < .001$ for locomotion; $r = -.04$ for assessment).

It is notable that both locomotion and assessment were reliably and positively associated with Type A orientation ($r = .56$, $p < .001$ for locomotion; $r = .25$, $p < .001$ for assessment). As expected, locomotion was significantly more positively associated with Type A than was assessment ($Z = 5.20$, $p < .001$). It is interesting to consider why, although smaller than the relation of locomotion and Type A, the relation of assessment and Type A was nonetheless significant and positive. There is evidence that Type A individuals are particularly concerned with obtaining social comparison information (Dembroski & MacDougall, 1978) despite the availability of clear personal standards for evaluation (Matthews & Siegel, 1983). Indeed, one current conceptualization of the Type A personality pattern proposes that Type A behaviors are "strategic attempts to render the appraisal of one's abilities less ambiguous" (Strube, 1987). Thus, Type A may correlate especially with locomotion because it involves chronic initiation and maintenance of achievement behavior, but may correlate to some extent with assessment as well because it also involves an emphasis on social comparison processes.

Measures of Big Five personality factors. Relating the locomotion and assessment scales to measures of the Big Five personality traits allows the opportunity to place our constructs within the broader context of personality theory. For example, to the extent that locomotion involves a heightened activity level and greater persistence in goal-directed activity, we would expect it to correlate positively with extroversion and conscientiousness (Cattell et al., 1993; Costa & McCrae, 1992). In addition, to the extent that assessment involves heightened self-consciousness, difficulty in decision making, and inclination to compare alternatives, we might expect it to correlate positively with the neuroticism (or emotional [in]stability) and openness dimensions.

Indeed, an examination of the correlations in Table 11 reveals that across two different measures of the Big Five traits, extroversion and conscientiousness were most strongly positively associated with locomotion, whereas these measures were rather unrelated to assessment. Specifically, the NEO and 16PF measures of extroversion were weakly to moderately positively correlated with locomotion ($rs = .38$ and $.17$, respectively, both $ps < .001$), and they were essentially unrelated to assessment ($rs = -.03$ and $-.08$, respectively, both ns). Similarly, the NEO and 16PF measures of conscientiousness were moderately to strongly positively correlated with locomotion ($rs = .56$ and $.25$, respectively, both $ps < .001$), and they were uncorrelated with assessment ($rs = -.04$ and $-.01$, respectively, both ns).

By contrast, neuroticism and openness were most strongly positively associated with assessment and were rather unrelated to locomotion. Specifically, assessment was relatively strongly correlated with NEO neuroticism ($r = .41$, $p < .001$) and 16PF emotional stability ($r = -.32$, $p < .001$), whereas locomotion showed the opposite pattern of relations ($rs = -.20$ and $.09$, $ps < .001$ and $.05$, respectively). Furthermore, whereas assessment was positively related to the NEO and 16PF measures of openness (both $rs = .16$, both $ps < .001$), locomotion was essentially uncorrelated with either measure ($rs = .05$ and $.04$, respectively).[2] Further work on discriminability of our measures from the Big Five is reported later.

Intrinsic and autonomous self-regulation. Recent literature on task motivation has focused on the role of intrinsic and extrinsic motivation in self-regulation (Amabile & Hennessey, 1992; Amabile, Hill, Hennessy, & Tighe, 1994; Boggiano, 1998; Elliot & Harackiewicz, 1996; Harackiewicz, Manderlink, & Sansone, 1992; Sansone & Harackiewicz, 1996; Thompson, Chaiken, & Hazlewood, 1993). People engage in activities that are intrinsically motivated because of the inherent pleasure they derive from simply performing them. In contrast, activities that are extrinsically motivated are experienced as involving a means-ends function; that is, they are seen as instrumental to achieving specific end-states such as compliance with powerful others, behaving in accordance with introjected dictives, or meeting valued life goals (Ryan, 1995). Whereas intrinsic motivation has been described as the purest case of autonomous self-regulation (Deci & Ryan, 1991), forms of extrinsic motivation are said to vary in the extent to which they are experienced as truly self-determined.

We hypothesized that because the assessment tendency involves evaluating how one engages in an activity in relation to discernible alternatives, high assessors would be more likely to experience their engagement in activities as instrumental means to achieving specific goals. Thus, we expected it to be related to extrinsic motivation but not to intrinsic motivation. We expected locomotion to be related to intrinsic motivation because locomotors' tendency to stay in motion naturally promotes a deeper sense of involvement with activities (Csikszentmihalyi, 1975). We also expected locomotion to be related to the more autonomous forms of extrinsic motivation that relate to continually learning and making progress, as described earlier, such as doing boring math problems because this is seen as important for learning needed concepts (Deci & Ryan, 1991; Vallerand et al., 1992).

To measure intrinsic and extrinsic motivational orientation, we administered the Work Preference Inventory (WPI; Amabile, Hill, Hennessy, & Tighe, 1994). The obtained correlations of locomotion and assessment with the measures of intrinsic and extrinsic motivation, need for cognition, relative autonomy, and goal orientations in Samples 2 and 4 are displayed in Table 11. As expected, higher locomotion predicted both more intrinsic motivation (average $r = .43$, $p < .001$) and more extrinsic motivation ($r = .29$, $p < .001$), as measured by the WPI. In contrast, assessment predicted only extrinsic motivational orientation (average $r = .36$, $p < .001$), but was unrelated to intrinsic motivation ($r = -.02$, ns).

Table 11 also displays the zero-order correlations between locomotion and assessment and the five subscales of Vallerand et al.'s (1992) Academic Motivation Scale (AMS) (Sample 4 only). Consistent with the prediction that a stronger locomotion tendency would predict more autonomous self-regulation, locomotion scores showed a pattern of correlations suggesting a linear increase in positive covariation from the least autonomous form of self-regulation (amotivated) to the most autonomous form (intrinsic). Furthermore, locomotion was positively related to the weighted Relative Autonomy Index (RAI; $r = .38$, $p < .001$). In contrast, assessment was positively associated only with the two least autonomous forms of extrinsic self-regulation (for external and introjected: $rs = .18$ and .13, respectively, both $ps < .05$) and was unrelated to the RAI overall ($r = .02$, ns). Multiple regression analyses were conducted separately for locomotion and assessment, in which each was predicted from the five AMS scales simultaneously. The most autonomous form of intrinsic self-regulation was positively associated with locomotion ($\beta = .30$, $p < .001$), and the least autonomous form of extrinsic self-regulation (external) was positively related to assessment ($\beta = .17$, $p < .01$).

Discriminant validity. To demonstrate the discriminant validity of a measure, one must show that it is uncorrelated with instruments tapping conceptually unrelated constructs. Across a number of samples, we found that both locomotion and assessment were essentially uncorrelated with participants' self-reported political orientation (1 = *strongly liberal*, to 6 = *strongly conservative*) and with Pratto et al.'s (1994) 16-item measure of social dominance orientation, the tendency to support anti-egalitarianism, and group-based dominance in social relations. Both measures were also uncorrelated with a measure of ingroup favoritism (attitude toward one's own racial/ethnic group minus mean attitude toward other racial/ethnic groups; e.g., "Asians," "Blacks," "Hispanics," "Whites"; see Shah, Kruglanski, & Thompson, 1998). Both locomotion and assessment were also uncorrelated with age and sex. Finally, though we found many correlations and regression coefficients supportive of the convergent validity of our new scales, it is important to note that no other measure accounted for more than 32% of the variance in either locomotion or assessment. Thus, neither appeared to be measuring previously identified individual difference variables, at least none that we have examined thus far.

Study 6: Locomotion, Assessment, and the Big Five

As noted earlier, in view of the breadth of psychological domains covered by the Big Five personality factors (Catell et al., 1993; Costa & McCrae, 1992; Goldberg, 1992), it was important to compellingly establish the discriminability of the Locomotion and Assessment Scales from these generally inclusive constructs. We have already reported the moderate to positive associations between locomotion and the NEO measures of extroversion (.38) and conscientiousness (.56), as well as the positive to moderate associations between NEO measures of assessment and neuroticism (.41) as well as openness to experience (.16). Though these correlations imply that our measures are not redundant with the pertinent Big Five dimensions, it was deemed prudent to conduct a more systematic investigation of their distinctiveness from the Big Five.

To that end, we used the Italian sample described earlier (see Study 3). Recall that participants in this sample ($N = 419$) filled out the Italian version of the Locomotion and Assessment Scales. They also responded to the 100 unipolar markers of the Big Five developed by Goldberg (1992). This is a commonly used measure of the Big Five that is relatively quick and easy to administer and hence is more convenient to use than the NEO-Personality Inventory. As Goldberg has shown, the factor scores based on participants' responses to these scales provide quite unequivocal markers for each of the Big Five domains. Consequently, Goldberg's measure is generally considered a reasonable alternative to the NEO-PI and the Hogan personality inventories.

For purposes of the following analysis, our entire sample of participants was divided into two subsamples. One subsample (hereinafter Sample 1, $N = 216$) completed additionally the Italian versions (Pierro et al., 1995) of the Need for Closure Scale (Webster & Kruglanski, 1994), the Personal Fear of Invalidity Scale (M. M. Thompson et al., 1989), and of the Goal Orientation Scale (Button et al., 1996). The second subsample (hereinafter Sample 2, $N = 203$) completed the Italian versions of the Attentional Control subscale of the Short Imaginal Process Inventory (Huba et al., 1981), the Functional Impulsivity Scale (Dickman, 1990), the Need to Evaluate Scale (Jarvis & Petty, 1996), and the Action–Decision Scale (Kuhl, 1985).

To investigate the discriminant validity of the locomotion and assessment scales with respect to the Big Five factors, we tested a first-order confirmatory factor model with 7 correlated latent variables. This analysis was performed on the entire sample. To carry it out, we combined the items of each scale (Locomotion, Assessment, Extraversion, Agreeableness, Conscientiousness, Neuroticism, and Openness) using a split-half procedure, forming two indicators for each construct. The rationale for this procedure was as follows: Because the Locomotion, Assessment, and the Big Five Scales together consisted of 124 items (12 + 12 + 100), a model expressing the relations among them would require the estimation of more than 250 parameters.

However, models with numerous parameters to estimate (more than 20) rarely fit the data (Bentler & Chou, 1987). Bagozzi and Heatherton (1994, p. 43) noted further that it is not uncommon to find an unsatisfactory fit when measurement models have more than four or five items for each factor and when sample sizes are large. In such cases, poor fit may be due to high levels of random error found in typical items, as well as to the large number of parameters to be estimated. To address this problem, several authors (cf. Bagozzi & Heatherton, 1994; Brooke, Russell, & Price, 1988) proposed that subsets of items within factors be summed to create aggregate variables. Furthermore, a ratio of at least five participants per parameter has been recommended to derive reliable estimates (Bentler & Chou, 1987). Our procedure reduced the number of indicators (items) from 124 to 14 (7 scales × 2), hence appropriately reducing the number of parameters to be estimated and allowing a reasonable ratio of participants per parameter (around 13).

The results of our analysis indicated that the fit of the overall 7-factor model was adequate. The relevant fit indexes for this model and its null counterpart are displayed in Table 10. Although this result conforms to our expectation, the fit of the overall model is a necessary but insufficient condition for claiming convergent and discriminant validity. In addition, it is necessary to examine the magnitude of the parameter estimates, particularly the factor loadings (the lambda matrix) to assess convergent validity and the matrix of correlations between latent factors (the phi matrix) to assess discriminant validity. The former estimates should be significant and at least .40, whereas correlations between latent factors should be less than 1.00 (Bagozzi, 1993).

The standardized parameter estimates for the confirmatory factor analysis (CFA) are displayed in Table 12. As can be seen, all factor loadings are significant and above .71. As for the intercorrelations among latent factors (see Table 13), the

Table 12 Parameter estimates for confirmatory factor analysis of the Seven-Factor Model (Locomotion, Assessment, and the Big Five): Matrix (λx) of factor loading

Item and sample	Locomotion	Assessment	Extroversion	Agreeableness	Conscientiousness	Neuroticism	Openness
Locomotion A	.80						
Locomotion B	.71						
Assessment A		.72					
Assessment B		.83					
Extroversion A			.83				
Extroversion B			.99				
Agreeableness A				.78			
Agreeableness B				.93			
Conscientiousness A					.80		
Conscientiousness B					.90		
Neuroticism A						.90	
Neuroticism B						.90	
Openness A							.71
Openness B							.97

Note. Sample A combines Individual Samples 1 and 2, and Sample B combines Individual Samples 3 and 5.

Table 13 Parameter estimates for confirmatory factor analysis of the Seven-factor Model (Locomotion, Assessment, and the Big Five): Intercorrelation matrix (Φ) of latent variables

	Item	α	1	2	3	4	5	6	7
1.	Locomotion	.73	—						
2.	Assessment	.73	.04 (.03)	—					
3.	Extroversion	.88	.50 (.44)	−.13 (−.10)	—				
4.	Agreeableness	.81	.39 (.32)	−.25 (−.20)	.33 (.36)	—			
5.	Conscientiousness	.91	.48 (.38)	−.05 (−.03)	.03 (.04)	.32 (.24)	—		
6.	Neuroticism	.86	−.27 (−.21)	.44 (.36)	−.23 (−.20)	−.39 (−.31)	−.48 (−.40)	—	
7.	Openness	.82	.32 (.28)	.36 (.28)	.36 (.28)	.12 (.15)	−.03 (−.03)	.05 (.02)	—

highest disattenuated correlations between the locomotion factor and the Big Five are with the extroversion (.50) and the conscientiousness (.48) factors, whereas the highest disattenuated correlation between the assessment factor and the Big Five is that with neuroticism (.44). Note that these correlations are very close in magnitude to those obtained with the American samples (see Table 11). Also note that although moderately high, these correlations are substantially less than 1.00 and therefore attain the criterion of discriminant validity. In this connection, note that the disattenuated correlations are generally higher than the raw coefficients (see Table 14) and that the test of discriminant validity via the CFA approach is a relatively stringent one.

Perhaps the most compelling evidence for the discriminant validity of the Locomotion and Assessment Scales with respect to the Big Five would be a demonstration that the relations of these scales with other theoretically relevant constructs remain unchanged while controlling for the Big Five factors. The results of these analyses are summarized in Tables 14 and 15. Note that the pattern of correlations between locomotion, assessment, and the several scales included with the Italian sample is remarkably similar to the correspondent correlation pattern obtained with our American samples (see Table 11). These data attest further that our scales and the theory they operationalize are generalizable across cultures (see Study 3). More to the present point, the correlations of locomotion with other pertinent individual difference measures, controlling for the Big Five and assessment, remain significant (compared with the zero-order correlations) and in the predicted direction, as do the correlations between assessment and pertinent

Table 14 Correlations of the Locomotion scale with other individual difference measures: Zero-order correlations and partial correlations controlling for the Big Five and the Assessment scale

				Locomotion	
Scale	Sample	N	α	r	Partial r
Need for Cognitive Closure	A	216	.86	.17***	.14
Decisiveness	A	216	.79	.29**	.15**
Preference for Order	A	216	.80	.16*	.09
Closed-Mindedness	A	216	.58	−.12	−.06
Preference for Predictability	A	216	.83	−.05	−.01
Discomfort with Ambiguity	A	216	.65	.16*	.21**
Fear of Invalidity	A	216	.73	−.31**	−.17**
Performance Goal Orientation	A	216	.83	.07	.06
Mastery Goal Orientation	A	216	.84	.47**	.31**
Attentional Control	B	203	.80	.35**	.15*
Need to Evaluate	B	203	.69	.36**	.18**
Functional Impulsivity	B	203	.73	.35**	.19**
Action–Decision	B	203	.66	.41**	.20**

Note: Sample A combines Individual Samples 1 and 2, and Sample B combines Individual Samples 3 and 5.
* p < .05. ** p < .01.

Table 15 Correlations of the Assessment scale with other individual difference measures: Zero-order correlations and partial correlations controlling for the Big Five and the Locomotion scale

Scale	Sample	N	α	Locomotion r	Partial r
Need for Cognitive Closure	A	216	.86	.05	.09
Decisiveness	A	216	.79	−.26**	−.19**
Preference for Order	A	216	.80	.09	.16
Closed-Mindedness	A	216	.58	−.06	−.13
Preference for Predictability	A	216	.83	.08	.11
Discomfort with Ambiguity	A	216	.65	.31**	.30**
Fear of Invalidity	A	216	.73	.40**	.35*
Performance Goal Orientation	A	216	.83	.33**	.32**
Mastery Goal Orientation	A	216	.84	.06	.08
Attentional Control	B	203	.80	−.25**	−.20**
Need to Evaluate	B	203	.69	.22**	.16*
Functional Impulsivity	B	203	.73	−.09	−.04
Action–Decision	B	203	.66	−.16*	−.10

Note: Sample A combines Individual Samples 1 and 2, and Sample B combines Individual Samples 3 and 5.
* $p < .05$. ** $p < .01$.

individual difference measures again controlling for the Big Five and locomotion. In summary, then, the results of our various analyses support the discriminability of the locomotion and assessment constructs from the Big Five.

Criterion-related validity

Study 7: Predicting students' academic achievement

We predicted that the locomotion and assessment scores would predict undergraduates' grade point averages (GPAs) and specifically that students scoring high on both dimensions would do better than those scoring high on only one or on neither dimension. Keeping blind to individual students' identities, we obtained from university records the GPAs for a sample of 655 University of Maryland, College Park undergraduates (359 women) who had completed the Locomotion and Assessment Scales. The sample was limited to sophomores, juniors, and seniors—that is, students who had, by the end of the Fall 1997 semester, completed either 3, 5, or 7 semesters of course work. Participants had completed the Locomotion and Assessment Scales either in the Spring 1996 semester (23%) or in the Fall 1996 or Spring 1997 semesters (50% and 27%, respectively).

We conducted a multiple regression analysis to predict participants' cumulative GPA scores ($M = 2.86$) from their locomotion scores, their assessment scores, and the Locomotion × Assessment interaction. From this analysis, which controlled for sex and Scholastic Aptitude Test (SAT) score, emerged significant main effects for sex ($\beta = .21$, $p < .001$), SAT score ($\beta = .42$, $p < .001$), and locomotion ($\beta = .12$, $p < .001$). Although the main effect of assessment did not achieve significance ($\beta = .06$, $p = .11$), a reliable Locomotion × Assessment interaction ($\beta = .07$, $p < .05$) revealed that the locomotion effect on GPA increased as a positive function of assessment. Indeed, for participants scoring below the median on assessment ($mdn = 4.05$), locomotion was unrelated to cumulative GPA ($\beta = .04$, ns). However, for high assessors (scoring >4.05), locomotion score was a reliable predictor of GPA, $\beta = .23$, $p < .001$. These results imply that, as predicted, optimal self-regulation occurs when both locomotion and assessment tendencies are relatively pronounced.

Study 8: Predicting successful completion of elite military training

The Locomotion and Assessment Scales were administered, along with a battery of other prescreening measures, to 490 applicants to an elite combat training unit in the U.S. Army, prior to onset of the training period. Applicants were all men ranging in age from 19 to 41, M = 26.06 years, all of whom were already in military service. Most were Caucasian (about 81%), and about 12% were commissioned officers. About 16% of the applicants had already completed a course of advanced training in the Army Rangers.

The program is highly selective and the training is extremely demanding. In fact, approximately 60% of the applicants in the current sample either withdrew voluntarily prior to the completion of training or else were removed for reasons of medical incapacity or unsatisfactory performance. In the current study, we attempted to predict successful completion of the training course from the locomotion and assessment scores and their interaction. We also controlled for several other predictor variables recommended by U.S. Army researchers who administered the precourse testing battery. These included applicants' scores from a general technical survey and from a spatial abilities test, whether applicants were commissioned officers or enlisted soldiers (0 = *enlisted*, 1 = *commissioned*), and whether applicants were "Ranger-qualified" (0 = *not qualified*, 1 = *qualified*). Because the primary dependent variable in question was dichotomous (0 = *did not complete the program*, 1 = *completed the program*), we used a logistic regression analysis, from which three significant effects emerged.

As expected, Ranger-qualified soldiers were more likely to complete the program than were nonqualified soldiers, $B = 1.36$, $Wald (1) = 16.91$, $p < .001$. In addition, higher locomotion scores predicted a higher likelihood of success, $B = 0.33$, $Wald (1) = 6.41$, $p < .02$. Finally, a reliable Locomotion × Assessment interaction, $B = 0.22$, $Wald (1) = 4.09$, $p < .05$, suggested that the impact of locomotion depended on level of the assessment tendency. Indeed, among soldiers scoring below the median in assessment ($mdn = 3.43$) locomotion had a negligible impact on program completion, $B = 0.06$, $Wald (1) = 0.14$, $p = .71$. However, among soldiers scoring above median assessment, locomotion score was a substantial predictor of success, $B = 0.58$, $Wald (1) = 8.06$, $p < .005$.

These results parallel precisely those found for college students' academic achievement. Although a tendency to locomote appears to be an important determinant of success at difficult endeavors requiring persistence and tenacity, it predicts success only when the individual's tendency to assess is relatively high as well. This interaction is quite notable. One might not find it surprising that individuals who describe themselves on a questionnaire as being a persistent, high energy go-getter and doer (high locomotors) are likely to be high performers. But the interaction shows that describing oneself in this way, by itself, does not in fact predict high success. Only high locomotors who are also high assessors are high performers.

Predictive validity

Study 9: Error spotting and completion time

According to our theory, assessors and locomotors should orient to different aspects of a task. High (vs. low) assessors may focus on the quality control aspect of task performance and may be highly critical and evaluative in their orientation. This critical stance might not only sensitize them to actual imperfections that an object or product may contain, but also lead to an exaggerated perception of errors and to "spotting" mistakes where none existed: Having discrepancies on one's mind, that is, positive (vs. null) outcomes of comparisons, may bias assessors to identify ambiguous stimuli as discrepancies. On the other hand, the assessment dimension should bear no direct relation to task-completion rate. There is little reason to suppose that high assessors should perform the task appreciably more rapidly or slowly than low assessors.

High (vs. low) locomotors, by contrast, should go swiftly through tasks, driven by their quest for palpable advancement. On the other hand, the locomotion tendency as such is not particularly relevant to error spotting. Thus, one's locomotion status shouldn't appreciably affect one's tendency to exercise tight quality control or to be vigilant with respect to imperfections. To test our hypotheses from the foregoing discussion, we used a proofreading task to see whether (a) the assessment, but not the locomotion, dimension would relate positively to finding errors, and (b) the locomotion, but not the assessment, dimension would relate positively to completion rate.

METHOD

Participants. Participants were 101 undergraduates at the University of Maryland, College Park; 55 men and 46 women who participated either in partial fulfillment of a course requirement or for a $7.00 payment.

Design and procedure. Participants were run in groups of one to eight. They were seated at individual desks, separated by tall partitions prohibiting communication and social comparisons. The experiment was described as a study about the ease of reading and the detection of spelling errors as a function of using different fonts. Participants were given a red pen and two five-page booklets with identical passages printed in different fonts. They were then asked to check one of the booklets, labeled Sample Copy, against the other, labeled Master Copy. Each booklet contained three passages on different topics, all extracted from introductory psychology texts. These topics were (a) TV violence, (b) linguistic ability of children raised by wild animals, and (c) the two halves of the brain. Participants were told to circle on the Sample Copy any differences found between it and the Master Copy. Such differences included the appearance of different words, numbers, or dates; different punctuation marks; and outright grammatical or spelling errors in one of the copies but not the other. There were a total of 63 differences between the two passages.

All participants were allowed as much time as needed to complete their booklet. The time to completion was measured surreptitiously by the experimenter. Following the proofreading task, participants responded to an eight-item filler questionnaire about such things as the clarity of fonts used in the passages, the difficulty and interest level of the task, and the participant's confidence in their performance. The filler activity continued with Zuckerman's (1971) Sensation-Seeking Scale, following which participants completed our Locomotion and Assessment Scales. At that point participants were debriefed and thanked for their participation.

RESULTS

Two participants had extreme scores on a Lie Scale, more than three standard deviations above the mean of 12.67 (26 and 31 within a possible scale range of 0 to 36). These participants' data were dropped, resulting in $N = 99$ (45 women) for subsequent analyses. Sex of participants did not exert significant effects on any of our dependent variables and is not discussed further.

Error spotting. Assessment scores were regressed onto the total number of errors circled, controlling for the locomotion scores. As expected, assessment scores significantly predicted the total number of errors circled, $F(1, 95) = 3.88, p < .05$. The errors total included both correct identifications and false hits. The latter constituted a very small percentage (.89%) of the total errors circled. When we excluded false hits from the errors measure, assessment scores still marginally predicted this variable, $F(1, 95) = 2.81, p < .10$. Furthermore, despite the very small number of false hits, this measure too was marginally predicted by the assessment scores, $F(1, 95) = 2.88, p < .10$. This evidence is consistent with our hypothesis that the assessment tendency is related to zealousness in finding errors. The locomotion scores did not significantly predict the number of errors spotted $(F < 1)$.

Completion time. To test our predictions about completion time, the locomotion scores were regressed on the time variable (its inverse transformation), controlling for assessment scores and instruction type. As hypothesized, the locomotion scores predicted the completion time, $F(1, 95) = 4.77, p < .04$. There was no significant relation between assessment scores and completion time $(F < 1)$.

Study 10: Selecting goals and generating means

GOAL CHOICE

As high (vs. low) locomotors are particularly concerned with progress, they may select their goals primarily on the basis of attainability information (Kruglanski, 1996). It follows, that high (vs. low) locomotors should adopt goals with high attainment expectancy. On the other hand, high (vs. low) locomotors should not differ much in the degree to which they select goals of considerable (vs. less pronounced) value, because locomotion is theoretically unrelated to comparing alternatives on merit or worth.

The very opposite can be expected of high (vs. low) assessors. High (more so than low) assessors should select goals of high perceived value or importance because concern with relative worthiness and excellence are quintessential features of the assessment dimension. We did not expect a significant relation between assessment and perceived goal attainability because ease of advancement seems unrelated to the evaluative essence of the assessment dimension.

MEANS GENERATION

High (vs. low) assessors may generate a greater number of means in order to have a suitable selection that affords evaluative comparison. On the other hand, high (vs. low) assessors should not predictably differ in how quickly they select the best means to attain their goals, because assessment is not directly related to the perceived urgency of commencing an activity. The opposite should hold for high (vs. low) locomotors, who should not particularly differ in the number of means they generate, because the issue of comparative evaluation is not directly relevant to locomotion. However, they should be quicker to select their best means in the interest of immediate activity engagement.

METHOD

In partial fulfillment of a course requirement, 63 University of Maryland, College Park, students, 22 men and 41 women, participated in the study. All participants were enrolled in an introductory psychology course, and each received one credit toward their experimental course requirement. Participants were run in groups of four or less.

Participants entered into a computer five personal attributes they wanted to attain. They listed attributes such as being or becoming "educated," "strong," 'fit," "knowledgeable," or "outgoing." After listing all five attributes, participants were asked to enter into a computer all the different means they might use to attain each attribute. Participants also rated the likelihood they would attain each attribute, as well as its perceived value. Both types of ratings were made on 7-point scales ranging from 1 (*not at all likely/valuable*) to 7 (*extremely likely/valuable*).

Participants then typed in as quickly as possible responses to a number of control questions, such as their first name and the last five digits of their social security number. They then typed in as quickly as possible the best means for attaining each of the attributes. The order of attributes was randomly generated by the computer for each participant. Following the entire procedure, participants filled out the Locomotion and Assessment Scales. This completed the experiment. Participants were debriefed and thanked for their participation. The following outcome variables were used in subsequent analyses.

Total attainment expectancy. Total attainment expectancy was calculated by summing up the expectancy ratings for each of the attributes. This measure indexed the degree to which one pursues goals whose attainment expectancy is high.

Total attainment value. Total attainment value was calculated by summing up the value ratings for each of the attributes listed. This total indexed the degree to which one pursues goals whose attainment is valued highly.

Total number of means. The number of means listed for each attribute was summed across the five attributes for a total number of means.

Speed of choosing the best means. Times taken to type in the best means for each of the attributes were submitted to a natural log transformation to lessen the impact of outliers. They were then summed across the five attributes to indicate the speed with which participants listed their best means.

Control speed. Times taken to type in the control questions were also submitted to a natural log transformation and totaled to control for general individual differences in response speed.

RESULTS

We carried out separate regression analyses to examine how differences in locomotion and assessment scores related to participants' tendencies to pursue valuable goals, attainable goals, or both. In conducting the analyses, attainment value was tested controlling for attainment expectancy and vice versa because the motivational literature postulates that the variables of value and expectancy are related to one another (see, for example, Atkinson, 1964), which means that a test of our two independent hypotheses requires controlling for one variable when testing the hypothesis about the other variable. A regression on participants' total attainment value, controlling for total attainment expectancy, found, as expected, that participants' assessment scores were positively related to value, $F(1, 55) = 8.85, p < .005$, whereas their locomotion scores were not, $F(1, 55) = 1.18, p > .25$. A regression on participants' total attainment expectancy, controlling for their total attainment value, found, as expected, that their locomotion scores were positively related to such expectancy, $F(1, 56) = 12.66, p < .001$. Also as expected, participants' assessment scores were not positively related to attainment expectancy, but were in fact negatively related, $F(1, 56) = 6.71, p < .01$. It is not clear why this negative relation was obtained rather than simply no relation. It could be that high assessors experience the process of goal attainment as difficult, as suggested by its extrinsic, demanding nature discussed earlier.

As expected, participants' assessment score was significantly and positively correlated with the number of means listed by participants, $F(1, 56) = 5.71$, $p < .05$, but their locomotion score was not, $F < 1$. As expected, participants' locomotion score was positively correlated with choice speed, $F(1, 54) = 4.10$, $p < .05$, but participants' assessment score was not, $F < 1$. A final analysis revealed that total means number and choice speed were not significantly correlated, $F < 1$.

General discussion

Beyond simple habits, most activities involve the copresence of two fundamental components, an evaluation that a particular activity is warranted and the commitment of energies to its initiation and maintenance. We refer to these functional ingredients as assessment and locomotion, respectively. One might think that the relative emphasis on assessment and locomotion should work in harmonious concert, jointly covarying with the perceived importance of a given self-regulatory activity. By contrast, we have theorized that, irrespective of specific tasks, individuals may differ on their assessment and locomotion tendencies independently of each other.

The research in this article reports our work with two scales designed to measure independently the assessment and locomotion functions. Our investigations encompassed a broad variety of samples (college students at various universities and with different majors, U.S. Army recruits and elite units) totaling over 5,000 participants. We also used heterogeneous methodologies to triangulate on the theoretically predicted properties of our scales. We used psychometric methods to determine their structural properties and we used the known-groups technique; convergent, discriminant and predictive validation methods; as well as additional correlational and experimental means to investigate a broad range of propositions implied by our theory.

On the basis of this research, it seems justifiable to conclude that (a) our theoretical notions about assessment and locomotion were strongly supported, and (b) our two scales constitute adequate measures of the assessment and locomotion tendencies. Specifically, we found that our Assessment and Locomotion Scales are unidimensional and possess satisfactory degrees of internal consistency and temporal stability. These properties were demonstrated across numerous replications, including a cross-cultural replication with an Italian sample. Our Locomotion and Assessment Scales satisfactorily distinguished between groups that on a priori grounds may be expected to emphasize one tendency more so than another. We also found support for the notion that successful outcomes on complex and difficult tasks depend on the joint presence of assessment and locomotion.

Our Locomotion and Assessment Scales related in a theoretically predicted way to several individual difference constructs and demonstrated discriminant validity in regard to other constructs including the Big Five personality factors. We also found that (a) the assessment tendency is related to zealousness in determining the right thing to do, whereas locomotion relates to the inclination to move quickly through one's tasks; (b) in the choice of goals, assessment relates positively to an emphasis on value, whereas locomotion relates positively to an emphasis on expectancy and attainment progress; and (c) in the generation of means aimed at goal attainment, the assessment tendency is positively related to the number of alternative means produced, whereas the locomotion tendency is related to quickly selecting a means for immediate engagement.

Antecedents and consequences

Antecedents

Whereas our findings thus far support the existence of two relatively independent functional dimensions of self-regulatory activities, important questions remain for further inquiry, principally, "What are the antecedents of an overemphasis on locomotion, assessment, or both?" and "What are its possible consequences?" For instance, it is of interest to ask what kinds of socialization patterns contribute to the development of locomotion and assessment inclinations and whether these are instigated by situational conditions as well. The notion that assessment activities are often prompted by failure experiences, for example, are suggested by findings of spontaneous attributional activity following failure (Weiner, 1985) or control deprivation experiences (Pittman & D'Agostino, 1985), as well as findings of enhanced counterfactual thinking following failure experiences (Nasco & Marsh, 1999; Roese & Olson, 1997). It seems plausible to assume that success experiences, to the contrary, may encourage locomotion.

Consequences

Potential consequences of locomotion and assessment are also worth exploring. For instance, responses to goal attainment may also differ as a function of the locomotion and assessment tendencies. It is likely that locomotors (i.e., persons emphasizing locomotion relative to assessment) may feel uncomfortable when a major goal has just been attained because this situation brings movement to a halt. Such people are likely to select a new goal to pursue as quickly as possible, much to the surprise of others who expected them to relax or take a break after having worked so hard for so long. Because locomotors are motivated to be in motion, rather than simply to attain their goals per se, such people may enjoy the fruits of their labor much less than would be expected from just their inherent value.

Social implications

Individuals' assessment and locomotion tendencies may have important social consequences. When locomotion (vs. assessment) predominates, for example, people may prefer hierarchical decision-making systems where the amount of collective debate, discussion, and examination of alternatives is minimal, and the amount of action is maximal. By contrast, when assessment prevails, people may prefer participatory decision-making systems endowed with the opposite features. Similarly, a locomotion emphasis should yield a preference for authoritarian leadership whereas an assessment emphasis should yield preference for democratic leadership. In regard to modes of power (see French & Raven, 1959; Raven & Kruglanski, 1970), a locomotion emphasis might yield a preference for authority figures or legitimate power whereas an assessment emphasis might yield a preference for informational power or expertise.

It is of interest to consider the potential effects of locomotion and assessment orientation in the context of close relationships. Specifically, a couple whose regulatory modes diverge in that one partner is a high locomotor (and moderate to low assessor) and the other a high "assessor" (and moderate to low locomotor) may experience a great deal of conflict at the local level. Yet, from a more general perspective, the partners may do well in attaining their joint goals because of the complementary nature of their regulatory propensities. Such "mixed" couples may represent an intriguing exception to Berscheid's (1983) generalization that successful couples experience little affect in their relationship because of the facilitating nature of their interaction. To the contrary, mixed locomotor-assessor couples may experience a great deal of (local) conflict capable of engendering intense affect, while at the same time their clashing, yet complementary, orientations contribute to their successful coping with the obstacles and challenges they face together. This brings us full circle to the conflicted spouses in our opening example. If our analysis is correct, despite the tension-inducing incident on the parking lot, their overall partnership might be highly successful as well as stimulating. As the great oceans illustrate, it is not only still waters that run deep.

Notes

1   One explanation for the high correlation between locomotion and the need to evaluate may be that appraisals of objects in the environment also serve as a basis for action by organizing one's responses in terms of objects and entities to approach versus objects and entities to avoid (see Eagly & Chaiken, 1998; Maio & Olson, 1999, for reviews of such basic functions). Jarvis and Petty (1996) originally identified two (highly correlated) factors in their instrument—one set of items measuring a need to evaluate, and another set of (mostly reverse-scored) items measuring a preference for neutrality. For exploratory purposes, we calculated separate indexes corresponding to both factors and used them as simultaneous predictors of locomotion and assessment in separate multiple regression analyses. The data set involved responses from both independent samples where the Need to Evaluate (NEV) Scale was administered (combined $N = 777$), and each analysis also controlled for the other self-regulation variable (locomotion or assessment). The results indicated that although both NEV indexes had small but reliable unique relations with locomotion (βs = .13 and .09, ps < .05, for the need to evaluate and preference for neutrality indices, respectively), only the need to evaluate index was uniquely and reliably associated with assessment ($\beta = .37$, $p < .001$; preference for neutrality index, $\beta = -.05$, ns). Thus, assessment was particularly strongly associated with those NEV items that most directly expressed a need for strong opinions and extreme evaluations.

2   There was a relatively high negative correlation between assessment and agreeableness as measured by Costa and McCrae's (1992) instrument, but this effect was not replicated with the Cattell et al. (1993) measure. If future studies obtain more consistent evidence of this relation, it might reflect a tendency for critical evaluation among individuals strong in assessment. Consistent with such an interpretation, Costa and McCrae (1992, p. 15) described low agreeableness as involving "skeptical and critical thinking."

References

Amabile, T. M., & Hennessey, B. A. (1992). The motivation for creativity in children. In A. K. Boggiano & T. S. Pittman (Eds.), *Achievement and motivation: A social-developmental perspective* (pp. 54–74). New York: Cambridge University Press.

Amabile, T. M., Hill, K. G., Hennessy, B. A., & Tighe, E. M. (1994). The Work Preference Inventory: Assessing intrinsic and extrinsic motivational orientations. *Journal of Personality and Social Psychology, 66*, 950–967.

Aspinwall, L. G. (1998). Rethinking the role of positive affect in self-regulation. *Motivation and Emotion, 22*, 1–32.

Atash, M. N. (1994). Assessing the dimensionality of the IEA reading literacy data. In M. Binkley, K. Rust, & M. Wingle (Eds.), *Methodological issues in comparative educational studies: The case of the IEA reading literacy study* (pp. 75–103). Washington, DC: National Center for Educational Statistics.

Atkinson, J. W. (1964). *An introduction to motivation*. Princeton, NJ: Van Nostrand.

Bagozzi, R. B. (1993). Assessing construct validity in personality research: Application to measures of self-esteem. *Journal of Research in Personality, 27*, 49–87.

Bagozzi, R. B., & Heatherton, T. F. (1994). A general approach to representing multifaceted personality constructs: Application to state self-esteem. *Structural Equation Modeling, 1*, 35–67.

Bentler, P. M., & Chou, C. P. (1987). Practical issues in structural modeling. *Sociological Methods & Research, 16*, 78–117.

Berscheid, E. (1983). Emotion. In H. H. Kelley, E. Berscheid, A. Christensen, J. Harvey, T. Huston, G. Levinger, E. McClintock, L. A. Peplau, & D. Peterson (Eds.), *Close relationships* (pp. 110–168). San Francisco: Freeman.

Boggiano, A. K. (1998). Maladaptive achievement patterns: A test of a diathesis-stress analysis of helplessness. *Journal of Personality and Social Psychology, 74*, 1681–1695.

Bollen, K. A. (1989). A new incremental fit index for general structural equation models. *Sociological Methods and Research, 17*, 303–316.

Brooke, P. P., Russell, D. W., & Price, J. L. (1988). Discriminant validation of measures of job satisfaction, job involvement, and organizational commitment. *Journal of Applied Psychology, 73*, 139–145.

Button, S. B., Mathieu, J. E., & Zajac, D. M. (1996). Goal orientation in organizational research: A conceptual and empirical foundation. *Organizational Behavior and Human Decision Processes, 67*, 26–48.

Carver, C. S., & Scheier, M. F. (1990). Origins and functions of positive and negative affect: A control process view. *Psychological Review, 97*, 19–35.

Cattell, R. B., Cattell, A. K., & Cattell, H. E. (1993). *Sixteen Personality Factor Questionnaire* (5th ed.). Champaign, IL: Institute for Personality and Ability Testing.

Costa, P. T., Jr., & McCrae, R. R. (1992). *Revised NEO Personality Inventory (NEO-PI-R) and NEO Five Factor Inventory (NEO-FFI) professional manual*. Odessa, FL: Psychological Assessment Resources.

Csikszentmihalyi, M. (1975). *Beyond boredom and anxiety*. San Francisco: Jossey-Bass.

Deci, E. L., & Ryan, R. M. (1991). A motivational approach to self: Integration in personality. In R. Dienstbier (Ed.), *Nebraska symposium on motivation* (Vol. 38, pp. 237–288). Lincoln, NE: University of Nebraska Press.

Dembroski, T. M., & MacDougall, J. M. (1978), Stress effects on affiliation preferences among subjects possessing the Type A coronary-prone behavior pattern. *Journal of Personality and Social Psychology, 36*, 23–33.

Dickman, S. J. (1990). Functional and dysfunctional impulsivity: Personality and cognitive correlates. *Journal of Personality and Social Psychology, 58*, 95–102.

Divgi, D. R. (1980, July). *Dimensionality of binary items: Use of mixed model*. Paper presented at the annual meeting of the National Council on Measurement in Education, Boston.

Duval, S., & Wicklund, R. A. (1972). *A theory of objective self-awareness*. New York: Academic Press.

Dweck, C. S. (1991). Self-theories and goals: Their role in motivation, personality and development. In R. Dienstbier (Ed.), *Nebraska symposium on motivation* (Vol. 38, pp. 199–235). Lincoln, NE: University of Nebraska Press.

Eagly, A. H., & Chaiken, S. (1998). Attitude structure and function. In D. Gilbert, S. Fiske, & G. Lindzey (Eds.), *Handbook of social psychology* (4th ed., Vol. 1, pp. 269–322). New York: McGraw-Hill.

Elliot, A. J., & Harackiewicz, J. M. (1996). Approach and avoidance achievement goals and intrinsic motivation: A mediational analysis. *Journal of Personality and Social Psychology, 70*, 461–475.

Fenigstein, A., Scheier, M. F., & Buss, A. H. (1975). Public and private *self-consciousness: Assessment and theory*. *Journal of Consulting and Clinical Psychology, 43*, 522–527.

French, J. R. P., Jr., & Raven, B. H. (1959). The bases of social power. In D. Cartwright (Ed.), *Studies in social power* (pp. 150–167). Ann Arbor, MI: University of Michigan Press.

Green, S. B., Lissitz, R. W., & Muliak, S. A. (1977). Limitations of coefficient alpha as an index of test unidimensionality. *Educational and Psychological Measurement, 37*, 827–838.

Goldberg, L. R. (1992). The development of markers for the Big Five factor structure. *Psychological Assessment, 4*, 26–42.

Gollwitzer, P. M. (1990). Action phases and mind-sets. In E. T. Higgins & R. M. Sorrentino (Eds.), *Handbook of motivation and cognition: Foundations of social behavior* (Vol. 2, pp. 53–92).

Gollwitzer, P. M., Heckhausen, H., & Stellar, B. (1990). Deliberative vs. implemental mind-sets: Cognitive tuning toward congruous thoughts and information. *Journal of Personality and Social Psychology, 59*, 1119–1127.

Harackiewicz, J. M., Manderlink, G., & Sansone, C. (1992). Competence processes and achievement: Implications for intrinsic motivation. In A. K. Boggiano & T. S. Pittman (Eds.), *Achievement and motivation: A social development perspective* (pp. 115–137). New York: Cambridge University Press.

Hattie, J. (1985). Methodology review: Assessing unidimensionality of tests and items. *Applied Psychological Measurement, 9*, 139–164.

Heckhausen, H., & Gollwitzer, P. M. (1987). Thought contents and cognitive functioning in motivational versus volitional states of mind. *Motivation and Emotion, 11*, 101–120.

Herman, W. E. (1990). Fear of failure as a distinctive personality trait measure of test anxiety. *Journal of Research and Development in Education, 23*, 180–185.

Higgins, E. T. (1987). Self-discrepancy: A theory relating self and affect. *Psychological Review, 94*, 319–340.

Higgins, E. T. (1989). Knowledge accessibility and activation: Subjectivity and suffering from unconscious sources. In J. S. Uleman & J. A. Bargh (Eds.), *Unintended thought* (pp. 75–115). New York: Guilford Press.

Higgins, E. T., & Kruglanski, A. W. (1995). *A theory of regulatory modes: When locomotion versus assessment is emphasized.* Unpublished manuscript, Columbia University, New York.

Higgins, E. T., Shah, J., & Friedman, R. (1997). Emotional responses to goal attainment: Strength of regulatory focus as moderator. *Journal of Personality and Social Psychology, 72,* 515–525.

Hill, C. A. (1987). Affiliation motivation: People who need people . . . but in different ways. *Journal of Personality and Social Psychology, 52,* 1008–1018.

Huba, G. J., Aneshensel, C. S., & Singer, J. L. (1981). Development of scales for three second-order factors of inner experience. *Multivariate Behavioral Research, 16,* 181–206.

Jackson, D. N. (1974). *Personality Research Form manual.* Goshen, NY: Research Psychologists Press.

Jarvis, W. B. G., & Petty, R. E. (1996). The need to evaluate. *Journal of Personality and Social Psychology, 70,* 172–194.

Jenkins, C. D., Zyzanski, S. J., & Roseman, R. H. (1979). *Jenkins Activity Survey, Form C.* New York: The Psychological Corporation.

Jöreskog, K. G., & Sörbom, D. (1993). *Lisrel 8: Structural equation modeling with the SIMPLIS command language.* Chicago: Scientific Software.

Kruglanski, A. W. (1996). Goals as knowledge structures. In P. M. Gollwitzer & J. A. Bargh (Eds.), *The psychology of action: Linking cognition and motivation to behavior* (pp. 599–619). New York: Guilford Press.

Kuhl, J. (1985). Volitional mediation of cognition-behavior consistency: Self-regulatory processes and action versus state orientation. In J. Kuhl & J. Beckman (Eds.), *Action control: From cognition to behavior* (pp. 101–128). Berlin, Germany: Springer-Verlag.

Leary, M. R. (1983). Social anxiousness: The construct and its measurement. *Journal of Personality Assessment, 47,* 66–75.

Lewin, K., Dembo, T., Festinger, L., & Sears, P. S. (1944). Level of aspiration. In J. McHunt (Ed.), *Personality and the behavior disorders* (Vol. 1, pp. 333–378). New York: Ronald Press.

Lumsden, J. (1961). The construction of unidimensional tests. *Psychological Bulletin, 58,* 122–133.

Maio, G. R., & Olson, J. M. (Eds.). (1999). *Why we evaluate: Functions of attitudes.* Hillsdale, NJ: Erlbaum.

Matthews, K. A., & Siegel, J. M. (1983). Type A behaviors for children, social comparison, and standards for self-evaluation. *Developmental Psychology, 19,* 135–140.

McNemar, Q. (1969). *Psychological statistics.* New York: Wiley.

Miller, G. A., Galanter, E., & Pribram, K. (1960). *Plans and the structure of behavior.* New York: Holt.

Mischel, W. (1974). Processes in delay of gratification. In L. Berkowitz (Ed.), *Advances in experimental social psychology* (Vol. 7, pp. 249–292) . New York: Academic Press.

Mischel, W. (1981). Metacognition and the rules of delay. In J. H. Flavell & L. Ross (Eds.), *Social cognitive development: Frontiers and possible futures* (pp. 240–271). New York: Cambridge University Press.

Moretti, M. M., & Higgins, E. T. (1990). Relating self-discrepancy to self-esteem: The contribution of discrepancy beyond actual self-ratings. *Journal of Experimental Social Psychology, 26,* 108–123.

Muliak, S. A. (1987). A brief history of the philosophical foundations of exploratory factor analysis. *Multivariate Behavioral Research, 22,* 267–305.

Nasco, S. A., & Marsh, K. L. (1999). Gaining control through counterfactual thinking. *Personality and Social Psychology Bulletin, 25*, 556–568.

Nunnaly, J. C. (1978). *Psychometric theory* (2nd ed.). New York: McGraw-Hill.

Pierro, A., Mannetti, L., Converso, D., Garsia, V., Miglietta, A., Ravenna, M., & Rubini, M. (1995). Caratteristiche strutturali della versione italiana della scala di bisogno di chiusura cognitiva (di Webster e Kruglanski) [Structural characteristics of the Italian version of the Need for Cognitive Closure Scale (of Webster and Kruglanski)]. *Testing, Psicometria, Metodologia, 2*, 125–141.

Pittman, T. S., & D'Agostino, P. R. (1985). Motivation and attribution: The effects of control deprivation on subsequent information processing. In J. H. Harvey & G. Weary (Eds.), *Attribution: Basic issues and applications* (pp. 117–141). New York: Academic Press.

Pratto, F., Sidanius, J., Stallworth, L. M., & Malle, B. F. (1994). Social dominance orientation: A personality variable predicting social and political attitudes. *Journal of Personality and Social Psychology, 67*, 741–763.

Pyszczynski, T., & Greenberg, J. (1987). Self-regulatory perserveration and the depressive self-focusing style: A self-awareness theory of reactive depression. *Psychological Bulletin, 102*, 122–138.

Radloff, L. S. (1977). The CES-D scale: A self-report depression scale for research in the general population. *Applied Psychological Measurement, 1*, 385–401.

Raven, B. H., & Kruglanski, A. W. (1970). Conflict and power. In P. Swingle (Ed.), *The structure of conflict* (pp. 69–109). New York: Academic Press.

Roese, N. J., & Olson, J. M. (1997). Counterfactual thinking: The intersection of affect and function. In M. P. Zanna (Ed.), *Advances in experimental social psychology* (Vol. 29, pp. 1–59). San Diego, CA: Academic Press.

Rosenberg, M. (1965). *Society and the adolescent self-image*. Princeton, NJ: Princeton University Press.

Ruble, D. N. (1983). The development of social comparison processes and their role in achievement-related self-socialization. In E. T. Higgins, D. N. Ruble, & W. W. Hartup (Eds.), *Social cognition and social development: A socio-cultural perspective* (pp. 134–157). New York: Cambridge University Press.

Ryan, R. M. (1995). Psychological needs and the facilitation of integrative processes. *Journal of Personality, 63*, 397–427.

Ryan, R. M., & Frederick, C. (1997). On energy, personality, and health: Subjective vitality as a dynamic reflection of well-being. *Journal of Personality, 65*, 529–565.

Sansone, C., & Harackiewicz, J. M. (1996). "I don't feel like it": The function of interest in self-regulation. In L. Martin & A. Tesser (Eds.), *Striving and feeling: Interactions between goals and affect* (pp. 203–228). Mahwah, NJ: Erlbaum.

Scheier, M. F., Carver, C. S., & Bridges, M. W. (1994). Distinguishing optimism from neuroticism (and trait anxiety, self-mastery, and self-esteem): A reevaluation of the Life Orientation Test. *Journal of Personality and Social Psychology, 67*, 1063–1078.

Shah, J. Y., Kruglanski, A. W., & Thompson, E. P. (1998). Membership has its (epistemic) rewards: Need for closure effects on intergroup favoritism. *Journal of Personality and Social Psychology, 75*, 383–393.

Strube, M. J. (1987). A self-appraisal model of the Type A behavior pattern. In R. Hogan & W. Jones (Eds.), *Perspectives in personality: Theory, measurement, and interpersonal dynamics* (Vol. 2, pp. 201–250). Greenwich, CT: JAI Press.

Tanaka, J. S. (1993). Multifaceted conceptions of fit in structural equation models. In K. A. Bollen & J. S. Long (Eds.), *Testing structural equation models* (pp. 10–39). Newbury Park, CA: Sage.

Taylor, S. E., & Brown, J. D. (1988). Illusion and well-being: A social psychological perspective on mental health. *Psychological Bulletin*, 103, 193–210.

Thompson, E. P., Chaiken, S., & Hazlewood, J. D. (1993). Need for cognition and desire for control as moderators of extrinsic reward effects: A Person × Situation approach to the study of intrinsic motivation *Journal of Personality and Social Psychology*, 64, 987–999.

Thompson, M. M., Naccarato, M. E., & Parker, K. E. (1989, June). *Assessing cognitive need: The development of the Personal Need for Structure and Personal Fear of Invalidity scales*. Paper presented at the annual meeting of the Canadian Psychological Association, Halifax, Nova Scotia, Canada.

Trope, Y., & Neter, E. (1994). Reconciling competing motives in self-evaluation: The role of self-control in feedback seeking. *Journal of Personality and Social Psychology*, 66, 646–657.

Vallerand, R. J., Pelletier, L. G., Blais, M. R., Briere, N. M., Senecal, C., & Vallieres, E. F. (1992). The academic motivation scale: A measure of intrinsic, extrinsic, and amotivation in education. *Educational and Psychological Measurement*, 52, 1003–1017.

Webster, D. M., & Kruglanski, A. W. (1994). Individual differences in need for cognitive closure. *Journal of Personality and Social Psychology*, 67, 1049–1062.

Weiner, B. (1985). Spontaneous causal thinking. *Psychological Bulletin*, 97, 74–84.

Zuckerman, M. (1971). Dimension of sensation-seeking. *Journal of Consulting and Clinical Psychology*, 36, 45–52.

9 To the fringe and back

Violent extremism and the psychology of deviance

Arie W. Kruglanski, University of Maryland
Katarzyna Jasko, Jagiellonian University
Marina Chernikova and Michelle Dugas, University of Maryland
David Webber, Virginia Commonwealth University

Editor's note. This article is one in a collection of articles published in a special issue of *American Psychologist* titled "Psychology of Terrorism" (April 2017). John G. Horgan served as guest editor with Anne E. Kazak as advisory editor. Neil D. Shortland provided scholarly lead.

Violent extremism (VE) counts among the most vexing challenges confronting the world today (Zarif, 2015). Experts increasingly agree, moreover, that there is no military solution to this problem, for no matter how many militants are killed or apprehended, scores of others rush to fill their place (Office of the Press Secretary, 2014). The perplexing question, therefore, is what prompts the massive volunteering of young men and women to violent organizations such as the Islamic State in Iraq and Syria (ISIS)? Equally important are the questions of how individuals who have radicalized already can be deradicalized and returned to moderation.

In this chapter, we offer a theory to address these issues. Though important recent work has examined VE (Atran, Axelrod, & Davis, 2007; Horgan, 2009; Sageman, 2004; Swann, Gómez, Seyle, Morales, & Huici, 2009), a number of fundamental issues on this topic remain unresolved concerning the motivational dynamics leading to extremism, the role of ideology in radicalization, the contribution to this phenomenon of social networks, and the place of personality predispositions in this process. We approach these issues within a broad analytic framework that treats VE as a special case of extremism writ large, distinguished by the unmitigated perpetration of aggression for a cause. Accordingly, we first discuss the general phenomenon of extremism as such, and then consider in depth the special case of VE.

What extremism is: Defining the phenomenon

The term *extreme* is defined as "exceeding the ordinary, usual, or expected" (Merriam-Webster, Inc., 1986, p. 441). To be sure, not every behavior that is unusual, or out of the ordinary, qualifies as extremist. An individual from a different culture may enact behaviors that are uncommon in a given setting, or a disabled individual may be prevented from acting in ways that characterize a majority of people, without such instances being considered extremist. Rather, we reserve the term *extremism* for a *willful deviation from the norms of conduct in a given context or situation*. Such norms describe what most people in a given society would do in the same circumstances.

According to the present definition, varied types of behavior are classifiable as extreme. Bungee jumping or wing-suit flying, for example, are "extreme" because they entail risks (to health and survival) that relatively *few* persons undertake. Anorexic diets are extreme because they involve acts of self-denial that most people eschew, and VE encompasses activities (e.g., the killing of innocents) that *deviate* from norms of conduct condoned in most civilizations and religions. Extreme actions that most people eschew may occur on the spur of the moment under the influence of intoxicating substances. Finally, not all extreme behaviors are violent or destructive. The humanistic works of Mother Theresa or of Albert Schweitzer, for instance, represent acts of self-denial that very few persons venture, which makes them extreme. In the present article, we cast a broad analytic net to capture all such diverse types of extraordinary behavior.

Why does extremism happen?

Any behavior, including its extreme forms, is a function of two general factors: *motivation* and *ability* (Kruglanski et al., 2012). Motivation represents the *internal* determinant of behavior. It contains the factors of value and expectancy that under proper circumstances translate into a goal (Kruglanski et al., 2014), which prompts the selection of a behavioral means to its attainment. Ability is the behavior's *external* determinant. It expresses the degree of actual control an individual has over the behavior in question (Fishbein & Ajzen, 2010). In the sections that follow, we consider how motivation and ability determine extreme behavior in general, and VE in particular.

Motivational balance and imbalance

A major determinant of extremism is *motivational imbalance*, the degree to which a given need comes to dominate the others. We assume that moderate behaviors, exhibited by majorities of people, are guided by a set of basic biological and psychogenic needs (cf. Deci & Ryan, 2000; Fiske, 2004; Higgins, 2012; Maslow, 1943); these reciprocally constrain behaviors enacted on their behalf. In other words, behaviors that satisfy one need while undermining another would tend to be avoided. For example, the need for esteem and admiration may be seen as best served by heroism in battle, yet concerns for safety and the survival instinct may prohibit such risky heroics. Because people generally strive to satisfy their fundamental needs, they tend to stay within a restricted behavioral range that these constrain; this results in the moderate pattern of conduct defining the behavioral norm displayed by majorities of persons. In this manner, motivational dynamics at the individual level translate into social patterns in which majorities of persons (the "mainstream") exhibit moderation and minorities (the "fringe") display extremism.

Psychological asymmetry of extremism and moderation

Empirical evidence supports the notion that people exhibit a preference for moderation over extremity. For example, average stimuli are liked more than extreme ones (e.g., Halberstadt & Rhodes, 2003), and traits of moderate intensity are liked better than ones that are very low or very high (Koch, Imhoff, Dotsch, Unkelbach, & Alves, 2016). Our motivational-imbalance assumption, whereby extremism involves partial oblivion to individuals' fundamental needs, explains not only why extreme behaviors are exhibited by a minority of people but also why extremism tends to be short-lived, relatively speaking, though different "extremisms" vary on the temporal scale of their duration. For example, membership in militant far-right organizations lasts on the average of 10 years (Bjorgo, 2002), the pursuit of criminal lifestyle is typically brief (Ridgeway, 2014), and revolutions often lead to counterrevolutions and end up with a "domestication" of erstwhile revolutionaries. Thus, there exists an asymmetry between extremism and moderation, in that the latter is more appealing overall and psychologically easier to sustain than the former.

How extremism starts and how it ends

Triggering motivational imbalance

For most persons, the initial point of departure is the mainstream. No one is born a revolutionary, a terrorist, or an extreme dieter. To become an extremist, something must transpire along the way to trigger the motivational imbalance that induces deviance. This may take place when persons realize on their own or are persuaded by others that their important need has been neglected, and that an opportunity presents itself to gratify it. Addressing the need in question may then assume high priority, overshadow other considerations, and allow the contemplation of extreme behavior. For instance, under intense hunger, individuals may carry out such counternormative acts as scavenging for food, stealing, or eating substances or articles considered disgusting or inedible.

Often, the frustrated need is social in nature. For instance, when frustrated, the need for love and relatedness (Baumeister & Leary, 1995) may drive individuals to so called "crimes of passion" in violation of societal norms and legal codes (Baumeister, Brewer, Tice, & Twenge, 2007). The desire to appeal to potential mates may promote the adoption of an extreme diet aimed to improve one's appearance, and so forth.

Extremism is a matter of degree, defined by the *extent* of motivational imbalance among individuals' basic needs. Where a given focal need looms considerably larger than its alternatives (vs. less so), it affords greater freedom from their constraints (Köpetz, Faber, Fishbach, & Kruglanski, 2011). In turn, liberation from constraints permits extreme behaviors that would be prohibited otherwise. For instance, volunteering to help out in a soup kitchen in order to feel good about oneself or making a monetary contribution to charity are less extreme than volunteering for the Peace Corps or devoting one's life to the poor. Simply, the former behaviors entail more limited degrees of self-sacrifice that allows one also to address one's selfish concerns (one's career, comfort, social relationships, or leisure).

Restoring motivational balance

The opposite journey, back to moderation, is prompted by the same general factors (albeit in reverse) that produced the shift to the extreme in the first place. Just as the motivational imbalance underlies a fringe-bound shift, restored motivational balance underlies abandonment of the fringe and a reversion to the mainstream. Such balance restoration may happen through weakening of a once-dominant need, the strengthening of alternative concerns, and/or a realization that the extreme means does not serve the dominant need the way it was supposed to. For instance, a change in one's life circumstances (e.g., marriage, family) might reduce one's concern about sexy appearance presumably served by an extreme diet. Also, one's overriding need for achievement may give way to concern about one's health if one was diagnosed with a life-threatening illness.

Cognitive representations and the role of narratives. Goals and means are cognitively represented (Fishbach & Ferguson, 2007; Kruglanski, 1996). Activation of the relevant cognitions may happen in various ways. Occasionally, one may form a goal–means schema on one's own, based on one's independent experience and assessment; more typically, such a schema is contained in a culturally approved narrative (or ideology) to which individuals have been exposed, and that they have internalized. A narrative that privileges one type of value (e.g., money) over competing values can induce the commitment to extreme behavior because it selectively activates certain goals while neglecting others. Similarly, the shift back to motivational balance might be based on one's own inferential process, but also on sociocultural narratives that advocate moderation. For instance, narratives that highlight the complexity of a value system (e.g., advocating work–life balance) may decrease the appeal of extreme behavior and restore moderation. Research by Tetlock (1984, 1986) has confirmed that moderate ideology was associated with a perception of multiple values as approximately equally important, whereas ideological extremism was associated with one value dominating over others.

The twin functions of social networks. Another factor that may contribute to initiation and maintenance of extreme behavior in service of a goal is social network. Social networks fulfill two motivationally relevant functions for their members: informational and normative (cf. Deutsch & Gerard, 1955; Kelley, 1952). The informational function consists of validating a given goal–means schema as worthy of adopting. The normative function consists of *rewarding* individuals for enacting the schema-implied behavior.

Informational influence. The networks' informational influence consists of serving an epistemic authority whose consensual support validates a given narrative (Hardin & Higgins, 1996; Kruglanski et al., 2005). Agreement of one's respected peers with its content is taken as evidence of its veracity, as does the charisma, credibility, and perceived expertise of a communicator who delivers the narrative. Just like extremist narratives, those that promote moderation often derive their persuasive power from the epistemic authority of their source, including the network of significant others whom the individual holds in high regard. Thus, a new friendship network may curb individuals' enthusiasm for extreme means and encourage them to embark on a renewed pursuit of mainstream activities. Similarly, extrication from the extremist network may facilitate leaving extremism behind, just as immersion in that network may have previously fostered a movement to the fringe.

It is noteworthy that the support of social networks or validation of given narratives by credible communicators, although often *helpful* in inducing a given motivational state, is not *essential* for that purpose. Specifically, individuals with high confidence in their own judgment, or with high self-ascribed epistemic authority, may not depend as much on others for validation of their goals and means; they are less impacted by social networks and persuasive communicators, as they feel confident in their own assessment and are in no need of external validation (Kruglanski et al., 2005).

Normative influence. A social network's normative influence resides in its power to reward the individual for subscribing to network-espoused goal–means schema and implementing the activities that it suggests. Such rewards may consist of bestowal upon the individual of the group's approval and according them the status and acceptance that approval begets.

The role of ability. Beyond the motivation to carry out extreme behavior in service of a predominant need, individuals must have the ability to do so. Ability has two aspects: subjective and objective. The subjective aspect has to do with the individual's *expectancy* to be able to carry out the (extreme) activities, that is, to implement the goal–means schema in the prescribed manner. In psychological models of motivation (Atkinson, 1964; Kruglanski, 1996; Kruglanski et al., 2014; Lewin, 1951), expectancy (attainability) combines with value (desirability) to determine the readiness to initiate goal-driven behavior. However, whereas subjective ability determines the initiation of an activity, its completion will not take place without objective ability to see it through. For instance, some persons may suffer physical limitations that preclude their pursuit of an extreme behavior that is physically taxing, or they may lack the required know-how for such pursuit—for instance, the military training required of a revolutionary fighter. Although existing research suggests that a reduction of individuals' energetic resources reduces their ability to control their urges and increases their vulnerability to temptations of various kinds (Baumeister, Bratslavsky, Muraven, & Tice, 1998; Muraven & Baumeister, 2000), including impulses to carry out extreme, socially unacceptable behaviors, the ability to *maintain* such extreme commitment most likely demands a high rather than low level of energetic resources.

Ability may also play a significant role in individuals' return to the mainstream. To leave the fringe behind, one may require the resolve and willpower to withstand the group pressure that often binds one to the extremist "attractor," and/or the competence to satisfy one's fundamental needs in the balanced ways prescribed by the mainstream. Thus, in order to be reintegrated into the society, a criminal may need to receive the appropriate vocational training and education, the drug addict may need to learn to subjugate her or his destructive habit, and the extreme dieter may need to acquire novel eating habits.

Distinct roles of motivation and ability. We finally assume that motivation and ability play distinct roles in extreme behavior. The degree of motivational imbalance determines the *degree* of extremism to which the individual may be ready to commit. In this sense, it sets an upper bound on potential extremism. In contrast, ability determines whether the individual is capable of reaching that upper point on the extremism continuum. Absent such an ability, people may need to resort to less extreme activities of which they are capable. Consider an individual who lacks the ability to pursue an extreme sport she/he is passionate about. In those circumstances, that person might instead become an extreme fan of a team in that athletic discipline, collect clippings about its champions and history, and so forth.

Personality predispositions. The process of initiating and maintaining a motivational imbalance or balance may be influenced by a host of stable individual differences. For instance, individuals who are chronically high on a given need (e.g., need for achievement, social approval, sensation seeking) should be predisposed to privilege it over others. Other personality factors may prompt persons to yield to the impetus to emit extreme behavior whenever it occurs. People high in the need for cognitive closure (Kruglanski, 2004) have been known to "seize and freeze" on accessible notions and to eschew weighing their alternatives. Thus, they may be more prone to remain committed to a focal goal even when it happens at the expense of other goals (Shah, Friedman, & Kruglanski, 2002). Highly acquiescent individuals may be more readily convinced than others by extremism-promoting narratives and networks, whereas individuals with a strong predisposition toward uniqueness may be more prepared than others to break out of the mainstream and explore the fringe, regardless of social support (Imhoff & Erb, 2009). Of special relevance, Vallerand's (2015) distinction between individuals who are *obsessive* versus *harmonious* in their passion for a given pursuit directly taps a personality predisposition toward motivational imbalance versus balance, respectively. Indeed, a recent study by Bélanger, Lafrenière, Vallerand, and Kruglanski (2013) found that obsessively passionate individuals were significantly more likely than harmoniously passionate individuals to select extreme means relevant to their passion.

Some personality traits may be relevant to the initiation of extreme behavior, but not necessarily to its maintenance. For instance, although *impulsive* individuals may act without much hesitation on their temporarily dominant need, it is unlikely that they will be able to maintain their commitment for very long. The same should be true of other psychological variables associated with impulsive behavior, such as low self-control (Tangney, Baumeister, & Boone, 2004) or low conscientiousness (Costa & McCrae, 1992), which may lead to increased appeal of extreme activities, but not necessarily to their maintenance.

In summary, the movement away from the mainstream and toward the fringe requires a shift toward a motivational imbalance wherein a given need dominates the others, and an extreme behavior is identified as the means of choice for satisfying that need. In addition to the motivational imbalance, extremism also requires an ability to carry out such deviant behavior. Similarly, the movement back to moderation requires a shift toward motivational balance and an ability to sustain such balance via appropriate activities. Next, we apply the analysis of extremism as a general phenomenon to the specific case of VE.

Violent extremism

The common features that VE shares with other forms of extremism are the shift toward *motivational imbalance* and the *ability* to sustain the extreme means to the dominant need. The features that characterize VE uniquely concern the specific need that animates it, and the use of violence as the extreme means for gratifying that need.

Shift toward motivational imbalance

Quest for significance. Earlier we posited that the move toward extremism is occasioned by a motivational shift in which a given need becomes dominant and trumps other common concerns. What might this need be in the case of VE? A considerable number of motivations relevant to VE have been identified in the literature (such as honor, vengeance, religion, loyalty to the leader, perks in the afterlife, feminism; e.g., Bloom, 2005; Stern, 2004). All of these are entirely appropriate descriptions of specific cases. But underlying them, there seems to exist a more general motivating force that we label the *quest for significance*. This is the fundamental desire to matter, to be someone, to merit respect (Kruglanski et al., 2013; Kruglanski, Chen, Dechesne, Fishman, & Orehek, 2009; Kruglanski et al., 2014). Psychological theorists have long realized that this quest constitutes a universal, human motivation variously labeled as the need for esteem, achievement, meaning, and control (Deci & Ryan, 2000; Frankl, 1969; Higgins, 2012; Maslow, 1943).

Triggering the significance quest. A major way to arouse a motivation is through *deprivation* of a need. Accordingly, the need for significance may be aroused via a perceived loss of significance, that is, through significance deprivation. Significance loss can sometimes happen due to *individual* humiliation, unrelated to any intergroup conflict. This is illustrated by cases of Palestinian women who volunteered for suicide missions after they had suffered a stigma in their personal lives (e.g., infertility, disfiguration, or allegation of an extramarital affair or divorce; Pedahzur, 2005). But humiliation can also arise in the context of intergroup conflict and result from personal losses perpetrated by the enemy. For instance, the Chechen "black widows" were rendered powerless, and thus were demeaned and humiliated by having their loved ones wrested from them by the Russian forces (Speckhard & Paz, 2012). Often, significance loss can stem from an affront to one's *social identity*. For instance, Muslim immigrants in Europe who encounter widespread "Islamophobia" on the part of native Europeans (Kruglanski, Crenshaw, Post, & Victoroff, 2008; Sageman, 2004) may pervasively experience this kind of "putdown." Discrimination against one's group and trampling of its sacred values (Atran et al., 2007) engenders a considerable significance loss by members of the group (e.g., all Muslims); this is often skillfully exploited by the propagandists of Al Qaeda and ISIS, for example.

Often, motivational priming stems from a perceived *opportunity* to gratify the motive in question (Shah & Kruglanski, 2003). The pursuit of violence and self-sacrifice can be portrayed as an *opportunity* for a vast significance gain, a place in history, and the status of hero or martyr (Post, 2006). Significance loss or threat of loss may be intertwined with the opportunity for significance gain through attempts to eradicate or prevent the loss. Thus, humiliation of one's group offers the possibility to strike back at the culprits, therefore leveling the playing field and demonstrating one's power and, hence, significance.

Willingness to use extreme means. The motivational shift toward the quest for significance entails the relative suppression of alternative, common concerns. This liberates individuals to use whatever means they perceive as effective to satisfying their dominant need, regardless of how extreme these might be. Research by Dugas et al. (2016) found that the experience of significance loss was related to expressed readiness to suffer pain and to sacrifice one's comfort for a significance-lending cause. Relatedly, research on sacred values repeatedly demonstrated that individuals were prepared to sacrifice material benefits on the altar of such values, which protection bestows the aura of significance on individuals (Atran et al., 2007).

Note that, in and of itself, the quest of significance does not necessarily promote violence as the means of choice. After all, some means to significance are quite socially accepted, namely, (a) moderate ones compatible with other common concerns, (b) extreme ones compatible with social norms, and (c) extreme ones that in fact *serve* major moral imperatives. In the category of moderate means belong routes to significance via the pursuit of excellence and achievements in various socially applauded domains such as science, art, and business. In the second category belong activities like extreme diets and extreme sports that involve self-denial that does not contradict important societal injunctions. Finally, in the third category belong self-sacrificial activities (e.g., those of missionaries and other humanitarians) that are venerated by the mainstream because they in fact serve cherished values. Nonetheless, as shown in the following section, violence appears to constitute a particularly common means to significance gain.

Violence as means to significance. There is something special about violence as a possible means to significance. It constitutes the primordial, raw, and direct use of power, inflicting hurtful *costs* on the targets of one's aggression (Raven, 1993).

Violence is the "great equalizer" capable of obliterating the significance of venerated individuals and turning them into disempowered victims. It is through violence or threatened violence that conflicts in the animal kingdom are typically resolved, and pecking order in animal hierarchies is established (Buss & Shackelford, 1997). To a large extent, the potential for violence (i.e., military might) also determines the standing (hence, significance) of nations in the world arena.

Ample empirical evidence suggests that violence is often employed in the effort to restore one's compromised significance. Case studies of 15 school shootings show that they often occurred in response to social rejection (Leary, Kowalski, Smith, & Phillips, 2003). In our own work, we have found that significance loss leads to the adoption of extreme, group-oriented ideology and the support for violence; this has been shown in culturally diverse samples, including American respondents, Muslims in Spain and the Philippines, and Tamils in Sri Lanka (Webber et al., 2016). In a sample of ideological extremists in the United States, we found that those who experienced abuse, social rejection, or failure were more likely to resort to ideologically directed violence (Jasko, LaFree, & Kruglanski, 2016). Analyses of the motivational patterns of suicide attackers revealed that the degree of violence in an attack was correlated with indicators of the attacker's motivation to gain significance (Webber, Klein, Kruglanski, Brizi, & Merari, 2015). Similarly, perceiving oneself as a victim of anti-Muslim discrimination was associated with support for suicide bombing in Muslim diaspora populations (Victoroff, Adelman, & Matthews, 2012), and economic discrimination against minorities has been found to be a substantive predictor of domestic terrorism (Piazza, 2011).

These various examples show that many instances of significance loss are perceived as a result of other people's actions. In such situations, when there is a clear target to blame for the experienced injustice, violence may be perceived as an appealing means with which to redress the undeserved harm. Indeed, analyses of violent acts have shown that their preponderance can be attributed to motives that—from the perspective of the perpetrator—are reactions to perceived unfairness that foster significance loss for the victims (Baumeister, 1999; Stillwell, Baumeister, & Del Priore, 2008). The determination to use violence in such situations might also serve to protect one from a future loss (Nowak, Gelfand, Borkowski, Cohen, & Hernandez, 2016), thus offering a valuable deterrence as bulwark against future humiliations.

To be sure, the use of violence has a serious drawback as well. It runs afoul of societal norms common in most civilizations that expressly prohibit violence; such prohibitions recognize the destructive potential of violence and its propensity to undermine the social order in the long run (Freud, 1930/1991; Pinker, 2012). In light of the pervasive injunctions against violence, its use by individuals and societies calls for special justification. The two factors reviewed next—ideological narratives and social networks—are particularly common sources of such justification.

Ideological narratives. By highlighting the discrepancy between the imperfect present and the utopian future (Jost, Federico, & Napier, 2009), an ideological narrative sustains the motivational imbalance that drives extreme actions. Because it depicts the cause in terms of grand and far-reaching goals (e.g., "Liberté, égalité, fraternité"), behavior in service of those goals is no longer influenced by a cost–benefit analysis (Ginges, Atran, Medin, & Shikaki, 2007) simply because the awoken quest for significance renders such costs irrelevant.

In addition to invoking a supreme, significance-promoting goal, an ideological narrative delineates a set of legitimate means to pursue it. By creating an association between an important goal and violent means, extremist ideologies facilitate translating motivation into action, because they significantly reduce the difficulty of coming up with a specific plan to pursue the cause (Gollwitzer, 1999). One example of such a strong goal–means association is found in *culture-of-honor* narratives (Nisbett & Cohen, 1996), whereby affronts must be countered with aggression against one's detractors. Research confirms that culture-of-honor states have more aggressive acts than non-culture-of-honor states (Brown, Osterman, & Barnes, 2009).

Finally, by identifying the culprits responsible for the unacceptable current state and depicting them as immoral and contemptible, ideological narratives eliminate another important constraint on violence: empathetic concern for the suffering of others. Two justificatory themes relevant to this strategy are particularly prevalent: (a) those based on employment of in-group/purity morality (Haidt & Graham, 2006), and (b) those based on the dehumanization of the intended targets of one's violence. The concept of in-group morality refers to the belief that whatever serves the group's interest is moral and ethically warranted (Haidt & Graham, 2006). In this manner, Islamic VE has stressed the notion that the West has been actively assaulting Islam and vying to eradicate it, and that, therefore, attacks against Westerners are morally justified and commanded by Allah (Al-Adnani, 2015). Moreover, justification of violence against civilians typically employs a language that delegitimizes them (Bandura, 1999), often by denying them human properties and portraying them as disgusting infrahuman creatures (e.g., cockroaches, rats, pigs, or apes) that do not merit the consideration generally extended to humans (Castano & Giner-Sorolla, 2006).

The role of social networks. Radical social networks can influence the intention to engage in violence by validating the importance of the goal and confirming that a violent means is an appropriate way to pursue it. Moreover, when important others are willing to engage in violent acts, they create a local norm, whereby violence is commendable, and its pursuit is rewarded by the group's esteem and reverence. Empirical research has confirmed that when a violent act is socially validated, people experience less guilt and distress than when it is questioned by important others (Webber, Schimel, Martens, Hayes, & Faucher, 2013). Finally, by offering significance and acceptance, belonging to a group may become an end in itself, and thus increase members' willingness to undergo sacrifices for a collective cause (Willer, 2009). Empirical research by Swann and colleagues attests to the notion that when the group constitutes an important part of the self-concept, individuals are more likely to engage in extreme pro-group behaviors (e.g., Swann, Gómez, Dovidio, Hart, & Jetten, 2010; Swann et al., 2009).

Note that validation of a justificatory narrative by a social network may not be absolutely essential for sustaining individuals' commitment to extreme violence.

Some individuals may have such a strong sense of their own *epistemic authority* that they do not require concrete validation of their views by others; furthermore, they may have such a confident sense of self that they have little need for others' approval. Ted Kaczynski, the infamous Unabomber (*Encyclopedia Britannica*, n.d.) was a loner who spun his justificatory narrative for violence on his own (Federal Bureau of Investigation, 2008). Similarly, Anders Breivik, the Norwegian who killed 77 persons in Oslo and on the island of Utoya in 2011 had no concrete network of social support and constructed his own justificatory narrative for the massacre (Knausgaard, 2016). Finally, the recent spate of "lone wolf" attacks in Israel, Europe, and the United States (Oliphant, 2016) suggest that the internet and social media may serve the function of (virtual) social networks by inducing and validating individuals' notions concerning the relative importance of specific goals (e.g., earning glory by fighting for a given cause) and the appropriateness of the extreme means for their pursuit.

Role of ability in turning to extremism

Skill. VE on behalf of an ideological cause may require corresponding competencies and abilities. For instance, participation of foreign fighters in the ongoing struggle in Syria and Iraq requires the ability to reach those locations and circumvent tight travel bans designed to stem the flow of recruits to the militant organizations. Over the years, the Islamist organizations ISIS and Jabhat al Nusra have managed to set up effective smuggling networks that facilitate travel of their would-be volunteers, even as states inside and outside the region have increased their efforts to tighten travel restrictions (Schmitt & Sengupta, 2015).

Targeting policies of extremist organizations also determines the level of difficulty that the required activities entail; this has direct implications for the ability level needed to carry them out. Whereas the original targeting policy of Al Qaeda involved high-profile objects such as the World Trade Center, the Pentagon, the USS *Cole*, or the U.S. embassies in Africa, the ISIS policy of inspiring attacks with minimal means (like hatchets, vehicles, or knives) and unleashed against anyone anywhere has made the acts of extremism considerably easier and less demanding.

Energy. Leaving the comfort zone of the mainstream and embarking on risky extremism requires considerable zest and energy. Indeed, in general, violent extremists tend to be young and energetic. An analysis of 350 known terrorists from Middle Eastern, Latin American, West European, and Japanese groups revealed that the "composite terrorist" is a single male in his early 20s (Russell & Miller, 1977). Other terrorist groups reveal similar patterns (Gunaratna, 2000; Ergil, 2000). It is difficult to isolate the variable of energy from the multiple factors correlated with age; nonetheless, given the challenges of VE, it seems plausible that youthful vigor and attendant optimism play a significant part in the relation between age and VE.

Entitlement. Finally, deviation from mainstream norms is easier for individuals with status and power, who often feel entitled to stray from the accepted patterns of behavior. Indeed, experimental studies suggest that when combined with frustration, a sense of one's own power increases the likelihood of aggressive behavior (Fast & Chen, 2009).

Back to moderation

Restoring motivational balance. Moving toward or away from VE are mirror images of each other, whether one or the other occurs depends on the field of driving and restraining psychological forces promoting extremism or moderation (Altier, Thoroughgood, & Horgan, 2014; Kruglanski et al., 2012). The allure of alternative means to significance and the relinquishment of VE may be prompted by the satisfaction of need for significance or resurfacing of alternative needs, such as those for affection, comfort, safety, and hedonic enjoyment that may have been suppressed to an appreciable extent during the individuals' active engagement in VE.

Case studies suggest that as extremists enter their 30s, front-line activism begins to feel forced and uncomfortable, especially once individuals have begun to seriously miss things such as a career, family, and a secure place to live (Dalgaard-Nielsen, 2013; Reinares, 2011). In addition, ideological justification for violence might "wear thin" in some cases, and individuals may be swamped by guilt about the mayhem they have perpetrated (e.g., Bubolz & Simi, 2015). All of these attest to different ways in which a motivational recalibration may take place and prompt individuals to abandon VE.

Alternative means to significance. There is evidence that relinquishment of VE is related to a shift in the individual's perception, whereby extremism no longer affords significance and/or alternative means to significance become available that seem superior to extremism. Illustrating the former process are numerous cases of exit from right-wing extremist groups, prompted by individuals' growing sense that life in the violent organization, far from the idealistic picture that the ideological narrative had painted, is rife with intrigue, back stabbing, and mutual suspicion (Dalgaard-Nielsen, 2013). Similarly, some foreign fighters who joined the "holy war" in Iraq and Syria found out that they were reduced to menial tasks such as cleaning the toilets, while also being treated with disrespect by ranking ISIS members (Tomlinson, 2014). A different road to significance is through a newly afforded opportunity for employment, affording the touted "dignity of work"; indeed, research found that participants in a terrorist rehabilitation program were more likely to disengage from terrorism if they were provided with such an opportunity (Abuza, 2009) or if they realized that their activist involvement jeopardized their ability to land or maintain certain types of jobs (Simi & Futrell, 2009).

The luster of violent struggle—hence, its efficacy as a means to significance—may be dimmed by *defeat* and the abject failure of aggression to bestow glory on its perpetrators. For instance, the significant decline in support for the Liberation Tigers of Tamil Eelam (LTTE), which we observed in an extensive survey carried out with samples of former LTTE members (cf. Kruglanski et al., 2014; Webber et al., 2016), could be partially explained by the 2009 defeat of the LTTE by the

Sri Lankan military. This effectively eliminated the option of continued struggle and the hope of a significance-enhancing victory.

Cognitive change and the role of narratives and networks. Increased loyalty to a *different group* (Demant & de Graaf, 2010), or embracement of a *different cause* that rejects violence, induces individuals to disengage from a terrorist group (Reinares, 2011). Realization that the extreme activity fails to satisfy one's quest for significance or a substitution of a univalent ideology by a narrative that embraces plural values (Tetlock, 1986) involves a change in the individual's beliefs. Such change is occasionally instigated by the individual's own reflections; often, however, it is carried by explicit counternarratives to which the extremist is exposed. A major component of terrorist deradicalization programs in Saudi Arabia, Singapore, or Iraq have been dialogues with imams and ulama (Islamic scholars) designed to convince detainees that their violent pursuits are contrary to the teachings of Islam (El-Said & Harrington, 2010). The ultimate effectiveness of these programs in changing detainees' beliefs about the legitimacy of violence has yet to be determined; nonetheless, the fact that thousands of their graduates were released into society implies that, at least in the organizers' judgments, they no longer posed acute danger (Angell & Gunaratna, 2012; El-Said & Harrington, 2010).

Reframing extremists' views about the justifiability of violence is often carried out by social networks that espouse contrary views on these matters. A significant role in this regard is played by the detainees' families. Families often oppose their relatives' involvement in extremism and are natural allies in the struggle for their deradicalization (Koehler, 2013). Recruitment of families to the deradicalization effort has been a staple of the Saudi and the Singaporean rehabilitation programs (Al-Hadlaq, 2011; El-Said & Harrington, 2010; Gunaratna & Hassan, 2015). In the Saudi case, for example, families are entrusted with responsibility for the released detainee and cooperation with the government as to prevention of their reconnection with their extremist ex-comrades (Al-Hadlaq, 2011).

Role of ability in returning to moderation

Skill. A return to the motivational balance of the mainstream requires the ability to gratify one's various needs in conventionally approved ways. Often, this necessitates the acquisition of a new skill set that would allow individuals to reintegrate into the mainstream society and become respected members of their community. An important aspect of various deradicalization programs, such as those in Saudi Arabia (Al-Hadlaq, 2011), Singapore (Gunaratna & Hassan, 2015), or Sri Lanka (Webber et al., 2016), was the provision of such skill sets via vocational education courses, general education courses, and language training.

Energy. The considerable demands of life on the fringe may reduce individuals' ability to sustain it for long (Aho, 1988; Horgan, 2009). Indeed, evidence suggests that the role of *exhaustion* as a consequence of engaging in violent behavior is an important facet of the exit process (Gallant, 2014). Declining energies may also partially explain why growing older appears to be an important predictor of the relinquishment of violent activism (Dalgaard-Nielsen, 2013).

Entitlement. To overcome the apprehensions that exiting the fringe may involve may require considerable personal confidence and fortitude. Such characteristics may characterize people in leadership positions, and with a sense of power and independence. In the same way that status and power enable individuals to initiate a violent movement that deviates from the mainstream, it may also enable them to return to moderation. The spontaneous 1997 deradicalization of the Egyptian Gammah Islamiyah, and the 2007 partial deradicalization of the Egyptian Al Jihad organization, were both initiated by the movements' leaders, as was the Armée Islamique du Salut deradicalization in Algier (Ashour, 2008).

To be sure, high-powered persons within a violent organization might be particularly *unmotivated* to carry out a policy reversal toward moderation for fear of losing status and being criticized for inconsistency and poor judgment. Yet should they decide to do so, they may be more capable of promoting a general deradicalization than individuals with lesser standing.

Personality characteristics. Individuals may vary in their sensitivity to affronts or rejections (Downey & Feldman, 1996) and, hence, to the extent to which their significance quest is aroused by perceived insults or discriminations. In that regard, rejection-sensitive (vs. less sensitive) individuals may be more prone to radicalization than ones who are less rejection-sensitive. Similarly, some individuals may be more attuned to a militant organization's *narrative*. Because the latter is typically cast in categorical "black versus white" (us vs. them) terms, individuals who are high on the need for cognitive closure may find such ideologies more appealing and, hence, are more likely to radicalize than individuals who are low on the need for closure (Webber et al., 2016). Finally, individuals who are dependent or conformist may be more attuned to the *network* pressures toward radicalization than individuals who are independent and nonconformists (Merari, 2010). Thus, even though there may not be a unique personality *profile* that characterizes violent extremists prone to volunteer to extremist organizations, certain individual characteristics relevant to determinants of the radicalization *process* may certainly contribute to those persons' likelihood of radicalizing under the proper circumstances.

Recapitulation and conclusion

The present theory

Because of its striking real-world manifestations, it is tempting to treat VE as a "one of a kind" phenomenon that is qualitatively distinct from other behavioral occurrences. But even though its specific combination of features is unique, VE shares significant psychological dynamics with other extremisms. Identifying those commonalities offers a general perspective on VE and promises new insights into its determinants. From the present perspective, extremism writ large has two fundamental components pertaining to *motivation* and *ability*, respectively. The motivational component is essential and unique to extremism. It involves a *motivational imbalance* in which a given need becomes dominant and suppresses other concerns. This removes the constraints that the latter typically impose on behavior and allows extreme actions to be contemplated as possible means to one's goals. For those behavioral means to be actually enacted, however, the individual must have the appropriate ability. In its objective sense, ability is related to the actual difficulty of carrying out the extreme activities, which, in turn, is significantly affected by staunch resistance to extremism by individuals and groups. The degree of motivational imbalance determines how far individuals are prepared to go on the extremism dimension. The ability component, in contrast, determines what degree of extremism is actionable, given the individual's competencies. In contrast to extremism, moderation is produced by a motivational balance in which individuals attend to their varied needs and select behaviors compatible with the constraints these impose.

Applying the foregoing general analysis to VE involved identifying the dominant motivation that undergirds its pursuit. Conceptual analysis, buttressed by empirical research (cf. Kruglanski et al., 2009, 2014; Webber et al., 2016), assigns this role to the quest for personal significance, and the desire to matter and to be recognized. The way of addressing the quest for significance (e.g., via violence) is cognitively represented in a goal–means narrative and appropriately validated. Some individuals construct their own narrative that they hold as valid. More typically, the relevant narratives are available in individuals' social environments (e.g., in social media, blogs, and chat rooms) and are supported by these persons' networks. Moreover, formation of extremist or moderate mind-sets is affected by a host of personality variables related, for instance, to individuals' tendency to prioritize momentarily salient needs over other concerns, susceptibility to persuasion, energy levels, and autonomy versus dependence. Whereas the motivational imbalance or balance and the ability to pursue those behaviorally are essential for development of the extremist and moderate mind-sets, their multiple determinants may partially substitute for each other so that none of them is completely necessary for their emergence. Our theoretical model is presented in Figure 1.

Alternative approaches

In recent decades, social scientists have approached the issue of VE from diverse angles. A well-known attempt grounds the VE in such root causes as poverty, political repression, poor education (e.g., Fearon & Laitin, 2003; Kennedy, 1998), or relative deprivation (Gurr, 1970). A different approach offers psychological models of VE that explain it in terms of personality characteristics such as narcissism (Crayton, 1983), paranoia (e.g., Robins & Post, 1997), or authoritarianism (e.g., Ferracuti & Bruno, 1981). The rational actor model purports to explain VE in terms of a calculus of costs and benefits that accrue from extremism versus moderation (e.g., Crenshaw, 1990; Enders & Su, 2007; Perry, Berrebi, Brown, Hollywood, & Jaycocks, 2013). Social movement theory (della Porta, 2013)

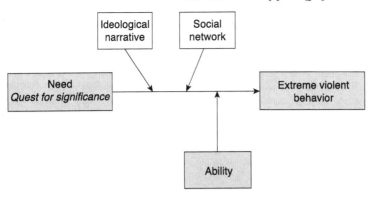

Figure 1 Model of underpinnings of violent extremism.

describes VE in terms of an unfolding processes of escalating policing, competitive escalation, and militancy. Finally, social network theory espouses the idea that radicalization and collective political action are intimately related to people's interpersonal relationships and connections to others committed to a violent ideology (e.g., Dean, 2007; Sageman, 2004).

Those various approaches to extremism share important elements in common with our analysis; in that sense, we build on past insights and "connect the dots" contributed by other scholars. Importantly, however, the present model offers a broader and more integrative conception than those of its predecessors. For instance, whereas some prior theories (the psychological models) focused on problematic personality development reducing individuals' sense of self-worth, we view developmental issues as one among several possible sources of feelings of humiliation and insignificance. Also, whereas some prior models highlighted one element in particular (e.g., the network element, the personality element, or the ideological element), the present model outlines how these different elements interact and come together. Thus, rational actor (cost–benefit) models address a motivational component without identifying the specific motivation underlying VE, and they do not relate it to the network or the ideological components as they may interact in promoting extremism. The root cause models specify conditions that might, under some conditions, lead to feelings of injustice and unfairness (cf. Gurr, 1970) without identifying the linkage of such feelings (of significance loss) or to the means of violence identified in a justifying narrative.

The present framework offers a general blueprint concerning possible interventions aimed to counteract or prevent VE. It suggests that (a) alternative, equally compelling means to significance must be identified and made available to radicalized individuals or those at risk of radicalization, (b) relevant *social support* against radicalization needs to be generated, (c) compelling counternarratives against the violence–significance link need to be generated, and (d) the ability of individuals to perpetrate violence for their cause must be thwarted by state policies (e.g., travel restrictions, elimination of funding sources) and military/policing actions aimed at defeating the extremists and causing them to fail.

Obviously, these general principles need to be carefully translated into specific policies and best practices in accordance with specific contexts of their application. Such translation should take into account whether a given project involves the deradicalization of *committed* extremists or a preventive counterradicalization for those *at risk* of succumbing to VE. Specific implementation of the general principles should be flexible enough to accommodate cultural variation, as well as for differences in age and socioeconomic status of targeted individuals. The translation efforts would likely require considerable ingenuity, dedication, and investment of time and material resources. Yet failure to undertake them would allow the current waves of extremism to grow unabated. Given the danger they pose to world stability and security, countering them head on, based on the best available science, constitutes a truly global imperative.

References

Abuza, Z. (2009). *Conspiracy of silence: The insurgency in southern Thailand*. Washington, DC: United States Institute of Peace Press.

Aho, J. A. (1988). Out of hate: A sociology of defection from neo-Nazism. *Current Research on Peace and Violence, 11*, 159–168.

Al-Adnani, A. M. (2015). Say, "Die in your rage." Al Hayat Media Centre. https://pietervanostaeyen.wordpress.com/2015/01/26/audio-statement-by-is-spokesman-abu-muhammad-al-adnani-as-shami-say-die-in-your-rage/

Al-Hadlaq, A. M. (2011). Terrorist rehabilitation: The Saudi experience. In L. Rubin, R. Gunaratna, & J. A. R. Jerard (Eds.), *Terrorist rehabilitation and counter-radicalisation: New approaches to counter-terrorism* (pp. 59–69). New York, NY: Routledge.

Altier, M. B., Thoroughgood, C. N., & Horgan, J. G. (2014). Turning away from terrorism: Lessons from psychology, sociology, and criminology. *Journal of Peace Research, 51*, 647–661. http://dx.doi.org/10.1177/0022343314535946

Angell, A., & Gunaratna, R. (2012). *Terrorist rehabilitation: The U.S. experience in Iraq*. Boca Raton, FL: Taylor & Francis.

Ashour, O. (2008, November). Islamist de-radicalization in Algeria: Successes and failures. *Middle East Institute Policy Brief, 2008*(21). www.mei.edu/content/islamist-de-radicalization-algeria-successes-and-failures

Atkinson, J. W. (1964). *An introduction to motivation*. London, UK: Van Nostrand.

Atran, S., Axelrod, R., & Davis, R. (2007). Sacred barriers to conflict resolution. *Science, 317*, 1039–1040. http://dx.doi.org/10.1126/science.1144241

Bandura, A. (1999). Moral disengagement in the perpetration of inhumanities. *Personality and Social Psychology Review, 3*, 193–209. http://dx.doi.org/10.1207/s15327957pspr0303_3

Baumeister, R. F. (1999). *Evil: Inside human violence and cruelty*. New York, NY: Freeman.

Baumeister, R. F., Bratslavsky, E., Muraven, M., & Tice, D. M. (1998). Ego depletion: Is the active self a limited resource? *Journal of Personality and Social Psychology, 74*, 1252–1265. http://dx.doi.org/10.1037/0022-3514.74.5.1252

Baumeister, R. F., Brewer, L. E., Tice, D. M., & Twenge, J. M. (2007). Thwarting the need to belong: Understanding the interpersonal and inner effects of social exclusion. *Social and Personality Psychology Compass, 1*, 506–520. http://dx.doi.org/10.1111/j.1751-9004.2007.00020.x

Baumeister, R. F., & Leary, M. R. (1995). The need to belong: Desire for interpersonal attachments as a fundamental human motivation. *Psychological Bulletin, 117,* 497–529. http://dx.doi.org/10.1037/0033-2909.117.3.497

Bélanger, J. J., Lafrenière, M.-A. K., Vallerand, R. J., & Kruglanski, A. W. (2013). When passion makes the heart grow colder: The role of passion in alternative goal suppression. *Journal of Personality and Social Psychology, 104,* 126–147. http://dx.doi.org/10.1037/a0029679

Bjorgo, T. (2002). *Exit neo-Nazism: Reducing recruitment and promoting disengagement from racist groups.* Working paper, Norsk Utenrikspolitisk Institutt, Oslo, Norway. https://brage.bibsys.no/xmlui/handle/11250/2394077

Bloom, M. (2005). *Dying to kill: The allure of suicide terror.* New York, NY: Columbia University Press.

Brown, R. P., Osterman, L. L., & Barnes, C. D. (2009). School violence and the culture of honor. *Psychological Science, 20,* 1400–1405. http://dx.doi.org/10.1111/j.1467-9280.2009.02456.x

Bubolz, B. F., & Simi, P. (2015). Leaving the world of hate: Life-course transitions and self-change. *American Behavioral Scientist, 59,* 1588–1608. http://dx.doi.org/10.1177/0002764215588814

Buss, D. M., & Shackelford, T. K. (1997). From vigilance to violence: Mate retention tactics in married couples. *Journal of Personality and Social Psychology, 72,* 346–361. http://dx.doi.org/10.1037/0022-3514.72.2.346

Castano, E., & Giner-Sorolla, R. (2006). Not quite human: Infrahumanization in response to collective responsibility for intergroup killing. *Journal of Personality and Social Psychology, 90,* 804–818. http://dx.doi.org/10.1037/0022-3514.90.5.804

Costa, P. T., Jr., & McCrae, R. R. (1992). Four ways five factors are basic. *Personality and Individual Differences, 13,* 653–665. http://dx.doi.org/10.1016/0191-8869(92)90236-I

Crayton, J. W. (1983). Terrorism and the psychology of the self. In L. Z. Freedman & Y. Alexander (Eds.), *Perspectives on terrorism* (pp. 33–41). Wilmington, DE: Scholarly Resources.

Crenshaw, M. (1990). Questions to be answered, research to be done, knowledge to be applied. In W. Reich (Ed.), *Origins of terrorism: Psychologies, ideologies, theologies, states of mind* (pp. 247–260). Cambridge, UK: Cambridge University Press.

Dalgaard-Nielsen, A. (2013). Promoting exit from violent extremism: Themes and approaches. *Studies in Conflict and Terrorism, 36,* 99–115. http://dx.doi.org/10.1080/1057610X.2013.747073

Dean, G. (2007). Criminal profiling in a terrorism context. In R. Kocsis (Ed.), *Criminal profiling: International perspectives in theory, practice & research* (pp. 169–188). Totowa, NJ: Humana Press. http://dx.doi.org/10.1007/978-1-60327-146-2_8

Deci, E. L., & Ryan, R. M. (2000). The "what" and "why" of goal pursuits: Human needs and the self determination of behavior. *Psychological Inquiry, 11,* 227–268. http://dx.doi.org/10.1207/S15327965PLI1104_01

della Porta, D. (2013). *Clandestine political violence.* New York, NY: Cambridge University Press. http://dx.doi.org/10.1017/CBO9781139043144

Demant, F., & de Graaf, B. D. (2010). How to counter radical narratives: Dutch deradicalization policy in the case of Moluccan and Islamic radicals. *Studies in Conflict & Terrorism, 33,* 408–428. http://dx.doi.org/10.1080/10576101003691549

Deutsch, M., & Gerard, H. B. (1955). A study of normative and informational social influences upon individual judgement. *The Journal of Abnormal and Social Psychology, 51,* 629–636. http://dx.doi.org/10.1037/h0046408

Downey, G., & Feldman, S. I. (1996). Implications of rejection sensitivity for intimate relationships. *Journal of Personality and Social Psychology, 70*, 1327–1343.

Dugas, M., Bélanger, J. J., Moyano, M., Schumpe, B. M., Kruglanski, A. W., Gelfand, M. J., Touchton-Leonard, K., & Nociti, N. (2016). The quest for significance motivates self-sacrifice. *Motivation Science, 2*, 15–32. http://dx.doi.org/10.1037/mot0000030

El-Said, H., & Harrington, R. (2010). *Globalisation, democratisation and radicalisation in the Arab world*. New York, NY: Palgrave Macmillan.

Encyclopedia Britannica. (n.d.). *Ted Kaczynski*. www.britannica.com/biography/Ted-Kaczynski

Enders, W., & Su, X. (2007). Rational terrorists and optimal network structure. *Journal of Conflict Resolution, 51*, 33–57. http://dx.doi.org/10.1177/0022002706296155

Ergil, D. (2000). Suicide terrorism in Turkey. *Civil Wars, 3*, 37–54.

Fast, N. J., & Chen, S. (2009). When the boss feels inadequate: Power, incompetence, and aggression. *Psychological Science, 20*, 1406–1413. http://dx.doi.org/10.1111/j.1467-9280.2009.02452.x

Fearon, J. D., & Laitin, D. D. (2003). Ethnicity, insurgency, and civil war. *The American Political Science Review, 97*, 75–90. http://dx.doi.org/10.1017/S0003055403000534

Federal Bureau of Investigation. (2008, April 10). *The Unabomber*. https://archives.fbi.gov/archives/news/stories/2008/april/unabomber_042408

Ferracuti, F., & Bruno, F. (1981). Psychiatric aspects of terrorism in Italy. In I. Barak-Glanatz & C. R. Huff (Eds.), *The mad, the bad and the different: Essays in honour of Simon Dinitz* (pp. 199–213). Lexington, MA: Lexington Books.

Fishbach, A., & Ferguson, M. J. (2007). The goal construct in social psychology. In A. W. Kruglanski & E. T. Higgins (Eds.), *Social psychology: Handbook of basic principles* (pp. 490–515). New York, NY: Guilford Press.

Fishbein, M., & Ajzen, I. (2010). *Predicting and changing behavior: The reasoned action approach*. New York, NY: Psychology Press.

Fiske, S. T. (2004). *Social beings: Core motives in social psychology*. New York, NY: Wiley.

Frankl, V. E. (1969). *The will to meaning: Foundations and applications of logotherapy*. New York, NY: Random House.

Freud, S. (1991). Civilization and its discontents. In A. Dickson (Ed.), *Sigmund Freud: 12. Civilization, society, and religion* (pp. 245–341). New York, NY: Penguin. (Original work published 1930.)

Gallant, D. (2014). *A "former's" perspective: Qualitative thematic exploration of the disengagement process from violent right wing extremism* (Unpublished master's thesis). University of Northern British Columbia, Canada. www.academia.edu/8138387/

Ginges, J., Atran, S., Medin, D., & Shikaki, K. (2007). Sacred bounds on rational resolution of violent political conflict. *Proceedings of the National Academy of Sciences of the United States of America, 104*, 7357–7360. http://dx.doi.org/10.1073/pnas.0701768104

Gollwitzer, P. M. (1999). Implementation intentions: Strong effects of simple plans. *American Psychologist, 54*, 493–503. http://dx.doi.org/10.1037/0003-066X.54.7.493

Gunaratna, R. (2000). Suicide terrorism: A global threat. *Jane's Intelligence Review, 12*, 52–55.

Gunaratna, R., & Hassan, M. F. B. M. (2015). Terrorist rehabilitation: The Singapore experience. In R. Gunaratna & M. B. Ali (Eds.), *Terrorist rehabilitation: A new frontier in counter-terrorism* (pp. 41–70). London, UK: Imperial College Press.

Gurr, T. (1970). *Why men rebel*. Princeton, NJ: Princeton University Press.

Haidt, J., & Graham, J. (2006). Planet of the Durkheimians, where community, authority, and sacredness are foundations of morality. In J. T. Jost, A. C. Kay, & H. Thorisdottir

(Eds.), *Social and psychological bases of ideology and system justification* (pp. 371–401). Oxford, UK: Oxford University Press. http://dx.doi.org/10.2139/ssrn.980844

Halberstadt, J., & Rhodes, G. (2003). It's not just average faces that are attractive: Computer-manipulated averageness makes birds, fish, and automobiles attractive. *Psychonomic Bulletin & Review, 10*, 149–156. http://dx.doi.org/10.3758/BF03196479

Hardin, C. D., & Higgins, E. T. (1996). Shared reality: How social verification makes the subjective objective. In R. M. Sorrentino & T. E. Higgins (Eds.), *Handbook of motivation and cognition* (Vol. 2, pp. 28–84). New York, NY: Guilford Press.

Higgins, T. E. (2012). *Beyond pleasure and pain: How motivation works*. Oxford, UK: Oxford University Press.

Horgan, J. (2009). *Walking away from terrorism: Accounts of disengagement from radical and extremist movements*. New York, NY: Routledge.

Imhoff, R., & Erb, H. P. (2009). What motivates nonconformity? Uniqueness seeking blocks majority influence. *Personality and Social Psychology Bulletin, 35*, 309–320. http://dx.doi.org/10.1177/0146167208328166

Jasko, K., LaFree, G., & Kruglanski, A. W. (2016). Quest for significance and violent extremism: The case of domestic radicalization. *Political Psychology*. Advance online publication. http://dx.doi.org/10.1111/pops 12376

Jost, J. T., Federico, C. M., & Napier, J. L. (2009). Political ideology: Its structure, functions, and elective affinities. *Annual Review of Psychology, 60*, 307–337. http://dx.doi.org/10.1146/annurev.psych.60.110707.163600

Kelley, H. H. (1952). Two functions of reference groups. In G. E. Swanson, T. M. Newcomb, & E. L. Hartley (Eds.), *Readings in social psychology* (2nd ed., pp. 410–414). New York, NY: Holt, Rinehart & Winston.

Kennedy, M. (1998). The 21st century conditions likely to inspire terrorism. In H. W. Kushner (Ed.), *The future of terrorism: Violence in the new millennium* (pp. 185–194). London, UK: Sage. http://dx.doi.org/10.4135/9781452243702.n10

Knausgaard, K. O. (2016, July 22). Inside the warped mind of Anders Breivik. *The Telegraph*. www.telegraph.co.uk/news/2016/07/22/anders-breivik-inside-the-warped-mind-of-a-masskiller/

Koch, A., Imhoff, R., Dotsch, R., Unkelbach, C., & Alves, H. (2016). The ABC of stereotypes about groups: Agency/socioeconomic success, conservative-progressive beliefs, and communion. *Journal of Personality and Social Psychology, 110*, 675–709. http://dx.doi.org/10.1037/pspa0000046

Koehler, D. (2013, August 3). Family counselling as prevention and intervention tool against "foreign fighters." The German "hayat" program. *Journal Exit Deutschland*. http://journals.sfu.ca/jed/index.php/jex/article/viewFile/49/83

Köpetz, C., Faber, T., Fishbach, A., & Kruglanski, A. W. (2011). The multifinality constraints effect: How goal multiplicity narrows the means set to a focal end. *Journal of Personality and Social Psychology, 100*, 810–826. http://dx.doi.org/10.1037/a0022980

Kruglanski, A. W. (1996). Goals as knowledge structures. In P. M. Gollwitzer & J. A. Bargh (Eds.), *The psychology of action: Linking cognition and motivation to behavior* (pp. 599–618). New York, NY: Guilford.

Kruglanski, A. W. (2004). *The psychology of closed mindedness*. New York, NY: Psychology Press.

Kruglanski, A. W., Bélanger, J. J., Chen, X., Köpetz, C., Pierro, A., & Mannetti, L. (2012). The energetics of motivated cognition: A forcefield analysis. *Psychological Review, 119*, 1–20. http://dx.doi.org/10.1037/a0025488

Kruglanski, A. W., Bélanger, J. J., Gelfand, M., Gunaratna, R., Hettiarachchi, M., Reinares, F., Orehek, E., Sasota, J., & Sharvit, K. (2013). Terrorism—A (self) love story: Redirecting the significance quest can end violence. *American Psychologist, 68*, 559–575. http://dx.doi.org/10.1037/a0032615

Kruglanski, A. W., Chen, X., Dechesne, M., Fishman, S., & Orehek, E. (2009). Fully committed: Suicide bombers' motivation and the quest for personal significance. *Political Psychology, 30*, 331–357. http://dx.doi.org/10.1111/j.1467-9221.2009.00698.x

Kruglanski, A. W., Crenshaw, M., Post, J. M., & Victoroff, J. (2008). Talking about terrorism. *Scientific American Mind, 19*, 58–65. http://dx.doi.org/10.1038/scientificamericanmind 1008-58

Kruglanski, A. W., Gelfand, M. J., Bélanger, J. J., Sheveland, A., Hetiarachchi, M., & Gunaratna, R. (2014). The psychology of radicalization and deradicalization: How significance quest impacts violent extremism. *Political Psychology, 35*, 69–93. http://dx.doi.org/10.1111/pops.12163

Kruglanski, A. W., Raviv, A., Bar-Tal, D., Raviv, A., Sharvit, K., Ellis, S., Bar, R., Pierro, A., & Mannetti, L. (2005). Says who? Epistemic authority effects in social judgment. In M. P. Zanna (Ed.), *Advances in experimental social psychology* (Vol. 37, pp. 345–392). San Diego, CA: Academic Press. http://dx.doi.org/10.1016/S0065-2601(05)37006-7

Leary, M. R., Kowalski, R. M., Smith, L., & Phillips, S. (2003). Teasing, rejection, and violence: Case studies of the school shootings. *Aggressive Behavior, 29*, 202–214. http://dx.doi.org/10.1002/ab.10061

Lewin, K. (1951). *Field theory in social science: Selected theoretical papers* (D. Cartwright, Ed.). Oxford, UK: Harpers.

Maslow, A. H. (1943). A theory of human motivation. *Psychological Review, 50*, 370–396. http://dx.doi.org/10.1037/h0054346

Merari, A. (2010). *Driven to death: Psychological and social aspects of suicide terrorism.* Oxford, UK: Oxford University Press.

Merriam-Webster, Inc. (1986). *Webster's ninth new collegiate dictionary.* Springfield, MA: Merriam-Webster.

Muraven, M., & Baumeister, R. F. (2000). Self-regulation and depletion of limited resources: Does self-control resemble a muscle? *Psychological Bulletin, 126*, 247–259. http://dx.doi.org/10.1037/0033-2909.1262.247

Nisbett, R. E., & Cohen, D. (1996). *Culture of honor: The psychology of violence in the South.* Boulder, CO: Westview.

Nowak, A., Gelfand, M. J., Borkowski, W., Cohen, D., & Hernandez, I. (2016). The evolutionary basis of honor cultures. *Psychological Science, 27*, 12–24. http://dx.doi.org/10.1177/0956797615602860

Office of the Press Secretary. (2014, August, 7). *Statement by the President.* www.whitehouse.gov/the-pressoffice/2014/08/07/statement-president

Oliphant, V. (2016, July 20). Terror warning: Lone Wolf attacks are on the rise, says Europol. *Sunday Express.* www.express.co.uk/news/world/691517/Terror-lone-wolf-attacks-rising-Nice-Bastille-Day-Germany-Orlando-Europol

Pedahzur, A. (2005). *Suicide terrorism.* Cambridge, UK: Polity Press.

Perry, W. L., Berrebi, C., Brown, R. A., Hollywood, J., & Jaycocks, A. (2013). *Predicting suicide attacks: Integrating spatial, temporal, and social features of terrorist attack targets.* Washington, DC: Rand Corporation.

Piazza, J. A. (2011). Poverty, minority economic discrimination and domestic terrorism. *Journal of Peace Research, 48*, 339–353. http://dx.doi.org/10.1177/0022343310397404

Pinker, S. (2012). *The better angels of our nature: Why violence has declined.* New York, NY: Penguin.

Post, J. (2006). *The mind of the terrorist: The psychology of terrorism from the IRA to Al Qaeda.* New York, NY: Palgrave Macmillan.

Raven, B. H. (1993). The bases of power: Origins and recent developments. *Journal of Social Issues, 49,* 227–251. http://dx.doi.org/10.1111/j.1540-4560.1993.tb01191.x

Reinares, F. (2011). Exit from terrorism: A qualitative empirical study on disengagement and deradicalization among members of ETA. *Terrorism and Political Violence, 23,* 780–803. http://dx.doi.org/10.1080/09546553.2011.613307

Ridgeway, G. (2014, May). *Criminal career patterns.* www.ncjrs.gov/pdffiles1/nij/242545.pdf

Robins, R. S., & Post, J. M. (1997). *Political paranoia: The psychopolitics of hatred.* New Haven, CT: Yale University Press.

Russell, C. A., & Miller, B. H. (1977). Profile of a terrorist. *Studies in Conflict and Terrorism, 1,* 17–34.

Sageman, M. (2004). *Understanding terror networks.* Philadelphia, PA: University of Pennsylvania Press. http://dx.doi.org/10.9783/9780812206791

Schmitt, E., & Sengupta, S. (2015, September 26). Thousands enter Syria to join ISIS despite global efforts. *New York Times.* www.nytimes.com/2015/09/27/world/middleeast/thousands-enter-syria-to-join-isis-despite-global-efforts.html

Shah, J. Y., Friedman, R., & Kruglanski, A. W. (2002). Forgetting all else: On the antecedents and consequences of goal shielding. *Journal of Personality and Social Psychology, 83,* 1261–1280. http://dx.doi.org/10.1037/0022-3514.83.6.1261

Shah, J. Y., & Kruglanski, A. W. (2003). When opportunity knocks: Bottom-up priming of goals by means and its effects on self-regulation. *Journal of Personality and Social Psychology, 84,* 1109–1122. http://dx.doi.org/10.1037/0022-3514.84.6.1109

Simi, P., & Futrell, R. (2009). Negotiating white power activist stigma. *Social Problems, 56,* 89–110. http://dx.doi.org/10.1525/sp.2009.56.1.89

Speckhard, A., & Paz, R. (2012). *Talking to terrorists: Understanding the psycho-social motivations of militant Jihadi terrorists, mass hostage takers, suicide bombers and martyrs to combat terrorism in prison and community rehabilitation.* McLean, VA: Advances Press.

Stern, J. (2004). *Terror in the name of God: Why religious militants kill.* New York, NY: HarperCollins.

Stillwell, A. M., Baumeister, R. F., & Del Priore, R. E. (2008). We're all victims here: Toward a psychology of revenge. *Basic and Applied Social Psychology, 30,* 253–263. http://dx.doi.org/10.1080/01973530802375094

Swann, W. B., Jr., Gómez, A., Dovidio, J. F., Hart, S., & Jetten, J. (2010). Dying and killing for one's group: Identity fusion moderates responses to intergroup versions of the trolley problem. *Psychological Science, 21,* 1176–1183. http://dx.doi.org/10.1177/0956797610376656

Swann, W. B., Jr., Gómez, A., Seyle, D. C., Morales, J. F., & Huici, C. (2009). Identity fusion: The interplay of personal and social identities in extreme group behavior. *Journal of Personality and Social Psychology, 96,* 995–1011. http://dx.doi.org/10.1037/a0013668

Tangney, J. P., Baumeister, R. F., & Boone, A. L. (2004). High self-control predicts good adjustment, less pathology, better grades, and interpersonal success. *Journal of Personality, 72,* 271–324. http://dx.doi.org/10.1111/j.0022-3506.2004.00263.x

Tetlock, P. E. (1984). Cognitive style and political belief systems in the British House of Commons. *Journal of Personality and Social Psychology, 46,* 365–375. http://dx.doi.org/10.1037/0022-3514.46.2.365

Tetlock, P. E. (1986). A value pluralism model of ideological reasoning. *Journal of Personality and Social Psychology, 50,* 819–827. http://dx.doi.org/10.1037/0022-3514.50.4.819

Tomlinson, S. (2014, December 1). How disenchanted Islamic fanatics are returning home because jihad isn't as glamorous as they hoped. *Daily Mail.* www.dailymail.co.uk/news/article-2855780/Indian-IS-recruit-goes-home-having-clean-toilets.html

Vallerand, R. J. (2015). *The psychology of passion: A dualistic model.* New York, NY: Oxford University Press. http://dx.doi.org/10.1093/acprof:oso/9780199777600.001.0001

Victoroff, J., Adelman, J. R., & Matthews, M. (2012). Psychological factors associated with support for suicide bombing in the Muslim diaspora. *Political Psychology, 33,* 791–809. http://dx.doi.org/10.1111/j.1467-9221.2012.00913.x

Webber, D., Chernikova, M., Kruglanski, A. W., Gelfand, M. J., Hettiarachchi, M., Gunaratna, R., Lafrenière, M-A. K., & Bélanger, J. J. (2016). *Deradicalizing the Tamil Tigers.* Unpublished manuscript, University of Maryland, College Park, MD.

Webber, D., Klein, K., Kruglanski, A. W., Brizi, A., & Merari, A. (2015). Divergent paths to martyrdom and significance among suicide attackers. *Terrorism and Political Violence.* Advance online publication. http://dx .doi.org/10.1080/09546553.2015.1075979

Webber, D., Schimel, J., Martens, A., Hayes, J., & Faucher, E. H. (2013). Using a bug-killing paradigm to understand how social validation and invalidation affect the distress of killing. *Personality and Social Psychology Bulletin, 39,* 470–481. http://dx.doi.org/10.1177/0146167213477891

Willer, R. (2009). Groups reward individual sacrifice: The status solution to the collective action problem. *American Sociological Review, 74,* 23–43. http://dx.doi.org/10.1177/000312240907400102

Zarif, J. (2015, June 17). The imperative of a comprehensive strategy to fight violent extremism. *Harvard International Review.* http://hir.harvard.edu/archives/11547

Index

Entries in *italics* denote figures; entries in **bold** denote tables.

AB (attitude toward the behavior) 276–7, 282–3
ability: and extremism 348–9, 354, 358; and returning to moderation 356–7
abortion 84, 130, 141, 276, 280
abstraction in language 25, *26*, 65, 82–8, *86*, **87**, 93, 98
Academic Motivation Scale (AMS) 325
accessibility: of constructs 77; of death 181; of goals 257; of knowledge structures 146–7; of liking 268; of rules 12, 35, 42, 50, 105, 108; *see also* attitude accessibility
accountability instructions 23, 28, 94
acculturation 111, 113
achievement orientation 320, 323, 349–50
ACT* model 33
action orientation 301
action phases, rubicon model of 300
Action-Decision Scale 322–3, 327
activity pace 304
ACT-R (Adaptive Control of Thought-Rational) theory 109
adaptive toolbox 105, **110**, 114
Adorno, Theodor 66–7, 69, 129, 140, 143
affectivity 302
affronts, sensitivity to 351, 353, 357
age, and extremism 354, 356–7
aggression: and conservatism 139–40, 155, 173–6; and entitlement 355; and mortality salience 183, 188; and personal significance 9
agreeableness 327, 339.n2; *see also* Big Five personality factors
Al Jihad 357
Al Qaeda 351, 354
alcohol intoxication 99.n1, 115, 146

Allport, Gordon 253
alternative goals: in goal systems 209; inhibition of 225–6; other people as 246; presence of 235–6; undermining focal goal 8, 215
ambient noise, impact on NFCC 22, 30, 62, 78, 80, **81**, 86–8, 90, **91**, 146
ambiguity *see* intolerance of ambiguity
ambiguous behavior 38
anchoring effects 74–5
anger, and conservatism 144–5, 153, 155, 173, 179–80
animal learning studies 2, 34, 222
anti-egalitarianism *see* inequality, acceptance of
anti-immigration views 30–1, 154
anti-Muslim discrimination *see* Islamophobia
anxiety, and conservatism 131, 134, 139, 145, 149, 180
Armée Islamique du Salut 357
Arrowood, John 2
artistic preferences, and uncertainty avoidance 167
assessment function 11, 299–301, 338; and agreeableness 339.n2; and Big Five personality factors 326; creating scale for 304–5; and decision-making systems 338; exaggerated 213; internal consistency of scale 313–14; items on scale for **309**, **311**; and other individual-difference measures 320–6, **330**; psychological characteristics of 302–4; and quality control 332–3; *see also* self-regulatory modes
association, strength of *see* strength of goals-means association

associative learning 32–3, 108
associative processes 108, 122.n2
attainability of goals: and accessibility 269–71; and goal commitment 214, 223–4; and liking and wanting 255, 274; as requisite for motivation 255–8, 262, 285–7, 348; and self-regulatory modes 303, 334–7
attainment, means of 209, 257
attainment expectancy *see* attainability of goals
attainment value 256, 335
attentional resources 8, 33, 115, 227
attitude accessibility: and attitude strength 265, 267, 273; measuring 258; temporary 187–8, 256; and valence 268–70, *272*
attitude attributions 76, 147
attitude change: and dissonance reduction 261; and information processing 36–8; motivation and cognition in 207
attitude extremity 255, 265
attitude strength 254, 264–8, 273–4
attitude valence 269–72
attitude-behavior relations 10; attainability and accessibility in 268–9, **270–1**; attitude strength model 265–74; behavior focus model 275–7; correspondence hypothesis 75; and goal systems 255–8, 284; mediation model of 279, *280*, *283*; in persuasion 37; research on 253–5, 264, 286; rocky road model 258–64, 287
attitudes: automatically activated 267, 273; concept of 37, 255–6, 275, 285, 288.n4; formation of 19, 47; general 130, 157, 265, 275–80, **279**, 285–6; relative 258
attribution theory 3, 11–12, 20
attributional categories 3
Attributional Style Questionnaire 82
authoritarian personality theory 67–8, 129, 140–2, 153, 179–80
authoritarianism: and conservatism 140–1; and dogmatism 157; dominance-submissive 142, 151; fear and aggression and 173–6; and intolerance of ambiguity 160; left-wing 143, 157; and mental rigidity 156; and need for order and structure 171; and NFCC 69; and resistance to change 138; as response to uncertainty 145; and self-esteem 172–3; and self-regulatory modes 338; and social crisis 183–4; and violent extremism 358; *see also* RWA

autocratic group structure 29–30, 50
automaticity 33, 227–8, 268, 285–6
autonomy: and closed-mindedness 67; as goal 222; and self-regulatory modes 303
availability heuristic 42, 109

background goals 211, 215, 232–4
bad news 61, 147
base rate rule 39–40, 119
basic needs 345–6
Bayes' rule 109
behavior *see also* attitude-behavior relation; TPB
behavior focus 254, 264, 276–7, 286
behavior identification 38–9
behavior processes, spontaneous and deliberative 267–8
behavioral intentions: and behavioral expectations 290.n18; determinants of 276–8, 281–2, 286–7, 290.n19; effects of reward and threat on 181; and goal activation 274; and instrumentality 282–3, 285
behavioral learning theory 2, 12
behavioral predictions 10; and attitudes 253–4, 265, 275, 277, 280; and equifinality 288; goal-systemic perspective on 287–8; of MODE model 273
belief bias 117–18
belief crystallization 65, 88, 93
belief formation, motivations for 131–3
belief strength 35, 82, 146
belief systems, closed 68, 143, 191.n1
beliefs: firm *see* belief strength; motivational underpinnings of 131; tendency to persevere 98
bias-variance dilemma 121
Big Five personality factors 164, 324, 326–30, **328**, 336, 340
Breivik, Anders 354
Bush, George W. 6, 160

caregivers, primary 44, 49
causal attribution 3–4, 98
central-systematic information processing 70
change: preference for 148; resistance to 135–8, 147, 153–4, 188, 190, 191.n3
children, attribution of epistemic authority by 44–5
churches, authoritarian 139, 184–5
classical conditioning 32–3, 108

closed-mindedness 20, 66–7, 69, 143, 153, 155
cognition, need for 70, 132
cognitive capacity: and cognitive inference performance 36, 39; core 105; identifying 35; and lay epistemics 146; limited 7, 115–16, 208, 213; and motivation 95–7; and NFCC 52.n2, 70; relative 99.n1; and strategy selection 120
cognitive change 65, 356
cognitive closure: avoidance of 63, 74; impulsive 146, 171–2; need for *see* NFCC; nonspecific 4, 21–2, 60, 132, 146; premature 62, 76, 79, 143
cognitive complexity 153, 155, 160, 162–3, 181
cognitive consistency 11–12, 20, 132
cognitive dissonance 98, 152
cognitive energetics 7
cognitive impatience 61
cognitive inconsistency 98
cognitive load: and attentional capacity 115; and judgment 38–40, *41*, 119
cognitive resources *see* cognitive capacity
cognitive rigidity 68–9, 171
cognitive sophistication 144, 156, 163
cognitive structure, and ideological content 191.n1
cognitive style: and conservatism 156, 160, 171; and NFCC 68
cold cognitive approach 133
communist countries 136–7
compatibility principle 254, 280
conditioning, as rule acquisition 112
confidence: initial 88–90, 93; subjective 72–3, 80–1; unfounded 98
confirmation bias 98
conjunction rule 109, 118
conscientiousness 323–4, 326–7, 329, 350; *see also* Big Five personality factors
consciousness, parsimony principle of 33
consensus: formation of 30, 32; preference for 65, 78–82, *80*, **81**, 84, 92–3
consensus heuristic 28, 41, 117
conservatism: core aspects of 135–6; ideological *see* political conservatism; measures of 130, 135, 137–9 (*see also* C-Scale; RWA Scale); and NFCC 30; psychological and political 130, 137, 167 (*see also* political conservatism); psychology of 139–49, 164, 187, 190–1; sociopolitical theories of 149–53; theories of 133–4 (*see also* motivated social cognition; personality theory of conservatism)
consideration set of rules 114–15
consistency, bias toward 65
constraints, liberation from 9, 346–7
construct accessibility effects 77
contempt, and conservatism 144–5, 155, 173, 179
context theory 163
control deprivation 337
control theories 300
convergent validity 304, 326–7
core capacities 111–12
correspondence bias 75–6, 98, 147
cost–benefit models: in deliberative process 267–8, 286; and extremism 353, 358–9; and NFCC 22, 28, 66, 68, 92–3, 95, 146
counterfactual thinking 337
counterfinality 7
covariation 4
C-Scale: and artistic preferences 167; and need for order 167; and openness to experience 164; and resistance to change 135, 138
cue utilization 64–5, 75, 95
cue weights 116, 121
cultural and social norms, and NFCC 63

dangerous world 176
death, fear of *see* mortality salience
death penalty 130, 139, 141, 151, 171–2, 183
decision-making styles 6
decision-making systems 337–8
decisiveness: on NFCC scale 30; and regulatory modes 302, 322–3
deductive ability, self-ascribed 5
deductive nomological framework 52.n3
default heuristics **110**, 111
dehumanization 353
deliberation function or mind-set 65, 300
deliberative judgments 104–6, 119
deradicalization 9, 356–7, 360
directional motives 131–2
discounting principle 72–3
discrepancy: ability to spot 303–4; in actual and desired attitudes 289.n6; and anxiety 180; in ideological narratives 352–3; motivating properties of 10–11, 88, 90, 208, 224, 240, 265; reducing 260; and self-regulatory modes 300, 322; types of 261
discriminant validity 141, 326–7, 329, 336
dispositional attributions 38–9

dissent, tolerance for 79–82
dissonance reduction 94, 134, 152, 207, 238, 261
diversity, intolerance of 30
dogmatism: and closed-mindedness 68, 143–4, 156; and conservatism 129, 153, 155–7, 186; and intolerance of ambiguity 160; and NFCC 69
Dogmatism Scale 143, 157
dopamine neurotransmission 259
dormant goals 262
dreams, and political ideology 176
dual-process theories: and dual-system formulations 122.n1; motivation and cognition in 207; and rule-following 109; and social judgment 36, 43; unimodel as alternative to 5, 104–5, 117

early cues, reliance on 64, 71, 74–6, 92
ease of retrieval effect 42–3
ecological approach 121
ecological rationality 105–7, 114–20, 122
economic conservatism 138–9, 172
economic system justification 135, 138–9, 164
elimination-by-aspects heuristic 120
emotional instability 302
emotional magnitude 220
emotions, political 179
empathy, and NFCC 27
endowment effect 181
entitlement 354–5, 357
environmental noise *see* ambient noise
epistemic authority 5, 20, 43–9; and attitude 256; for extremism 52, 348, 354; hierarchy of 45, 51; inequality in 192.n7; and lay epistemics 21–2; and rule conflict 117; self-ascribed *see* SAEA; and social development 113
epistemic machinery 5
epistemic motivations 4, 7; and conservatism 130, 153–4, 156, 171–2; in lay epistemic theory 146; NFCC as 92; rigidity and closed-mindedness 155
epistemic processes 19, 21, 32, 98, 146
epistemic sequence, end of 21–2
epistemic stability 147
equality (1/N) heuristic **110**, 111
equality, opposition to *see* inequality, endorsement of
equifinality 7, *210*, 212, 231, 234–7, 247, 277, 288
error spotting 332–3
errors, good 107

ethnocentrism 145, 150–1, 160, 173
evaluation apprehension *24*, 45–6, 74–5, 94, 322
evaluative conditioning 33, 108
evidence, in lay epistemics 21, 32, 34, 43, 49–51
existential motives, and conservatism 153–4, 172
experience: learning from 46–7, 49, 265–7; openness to 70–1, 155, 164, **165–6**, 186, 326–7; and rule acquisition 112
Experience Inventory Scale 164
expertise, and epistemic authority 5, 43–4
expertise heuristic 119
extensional rules 119
external attributions 3
extraversion 164, 327
extreme sports 9, 349, 351
extremism: beginnings and ends of 346–50; and cognitive complexity 160, 163; determinants of 345–6; and NFCC 171; use of term 8–9, 344–5; *see also* violent extremism
extrinsic motivation 281, 325
extroversion 324, 326, 329; *see also* Big Five personality factors

failure: attributions for 82–3, 93, 337; and violence 352
failure-induced threat 146
faking scores 319
false consensus effect 98
fan effect 210
fascism 67, 129, 140, 191.n1; *see also* F-Scale
fatigue, and NFCC 62, 95
fear, and conservatism 139–40, 145, 153–5, 173–9, **177–8**, 183, 186
Fear of Failure Scale 320
fear of invalidity: and attributions for failure 82–3; and conservatism 132; and NFCC 25, 62–3, 89
"feelings as information" model 34
Feyerabend, Paul 4, 20
"fight rather than switch" paradox 91–2, 98
fit index 327
floor control, asymmetry of *29*
fluency heuristic **110**, 111, 114–15
focal goal: and alternative goals 8, 215, 224, *225–6*, 232, 236–7, 247; means supplementing 263; number of means to *235*, 236
focal rules 118

Frankfurt School 140
freezing: and empathy 27; and resistance 65; *see also* permanence tendency
Freud, Sigmund 2, 23, 66, 140, 142, 237
friendship, and goal systems 243–4, *245*
F-Scale: attitudes measured in 138; criticisms of 143; and mental rigidity 156; and NFCS 69; and self-esteem 173
Functional Impulsivity Scale 320, 322–3, 327

Gammah Islamiyah 357
gaze heuristic 112
gender, and epistemic authority assignments 45
General Conservatism Scale 139
Gigerenzer, Gerd 5, 105
gist-guided approach 11–12
goal accessibility 242
goal attainment: and behavioral intention 281–2; delegation to others 262; emotions following 221; and goal commitment 215; and inter-goal association *224*; and self-regulatory modes 303, 336–7; social means to 240, 243; *see also* attainment expectancy
goal commitment: importance of 247; and inter-goal association *224–6*, 262–3; relationship to means 219–23, *220*; and social primes *241*; use of term 214–15
goal concept 10, 256–7, 283, 289.n15
goal conflict 215–16, 262
goal formation: and attainability 262, 268; and attitudes 254, 258, 285; liking and wanting in 10, 259, 262–3; measuring 287
Goal Orientation Scale 321, 327
goal priming 212, *218*, 256, 258
goal pursuit, resources allocated to 8, 213
goal shielding 8, 226
goal striving 214–16, 225
goal systems *209*, 246–7; allocational properties of 209, 213; associative links within 217–30; configurational patterns of 231–40; interpersonal implications of 240–6; motivational properties of 213–16; structural properties of 208–13; theory of 7–8, 216
goal-commonality *238*
goal-facilitative relations *224*
goal-gradient phenomenon 222
goal-means association 7, 209–10, *211*, 216–18, *223*, *280*; *see also* equifinality; multifinality; strength of association; uniqueness of association
goal-means transfer: of affective quality 220; of commitment 211, 218–22, *221*
goals: active 213, 228, 234–5, 258, 263–4, 281–4; and attitudes 266, 278–9, 290. n21; cognitive representation of 347; desirability and attainability of 256–7, 262, 269 (*see also* attainability of goals); as determining behavior 254–5, 258, 262–3, 274, 277, 281–2, 285, 300; ideal and "ought" 148, 220–1; mediation of 278, 280; other people as 245–6; performance and mastery 208, 321
group conflict, minimizing 150
group dominance 138–9, 150–1, 153, 190, 326
group identification *233*, 234
group permeability *31*
group-centrism 6, 28–31, 50–2

Heider, Fritz 3
hero status 351
heuristic cues 36, 39, 41, 45–6, 50, 207
heuristics: accuracy of 120–1; in adaptive toolbox **110**; selection of 114–16, 119; in unimodel 105; use of term 109
Hierarchy of Epistemic Authorities Test 45
Hitler, Adolf 135, 142, 191.n4
Hogan personality inventory 326
hot cognitive approaches 133
humiliation, and extremism 350–2, 359
hypothesis generation: extent of 63–4, 72–3; length of sequence 21–2
hypothesis testing 52.n1
hypothetical constructs 94–5

ideo-affective polarity 144–5, 179–80
ideological and political beliefs: psychological theories of 129, 132, 154; rigidity of 147; in social dominance theory 150; *see also* political attitudes
ideological motives, and conservatism 134, 136, 153, 155, 188
ideology: core and periphery of 190, 191. n2; Marxist and feminist notions of 140, 152
"if–then" sequences: assumptions about 4, 43, 108; and equivalence 34; and inference 52.n3; and judgements 35, 106; and knowledge formation 21, 51; routinization of 113
imagination, political 179
imitation heuristics **110**, 111

implemental function or mind-set 65, 300–1
impression formation: and epistemic processes 19; primacy effects in 147
impression management 132, 240
individual-differences variables: assessment and locomotion modes 11; attitude-behavior relation as 274, 290.n21; conservatism as 129–30, 133, 140; epistemic authority effect 44–5; NFCC as 63, 66, 73, 85, 94, 97; openness to experience 70; physical impact of uncertainty 22; and self-regulatory mode scales **316–18**, 320, 329
individuating information 39, 64, 77
inequality, support for 131, 135–9, 141, 150–4, 188, 190–1, 191.nn1–2, 326
inference: accuracy of 121; and experience 49; unconscious 33–4
inference rules 52.n1; and judgments 42, 109; and knowledge formation 21, 32, 34–5, 50–1; and visual illusions 107
inferential process 2–5, 7, 347
inferential task demands 35, 39–40
information: attitudes to new 66; and belief formation 132; contextually activated 23; diagnostic or prototypical 73–4; selective exposure to 132
information given 34–5
information processing: and difficulty of rules 105–6; extent of 5, 71–3, 95, 132–3, 146, 208; motivation for 7, 39, 41, 95–6, 115, 207; and NFCC 62, 64, 69–70; potential 115, 119–20; resources for 35–6, 39–40, 44–6, 119
information seeking: latency of 88–9, 93; and validity concerns 63
information sources 5, 42; credibility of 43–4, 47 (*see also* epistemic authority); diversification of 49; information about 36–7, *38*
informational impact, parametric determinants of 35–43
informational influence, referent 132
informational search 65, 72, 88–9, 146
in-group favoritism 52, 83–4, 86, 93, 353
instability, and conservatism 134, 147, 153, 184
instantiation difficulty 114, 119
instrumentality 263, 282–3, 286
insufficient adjustment process 75
integrative complexity 144, 156, 160–4, **161–2**, 186
intelligence, and NFCC 69

interconnectedness, goals and memes 209–10, 216
inter-goal associations *224*, 226–7
intergroup bias, linguistic 83–5, 93
internal attributions 3
Interpersonal Orientation Scale 320–1
interpersonal relations: as feminine sphere 45; goal-systemic conceptions of 243–7
intolerance, political 183
intolerance of ambiguity: and conservatism 139, 142–3, 153, 155–60, **158–9**; and NFCC 69; and self-regulatory modes 320, 323; use of term 66
intrinsic motivation 6–7, 12; and goals-means association 221–2, 246; and self-regulatory modes 303, 325
intuitive judgments 104, 106–7, 119
Iraq, foreign fighters in 354–6
ISIS (Islamic State in Iraq and Syria) 344, 351, 354–5
Islamist extremism 351, 353–4, 356–7
Islamophobia 351–2

Jabhat al Nusra 354
James, William 6, 33
Jones, Edward (Ned) 3
Jost, John 6
judgmental confidence 72, 82, 88, 97
judgments: accuracy of 120; intuitive and deliberate 104–5, 109–11, 117, 122; motivation and cognition in 207; and routinization 113–14; as rule-based 32–4, 106, 108–9, 122
just world theory 152

Kaczynski, Ted 354
Kelley, Harold 2–3, 12
Kierkegaard, Søren 246
knowledge: desire for 60; general 65; stable 4, 21, 26, 47, 50–1, 65, 82; subjective 3, 20–1, 62
knowledge formation: motivation for 7, 22, 32, 60; process of 4–5, 19–20; social and development aspects of 49–50, 60–1; syllogistic structure of 20–1, 35
knowledge validation 11–12
known-groups analysis 315–19
Kruglanski, Arie, personal history of 1–2
Kuhn, Thomas 4

Lakatos, Imre 4, 20
lay epistemics: and conservatism 146–7; and epistemic authority 43–9; and

NFCC 22–32; theory of 20–2, 49–52; and unimodel of judgment 32–43
left-wing ideology: and conservatism 148; and dogmatism 143, 156–7, 160; and egalitarianism 135–6; ideo-affective posture of 144
legitimizing myths 150, 152
Lennon, John 192.n12
less-is-more effects 121
Lewin, Kurt 94, 243–5
LIB (linguistic intergroup bias) 25–6
liberalism: and change 136; self-definition of 135
Lie Scale 307–8, 333
liking 288.n2: and attitude strength 265–7; latency of 268; and wanting 10, 258–60, *261*, 285, 288 (*see also* relative liking)
linguistic expression, and NFCC 25–6
locomotion function 11; and Big Five personality factors 326; creating scale for 304–5; and decision-making systems 337–8; and goal selection 334–5; internal consistency of scale 313; items on scale for **309**, **311**; and need to evaluate 338.n1; and other individual-difference measures 320–6, **329**; psychological characteristics of 214, 302–4; and speed of task completion 332–3; undermined by assessment 213
lone wolf attacks 354
long-term memory 112
loss, threat of 155, 180–1, 215, 351
low-status group, conservatism in 134, 152
LTTE (Liberation Tigers of Tamil Eelam) 355–6

martyrdom 9, 351
Marxism 140, 152
mastery orientation 321
means: choice and substitution of 215; (*see also* substitutability); cognitive representation of 347; commitment to 218, *219*; generating and selecting 224, 303, 334–5, 337; instrumentality and supplementarity of 263, 286; negative 247
means-ends fusion model 12
memory, organization of concepts in 213
memory constraints, and rule selection 114–15
mental fatigue 27, 74, 94, 96, 115, 146
mental resources *see* cognitive capacity
mental rigidity 136, 143, 155–7, 163, 181
mental-contrasting procedure 223–4

message arguments 36–7, 40–1, 207–8
metacognitive inferences 41–2
micro-cognitive priming techniques 216
minority groups 138, 183, 275
MODE model 267, 272–3
moderation, and extremism 9, 344–8, 350, 355–8
Moebius strip of motivation and cognition 6, *7*
mortality salience, and conservatism 139, 145, 149, 154–5, 181–3, **182**, 186, 188
motivated social cognition: differences from other theories 133; as theory of conservatism 130–4, 140, 145, 149, 153–5, 176, *186*, 187
motivation *see also* extrinsic motivation; intrinsic motivation
motivation and cognition paradigm 6–7, 133, 207–8, 246–7
motivational balance and imbalance 345–7, 349–52, 355–6, 358
motivational entities 7
motivational proclivities 115
motivational properties, transfer of 211
multifinality 7, *210*; as determinant of choice *231–2*, 263, 284–5, 287; and expectancy 215; and friendship 243–4, *245*; and number of goals 234–6, 288; and substitution effects 238–40; in unconscious choice 232–4, *233*
Mussolini, Benito 135, 142

narratives, and extremism 9, 347–9, 352–3, 356–8
need to know 132
negative affectivity, and self-regulatory modes 322
negotiation behavior 25, 27, *28*, 32
NEO Personality Inventory 320, 324, 326; *see also* Big Five personality factors
neuroticism: and conservatism 176; and self-regulatory modes 320, 324, 327, 329; *see also* Big Five personality factors
NEV (Need to Evaluate) Scale 320–2, 327, 338.n1
Neyman-Pearson decision theory 109
NFCC (Need for Cognitive Closure): consequential tendencies of 63–6 (*see also* seizing and freezing); conservatism and 6, 129, 139, 146–7, 155, **169–70**, 171–2, 186; and epistemic authority 46, 50–1; and extremism 349, 357; historical precursors of theory 66–9; interpersonal effects of 24–31, *28–9*, *31*; intrapersonal

effects of 22–4, *24–5*; motivating knowledge formation 31–2, 61–3, 92; nonspecific and specific 21; operationalization of 74, 91; relationship to alternative constructs 69–71; and rule selection 116; and rule-following 50, *51*; scientific value of theory 94–8; situational manipulations of 22, 52.n2, 76; and unconscious choice 232, *233*; work on theory 4–5

NFCS (Need for Closure Scale) 22, 74, 76, 78, 146–7; and conservatism 171–2; and F scale 69; and self-regulatory mode scales 320, 322–3

non-directional motives 132

object attitudes 254–5, 265–6, 273–8, 280, 286
openness *see* experience, openness to
optimism 21, 179–80, 302, 322, 354
optimizing rules 109
order, need for 132, 137, 146–7, 153, 155, 167, **169–70**, 186
outcome dependency 62
out-group derogation 30, 52, 151, 172, 188
overinclusiveness 95

parenting styles, and conservatism 140, 148, 150, 179–80
parents: epistemic authority of 44–5, 47, 113, 138; heuristics used by 111; political influence on children 132, 134; and transference 23
passion, crimes of 346
paternalistic myths 150
PBC (perceived behavioral control) 276–7, 281–3, 286, 289.n13, 290.nn19–20
peer groups, as epistemic authorities 45
perception, active and passive 121
perceptual inferences 106–8, *107*, 114
performance orientation 321
peripheral-heuristic information processing 70
permanence tendency 63–5, 71, 74, 92; boundaries with urgency tendency 88; manifestations of 78–84, 86, 92–3; *see also* freezing
Personal Fear of Invalidity Scale 320, 322–3, 327
personal mattering 9
personal scripts 144
personality, Big Five dimensions of *see* Big Five personality factors

personality theories of conservatism 129–30, 133, 140, 151–2
personality typologies 66, 68
persuasion: instantiation difficulty in 119; motivation and cognition in 207; negative and positive frames of 180–1; and NFCC 26–7, 98, 147; peripheral cues and message arguments in 36–7, *38*; seizing and freezing in 65, 89–90, 93
pessimism, and conservatism 153–5, 179–80, 192.n6
philosophy of science 4
planned behavior, theory of *see* TPB
Polarity Scale 144–5, 179
political attitudes: motivational basis of 189–90; and NFCC 30; parents as models of 134; psychological motives for 129–30, 188; self-reported 139; socially representative surveys of 188–9
political conservatism: and the arts 167; and fear of death 181, **182**; and integrative complexity **161–2**, 162–4; and mental rigidity 155–6; motivational underpinnings of 132–3, 153–5, 186–7, 190–1, 191–2.n5; and need for order and structure **169–70**; and negative emotions **177–8**, 179–80; and NFCC 30, 172; and openness to experience **165–6**; psychological study of 129–31, 139–40, **156**, 189; and self-esteem 173, **174–5**; situational determinants of 187–8; and system instability **185**; and uncertainty tolerance **168**; *see also* right-wing conservatism
political elites, thinking styles of 160, 163
Political-Economic Conservatism Scale 139
Popper, Karl 4, 20, 52.n1
postcrystallization phase 88–90, 93; *see also* freezing
precrystallization phase 71, 88–90, 93; *see also* seizing
premises, of syllogisms 21, 33, 35–6, 42, 50, 52.n3, 106, 114–15
prevention system 132, 148, 181, 192.n6, 214, 220, 237; *see also* RLPREV
primacy effects 23, 64, 74, 95, 98, 147
probability, conditional 264
promotion system 148, 181, 214, 220, 237; *see also* RLPROM
punishment, capital *see* death penalty
punitiveness 140, 145, 179, 183

racism 150–1, 172
RAI (Relative Autonomy Index) 325

rationalizations, individual and collective 131, 149–50, 155
reaction time (RT): and goal systems 217, *218*, 228, *242*; in process of recognition 110
reasoning: and emotions 131; rules and similarities in 123.n6
recall memory 112
recency effects 74
reciprocal myths 150
recognition heuristic 109, **110**, 114
recognition memory 105, 112
recognize–act cycle 32
redundancy 116
regulatory focus: and parental punitiveness 179; prevention-oriented 139, 148
regulatory focus theory 147–8, 180–1
regulatory mode theory *see* self-regulatory modes
rejecting the deviate 78–82, 96–7, 147
rejection, sensitivity to 357
relative liking (RL) 259–63, 265, 268, 286–7, 289.n9
relevance, subjective 35, 39–40, 43
religion: attitude and behavior in 280; as response to adversity 192.n12
religious dogmatism 138, 145
religious goals 227, *228*
representativeness heuristic 109, 113, 118
response latencies 50, *51*, 176, 268, 273
reverence effect 47, 49
right-wing authoritarianism *see* RWA
right-wing conservatism 138, 147, 184
right-wing extremism 346
right-wing politics: and cognitive sophistication 163; definitions of 135; and dogmatism 157; emotional resonances of 179–80; following terrorist attacks 192.n11; ideo-affective posture of 144; measures of 138; and mortality salience 183; motivations for 134; and NFCC 171–2; psychology of 137
RLPREV (Relative Preventive Liking) 261, 263, 266
RLPROM (Relative Promotive Liking) 261, 263, 266
Rogers, Carl 46
rule acquisition 112–13
rule activation 35–6
rule conflict 105, 117–18
rule conforming 108–9
rule following: and conservatism 139; and judgment formation 106–7; in lay epistemics 32–4; and rule conforming 108–9
rule instantiation 106, 119
rule selection 105, 116, 122
rules: origins of 111–12; routinization of 33, 36, 105, 113–14; use of term 106
RWA 30, 129, 151, 162, 166, 170, 175–6, 178, 193, 204
RWA (right-wing authoritarianism) 140–2; asymmetrical focus on 129; fear and aggression and 176; and SDO 151; and self-esteem 173
RWA Scale: predictive value of 141–2; resistance to change on 135, 138

sacred myths 150
SAEA (self-ascribed epistemic authority) 5, 45–50, *48*, 348
SAT (Scholastic Aptitude Test) 60, 331
satisficing heuristic 105, 109, **110**
scapegoats, socially sanctioned 142, 176
SDO (social dominance orientation): and conservatism 129; measuring 135; motivational base of 151; and NFCC 30; and self-esteem 173
SDO Scale 150; attitudes measured in 138; and conservatism 151; and openness to experience 164; and self-regulatory mode scales 320, 326
secondary reinforcement 12
seizing *see also* urgency tendency
seizing and freezing 22–4, 30, 32, 63–5, 92, 349; boundary conditions between 88–9, **90–1**, 93; empirical evidence for 71–7; separating 65, 77
self-awareness 274–5
self-consciousness 320–1, 324
self-denial 345, 351
self-enhancement 61, 132, 288
self-esteem: and conservatism 132, 172–3, **174–5**; enhancement 238, *239*; low 145, 155, 173, 192.n10, 322; and self-regulatory modes 302, 322
self-esteem scales 173, 320
self-evaluation, focus on 302, 320
self-interest theory of conservatism 133–4, 153, 192.n5
self-monitoring 274–5
self-promotion bias 319
self-regulation: in goal systems 207, 226–30, 246–7; intrinsic and autonomous 325–6; motivation and cognition in 215–16; in regulatory focus theory 148

self-regulatory emphasis 303
self-regulatory function, centralized 263, *264*
self-regulatory mode scales: and Big Five personality factors 326–9, **328**; coefficient alpha for **312**; construct validity of 315–19; constructing 304–5; convergent-discriminant validity 319–20, 326; correlation between pairs of items **313**; correlations with individual-difference measures **316–18**, 320–6; cross-cultural validation of 314–15; implications of 336–8; model fit for **312**, **315**; predictive validity of 332–6; as predictors of success 330–2; structural validity of 309–11; temporal stability of 314; testing 305–9, **306**, **308**; variance explained in **314**
self-regulatory modes 10–11, 299–302, 338; *see also* assessment function; locomotion function
self-righteousness 176
self-sacrifice 347, 351
self-verification 61, 98
sensation seeking 164, 333, 349
September 11, 2001 attacks 52, 154, 181, 184, 192.n11
sexism 150–1
shared realities 28–30, 32
shared reality 30
Short Imaginal Process Inventory 320, 327
signal detection theory 109, 148
significance, quest for 350–3, 355, 358–9
sins of omission 121
situational conservatism 135, 152
situational demands, and NFCC 50, 95–9
Sloman's S-criterion 118
SN (subjective norms) 276–7, 281–3, 290. nn19–20
social change 135, 138, 145, 150
social cognition, simple rules in 121
social comparison: and knowledge construction 61; and self-regulatory modes 320–1, 324, 332
social comparison processes 20
social convention 138, 141, 164
social development, and rule acquisition 111–13
social dominance theory 141–2, 150–2; *see also* SDO
social identity 262, 351
social information 88, 90
social innovation, hostility to 135
social interactions, and prior knowledge 19

social intolerance 149
social judgment: dual mode perspective 36; and knowledge construction 31; as procedural learning 33; transference in 23–4; unimodel of 22
social learning 57, 134
social movement theory 358–9
social networks: and extremism 9, 344, 353–4, 359; twin functions of 347–8
social primes 240–3, *241*
social psychology: importance of NFCC theory for 98; Kruglanski's introduction to 2; motivation and cognition in 208; of science 20
social stability, threats to 130, 155, 183–6, **185**
socially desirable responding 319
source expertise 38, 132
source rules 113
spontaneous trait inferences 34
Stalin, Josef 135, 191.n4
state orientation 301, 322
status quo: inequality as 138; left-wing as 136, 148, 189; preserving 151–3, 172, 261
stereotypes: and fear of death 183; and NFCC 24, 76–7, 92, 147
stimuli, proximal and distal 108, 123.n5
strategy selection theory 116–17, 120
strength of goals-means association 210, *211*, 213, 217–23, *218*, 246
structure, need for 82–3, 132, 139, 146, 153, 155–6, 167, **169–70**, 186
subconscious impact, of goals 211–12, 256, 258
suboptimal heuristics hypothesis 44–6
substance abuse 9
substitutability: of means 210, *213*, 237–8; in self-esteem enhancement 238–9, *240*
sufficiency threshold 44
suicide attackers 350, 352
superordinate goals 209, 273
superstition 67, 145, 184
supplementarity 263, 282, 286
syllogistic reasoning: inference as 32–4; and judgment formation 106; motivations for 131; structure of 21, 35
Syria, foreign fighters in 354–5
system justification theory 139, 141, 151–3, 184

take-the-best heuristic **110**, 111, 115–16, 120–1
tallying heuristic **110**, 111, 115–16, 121

Index 377

task completion time 332–3
task orientation 302, 320, 323
task performance: and NFCC 52.n2; speed and quality control in 304, 332–3
temptations, and goals 208, *227*, 228, *229*, 230, 236, 246–7
terror management, and mortality salience 181, 183
terror management theory 130, 149, 153, 188
terrorism: and conservatism 181; and deradicalization 356; narrative justifying 9; and NFCC 52; personality profile of 354; *see also* violent extremism
thinking: as end in itself 70; fast and slow 5
thinking styles *see* cognitive style
threat, and conservatism 155
time pressure: and epistemic authority 46; and NFCC 22–3, 30, 74, 77, 79, 94–5, 146, 232–3
tit-for-tat heuristic **110**
tolerance, and mortality salience 183
Tolman, Edward 108
total evidence, principle of 121
TPB (theory of planned behavior) 275–7, 281–2, 284–7, 289.n13
TRA (theory of reasoned action) 275–7, 281–3
traditionalism 135
trait labels 65, 83, 93
transference 23–4
transformational impact 289.n14
transsituational consistency 78, 84, 93
trust, basic 66
Type A personalities 324

uncertainty: judgment under 19; and NFCC 51–2; savoring 62
uncertainty avoidance: and conservatism 129–30, 132, 139, 145–6, 153–5, 167, **168**, 184, 186, 190; and intolerance of ambiguity 142–3; and mental rigidity 156; and parental punitiveness 179; psychodynamic theories of 66–7, 69; and self-esteem 172
unconscious impact *see* subconscious impact
unifinality 243–4, 288
unimodel of judgment 5, 20, 32–43, 105–6; motivation and cognition in 207–8; novel findings of 118–21; struggle for acceptance 12
uniqueness of goals-means association 210, *211*, *218*
United States, conservatism in 137
University of Toronto 1–2
urgency tendency 63–4, 71, 74, 88–9, 92
utility: maximizing 109; subjective 214–16, 223–4, 231

validity *see* fear of invalidity
value systems, complexity of 347
values: plural 356; religious 137, 351
variance, overlapping 319
vested interest 265, 284
violence: ideological justifications for 9, 352, 355–6, 359; as means to significance 351–3
violent extremism 8–9, 344, 350–1; alternative approaches to 358–9; ideological narratives of 353; model of underpinnings *359*; motivation and ability in 354–5, 358; moving away from 355–7, 359–60
visual illusions 106, *107*
vitality, psychological 320, 323

Wason's selection task 34, 113, 118
weighted additive rule 116
Whitehead, Alfred North 114
Will, George F. 129, 137, 179
Work Preference Inventory 325
working memory 273